ANNUAL E

Macroeconomics 00/01
Thirteenth Edition

EDITOR

Don Cole
Drew University

Don Cole, Professor of Economics at Drew University, received his Ph.D. from Ohio State University. He has served as consultant to a variety of public and private organizations, and is cofounder of the Drew University Semester on the European Union in Brussels, Belgium. An innovator in the use of computer-assisted instruction in the teaching of economics, Dr. Cole is the author of articles on various subjects, including economic policy, monetary theory, and economic education. He is also the editor of other Dushkin/McGraw-Hill publications, including *The Encyclopedic Dictionary of Economics* and two other *Annual Editions* anthologies, *Economics* and *Microeconomics*.

Dushkin/McGraw-Hill
Sluice Dock, Guilford, Connecticut 06437

Visit us on the Internet
http://www.dushkin.com/annualeditions/

Credits

1. Introduction to Macroeconomics
Unit photo—Dushkin/McGraw-Hill illustration by Mike Eagle.
2. Measuring Economic Performance
Unit photo—© 1999 by PhotoDisc, Inc.
3. Fiscal Policy and the Federal Budget
Unit photo—courtesy of The Federal Reserve Bank of Boston.
4. Money, Banking, and Monetary Policy
Unit photo—courtesy of the New York Stock Exchange.
5. Employment, Prices, and the Business Cycle
Unit photo—courtesy of United Automobile Workers.
6. International Economics
Unit photo—© 1999 by PhotoDisc, Inc.

Copyright

Cataloging in Publication Data
Main entry under title: Annual editions: Macroeconomics. 2000/2001.
  1. Macroeconomics—Periodicals. 2. Economics—Periodicals. 3. United States—Economic Conditions—Periodicals. I. Cole, Don, comp. II. Title: Macroeconomics.
ISBN 0–07–039382–6   339'73'05   75-20753   ISSN 1096–424X

© 2000 by Dushkin/McGraw-Hill, Guilford, CT 06437, A Division of The McGraw-Hill Companies.

Copyright law prohibits the reproduction, storage, or transmission in any form by any means of any portion of this publication without the express written permission of Dushkin/McGraw-Hill, and of the copyright holder (if different) of the part of the publication to be reproduced. The Guidelines for Classroom Copying endorsed by Congress explicitly state that unauthorized copying may not be used to create, to replace, or to substitute for anthologies, compilations, or collective works.

Annual Editions® is a Registered Trademark of Dushkin/McGraw-Hill, A Division of The McGraw-Hill Companies.

Thirteenth Edition

Cover image © 1999 PhotoDisc, Inc.

Printed in the United States of America   1234567890BAHBAH543210   Printed on Recycled Paper

Editors/Advisory Board

Members of the Advisory Board are instrumental in the final selection of articles for each edition of ANNUAL EDITIONS. Their review of articles for content, level, currentness, and appropriateness provides critical direction to the editor and staff. We think that you will find their careful consideration well reflected in this volume.

EDITOR

Don Cole
Drew University

ADVISORY BOARD

Frank J. Bonello
University of Notre Dame

Sarah J. Bumgarner
University of North Carolina

Robert B. Catlett
Emporia State University

Lucinda Coulter-Burbach
Seminole Community College

Eleanor D. Craig
University of Delaware

Lawrence Frateschi
College of DuPage

Jo-Anne Gibson
Southeastern Louisiana University

Stephen K. Happel
Arizona State University

Matthew R. Marlin
Duquesne University

Joseph W. Meador
Northeastern University

Marshall D. Nickles
Pepperdine University

Kostis Papadantonakis
Essex Community College

Arthur J. Raymond
Muhlenberg College

Rolando A. Santos
Lakeland Community College

Howard Stein
Roosevelt University

Evert Van Der Heide
Calvin College

David B. Yerger
Lycoming College

EDITORIAL STAFF

Ian A. Nielsen, Publisher
Roberta Monaco, Senior Developmental Editor
Dorothy Fink, Associate Developmental Editor
Addie Raucci, Senior Administrative Editor
Cheryl Greenleaf, Permissions Editor
Joseph Offredi, Permissions/Editorial Assistant
Diane Barker, Proofreader
Lisa Holmes-Doebrick, Program Coordinator

PRODUCTION STAFF

Brenda S. Filley, Production Manager
Charles Vitelli, Designer
Lara M. Johnson, Design/Advertising Coordinator
Laura Levine, Graphics
Mike Campbell, Graphics
Tom Goddard, Graphics
Eldis Lima, Graphics
Juliana Arbo, Typesetting Supervisor
Jane Jaegersen, Typesetter
Marie Lazauskas, Typesetter
Kathleen D'Amico, Typesetter
Larry Killian, Copier Coordinator

To the Reader

In publishing ANNUAL EDITIONS we recognize the enormous role played by the magazines, newspapers, and journals of the public press in providing current, first-rate educational information in a broad spectrum of interest areas. Many of these articles are appropriate for students, researchers, and professionals seeking accurate, current material to help bridge the gap between principles and theories and the real world. These articles, however, become more useful for study when those of lasting value are carefully collected, organized, indexed, and reproduced in a low-cost format, which provides easy and permanent access when the material is needed. That is the role played by ANNUAL EDITIONS.

New to ANNUAL EDITIONS is the inclusion of related World Wide Web sites. These sites have been selected by our editorial staff to represent some of the best resources found on the World Wide Web today. Through our carefully developed topic guide, we have linked these Web resources to the articles covered in this ANNUAL EDITIONS reader. We think that you will find this volume useful, and we hope that you will take a moment to visit us on the Web at **http://www.dushkin.com** to tell us what you think.

Annual Editions: Macroeconomics is an anthology that provides up-to-date readings on contemporary macroeconomic issues. In view of the recent explosion of interest in economics, it is essential that students are given opportunities to observe how economic science can help them to understand major economic events in the real world. *Annual Editions: Macroeconomics 00/01 is designed to meet such a need.*

This anthology is divided into six sections, which generally correspond to the typical sequence of topics in macroeconomic textbooks:

Introduction to Macroeconomics. Macroeconomics involves the study of the economy "in the large"; it concerns such broad issues as how gross domestic product, economic growth, unemployment, and inflation are determined. As articles in this section indicate, macroeconomic reasoning can be applied to a vast assortment of "real world" problems.

Measuring Economic Performance. Economists use economic data for the purpose of judging an economy's general health and making informed choices among policy alternatives. This section examines various problems associated with the gathering and interpretation of such data.

Fiscal Policy and the Federal Budget. Articles in this section deal with ways in which the federal government might use its spending and tax programs to achieve various macroeconomic goals. Major emphasis is placed upon issues of tax and budgetary reform.

Money, Banking, and Monetary Policy. Monetary policy involves deliberate changes in the money supply and credit availability for the purpose of achieving macroeconomic goals. This section provides an overview of the U.S. banking system and an assessment of the effectiveness of monetary policy.

Employment, Prices, and the Business Cycle. A major goal in the implementation of macroeconomic policy is the simultaneous achievement of high employment, stable prices, and vigorous economic growth. Articles selected for this section discuss some theoretical and policy issues involved in improving the economy's performance in these areas.

International Economics. In recent years the global economy has experienced a series of dramatic events unforeseen even a decade ago: the end of the cold war; ambitious market reforms in what were formerly centrally planned economies; an acceleration of the process of economic integration in the Americas, Western Europe, and the Pacific Rim; and increased use of protectionist measures by most major traders. This section examines key aspects of these developments.

Whether you are someone who is currently pursuing studies in economics, or just a casual reader eager to learn more about some of the major economic issues of the day, you will find *Annual Editions: Macroeconomics 00/01* to be one of the most useful and up-to-date anthologies available. Your comments can be very valuable in designing the next edition. Please complete and mail the postpaid rating form at the conclusion of this book and let us know your opinions.

Don Cole
Editor

Contents

To the Reader iv
Topic Guide 2
⊚ Selected World Wide Web Sites 4
Overview 6

1. **Meeting the Challenge of the New Economy,** Michael J. Mandel, *Blueprint*, Winter 1998. 8
   The editor of *Business Week* argues that a **New Economy** has been born, which is transforming America and much of the world at a pace that is scarcely imaginable. How the United States responds to the twin forces of **globalization** and the **information revolution** will help to shape the world economy in the twenty-first century.

2. **The Accidental Inventor of Today's Capitalism,** Louis Uchitelle, *New York Times*, February 21, 1998. 13
   Although he may never have actually used the words "supply creates its own demand," the French historian Jean-Baptiste Say invented a concept (known as **Say's Law**) that continues to influence economic reasoning to the present day. Louis Uchitelle traces the origin and development of this important principle.

3. **Economic Possibilities for Our Grandchildren,** Elizabeth Johnson and Donald Moggridge (eds.), from *Collected Writings of John Maynard Keynes*, Vol. 9, 1978. 16
   In this essay, originally written in 1930, the father of modern macroeconomics predicts the **demise of the economic problem** 100 years from now. Filling leisure time in a meaningful way, John Maynard Keynes contends, will prove to be our grandchildren's chief concern.

4. **What in the World Happened to Economics?** Justin Fox, *Fortune*, March 15, 1999. 19
   Economics is a subject rich in **controversy**. Although most economists speak the same language, disagreements often do occur. More often than not these disagreements involve the global economy. According to Justin Fox, most economists no longer seem to believe that there are single answers to the big global issues.

5. **Statistics and Even Lore of the Dismal Science,** David Cay Johnston, *New York Times*, September 15, 1997. 24
   A vast and growing trove of online information is available to track both the domestic and world economies. David Johnston shows how **to use the Internet** effectively.

Overview 26

6. **State of the Union: Black Holes in the Statistics,** Robert Eisner, *Challenge*, January/February 1997. 28
   How reliable are official U.S. government statistics? Robert Eisner believes that they are deeply flawed. This applies to measures of GDP, public deficits and debt, domestic and foreign investment and saving, productivity, real wages, and the distribution of income and wealth.

7. **The Economy You Can't See,** Paul Starobin, *National Journal*, June 18, 1994. 31
   A large share of economic activity occurs in the **underground economy,** where goods and services—some legal, some not—are produced but not reported. Paul Starobin considers possible implications of proposals for regulating such activity.

UNIT 1

Introduction to Macroeconomics

Five articles examine some of the controversies that lie at the heart of macroeconomics.

UNIT 2

Measuring Economic Performance

Four articles consider the dynamics of the measurement and interpretation of economic indicators. Subjects examined include the validity of government statistics, productivity, and sustainable development.

The concepts in bold italics are developed in the article. For further expansion please refer to the Topic Guide, the Glossary, and the Index.

8. **How Fast Can the U.S. Economy Grow?** Paul Krugman, *Harvard Business Review*, July/August 1997. 34

According to the so-called **new economic view**, rapid technological change and global competition have created an environment in which the old speed limits on economic growth no longer apply. Advocates of this view foresee an economy in which faster growth, without inflation, is likely. Paul Krugman examines their arguments.

9. **Hell No, We Won't Save!** Robert J. Samuelson, *Newsweek*, February 22, 1999. 41

As the American economy continues to zip along, defying predictions that it would slow down or crash, a potentially troublesome problem has developed—**U.S. personal saving** has virtually disappeared. Robert Samuelson asserts that low personal saving is an essential catalyst of the current boom. If somehow it were to rise, the United States and the rest of the world would face even greater peril.

Overview 42

10. **The Economic Report of the President for 1998: A Review,** James Galbraith, *Challenge*, September/October 1998. 44

The Council of Economic Advisers argues that the present economic expansion can be sustained without a significant **increase in public spending.** James Galbraith asks: Can a long recovery rely entirely on the growth of private-sector investment and consumption with no contribution from government?

11. **Reflections on the Balancing Act,** George Brockway, *Challenge*, January/February 1998. 48

Economic theory suggests that a **balanced budget will bring interest rates down.** Now that the federal budget has finally come into balance, the time has come to put this theory to the test of practice. George Brockway warns that the theory may not work as stated.

12. **The Tax Man Cometh: Consumer Spending and Tax Payments,** Peter S. Yoo, *Review (Federal Reserve Bank of St. Louis)*, January/February 1996. 50

How do consumers respond to changes in income tax rates? Peter Yoo examines several episodes in U.S. history when tax payments changed noticeably. He finds that the response of households was rather modest.

13. **The Flat Tax in Theory and Practice: Simple, Efficient, Fair. Or Is It?** William G. Gale, *Brookings Review*, Summer 1998. 58

Fundamental tax reform—replacing the present income tax with a new tax system—continues to attract national attention. However, as William Gale demonstrates, none of the current proposals for reform (including the flat tax) is a panacea, and each is flawed in some important way.

UNIT 3

Fiscal Policy and the Federal Budget

Seven selections discuss the state of the federal budget. Topics include the current budget predicament, the dynamics of the deficit, balancing the budget, federal tax policy, and Social Security.

The concepts in bold italics are developed in the article. For further expansion please refer to the Topic Guide, the Glossary, and the Index.

14. **Why Are Taxes So Complicated, and What Can We Do about It?** William Gale, *Brookings Review*, Winter 1999. — 63

Since virtually everyone agrees that taxes should be easy to understand, administer, and enforce, **why are taxes so complicated?** The author suggests that the answer is that people also agree that taxes should be fair, should be conducive to economic prosperity, should raise sufficient revenue to finance government spending, and should respect the privacy of individuals.

15. **Are Americans Really Overtaxed?** William G. Gale, *Los Angeles Times*, February 24, 1999. — 66

Are U.S. taxes too high? Tax-cut advocates maintain that taxes are at record high levels and are imposing increasingly crushing burdens on American families. William Gale says that the first claim is correct, while the second is simply wrong.

16. **Should We Retire Social Security?: Grading the Reform Plans,** Henry J. Aaron and Robert D. Reischauer, *Brookings Review*, Winter 1999. — 68

Most Americans understand that **Social Security** faces a long-term imbalance between the cost of benefits promised under current law and the program's projected income. The authors evaluate some of the major proposals for Social Security reform.

Overview — 74

17. **U.S. Monetary Policy: An Introduction,** *FRBSF Economic Letter (Federal Reserve Bank of San Francisco)*, January 1, 1999. — 76

In this essay insights into the major dimensions of **U.S. monetary policy** are provided. What are the ultimate goals of the Federal Reserve? What happens when these goals conflict? How does the Fed formulate its strategies, and how do its policies affect the economy?

18. **Central Banking in a Democracy,** Alan S. Blinder, *Economic Quarterly (Federal Reserve Bank of Richmond)*, Fall 1996. — 83

A former vice chairman of its Board of Governors asks, **who does the Federal Reserve serve?** Alan Blinder argues that it is not the U.S. president, or the Congress, or the banks, or the financial system. The Fed's true constituency is the entire nation.

19. **Is the Fed Slave to a Defunct Economist?** Evan F. Koenig, *Southwest Economy (Federal Reserve Bank of Dallas)*, September/October 1997. — 91

Some commentators have recently accused the Federal Reserve of pursuing a **Keynesian policy of "fine tuning" the economy.** As an alternative they advocate a policy of allowing output and employment to range freely, as long as inflation holds steady. Evan Koenig argues that the Fed has, in fact, steered a middle course between these extremes.

UNIT 4

Money, Banking, and Monetary Policy

Seven articles analyze the accountability of central banking, how politicians influence federal policy, and the money movement.

The concepts in bold italics are developed in the article. For further expansion please refer to the Topic Guide, the Glossary, and the Index.

20. **Should the Fed Care about Stock Bubbles?** Paul Krugman, *Fortune*, March 1, 1999. 95
Several years ago, when the Dow Jones Industrial Average stood at 6500, Fed Chairman Alan Greenspan warned about "irrational exuberance." Today, with the stock market at record highs, the question may be even more urgent than it was then: ***Should the Federal Reserve care when stock prices soar?***

21. **Bank Mergers and the Big Money,** Charles Geisst, *Newsday*, April 19, 1998. 97
Since the 1933 passage of the ***Glass-Steagall Act,*** commercial banks have been prevented from providing services in either investment banking or real estate and insurance. Yet, recent mergers within the banking and securities businesses are clearly in violation of the spirit of Glass-Steagall, if not its text. Charles Geisst cautions of the dangers of this arrangement.

22. **The Stepchildren of Banking,** Richard A. Oppel Jr., *New York Times*, March 26, 1999. 99
Many people, especially in low-income neighborhoods, shy away from banks. Claiming poor location, high fees, and other obstacles as excuses against owning a bank account, they turn to expensive check-cashing outlets. Richard Oppel examines possible ways in which these individuals might be given ***better access to banking services.***

23. **Electronic Cash and the End of National Markets,** Stephen J. Kobrin, *Foreign Policy*, Summer 1997. 102
"E-cash" (or electronic money) is money that moves along multiple channels largely outside the established network of banks, checks, and paper currency overseen by the Federal Reserve. Stephen Kobrin considers what the development of E-cash might mean for the future of banking and the monetary system.

Overview 108

24. **Learning from the Big Booms,** Louis Uchitelle, *New York Times*, June 28, 1998. 110
The ***"Soaring Nineties"*** invites comparison with other great periods of prosperity in modern history. What is striking is that each of them—the Gilded Age in the late nineteenth century, the Roaring Twenties, the Fabulous Fifties and Sixties—ended suddenly, and in each case the end came as a shock. This article offers some historical perspective on the current economic expansion.

25. **Yes, Virginia, There Will Be Recessions,** *Business Week*, August 31, 1998. 112
The dawning of the twenty-first century doesn't mean that we have seen our last ***recession.*** If productivity falls sharply during the next downturn, that will suggest that recent gains were only a temporary spike. But if productivity continues to rise, it may be a clear sign that the twenty-first century economy is a good bet.

UNIT 5
Employment, Prices, and the Business Cycle

Six selections examine the interaction between employment and inflation. Specific topics discussed include employment rates, our standard of living, and inflation cycles.

26. **Productivity Gains Help Keep Economy on a Roll,** 113
Louis Uchitelle, *New York Times,* March 22, 1999.
Eight years into the current recovery, the U.S. economy is experiencing labor shortages and rising wages. Such conditions normally lead to an acceleration of inflation or shrinking profits. Yet neither is happening. Louis Uchitelle traces events that have led to recent developments in ***labor productivity.***

27. **Calculating the Price of Everything: The CPI,** 117
Daniel Mitchell, *Challenge,* September/October 1998.
Recently, a debate has developed among many economists and politicians over the usefulness of the ***Consumer Price Index (CPI)*** as the single most important measure of price movements. In this article, Daniel Mitchell suggests that there are many plausible and reasonable versions of the CPI. A variety of alternatives should be offered to meet the preferences of the CPI users.

28. **Overworked *and* Underemployed,** Barry Bluestone 122
and Stephen Rose, *The American Prospect,* March/April 1997.
At least since the 1980s, people have said that they work "too hard"—that they are spending too much time on the job, with too little left for family, chores, or leisure. At the same time there has been a marked increase in part-time work by those who can't find full-time work. Can Americans be simultaneously ***"overworked"*** and ***"underemployed"***? Barry Bluestone and Stephen Rose investigate this apparent paradox.

29. **The Age-Adjusted Unemployment Rate: An Alternative Measure,** Robert Horn and Philip Heap, *Challenge,* January/February 1999. 132
The ***U.S. unemployment rate*** is low by recent historical standards. However, the official rate does not take into account the fact that the age and sex composition of the labor force changes over time. Robert Horn and Philip Heap show how, once such adjustments are made, today's unemployment rate does not look low at all.

Overview 134

30. **Globalization and Its Discontents: Navigating the Dangers of a Tangled World,** Richard N. Haass and Robert E. Litan, *Foreign Affairs,* May/June 1998. 136
The ***global liberalization of trade*** has reduced barriers to the movements of goods and capital across national boundaries. But globalization has also created a series of problems, including job losses, increasing income inequality, and stagnant or deteriorating real wages. The authors examine three fundamentally different approaches to addressing recent developments in the global economy.

31. **Why Trade Is Good for You,** *The Economist,* October 3, 1998. 140
If countries specialize according to their ***comparative advantage,*** they can prosper through trade regardless of how inefficient, in absolute terms, they may be in their chosen specialty. This article demonstrates how this principle can be used to support the case for free trade.

UNIT 6

International Economics

Thirteen articles consider how free trade, protectionism, trade deficits, the European Union, the emergence of Central Europe, and NAFTA affect the world economy.

32. **Could It Happen Again?** *The Economist*, February 20, 1999. **143**

The Economist maintains that for the past 25 years, the biggest economic enemy in most countries has been inflation. Now, however, the world economy is precariously balanced on the edge of a deflationary precipice. Does this mean that today, in most of the world, a greater danger is ***deflation***?

33. **Will Fair Trade Diminish Free Trade?** David M. Gould and William C. Gruben, *Business Economics*, April 1997. **146**

While trade agreements have reduced tariffs dramatically since the end of World War II, ***new forms of protection*** have exploded. The authors ask why fair trade laws don't always work.

34. **The Spotlight and the Bottom Line: How Multinationals Export Human Rights,** Debora L. Spar, *Foreign Affairs*, March/April 1998. **153**

Traditionally, U.S. manufacturers of consumer products targeted for ***human rights violations*** abroad have turned the blame over to foreign subcontractors. These corporations have begun to acknowledge responsibility for such violations and have created voluntary codes of conduct. Debora Spar assesses their effectiveness.

35. **NAFTA: How Is It Doing?** Joe Cobb and Alan Tonelson, *The World & I*, October 1997. **158**

The formation of the ***North American Free Trade Association (NAFTA)*** in 1994 was marked both by extravagant promises about its benefits and by bloodcurdling warnings about its costs. Now that some time has passed, the authors ask: How is NAFTA doing?

36. **Trade Policy at a Cross Roads,** I. M. Destler, *Brookings Review*, Winter 1999. **164**

Anxieties over globalization have brought the ***U.S. trade policy agenda*** to a stalemate. But the exceptional current condition of the American economy offers an unusually favorable climate for addressing these anxieties. I. M. Destler suggests a new approach.

37. **The United States Is Not Ahead in Everything That Matters,** John Schmitt and Lawrence Mishel, *Challenge*, November/December 1998. **168**

Many people now argue that ***labor market rigidities*** are making Western Europe less competitive. The authors use key measures of economic strength, including GDP per capita and productivity, to assert that Europe is doing as well as the United States in the 1990s.

38. **The Euro: Who Wins? Who Loses?** Jeffry Frieden, *Foreign Policy*, Fall 1998. **175**

With the end of the battle over a ***common currency***, Europeans have a more momentous task before them: to agree on a common monetary policy for Europe's disparate countries and to manage the political clashes that this process of agreement will unleash. Jeffry Frieden sorts out the potential winners and losers.

39. **Russia Is Not Poland, and That's Too Bad,** Michael M. Weinstein, *New York Times*, August 30, 1998. **183**

Both ***Poland*** and ***Russia*** began the 1990s saddled with paltry living standards left by a sclerotic, centrally controlled economy. Poland now ranks among Europe's fastest growing economies; the Russian economy stagnates. This article tells what went wrong.

The concepts in bold italics are developed in the article. For further expansion please refer to the Topic Guide, the Glossary, and the Index.

40. **Japan's Economic Plight: Fallen Idol,** *The Economist,* 185
June 26, 1998.
Japan was once feared for its economic might. Today it is feared for its economic weakness. *The Economist* examines the harm its ailing system might do to the rest of Asia and the world.

41. **The Other Crisis,** James D. Wolfensohn, *Across the* 188
Board, February 1999.
The head of the World Bank asserts that we must look beyond the *global financial crisis* to seek the long-term structural reforms necessary to put the world's troubled economies back on the road to recovery. Ultimately, the real issue is the state in which the world finds itself in terms of environment, humanity, and peace and stability.

42. **Changing Today's Consumption Patterns—for To-** 192
morrow's Human Development, United Nations Development Programme, *Human Development Report,* May 1998.
World consumption has expanded at an unprecedented pace over the twentieth century, and its benefits have been spread far and wide. Yet, as this United Nations report shows, competitive spending and conspicuous consumption have turned the affluence of some into the social exclusion of many.

Documents*

The following is a list of documents that appear in this edition of **Annual Editions: Macroeconomics.**

Total Output, Income, and Spending	**205**
Disposition of Personal Income	**206**
Sources of Personal Income	**207**
Corporate Profits	**207**
Consumer Prices—All Urban Consumers	**208**
Real Personal Consumption Expenditures	**209**
Consumer Credit	**209**
Share of Aggregate Income and Mean Income in 1977 to 1996	**210–211**
Employment, Unemployment, and Wages	**212**
Average Weekly Hours, Hourly Earnings, and Weekly Earnings	**213**
Employment Cost Index—Private Industry	**213**
Federal Receipts, Outlays, and Debt	**214**
U.S. International Transactions	**215**

Glossary	**216**
Index	**225**
Article Review Form	**228**
Article Rating Form	**229**

*****The Economic Indicators** are prepared and published monthly for the Joint Economic Committee by the Council of Economic Advisers. They can be contacted by phone at (202) 512-1530, FAX at (202) 512-1262, or through the World Wide Web at http://www.access.gpo.gov.

The concepts in bold italics are developed in the article. For further expansion please refer to the Topic Guide, the Glossary, and the Index.

Topic Guide

This topic guide suggests how the selections and World Wide Web sites found in the next section of this book relate to topics of traditional concern to macroeconomics students and professionals. It is useful for locating interrelated articles and Web sites for reading and research. The guide is arranged alphabetically according to topic.

The relevant Web sites, which are numbered and annotated on pages 4 and 5, are easily identified by the Web icon (◎) under the topic articles. By linking the articles and the Web sites by topic, this ANNUAL EDITIONS reader becomes a powerful learning and research tool.

TOPIC AREA	TREATED IN	TOPIC AREA	TREATED IN
Asian Economies	40. Japan's Economic Plight 41. Other Crisis ◎ **21, 28, 30, 33, 34, 36, 37**		16. Should We Retire Social Security? ◎ **2, 7, 12, 14, 15, 17**
Banking Industry	17. U.S. Monetary Policy 18. Central Banking in a Democracy 21. Bank Mergers 22. Stepchild of Banking 23. Electronic Cash ◎ **12, 18, 19, 20, 21**	**General Agreement on Tariffs and Trade (GATT)**	30. Globalization and Its Discontents 33. Will Fair Trade Diminish Free Trade? 36. Trade Policy at a Cross Roads ◎ **28, 36**
Business Cycles	1. Meeting the Challenges 4. What in the World Happened to Economics? 5. Statistics and Even Lore of the Dismal Science 24. Learning from the Big Booms 25. Yes, Virginia, There Will Be Recessions 26. Productivity Gains Help ◎ **4, 22, 24, 26**	**Government Spending**	5. Statistics and Even Lore of the Dismal Science 6. State of the Union 10. Economic Report of the President for 1998 11. Reflections on the Balancing Act 16. Should We Retire Social Security? ◎ **14, 15, 16, 17, 18**
Comparative Advantage	6. State of the Union 12. Tax Man Cometh 27. Calculating the Price 42. Changing Today's Consumption ◎ **2, 7, 9, 17, 23**	**High Technology Industries**	1. Meeting the Challenges 24. Learning from the Big Booms 25. Yes, Virginia, There Will Be Recessions 32. Could It Happen Again? ◎ **2, 6, 11, 12, 18, 21**
Economic Growth	1. Meeting the Challenges 8. How Fast Can the U.S. Economy Grow? 9. Hell No, We Won't Save! 13. Flat Tax 24. Learning from the Big Booms 25. Yes, Virginia, There Will Be Recessions 26. Productivity Gains Help 32. Could It Happen Again? 37. United States Is Not Ahead 42. Changing Today's Consumption ◎ **2, 7, 8, 9, 10, 13, 15, 23**	**Inflation**	8. How Fast Can the U.S. Economy Grow? 17. U.S. Monetary Policy 18. Central Banking in a Democracy 19. Is the Fed Slave to a Defunct Economist? 24. Learning from the Big Booms 26. Productivity Gains Help 27. Calculating the Price 32. Could It Happen Again? ◎ **9, 11, 12, 14, 15, 16, 18**
Economic Indicators	6. State of the Union 7. Economy You Can't See 17. U.S. Monetary Policy 27. Calculating the Price 29. Age-Adjusted Unemployment ◎ **2, 7, 8, 9, 10, 15, 18, 19**	**Interest Rates**	11. Reflections on the Balancing Act 17. U.S. Monetary Policy 18. Central Banking in a Democracy ◎ **19, 20, 21**
Economic Research	5. Statistics and Even Lore of the Dismal Science 6. State of the Union 12. Tax Man Cometh ◎ **6, 7, 8**	**International Trade and Finance**	6. State of the Union 30. Globalization and Its Discontents 31. Why Is Trade Good for You? 33. Will Fair Trade Diminish Free Trade? 34. Spotlight and the Bottom Line 35. NAFTA: How Is It Doing? 36. Trade Policy at a Cross Roads 37. United States Is Not Ahead 39. Russia Is Not Poland 40. Japan's Economic Plight 41. Other Crisis 42. Changing Today's Consumption ◎ **2, 27, 28, 29, 30, 31, 32, 33, 34, 36, 37**
European Union	37. United States Is Not Ahead 38. Euro: Who Wins? Who Loses? ◎ **27**		
Federal Deficit/Surplus	6. State of the Union 9. Hell No, We Won't Save! 11. Reflections on the Balancing Act	**Internet**	5. Statistics and Even Lore of the Dismal Science ◎ **11**

TOPIC AREA	TREATED IN	TOPIC AREA	TREATED IN
Keynesian Economics	2. Accidental Inventor 3. Economic Possibilities for Our Grandchildren 4. What in the World Happened to Economics? 10. Economic Report of the President for 1998 19. Is the Fed Slave to a Defunct Economist? ○ **1, 2, 4, 15**	**Russian Economy**	39. Russian Is Not Poland 41. Other Crisis ○ **28, 30, 36, 37**
		Say's Law	2. Accidental Inventor 4. What in the World Happened to Economics? ○ **1, 2, 4**
Less Developed Countries	34. Spotlight and the Bottom Line 41. Other Crisis 42. Changing Today's Consumption ○ **29, 31, 32, 33, 34**	**Social Security System**	16. Should We Retire Social Security? ○ **14, 15, 16, 17**
Monetary Policy	5. Statistics and Even Lore of the Dismal Science 8. How Fast Can the U.S. Economy Grow? 17. U.S. Monetary Policy 18. Central Banking in a Democracy 19. Is the Fed Slave to a Defunct Economist? 20. Should the Fed Care about Stock Bubbles? 21. Bank Mergers 23. Electronic Cash 24. Learning from the Big Booms 38. Euro: Who Wins? Who Loses? ○ **18, 19, 20, 21**	**Stock Market**	9. Hell No, We Won't Save! 20. Should the Fed Care about Stock Bubbles? 21. Bank Mergers 26. Productivity Gains Help ○ **5, 12**
		Taxation	5. Statistics and Even Lore of the Dismal Science 7. Economy You Can't See 12. Tax Man Cometh 13. Flat Tax 14. Why Are Taxes So Complicated? 15. Are Americans Really Overtaxed? 16. Should We Retire Social Security? ○ **14, 16, 17, 18**
New Economy View	1. Meeting the Challenges 8. How Fast Can the U.S. Economy Grow? 24. Learning from the Big Booms 26. Productivity Gains Help ○ **18, 19, 20, 21**	**Underground Economy**	6. State of the Union 7. Economy You Can't See ○ **1, 2, 4, 5, 9, 12**
Nonaccelerating-Inflation Rate of Unemployment (NAIRU)	10. Economic Report of the President for 1998 19. Is the Fed Slave to a Defunct Economist? 29. Age-Adjusted Unemployment ○ **23, 25, 26**	**Unemployment**	17. U.S. Monetary Policy 18. Central Banking in a Democracy 19. Is the Fed Slave to a Defunct Economist? 26. Productivity Gains Help 28. Overworked *and* Underemployed 29. Age-Adjusted Unemployment 37. United States Is Not Ahead in Everything That Matters ○ **25, 26**
North American Free Trade Agreement (NAFTA)	35. NAFTA: How Is It Doing? 36. Trade Policy at a Crossroads ○ **31**	**U.S. Income Distribution**	1. Meeting the Challenges 6. State of the Union 16. Should We Retire Social Security? 22. Stepchild of Banking 28. Overworked *and* Underemployed ○ **1, 2, 4, 5, 8, 10, 17**
Organization for Economic Cooperation and Development (OECD)	5. Statistics and Even Lore of the Dismal Science 42. Changing Today's Consumption ○ **32**	**World Trade Organization (WTO)**	30. Globalization and Its Discontents 33. Will Fair Trade Diminish Free Trade? 36. Trade Policy at a Cross Roads ○ **37**
Phillips Curve	4. What in the World Happened to Economics? 19. Is the Fed Slave to a Defunct Economist? 26. Productivity Gains Help ○ **1, 2, 4, 9**		
Protectionism	30. Globalization and Its Discontents 33. Will Fair Trade Diminish Free Trade? 35. NAFTA: How Is It Doing? 36. Trade Policy at a Cross Roads 41. Other Crisis ○ **27, 28, 29, 31, 36**		

AE: Macroeconomics

The following World Wide Web sites have been carefully researched and selected to support the articles found in this reader. If you are interested in learning more about specific topics found in this book, these Web sites are a good place to start. The sites are cross-referenced by number and appear in the topic guide on the previous two pages. Also, you can link to these Web sites through our DUSHKIN ONLINE support site at *http://www.dushkin.com/online/*.

The following sites were available at the time of publication. Visit our Web site—we update DUSHKIN ONLINE regularly to reflect any changes.

General Sites

1. AmosWorld
http://amos.bus.okstate.edu
Here is a premiere Internet site for instructional economic information whose main features include a glossary of over 500 economic terms and concepts, a reading room, and an interactive question-and-answer resource.

2. The Dismal Scientist
http://www.dismal.com
Often referred to as the "best free lunch on the Web," this is an excellent site with many interactive features. Provides access to economic data, briefings on the current state of the economy, and original articles on economic issues.

3. Fairmodel
http://fairmodel.econ.yale.edu
This site brings the power of large-scale macroeconomic analysis to anyone with access to the Internet.

4. MBA Lectures in Macroeconomics
http://www.stern.nyu.edu/~nroubini/LNOTES.HTM
Lectures in macroeconomics prepared by Professors Nouriel Roubini and David Backus of the Stern School of Business at New York University are available at this site.

5. The Mining Company
http://economics.miningco.com
This frequently updated source "mines the Net" for information on economic subjects. Major features include a very large number of Net Links.

6. Resources for Economists on the Internet
http://econwpa.wustl.edu/EconFAQ/EconFAQ.html
This resource of the WWW Virtual Library on Economics is an excellent starting place for any research in economics.

Measuring Economic Performance

7. Bureau of Economic Analysis
http://www.bea.doc.gov
Part of the U.S. Department of Commerce, the BEA is the nation's accountant. It issues the Survey of Current Business and is a good data source.

8. Bureau of Labor Statistics
http://stats.bls.gov
The home page of the BLS, an agency of the U.S. Department of Labor, offers Data, Economy at a Glance, Keyword Searches, Surveys and Programs, other statistical sites, and more.

9. Dr. Ed Yardeni's Economics Network
http://www.yardeni.com
Prepared by the Chief Economist of Deutsche Bank Securities, this site provides chartbooks and studies on such topics as economic indicators, public policy, and global trade.

10. Economic Statistics Briefing Room
http://www.whitehouse.gov/fsbr/esbr.html
This site has easy access to current federal economic indicators. It provides links to information from a large number of federal agencies.

11. Internet Public Library: Business and Economics Reference
http://ipl.org/ref/RR/static/bus0000.html
A comprehensive reference library on matters involving the production, distribution, and consumption of goods and services, this site includes many subtopics, including consumer issues and labor and work place.

12. New York Times Business Connections
http://www.nytimes.com/library/cyber/reference/busconn.html
This page of links to business and economics sites on the Web was prepared for use by journalists of the *New York Times* for their own research purposes. It includes links to such categories as markets, companies, business news, banking and finance, and government.

13. WebEc-WWW Resources in Economics
http://netec.wustl.edu/WebEc.html
A most complete virtual library of economics facts, figures, and ideas can be found here.

Fiscal Policy and the Federal Budget

14. Center on Budget and Policy Priorities
http://www.cbpp.org
The Center on Budget and Policy Priorities is a nonpartisan research organization and policy institute that conducts research and analysis on a range of government policies and programs, with an emphasis on those affecting low- and moderate-income people.

15. Economic Report of the President
http://www.whitehouse.gov/WH/EOP/CEA/html/CEA.html
This is the Web page of the Council of Economic Advisers. A copy of the latest *Economic Report of the President* is available here.

16. The Public Debt
http://www.publicdebt.treas.gov/opd/opd.htm
Here you will find links to The Public Debt of the United States to the Penny, Historical Debt, Interest Expense and the Public Debt, and Frequently Asked Questions.

17. Tax Wire
http://www.tax.org/TaxWire/taxwire.htm
Created by Tax Analysts, this site provides forums for discussion of a wide variety of tax ideas. It provides up-to-the-minute news on tax development.

Money, Banking, and Monetary Policy

18. Alan Greenspan's Tradeoff
http://www.pathfinder.com/fortune/1997/971208/fst5.html
This page from *Fortune* magazine leads to an extensive discussion of the Fed and its chairman, Alan Greenspan.

19. Federal Reserve Board
http://www.bog.frb.fed.us
This is the Web site of the Federal Reserve Board (the Fed), which governs the 12 Federal Reserve banking districts. The site includes links to all the Federal Reserve Banks and other federal agencies. It provides access to the Fed's Beige Book, a report published eight times each year on current economic conditions by the Federal Reserve district.

20. History of Money
http://www.ex.ac.uk/~RDavies/arian/llyfr.html
This award-winning site provides a comprehensive chronology of money from ancient times to the present day. It also includes articles on such topics as the Origins of Banking, Money in North American History, and Third World Debt.

21. Mark Bernkopf's Central Banks of the World: Central Banking Resources Center
http://patriot.net/~bernkopf
Interesting papers on electronic money and its effect on the banking world are available at this Web site.

Employment, Prices, and the Business Cycle

22. Business Cycle Indicators
http://www.globalexposure.com
This site leads to the 256 data series known as the U.S. Business Cycle Indicators, which are used to track and predict U. S. business activity.

23. What's a Dollar Worth? CPI Calculation Machine
http://minneapolisfed.org/economy/calc/cpihome.html
This interactive site demonstrates how the Consumer Price Index is used to calculate how prices have changed over the years. It includes CPI data from 1913 to 1998.

24. Economic Cycle Research Institute
http://www.businesscycle.com
The Economic Cycle Research Institute represents over 60 years of business cycle research covering all major market economies. The focus of its work is business cycle forecasting.

25. Employment Policy Foundation
http://www.epfnet.org
The EPF provides policymakers and the public with analysis and commentary on U. S. employment policies affecting businesses and their employees.

26. WorkIndex
http://workindex.com
This annotated guide to Internet resources in human resources, labor relations, benefits, training, technology, recruiting, leadership, and more is sponsored by the School of Industrial Relations at Cornell University.

International Economics

27. European Union in the U.S.
http://www.eurunion.org
This is a comprehensive Web site for the European Union. Topics include EU policies and legislation, information on member states, and EU-US relations. Online access to *Europe Magazine* is also provided.

28. Institute for International Economics
http://www.iie.com
The site of this nonprofit, nonpartisan research institution is devoted to the study of international economic policy, contains news, views, reviews, working papers, publications, and press releases, plus links to related sites.

29. Inter-American Development Bank
http://www.iadb.org
The Inter-American Development Bank was established in 1959 to help accelerate economic and social development in Latin America and the Caribbean. This site offers access to IDB reports and information on member countries.

30. International Monetary Fund (IMF)
http://www.imf.org
The IMF is a cooperative institution involving 182 countries that consult each other "for the purpose of maintaining a stable system of buying and selling their currencies."

31. North American Free Trade Association (NAFTA)
http://www.itaiep.doc.gov/nafta/nafta2.htm
This is the home page of the North American Free Trade Association. NAFTA's stated objective is "to provide accurate and timely information to U. S. exporters experiencing market access barriers in Canada or Mexico."

32. Organization for Economic Cooperation and Development (OECD)
http://www.oecd.org
This Web site of OECD provides information on OECD activities, news, documentation, and related links. One interesting feature is a link to the Centre for Cooperation with Nonmembers.

33. Sustainable Development Organization
http://www.sustainabledevelopment.org
This site provides a resource center for investigating issues of sustainable development. Extensive links lead to such sustainable development categories as agriculture, energy, environment, finance, health, microenterprise, public policy, and technologies.

34. UNCTAD
http://www.unctad.org
The main task of the United Nations Conference on Trade and Development (UNCTAD) is to accelerate economic growth and development, particularly that of the least developed countries (LDCs).

35. WORLDLINK Glossary and Acronyms
http://www.worldlinkinternational.com/gloss.htm
This WORLDLINK glossary includes definitions of many terms and acronyms encountered in international trade and finance, which has developed its own distinctive vocabulary.

36. World Policy Institute
http://www.worldpolicy.org
The WPI publishes an online version of the *World Policy Journal*, which focuses on core policy issues, with an emphasis on international economic affairs and the requirements for a civil society.

37. World Trade Organization (WTO)
http://www.wto.org
The WTO facilitates the working of the multilateral trading system. It negotiates agreements among trading nations that guarantee member countries important trade rights.

We highly recommend that you review our Web site for expanded information and our other product lines. We are continually updating and adding links to our Web site in order to offer you the most usable and useful information that will support and expand the value of your Annual Editions. You can reach us at:
http://www.dushkin.com/annualeditions/.

Unit 1

Unit Selections

1. **Meeting the Challenge of the New Economy,** Michael J. Mandel
2. **The Accidental Inventor of Today's Capitalism,** Louis Uchitelle
3. **Economic Possibilities for Our Grandchildren,** Elizabeth Johnson and Donald Moggridge (eds.)
4. **What in the World Happened to Economics?** Justin Fox
5. **Statistics and Even Lore of the Dismal Science,** David Cay Johnston

Key Points to Consider

❖ What is meant by the "New Economy?" How should America confront the macroeconomic challenges of the twenty-first century?

❖ Is Say's Law relevant to the present? Do you agree with John Maynard Keynes's forecast of economic life in the year 2030? Why or why not?

❖ How does one use the Internet for the purpose of learning about macroeconomic issues?

 **Links**   www.dushkin.com/online/

1. **AmosWorld**
   http://amos.bus.okstate.edu
2. **The Dismal Scientist**
   http://www.dismal.com
3. **Fairmodel**
   http://fairmodel.econ.yale.edu
4. **MBA Lectures in Macroeconomics**
   http://www.stern.nyu.edu/~nroubini/LNOTES.HTM
5. **The Mining Company**
   http://economics.miningco.com
6. **Resources for Economists on the Internet**
   http://econwpa.wustl.edu/EconFAQ/EconFAQ.html

These sites are annotated on pages 4 and 5.

Introduction to Macroeconomics

Economics is a science of thinking in terms of models joined to the art of choosing models which are relevant to the contemporary world. —John Maynard Keynes

This reader is about the ways in which economists think about economic problems and the advice they give to those who make economic policy. Its focus is on macroeconomics, the branch of economics that provides an overview of the ways in which an economy's major components—households, businesses, and governments—are related. Topics of investigation include such large, economy-wide variables as national output, the extent of unemployment, the general level of prices, and the rate of economic growth. Also considered are ways in which government policies might be used to promote various national goals, including high levels of employment, price stability, and an adequate expansion of output over time.

If you are a newcomer to the study of economics, you may be confused and dismayed by what you hear economists say about economic problems and policies. Someone once summed this up with the observation that "if all economists were laid end-to-end, they would never reach a conclusion." Outside observers want agreement on economic issues, and they are often discontent when they find that deep divisions exist within the economics profession. Why can't economists agree? they ask. The simplest answer is that economists, like other human beings, often have strongly held political and social beliefs. Professional quarrels are not primarily over scientific issues—in fact, most economists use the same scientific language in their debates. Rather, the disagreements among economists frequently reflect fundamental differences in value systems. This is particularly true where macroeconomics is concerned.

This is an exciting time to begin a study of economics. The last few decades have witnessed major changes in both the U.S. and the global economy. As they look back on this period of turbulence, today's economists—perhaps reflecting a more pragmatic, less ideological position—are asking: What have we learned from this experience that will guide us in understanding what needs to be done at the dawn of a new century? Like bruised combatants after a lengthy battle, they may be somewhat more tolerant of opposing views.

The U.S. economy has done far better in recent years than anyone ever predicted. More than 7 years of strong economic growth with little unemployment and low inflation have led many economists to ask: How did this happen, and is such performance sustainable? A handful of economists (including Michael Mandel, author of the first article in this unit) trace this development to the emergence of a "New Economy." In such an economy those nations which stay ahead of the wave of technological innovation and remain competitive in the global economy will succeed in the twenty-first century. Mandel considers what the United States must do to remain among this group of countries.

In the next article, Louis Uchitelle assesses the role played by the nineteenth century French historian, Jean-Baptiste Say, in the history of macroeconomics. Inventor of a law bearing his name, Say provided the theoretical foundation for the view that economies were self-regulating and without need of government intervention. Say's Law served as an explanation of macroeconomic performance until the early 1930s, when—during the Great Depression—the British economist John Maynard Keynes challenged the Saysian view. Keynes's ideas dominated economic thought through the early 1980s, as a "mixed economy" became the standard—part free market, part government intervention. Since then, however, Say's Law has reasserted itself.

The unit continues with "Economic Possibilities for Our Grandchildren," an essay written by Keynes in 1930, which offers a fascinating perspective on the future. Keynes's comment that "we are suffering now from a bad attack of economic pessimism" seems prophetic, given the Great Depression and the economic difficulties of subsequent decades. Yet, Keynes urges us to take a longer view, and he offers some much-needed hope. In 100 years he foresees the demise of the economic problem as we presently understand it. Instead, Keynes contends, filling leisure time in a meaningful way will prove to be our grandchildren's chief concern.

Next, in "What in the World Happened to Economics?" Justin Fox traces some recent developments in macroeconomic thinking. Economics is a subject rich in controversy. Although most economists speak the same language, disagreements frequently occur, and these more often than not involve explaining the behavior of the global economy. In fact, as Fox observes, most economists no longer seem to believe there is a single correct explanation.

The unit concludes with an article about economics and the Internet, the fastest growing repository of information in history. David Cay Johnston shows how, with a personal computer and a modem, you can put the Internet to work for you as you begin your study of macroeconomics. You will notice that listed throughout this anthology are a large number of Internet addresses which pertain to subjects discussed in the readings. Using them will greatly enhance your understanding of these issues.

Article 1

MEETING THE CHALLENGE OF THE NEW ECONOMY

BY MICHAEL J. MANDEL

It is the dawn of a new era. Technology is opening the doors for a prodigious burst of national creativity, as new industries spring up seemingly overnight. Global trade is pouring a flood of ideas and commerce across national boundaries, helping to spur innovation. Companies are restructuring themselves—laying off some workers, while giving others much greater responsibility. American manufacturers, left for dead in the 1980's, are roaring back to life with new ways of working and new technologies. Inflation, once out of control, is now dormant.

This transformation has profound implications—for the economy, for policy, for politics. Some skeptics maintain that all is the same. But with each passing day, it becomes harder to ignore the signs that something very real has changed. The New Economy has been born—and it is transforming America and much of the world at a pace that is scarcely imaginable.

The twin motive forces of this New Economy are technological innovation and globalization. The Information Revolution is transforming virtually every sector of the economy. And the U.S. economy's openness to the free flows of trade, money, and ideas has reinforced the country's position as the financial and economic capital of the world.

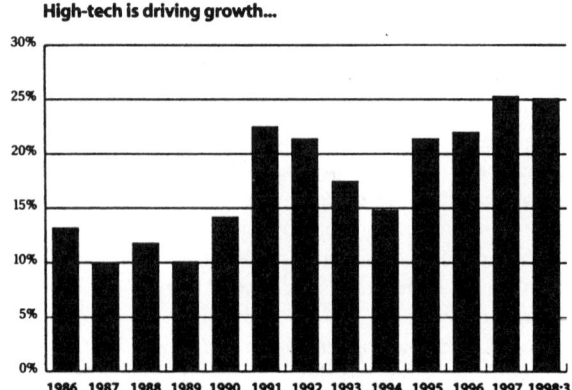

High-tech is driving growth...

Share of growth coming from high-tech sector over previous 12 years*

*Fourth quarter to fourth quarter, except for 1998. High-tech spending primarily includes business and consumer spending on information technology hardware and consumer spending on telephone service, adjusted for exports and imports of information technology equipment.

Data: Commerce Department and author calculations

Michael J. Mandel is economics editor at Business Week, where he won the 1998 Loeb Award for his coverage of the New Economy. Mandel holds a Ph.D. in economics from Harvard University.

1. Meeting the Challenge of the New Economy

...patent activity is rising...

Utility patents of U.S origin, three-year average

Data: U.S. Patent and Trademark Office

The New Economy is not simply an abstraction—it touches every person, from every walk of life. It is the 70-year-old who can walk because of an artificial knee made out of high-tech materials. It is the network technician who becomes the first community college graduate from a poor immigrant family. It is the worker at the small steel company that employs sophisticated technology to deliver better steel faster. It is the parent who uses e-mail and fax machines to work from home.

And not the least, the New Economy is vibrant and vital. Since 1994—roughly coinciding with the arrival of the Internet on the scene—the U.S. economy has performed better than expected on virtually every measure. Since 1994, the economy has grown at a 3.3 percent rate, a full percentage point above what most forecasters expected. Both unemployment and inflation have fallen, while real wage growth has accelerated. The statistics tell only the beginning of the promise the New Economy holds to improve the lives of the American people.

Yet if we are to seize the promise, Americans—and America—must rethink some old assumptions and meet three big challenges posed by the New Economy:

Growth

The first challenge is to put in place policies that can keep U.S. growth strong over the long run, not just for a few years. There are far too many examples of countries once regarded as paragons of economic virtue, such as Japan in the 1980's, that were brought crashing to the ground by complacency and bad decisions. We must pay attention to the basics: establishing sound macroeconomic policies and encouraging technological innovation.

As this decade began, many economists accepted as gospel the proposition that, after two decades of stagnation, America would never again be a fast-growth economy. The consensus—held by virtually all respectable forecasters—was that the United States could at best eke out two percent or 2.5 percent annual growth for the foreseeable future. Anything more was wishful thinking.

This assumption of slow growth, found in virtually every government economic projection, dictated the terms of the ongoing policy and political debates. Under this conventional view, living standards were expected to rise very slowly—if at all. One example: As of the middle of 1998, Standard & Poor's DRI, a leading economic forecasting firm, was predicting that real wages would rise by a grand total of two percent over the next 10 years (based on a forecast of 2.3 percent annual growth).

This slow-growth world would have been one in which the United States would be doomed to watch younger, more vibrant economies catch up and surpass it. It would be a gray, bleak place, very different from the country's first 200 years. No wonder Americans felt despondent about their future and the future of their children.

But, while no one wants to start a premature celebration, the U.S. economy has surprised the pessimists in recent years. The strength and energy of the New Economy are directly reflected in faster growth and lower rates of inflation. What's more, this powerful performance may turn out to be more than simply a short-run phenomenon. With a combination of good luck and good policy, the United States could be in the early stages of a long period of strong growth, with annual growth of three percent or more well within reach—at least a half percentage point higher than current projections.

Such growth, if sustained, would rewrite the political and economic rule book. Rather than watching stagnation, Americans would see real wages and living standards rise for themselves and for their children. Faster growth would also mean more resources available for crucial investments in education and training. And a bigger economy would mean that the problems of financing Social Security and the retire-

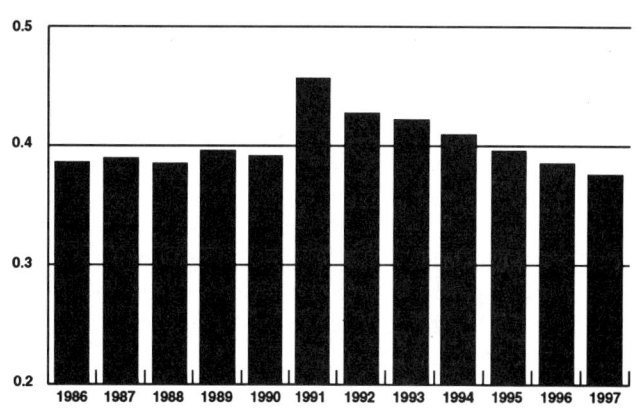

...but basic research is not keeping up.

Public and private basic research spending as share of GDP*

Survey methodology changed in 1991
Data: National Science Foundation

1 ❖ INTRODUCTION TO MACROECONOMICS

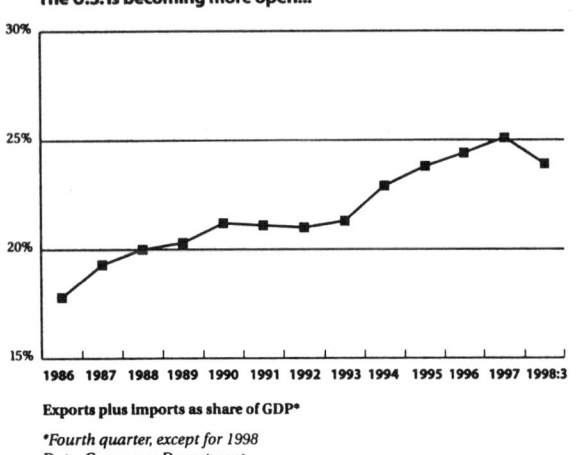

The U.S. is becoming more open...

Exports plus imports as share of GDP*

*Fourth quarter, except for 1998
Data: Commerce Department

ment of the baby boomers would become much easier to solve.

To be sure, it is important to remember that even a resurgent New Economy will not mean an end to recession and other economic ills. History shows that periods of fast growth have never been immune to downturns. Quite the contrary: The forces propelling growth—technological innovation and globalization—may well add to economic and financial volatility. To put it another way, high returns bring high risks.

Many economists have a more fundamental problem with the New Economy: They simply are not convinced that it even exists. From their offices in Wall Street firms, universities, or government buildings, these skeptics see no persuasive evidence that much has changed in the 1990's.

Yet the transformation in the economy should be obvious for all to see. Most striking are the changes wrought by the Information Revolution, which affects how we work, how we shop, how we play. It is especially amazing just how quickly the Internet—with its e-mail and its websites—has been incorporated into the daily thread of our lives, given that few had heard of it four years ago.

History suggests that it is exactly this sort of pervasive technological innovation that propels long-run growth. Look back a hundred years. Starting in the 1890's, the United States moved into a 70-year period of innovation-driven growth that saw living standards and incomes lifted by a series of breakthroughs, including electricity, the automobile, television, and jet travel. From the 1890's to the 1960's, real per capita income quadrupled and life expectancy soared, from under 45 years to about 70 years. The very texture of American life changed.

On the other hand, the slowdown of the 1970's and 1980's can be traced directly to a lack of economically useful technological innovations. Indeed, according to calculations by the Bureau of Labor Statistics, technological change contributed almost nothing to growth in those two decades.

But the 1990's have seen a revival of technological innovation. In part, this has manifested itself in the explosion of the information technology industry. Over the last three years, high-technology alone has accounted for fully 25 percent of growth and added about 0.7 percentage points to the overall growth rate.

In particular, biotechnology seems to be finally coming of age. The first successful gene-splicing experiment was done in 1973, but it is only now that large numbers of commercial products are finally coming on the market. Indeed, biotech is in part riding on the shoulders of the Information Revolution. Fast computers make possible much of the sophisticated techniques underlying biotechnology, including the sequencing of the human genome.

Conversely, biotech will be an essential complement to information technology in boosting growth. Advances in computers and communications directly affect industries that move and process information, such as finance, media, and entertainment. Together these make up about one quarter of the economy. Biotech, by contrast, will transform industries such as health care and agriculture, an additional 15 percent of the economy. So just as the growth surge of the early 20th century was fueled by whole clusters of innovations—not just one—so will the New Economy be propelled by more than one major technology.

If strong economic growth is to be part of American life in the New Economy, we must continue to spur and power innovation. That is why it is so worrisome that public and private spending on basic research—which provides the foundation for future innovations—has not kept up in the 1990's with the growth of the economy (*see chart*, "... but basic research is not keeping up."). Our first challenge must be to turn that trend around.

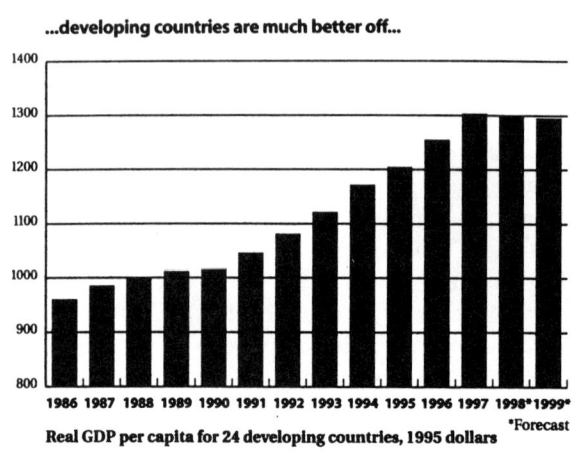

...developing countries are much better off...

Real GDP per capita for 24 developing countries, 1995 dollars
*Forecast
Data: Standard and Poor's DRI

...but Asia is heading downwards.

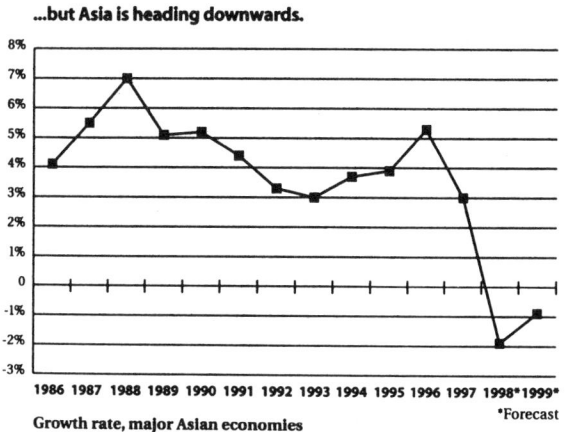

Growth rate, major Asian economies
*Forecast
Data: Standard & Poor's DRI

1. Meeting the Challenge of the New Economy

Globalization

Along with fostering economic growth at home, the United States faces the challenge of helping continue the growth of the world economy. That means reforming the global financial system to lessen the chance of a crisis like the Asian meltdown. It also means supporting pro-growth policies in developing countries and working to ensure that free trade policies are continued around the globe.

For along with technological transformation, the indisputable change in the New Economy is the United States' integration into the global economy. Since the mid 1980's, exports plus imports, as a share of the gross domestic product, have risen from 18 percent to 24 percent. Many U.S. companies now get a substantial portion of their profits from overseas. And even though exports have dropped because of the troubles overseas, they are still almost double what they were at the beginning of the 1990's.

Yet the rule of globalization in the New Economy is more subtle and elusive than the impact of technology. The trade deficit does not go away in the New Economy. Indeed, in recent years, the direct effect of foreign trade on growth has been negative, as the trade deficit has widened to historic proportions. Over the last three years, foreign trade has cut almost a half a percentage point off growth, as strong growth in the United States has kept demand high for imported consumer goods and capital equipment. Meanwhile, the depressed Asian economies are buying fewer U.S. exports.

But these narrow numbers—though easily seized upon by the opponents of trade—are misleading. For the growth numbers do not capture the impact of trade in driving the innovation and cost-cutting that have been so important in America's recent economic success. The benefits of openness come through other channels. For one, increased globalization accelerates the rate at which innovations are made and brought to market. Facing intense foreign competition, U.S. corporations are being forced to actively embrace change. In the past, many large companies intentionally slowed down the introduction of new products and innovations in order to milk additional profits from existing products. This approach worked for companies that dominated the U.S. market. Today, however, such a strategy would be suicide.

That's the stick of globalization—but there's a carrot as well. With global markets growing ever bigger, a company that innovates successfully can reap enormous rewards. Despite the fall in Asia, real incomes in developing countries are still 50 percent higher than they were 15 years ago. As a result, U.S. companies have a far greater incentive to look for breakthroughs that can win them a profitable share of these markets.

Technology companies, in particular, thrive on large markets—the larger the better. The R&D required to create a computer chip or an airplane is enormous. The bigger the potential market is, the greater the incentive is to innovate and the more likely it is that the research will be undertaken.

And last but not least, the flow of inexpensive imports has played a major role in holding down inflation. This is, of course, a mixed blessing, as the latest

```
Global trade is
pouring a flood
of ideas and
commerce across
national boundaries
helping to spur
innovation.
```

surge of imports has eroded U.S. manufacturing jobs. Nevertheless, falling prices for things such as cars and clothing have benefitted many Americans.

Helping Americans Succeed in the New Economy

The third big challenge we face is helping Americans adjust to the rapid pace of change in the New Economy. Technological change and globalization boost growth, but they do so at the cost of creating enormous upheaval in the labor markets. In the first 10 months of 1998, for example, American companies

1 ❖ INTRODUCTION TO MACROECONOMICS

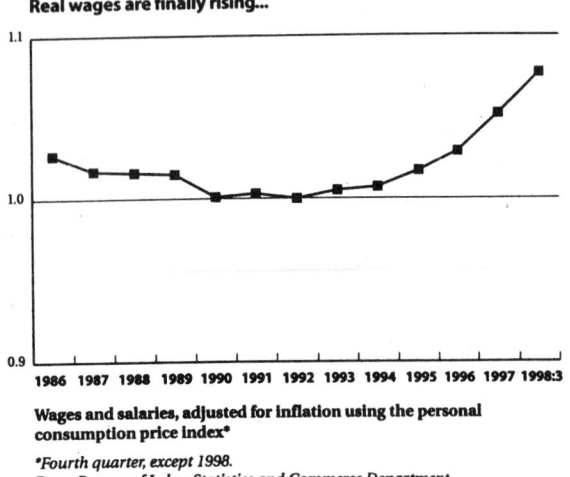

Real wages are finally rising...

Wages and salaries, adjusted for inflation using the personal consumption price index*

*Fourth quarter, except 1998.
Data: Bureau of Labor Statistics and Commerce Department

announced plans to eliminate 523,000 jobs, 60 percent above the pace of the previous year. Yet during those same 10 months, 2.2 million new jobs were created overall—an example of the pluses and minuses of the New Economy.

Indeed, there is little doubt that the New Economy, if it continues, will substantially ease some of the problems that have dogged the U.S. economy for the last two decades. The most obvious gain is on the wage side: Since the last recession ended in March 1991, real wages have risen at an annual rate of 1 percent. In the expansion of the 1980's, by comparison,

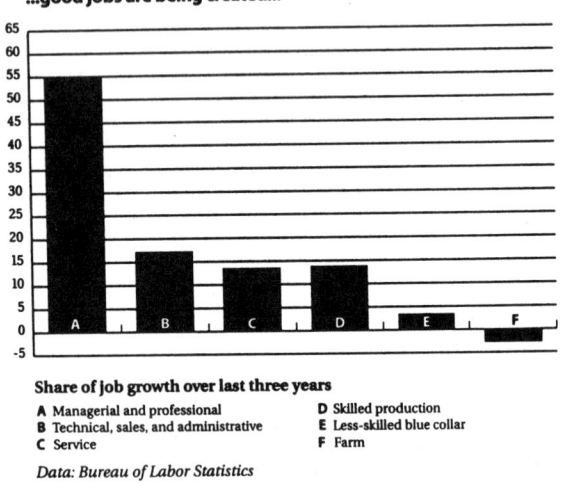

...good jobs are being created...

Share of job growth over last three years
A Managerial and professional
B Technical, sales, and administrative
C Service
D Skilled production
E Less-skilled blue collar
F Farm

Data: Bureau of Labor Statistics

real wages rose at a rate of only 0.2 percent—a big difference. Incomes are rising for everyone. The government's numbers show a sharp increase in real hourly wages for production and non-supervisory workers over the last two years, helped partly by an increase in the minimum wage. The benefits are especially apparent for young people graduating from college, who are coming into a world of soaring salaries rather than dim prospects many had expected.

But the New Economy is widening the income gap by rewarding people with higher levels of education and skills. The share of personal income going to the top 5 percent of households is still rising and is now almost 22 percent, as earnings for the best jobs and for the best educated workers continues to go up faster than for the rest of the population. Over the last year, wages and salaries for managers and executives have increased by 5.2 percent, compared to four percent for the rest of the population. Moreover, the top-tier workers are more likely to have stock options or money invested in the stock market, which means that they have reaped the gains of the stock market's rise.

The U.S. cannot accept an economy divided between education haves and have-nots. Nor can workers expect a return to job stability, with corporations more willing than ever to reorganize their operations. What's needed are policies that will give all Americans the tools to find upward mobility at every stage of their lives. What's more, today's unemployment insurance safety "net" needs to be replaced with a system that will help Americans get the skills and security they need as they hop from job to job.

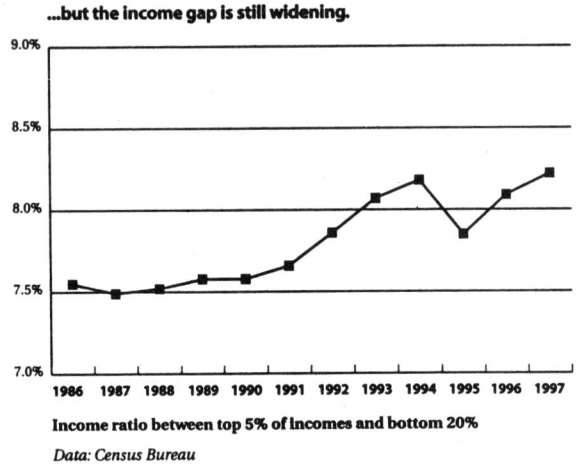

...but the income gap is still widening.

Income ratio between top 5% of incomes and bottom 20%
Data: Census Bureau

Perhaps the hardest task is balancing hope with realism. The U.S. economy was so sluggish for so long that many people accepted that as the norm. Now it's hard for them to realize that strong growth is possible again. But it's equally dangerous to go to the other extreme and believe that the New Economy is a panacea. The New Economy can be a time of great progress and prosperity for the American people. But it will only be so if we address the challenges it presents. That will be the major task ahead of us in the 21st century.

The Accidental Inventor of Today's Capitalism

Jean-Baptiste Say, No Longer a Villain, Stands Guard Over Free Markets

By LOUIS UCHITELLE

He came of age in the French Revolution. In the spirit of the times, he greatly admired Benjamin Franklin and Thomas Jefferson. And when the Bourbons managed to get their throne back in 1814, a discouraged Jean-Baptiste Say almost emigrated to America. He even wrote to Jefferson, asking how much he would have to pay to purchase a working cotton farm near Jefferson's own Virginia spread.

"I specify the neighborhood of Charlottesville," Say wrote from his home in Paris, "because it is neither so close to the seaports to make the land too expensive, nor so distant as to present the rigors of a new settlement."

The Say family—there were five children—never came to America. Say considered himself too old, at 47, to go through such a stressful relocation. (Jefferson agreed.) But the economic theory he popularized in a French best seller eventually made the journey. And today a pithy "law of markets" that bears Say's name has become American capitalism's guiding aphorism. It stands as a warning against undue tinkering with markets, even when they are out of whack, as they are now, in Asia, in a particularly Saysian way.

What is arguably the most famous "law" in economics is just five words: "Supply creates its own demand." Build a field and the players will come. Manufacture 10 cars and the buyers will materialize. That is how markets work. Just leave them alone, let them be free, and demand will automatically meet supply at a robust level. The people who make the 10 cars, or supply the metal and parts that go into the cars, earn from their efforts the income to then buy the cars.

Say certainly believed this. So did most of the other great thinkers in the early days of the Industrial Revolution, before recessions and slumps had been recognized as the downside of capitalism or had entered very much into anyone's thinking. In the opening sentence of "The Wealth of Nations," Adam Smith, the father of free market capitalism, laid down virtually the same "law" as Say—although taking 48 words to make the point.

Say, who died in 1832 at age 65, is one of the stranger figures in economic history. He never actually wrote "supply creates its own demand." His best seller, the "Treatise on Political Economy," published in 1803—seven years after Smith's great work—is full of the concept, but not the famous five words.

"I do not see how the products of a nation in general can ever be too abundant, for each such product (through payment of wages, profits, etc.) provides the means for purchasing another," Say wrote. "The mass of products composes the mass of a nation's wealth, and wealth is no more inconvenient to nations than it is to private persons."

A century after the Frenchman's death, John Maynard Keynes attributed Say's law to Say, and made him famous. It was the Great Depression of the 1930's, and free market concepts were ripe for attack. Supply certainly was not creating its own demand. There was supply, but no buyers. And Keynes singled out Say, making him the foil for his own view of how markets work and the role government should play in keeping markets on track. Keynes was successful, but in making his case, he may have cut a corner or two, perhaps editing Say to suit his needs.

"Before Keynes, the way I would have heard about Say is not that supply creates its own demand but that overproduction is not possible," Paul Samuelson, the Nobel laureate in economics, said in an interview. He was a graduate student in 1936, the year that Keynes published his most famous work, "The General Theory of Employment, Interest and Money," the book that elevated Jean-Baptiste Say to star villain status.

Mark Blaug, a British economist, agreed. "Say seems to us a tremendously important figure, but it is a case in which Keynes really elevated him," Mr. Blaug said. "What he was was a very good teacher of Adam Smith to French readers. In the 19th century, the French learned their Smith by reading Say. He was mainly a popularizer."

In Reality, a Model of Flexibility

The irony is that of all the early 19th-century thinkers, Say was perhaps the most flexible. David Ricardo and James Mill were more dogmatic in their adherence to what is now known as Say's law of markets. And when Thomas Malthus objected to that law, Ricardo took him on far more than did Say, who could see two sides of an argument.

"If in a society composed of 10,000 families," Say wrote, "5,000 engaged in making crockery vases, and 5,000 in making shoes, this society would undoubtedly have too many vases and too many shoes, and would lack many things no less favorable to its well being. But it is also evident that this inconvenience would arise not from producing too much, but from not producing exactly what is wanted."

Say thought such distortions could occur, but not for long, not when people lack so much of everything. "I live at this moment in one of the richest regions of France," he wrote. "Yet of 20 houses there are 19 in which, on entering them, I see none but the coarsest food, nothing to serve the well being of families, none of the things that the English call comfortable; not enough beds for all members of the family to lie on, not enough furniture for them to sit at ease at their meals; not enough linen, nor of soap, for proper laundering, etc."

Malthus, the gloomiest thinker of his generation, is a pivotal figure in economic history, a sort of early Keynesian. He is most famous for his prediction that the demand for food would outrun the supply. He also argued that the supply of goods could outrun the demand for them, resulting in unemployment among the suppliers. Say eventually found some merit in Malthus's argument, and that angered Ricardo.

"The aphorism attributed to Say probably evolved over the decades after Say's lifetime," William Baumol, a Princeton economist and historian, said. "There is no one villain. But what is becoming increasingly clear to people who write about the history of ideas is that Keynes overstated what Say thought. Say in some sense is a victim of history."

Whatever the case, Ricardo won the great debate with Malthus. But nearly 200 years later, nothing is resolved. The central issue in economics is still this question: Will supply and demand balance on their own at a high enough level to put everyone to work? Or can the balance come at a much lower level, requiring government to step in with job-creating measures?

The 20th century opened with the Saysians in the great majority. From the early 1930's to the early 1980's, Malthus and Keynes, his spiritual descendant, held sway. A "mixed economy" became the standard—part free market, part government intervention. Since then, however, Say's law has reasserted itself. Ricardo's initial victory is reflected today in deregulation, in the privatization of state enterprises, in the expanding global market and, most recently, in the commentary on the Asian crisis.

The Asian collapse is a result of too much government meddling, modern Saysians argue. The Korean Government, for example, pushed companies to borrow when they should not have borrowed and to manufacture too many cars, semiconductors, steel products and other things when there was no ready market for them. The markets, left to themselves, would have balanced supply and demand at a healthy level and Asia would not be in crisis today, the Saysians hold.

"If business people persist in producing the wrong things, for whatever reason, then you can have a situation where they cannot sell what they make," said Deirdre N. McCloskey, an economic historian at the University of Iowa.

Adjustments Made by Keynes

Still, Keynes made a permanent dent in Saysian thinking. The argument evolved in this fashion:

Supply does create its own demand, as Say maintained, but under limited circumstances. When a farmer comes to market with a basket of eggs, a weaver with a bolt of cloth and a potter with a vase, each is offering his own "income" for sale to the others, in exchange for their incomes. Supply and income are interchangeable, and there cannot be too much supply, because the supply always generates the income to purchase it.

"For professional economists, there is this marvelous appeal of the nicely working model, the clockwork economy in which everything matches everything else," said Robert M. Solow, a Nobel laureate in economics. "If you believe in Say's law, then you can believe that there is no need for public policy, for a government role in the economy. Just stay out of the market's way."

The Saysian model assumes, however, that people accumulate income with the intention of spending it right away, if not on consumer goods, then on investment in a new loom, for instance, or a new factory—another form of spending, financed through savings. There are other built-in assumptions. Lacking a role of its own, money is mainly a reflection of the value of goods and services. And interest rates adjust to the needs of the marketplace with its automatic matching of supply and demand.

Keynes changed the assumptions. Money, he argued, does have a role, and spending isn't automatic. When people become uncertain, or panicky, they keep their money, their incomes, in their pockets. And investors hold back when they don't anticipate an adequate return on their investments, even if savings are plentiful and interest rates low. Indeed, investment is independent of savings, in Keynes's view, coming first and generating income and savings in its wake.

What if Spenders Don't Spend?

Supply, in any case, exceeds demand when spenders hold back. Prices can drop to offset this reluctance, and supply and demand can once again move into equilibrium. But if prices get so low that they wipe out profits and fail to cover costs, the new equilibrium will foster layoffs, cost-cutting, bankruptcy and unemployment.

Out of this thinking came a role for government. The Federal Reserve's periodic adjustments of the nation's interest rates are a now standardized meddling in the marketplace with the stated intention of promoting full employment, among other goals. And for all the cutbacks in welfare and other public programs, the Federal Government, not the marketplace, is still entrenched as the provider of unemployment pay for the jobless, numerous subsidies for business, and health insurance for the poor and elderly.

Say would have been surprised. Government had become an obstacle for him. While he welcomed the French Revolution and the new freedom it brought, Napoleon was trouble. The two men differed on taxes and tariffs, both of which Napoleon imposed, and on trade, which Napoleon restricted over Say's objections. When Say's famous "Treatise on Political Economy" appeared, Napoleon suppressed it for a while.

The return of Louis XVIII to the throne, after Napoleon's defeat, seemed to promise more government meddling, and a discouraged Say thought of emigration to America. "I would rather live in a free country," he wrote to Jefferson, "and can hardly flatter myself that this country will ever become such."

Economic Possibilities for Our Grandchildren*

John Maynard Keynes

We are suffering just now from a bad attack of economic pessimism. It is common to hear people say that the epoch of enormous economic progress which characterised the nineteenth century is over; that the rapid improvement in the standard of life is now going to slow down—at any rate in Great Britain; that a decline in prosperity is more likely than an improvement in the decade which lies ahead of us. . . .

My purpose in this essay, however, is not to examine the present or the near future, but to disembarrass myself of short views and take wings into the future. What can we reasonably expect the level of our economic life to be a hundred years hence? What are the economic possibilities for our grandchildren?

From the earliest times of which we have record—back, say, to two thousand years before Christ—down to the beginning of the eighteenth century, there was no very great change in the standard of life of the average man living in the civilised centres of the earth. Ups and downs certainly. Visitations of plague, famine, and war. Golden intervals. But no progressive, violent change. Some periods perhaps 50 per cent better than others—at the utmost 100 per cent better—in the four thousand years which ended (say) in A.D. 1700.

This slow rate of progress, or lack of progress, was due to two reasons—to the remarkable absence of important technical improvements and to the failure of capital to accumulate. . . .

For the moment the very rapidity of these changes is hurting us and bringing difficult problems to solve. Those countries are suffering relatively which are not in the vanguard of progress. We are being afflicted with a new disease of which some readers may not yet have heard the name, but of which they will hear a great deal in the years to come—namely, *technological unemployment.* This means unemployment due to our discovery of means of economising the use of labour outrunning the pace at which we can find new uses for labour.

But this is only a temporary phase of maladjustment. All this means in the long run *that mankind is solving its economic problem.* I would predict that the standard of life in progressive countries one hundred years hence will be between four and eight times as high as it is to-day. There would be nothing surprising in this even in the light of our

From *Collected Writings of John Maynard Keynes,* Vol. 9, 1978, *Essays in Persuasion,* edited by Elizabeth Johnson and Donald Moggridge. © 1978 by John Maynard Keynes. Reprinted by permission of Cambridge University Press.

3. Economic Possibilities

present knowledge. It would not be foolish to contemplate the possibility of a far greater progress still. . . .

Now it is true that the needs of human beings may seem to be insatiable. But they fall into two classes—those needs which are absolute in the sense that we feel them whatever the situation of our fellow human beings may be, and those which are relative in the sense that we feel them only if their satisfaction lifts us above, makes us feel superior to, our fellows. Needs of the second class, those which satisfy the desire for superiority, may indeed be insatiable; for the higher the general level, the higher still are they. But this is not so true of the absolute needs—a point may soon be reached, much sooner perhaps than we are all of us aware of, when these needs are satisfied in the sense that we prefer to devote our further energies to non-economic purposes.

Now for my conclusion, which you will find, I think, to become more and more startling to the imagination the longer you think about it.

I draw the conclusion that, assuming no important wars and no important increase in population, the *economic problem* may be solved, or be at least within sight of solution, within a hundred years. This means that the economic problem is not—if we look into the future—*the permanent problem of the human race*.

Why, you may ask, is this so startling? It is startling because—if, instead of looking into the future, we look into the past—we find that the economic problem, the struggle for subsistence, always has been hitherto the primary, most pressing problem of the human race—not only of the human race, but of the whole of the biological kingdom from the beginnings of life in its most primitive forms.

Thus we have been expressly evolved by nature—with all our impulses and deepest instincts—for the purpose of solving the economic problem. If the economic problem is solved, mankind will be deprived of its traditional purpose.

Will this be a benefit? If one believes at all in the real values of life, the prospect at least opens up the possibility of benefit. Yet I think with dread of the readjustment of the habits and instincts of the ordinary man, bred into him for countless generations, which he may be asked to discard within a few decades.

To use the language of to-day—must we not expect a general "nervous breakdown"? We already have a little experience of what I mean—a nervous breakdown of the sort which is already common enough in England and the United States amongst the wives of the well-to-do classes, unfortunate women, many of them, who have been deprived by their wealth of their traditional tasks and occupations— who cannot find it sufficiently amusing, when deprived of the spur of economic necessity, to cook and clean and mend, yet are quite unable to find anything more amusing.

To those who sweat for their daily bread leisure is a longed-for sweet—until they get it.

There is the traditional epitaph written for herself by the old charwoman:—

Don't mourn for me, friends, don't weep for me never,
For I'm going to do nothing for ever and ever.

This was her heaven. Like others who look forward to leisure, she conceived how nice it would be to spend her time listening-in—for there was another couplet which occurred in her poem:—

With psalms and sweet music the heavens'll be ringing,
But I shall have nothing to do with the singing.

Yet it will only be for those who have to do with the singing that life will be tolerable—and how few of us can sing!

Thus for the first time since his creation man will be faced with his real, his permanent problem—how to use his freedom from pressing economic cares, how to occupy the leisure, which science and compound interest will have won for him, to live wisely and agreeably and well.

The strenuous purposeful money-makers may carry all of us along with them into the lap of economic abundance. But it will be those peoples, who can keep alive, and cultivate into a fuller perfection, the art of life itself and do not sell themselves for the means of life, who will be able to enjoy the abundance when it comes.

Yet there is no country and no people, I think, who can look forward to the age of leisure and of abundance without a dread. For we have been trained too long to strive and not to enjoy. It is a fearful problem for the ordinary person, with no special talents, to occupy himself, especially if he no longer has roots in the soil or in custom or in the beloved conventions of a traditional society. To judge from the behaviour and the achievements of the wealthy classes to-day in any quarter of the world, the outlook is very depressing! For these are, so to speak, our advance guard—those who are spying out the promised land for the rest of us and pitching their camp there. For they have most of them failed disastrously, so it seems to me—those who have an independent income but no associations or duties or ties—to solve the problem which has been set them.

I feel sure that with a little more experience we shall use the new-found bounty of nature quite differently from the way in which the rich use it to-day, and will map out for ourselves a plan of life quite otherwise than theirs.

For many ages to come the old Adam will be so strong in us that everybody will need to do *some* work if he is to be contented. We shall do more things for ourselves than is usual with the rich to-day, only too glad to have small duties and tasks and routines. But beyond this, we shall endeavour to spread the bread thin on the butter—to make what work there is still to be done to be as widely shared as possible. Three-hour shifts or a fifteen-hour week may put off the problem for a great while. For three hours a day is quite enough to satisfy the old Adam in most of us!

There are changes in other spheres too which we must expect to come. When the accumulation of wealth is no longer of high social importance, there will be great changes in the code of morals. We shall be able to rid ourselves of many of the pseudo-moral principles which have hag-ridden us for two hundred years, by which we have exalted some of the most distasteful of human qualities into the position of the highest virtues. We shall be able to afford to dare to assess the money-motive at its true value. The love of money as a possession—as distinguished from the love of money as a means to the enjoyments and realities of life—will be recognised for what it is, a somewhat disgusting morbidity, one of those semi-criminal, semi-patho-

17

logical propensities which one hands over with a shudder to the specialists in mental disease. All kinds of social customs and economic practices, affecting the distribution of wealth and of economic rewards and penalties, which we now maintain at all costs, however distasteful and unjust they may be in themselves, because they are tremendously useful in promoting the accumulation of capital, we shall then be free, at last, to discard.

Of course there will still be many people with intense, unsatisfied purposiveness who will blindly pursue wealth—unless they can find some plausible substitute. But the rest of us will no longer be under any obligation to applaud and encourage them. For we shall inquire more curiously than is safe to-day into the true character of this "purposiveness" with which in varying degrees Nature has endowed almost all of us. For purposiveness means that we are more concerned with the remote future results of our actions than with their own quality or their immediate effects on our own environment. The "purposive" man is always trying to secure a spurious and delusive immortality for his acts by pushing his interest in them forward into time. He does not love his cat, but his cat's kittens; nor, in truth, the kittens, but only the kittens' kittens, and so on forward for ever to the end of cat-dom. For him jam is not jam unless it is a case of jam to-morrow and never jam to-day. Thus by pushing his jam always forward into the future, he strives to secure for his act of boiling it an immortality. . . .

I see us free, therefore, to return to some of the most sure and certain principles of religion and traditional virtue—that avarice is a vice, that the exaction of usury is a misdemeanour, and the love of money is detestable, that those walk most truly in the paths of virtue and sane wisdom who take least thought for the morrow. We shall once more value ends above means and prefer the good to the useful. We shall honour those who can teach us how to pluck the hour and the day virtuously and well, the delightful people who are capable of taking direct enjoyment in things, the lilies of the field who toil not, neither do they spin . . . .

This essay was originally written in 1930 to predict the demise of the economic problem. Ed.

What in the world happened to economics?

Economists are all finally speaking the same language, but they still can't answer the big questions. **By Justin Fox**

Economists rule the world. This is not a new phenomenon. "The ideas of economists and political philosophers, both when they are right and when they are wrong, are more powerful than is commonly understood," John Maynard Keynes wrote in 1935, in the famous conclusion to his *General Theory of Employment, Interest, and Money.* "Indeed, the world is ruled by little else. Practical men, who believe themselves to be quite exempt from any intellectual influences, are usually the slaves of some defunct economist." The world went on to prove Keynes right: His *General Theory* became the basis of economic policymaking in the U.S. and Europe for decades after his death.

Now the undisputed role of Keynesianism is long past, but the work of economics professors still rules. When we talk about emerging-markets currency crises, about Japanese stagnation, about European unemployment, about U.S. prosperity, the words we use and the framework that shapes our thinking come from Adam Smith, from Keynes, from Milton Friedman, from other academics we may never have heard of.

These days, in fact, it's not just the economists' *ideas* that have power. Of the three men who, by most accounts, currently run the world—Federal Reserve Chairman Alan Greenspan, Treasury Secretary Robert Rubin, and Rubin's deputy and likely successor, Larry Summers—two have economics Ph.D.s. And while Greenspan has spent his career outside academia, Summers is a former Harvard and MIT professor of impeccable academic-economist

The pragmatist

Academic-turned-power-broker **Larry Summers** says that economics provides a framework for making decisions. It doesn't give him answers.

stock—son of two professors, nephew of two Nobel laureates, and himself the 1993 recipient of the John Bates Clark Medal as the top under-40 American economist.

Sitting in his office overlooking the Washington mall, Summers proudly reels off the names of other powerful products of the Cambridge, Mass., economics tradition whence he sprang: IMF deputy director Stanley Fischer; former finance ministers Pedro Aspe of Mexico and Domingo Cavallo of Argentina; current Finance Minister Eduardo Aninat of Chile; Japanese vice minister of finance Eisuke Sakakibara (a stretch, although Sakakibara did *teach* at Harvard for a year in the 1980's); globetrotting adviser-to-governments Jeffrey Sachs. This isn't a matter of politics. If the next President in Republican, he'll likely turn for advice to Summers' academic mentor, Harvard professor Martin Feldstein. It is all, Summers concludes, "evidence of the triumph of a more analytically oriented approach."

This is an interesting claim. The field of economics—or at least *macro*economics, the

1 ❖ INTRODUCTION TO MACROECONOMICS

study of big issues like inflation, unemployment, and the business cycle—has been the scene of some very public battles over the past half-century. Is Summers saying somebody won? Also, the world economy is in a scary state these days. Politicians don't know what to do about it; the hedge fund managers who a couple of years ago seemed to be running the show don't have a clue. Is Summers saying the economists have an answer?

No, and no again. The pitched battles of years past are over, but nobody really won. Academic economists have indeed attained a state of relative peace and consensus, but they have done so by diminishing their expectations. They use similar analytical tools and come up with similar answers to narrow questions. But when it comes to explaining the behavior of the global economy, economists can't agree—in fact, most of them no longer seem to believe there is a single correct explanation. Economists rule the world, but they aren't quite sure what to do with it.

It wasn't always this way, of course. To understand how economics went from warring dead certainties to peaceful confusion, one has to go back a few decades. Back to the 1960s, when most everybody was sure there *was* one obviously correct explanation for the workings of the economy. And back even further, to when the previous economic orthodoxy—which held that if the laws of supply and demand were allowed to work their magic, everything would turn out okay in the end—ran into the messy reality of the Great Depression.

In the U.S. in the 1930s, the financial system essentially stopped functioning, the market for real estate and other assets dried up, and unemployment remained stubbornly high. "Nothing in what I was taught from nine o'clock to ten o'clock in economic theory had any room to explain that," says Paul Samuelson, then an undergraduate at the University of Chicago and now one of Larry Summers' Nobel laureate uncles. "Finally, I heard [Chicago professor] Frank Knight say normal economics applies in normal times, but when it comes to really pathological times, it doesn't apply."

The job of designing an economics for pathological times fell to none other than John Maynard Keynes. Keynes—a lecturer at England's Cambridge University as well as a journalist, an adviser to governments, an insurance company executive, a commodities speculator, and husband of a famous ballerina—had, like every other economist of his time, internalized the "classical" truisms that the laws of supply and demand interact to set prices at the appropriate level and that something called Say's law decrees that every penny saved is automatically converted into investment. In the alternative economics Keynes proposed in the mid-1930s, however, savings sometimes gets stuffed in mattresses, prices and wages don't always adjust to falling demand, and it's perfectly possible for an economy to get stuck in a slump unless the government acts to stimulate demand.

By the 1950s this Keynesian economics had become the new orthodoxy—with first Cambridge University in England and then the Cambridge, Mass., neighbors Harvard and MIT as its temples. At MIT the high priest was Samuelson, whose best-selling introductory textbook, *Economics,* first published in 1948, introduced Keynesian ideas to generations of college students. Of course, by the 1950s the U.S. economy was no longer the pathological wreck that Keynes was trying to repair in the 1930s. But Samuelson and his fellow Keynesians figured they could banish economic downturns and mass unemployment by tweaking government fiscal and monetary policy. In the early 1960s, Samuelson and another MIT star and future Nobelist, Robert Solow, were able to put their ideas into practice as advisers to President Kennedy. The U.S. economy responded with the longest expansion in history. "It seemed an economics as free of ideological difficulties as, say, applied chemistry or physics, promising a straightforward expansion in economic possibilities," wrote economists Robert Lucas and Thomas Sargent years later. "One might argue about how this windfall should be distributed, but it seemed a simple lapse of logic to oppose the windfall itself."

A few economists weren't so sure. The most notable dissenter was Milton Friedman of the University of Chicago. Friedman had been a graduate student at Chicago during the same troubled times that Samuelson was there as an undergrad, but he never shared Samuelson's conviction that the Chicago economics they learned had failed. In the epic *Monetary History of the United States* he co-authored with Anna Schwartz in 1961, Friedman argued that the best explanation for the Great Depression was not market pathology but the failure of the Federal Reserve to keep the money supply from shrinking in the early 1930s.

The dean

Almost every road modern economics has taken can be traced back to **Paul Samuelson**. That doesn't mean he's always been right.

Friedman's emphasis on monetary policy—which had been deemed by Keynes to be impotent in times of true economic crisis and was thus long ignored by his disciples—had a big impact on economic discourse. But at first most economists adopted monetary policy as a way to keep the economy running on high-employment overdrive. Samuelson and Solow had brought to the U.S. the empirical evidence, first compiled by a British economist named A. W. Phillips, that there was a tradeoff between inflation and unemployment— that is, higher inflation meant lower unemployment. Allowing prices to rise seemed the only humane thing to do. Friedman argued that the unemployment/inflation tradeoff was temporary, and he also pointed out that using fiscal and monetary policy to avert recessions was a lot harder than it looked. These arguments weren't ignored: For years Friedman and Samuelson wrote dueling columns for *Newsweek;* in 1967 Friedman was president of the American Economic Association. But his thinking wasn't mainstream, either among Americans at large or within the economics profession.

That changed in the 1970s when the Mideast oil crisis hit the U.S. with both high inflation and high unemployment. Friedman won the Nobel Prize (six years after Samuelson) and became a best-selling author, TV personality, and revered adviser to free-market-oriented politicians around the world. Within the economics profession, however, the deathblow to the old ways came from the above-mentioned Robert Lucas, a Friedman student at the University of Chicago who had gone on to teach at what is now Carnegie Mellon University. Lucas wrote a series of articles in the 1970s hammering away at the theoretical underpinnings of Keynesian thought. He argued that if people are rational—a basic tenet of economics that we'll discuss in more depth later—they can form rational expectations of predictable future events. So if the government gets in the habit of boosting spending or increasing the money supply every time the economy appears headed for a downturn, everybody will eventually learn that and adjust their be-

4. What in the World Happened to Economics?

havior accordingly. Which means that regular government efforts to control the business cycle simply cannot work.

By 1980, Lucas was able to claim—with some justification—that "one cannot find good, under-40 economists who identify themselves or their work as 'Keynesian.'" For a while it looked as if Lucasism was the wave of the future and the University of Chicago (to which Lucas returned in 1974) had supplanted MIT and Harvard as the world's center of economic thought. But the deductive logic of Lucas and other "new classical" economists led them to the stark conclusion that government monetary and fiscal policy should have *no* effect on the real economy. Even Lucas never really believed that, and the two early 1980s recessions brought on by the Federal Reserve convinced most economists that monetary policy could in fact have a real impact.

Lucas, who won the 1995 Nobel Prize for his critique of Keynesianism, has never come up with a viable alternative macro theory. One of his former students, Edward Prescott of the University of Minnesota, has proposed that recessions and booms could be explained as the stops and starts of technological process. But this "real business cycle" school has yet to deliver anything of much use to economic policymakers. So Cambridge, Mass., home of the discredited Keynesian orthodoxy, got the opportunity to come up with a credible replacement. And in a way, it did.

The process started in 1973 when Stanley Fischer returned to MIT. Fischer had been a star student of Samuelson's in the late 1960s, but MIT had a policy of not hiring its own newly minted Ph.D.s, so he ended up at the University of Chicago. By the time MIT called with a job offer several years later, Fischer had acquired both an appreciation for Friedman's real-world approach to economics and an interest in Lucas' theoretical critique of Keynesianism. Fischer brought over another Chicagoan, international economist Rudiger Dornbusch, and the pair came to dominate MIT economics for two decades. "They were bringing the latest thinking in," recalls Columbia professor Frederic Mishkin, one of Fischer's first students at MIT. "They had absorbed a lot of the Chicago approach, but had very open minds." They also had open doors, and before long Fischer and Dornbusch had become MIT's dissertation advisers of choice.

Across town at Harvard, the agent of change was Martin Feldstein. Feldstein, an Oxford Ph.D. who joined the Harvard faculty in 1967, specialized in investigating how the incentives created by government taxing and spending change the behavior of people and firms—an area that had been given short shrift by the Keynesians but that became, in cruder form, the heart of Reagan-era supplyside economics. His biggest impact on the study of economics, though, may have been his transformation of the National Bureau of Economic Research. The bureau, a private think tank, had been founded in 1920 by one of the most prominent economists of the day, Columbia's Wesley Mitchell, to offer "scientific determination and impartial interpretation of facts bearing upon economic, social, and industrial problems." Over the years it had sponsored some landmark research—including Milton Friedman's monetary history—but by the late 1970s it was a fusty place known mainly as the official arbiter of when recessions start and end. Upon being named president of the NBER in 1977, Feldstein moved it from New York to Cambridge and brought in top academics like Fischer and Dornbusch, and their students, to churn out working papers using cutting-edge theory to examine real-world problems.

The products of this atmosphere include a disproportionate number of the world's most prominent economists. There are the policymakers listed above; the chairmen of three top economics departments, Olivier Blanchard of MIT, Maurice Obstfeld of Berkeley, and Ben Bernanke of Princeton; the many Romers: Stanford growth-theorist Paul (who started his Ph.D. training at MIT but finished at Chicago), Berkeley economic historian Christina (no relation to Paul), and Berkeley macroeconomist David (married to Christina, not related to Paul); Columbia's Mishkin, the former chief economist of the New York Fed; industrial organization guru Jean Tirole of the University of Toulouse; and, most familiar to readers of this magazine, FORTUNE columnists Greg Mankiw of Harvard and Paul Krugman of MIT. The members of this group don't fit into any neat ideological or doctrinal category, but they are generally skeptical of both unfettered capitalism and government efforts to fetter it. They share Keynes' conviction that markets can go wrong (some of the younger ones even call themselves new Keynesians) but have also accepted the criticisms of Friedman and Lucas.

To a casual observer this may sound like plain old common sense, and to a certain extent that's what it is. But when these economists communicate with one another, it's not in the language of common sense but in a jargon that has its roots in the work of 18th-century Scotsman Adam Smith. Smith's masterpiece, *An Inquiry Into the Nature and Causes of the Wealth of Nations,* introduced the then-radical notion that selfish, greedy individuals, if allowed to pursue their interests largely unchecked, would interact to produce a wealthier society as if guided by an "invisible hand." Smith never worked out a proof that this invisible hand existed, and not all subsequent economists agreed with his optimistic assessment—Thomas Malthus thought people would have too many children and overpopulate the world; Karl Marx thought capitalists would be so greedy they would bring down the system. But they all shared Smith's view of economics as the study of people trying to maximize their material well-being.

This assumption of rational, maximizing behavior won out not just because it often reflected reality but because it was useful. It enabled economists to build mathematical models of behavior, to give their discipline a rigorous, scientific air. This process started in the mid-1800s, evolving by the end of the century into the approach known today as neoclassical economics (Marx having assigned the term

---

The dissident

For decades, **Milton Friedman** challenged conventional economic wisdom. Eventually the conventional wisdom collapsed.

The critic

Robert Lucas picked apart the inconsistencies of Keynesianism so convincingly that it died. But he hasn't come up with a replacement.

1 ❖ INTRODUCTION TO MACROECONOMICS

"classical" to Smith and his immediate successors). And while 20th-century critics like the University of Chicago's Thorstein Veblen and Harvard's John Kenneth Galbraith argued that people are also motivated by altruism, envy, panic, and other emotions, they failed to come up with a way to fit these emotions into the models that economists had grown accustomed to—and thus had little impact.

Keynes, to get at his explanation for slumps, did have to assume that economic actions were sometimes motivated by "animal spirits" rather than by pure rationality. But he never tried to work this into a full-blown behavioral theory. After Keynes, in fact, economics came to be split into two parts. There was macroeconomics, which used broad strokes to depict the big things that Keynesians cared about: unemployment, inflation, and the business cycle. Then there was microeconomics, which examined how the interactions of rational individuals led to market outcomes. Macroeconomics described how economies malfunctioned; microeconomics described how they worked.

These two sides of economics coexisted uneasily in the same academic departments, sometimes in the same people. In his advice to President Kennedy and in his undergraduate textbook, MIT's Samuelson offered thoroughly Keynesian explanations of macroeconomic phenomena; meanwhile, Samuelson's landmark 1947 book, *Foundations of Economic Analysis*, taught generations of graduate students how to approach microeconomics as a set of mathematical models featuring rational actors. One of those students was Robert Lucas, who worked through *Foundations*, calculus textbook in hand, the summer before he started grad school at Chicago. Lucas' subsequent theoretical work essentially forced Keynes' (and Samuelson's) macroeconomics to submit to the same relentless mathematical logic as Samuelson's microeconomics—a test it couldn't pass.

Microeconomics, however, was beginning to change. The neoclassical tradition reached an apotheosis in 1951 when future Nobel laureates Kenneth Arrow (another Summers uncle) and Gerard Debreu published an article that in essence mathematically proved the existence of Adam Smith's invisible hand. This "general equilibrium" proof has been a mainstay of graduate-level economics training ever since. But Arrow soon moved on; he and other economists began working out ways in which rational behavior could lead to less-than-optimal market outcomes.

The most important tool in this analysis was game theory—the study of situations, like poker or chess games, in which players have to make their decisions based on guesses about what the other player is going to do next. Game theory was first adapted to economics in the 1940s by mathematician John von Neumann (the same von Neumann whose theoretical insights made the computer possible) and economist Oskar Morgenstern. But it took a while to catch on.

In 1963, Arrow was first to hint at the game-theory implications of situations in which different parties to a transaction possess different amounts of information. But "asymmetric information" really came into its own in the 1970s as a way to explain the behavior of financial markets—which are extremely susceptible to information difficulties. Its leading theorist was probably Joseph Stiglitz, a 1966 MIT Ph.D., now the World Bank's chief economist.

Another long-neglected aspect of microeconomics that Stiglitz and others began to study in the 1970s was increasing returns. To work out to equilibrium, models of economic behavior always had to assume that at a certain point makers of a product would be faced with diminishing returns: The more they produced, the less profit per piece. It had long been clear that this didn't always reflect reality, but new math techniques and the growth of the software industry—a business in which making additional copies of a product costs virtually nothing—led economists to finally take increasing returns seriously.

This was the context in which the young scholars of Harvard and MIT learned economics in the late 1970s and early 1980s. Keynesian macroeconomics was dead, but nothing had sprung up in its place. Microeconomics, meanwhile, had moved away from the dead certainties of the past into a much more interesting thicket of research possibilities. The mathematical models that had come to form the basis of academic economics were shifting from general equilibrium, in which everything worked out for the best, to multiple equilibriums, in which it might not. "That was kind of a golden age for economic theorizing," says Krugman.

Different people took to the atmosphere in different ways. Larry Summers became a master debunker, using theory and data to poke holes in new-classical certainties. Paul Romer moved macroeconomics away from its business-cycle orientation to devise a new theory of long-term economic growth. And Krugman, whose academic work probably best represents the direction

The model builder

Paul Krugman became a star by fitting the real world into elegant mathematical models. But he doesn't always trust the results.

economics has taken, built lots of mathematical models of real-world economic phenomena.

The models, Krugman says, are constructed upon a couple of basic principles: "self-interested behavior and interaction—$100 bills don't lie in the street for very long, and you don't have sales that aren't purchases." Beyond that there are no clear rules. "What you end up looking for is a specific set of strategic simplifications," he says.

The two models that made Krugman's name in the late 1970s both involved international economics. One concluded that currency crises were rational, inevitable reactions to untenable government policies. The other overturned the conventional economic wisdom that countries could gain an advantage in trade only because of better technology or greater resources—by showing that the increasing returns inherent in making huge quantities of a product can lock in an advantage.

These two models shared no grand theme or ideology, and matters got even murkier when Krugman tried to draw policy conclusions from them. He gradually came over to the view that currency collapses can also result from self-fulfilling investor panics that overrun even countries with sensible economic policies. This has led him to conclude that controls on capital flows sometimes make sense. But he does not believe in restricting trade, even though his increasing-returns model seems to suggest advantages for the sort of protectionist, volume-building tactics used by Japanese industries in the 1980s.

Herein lies the dilemma of modern economics. Analytical techniques are becoming ever more sophisticated, but it is looking ever less likely that they'll someday add up to a coherent, reliable *science* of economics. "If you ask grand questions of economic theory, you come up with garbage," says

4. What in the World Happened to Economics?

David Colander, a historian of economic thought at Middlebury College. Most economists have come to agree. As a result they are staying away from grand questions and sticking to narrower ones.

It's not that economists can't agree on *any* big issues. The experience of the 1970s, plus the articles of Robert Lucas, appears to have banished from the economic mainstream all hankering for inflationary Fed policy—although there is debate over whether the optimal inflation rate is 3% or 2% or 0. There's also consensus about what facilitates long-term growth: transparent financial markets; well-capitalized, well-regulated banks; free trade; educated workers; a reliable but not inflexible legal system; taxes and welfare benefits low enough to avoid disincentives to work.

The trouble comes when there's trouble. In dealing with the impact of financial crises on the real economy, with downturns in the business cycle, with interactions between nations, the mathematical models of modern economics come up short. So economists make substitutions: guesswork, judgment, experience, ideology.

Which leads to large differences of opinion. Witness the response to the recent emerging-markets economic crises. Economists who use the same techniques, believe in the same principles, and studied under the same teachers are coming up with wildly different responses. Summers and Fischer have backed a tough-love policy of advancing IMF loans to countries in crisis but demanding that those countries shut down reckless banks, raise interest rates, and cut government spending. Stiglitz wants more generous lending and reregulation of global capital flows. Sachs favors creation of an international bankruptcy code under which troubled countries could seek protection. Krugman has urged countries to impose capital controls. Dornbusch, who taught Krugman international economics, says that's nuts.

A big help, these economists are. Says Krugman: "I've got a guess, Jeff Sachs has a guess, and Larry Summers is ruling the world." Summers has a slightly more reassuring take: "Ultimately there's no alternative to judgment—you can never get the answers out of some model. But the reason there are many, many more good economists in positions of influence in the world is that one can understand the issues more sharply and clearly, and can pose the trade-offs and can make more accurate judgments within a clear analytic framework."

That's a long way from saying economics has all the answers. But it's about all any economist can honestly claim.

Article 5

Taking In the Sites

Statistics and Even Lore Of the Dismal Science

By DAVID CAY JOHNSTON

Should you wake up in the middle of the night wondering whether Americans or Norwegians have a bigger per-capita gross domestic product, there is no need to lose sleep. You can find the answer, quickly and free, on the World Wide Web.

A rapidly proliferating number of Web sites are filled with economic statistics on everything from the lat-

---

Hey, did you hear the joke about the two-handed economist?

---

est official estimate of inflation by the Bureau of Labor Statistics to details of the Turkish budget.

Other sites let you manipulate data, such as easy-to-use sites that adjust dollars for inflation.

Economic Web sites can be valuable to businesses that are trying to decide on new investments or marketing, to students, and to anyone who needs answers to questions like how many Americans use wheelchairs (answer: 1.4 million) and the percentage of residents of every county who are children between the ages of 5 and 17.

Perhaps the most comprehensive site is Resources for Economists on

WHERE TO GO

- FEDSTATS, http://www.fedstats.gov
- FEDERAL RESERVE, http://www.bog.frb.fed.us
- CENSUS BUREAU, http://www.census.gov.
- BUREAU OF LABOR STATISTICS, http://stats.bls.gov/blshome.html
- BUSINESS CYCLE INDICATORS, http://www.globalexposure.com
- ECONOMICS OF NETWORKS, http://raven.stern.nyu.edu/networks
- FAIR MODEL (MACRO ECONOMIC MODELING), http://fairmodel.econ.yale.edu
- ECONOMIST JOKE, http://netec.wustl.edu/JokEc.html
- INTERNAL REVENUE SERVICE, http://www.irs.ustreas.gov/prod/tax_stats/index.html
- BILL GOFFE'S RESOURCES FOR ECONOMISTS, http://econwpa.wustl.edu/ EconFAQ.html
- INFLATION ADJUSTERS, http://www.orst.edu/Dept/pol_sci/sahr/cpi96.htm http://www.NewsEngin.com/neFreeTools.nsf/CPIcalc
- ORGANIZATION FOR ECONOMIC COOPERATION AND DEVELOPMENT, http://www.oecd.org
- DETAILED EXCHANGE RATE DATA FROM OLSEN & ASSOCIATES, http://www.oanda.com/cgi-bin/ncc
- WHITE HOUSE ECONOMIC STATISTICS BRIEFING ROOM, http://www.whitehouse.gov/fsbr/esbr.html
- CONGRESSIONAL BUDGET OFFICE ECONOMIC REPORTS, http://gopher.cbo.gov:7100/1/reports/online
- FEDERAL BUDGET, http://www.access.gpo.gov/su_docs/budget98/maindown.html
- FEDERAL FUNDS REPORTS (FEDERAL SPENDING AT STATE AND COUNTY LEVELS), http://govinfo.kerr.orst.edu/cffr-stateis.html

5. Statistics and Even Lore of the Dismal Science

the Internet, created by Bill Goffe, a University of Southern Mississippi economist, who has found enough links to fill 24 screens.

Most of these sites are easy to use, even by those who never took Economics 101 and do not care what price elasticity means.

You can find out how much the Federal Government spends per capita in every county, which turns up some curious figures. For example, the House Speaker, Newt Gingrich, represents two Georgia counties where Federal spending is more than $7,000 per person, while Federal per-capita spending is less than half that level in two Missouri counties represented by Richard A. Gephardt, the House's Democratic minority leader.

The White House Economic Statistics Briefing Room has pages of color charts, some of them backed up by tables on income, crude oil, farm prices and household wealth. But the site's creators have a curious lack of consistency about chronology. You can trace poverty rates back to 1959, but median household income data to 1970 and disposable personal income only to January 1995.

At the site maintained by the Paris-based Organization for Economic Cooperation and Development, which posts comparative statistics from 25 advanced nations, you can answer the question about whether Americans or Norwegians are better off. The answer, as of the last time the Web site was updated, is both. Norwegians are 26 percent better off than Americans based on currency-exchange rates. On the other hand, in terms of purchasing power, Norwegians have only 85 percent as much as Americans.

Ever wonder what would happen if gasoline prices doubled, Pentagon spending was cut by a third or a flat 27 percent income tax was adopted? You can find out using Fairmodel, a model of the United States economy created by Ray C. Fair, a Yale University professor. The model is easy enough that social studies students use it during their nine weeks of economics instruction at Palatine High School outside Chicago. Advanced students manipulate the model on their own, while lower-level students sit around as their teacher, Robert Gilbert, punches in their proposed changes to fiscal and monetary policies.

"Instead of hearing a lot of theory, my students actually put their hands on the valves of the economy," Mr. Gilbert said. "And it turns out to be a great tool for building self-esteem because I have them work with a 20-year period; they just don't know what the period was because I remove the years, and their decisions usually produce better results than the actual results of what Presidents and the Congress did."

There are even sites with a touch of whimsy, like Ken White's coin-flipping page, where with the stroke of a key you can demonstrate what happens if you flip 100 dimes (heads American, tails Canadian).

And one site is filled with jokes about the dismal science created by Pasi Petteri Kuoppamki, a research fellow at the Finnish Ministry of Trade and Industry, with a United States mirror site for faster downloading.

Among its jokes is this one, edited to its essence from the shaggy-dog version on the Web:

A man comes upon a shepherd and his flock, and proposes a wager.

"I will bet you $100, against one of your sheep, that I can tell you the exact number in this flock," the man says.

The shepherd accepts.

"973," says the man.

The shepherd, astonished at the accuracy, says "I'm a man of my word; take an animal."

The man picks one up and begins to walk away.

"Wait," cries the shepherd, "Let me have a chance to get even. Double or nothing that I can guess your exact occupation."

"Sure," the man replies.

"You are an economist for a government think tank," says the shepherd.

"Amazing!" responds the man, "how did you deduce that?"

"Well," says the shepherd, "if you will first put down my dog..."

Unit 2

Unit Selections

6. **State of the Union: Black Holes in the Statistics,** Robert Eisner
7. **The Economy You Can't See,** Paul Starobin
8. **How Fast Can the U.S. Economy Grow?** Paul Krugman
9. **Hell No, We Won't Save!** Robert J. Samuelson

Key Points to Consider

❖ Why are reliable statistics essential for good economic policy making?

❖ What is the underground economy, and why is it a troubling issue for policymakers?

❖ How fast can the U.S. economy grow? Why has the U.S. personal saving rate declined, and should we be concerned about it?

 **Links**   www.dushkin.com/online/

7. **Bureau of Economic Analysis**
   http://www.bea.doc.gov
8. **Bureau of Labor Statistics**
   http://stats.bls.gov
9. **Dr. Ed Yardeni's Economics Network**
   http://www.yardeni.com
10. **Economic Statistics Briefing Room**
    http://www.whitehouse.gov/fsbr/esbr.html
11. **Internet Public Library: Business and Economics Reference**
    http://ipl.org/ref/RR/static/bus0000.html
12. **New York Times Business Connections**
    http://www.nytimes.com/library/cyber/reference/busconn.html
13. **WebEc-WWW Resources in Economics**
    http://netec.wustl.edu/WebEc.html

These sites are annotated on pages 4 and 5.

Measuring Economic Performance

Data! Data! Data! I can't make bricks without clay.—Sherlock Holmes ("The Adventure of the Copper Beeches")

Economic decision making involves an assessment of the economy's general health and the informed selection of policies from among many alternatives. Economic analysts, in both the public and private sectors, regularly watch such measures as gross domestic product (GDP), unemployment, and inflation. You are probably familiar with these terms, since they are frequently mentioned in news broadcasts and daily newspapers. However, the popular understanding of economic data is sometimes flawed, partly because the formulation and use of economic statistics is a normative process influenced by value judgments. Arthur Ross summarizes this point quite well:

> Let us recognize candidly that statistical truths, like the other truths about man's social life, are created rather than discovered. It may well be different when it comes to measuring the amount of rainfall or the population of redwood trees. These are physical phenomena. It is man who invents and defines these categories. It is man who selects a few dimensions that are capable of measurement and uses them to characterize complex social conditions and relationships. It is man who decides how much effort should be expended in measuring these dimensions or others that might be selected. ("Living with Symbols," *American Statistician,* June 1966)

The articles in this section address a number of important issues involving the measurement and interpretation of macroeconomic data. Policymakers must be concerned with the relevance and reliability of the statistical truths upon which they base their decisions. This presupposes a knowledge not only of the way in which government statisticians structure their data, but also of the official meaning of these statistics. Beyond this, policymakers need to develop a sensitivity to at least three issues: that economic data are often subject to wide margins of error (which sometimes cast doubt upon the reliability of such data); that discrepancies between different sets of statistics are common (thereby requiring policymakers to make choices about the relative importance of one sort of data over another); and finally, that not all economic phenomena can be measured (particularly where such issues as the quality of economic life are concerned). In the end, good policy making mandates a careful consideration of these issues.

This section begins with a discussion by Robert Eisner of the reliability of economic data. He cites a large number of flaws in official government statistics. Recent federal attempts at cutting costs have seriously impaired the process through which data are collected. As a result, policymakers often must depend on unreliable information.

Then, Paul Starobin explores the "underground economy," where goods and services—some legal, some not—are produced and exchanged but not reported. He contends that this hidden economy has become a permanent fixture of post-industrial American capitalism, acting as a useful safety valve, capable of generating jobs and business opportunities that hold otherwise frayed communities together.

Those who hold the "New Economy" view assert that rapid technological change and global competition have qualitatively altered the old rules of the game. But, in the next article, Paul Krugman argues that the new view just doesn't make sense. A careful examination of recent evidence suggests that—globalization and innovation aside—every economy has a speed limit. According to Krugman, advocates of the New Economy view are engaged in some wishful thinking.

The unit concludes with an article in which Robert Samuelson examines a puzzling development— as the American economy continues to zip along, personal saving has virtually disappeared. This has given rise to a debate among macroeconomists on the implications of savings trends for future economic growth. Samuelson sides with those who maintain that low personal saving is an essential catalyst of the current boom. If somehow savings were to rise, both the United States and the world would face even greater peril.

STATE OF THE UNION:
Black Holes in the Statistics

Robert Eisner

ROBERT EISNER is Professor of Economics, Emeritus, at Northwestern University. This article was originally a luncheon address delivered at an international conference in Washington, September 9, 1996. It will also be published in Accuracy, Timeliness and Relevance of Economic Statistics, ed. Zoltan Kenessey (Washington, 1997).

Most of you have probably heard the story of the drunk stumbling around a street lamp. When a policeman asked him what he was doing, he said he was looking for his lost wallet. "Where do you think you lost it?" asked the officer. "I haven't the foggiest idea," was the reply. "Then why are you looking here?" "Because it's light here," the drunk replied.

The moral of the story is, obviously, that restricting our measurement to areas where there is the most light may not be optimal. And although it would be nice to have more light everywhere, we can at least try to cast light—and measure—in areas that economic theory indicates are relevant to resolving critical policy issues. While always striving to be as accurate as possible, we must not shirk from working in relatively dark places. What we find in those dark places should be prominently displayed with whatever caveats are appropriate.

Let me apply this moral to our measures of GDP, public deficits and debt, domestic and foreign investment and saving, productivity, real wages, and the distribution of income and wealth.

Understanding GDP

To many, the single most important measure of the economy is real GDP and its rate of growth. GDP essentially measures the market value of goods and services produced for the market. A huge amount of output—estimated at more than half of conventional GDP—is not produced for the market. This includes almost all of household and government output (Eisner 1989, Tables 1 and 5). The non-market output of households is generally not counted in GDP. Government output in the United States until recently was valued as only the compensation of government employees. That has now been extended to include capital consumption allowances on fixed capital but still lacks any item corresponding to the substantial net profits earned in private production.

The problem is not merely the extent of understatement of total output of the economy; it includes the measurement of rates of growth and major policy issues. Thus, more and more women have gone to work in the market. Home cooking is being replaced with TV dinners and restaurants. Maternal home nurture of children is being replaced with day-care centers, and, conversely, domestic servants and commercial laundries are being replaced with washers and dryers in the basement. We have also moved from movie houses to television and VCRs in the home and from public transportation to private automobiles. These shifts and the privatization of government activity entail moves between non-market and market output and across the conventional line separating final and intermediate product.

Non-market output of households and government is generally harder to measure, without the concrete numbers from market transactions. But we need comprehensive measures of output of all sectors, market and non-market, if we are to get a meaningful picture of what is happening to the economy and what we should be doing to make it better. We may not want to pursue policies that bring increases in market output accompanied by greater decreases in non-market output, and we need measures to inform us.

What Is the Deficit Anyway?

Almost everyone attacks "the deficit," but almost no one knows how it is measured or what it really is. The presumed federal budget deficit in the United States bears little resemblance to any meaningful economic concept. It violates key rules of private accounting in not distinguishing between current and capital outlays. It includes in expenditures the purchase of financial and real assets and counts the sale of assets as negative outlays, akin to receipts. The deficit could be eliminated for many years by selling off federal assets—perhaps in a lease-back arrangement (we could begin with the Capitol, the White House, the entire defense arsenal, and our interstate highway system). And our so-called unified budget—as argued about in Congress—makes no adjustment for inflation. It lumps together the underlying structural or exogenous deficit and the effects of cyclical variations of economic activity.

The U.S. Bureau of Economic Analysis (BEA) does considerably better in its government deficits on national income and product account. Following the internationally formulated and recommended System of National

Accounts and the practice of most other countries, it has finally separated investment in physical assets from current expenditures. The BEA also does not count purchases and sales of financial assets. Thus, the savings and loan (S&L) fiasco in the United States did not alternately raise and lower the national income account deficits, as it did the unified budget deficits when the Treasury bought and then sold assets of bankrupt S&Ls. The BEA does not, however, include any of the massive investments by government in education, research, and health. And pressures on its own budget has led the BEA to abandon measures of the high-employment or cyclically adjusted budget, so vital for the measurement and analysis of the impact of the deficit on the economy.

Also largely ignored are measures that offer meaningful evaluation of the deficit in a growing economy with a rising price level. The deficit is meaningful largely because it adds to the financial liabilities of the government and, correspondingly, to the financial assets held outside the government. But surely the major impact of changes in the values of these liabilities and assets must stem from real, not merely nominal, changes. The unified budget deficit in the United States, which was $290 billion in fiscal year 1992, this year is $107 billion (*Economic Indicators*, October 1996, p. 32). But with a federal debt of about $3.7 trillion, even our modest inflation rate of around 2.2 percent implies a reduction in the real value of the debt of $82 billion due to inflation. Counting this "inflation tax" reduces the deficit to about $25 billion—all of one-third of 1 percent of GDP.

A still more comprehensive measure would show the change in the ratio of the federal debt to GDP. Now hovering at about 50 percent, it is actually being reduced. We might thus appropriately report a 1996 *surplus* equal to the amount that the increase in the debt falls short of keeping that ratio constant.

What About National Saving?

Another major concern, in the United States at least, is a purportedly inadequate rate of national saving. But what is national saving? Steve Landefeld notes the vast discrepancy between saving measures in the national income and product accounts and those found in the Federal Reserve Flow of Funds reports (1996). In principle, national saving should correspond to increases in a nation's real wealth. In practice, the two are only barely related.

Our measures of investment, the aggregate of which is equal to saving, include only a very poor and misleading count of net foreign investment, business and non-profit institution acquisition of structures and equipment, business investment in inventories, and government acquisition of structures and equipment—only recently measured in the United States. Omitted are all investment by households in durable goods: If Hertz buys a car, which a household rents, it is counted as investment, while if the household buys a car it is counted as consumption!

Also omitted are all investment in research and development in any sector (other than that already counted in physical capital) and investment in the human capital of education, training, and health. In addition, we ignore most investment in preserving our land, air, and water, as well the capital consumption of these vital assets.

The U.S. Office of Management and Budget estimate of our national wealth at the end of fiscal year 1995, including publicly and privately owned physical assets and education and R&D capital, was $54.1 trillion (1996, p. 27, Tables 2–4). Of that, only $16.5 trillion consisted of structures and equipment included in our measures of investment. The 1995 increase in national wealth in constant 1995 dollars was estimated at $1.2 trillion; net saving (gross saving minus capital consumption allowances) in the national income and product accounts was $316 billion.

And That Net Foreign Investment Figure!

Politicians—and even some economists—often claim that we have become "the world's greatest debtor nation." They base this claim on a misinterpretation of the BEA's bottom line, based on reports of the net international investment position of the United States, as relating to debt rather than total net claims, including equity and direct foreign investment. But it was also based in part on a failure of the BEA, since corrected, to offer some estimates, however imperfect, of the relevant market or replacement-cost values of investment. The net foreign investment in the income and product accounts still includes no adjustments for changes in the value of existing assets, vast as these have been as national economies and their currencies wax and wane.

The direct investment figures themselves are suspect in much of the world, with startling differences between the amounts of the same investment as reported by the investing and receiving countries. Moreover, in a world of multinational companies and substantial migration, are we correctly measuring the nationality of assets? If a wealthy Latin American moves to Miami while maintaining assets in his country of origin, the United States, and Switzerland, should those assets be counted as U.S. assets or foreign claims?

Finally, is it clear that the most recent net negative international investment position of the United States, estimated at $800 billion (Scholl 1996, p. 42, Table 1), is less than 2 percent of the national wealth total of $54 trillion just mentioned? Indeed, if net foreign investment, as officially measured, continues indefinitely at its most recent proportion of negative $140 billion, or 0.3 percent of national wealth, while the national wealth continues to grow even at its modest recent rate of about 5 percent per annum, the ratio of net foreign claims to U.S. national wealth would approach only 6 percent. At a real rate of return of even 4 percent that would mean net payments by the United States to foreigners equal to 0.24 percent of U.S. wealth or, assuming that income–wealth ratios remain about the same, less than 2 percent of GDP.

Measuring Changes in Productivity

I will not try to explain growth in market productivity but would like to suggest one major matter usually overlooked because of our focus on market output. Can we not infer something from the revealed preferences of the millions who have moved from non-market, household production into the labor force? Should we not assume that they moved in large part because the income they could earn in the market, and therefore the output they would be producing in the market, was more than the value of the output they were producing at home? To the extent that they moved into lower-paying and less-productive market jobs than the average for market work, they would be lowering measured *market* output per worker. But if their new, market output exceeded the value of the non-market production they left, total output—market and non-market—must have risen.

Measures of real wages are related to measures of productivity. Here again, political rhetoric has at times obscured reality and our statistics-gathering agencies have generally failed to correct popular misconceptions. International comparisons of real wages have been particularly faulty, with many presented on the basis of foreign exchange rates that bear little relation to relative domestic purchasing power and indeed fluctuate greatly from year to year. In the presidential campaign of four years ago we heard repeated assertions that the United States had fallen and was only fourteenth in the world in terms of real wages. The correct statement would certainly be that U.S. real wages, on the basis of purchasing-power parity, were easily the highest among major industrial nations.

The Growing Inequality in the Distribution of Income and Wealth

The growing inequality in the distribution of income and wealth in much of the advanced world and most sharply in the United States may be contributing several factors that are biasing our measures. First, again, we often fail to take into account non-market output. The poor may be increasingly less able to afford a movie, but they can generally watch television at home. Their health services may be inadequate, but the value of what they receive from public hospitals may be more than we measure.

Second, the deterioration of the environment for many of the poor, the loss in security as massive crime invades neighborhoods, and the breakdown of public education in inner cities all suggest that the poor have become even poorer than indicated by our conventional measures.

Third, we have probably underestimated the inequality by failing to take into account the "perks" and non-wage benefits enjoyed by those high on corporate ladders, as well as the free or reimbursed lunches at gatherings like this.

Fourth, our measures of personal income and income distribution exclude the real value of capital gains. The theoretical measures of income, modeled after the Hicksian concept of the amount that we can consume while keeping our real wealth intact, would certainly include these capital gains. But unequal as the income distribution may be by conventional measures, the distribution of wealth is far more skewed. The rich have been getting *much* richer, and much of their new wealth has come from capital gains. Bill Gates, Warren Buffett, Ross Perot, and Donald Trump accumulated their many billions from capital gains, not personal income. My namesake, Michael Eisner, despite his top salaries from the Disney enterprises, must impute most of his enormous wealth to the increases in the value of his assets.

The moral again? Spread the light as far as we can and try to measure what counts, even if it goes beyond areas where precise numbers are easy to come by. Economic theory, which is a vital guide, indicates that God did not limit consumption, investment, and output and income to what is produced by business and can be measured by market transactions. As we recognize this, we realize that the task of statistics gatherers and analysts the world over is that much harder.

So let us tell all our governments to measure their budgets better and to stop squeezing *our* budgets. They should give us more information so that we can determine the status of our economies and where we are really headed.

For Further Reading

Council of Economic Advisers. 1996. *Economic Indicators*. October.
Eisner, Robert. 1989. *The Total Incomes System of Accounts*. Chicago and London: University of Chicago Press.
Kenessey, Zoltan, ed. *Accuracy, Timeliness and Relevance of Economic Statistics*. Materials of a conference of the International Statistical Institute, the Statistical Office of the European Communities, and the Bureau of Economic Analysis of the U.S. Department of Commerce, Washington DC, 1997.
Landefeld, Steven J. 1996. In Kenessey, *Accuracy, Timeliness and Relevance of Economic Statistics*.
Office of Management and Budget. 1996. *Budget of the United States Government, Analytical Perspectives*. Fiscal Year 1997.
Scholl, Russell B. 1996. *Survey of Current Business* (July): 36–44.

THE ECONOMY YOU CAN'T SEE

PAUL STAROBIN

Last year, the American economy produced $6.37798 trillion worth of goods and services, according to the Commerce Department's Bureau of Economic Analysis (BEA), the federal agency responsible for wrapping a tape measure around the economy.

Yeah, right. Don't be gulled: The precise-sounding number is as suspect as a Chesapeake Bay oyster left on the dock at midday. The truth is that nobody knows how big the economy is. Pressed by an interviewer, BEA director Carol S. Carson declined even to hazard a guess.

Nor does anyone know the level of family income in the United States, the extent of poverty or how many people lack jobs. And because nobody knows how much Americans earn and spend, nobody knows how much they save. Never mind that the government and others collect and publish statistics on every conceivable form of economic activity; that merely speaks to a modern society's wish for precision—or the illusion of precision. If you're looking for a reliable body of data, try baseball batting averages instead.

The main reason for the statistical squishiness is that murky mudpile known as the underground economy. BEA bean counters can count only the economic transactions that are reported to the government. That leaves out the zillions of transactions for which there isn't a paper (or electronic) trail. These include illegal activities, such as drug-peddling, as well as legal ones, such as babysitting, on which taxes or regulations are frequently evaded.

The underground sector wasn't born yesterday: Before America was even America, pirates were running West Indies rum past the colonial customs authorities. Tax evasion has been around as long as the tax man has—and prostitution and illicit gambling longer still. Nevertheless, there are many reasons to think that over the past quarter-century, the underground economy has grown at a faster pace than the above-ground economy has, and there's almost no reason to think this trend will slacken over the next 25 years.

Seismic changes in the nation's economy and its culture—such as a shift from manufacturing to services and increased popular discontent with government—favor the continued growth of the underground sector. This may be an uncomfortable truth for an often-moralistic society, but an underground economy has become a permanent fixture of post-industrial American capitalism, as much a part of the economic infrastructure as Wall Street's gleaming skyscrapers. It's as if a seedling from Nairobi or some other Third World spot has taken root in the sidewalk cracks of the world's most sophisticated economy.

A SAFETY VALVE?

If the underground economy is viewed as some sort of out-of-control dandelion, then the solution might be to redouble enforcement efforts to eradicate tax dodging and the like. But aside from certain predatory activities, such as drug dealing, the shadow sector may not be all bad. Many analysts are coming to view it as a safety valve, a generator of jobs and business opportunities that holds frayed communities together.

In a public housing tenement on the South Side of Chicago, for example, welfare mothers get together on Sunday nights and bake breakfast rolls for sale to schoolchildren. They don't declare the income to Uncle Sam because if they did, they wouldn't get their welfare checks, according to John Kretzmann, a Northwestern University social policy analyst who has surveyed the housing project residents about their off-the-books-activities. "Almost everybody has some [underground] economic activity going on," Kretzmann said. "I think it's absolutely necessary for people's survival that they have these activities."

As usual, California seems to be leading the way. A recent study by economists at San Francisco-based Wells Fargo Bank concluded, "California's underground economy has taken its place with foreign trade, biotech, entertainment and health services as one of the few growth industries during the worst recession to hit the state since the 1930s."

New York, however, probably isn't far behind. Last year, a six-part series in *The New York Times* revealed a dizzying breadth of underground activities in New York City—such as illegal immigrants peddling T-shirts and mood rings on the sidewalks in front of the Immigration and Naturalization Service office in lower Manhattan.

The United States has plenty of company: Shadow economies are flourishing in Eastern Europe and in such supposedly law-abiding places as Canada, where a surge in tax cheating and cigarette smuggling has ignited a national soul search on the ethics of economic disobedience. Canada's finance minister, Paul Martin, recently declared: "The underground economy is not all smugglers. . . . It's hundreds of thousands of otherwise honest people who have withdrawn their consent to be governed, who have lost faith in government." Sound familar?

Common sense suggests that data on the reported economy not only understate the true scale of U.S. economic output, but also overstate the amount of unemployment. If nearly everyone on government relief earns off-the-books income, then alarmist reports on a widening income gap between rich and poor may need to be toned down—except, of course, if the wealthy are heavily misreporting income. No doubt there are plenty of fat cats who don't report capital-gains income on some spectacular investments. (Illegal misreporting shouldn't be confused with legal tax avoidance, everyone's favorite sport in America.)

But don't put much stock in any of the estimates of the size of the underground economy. After all, secrecy and disguise are its defining characteristics.

The Wells Fargo analysis pegged California's underground sector at 18 per cent of the state's above-ground economy—but the author of the study, economist Gary Schlossberg, confessed in an interview that that number was no more than "a conjecture" based on a very crude analysis of the level of cash transactions in the economy. (Drug dealers, prostitutes and off-the-books carpenters usually don't take MasterCards.)

Using the same rubbery yardstick, Schlossberg estimated the national underground economy at about $1 trillion in 1993; that's nearly 17 per cent of the officially reported gross domestic product. Over the past two decades, other economists have produced guesstimates of the underground economy ranging from 1.4 per cent of the reported economy to 28 per cent. *(For a range of such estimates, see table.)*

The Internal Revenue Service (IRS) has thrown up its hands. Asked for an estimate of the underground economy, a spokeswoman said the IRS had long ago stopped trying to make any calculations. (Back in 1976, the IRS estimated the shadow sector at 8 per cent of reported economic output.) "It's too nebulous," the spokeswoman said. "You can't get a figure on it." One number that the IRS does spit out is the so-called tax gap—an estimate of the difference between what taxpayers should pay if they fully report all income from legitimate activities, and what they actually pay. For 1992 alone, the gap was pegged at $90 billion. (The BEA takes account of this estimate when it comes up with its economic-output calculation.)

THE PAPER MONEY TRAIL

With all the fuzziness, why do many analysts say the underground economy has grown rapidly over the past few decades? And why is it widely assumed that this trend will accelerate?

One clue is the curious staying power of paper money, just about the only acceptable means of payment, other than barter, in the underground economy. A little more than a decade ago, experts were hailing the arrival of the cashless society: "Paper currency will give way to electronic impulses," a soothsayer predicted. And in fact, the proliferation of plastic-money credit cards and bank debit cards now allows consumers to fill their carts at the grocery store and their cars at the service station without ever removing a bill from their wallets. But cash hasn't disappeared: In fact, on a per person basis, paper-money holdings rose from $179 in 1950 to $1,142 in 1990, a 538 per cent increase that surpassed the 440 per cent increase in inflation over this period. The underground economy isn't the only reason for the persistence of cash—some people just can't leave their homes without that $10 bill in their side pocket—but it is certainly a very prominent one. The illegal drug economy alone probably accounts for a good deal of the continued popularity of $100 bills.

And how could the numbers racketeers ply their trade without cash? Despite the spectacular growth of legal gambling outlets all over the country, many people still prefer to take their winnings in nontaxable form. A few months ago, Manhattan prosecutors busted "Spanish Raymond" Marquez—a legendary numbers king with a fiefdom of 41 betting parlors that reportedly grossed $30 million annually.

Another spur to the underground economy is illegal immigration. Illegals are heavily employed in activities that can easily be conducted off the books, such as peddling, taxi driving, day care and construction work. In New York City alone, unregulated garment sweatshops, drawing on a pool of cheap, often illegal immigrant labor, have multiplied from the hundreds to the thousands over the past 20-odd years, according to labor union estimates.

Then there are the changes that have rippled through the economy over the past quarter-century. The most important trend is a shift away from the production of tangible goods, such as automobiles and screwdrivers, toward the production of not-so-tangible services, such as business consulting and health care. It's usually easier for service providers than it is for manufacturers to conduct business without leaving a paper or electronic trail. (An important exception is financial services, which often do leave a trail.)

And with the decline of a manufacturing-based economy has come the decline of labor unions, which historically have offered protections against off-the-books business operators. What's more, jobs in the economy have been shifting away

THE SIZE OF THE UNDERGROUND ECONOMY

Estimates of how large the underground economy is vary widely, as shown by this comparison of studies over the past two decades by the Internal Revenue Service (IRS), academic economists Edgar L. Feige and Vito Tanzi, Federal Reserve Bank of Philadelphia economist Joel F. Houston, the Commerce Department's Bureau of Economic Analysis (BEA), U.S. Trust Co. economic consultant James J. O'Leary, author Harry I. Greenfield (from his book *Invisible, Outlawed and Untaxed*), the Labor Department and Wells Fargo Bank.

Study	Estimate (in billions)	Per cent of GNP*	Year of estimate
IRS	$145	8%	1976
Feige	600+	27	1979
Tanzi	118-159	4.5-6	1980
Houston	400	14.7	1980
BEA	184	5.4	1983
O'Leary	432	15.2	1985
Greenfield	350	6.7	1990
Labor	500	10	1992
Wells Fargo	1,000+	16.8	1993

*all estimates stated as a share of gross national product except Wells Fargo's, which is a share of gross domestic product

SOURCES: Federal Reserve Bank of Philadelphia (except for Wells Fargo data)

from large firms to small ones, including sole proprietorships, that can more easily disguise their books.

SORRY, BIG BROTHER

Also nurturing the underground economy is the growth of a postindustrial regulatory regime that has put all sorts of business activities under some form of government control. Keep in mind that some economic actors operate underground principally to escape burdensome requirements—restrictions against pollution, for example.

The tighter the clamps, the greater the incentive for underground activity. Many analysts predict that increased government controls on the health care sector, now being considered by Congress, will spur the growth of off-the-books activities by doctors and others subject to new rules.

The White House has tried to deal with this possibility by calling for tough penalties—including prison terms—for doctors and patients who don't abide by new regulations. And yet, the Congressional Budget Office (CBO) didn't address the potential resort to underground activities as part of its economic and budgetary analysis of the Administration's health care bill. "I don't have any idea what the magnitude of this incentive might be," CBO director Robert D. Reischauer told a researcher for the Federal Reserve Bank of Minneapolis who recently published a lengthy piece on the underground economy.

Likewise, efforts to set tighter controls on the gun market could drive a lot of the activity underground—and not necessarily prevent criminals from getting their hands on weapons.

For evidence of the power of economic incentives—the law be damned—consider the drug trade. The inner-city toughs who peddle crack cocaine are, in a sense, following a basic law of economics. "Returns in the regular [legal] sector can't match the returns in the illegal sector," observed economist Harry J. Holzer of Michigan State University, who has long studied the employment market for minority youths. "These people are making a fairly straightforward economic calculus." A rational actor, of course, might also weigh the short-term rewards against the long-term odds of survival. But the dealers behave according to a famous maxim of British economist John Maynard Keynes: In the long run, we're all dead.

Although the drug trade has thwarted every attempt to eradicate it, there's not much popular support for legalizing drug use. Nor does there appear to be much support for legalization of prostitution—a first step toward bringing it into the above-ground economy.

7. Economy You Can't See

Many analysts and ordinary citizens say that the solution to evasion of taxes on legitimate activities is stepped-up enforcement by the authorities. And why not crack down on all those unlicensed peddlers in New York City?

But before the enforcement squad is doubled and given loads of fancy new equipment, the side effects should be contemplated. "A world of perfect enforcement could be an intolerable place," economist Frank A. Cowell warned in an essay published last year by the Washington-based Institute for International Economics. Think of the shadow sector, Cowell suggested, as "an economic ventilation shaft to enterprises in danger of suffocation. Plumbing, decorating and vehicle repair jobs may get done that would otherwise be unprofitable under an inappropriately austere tax regime."

On the principle that it is more difficult to disguise spending than to disguise income, Uncle Sam may want to consider a shift away from the income tax to a value-added consumption tax. Some economists already back this step as a way to encourage more saving. If the underground economy can't be legislated, moralized or otherwise Big Brothered into oblivion, maybe it's time to reconcile ourselves to its stubborn presence.

How Fast Can the U.S. Economy Grow?

Not as fast as "new economy" pundits would like to think.

by Paul Krugman

Most economists believe that the U.S. economy is currently very close to, if not actually above, its maximum sustainable level of employment and capacity utilization. If they are right, from this point onward growth will have to come from increases either in productivity – that is, in the volume of output per worker – or in the size of the potential workforce; and official statistics show both productivity and the workforce growing sluggishly. So standard economic analysis suggests that the United States cannot look forward to growth at a rate of much more than 2% over the next few years. Furthermore, such analysis indicates that if the Federal Reserve Bank tries to force faster growth by keeping interest rates low, the main result will merely be a return to the bad old days of serious inflation.

However, many influential people – business leaders, journalists, and even a few reputable economists – do not accept that dreary verdict. They believe that the old speed limits on growth have been repealed, perhaps even that the whole idea of speed limits is obsolete. The conceptual basis for their optimism is sometimes referred to as the *new economy view*, sometimes more grandly as the *new paradigm*. Whatever one calls it, this new view of the economy has spread with a rapidity rare in the annals of economic thought. One would have to go back to the rise of supply-side economics in the 1970s to find a case in which a radical economic theory has so quickly become conventional wisdom among a large group of opinion leaders.

The essence of the new paradigm is the claim that the changes everyone can see in the U.S. economy – the rise of digital technology and the growing volume of international trade and investment – have qualitatively altered the rules of the game. Rapid technological change, the new paradigmatics claim, means that the economy can grow much faster than it used to; global competition means that an overheating economy will not produce high inflation. That is obviously an attractive view to anyone who would like to see more rapid growth than the disappointing 2-point-something percent offered by conventional economists; it is also a view that many businesspeople insist corresponds to what they see happening in their own industries. So we should not be surprised at the popularity of this view in the business community.

There is only one problem: when you think about it carefully, you realize that the new paradigm simply does not make sense.

For some reason, the presence of gaping conceptual and empirical holes in the new paradigm – holes that seem obvious to many economists – has

Paul Krugman is the Elizabeth and James Killian Professor of Economics at the Massachusetts Institute of Technology in Cambridge.

not been effectively communicated to a broader audience. Yet the issue is not really difficult or technical: all it takes to see the trouble with the new paradigm are a few thought experiments and some simple arithmetic.

Why Does the Economy Have a Speed Limit?

With the decline of the traditional extended family, in which relatives were available to care for children, many parents in the United States have sought alternative arrangements. A popular scheme is the baby-sitting cooperative, in which a group of parents agree to help one another out on a reciprocal basis.

Any such co-op requires rules to ensure that all members do their fair share. One natural way to ensure fairness, at least for people accustomed to a market economy, is to use some kind of token or marker system. Parents earn tokens by baby-sitting, then in turn hand over the tokens when their own children are minded by others. For example, a recently formed co-op in western Massachusetts uses Popsicle sticks, each representing one hour of baby-sitting. When a new parent enters the co-op, he or she receives an initial allocation of ten sticks. This system is self-regulating, in the sense that it automatically ensures that over any length of time a parent will put in roughly the same amount of time that he or she receives.

It turns out, however, that establishing such a token system is not enough to make a co-op work properly. It is also necessary to get the number of tokens per member more or less right.

To see why, suppose that there were very few tokens in circulation. Parents would want on average to hold some tokens in reserve – enough to deal with the possibility that they may want to go out a few times before they have a chance to baby-sit themselves and earn more tokens. Any individual parent could, of course, try to accumulate more tokens by baby-sitting more and going out less. But what happens if almost everyone is trying to accumulate tokens – as they will be if there are very few in circulation? One parent's decision to go out is another's opportunity to baby-sit. So if everyone in the co-op is trying to add to his or her reserve of tokens, there will be very few opportunities to baby-sit. That in turn will make people even more reluctant to go out and use up their precious reserves, and the level of activity in the co-op may decline to a disappointingly low level.

The solution to this problem is simply to issue more Popsicle sticks. But not too many, because an excess of sticks can pose an equally severe problem. Suppose that almost everyone in the co-op has more sticks than they need. People will be eager to go out but reluctant to baby-sit. It will therefore become hard to find baby-sitters, and because opportunities to use their sticks will become rare, people will become even less willing to spend time and effort earning them. Too many tokens in circulation can be just as destructive as too few.

What on earth does all this have to do with the new paradigm? Well, a baby-sitting co-op is a kind of miniature macroeconomy: a system in which individual decisions to spend and save are crucially interdependent because your spending is my income and vice versa. The depressed state of a baby-sitting co-op with too few tokens in circulation is essentially the same as that of the U.S. economy as a whole when it slips into a recession. And the ability of a Paul Volcker or an Alan Greenspan to engineer a recovery from such a recession rests on his control over the money supply – which is to say, over the number of Popsicle sticks.

There are, of course, some important differences between the full-scale economy and a baby-sitting co-op with a few dozen members. One difference is that the big economy has a capital market: individuals who are short of cash can borrow from others who are cash rich, so the effects of an overall shortage or abundance of money are mediated by the level of interest rates.

An even more important difference involves prices. In the typical baby-sitting co-op, prices are fixed: one Popsicle stick buys one hour of baby-sitting, and that's that. In the big economy, companies are free to cut prices if they are having trouble selling their product and to increase them if they think it will not hurt their sales. As a practical matter, companies are quite reluctant to cut prices – and workers are very reluctant to accept wage cuts. Although prolonged recessions do eventually lead to price reductions, they do so only gradually and painfully. Companies have, however, historically been less reluctant to raise prices in boom conditions. For this reason, the kind of labor shortage a

Have rapid technological change and global competition qualitatively altered the rules of the game?

co-op gets into when there are too many tokens in circulation is rarely severe in market economies; an excessive supply of money gets dissipated by inflation instead.

Still, the Popsicle-stick economy may help us to dispel some commonly held misconceptions about

2 ❖ MEASURING ECONOMIC PERFORMANCE

why economists generally think that there are limits to how fast the economy can grow.

First, nobody claims that the economy has a 2-point-something percent speed limit under all circumstances. When a baby-sitting co-op is in a depressed state because of an insufficient supply of Popsicle sticks, its GBP (gross baby-sitting product) can rise very quickly when that supply is increased. Thus there is nothing puzzling about the ability of the U.S. economy to grow at a rate of more than 3.5% from 1982 to 1989: thanks to expansionary monetary policy, the economy was rebounding from a recession that had raised the unemployment rate to 10.7% and left output probably 10% below capacity. The speed limit applies only when the economy has expanded as much as it can by taking up slack through the use of unemployed resources.

Second, economists don't argue against overambitious growth targets because they believe that any and all growth causes inflation. That is a misleading caricature of what economists are saying, and like all caricatures it is easy to ridicule. To return to our example, no economist would argue that our baby-sitting co-op would suffer inflationary pressures if it grew by adding new members or if current members became more efficient at child care and were therefore able to do more baby-sitting. The limits to growth apply only to growth achieved by expanding demand – say, by issuing more Popsicle sticks – and not to growth achieved by productivity improvements or increases in the number of workers.

So if excessive expansion in demand is the real culprit, how much expansion is too much? Again, return to the baby-sitting economy. How would you know when there were too many Popsicle sticks in circulation? One useful indicator would be the frequency with which parents sought but could not find opportunities to baby-sit, which would essentially be the co-op's unemployment rate. Another indicator would be the frequency with which parents sought but could not find baby-sitters. That figure would more or less correspond to the U.S. economy's vacancy rate – the number of jobs offered by business that have not been filled. Very low unemployment and a high vacancy rate would indicate that the co-op was suffering from excessive demand. In the full-scale economy, it turns out that the vacancy rate and the unemployment rate are closely (inversely) correlated, but data on unemployment are collected more regularly and systematically. We can use the more readily available unemployment rate as a pretty good indicator of labor-market tightness.

How low an unemployment rate is too low? There is, to be honest, a fair amount of uncertainty about that question. Evidence collected before 1990 suggested to most economists that inflation would begin to accelerate when the unemployment rate fell below about 6%; the failure of inflation to show any discernible increase with the rate barely above 5% has been something of a surprise. However, wage increases have begun to accelerate, and stories about labor shortages – usually rare in the U.S. economy – have become common. (In the last six months of 1996, such stories were about three times as common as they had been a year earlier.) In such a tight job market, it seems unlikely that the Fed could cut unemployment further merely by increasing demand. Perhaps policy initiatives such as training programs, which might make more people employable, could give the economy more running room. But the new paradigmatics want the Fed to adopt higher growth targets *now*, without any preconditions of that sort.

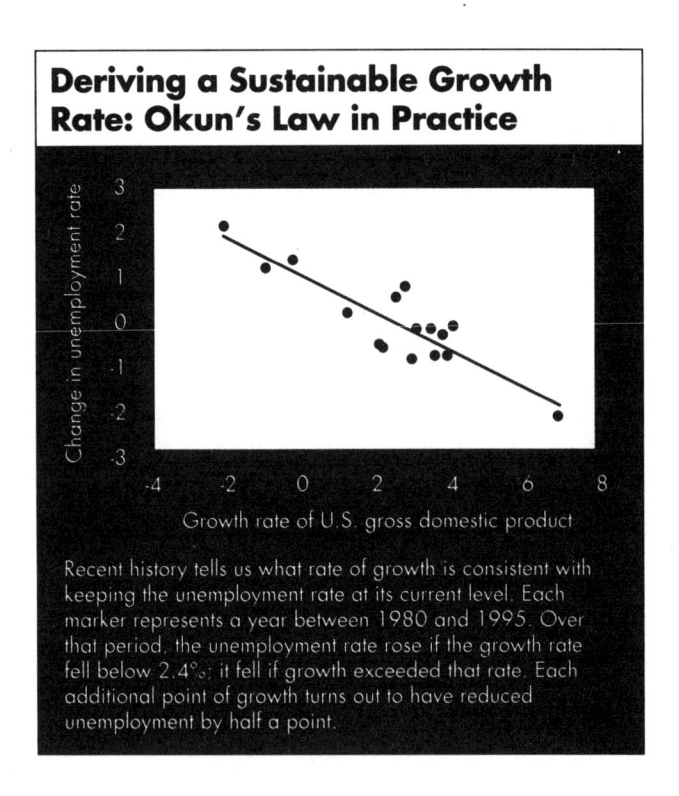

Deriving a Sustainable Growth Rate: Okun's Law in Practice

Recent history tells us what rate of growth is consistent with keeping the unemployment rate at its current level. Each marker represents a year between 1980 and 1995. Over that period, the unemployment rate rose if the growth rate fell below 2.4%; it fell if growth exceeded that rate. Each additional point of growth turns out to have reduced unemployment by half a point.

Although economists may not be able to say with great certainty how low an unemployment rate is too low (or, to put it another way, at what level we would expect increases in demand to trigger inflation), we do know reasonably well what growth rate will keep the unemployment rate at roughly its current level. There is a strikingly close relationship between the economy's growth rate and the rate of change in the unemployment rate; indeed, it is one of the few things economists are willing to call a "law" (Okun's Law) with a straight face. Between 1980 and 1995, the rate of growth consistent with a steady unemployment rate was about 2.4%. (See the graph "Deriving a Sustainable Growth Rate: Okun's Law in Practice.")

Nor is there any evidence to show that the growth rate consistent with a constant unemployment rate – which is the maximum growth rate that can be sustained once the economy has taken up all of its slack – has increased in the last few years. The unemployment rate in 1995 averaged 5.6%, about the same as the rate in 1990. The average growth rate over those five years was 1.9%, which is lower than the estimate of the sustainable growth rate based on the scatterplot in the graph.

Why does the sustainable growth rate seem to be so low? There are two main reasons. First, the U.S. labor force is no longer growing as fast as it did in the years when the baby boomers were growing up and women were moving into paid employment. In the 1990s, the number of people working or looking for work has grown at an annual rate of only about 1%. Second, according to the official numbers, productivity – output per worker – has also grown at a sluggish annual rate of only 1%. The sum of these two numbers is 2%: the growth in the economy's productive potential.

All of this seems pretty well established. How, then, can the new paradigmatics claim that the economy is capable of much faster growth?

In part, they simply do not believe the official numbers: they believe that outdated statistics are greatly understating productivity growth. But is that true? More important, does it matter?

Productivity Paradoxes

It is a truism that increases in productivity are the key to long-term economic growth. It is therefore a cause for concern that official numbers show that the United States remains in the productivity slow lane, which it has occupied since the early 1970s. The annual increase in output per worker-hour is in the vicinity of 1% per year, far below the nearly 3% annual rate of the 1950s and 1960s.

Many business leaders, however, find these official statistics hard to credit. For one thing, they find it implausible that the digital revolution, which has had so much impact on the way business is conducted, should not have produced a more visible payoff. Furthermore, many executives believe that intense competition has forced them to engage in radical measures to increase productivity; again, they cannot believe that these measures have not paid off for the economy as a whole.

To those who believe that dreary official statistics on productivity are wrong, it seems obvious that dreary conventional views about the limits to growth are also wrong. Suppose, after all, that

8. How Fast Can the U.S. Economy Grow?

actual productivity growth in the 1990s has been more than twice as high as the official number – say 2.5%. Then the economy's potential growth, the sum of its labor-force growth and productivity growth, is actually 3.5% rather than 2%. So shouldn't the Fed let the economy rip?

Let's take this in stages.

First, although the critics of official productivity statistics have a case, there are counterarguments. Techno-skeptics point out that digital technology, though flashy, arguably does less for the actual productivity of workers than many less glamorous innovations of the past. (My own favorite example of an utterly unglamorous technology that had a profound effect on the economy was freight containerization, which was introduced in the 1960s and eliminated the need for literally hundreds of thousands of longshoremen and other freight handlers.) And businesses have found that some new technologies – the desktop computer among them – have large hidden costs.

Critics have also pointed out that much business restructuring does not eliminate jobs; it merely outsources them from large corporations that pay high wages to smaller suppliers that often pay less. From the point of view of the restructured company, it may seem as if the same work is being done with far fewer people; from the point of view of the economy as a whole, output per worker may not have increased much, if at all.

For what it is worth, economists who try to estimate productivity growth are thoroughly divided over the issue. A few believe that productivity has been greatly understated, and many believe that it has been at least mildly understated. But a substantial number believe that the official numbers are more or less right.

However, this discussion is really a side issue, because if we are asking what growth target is appropriate, it doesn't matter whether the official numbers are right.

The important point to remember is that productivity, by definition, is measured as output per worker. When we talk about productivity in the U.S. economy as a whole, we are talking about real gross domestic product per worker employed in the United States – nothing more, nothing less. (It is worth remembering that neither the output generated nor the workers employed by U.S.-based companies outside the United States plays any role in the calculation of either GDP or productivity.)

Now suppose that it were true that productivity has actually grown at 2.5% since 1990. Would that mean the Fed should have set a growth target of 3.5% over that period, and that by allowing GDP to grow at only 2% it has stifled the economy's potential? Not at all. After all, nobody is claiming that

For the economy as a whole, business restructuring may not have increased productivity much, if at all.

the numbers on employment are wrong (job growth has been about 1% per year), and the dollar value of GDP is not in question. So a claim that true productivity growth has actually been 1.5% higher than the statistics say is necessarily also a claim that true GDP growth has been higher by exactly the same amount; that is, any understatement of real growth must be a result of an overstatement of inflation. You should therefore not fault the Fed for failing to give the economy the 3.5% growth it deserved. Instead, you should congratulate it for getting the growth rate exactly right!

Or put it a bit differently: if the Fed had tried to achieve a growth rate of 3.5% - measured using our current yardsticks - it would have in fact been seeking a true growth rate of 5%, well above the economy's potential. And to have tried that over the period from 1990 through 1996 would have meant driving the unemployment rate down far below current levels, to roughly 2%. Few people think that is a feasible rate.

The question of whether official statistics about the U.S. economy are understating productivity growth is an important one for many issues. It is irrelevant, however, to the question of whether the target growth rate as measured using those same statistics should be higher.

Globalization and Inflation

The claim that the U.S. economy, despite the drab statistics, is actually experiencing a high rate of productivity growth is one of the two main planks of the new paradigm. The other is the claim that expanding demand will not lead to inflation, even at very low unemployment rates, because of the new importance of global competition. Unlike in the past, the story goes, U.S. companies today have to face actual or potential competition from rivals in Europe and Asia; thus even in the face of strong demand they will not dare raise prices, for fear that these rivals will seize the market.

As in the case of the claim of understated productivity growth, this assertion is open to attack. Without question, many U.S. companies are facing international competition to an unprecedented degree. However, such global competition mainly occurs in the goods-producing sector - very few services are traded on international markets - and even within manufacturing many industries remain largely isolated from foreign competitors. (Seen any Chinese refrigerators lately?) Because the United States is mainly a service economy, no more than 25% and probably less than 15% of employment and added value are actually subjected to the kind of global market discipline that the new paradigm emphasizes.

But discussion of the true extent of globalization, like discussion of the true rate of productivity growth, is beside the point. Even if global competition played a bigger role in the U.S. economy than it actually does, it would not raise the economy's speed limit. That's because no matter how big the world economy may be, the maximum possible growth rate of any piece of that economy, once any economic slack has been taken up, is still equal to the sum of productivity growth and labor-force growth in that piece.

That seems to be a tricky point to grasp, perhaps because many people wrongly suppose that a global economy is somehow more than the sum of the national economies of which it is composed. One way to correct this impression is to recall a parable introduced by MIT's Paul Samuelson more than 30 years ago; I refer to this as the story of Samuelson's angel.

Globalization has not changed in any important way the rules about how fast the U.S. economy can grow.

Samuelson's idea was, roughly speaking, to imagine history running backward. We usually think of the global economy as coming about through greater economic integration - which is indeed the way we actually got to where we are. But Samuelson suggested imagining what would happen if the world started with a unified economy and then split it apart. Specifically, he suggested the following parable: Imagine that initially neither distance nor national boundaries separated the world's resources. But then an angel descended and scattered the resources to many lands; thereafter, the nations could trade with one another, but some resources - such as labor - became immobile. (This parable is clearly inspired by Genesis 11:1-9, the story of the Tower of Babel; presumably, the factors of production had dared to challenge heaven.)

The parable's point is that the resulting global economy - produced by pulling apart a system that had no international trade because there was nobody to trade with - would be indistinguishable from a global economy produced, as happened in fact, by partly joining together previously separate national economies through trade. Now it is easy to fool yourself into thinking that joining economies together somehow changes the rules, that it removes old constraints on economic policy. One would hardly expect, however, to gain freedom from policy constraints by pulling an integrated economy apart. Thus there is no reason to expect economies in our imperfectly integrated world to be free from the limits that would apply even to a more perfect global union.

What the new paradigmatics claim, once again, is that because of globalization monetary expansion can now be pursued without risk of inflation. Can that be right? Let's think it through with the help of the angel.

First, imagine a world before the angel in which all resources can work together, a world with a single language and a single currency—say, one consisting of red banknotes. This world's economy would be one big baby-sitting co-op; therefore, expanding the quantity of money could boost output up to a point, but beyond that point such expansion would be counterproductive and would usually be dissipated in inflation. (True, the actual world economy is unthinkably immense—gross world product is probably about $25 trillion. The U.S. economy, with its $7 trillion GDP, is unthinkably immense even by itself—yet it can usefully be thought of as a baby-sitting co-op. It is hard to see that going up a notch in scale would make a qualitative difference.)

Now suppose the angel descends and divides the world into two nations, each with its own resources and currency, so that one country now uses blue notes and the other uses green. And suppose that the world as a whole is close to full employment and that both countries simultaneously expand their money supplies by doubling the number of notes in circulation. Clearly, the result would be no different from what would happen if the economy increased its money supply in the same proportion before the angel's visit; once the slack in the world economy had been taken up, further expansion would lead to inflation.

Matters would be somewhat different if only one country tried to expand its money supply. In that case, it might seem that competition from the non-inflating country would limit price rises in the expansionary economy. So perhaps the world as a whole is not exempted from speed limits, but at least the inflationary consequences of a unilateral expansion would be muted.

Still, there is a problem with this line of argument, too. If the exchange rate is floating, an increase in the number of green notes would lead to a depreciation of green currency against blue. That would lead directly to an increase in the prices of goods that the expanding nation imports (when measured in green currency); it would also lead to a rise in the prices of blue-currency products that compete with green goods, presumably giving those companies using green currency room to raise prices. (In fact, until the rise of the new paradigm the conventional wisdom held that monetary expansion leads to more inflation or at least feeds into inflation more quickly when a single country undertakes such expansion unilaterally rather than when many nations do so at the same time.) And the United States has a floating exchange rate: the dollar rises or falls promptly on indications that the Fed is likely to tighten or loosen its policies.

This is not just a conceptual argument. It is worth remembering that although large-scale international trade may still seem somewhat novel in the United States, most other countries have long been highly dependent on foreign trade. Even now, the share of exports and imports in U.S. GDP remains well below levels that have been commonplace elsewhere for many decades. Yet international evidence shows without question that excessive monetary expansion leads to inflation just as surely in highly open economies as it does in ones that do little trade.

All of this is not meant to downplay the importance of globalization for many economic issues. For example, growing world trade has unquestionably been an important factor in sparking economic development in many poor nations; less happily, it has played at least some role in the growing inequality of incomes in advanced countries. One thing globalization has not done, however, is to change in any important way the rules about how fast the U.S. economy can grow. Globalization or no globalization, if the Fed tries to expand the economy faster than the sum of labor-force growth and productivity growth, inflation will follow.

A Paradigm's Popularity

The popularity of the new paradigm poses something of a puzzle. The two key arguments in its favor are that high productivity growth justifies higher growth targets for the economy as a whole and that global competition prevents inflation. As we have seen, however, both arguments collapse—indeed, look quite silly—when given even a cursory critical examination. Moreover, the criticisms offered in this article are neither deep nor unusual: my own experience is that when one tries to explain the new paradigm to an academic macroeconomist who is unaware of the doctrine's growing influence, he or she produces essentially the same critique you have just read within a minute or two and finds it hard to believe that anyone would take the doctrine seriously.

But as I have pointed out, many people, especially in the business community, do take the doctrine very seriously indeed. Why?

One answer is that the critiques described here do not come naturally to businesspeople. The business of doing business is essentially microeconomic: it involves understanding how an individual market works, not the way all markets interact. A business leader in general has no need to understand macroeconomic issues, in which the interaction of markets is of the essence. Why should a CEO know or care about how an increase in the money supply affects GDP or how that effect changes when an economy has a floating as opposed to a fixed exchange rate?

A second reason for the broad popularity of the new paradigm is that it tells businesspeople what they would like to hear about growth. Who would not be attracted to a doctrine that promises that the economy can expand without limit for the indefinite future?

There is, however, one more reason for the special appeal of the new paradigm: it is extremely flattering to the businesspeople who constitute its audience. Imagine an advocate of the new paradigm speaking to a group of, say, several hundred top executives. The new paradigmatic tells the executives that their tough new management style and application of cutting-edge technology have brought a productivity revolution; meanwhile, they all know that they can't raise prices because they must now face intense global competition. Now in that group there will surely be at least a few executives whose honest reaction should be: "Well, that may be the way it is in other lines of business. In my industry, however, the truth is that we haven't made great strides in productivity lately. But that hasn't really hurt our bottom line: the fact is that there isn't much international competition in the stuff we sell, and my domestic rivals and I have a tacit understanding that it's in all of our interests not to get into price wars." Realistically, how likely is it that anyone will actually stand up and say this?

Perhaps we should not be surprised that the new paradigm, which makes businesspeople feel good both about their economic prospects and about themselves, has spread so rapidly. But it is time to get serious: an economic doctrine, no matter how appealing, must be rejected if it cannot stand up to well-informed criticism. We would like to believe that the U.S. economy can grow much faster if only the Fed would let it. But all the evidence suggests that it cannot.

'HELL NO, WE WON'T SAVE!'

Americans seem to have rejected thrift yet are wealthier than ever. Can this be? Can it last?

BY ROBERT J. SAMUELSON

THE AMERICAN ECONOMY CONTINUES TO ZIP ALONG, defying—so far—predictions that it would slow down or crash. In the last quarter of 1998, output (gross domestic product) raced ahead at a blistering annual rate of 5.6 percent, much faster than most economists had predicted. We seem to have created a perpetual-motion machine, but behind this remarkable performance is a puzzling phenomenon: the virtual disappearance of personal saving.

It's as if the entire country had chanted in unison, "Hell no, we won't save." By now, the official savings statistics are no secret. In 1998, Americans' personal-savings rate fell to a post-World War II low of 0.5 percent of disposable income: we spent 99.5 percent of our after-tax income. The apparent paradox is that even though we're saving less than ever, we feel—mostly as a result of the stock market—wealthier than ever.

Anyone who doubts that the falling savings rate has propelled the economic boom should do some arithmetic. In 1998, Americans' after-tax income totaled about $6 trillion. The personal-savings rate in 1997 was 2.1 percent of income; so the drop to 0.5 percent represents a decline of 1.6 percentage points. On $6 trillion, that's almost $100 billion of extra spending.

Richer Than Ever
Household wealth has grown much more than debts.

$ TRILLIONS	1987	1998
Total assets	**$19.6**	**$41.3**
Tangible assets	7.7	12.5
Financial assets	11.9	28.8
Total liabilities	**$2.8**	**$6.3**
Mortgages	1.8	4.1
Other debt	1.0	2.2
Net worth	**$16.8**	**$35.0**

SOURCES: FED. RESERVE, PRUDENTIAL SECURITIES

This meant, in practice, that Americans spent another $100 billion on computers, vacations, fast food, cars and toys, among other things. Strong consumer buying in turn bolstered business investment. These twin spending streams have carried the economic expansion and offset the huge drag of an ever-widening trade deficit (in 1998 it rose by 1.4 percent of GDP). The dissaving of American consumers has spared the U.S. economy a recession and—through higher imports—aided the ailing global economy.

But can it continue? The plunge in personal savings surprised economists and has triggered intense debate. If it doesn't last, prospects for the U.S. and world economies would worsen. So let's examine the debate.

The dominant view holds that, on inspection, lower savings make sense and need not change soon. To understand why, glance at the table above. It's adapted from a study ("There Is No Savings Crisis") by economist Richard Rippe of Prudential Securities. The table depicts the vast increase in the wealth of the household sector (including nonprofit organizations). Since 1987 Americans' net worth (assets minus liabilities) has roughly doubled to about $35 trillion. Higher tangible assets (homes, cars, furniture) account for some gain. But financial assets (savings accounts, stocks, bonds) represent most of the gain; perhaps $8 trillion of it is in stocks.

Rippe's argument is not simply that Americans, having won big in the stockmarket lottery, are entitled to splurge. The logic is more subtle. As he points out, personal savings make up only one part of national saving. Businesses do most national saving through retained profits and depreciation (the cost of replacing obsolete investment). And business saving has increased. But businesses are owned by shareholders: individuals, pension funds, mutual funds. If companies save and invest wisely, their profits and stock prices rise. Whats wrong with individuals (the real owners) skimming off some gains to augment spending?

Nothing, it would seem, as long as companies save, invest and achieve high-profit growth. The paradox of less saving and greater wealth is resolved. People continue the rituals of saving. They make, say, regular deposits into retirement accounts. But gains are so huge that investors decide they can spend against a bit of their profits. So people sell stocks or borrow. The extra spending drops their reported savings close to zero (spending equals current income). But their wealth—the value of their accumulated savings—is still rising rapidly.

Case closed? Not exactly. Consider now another study ("How Negative Can U.S. Saving Get?") from economists Wynne Godley of The Jerome Levy Economics Institute of Bard College and Bill Martin of Phillips & Drew, a London investment-management company. What bothers them is not the low savings rate by itself. The real problem (they say) is that the savings rate must continue to go lower. The other drags on the economy—the rising trade deficit and the government budget surplus—mean that growth depends on an ever-larger counterthrust from consumer spending.

Well, the savings rate has continually dropped. In 1992 it was 5.7 percent of income. Now it's zero. But will people overspend their incomes by 1 percent, 2 percent, 5 percent? To coax Americans to do that, the stock market must not just stay where it is, say Godley and Martin. It must leap forward in great strides to create ever more wealth for consumers to skim. Sooner or later the process must choke on itself, they say (though they don't say when). Then the U.S. economy would stagnate or decline. The aftershock would hit Asia and Latin America the hardest, because these regions send a quarter and two thirds, respectively, of their exports to the United States.

Who's right? My bias lies with the pessimists. The U.S. economy may be surfing on its own euphoria. Overpriced stocks cause consumers to overspend and businesses to overinvest—and none of it can last. The optimistic interpretation is that we're merely witnessing the advent of a new, unfamiliar pattern of thrift. Either way, low personal saving is an essential catalyst of the present boom. If somehow it were to rise, the American and world economies would face even greater peril.

From *Newsweek*, February 22, 1999, p. 42. © 1999 by The Washington Post. Reprinted by request.

Unit 3

Unit Selections

10. **The Economic Report of the President for 1998: A Review,** James Galbraith
11. **Reflections on the Balancing Act,** George Brockway
12. **The Tax Man Cometh: Consumer Spending and Tax Payments,** Peter S. Yoo
13. **The Flat Tax in Theory and Practice: Simple, Efficient, Fair. Or Is It?** William G. Gale
14. **Why Are Taxes So Complicated, and What Can We Do about It?** William Gale
15. **Are Americans Really Overtaxed?** William G. Gale
16. **Should We Retire Social Security?: Grading the Reform Plans,** Henry J. Aaron and Robert D. Reischauer

Key Points to Consider

❖ What role do public spending and private investment play in the current economic expansion?

❖ How do taxes affect household consumption and saving? Which of the major proposals for tax reform do you favor, and why?

❖ What should be done to solve financial problems in the Social Security system?

DUSHKIN ONLINE Links www.dushkin.com/online/

14. **Center on Budget and Policy Priorities**
    http://www.cbpp.org
15. **Economic Report of the President**
    http://www.whitehouse.gov/WH/EOP/CEA/html/CEA.html
16. **The Public Debt**
    http://www.publicdebt.treas.gov/opd/opd.htm
17. **Tax Wire**
    http://www.tax.org/TaxWire/taxwire.htm

These sites are annotated on pages 4 and 5.

Fiscal Policy and the Federal Budget

Discussion of federal budget policy in the United States has fallen to an abysmally low level. It consists wholly of bumper-sticker slogans, sound bites, lip reading. It finds public expression in shibboleths like no new taxes, balance the budget, don't raid Social Security. Prescriptions for dealing with the budget evade the central problem, which is making choices. —Herbert Stein ("Governing the $5 Trillion Economy," *The Brookings Review*)

Prior to the 1930s, fiscal policy—changes in taxes and government spending for the purpose of smoothing out the business cycle—was not used explicitly by policymakers in their pursuit of macroeconomic goals. In fact, the conventional wisdom of the day held that the best fiscal policy was a balanced budget. Most economists (known as *classicists*) maintained that a market economy had enough built-in mechanisms so that any downturns in economic activity would be quickly reversed. According to this line of reasoning, recessions were temporary departures from an economy's normal state of affairs, which was noninflationary full employment. In the classical view, since the economy would perform better if the government did not intervene, annually balanced budgets—which served to constrain government—were a good idea.

Classical reasoning was shattered by the events of the Great Depression, a period of prolonged and widespread joblessness, falling incomes, bankruptcies, and political turmoil. In 1936 the British economist John Maynard Keynes attacked the classical view in his *General Theory of Employment, Interest, and Money*. Keynes demonstrated how market economies could normally produce less than acceptable levels of employment and output. In Keynes's view, a healthy economy (operating at full employment and full production) could only come about if fiscal policymakers were permitted to administer the right medicine (in the form of carefully unbalanced budgets). As Keynes's ideas gained general acceptance over the next few decades, a national consensus emerged on the need for the federal government to intervene actively in the pursuit of macroeconomic goals. This view was officially sanctioned in the Employment Act of 1946 (which established a federal commitment to policies aimed at achieving "maximum production, employment, and purchasing power").

Although the goals mandated by the 1946 act are relatively clear-cut, actual policy-making experience since World War II demonstrates the difficulties the United States faces in implementing them. It also reflects the limitations of both economic ideology and the political system. Curiously, the late-1990s echo with the same question originally raised by Keynes and the classicists more than a half century ago: Are balanced federal budgets a good idea? Should federal surpluses be used to pay for such pressing programs as public education and Social Security reform? Or should they be used to cut personal income taxes? The challenge to fiscal policy is that there is no single, generally accepted answer to such questions.

This unit begins with a review by James Galbraith of "The Economic Report of the President for 1998." The report poses a critical question: Can the present U.S. economic recovery survive? The authors of the report (the Council of Economic Advisers) appear to trace the expansion primarily to private business investment rather than public spending. Galbraith challenges this interpretation. He says that all the long and strong expansions of the present era (including those of both the Kennedy-Johnson and Reagan years) were based on approximately equal increases of public spending and private investment.

Economic theory suggests that a balanced budget will bring interest rates down. Now that the federal budget has finally come into balance, the time has come to put this theory to the test of practice. In the next article George Brockway warns that the theory may not work as stated.

Few would doubt that the federal tax system contains serious flaws, particularly to the extent that taxes may discourage saving and investment. Then, in "The Tax Man Cometh," Peter Yoo considers evidence on ways in which income tax changes might alter savings and consumption. Next, William Gale asks a series of questions: Why are taxes so complicated? (The reason lies in the fact that we want the tax system to accomplish so many things at the same time.) Are Americans really overtaxed? (U.S. taxes are at record levels, but evidence of crushing tax burdens is missing.) Can some simple way be found to replace the income tax with a new tax system, such as the "flat tax"? William Gale explores various proposals for reforming federal taxes. He shows that none of these proposals is a panacea and that each is flawed in some way.

One of the major items in the federal budget is social insurance. The Social Security system has come under increased scrutiny recently. The program currently faces a long-term imbalance between the cost of benefits promised under current law and the program's projected income. In the final article in this unit Henry Aaron and Robert Reischauer evaluate some of the major proposals for Social Security reform.

The Economic Report of the President for 1998: A Review

James Galbraith

The Council of Economic Advisers argues that the economic expansion can be sustained without a significant increase in public spending. The author has his doubts.

It has been a long time since the pleasures of full employment have made their way into an *Economic Report of the President* or, under the circumstances, could have done so. But in the 1998 report we find that the time has once again come around:

> A high-employment economy brings enormous economic and social benefits. Essential to personal economic security is the knowledge that work is available to those who seek it, at wages sufficient to keep them and their families out of poverty. A tight labor market increases the confidence of job losers that they will be able to return to work, lures discouraged workers back into the labor force, enhances the prospects of those already at work to get ahead, enables those who want or need to switch jobs to do so without a long period of joblessness, and lowers the duration of a typical unemployment spell.... Wasted resources from not producing at potential, together with the human cost of unemployment, are intolerable; the elimination of this waste is the principal benefit of a sustained return to full employment.

Nor is this all. The 1998 report goes on to link macroeconomic performance and income distribution, a logical and empirical connection of profound importance. Not only does a full-employment economy reduce poverty by providing jobs to those who would otherwise not have them, it also raises the relative wages of those at the bottom of the earnings scale.[1] As the report rightly states:

> Since 1993, household income has grown in each quintile of the income distribution, with the largest percentage increase going to the poorest members of our society. Maintaining a full-employment economy is essential if this progress is to continue.

The emergence of a frankly Keynesian commitment to sustained full employment with reasonable price stability is the most important and the most heartening thing in the 1998 *Economic Report of the President*, the first under the leadership of Janet Yellen, who last year became the first macroeconomist and the first even approximate Keynesian in nearly twenty years to chair the Council of Economic Advisers (CEA).[2] And the analytical sections in the front of the present document that defend that commitment are its most challenging passages. After all, they pose the critical question: Will this recovery survive?

In delivering its answer, the 1998 report shies away from last year's "new vision economics," an empty set of effusions left behind by the departing Joseph Stiglitz. Indeed, without invoking that aberration directly, Yellen rejects calls for a "new paradigm" on the ground that "many such assessments are extreme and unsupportable." She then proceeds to marshal the case that deep economic changes have, in fact, made a sustained period of full employment possible under policies as they are. There are three main arguments:

- Improved competitive conditions in diverse markets, including traded manufactures but also transportation, communications, electricity, and banking, may have speeded the pace of technological innovation.

- Declining unionism (not an "unalloyed boon" as a later paragraph tardily adds) may have produced more flexible labor markets.

- The public sector has become smaller and more efficient, which, alongside reduced deficits, means that the private economy is better able to bear the burden of promoting and sustaining growth. This report specifically demonstrates that

---

JAMES GALBRAITH is the author of Created Unequal: The Crisis in American Pay *(New York: Free Press, a Twentieth Century Fund book, 1998). He is professor at the LBJ School of Public Affairs and senior scholar at the Levy Economics Institute.*

10. Economic Report of the President for 1998

since 1991 we have seen the strongest relative contribution of private investment to economic growth in any recovery since 1954; there has been no contribution from the growth of government. As a result, the council argues, the fundamentals are right, and the "economy is remarkably free of the symptoms that often presage an economic downturn—such as an increase in inflation, an accumulation of inventories, or evidence of financial imbalance." The council does note the very large increase in private debt burdens, but argues that, since private asset values have also increased, balance sheets are sound and the rise in household liabilities need not be a concern.

This case mixes non-Keynesian and Keynesian arguments. Unfortunately, insofar as it attempts to show that the expansion can be sustained with no changes in policy, it is not convincing in either mode. To begin with, the non-Keynesian arguments are hollow. There is no actual evidence of accelerated technological development, nor is there any reason to think that an increase of "creative destruction" would promote more rather than less stable growth if it occurred. There is equally no evidence linking "flexible labor markets" to the fall in unemployment. On the contrary, the approach to full employment has been a macroeconomic phenomenon from beginning to end, and it is associated with *decreasing* wage flexibility, stronger unions, and a compression of wage structures, as the council itself shows.

But the most important questions of sustainability stem from the Keynesian issue of macroeconomic balance. Can a long recovery rely entirely on the growth of private-sector investment and consumption, with no contribution from government? Can the associated accumulation of private debts go on indefinitely? Or, on the contrary, is a purely private-sector expansion likely to prove unsustainable, precisely because households and businesses become increasingly vulnerable to a collapse of creditworthiness and financial crisis as time goes on?

All the long and strong expansions of the present era were based on approximately equal increases of public spending and private investment.

On these points, the council's own evidence undermines the conclusions it would like to have us draw. The report produces a chart to show the singular reliance of the present expansion on private business investment rather than public spending. But the chart also shows two earlier expansions that exhibited a similar pattern—those of 1954–57 and 1970–73—each of which ended in a nasty recession after a short time. True, the present expansion has already lasted twice as long as those did—but it has also been only about half as strong. All the *long and strong* expansions of the present era, including both the Kennedy–Johnson boom of the 1960s and the Reagan expansion of the 1980s, were based on approximately equal increases of public spending and private investment.

The council's argument that the risk of rising debts in the household sector is offset by the rising value of assets is also flawed. Assets tend to be flexibly priced; liabilities are not. It is true that a rise in the stock market and in property values permits the assumption of ever-greater volumes of mortgage and consumer debt while actually improving household balance sheets. But if the asset prices were suddenly to collapse, the debts would still be there. It is at that point, and not before, that financial instability characteristically brings capitalist expansions to an end.

What is the likelihood that the turmoil in Asia will force a major drop in U.S. asset prices, exposing the naked vulnerability of the hyper-indebted American household? The council does not know, and neither do I. But I am quite sure that the danger exists, that efforts of the International Monetary Fund to restore stability in Asia will not succeed, and that fundamental changes in the U.S. approach to the crisis, including cuts in interest rates, are needed *now* to reduce the risks here at home. I do not want to read, retrospectively, of the correctness of this position in next year's economic report.

The Last Gasp of NAIRU

Although Keynesian arguments have reappeared in the 1998 *Economic Report of the President*, they do not yet predominate.[3] Instead they now coexist, in uneasy juxtaposition, with the anti-Keynesian views that have dominated the reports of past Clinton councils.

Thus, while the council has shed the inflation fears that once were associated with the concept of a non-accelerating inflation rate of unemployment (NAIRU), it still cannot muster the intellectual decisiveness required to ditch the idea completely. The council notes that last year's midpoint estimate of NAIRU, 5.5 percent unemployment, should have led to a 0.3 percent increase in core Consumer Price Index (CPI) inflation instead of to the 0.4 *decline* that actually occurred. It concedes that these events "would appear to pose a challenge to models of price inflation based on the concept of a NAIRU" (p. 57). This may be the macroeconomic understatement of the decade.

Yet the council makes a last-ditch effort to save NAIRU. It suggests that a special factor has depressed an otherwise rising inflation rate, namely, a sharp 40 percent a year reduction in the price index for computers. A figure on page 58 suggests that inflation would have risen sharply over the past several years, rather than declined, had it not been for this development.

The argument, and the figure, are in error. As Dean Baker of Washington's Economic Policy Institute has pointed out to Yellen in a letter, the council's statisticians apparently weighted the computer sector using a methodology appropriate for fix-weighted price statistics but not for the chain-weighted deflators actually in use. The result was that the contribution of computers to declining prices is overstated by a factor of about three. A corrected calculation would not show sharply rising inflation in the absence of falling computer prices. As Baker wrote to Yellen, the point is not an important one in itself, but it undermines—actually, it destroys—this bit of evidence for the survival of NAIRU.[4]

The International Dangers

It is normal that the *Economic Report of the President* should contain a measure of cheerleading for the declared policies of the

3 ❖ FISCAL POLICY AND THE FEDERAL BUDGET

administration. The present document is no exception; one finds the usual encomiums to free markets, free trade, deregulation, and small government that have marked the Clinton administration's persistent campaign to deny all rhetorical high ground to the Republican Party. For the most part, this sort of thing is harmless. And for the most part, in the present report, an experienced reader can distinguish between fluff and substance without too much trouble.

The major exception to this comes in the sections devoted to the international economy and its effect on the U.S. balance of trade. The report's take on the large trade deficit the United States is currently running is resolutely upbeat: The trade deficit exists only because domestic investment is outrunning domestic saving. Thus, although the once-vaunted "twin deficits" have disappeared, we need not be concerned with a large external imbalance because it reflects foreign confidence in the future of our economy. At one point, the Council even compares the present period to the late nineteenth century, when the United States was the world's developing country, a powerful newcomer with an unlimited potential.

One can understand the motivation. From a domestic and a political standpoint, the economy is performing well. To panic over the trade deficit per se would be foolish; to cut the trade deficit by slowing economic growth and so reducing imports would be a cure much worse than the disease.

But, on the other hand, what is the evidence that the surplus of investment over saving in this expansion is in any way more virtuous, or sustainable, than the same phenomenon during the boom phase of the Reagan expansion in the mid-1980s? Having accused the Reagan administration of a "consumption binge" (on p. 40), the Council presents (on p. 247) a chart showing that "net national investment" more than doubled from 4 to 10 percent of gross domestic product (GDP) between 1982 and 1984. The resulting gap between investment and savings, which widened to about 4 percent of GDP by 1986 and produced a comparable current-account deficit, are the exact counterparts, so far as one can tell, of the present 2 percent gap and current-account deficit. If there was something distinctively consumption binge-ish about Reaganism, or distinctly pro-investment about the Clinton policy, this report does not tell us what it is.

Does the fact that the federal budget was in deficit under Reagan and in balance today make any material difference to the relationship between the savings–investment imbalance and the current account? The answer is surely *not* that budget balance produces a better mix of consumption and investment. The Council's own data show that the investment share of GDP was actually higher under Reagan—which can hardly be surprising when one remembers the vast subsidies to business equipment purchases that were built into the Reagan tax cuts. There is also no evidence that the business investments of the Clinton era were more productive than those under Reagan and certainly no reason to think that foreigners have swooned over some such categorical change in fundamentals.

Instead, Clinton's advantage over Reagan lies mainly in the climate of lower interest rates with which Alan Greenspan chose to favor him. There is, of course, a relationship between interest rates and the budget, but it is not the one usually stated. We do not have low interest rates because we have budget balance. Rather, we have budget balance because Greenspan has kept interest rates comparatively low, allowing the economy to grow and tax revenues to rise by unexpectedly large amounts. Budget balance is an effect of this fundamental difference in monetary policies. In itself, and otherwise, it is not very important.

Paradoxically, it is monetary policy that is now giving us problems on the current account. Although interest rates have been low enough to maintain domestic growth and progress toward full employment, they have been too high in the international context. Indeed, rising *real* and *relative* short-term rates of interest in 1997 attracted vast flows of foreign capital to the United States—most of it in the form of liquid portfolio investments that can be just as easily moved out in a crisis. These funds pushed up the dollar and came to perch in our stock market, with predictable consequences in the form of a bubble in stock prices and a corresponding decline in the real economies of the (mainly Asian) sources of the capital flight.

In some ways, therefore, the summer of 1998 is emerging as a light version of the summer of 1982, with rising real interest rates, a rising dollar, financial instability, and a severe collapse in major U.S. export markets—Asia today, Latin America sixteen years ago. The sooner that the experts at the council and elsewhere in this administration come down from the clouds and see this parallel, the greater the hopes that strong actions can be taken to avert a repeat of the "lost decade" in the world economy as well as an end to the expansion and to the present period of full employment and growth-generated budget balance in the United States. One suspects that the Treasury's deputy secretary Lawrence Summers, who worked for Reagan's CEA in 1983 and who also became the architect of the one timely and successful bailout of our time, that of Mexico in 1995, has seen it. But Summers could definitely use some help.

What is now required to deal with the Asian depression? I am hoping for a detailed chapter in the next *Economic Report of the President*.[5] It should explain why the Asian economies collapsed after taking U.S.-prescribed medicine to liberalize their capital markets. It should give the brutal truth as to why the International Monetary Fund's prescriptions for stabilization and turnaround have failed. Indeed it should explain just how the ideologues at the IMF turned the crisis into panic, notably in Indonesia, by forcing bank closures. It should firmly renounce the untenable goal of open capital markets, as embodied in the proposed multilateral agreement on investments (MAI), and acknowledge the fundamental right of every state to control capital flows. It should embrace the Tobin Tax on foreign exchange transactions as a bare first step toward regaining control of global speculation. And it should also explain how, in the second half of 1998, Alan Greenspan seized control of a passive Federal Reserve Board and once again saved the world economy by dropping interest rates and flooding the globe with liquidity.

But I digress.

Social, Environmental, and Antitrust Policy

The 1998 report contains two competent chapters on social policy, no doubt reflecting in part the addition of Rebecca M. Blank as a member-nominee to the CEA. One of them deals with the well-being of children, and the other with income inequality across racial and ethnic groups. Both should serve students and teachers of these subjects as useful guides to basic facts, which are well-presented in diagrams. These chapters are, however, distinctly academic. Apart from a defense of affirmative action there is little policy content for the depressing reason that the administration has little policy to offer.[6] The inclusion of the 1996 "welfare reform"—the abolition of Aid to Families with Dependent Children (or welfare)—among a list of "policy initiatives to support family incomes" (p. 98) is enough to make one sick.

A chapter on environmental and health issues follows. The environmental section emphasizes incentive plans and market schemes to reduce pollution emissions, a staple of economistic interventions in this area. One can only wish for the first dispassionate analysis that will show that these schemes actually work. This chapter makes an effort to show that the sulfur dioxide permit-trading program has produced a more efficient mix of stack-gas scrubbers and low-sulfur coal inputs in electric power plants. But then it turns out that a high initial price of permits engendered *excessive* investment in stack-gas scrubbers, while the shift to low-sulfur coal is due to a fall in railroad freight rates from the Powder River Basin. The statement that "had regulators simply required all utilities to install scrubbers, they would not have been able to take advantage of the new availability of cheap, low-sulfur coal" (p. 161) is the purest non sequitur. Unwitting and undeterred, the CEA goes on to discuss similar schemes for nitrogen oxides and greenhouse gases, but it is obvious that the large technical problems in these areas will not be overcome.

Readers should not omit the short chapter on antitrust policy that rounds out the 1998 report. It is written by someone with a detailed knowledge of recent case law and no very serious commitment to rigid principle. Instead, one sees in this chapter the rare application of discretion and intelligence to the relationship between business and government, with government agencies frankly asserting their judgment about what will and will not unduly restrict competition. They may be right, and they may be wrong; complicated questions of market definition inevitably bedevil the measurement of monopoly power. But the contrast to the one-size-fits-all marketizing approach that some economists take to environmental questions is very sharp, and a frank recognition that the problems are complicated is, to this economist, a reassuring sign.

10. Economic Report of the President for 1998

Summary

In general, President Clinton's three chairs of the Council of Economic Advisers have begun their tenure with a good report, and Janet Yellen has the particular distinction of beginning to restore macroeconomic issues to their central place in the policy discussion. Moreover, there is clearly an evolution here toward a reassertion of core Keynesian principles and commitments. One can hope that the next report will complete the transition by, among other things, finally purging NAIRU.

There are, however, serious omissions. The present document fails to add anything to last year's defense of social security, which suggests that the council is not going to be a player in that debate as it unfolds. It fails to speak up for a higher minimum wage, even though the president has said he supports one. It asserts no responsibility for finding solutions to the serious international crisis we now face, but instead offers only bland assurances that further progress toward free trade and capital markets and support for the IMF will solve the problems of the Washington consensus. Like all Clinton-era reports since the ill-fated 1994 Laura Tyson effort, it also avoids any serious discussion, let alone criticism, of monetary policy. To try to deal with macroeconomic policy in this way is, of course, entirely like writing *Hamlet* without the prince.

Notes

1. A confession: This is the major theme of my new book.
2. A second confession: Assistant Professor Janet Yellen was my first macroeconomics instructor, at Harvard in 1970. I was then and remain today an admirer of her work.
3. There remains also a shifty unwillingness of the report to acknowledge that the achievement of full employment with reasonable price stability vindicates the Humphrey-Hawkins Full Employment and Balanced Growth Act of 1978, that oh-so-embarrassing legal charter of the council itself. In a mush-mouthed passage, the report refers to "the Employment Act of 1946 . . . , together with its later amendments" that supposedly "gave the Federal Government responsibility for stabilizing short-run economic fluctuations." In fact the 1946 act called ringingly for "maximum employment, production and purchasing power," while the full-employment act sets the higher goals of "full employment," "balanced growth," and "reasonable price stability." It would be nice if economists responsible for implementing this law stopped pretending that it says something other than what it does.
4. Baker tells me that the CEA has acknowledged his point.
5. Unlike this year's offering, it should not be a sermon entitled "The Benefits of Market Opening," a title designed to prejudge the issue it is supposed to discuss.
6. And, to be fair, even less likelihood of getting it enacted.

Budget Surplus?

Reflections on the Balancing Act

George Brockway

This former CEO finds no firm historical relationship between high interest rates and a widening federal budget deficit. If rates do not fall sharply by 2002, he says, we will have been shamefully misled.

It is fashionable to complain that economists do not (or cannot) put their theories to the test of practice. But an unexpected bonus of the nonpartisan budget-balancing agreement is that it will soon provide such a test, for our generation, of the theory that a balanced budget brings interest rates down.

Of course, we have had similar tests before. From 1942 to 1951 the Federal Reserve Board and the Treasury worked to maintain a "pattern of rates," whereby ninety-day Treasury bills paid 0.375 percent, the long bond paid 2.5 percent, and until 1947 the prime interest rate kept step at 1.5 percent. These rates are lower than most economists today consider feasible, and the budget then was as far from being balanced as it has ever been. But most of the time there was a war on, so the test is not altogether conclusive.

GEORGE BROCKWAY, the economic columnist for The New Leader, *is the author of* The End of Economic Man *and* Economists Can Be Bad for Your Health.

From *Challenge*, September/October 1998, pp. 55-58. © 1998 by M. E. Sharpe, Inc., Armonk, NY 10504. Reprinted by permission.

11. Reflections on the Balancing Act

Since the war—since 1929, actually—we have managed to balance the budget only eight times: four times under President Harry Truman, three times under President Dwight Eisenhower, and once under President Lyndon Johnson. The possibly astonishing fact is that in every one of these eight balancing years the prime rate went up, not down. Again, however, there were extenuating or confusing circumstances (mainly war or recovery from war). In addition, the last time it balanced (1969) was almost three decades ago. Conditions today are surely different in many ways.

It is also possible that the connection between low interest and a low or nonexistent deficit is not immediate but shows itself only over a stretch of years. But there have been puzzling

It is possible that the connection between low interest and a low or nonexistent deficit is not immediate but shows itself only over a stretch of years.

stretches. Since World War II, the most dramatic rise in the annual deficit was from $73.9 billion in 1981 to $237.5 billion in 1986. This record-breaking rise in the deficit was accompanied by an equally record-breaking fall in the prime rate, from 21.5 percent in January 1981 to 7.5 percent in August 1986. (Interestingly enough, the annual change in the Consumer Price Index declined from 10.3 percent in 1981 to 1.9 percent in 1986, roughly paralleling a fall in the federal funds rate.) These figures are from the time of President Ronald Reagan and Federal Reserve Board Chairman Paul Volcker, which was not so long ago, but may for some reason no longer be relevant.

There is, nevertheless, a more recent example. In 1989 the deficit was $152.5 billion, while the prime rate was 10.87 percent. Four years later, in 1993, the deficit rose to $255.0 billion, while the prime rate fell to 6 percent (inflation also fell).

During the 1996 election campaign, President Clinton repeatedly took credit for reducing the federal deficit and thus lowering interest rates. He continues to make the claim. It is a pretty story, but actually only half true. It is indeed true that the Clinton budgets have all shown a reduction of the deficit. The Republicans, as one might expect, claim responsibility for the reductions, but that is not what is false about the president's story. Neither side seems to have looked at the record. President Clinton's indisputable error is that whereas the deficit fell in all six years, the interest rate rose in 1994, 1995, and now 1997. In addition, despite the six declining deficits, and with the long-sought zero deficit in sight, the prime rate today is two full points higher than it was at the end of the Bush administration.

As a further conundrum, we may consider the fact that the Bank of England last month raised the British interest rate for the sixth time since the May elections, although the deficit has been reduced to less than 1 percent of GDP. Britain now has the highest interest rate of any European nation—and the lowest deficit.

We may have enough experience to anticipate what our leaders and their economic advisers may make of the foregoing figures. The obvious explanation is that the contrary behavior of the interest rate is attributable to the Federal Reserve Board's attempts to control inflation. The Board, the story goes, is forced by economic law to raise the interest rate from time to time to keep the economy from overheating.

Anyone questioning current policies may accept this explanation for two reasons: First, as Huck Finn said of *The Adventures of Tom Sawyer*, it tells the truth, mainly. And second, it makes the doubters' case. It is the truth that the Federal Reserve Board

To balance the budget by 2002, we have ripped holes in our social and cultural fabric.

controls the interest rate, though perhaps not always wisely. And since it is the Federal Reserve that controls the interest rate, then the turmoil, the destructiveness, and the grief of the budget-balancing hurrah have been misconceived and misdirected.

In order to balance the budget by 2002, we have ripped holes in our social and cultural fabric, allowed the decay of our infrastructure and public amenities, and abandoned much promising artistic, scholarly, and scientific work. These sacrifices we have made for low interest rates.

At present, interest rates are considerably higher than what forty years ago would have been judged usury or loan-sharking and prosecuted as violations of the law. If the rates do not fall substantially by 2002, we shall have been shamefully misled, not only by our political leaders but chiefly by the economists who have so confidently dispensed their advice. What actually happens when the budget is finally balanced will be the test of the economists' theories. Given this record of the past sixty or seventy years, it's no wonder that there has been little professional or political demand for rushing to judgment and balancing the budget this year or even the next or the next.

Despite the six declining deficits, and with the long-sought zero deficit in sight, the prime rate today is two full points higher than it was at the end of the Bush administration.

The Tax Man Cometh: Consumer Spending and Tax Payments

Peter S. Yoo

April 15. It causes much anxiety, with last-minute rushing to the post office. Of course tax day also spurs anger, especially in Americans who owe the government money. Surprisingly, people put themselves through this ritual year after year, undoubtedly promising themselves that they will never again wait until the eleventh hour. Paying taxes is after all one of life's certainties.

Unfortunately, the disruptions tax payments cause may go beyond mere annoyance. Early in 1995, the growth of personal spending—as measured by personal consumption expenditures—slowed sharply, increasing a meager 0.1 percent in April. Analysts immediately blamed tax payments for the slowdown in consumer spending. "One of the major reasons for the weakness in consumer spending this spring was the sharp rise in payments among many homeowners and affluent taxpayers to cover their unexpectedly high 1994 income tax obligations.... Many economists have cited the slow pace at which the Internal Revenue Service [IRS] issued tax refunds this year as a chief culprit for weak consumer spending."[1]

Indeed, certain circumstances increased individual tax liabilities in April 1995. High-income taxpayers saw their taxes rise as a result of the Omnibus Budget Reconciliation Act (OBRA) of 1993, which increased their taxes retroactively. The act gave them the option of distributing their increased tax bill over three years. The second installment was due in April 1995. In addition, the IRS was more careful in its review of tax returns, delaying some tax refunds.[2] Both of these factors increased individual tax payments in April, even though the increase attributable to refund delays was temporary. The story for the analysts, therefore, was simple: Tax payments went up, disposable income fell, and so consumer spending fell.

Is the story so simple? Does consumer spending change when tax payments change? To answer this, I present several episodes in which tax payments changed noticeably.

TAXES AND CONSUMER SPENDING

Traditional economic models present consumer spending as a function of disposable personal income. So any change in tax payments directly affects disposable personal income, thereby changing consumer spending. Typically, these models do not include expectations about future income. Because changes in tax payments reduce current disposable personal income dollar for dollar, the models predict that such changes contemporaneously have a large effect on consumer spending.

Recent models of consumer behavior, however, are more ambiguous about the contemporaneous link between tax payments and consumer spending. These models argue that people consider their lifetime resources when making spending decisions. If this indeed is the case, individuals should adjust their savings, thereby spreading the impact of tax liability changes over a longer period. In essence, these models assert that people have other and possibly better alternatives to merely changing their spending dollar for dollar because they can adjust their mix of consumption expenditures and savings.

[1] See Johnston (1995).

[2] Berry (1995) and Hershey (1995) reported that some economists attributed the slowdown in February's retail sales to the slow refunds.

Table 1

Changes in Individual Tax Liabilities

Act/Event	Month Enacted	Effective Date	Description
Revenue Act of 1964	February 1964	March 1964	$11 billion tax cut
Revenue and Expenditure Control Act of 1968	June 1968	April 1968	10 percent surcharge
Tax Reform Act of 1969	December 1969	January 1970	Extended surcharge
Revenue Act of 1978	November 1978	January 1979	$19 billion tax cut
Economic Recovery Act of 1981	August 1981	October 1981	25 percent cut in tax rates
Tax Reform Act of 1986	October 1986	January 1987	Major tax code overhaul
OBRA 1990	October 1990	January 1991	Tax increase on high income
OBRA 1993	August 1993	January 1993	Tax increase on high income
Tax Rebate 1975	March 1975	May 1975	Up to $200 tax rebate
Refund Delays*			

*Delays in tax refunds starting in March 1985, mostly reversed by May 1985.

Another reason to be wary of analyses that attribute changes in consumer spending to changes in tax payments is that changes in personal income, also induce dollar-for-dollar changes in disposable personal income. (The two measures of income are related by the following national income accounting identity: disposable personal income = personal income—personal tax and nontax payments.) So there may be periods when changes in consumer spending are in response to changes in personal income and not to changes in tax payments. That is what most likely happened early in 1995. As the growth of personal consumption expenditures fell, personal income growth also fell. Personal income grew 0.5 percent in March 1995 but rose only 0.2 percent in April 1995. It is likely, therefore, that the slowdown in personal income growth accounted for the slowdown in consumer spending.

Any examination of the relationship between changes in tax liabilities and changes in consumer spending, therefore, should consider a wide time frame, changes in personal income, and the possibility that individuals diffuse the impact of such changes by altering their savings. First, in my analysis, I use a 12-month window surrounding the changes in tax payments. This provides a time frame in which to observe the response of consumer spending beyond the period when a change in tax payment occurred.

Second, the analysis asks how much individuals spent out of every dollar of personal income and disposable personal income. Economists call this measure of spending *the average propensity to consume*—merely a ratio of consumer spending to a measure of personal income:

(1) $$APC \text{ out of } PI = \frac{PCE}{PI}$$

(2) $$APC \text{ out of } DPI = \frac{PCE}{DPI(= PI - T)},$$

where *APC* is average propensity to consume, *PI* is personal income, *DPI* is disposable personal income, *PCE* is personal consumption expenditures, and *T* is tax and nontax payments.

Figure 1

Personal Tax and Nontax Payments

Seasonally Adjusted Annual Rates ($Billions)

[Chart showing personal tax and nontax payments from 1959 to 1995, with annotations for: Revenue Act of 1964; Revenue and Expenditure Control Act of 1968; Tax Rebate, 1975; Refund Delays, March–May 1985]

Typically, these two measures of *APC* move in tandem, but there are occasions when the relative movements diverge. The divergences occur because any change in tax payments affects *disposable* personal income dollar-for-dollar but has no effect on personal income. Since changes in tax liabilities do not affect personal income, *APC* out of personal income will reflect the response of consumer spending to changes in tax payments. Changes in tax liabilities do affect disposable personal income, however. So, if consumer spending does not react to a change in tax payments, *APC* out of disposable income will move in the [same] direction of the change in tax liabilities. If consumer spending is not responsive to changes in tax liabilities, the two ratios will thus behave differently.

Finally, in my analysis I track the behavior of personal saving because individuals may use their savings as a buffer against changes in tax liabilities, increasing the amount saved if tax payments fall and reducing the amount saved or borrowed if tax payments increase. I therefore examine the behavior of personal saving rates, ratios of personal saving to personal and disposable personal incomes.

IDENTIFYING CHANGES IN TAX LIABILITIES

To examine the relationship between taxes and consumer spending, I first had to identify periods in which tax payments increased or decreased. The personal income tax rate changed at least eight times from 1959 through 1995 because of the Revenue Act of 1964, Revenue and Expenditure Control Act of 1968, Tax Reform Act of 1969, Revenue Act of 1978, Economic Recovery Act of 1981, Tax Reform Act of 1986, OBRA 1990, and OBRA 1993.[3] Table 1 provides a brief summary of these tax law changes. Pechman (1987), Hakkio et al. (1993) and *Congress and the Nation* provide more comprehensive summaries about the changes in the tax code.

The Department of Commerce publishes seasonally adjusted, monthly estimates of personal tax and nontax payments.[4] These estimates include federal, state, and local taxes, as well as nontax payments. Figure 1 shows the path of monthly personal tax and nontax payments since 1959, and it indicates that some of the changes in federal tax laws had identifiable effects on this series. Figure 1 also shows few prominent spikes that do not correspond to one of the noted changes in tax law. Personal tax and nontax payments show a sharp drop in 1975. This is attributable to a tax rebate offered in May 1975. The series also behaved oddly in early 1985 because there was a delay in tax refunds. Table 1 briefly describes these two special cases as well.

As you can see in Figure 1, not all tax law changes noted in Table 1 show changes in personal tax payments. This is probably

[3] I examined this period because personal consumption expenditure data are available back to January 1959.

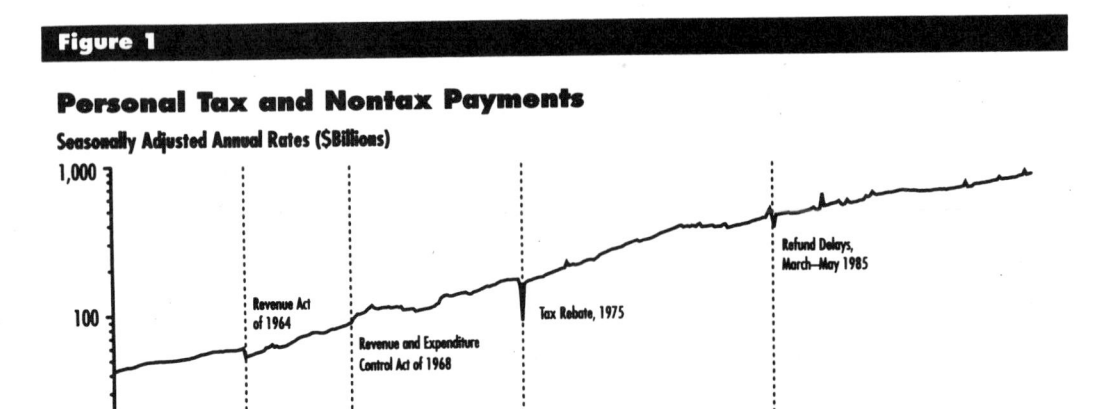

[4] Nontax payments include passport fees, fines and penalties, donations, and tuitions and fees paid to government-operated schools and hospitals. See Byrnes et al. (1979) for a discussion of the construction of the personal income statistics.

12. Tax Man Cometh

Figure 2

Revenue Act of 1964

Income and Consumption
Seasonally Adjusted Annual Rates ($Billions)

[Line chart showing Personal Income, Disposable Personal Income, and Personal Consumption Expenditures from 9/63 to 8/64, with Tax and Nontax Payments and Personal Saving, Net Interest Payments and Transfers Abroad labeled]

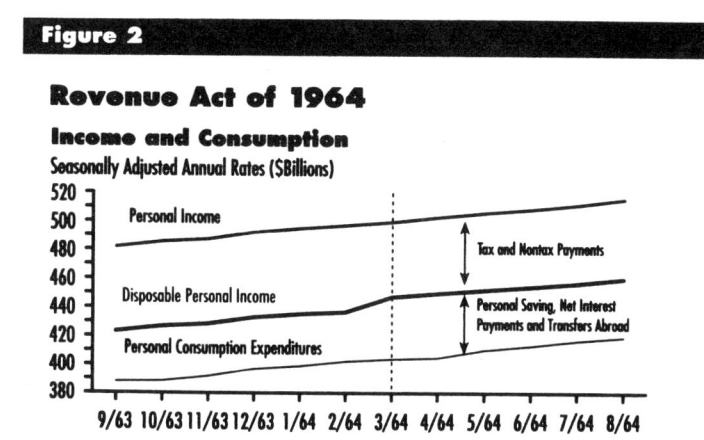

Average Propensitites to Consume

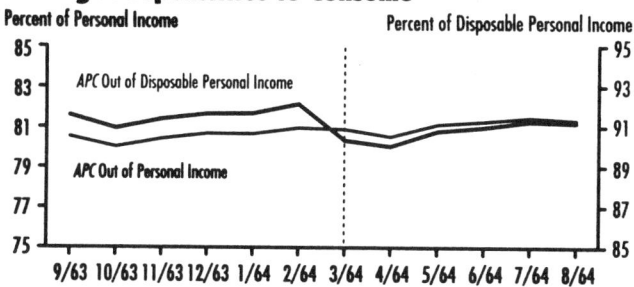

[Line chart showing APC Out of Disposable Personal Income and APC Out of Personal Income from 9/63 to 8/64]

Personal Saving Rates
Percent

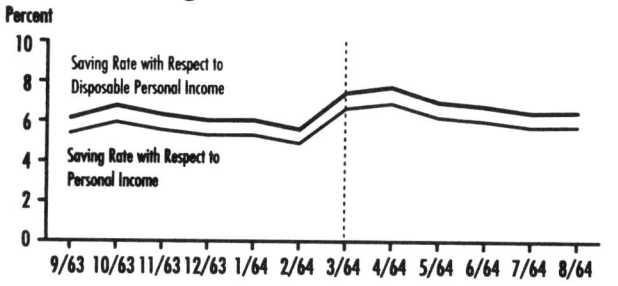

[Line chart showing Saving Rate with Respect to Disposable Personal Income and Saving Rate with Respect to Personal Income from 9/63 to 8/64]

because of changes in economic conditions or because individuals altered their behavior to circumvent the changes in the tax code. This presents a problem with the simple analysis I have proposed. Therefore, I focus on one tax cut (the Revenue Act of 1964) and one tax increase (the Revenue and Expenditure Control Act of 1968). I also examine two other episodes—the tax rebate of 1975 and the refund delays of 1985. Unlike the first two episodes, these two were unexpected or nearly unexpected. An episode's forecastability is important because modern consumption theory states that individuals adjust their behavior to minimize the disruptive nature of predictable future events. It is possible, therefore, that consumer spending did not respond contemporaneously to changes in taxes because consumers had adjusted their behavior well in advance of the changes taking effect. All four episodes show observable changes in personal tax and nontax payments.

WHAT HAPPENED TO CONSUMPTION?

Revenue Act of 1964

Congress passed the Revenue Act of 1964 in February of that year, and the changes took effect that March. The act substantially reduced individual taxes, decreasing personal tax and nontax payments by $8.1 billion between February and March.

So how did consumers react to this tax cut? Consumer expenditures, as illustrated in Figure 2, suggest consumers did not react during the 12 months surrounding the tax cut. Table 2 summarizes the behavior of tax and nontax payments, personal consumption expenditures, and personal saving near the effective dates of the four episodes.

The path of consumer spending shows little discernable movement between February and March of 1964. The change in personal consumption expenditures between the two months was merely $1.6 billion. It is possible, however, that other factors (like changes in personal income) may be distorting the picture. The top panel of Figure 2 also shows that personal income growth was relatively constant during the sample period. In contrast, disposable personal income rose noticeably when the tax cut took effect.

Disposable income rose, and consumer spending did not change. What happened to the extra money? Most likely, people saved it. Personal saving rose by $8.8 billion between February and March, very close to the reduction in tax payments between the same two months. The difference between disposable personal income and personal consumption expenditures

Table 2

Impact of Changes in Tax Liabilities*

	Tax and Nontax Payments	Personal Consumption Expenditures	Personal Saving
Revenue Act of 1964 (February–March)	−8.1	1.6	8.8
Revenue and Expenditure Control Act of 1968 (June–July)	6.0	6.8	−7.1
Tax Rebate of 1975 (April–May)	−60.1	24.2	49.0
Refund Delays of 1985 (February–March) (April–May)	30.1 −66.6	6.2 35.2	−16.2 21.3

* Changes in seasonally adjusted annual rates ($ billions).

(personal saving, net interest payments, and transfers abroad) rose sharply once the tax cut took effect, corresponding to the increase in personal saving.[5] The sharp increase in personal saving of nearly the same magnitude as the drop in personal tax and nontax payments suggests that the tax cut that took place in 1964 did not affect consumer spending near the time the cut took place, but rather led individuals to save more.

Figure 2 provides another way to see what happened to consumer spending's response to the change in tax liabilities. The middle panel shows the two measures of *APC* out of income. *APC* out of personal income shows little change during the 12 months, but *APC* out of disposable personal income shows a noticeable drop between February and March of 1964. The divergence of the two ratios is consistent with the hypothesis that the tax cut did not coincide with a change in consumer spending in the short run. *APC* out of personal income did not change because neither personal consumption expenditures nor personal income changed, whereas *APC* out of disposable personal income decreased because disposable personal income increased when tax payments fell. People responded by increasing their saving rates as indicated by the rise in the two personal saving rates between the two months in the third panel of Figure 2.

Revenue and Expenditure Control Act of 1968

The Revenue and Expenditure Control Act of 1968 provides an opportunity to see the response of consumer spending to increased tax payments. The act, established in June 1968, called for a 10 percent income-tax surcharge, retroactive to April 1968. The effect on personal tax and nontax payments began in July of the same year. Personal tax and nontax payments increased by $6 billion between June and July 1968.

How did individuals respond to the increase in tax payments? Personal consumption expenditures increased $6.8 billion between June and July, not at all consistent with the traditional theory that higher taxes reduce consumer spending. Moreover, the relative stability of personal income and personal consumption expenditures occurring at a time of increased tax payments produce the divergence of the two measures of *APC*, as shown in Figure 3. *APC* out of personal incomes shows little change during the 12 months, but *APC* out of disposable personal income shows a noticeable increase between June and July because disposable personal income fell as a result of the tax increase. This is consistent with the hypothesis that the tax increase did not affect personal consumption expenditures. How then did they pay

[5] Although personal saving is only a part of this sum, it is the largest of the three components. Furthermore, net interest payments and transfers abroad did not change much during the period.

Figure 3

Revenue Act of 1968

Income and Consumption
Seasonally Adjusted Annual Rates ($Billions)

- Personal Income
- Disposable Personal Income
- Personal Consumption Expenditures
- Tax and Nontax Payments
- Personal Saving, Net Interest Payments and Transfers Abroad

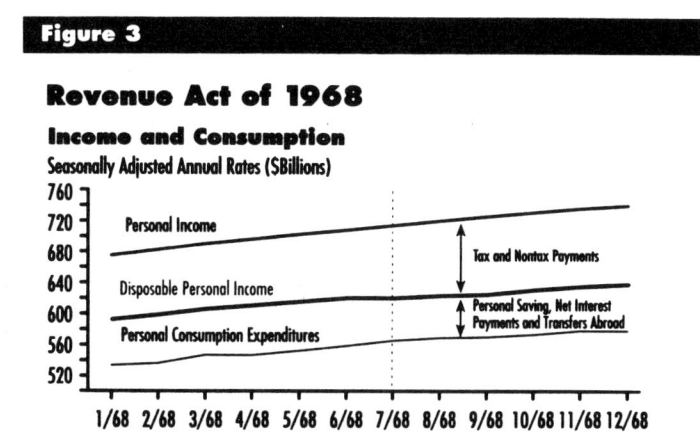

Average Propensities to Consume
- APC Out of Disposable Personal Income
- APC Out of Personal Income

Personal Saving Rates
- Saving Rate with Respect to Disposable Personal Income
- Saving Rate with Respect to Personal Income

---

amount, but less than half the reduction in tax payments.[6] Therefore, the upward tick in *APC* out of personal income reflects an increase in consumption. The sharp drop in *APC* out of disposable income and the increase in *APC* out of personal income is consistent with the hypothesis that people spent some of, but not all, the extra money they received from the rebate. The rebate increased *disposable* personal income but did not affect personal income, as shown in Figure 4.

What was not spent was saved. Personal saving increased $49 billion, which more than accounts for the difference between the drop in tax payments and the increase in spending. The higher saving increased personal saving rates with respect to personal and disposable personal incomes. So unlike the revenue acts discussed earlier, the data indicate that there was some contemporaneous movement of consumer spending to a change in tax liabilities; however, individuals absorbed most of the impact of the tax change by modifying their saving.

Refund Delay of 1985

In 1985 the IRS fell behind in issuing refunds because it was updating its computers. This caused an initial rise in tax payments in March. By May, however, refunds were back on track, depressing tax payments. The initial delay coincided with an increase in personal tax and nontax payments of $30.1 billion between February and March. Once the IRS resolved its problems, tax payments dropped $66.6 billion between April and May.

So what did consumers do when their promised checks were late? Personal consumption expenditures increased $6.2 billion during the delay; a $35.2 billion increase in consumer spending coincided with the reversal. The initial increase is once again contrary to the reaction typically attributed to increases in tax payments. The latter increase accounts for nearly half of the reversal in refund delays. A delay in refunds first increases net tax payments, reducing disposable income, as shown in Figure 5.

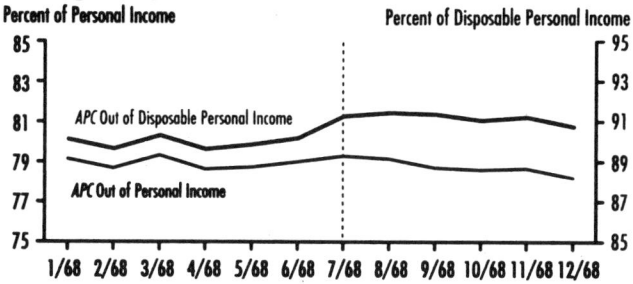

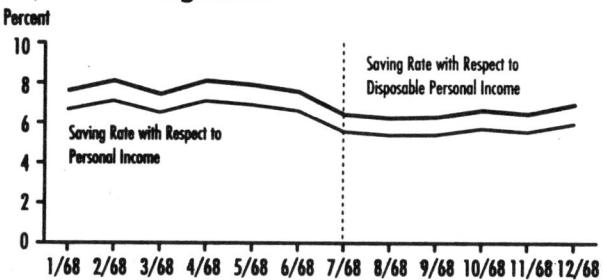

[6] Shapiro and Slemrod (1995) used survey data to analyze the impact of the 1992 reduction in withholding. They found that the temporary tax cut affected consumer spending among some individuals, increasing consumer spending 43 cents for every dollar reduction in withholding. Their number shows what happened to an average dollar of additional income. A crude, comparable number is a ratio of the change in personal consumption expenditures to the change in tax payments. That ratio is 40.3 cents.

for the additional taxes? Personal saving fell by $7.1 billion between the two months, an amount more than enough to pay for the higher tax payments. This drop in saving accounts for the fall in the two measures of personal saving rates shown in the bottom panel of Figure 3.

Tax Rebate of 1975

As a result of the tax rebate bill enacted in March 1975, the IRS issued rebate checks. This reduced personal tax and nontax payments by $60.1 billion between April and May 1975. Consumers reacted by increasing personal consumption expenditures by $24.2 billion—a large

So if consumer spending does not change, the ratio of consumption to personal income does not move because movements in tax payments do not affect personal income. In contrast, the ratio of consumption to disposable income rises as disposable income falls. Once refunds arrive, consumers have more disposable income, but if they have not altered their spending, their *APC* out of disposable personal income falls while their *APC* out of personal income remains constant.

Figure 5 indicates that people reacted somewhat to the timing of refunds because *APC* out of personal income shows a small decrease in March and a large increase in May. This is consistent with an initial drop followed by a rise in consumer spending in response to the timing of the refunds. The behavior of *APC* out of disposable personal income is also consistent with consumers' slight reaction to the timing of refunds. *APC* out of disposable income rose between February and March 1985 and then fell between April and May.

Again, data are consistent with the hypothesis that individuals used their savings to absorb most of the changes in tax payments. As net tax payments increased between February and March, personal saving fell $16.2 billion, then as net tax payments decreased between April and May, personal saving rose $21.3 billion. Although these figures are not as large as the changes in personal tax and nontax payments, they account for a sizable portion of the changes in taxes. Figure 5 indicates that personal saving rates with respect to personal and disposable personal incomes decreased then increased as net tax payments rose and fell.[7] It appears that individuals thus offset the negative impact of refund delays with reduced spending and saving. They then reversed their actions once they received their refunds.

CONSUMERS REACT— SOMEWHAT

My analysis suggests that consumers react only somewhat to changes in tax liabilities. The tax cut of 1964 and the tax hike of 1968 produced very little response in consumer spending. Moreover, accounting for individuals' ability to adjust to predictable events does not significantly change the conclusion about consumer sensitivity. The four cases suggest that consumers are reluctant to change their spending patterns and thus alter their savings to compensate for changes in their tax payments. If any sensitivity exists, it appears to be more in response to unexpected, rather than expected, events—even then the reaction is not large.

Figure 4

Tax Rebate of 1975

Income and Consumption
Seasonally Adjusted Annual Rates ($Billions)

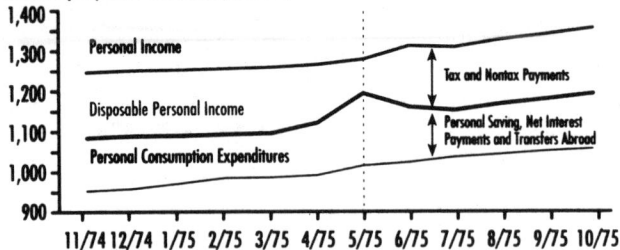

Average Propensities to Consume

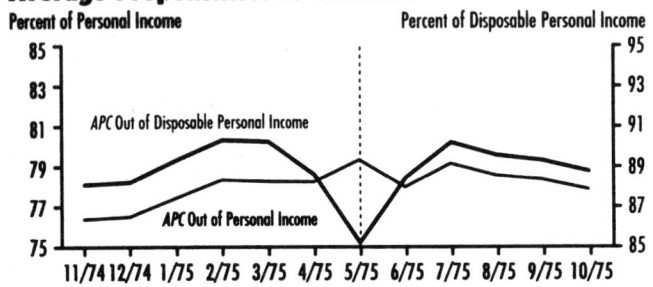

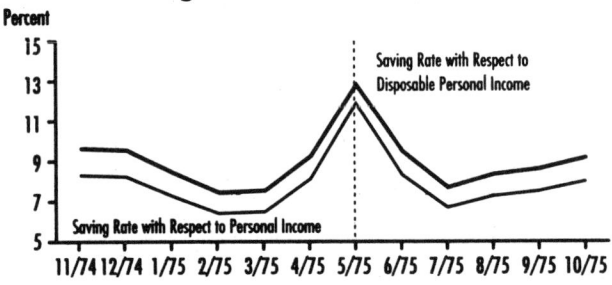

Personal Saving Rates

[7] Wilcox (1990) studied the effects of the timing of tax refunds on consumer spending, including the 1985 delay. He found that a dollar of received tax refunds translates into 7.5 cents of additional spending.

Figure 5

Refund Delays of 1985

Income and Consumption

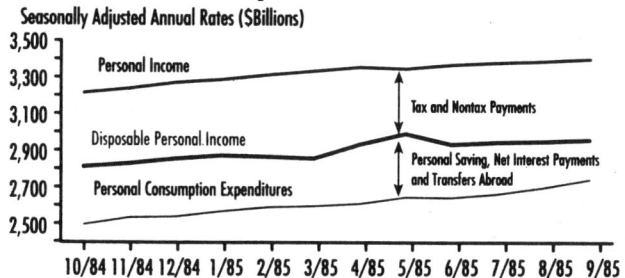

Seasonally Adjusted Annual Rates ($Billions)

[Line chart showing Personal Income, Disposable Personal Income, and Personal Consumption Expenditures from 10/84 to 9/85, ranging from 2,500 to 3,500. Annotations indicate "Tax and Nontax Payments" and "Personal Saving, Net Interest Payments and Transfers Abroad".]

Average Propensitites to Consume

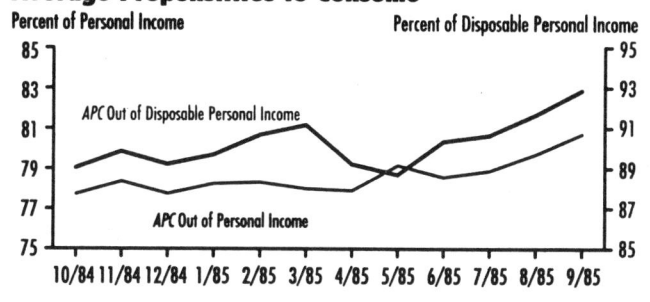

Percent of Personal Income (left axis: 75–85) / Percent of Disposable Personal Income (right axis: 85–95)

[Line chart showing APC Out of Disposable Personal Income and APC Out of Personal Income from 10/84 to 9/85.]

Personal Saving Rates

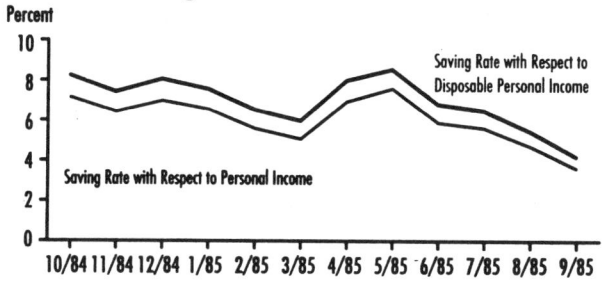

Percent (0–10)

[Line chart showing Saving Rate with Respect to Disposable Personal Income and Saving Rate with Respect to Personal Income from 10/84 to 9/85.]

REFERENCES

Berry, John M. "Retail Sales Fell 0.5% in February," *Washington Post,* March 15, 1995.

Byrnes, James C., et al. "Monthly Estimates of Personal Income, Taxes, and Outlays," *Survey of Current Business* (November 1979), pp. 18-37.

Congressional Quarterly Service, Inc. *Congress and the Nation* (various issues).

Hakkio, Craig S., Mark Rush, and Timothy J. Schmidt. "The Marginal Income Tax Rate Schedule from 1930 to 1990," Federal Reserve Bank of Kansas City *Research Working Paper 93-12* (October 1993).

Hershey, Robert D., Jr. "February Retail Sales Had Surprising Slide," *New York Times,* March 15, 1995.

Johnston, David Cay. "Weak Consumer Spending is Linked to Tax Bite," *New York Times,* June 2, 1995.

Pechman, Joseph A. *Federal Tax Policy.* The Brookings Institution, 1987.

Shapiro, Matthew D., and Joel Slemrod. "Consumer Response to the Timing of Income: Evidence from a Change in Tax Withholding," *American Economic Review* (March 1995), pp. 274-83.

Wilcox, David W. "Income Tax Refunds and the Timing of Consumption Expenditure," Board of Governors of the Federal Reserve System *Working Paper Series No. 106* (April 1990).

Peter S. Yoo is an economist at the Federal Reserve Bank of St. Louis. Richard D. Taylor provided research assistance.

THE FLAT TAX

Simple, Efficient, Fair. Or Is It?

by William G. Gale

The U.S. tax system remains continually, and deservedly, under attack. Many people find taxes too complex. Analysts blame the tax system for depressing saving, entrepreneurship, and economic growth. Few people believe it to be entirely fair or transparent.

Members of both political parties have put forth plans to overhaul the current tax system. The best known is the "flat tax." Conceived by Stanford economist Robert Hall and political scientist Alvin Rabushka in the early 1980s, the flat tax has been given legislative form in the past few years by Rep. Richard Armey (R-TX) and Sen. Richard Shelby (R-AL).

The flat tax would replace taxes on personal and corporate income and estates. Households would pay taxes on wages and pension income in excess of substantial personal and child allowances. Businesses would pay taxes on their sales less their wage and pension payments, input costs, and capital purchases. No other income would be taxed, no other deductions allowed. Businesses and individuals would face the same flat tax rate.

Proponents have made strong claims for the flat tax: it would be so simple that the tax form could fit on a postcard; it would take tax considerations out of people's economic decisionmaking, thereby increasing efficiency and revitalizing the economy; it is a fair and airtight system.

In theory, the flat tax is, indeed, a clever, principled approach to changing the nature of federal taxation. Whether it could satisfactorily meet the competing demands placed on the tax system—fairness, simplicity, growth—and the transition to the real world is an open question.

William G. Gale is a senior fellow in the Brookings Economic Studies program. He is the author, of a 1997 Brookings book on tax policy.

FLAT TAX

IN THEORY AND PRACTICE

Just What Is the Flat Tax?

The flat tax is not an income tax, but a consumption tax. The simplest form of consumption tax is a tax on retail sales. If we switch to a consumption tax, why not just adopt the simplest?

Implementing a national retail sales tax would be problematic for several reasons. First, it would be regressive. Poor households consume a much greater share of their income than do other households. Taxing their total consumption would be a large burden, especially compared with the current income tax system, which channels money to many poor working households via the earned income tax credit. In addition, as the sales taxes that now exist in 45 states have shown, it is often hard to distinguish business-to-business sales from business-to-household sales. But if each sale from business to business is taxed, the eventual product is taxed several times, resulting in "cascading," a problem that encourages firms to integrate vertically and also creates capricious redistributions of tax burdens across goods and people. Most important, though, a retail sales tax with a rate high enough—well over 30 percent—to replace existing federal taxes would be very hard to enforce. European countries that have tried to raise significant revenue by retail sales taxes have found that they become unadministrable at rates as low as 10–12 percent. They have therefore shifted to a different form of consumption tax, a value-added tax (VAT).

A sales tax and a VAT differ in the point at which they are exacted: a sales tax, on the final sale price; a VAT, at each stage of production. Under a VAT, each business pays a tax on the difference between gross revenues from all sales (including business-to-business sales) and the cost of materials, including capital goods. Thus it pays taxes on wages, interest, and profits, the sum of which represents the value added by the firm in providing goods and services.

The VAT avoids cascading because sales between businesses wash out. The baker who sells bread to the grocer pays VAT on the sale, but the grocer deducts the purchase in calculating his VAT. The VAT is also easier to enforce. One reason is that the seller, in trying to decide whether to report a transaction to the tax authorities, knows that the buyer will file the transaction with the tax authorities to claim the deduction for funds spent.

Like the sales tax, however, the VAT is regressive. Governments can address that problem by exempting from taxation, say, the first $20,000 of consumption by sending each family a check for $5,000 (assuming a 25 percent tax rate). But financing such transfers requires higher tax rates. Targeting the transfers to the poor would mean that rates would not have to be raised as much, but it would require all households to file information on income, thus sacrificing some of the simplicity gain.

The flat tax is a VAT, with two adjustments that help address the regressivity problem. First, businesses deduct wages and pensions, along with materials costs and capital investments. Second, the wages and pensions that businesses deduct are taxed at the individual (or household) level above a specified exemption. Dividing the VAT into two parts, one for businesses and one for households, makes possible the family exemptions that can ease the burden of the consumption tax for lower-income households.

How Does the Flat Tax Differ from the Current System?

Today's federal "income" tax is actually a hybrid between an income and a consumption tax. A pure income tax would tax all labor earnings and capital income, whether realized in cash, in kind, or accrued. But the current system does not tax certain forms of income, such as employer-provided health insurance or accrued gains on unsold assets. And it taxes some income more than once: in the case of corporate earnings, once at the corporate level and again at the individual level when distributed as dividends. It also taxes some items not properly considered income, such as the inflationary components of interest payments and realized capital gains. The flat tax would not tax capital income—such as interest, dividends, and capital gains—at the household level, or financial flows at any level. On the other hand, most saving—in pensions, IRAs, and so forth—is already taxed as it would be under a consumption tax.

Unlike the flat tax, the current income tax also permits dozens of allowances, credits, exclusions, and deductions. Taken together these "loopholes" reduced personal tax collections by some $1.3 trillion in 1993, about 50 percent of the actual tax base. Eliminating them all would make it possible to reduce tax rates across the board, or set rates as low as 13.5 percent.

The income tax is graduated: its six rates—0, 15, 28, 31, 36, and 39.6 percent—rise with taxable income. Multiple tax rates increase progressivity, but raise compliance and administrative costs and the importance of the deductions. A deduction that matters little when the tax rate is 10 percent is of much more consequence when the rate is 40 percent.

> Tax reform that collects the same amount of revenue in a new way will necessarily redistribute tax burdens among taxpayers. Those who stand to lose often try to prevent reform or to secure "transition relief" to avoid or delay the full brunt of the new law.

But the biggest differences between the existing system and the flat tax arise not because of large inherent differences in the underlying tax base. In fact, if the flat tax allowed firms to deduct investment expenditures over time, in accordance with the economic depreciation of their assets, instead of allowing them to deduct all investment expenses the year they are made, the flat tax would then be a flat income tax.

Rather, the key point is that the differences arise because, in response to a variety of political pressures, the existing tax system has strayed from a pure income tax structure. Indeed, perhaps the crucial question about the flat tax is how it would respond to those same pressures if it were to move from idea to reality.

The Armey-Shelby flat tax proposal features a $31,400 exemption for a family of four and a 20 percent tax rate. After two years the exemption would rise to $33,300 and the rate would fall to 17 percent. (The low tax rate is possible because the proposal is not "revenue neutral"; that is, it combines tax reform with a tax cut.)

But in recent years, different variants of the flat tax have begun to take on some features of today's income tax. Sen. Arlen Spector's (R-PA) proposal would reinstate the mortgage and charity deductions. So would Pat Buchanan's, which would also tax at least some capital income at the household level. The Kemp Commission favored deductions for payroll taxes and for mortgage interest and charity. Robert Dole voiced a wish to protect deductions for mortgages, charity, and state and local taxes.

These cracks in the flat tax armor, appearing long before serious legislative action takes place, suggest that the pressures that led to an impure income tax are likely to affect the flat tax as well.

Political and Economic Dilemmas in Tax Reform

Richard Armey, like some other advocates of the flat tax, candidly links his proposal to big tax cuts (although he does not specify how he would cut government spending to make up for the lost revenue). Because it is misleading to compare a plan that simultaneously reforms the tax structure and cuts taxes with the existing system, I will lay out the issues raised by the flat tax without the confounding effects of tax reduction.

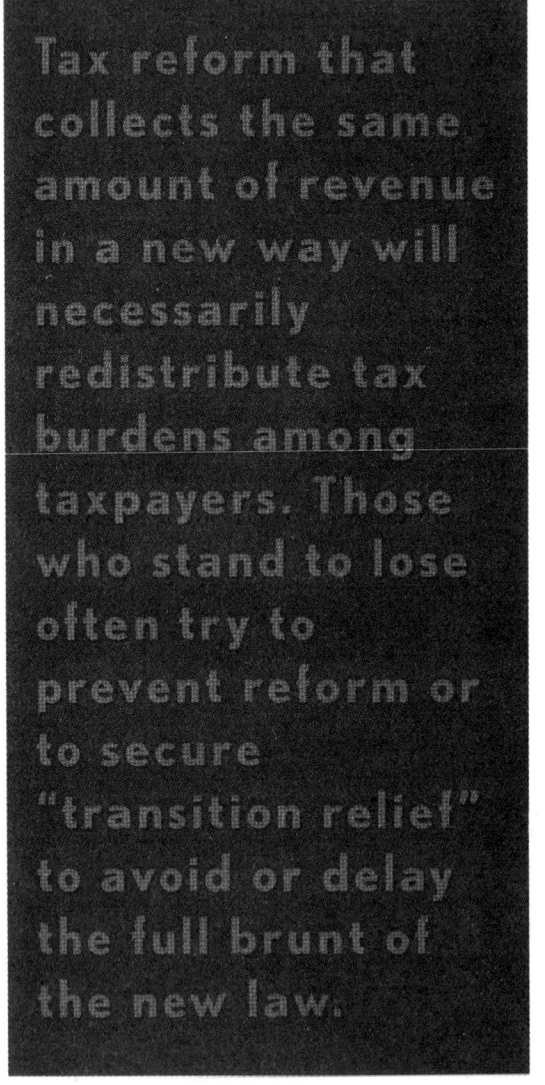

Tax reform that collects the same amount of revenue in a new way will necessarily redistribute tax burdens among taxpayers. Those who stand to lose often try to prevent reform or to secure "transition relief" to avoid or delay the full brunt of the new law. The flat tax embodies this problem in stark form, because it proposes a single rate on businesses and on household money wages above a threshold, with no deductions and no transition relief.

The biggest transition problem for the flat tax involves business. Under the current system, businesses may deduct depreciation, the loss of value of capital assets over their useful lives, in computing taxable business income. Under the flat tax, businesses can deduct the full value of the asset the year it is purchased. The practical problem is what to do about assets that have not been fully depreciated when the new tax takes effect.

The pure flat tax would allow no deductions for depreciation on existing assets. But companies that lose their existing depreciation deductions will claim unfair treatment. And the stakes are high. In 1993, corporations claimed $363 billion in depreciation deductions, unincorporated businesses about one-third that.

Similarly, under the current system many businesses have net operating losses that they can carry forward as offsets against future profits. And businesses' interest payments are deductible because they are a cost of earning income. The flat tax would disallow both the carryforwards and the deduction for interest payments. Firms that depend on those provisions will press for transition relief under the flat tax.

Flat tax advocates have already acknowledged the need for transition relief. The Kemp Commission, for example, recommended that policymakers "take care to protect the existing savings, investment, and other assets" during a transition to a new tax system. But these political concessions carry a big price tag. Transition relief will reduce the size of the tax base and therefore require higher tax rates on the rest of the base. Policymakers will have to choose: the more transitional relief they provide, the less efficient the new tax system.

What about the Existing Deductions?

Many prominent features of the income tax have long been a part of American economic life. The original (1913) income tax allowed deductions for mortgage interest and for state and local income and property taxes. Deductions for charity and employer-financed health insurance followed by 1918.

A pure flat tax would scrap these longstanding provisions. Without question, doing so would hurt the affected sectors of the economy. That, after all, is one of the points of tax reform: using the tax code to subsidize these sectors has channeled too many of society's resources to them. Removing the subsidy would make for a more efficient overall allocation of resources across sectors. But the affected groups are not likely to see things that way.

Under current tax law, for example, owner-occupied housing enjoys big advantages over other investments. Homeowners may deduct mortgage interest and property taxes without being required to report the imputed rental income they receive as owners. These deductions increase demand for owner-occupied housing and boost the price of housing and land. By treating owner-occupied housing and other assets alike, the flat tax would reduce the relative price of housing. Estimates of how much range widely, but even declines as low as 5–10 percent would hurt homeowners and could affect lending institutions through increased defaults.

Confronted with these realities, is Congress likely to end the tax advantages of owner-occupied housing? Perhaps not. But retaining the mortgage interest deduction means that tax rates would have to be higher to replace revenue lost from the deduction.

The same story would unfold with each of the other long-standing deductions. Under the flat tax, health insurance would no longer be deductible by businesses and would become taxable at the flat tax rate. Jonathan Gruber and James Poterba calculate that the change would boost the price of health insurance by an average of 21 percent and reduce the number of people who are insured by between 5.5 million and 14.3 million people. Pressure to keep the deduction would be strong. But if Congress were to retain it, the flat tax base would shrink, and rates would have to rise to maintain revenues.

Likewise, terminating the charitable contributions deduction would reduce charitable giving—and at a time when cuts in government spending are being justified on the grounds that private philanthropy should pick up the slack. But retaining the deduction means a higher tax rate to maintain revenues.

Flat Tax Trade-Offs: How Much?

In short, the flat tax is unlikely to be adopted in its pure form. What are the budget implications of various policy changes to the pure flat tax structure?

By my calculations, the Armey-Shelby plan with a 17 percent rate would have raised $138 billion less in 1996 than the current system. Even a 20 percent rate, which Jack Kemp referred to as the maximum acceptable flat tax rate in press conferences after the Kemp Commission report was released, would result in a shortfall of $29 billion. Allowing businesses to grandfather existing depreciation deductions—one form of transition relief—would raise the required rate to 23.1 percent. Allowing deductions for mortgage interest payments, as well as transition relief, would raise the required rate to 24.4 percent. If the deduction for employer-provided health insurance were also retained, the rate would rise to 26.5 percent. Adding in deductions for charitable contributions, individual deductions of state and local income and property tax payments, and the earned income tax credit would raise the rate to 29 percent. With all these adjustments, a tax rate of 20 percent would generate a revenue loss of well over $200 billion. Even with a flat tax rate of 25 percent, the revenue loss would be just over $100 billion.

Finally, retaining current payroll tax deductions for businesses would raise the required rate to 32 percent. The revenue shortfall, at a 20 percent tax rate, would be a whopping $280 billion a year. Even at a 25 percent tax rate, the revenue shortfall would be about $163 billion.

Politicians might find it hard to support a flat tax with these rates, since more than three-quarters of taxpayers now face a marginal tax rate of 15 percent or less, and less than 4 percent pay more than 28 percent on the margin. On the other hand, capping the rate at 20 percent or 25 percent would generate large losses in tax revenues that might also be hard to support.

One thing is clear. The flat tax is considered a simple tax with a relatively low rate in large part because it eliminates, on paper, deductions and exclusions that no Congress has dared touch.

The Flat Tax and Economic Growth

Retaining existing deductions and providing transition relief will also eat into the economic growth that flat tax advocates claim the tax will spur.

The most complete economic model that generates realistic estimates of the impact of the flat tax on growth, developed by Alan Auerbach of the University of California, Laurence Kotlikoff of Boston University, and several other economists, finds that moving from the current system to a pure, flat rate, consumption tax, with no exemptions, no deductions, and no transition relief or other adjustments, would raise output, relative to what it would have been under the income tax, by 6.9 percent after the first 2 years, 9 percent after 9 years, and almost 11 percent in the long run. These are remarkably large gains, but they vanish as the tax plan becomes more realistic.

For example, if the personal exemption is set at $9,000, somewhat less than the $11,000 personal exemption in the Armey-Shelby plan, and transition relief is provided for existing depreciation deductions, the economy would grow by only 0.6 percent over 2 years, 1.8 percent after 10 years, and 3.6 percent in the long run. Adding exemptions for children (which the Armey plan now provides) would drive these estimates to zero. Adding transition relief for interest deductions and retaining the earned income credit and deductions for mortgages, health insurance, taxes paid, and charity would reduce growth further. Thus, implementing realistic versions of the flat tax could even slow economic growth.

Tax Reform in the Real World

Good tax reform requires discipline. It is not hard to look at the U.S. tax code and see the need for a simpler, cleaner tax. But it is hard to look at the 1997 Taxpayer Relief Act, passed by Congress and signed by the president, and believe that the political system has the discipline to pass broad-based fundamental reform. After all, there is nothing—other than political forces and views of social equity—stopping our political leaders right now, or in any other year, from passing legislation that would broaden the tax base, close loopholes, and reduce tax rates. Those political forces and views of social equity will not vanish when the flat tax is passed. As one congressman noted, "You can't repeal politics."

The flat tax is a simple and thoughtful response to many of the problems in today's tax system. But tax reform is not a free lunch: we can't get everything we might want.

There are two ways out of this quandary. One would start with the flat tax proposals and make them less pure. For example, holding personal exemptions at about their current level would generate added revenue. And coupling the lower exemption levels with a two-tier tax rate system (similar to the 15 percent and 28 percent brackets that now apply to the vast majority of taxpayers) would raise revenue, enhance progressivity, and maintain many benefits of the flat tax.

The less radical alternative would be to start with the existing income tax system and simplify, streamlining the tax treatment of capital income, reducing the use of the tax code to run social policy, and reducing and flattening the rates. That would be an extension of the principles developed in the Tax Reform Act of 1986. Either alternative would place the resulting system somewhere between the current tax system and the flat tax on simplicity, efficiency, and equity—the three primary issues under debate.

The flat tax is an important advance in tax policy thinking and represents a thoughtful approach to several problems in the tax code and the economy. But removing the entire body of income tax law and starting over with a whole new system is a monumental task. We should approach the issue with our eyes open concerning the likely benefits, costs, and practical issues that would arise in adopting a flat tax.

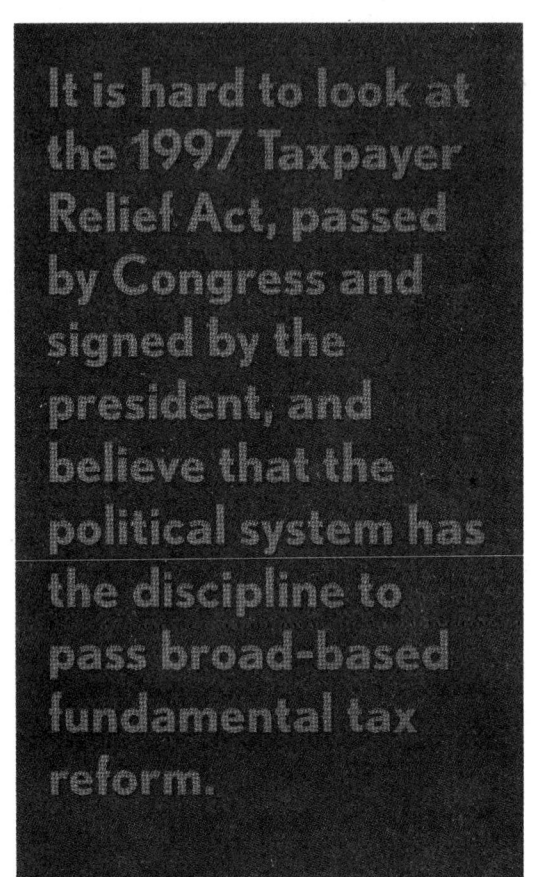

> It is hard to look at the 1997 Taxpayer Relief Act, passed by Congress and signed by the president, and believe that the political system has the discipline to pass broad-based fundamental tax reform.

WHY ARE TAXES SO COMPLICATED

AND WHAT CAN WE DO ABOUT IT?

BY **WILLIAM GALE**

The time, money, and aggravation that tens of millions of Americans expend to understand and comply with the income tax is, it turns out, nothing new. In his 1776 *The Wealth of Nations,* Adam Smith noted that "subjecting the people to the frequent visits and the odious examination of the tax gatherers ... may expose them to much unnecessary trouble, vexation, and oppression: and though vexation is not, strictly speaking, expence, it is certainly equivalent to expence at which every man would be willing to redeem himself from it." For Americans today, the "expence" includes maintaining records, learning the law, preparing the return or hiring a preparer, corresponding with the IRS, and learning how to reduce (or cheat on) taxes.

How Bad Is It?

For low-income households, headaches can arise from issues regarding filing status, abandoned spouses, dependency tests, the child and dependent care tax credit, and the earned income tax credit. For individuals with higher income, complexity arises in itemizing deductions, the treatment of capital income (particularly capital gains, interest deductions, and passive losses), and the alternative minimum tax. For small business owners, issues relating to inventory, depreciation, and distinguishing various expenses can be complicated. For large corporations, tax complexity is centered on depreciation, international income, the alternative minimum tax, and coordinating with state taxes. In addition, large firms are almost continually audited; one tax expert has described the basic corporate tax return as nothing more than an "opening bid."

Stories of income tax complexity are legion. The internal revenue code contains more than five million words. In *Money Magazine*'s recent surveys, every one of 40 to 50 tax preparers came up with a different estimate of the tax liability due on a complex, hypothetical return. The share of taxpayers who pay tax professionals to complete their tax returns rose from 42 percent in 1981 to 51 percent in 1997.

Yet the costs can easily be overblown or distorted. For many people, the tax system is not that complicated. Almost 40 percent file simplified 1040A or 1040EZ forms, and about 18 percent file the 1040 but have no itemized deductions or business income. Many people go to preparers to expedite refunds or because they prefer to spend their time on other things rather than on preparing taxes. Marsha Blumenthal and Joel Slemrod found that while the average taxpayer spent 27.4 hours on filing income tax returns and related activities, 30 percent spent less than 5 hours, and another 15 percent spent between 5 and 10 hours. About 11 percent spent 50–100 hours, and 5 percent spent more than 100 hours. About half had no out-of-pocket expenses, and 17 percent paid less than $50. Costs were highest among high-income and self-employed taxpayers.

Estimates of the total cost of complying with and running the individual and corporate income tax systems in 1995 go as high as $600 billion, but the most reasonable estimates range between $75 billion and $150 billion, or about 10–20 percent of income tax revenue. Even at $75 billion—or $386 per adult per year—tax complexity imposes significant costs. Resources lost to compliance and administrative costs could be productively devoted to other activities. Complexity also generates confusion and aggravation among taxpayers, which can reduce confidence in the system. Thus, *other things equal,* social welfare would be improved by having a tax system that is simpler to comply with, administer, and enforce. Of course, other things are never equal.

Tax Trade-offs

Since virtually everyone agrees that taxes should be easy to understand, administer, and enforce, why are taxes so complicated? The answer is that people also agree that taxes should be fair, should be conducive to economic prosperity, should raise sufficient revenue to finance government spending, and should respect individuals' privacy. Many people also think tax incentives should be used to pursue social or economic policies for the poor, housing, health, the environment, and small businesses.

Trading off these goals is difficult. Sometimes the meaning of a goal is unclear. Fairness, for example, is clearly "in the eyes of the beholder." Sometimes people differ about the best way to reach a goal. Is it best to help the poor via cash payments, tax incentives to work, direct provision of health care and education, or some other way? Finally, and most importantly, the goals are mutually inconsistent, and people disagree about which goals deserve the greatest weight.

As a result, tax policy involves trade-offs—and complexity is the result. In the end, complexity resembles pollution. Some of it is undoubtedly unnecessary, but much of it is the unfortunate byproduct of the production of goods that many people want.

For reasons of fairness, most tax systems tailor tax burdens to depend on individual characteristics. This creates complexity in several ways. It requires tracing income from the business sector to individuals. It requires reporting and documenting individual characteristics such as marital status, dependents, each person's level and composition of income and spending, and so on. And it requires tax rates that vary with individual characteristics, creating incentives to shift income to other people with lower income, such as children, or to other time periods when income might be lower.

Complexity also derives from using the tax system to house social programs that subsidize what Congress and a significant portion of the population consider to be desired activities: housing, charity, health insurance, higher education, child care, state and local governments, retirement saving, entrepreneurial activity.

Closing tax loopholes also increases complexity. Any time a provision for special treatment or social engineering arises, it must be limited. If the child care credit, for example, is not intended to subsidize ski lessons in Aspen, some line has to be drawn concerning what is allowed and what is not. The taxation of financial income is particularly difficult in this regard.

Clamping down on tax evasion often increases complexity. Given the opportunity, people sometimes cheat on their taxes. Taxes on income from wages, for example, are withheld and sent to the government by the employer. The evasion rate is around 1 percent. Taxes on income from sole proprietorships are neither withheld nor sent in by a third party. The evasion rate here exceeds 30 percent. Many tax complexities exist to limit opportunities to cheat. In the late 1980s, a new law required people who claimed the child care credit to provide the Social Security number of the care provider. This both reduced the number of child care credit claims and raised by 65 percent the amount of income reported by child care providers.

While trade-offs among consensus policy goals are an important source of complexity, political factors are another. That is, complexity can also be the result of the production of goods that only a few of us want. Politicians and interest groups have a vested interest in certain types of subsidies that reduce taxes on favored constituencies. The lavish campaign contributions received by members of the House Ways and Means Committee do not come from lobbyists deeply respectful of a tax code clean of special subsidies. There is no lobby for simplicity.

> Campaign gifts received by members of the House Ways and Means Committee do not come from lobbyists respectful of a tax code clean of special subsidies.

Sometimes the tax code is used to hide subsidies that would not be supported as outright spending. Consider a "homeowner welfare program" in which taxpayers earned an entitlement to help pay their mortgages. The entitlement grew in proportion to mortgage size, interest rate, and tax rate, but anyone whose entitlement was less than $6,000 received nothing from the program. Obviously, not a very appealing idea, but not that different from the mortgage interest deduction.

And let's face it: taxpayers *like* complexity that reduces their taxes. It's just complexity that raises taxes that annoys. Thus, people will grump about the new filing requirements for capital gains or child credits, but few will volunteer to give up those cuts.

The real question is not the total amount of compliance costs, but whether society gets good value for income tax complexity. My view is that, generally, we do not. The economy-wide perspective is important here. Suppose people had to fill out ten extra lines of the tax form to receive a $1,000 tax cut. Each might regard that as "good complexity," well worth the added cost of providing a few extra pieces of information. But in the aggregate, the revenues would have to [be] raised from taxpayers, so everyone's tax "cut" would be from a higher initial tax liability and net taxes would be the same. Thus, from a social perspective, the sum of all individuals' "good complexity" would be zero or negative.

Many existing provisions designed to encourage certain activities end up either largely subsidizing activity that would have occurred anyway or creating new problems. Many of the reasons for complexity are completely inappropriate: hiding unpopular programs, special loopholes that fuel campaign contributions. It is hard to see any impact on economic growth, and the "fairness" that occurs is a very strange kind. The subsidies help one group, but at the expense of all others.

Fundamental Tax Reform and Simplicity

The complexity of existing taxes is a powerful force behind the movement to replace the income tax with a flat tax or sales tax. The new systems would shift the tax base to consumption, rather than income, flatten tax rates, eliminate all deductions and credits, and collect most or all taxes at the business level. Plan advocates promise great simplification, and it is clear that pure versions of either plan would be much simpler than the existing system. But, well, it's not that simple.

Just as the income tax has deviated from a low-rate tax, with a one-page form and three pages of instructions, the flat tax or sales tax would also be under pressure to depart from its pure form. The thousands of lobbyists now working in Washington are unlikely to pack up and go home. In short, you can repeal the tax code, but you can't repeal politics.

On paper, for example, the sales tax would be vastly simpler than the current system. But the 45 existing state sales taxes are nothing like the single-rate, no-exemption sales tax that is proposed at the national level. The states feature numerous exemptions for goods and especially services, as well as different rates for different goods.

Moreover, as Joel Slemrod has shown, it is inappropriate to analyze simplicity independently of evasion and enforcement. The sales tax rate required to replace federal taxes would be well above the 23 percent rate claimed by advocates. After correcting for mistakes in the way the proposal treats government spending, and adjusting for political factors that would erode the tax base and for a reasonable amount of tax avoidance activity, a federal sales tax could result in mark-ups at the cash register in excess of 70 percent. At these rates, the incentive to evade sales taxes (which, unlike the income tax, feature no third-party withholding to aid in compliance) and the political pressure to exempt certain goods from taxes would be strong.

No country has ever successfully run a high-rate national retail sales tax. Many have tried to implement some variant of a sales tax and have given up. European governments, and numerous conservative and liberal scholars, have concluded that sales taxes at the required rates would be unworkable.

How about the flat tax? Under such a tax, businesses pay taxes on gross sales minus the cost of materials, services, capital goods, wages, and pension contributions. Individuals pay taxes on wages and pensions, less personal exemptions. No other income is taxed, and no other deductions are allowed. Flat tax advocates claim that individual and business returns will fit on a post card. In theory, the flat tax promises to be as simple as the sales tax.

But flat tax proponents have already acknowledged the need to provide transition relief to businesses that bought assets under the old system. Various flat tax plans include deductions for mortgage interest, charity, and payroll taxes. Deductions for health insurance and state and local taxes, the earned income credit, and graduated tax rates on wage income cannot be far behind. Allowing for these items would raise the required flat tax rate to about 32 percent and complicate taxes.

More fundamentally, the flat tax makes different distinctions than the existing system does. This will create new "pressure points," and so could create a host of new compliance and sheltering issues and accentuate problems created by existing regulations. For example, the differential treatment of "interest income" and "sales" under the flat tax has led tax experts Charles McLure and George Zodrow to conclude that the business tax "contains unacceptable opportunities for abuse." As attorney Alan Feld notes, the flat tax will either generate complicated business transactions (to skirt the simple rules) or complicated tax laws (to reduce the gaming possibilities), or both.

The flat tax would cause huge changes in tax liabilities for businesses across the country. It would create situations where some businesses with large economic profits would pay no taxes and others with economic losses would face steep taxes. Amending the tax to address these issues would create complexity.

At the individual level, the flat tax would renegotiate every alimony agreement in the country. Under the flat tax, alimony payments would no longer be deductible and receipts would no longer be taxable. Another difficulty would arise from earnings that are subsequently stolen. Under the flat tax, a robbery victim is still liable for taxes—and the robber is not. Under the income tax, it is the other way around. Additional anomalies will no doubt be discovered. Each of these problems with the individual tax could be fixed—but each solution would require a bigger postcard. Even a flat tax modified along these lines would be simpler than the current system. But with a rate of 30 percent or more, a realistic flat tax may not be politically appealing.

Simplifying the Income Tax

What about tax simplification options in the existing system? To begin with, procedural changes could raise the visibility and explicit consideration of simplicity and enforcement issues in the making of tax policy. For example, the recent IRS restructuring legislation requires the IRS to report to Congress each year regarding sources of complexity in the administration of federal taxes. The Joint Committee on Taxation is required to prepare complexity analysis of new tax legislation that affects individuals or small businesses.

It is also possible to eliminate the need for certain taxpayers to file tax returns. Thirty-six countries already use a return-free system for some of their taxpayers, replacing end-of-year filing requirements with withholding throughout the year and end-of-year reconciliation by the tax agency. In recent work, Janet Holtzblatt of the Treasury Department and I found that 52 million U.S. taxpayers could be placed on a return-free system with minor changes in the structure of taxes. These families have income only from wages, pensions, Social Security, interest, dividends, and unemployment compensation; they do not itemize deductions; and they face at most a 15 percent tax rate. Although the net compliance and administrative savings may not be great (because these people already have simple returns), a return-free system could reduce the psychic costs (fear and aggravation) associated with tax filing for the affected taxpayers.

Structural reforms could also reduce complexity. Broadening the tax base by eliminating deductions and preferences and taxing capital gains as ordinary income directly removes complexity. Increased standard deductions remove many people from the tax system. Lower tax rates would reduce the value of sheltering and cheating. Increasing the number of people who face the same "basic" rate facilitates the withholding of taxes on interest and dividends at the source, further simplifying taxes and increasing compliance. In short, broadening the base and reducing the rates can be revenue-neutral, fair, and efficient, as well as simplifying. Such reforms make taxes simpler for many taxpayers and could reduce compliance costs by 10–15 percent.

Getting Serious about Simplicity

We could have much simpler taxes if we were willing to change our preferences and forgo common notions of fairness, reduce our concern with tax evasion and loopholes, eliminate a raft of targeted social and economic incentives, and reduce the extent to which taxes depend on individual characteristics. Retaining those preferences, however, does not condemn us to much of the seemingly needless complexity of the current code. While the goal of fundamental tax reform is both more distant and less likely to resolve current problems than its advocates might care to admit, the existing system could be improved and simplified with a concerted effort to take simplicity seriously as a distinct policy goal.

Are Americans Really Overtaxed?

Studies show that the burden is the lowest in decades and proposed cuts are not warranted.

By WILLIAM G. GALE

Abstract:
The misleading estimate comes from a study by the Tax Foundation, a Washington organization that tracks tax policy. In fairness, the conceptual issues surrounding what is a "tax" or "income" and how to determine who bears the ultimate burden of taxes paid by businesses can be surprisingly complex and require judgment as well as rigor. But close inspection of the Tax Foundation's study, by the Center on Budget and Policy Priorities and others, reveals several problems. The foundation's tax measure does not include adjustments for popular deductions like child credits or flexible spending accounts. The measure of income overlooks pension contributions and health insurance. The study imputes some estate-tax liability to the typical two-earner household, even though only a tiny proportion—1.5%—of people who die face any estate tax liability. The foundation adds corporate taxes to families' tax burdens but does not add corporate earnings to families' income.

As President Clinton and congressional Republicans dicker about how to use the projected budget surpluses, a near constant drumbeat emanates from tax-cut advocates: Taxes are at record high levels and are imposing increasingly crushing burdens on American families.

The first claim is right: Federal, state and local taxes comprised just under a third of all income generated in 1998, the highest level ever. But the second claim is wrong. In fact, for the vast majority of families, taxes are as low or lower than they have been in the past 20 to 30 years. Overall tax payments have risen because the rich have gotten richer at an impressive rate and because they have faced higher tax rates due to policy changes in 1990 and 1993.

Tax-cut advocates like to report that the typical two-earner family paid nearly 40% of its income in taxes last year. This claim has acquired a life of its own, but it is flawed and vastly overstates tax burdens faced by most households.

The misleading estimate comes from a study by the Tax Foundation, a Washington organization that tracks tax policy. In fairness, the conceptual issues surrounding what is a "tax" or "income" and how to determine who bears the ultimate burden of taxes paid by businesses can be surprisingly complex and require judgment as well as rigor. But close inspection of the Tax Foundation's study, by the Center on Budget and Policy Priorities and others, reveals several problems. The foundation's tax measure does not include adjustments for popular deductions like child credits or flexible spending accounts. The measure of income overlooks pension contributions and health insurance. The study imputes some estate-tax liability to the typical two-earner household, even though only a tiny proportion—1.5%—of people who die face any estate tax liability. The foundation adds corporate taxes to families' tax burdens but does not add corporate earnings to families' income.

Other studies that avoid these flaws yield dramatically different conclusions about family tax burdens. A Treasury Department study, using a methodology that has not changed over the course of several administrations, shows that across a wide range of income levels, federal income taxes as a share of earnings are down. A four-person family with earnings of about $55,000 will pay 7.5% of that amount in federal income taxes

From the Los Angeles Times, *February 24, 1999. © 1999 by the Los Angeles Times. Reprinted by permission.*

15. Are Americans Really Overtaxed?

in 1999, the lowest rate since 1966. For families with earnings half as large, the 1999 income tax rate is the lowest since 1955. Families with earnings of almost $110,000, who are in the top 10% of the income distribution, will pay a projected 1999 income tax burden of 14.1%, the lowest rate since 1972.

Adding Social Security and Medicare taxes to the Treasury income tax estimates raises the estimated tax burden, but does not change the conclusion that taxes are low relative to previous years. Congressional Budget Office estimates show that, for households in the bottom 60% of the income distribution, the burden of all federal taxes is at a 20-year low. Only among the top 20% of households did total federal taxes rise in the last 15 years, and only back to 1970s levels. The Joint Tax Committee estimates federal burdens that are even lower than CBO's.

These studies suggest that a reasonable estimate is that all federal, state and local taxes account for about 26% to 30% of income for families in the middle fifth of the income distribution. This figure overstates the true tax burden, though, because about two-fifths of the total represents Social Security and Medicare contributions that entitle workers to future benefits. Many families pay substantially less: A family of four can earn more than $28,200, or about $540 per week, and pay no federal income taxes.

American tax burdens are also low compared with those in other industrialized countries—among the 20 largest in 1996, the U.S. had the lowest ratio of taxes to gross domestic product.

Ultimately, whether Americans are overtaxed is a judgment call. The measure of appropriate tax levels depends on many factors, including an analysis of how the money is used. But the evidence speaks clearly in at least two dimensions: The vast majority of American families pay nowhere near 40% of income in taxes, and they forfeit a smaller share of their income to taxes today than they would have in the past with the same income. Advocates might have other reasons to urge a cut in tax rates, but the debate over their plans should begin with facts rather than fantasy.

William G. Gale is a senior fellow at the Brookings Institution

Article 16

SHOULD WE RETIRE SOCIAL SECURITY?
Grading the Reform Plans

BY HENRY J. AARON AND ROBERT D. REISCHAUER

Most Americans understand that Social Security faces a long-term imbalance between the cost of benefits promised under current law and the program's projected income. They realize that the looming deficits arise from the coming retirement of the large baby boom cohort, the steady increase in life expectancies, and the reduction in fertility rates, not from program mismanagement.

Nevertheless, many wonder whether Social Security, devised during the Great Depression, amidst double-digit unemployment, pervasive poverty, and the inability of all but a few to save for retirement, is suitable for today's vastly changed economic, social, and financial conditions.

Today, policymakers and the public face a bewildering array of proposals to reform or replace the nation's public pension system. Fortunately for the interested citizen, most proposals take one of three approaches to reform. Some replace the current public system with private accounts. Others supplement the current system with private accounts. Still others strengthen and modernize the current system. In what follows we evaluate several prominent plans from each of the three major reform approaches, as well as sketch out one of our own. All the plans would restore financial balance to the nation's basic retirement system.

Criteria for Reform

We evaluate each plan on four criteria: benefit adequacy, protection against risk, administrative efficiency, and effect on national saving.

In our view a successful plan should, first, ensure adequate benefits that are equitably distributed to maintain protection for low earners and other vulnerable people. Current Social Security benefits are not unduly generous.

Henry J. Aaron and Robert D. Reischauer are senior fellows in the Brookings Economic Studies program and the authors of Countdown to Reform: The Great Social Security Debate *(A Century Foundation Book, 1998), from which this article is drawn.*

Benefits of average earners who retire in the United States at age 65 are less than 1.5 times the U.S. poverty threshold. U.S. benefits replace significantly less of pre-retirement earnings than do public pension benefits in Europe. Large benefit cuts would leave retirees, the disabled, and survivors inadequately protected. At the same time, overall benefit increases are also undesirable because they would push costs, which will grow as baby boomers retire, to very high levels.

Second, the plan should spread broadly the unavoidable risks of long-term pension commitments, not place them on the shoulders of individual workers. Third, administrative costs should be low, and the plan should not be unduly complex for

SOCIAL SECURITY REPORT CARD

Criteria	Grade
Adequacy, equity, and a fair return	C+
Protection against risk	C
Administrative efficiency	F
Increased national saving	B-
Overall grade	C

THE PERSONAL SECURITY ACCOUNTS PLAN

16. Should We Retire Social Security?

private businesses, workers, and the government. Finally, the plan should raise national saving by adding to reserves held in the Trust Fund or individual accounts (less any reductions in private saving or government surpluses outside of the retirement system).

Retiring Social Security

Two prominent plans would replace the current Social Security system with individual retirement accounts.

The Personal Security Accounts Plan

The Personal Security Accounts (PSA) plan, advanced by five members of the 1994–96 Advisory Council on Social Security, would gradually replace Social Security with a two-tier system—a flat benefit based on years worked and the age at which benefits are first received and a benefit based on balances accumulated in mandated personal savings accounts. The flat benefit for workers and their spouses, as well as disability and survivor benefits that would be retained but scaled back, would be financed by a payroll tax of 6.2 percent for employers and 1.2 percent for employees; 5 percent of each worker's earnings, up to the maximum subject to the payroll tax, would go into his or her personal account. (The Social Security payroll tax is 12.4 percent of taxable wages—6.2 percent on the employer, 6.2 percent on the worker.)

The PSA plan would be phased in over many years. Retirees and workers over age 55 would remain under the Social Security system. Workers between 25 and 55 would receive a blend of benefits under the new and old systems. Workers under age 25 would receive benefits only under the new system. The new system would run a deficit for the first few decades, forcing the government to borrow some $2 trillion (in 1998 dollars). Payroll tax rates would jump 1.52 percentage points—0.76 points for the employer, 0.76 points for the worker—for about seven decades to pay the interest costs and repay the principal on that borrowing. Eventually, as Social Security phases out, revenues would exceed costs and the debt would be paid off. When all borrowing had been repaid, the supplemental payroll tax could be repealed.

The PSA flat benefit would guarantee inflation-protected payments (of roughly 75 percent of the current Social Security benefit to low-wage workers) until the worker and his or her spouse died. The personal account benefit would not provide financial protection against inflation (or a long life) unless the worker chose to buy an inflation-indexed annuity with his or her personal account balance. All of the flat benefit, but none of the personal account benefit, would be subject to income tax, a change that would raise taxes on low- and moderate-income retirees and lower taxes on retirees with higher incomes.

Benefit adequacy and equity. The PSA plan promises good benefits for retirees on average but fails to protect certain vulnerable groups. For example, it cuts disability benefits (now provided by Social Security) as much as 30 percent. Because workers would be able to invest their personal accounts in a wide range of assets, some would do well, but others would do poorly and suffer reduced benefits.

Protection against risk. The inflation-adjusted flat benefit would provide excellent protection against risk. Personal account returns would be risky, however, since they would depend on how funds were invested, what administrative fees were imposed by fund managers, how high asset values were when balances were withdrawn, and whether pensioners bought annuities when they retired.

Administrative efficiency. The PSA plan does poorly on this criterion. The Social Security administrative structure would have to be maintained for many years, and two new systems would have to be set up: one to administer the flat benefit and another to see that employers made timely and accurate deposits into personal accounts and that the financial institutions managing personal accounts complied with the unavoidable regulations. The administrative burdens on small employers might be so onerous as to make the plan unworkable. Finally, dramatically higher administrative costs would lower net returns to workers, compared with plans that managed similar investments centrally.

National saving. The PSA plan adds to national saving by raising payroll taxes. But the personal accounts would be so similar to existing IRAs and 401(k) plans that workers might reduce other private saving or increase borrowing. Congress would also come under pressure to give workers access to their accounts—for medical emergencies, say, or college tuition—before retirement. Yielding to such pressure would diminish both the resources for retirement and any positive effect on national saving.

The Feldstein Plan

The second proposal to replace Social Security was crafted by Martin Feldstein, a Harvard economist and former chairman of the Council of Economic Advisers. Under his plan each worker would deposit 2 percent of earnings, up to the maximum subject to the payroll tax, in a personal retirement account. To offset the cost of these deposits, workers would receive an income tax credit financed by the projected federal budget surpluses. Once the surpluses ended, increased federal borrowing, tax increases, or spending cuts would be required.

The personal retirement accounts would be invested in regulated stock and bond funds chosen by the worker and administered by private fund managers. When workers began to draw pensions from their accounts, their Social Security benefits would be reduced by $3 for every $4 withdrawn. In effect, the benefits promised by the current Social Security program would become a floor under pensions. Overall, retirees would receive about 60 percent of their benefits from Social Security and 40 percent from personal accounts. Higher earners would depend more on their personal accounts; some would receive nothing from Social Security. The cuts in Social Security benefits would eventually close the projected long-term Social Security deficit.

Benefit adequacy and equity. By tapping into the projected federal budget surpluses, the Feldstein plan would be able to raise pensions—a feature we regard as imprudent in light of the sizable cost of pensions for retiring baby boomers. It would raise benefits more for high earners than low earners. A typical low earner, with average monthly earnings of $1,000, would, at retirement, receive a Social Security pension of $560 and an individual account pension of $240. When Social Security benefits are reduced by three-quarters of the individual account pension, the low earner's total pension would be $620, an increase of 11 percent over the current Social Security benefit. A high earner, with average monthly earnings of $5,600, would receive a Social Security pension of $1,375 and an individual account pension of $1,340. The total pension, once Social Security benefits are reduced by three-quarters of the individual account pension, would be $1,720, an increase of 25 percent. Because high earners are likely to select higher-yielding, albeit riskier, portfolios, their benefits are likely to increase even more.

SOCIAL SECURITY REPORT CARD

Criteria	Grade
Adequacy, equity, and a fair return	B+
Protection against risk	B-
Administrative efficiency	F
Increased national saving	D
Overall grade	C

THE FELDSTEIN PLAN

Protection against risk. The Feldstein plan provides substantial protection against market risk because it guarantees a pension at least as large as that promised by the current benefit formula. But the plan is likely to undermine political support for a defined-benefit guarantee like Social Security among high and moderate earners, most of whose pensions would be based on their personal accounts. The plan also poses major fiscal risks because the commitment to increased pensions would generate severe budget pressures, particularly after currently projected surpluses end, that would affect all government spending and taxes.

Administrative efficiency. The Feldstein plan would be complex and costly to administer. Administrative and investment management fees will eat into returns on personal account balances. And the Social Security Administration would have to design and operate a system to make the three-quarter reductions in Social Security benefits based on withdrawals from personal accounts.

National saving. The effects of the Feldstein plan on national saving are complicated and unclear. Initially saving would not be affected at all, as the deposits in individual accounts would be funded by budget surpluses. The longer-run effect on saving depends on how successive Congresses and presidents react when the surpluses can no longer sustain the required individual account deposits, as well as on the extent to which workers cut back on other saving.

Reform Social Security and Add Personal Accounts

Another group of proposals would supplement a reduced Social Security system with small defined-contribution personal retirement accounts.

The Individual Account Plan

The Individual Account plan, proposed by Edward Gramlich, chairman of the 1994-96 Advisory Council on Social Security, would gradually cut Social Security benefits to allow the current 12.4 percent payroll tax to cover future program costs. Cuts would be small for low earners but up to more than 25 percent for high earners. A 1.6 percentage point increase in the employee payroll tax would finance small personal retirement accounts to be invested in a limited number of index mutual funds managed by a government agency. Balances would be converted into inflation-protected annuities at retirement.

The annuities would be small. A worker with median covered earnings who was 40 years old when the plan was implemented would receive, at age 65, monthly benefits of $125 (in 1998 dollars), about 13 percent of expected Social Security benefit under the current system. Older workers would start contributing at a later age, contribute for fewer years, and receive less; younger workers would participate longer and receive larger pensions. Because payroll taxes would fully finance the new individual accounts, the plan would require no other transitional taxes or borrowing.

Benefit adequacy and equity. The Individual Account plan would continue to rely heavily on Social Security, although benefits would be cut significantly. On average, pensions financed by individual accounts would fill in this gap for people of retirement age. But disabled workers would suffer reduced benefits until they reached retirement age, and workers who became disabled when young would have little in their individual account even then.

Protection against risk. The individual accounts would be subject to market risk, but the risk would be moderate because investments would be limited to a few centrally managed index funds. The pensions based on individual accounts would form a small portion of future retirees' pensions—about 30 percent for an average earner and 20 percent for a low earner. Both the scaled-back Social Security pension and the individual account pension would be inflation-protected annuities.

Administrative efficiency. Central administration and the limited number of indexed investments would hold down administrative costs. Nevertheless, these costs would be somewhat higher than those under Social Security because the fed-

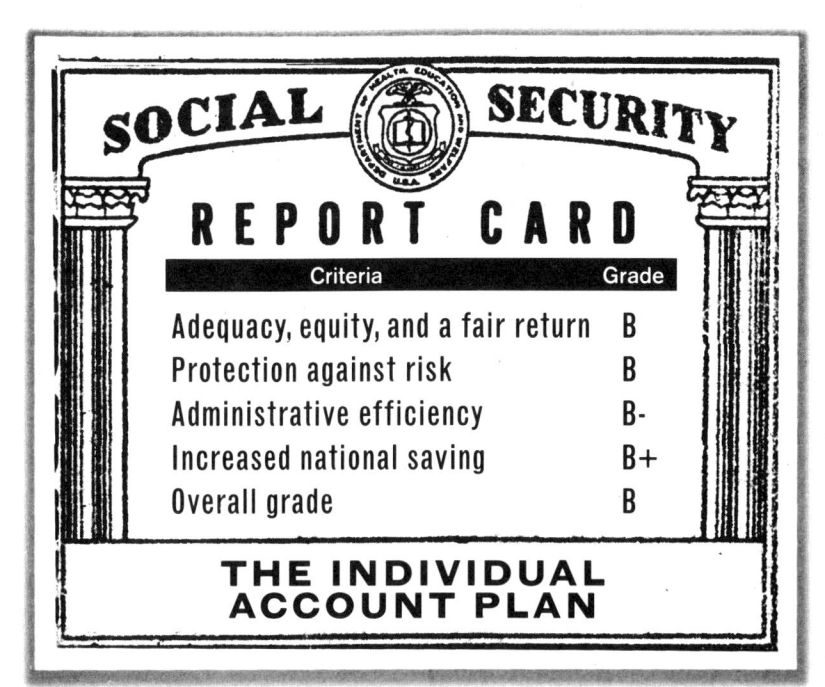

SOCIAL SECURITY REPORT CARD — THE INDIVIDUAL ACCOUNT PLAN

Criteria	Grade
Adequacy, equity, and a fair return	B
Protection against risk	B
Administrative efficiency	B-
Increased national saving	B+
Overall grade	B

---

eral government would have to deposit funds in accounts of each worker's choice, educate workers about the options, and respond to questions.

National saving. The increased payroll tax and the benefit cuts would both raise national saving. The centrally held individual accounts would probably add to saving because they would not be viewed as good substitutes for IRAs or 401(k) plans.

The Moynihan Plan

Senator Daniel Patrick Moynihan (D-NY) proposes to cut both payroll taxes and Social Security benefits and to authorize—but not require—workers to set up individual accounts. Retirement, survivors, and disability benefits would fall an average of about 20 percent. Payroll taxes would be cut 2 percentage points—1 point for workers and 1 point for employers—until 2025. Workers could spend their share or save it, either in personal accounts administered by a new government board or in special Individual Retirement Accounts managed by financial institutions of their choosing. Contributions of workers who chose to set up personal accounts would have to be matched by their employers. Withdrawal from the account at retirement would be unrestricted; it need not be in the form of an annuity.

From 2025 to 2060 the payroll tax rate would rise gradually to keep program revenues in line with benefit payments. In 2060 the payroll tax rate (by then 13.4 percent), together with contributions to personal accounts, would claim 15.4 percent of covered earnings, 3 percentage points above the current payroll rate. Over time the Moynihan plan would return Social Security to a pay-as-you-go system, with a contingency reserve sufficient to tide the system over a severe economic downturn.

Benefit adequacy and equity. This plan would steeply erode benefits and in ways that could hurt vulnerable groups the most. Because benefits would be reduced by holding the annual inflation adjustments 1 percentage point below the Consumer Price Index, those who received benefits the longest—the very old and the long-term disabled—would suffer the largest cuts.

Protection against risk. Because workers could choose how to invest their voluntary accounts, they would be exposed to investment risk. Social Security would provide only partial protection against inflation; pensions derived from the voluntary accounts would offer none. With no restrictions on when or how to convert their account balances into retirement income, some retirees could outlive the pensions based on their personal accounts.

Administrative efficiency. Government administrative costs would rise. The Social Security Administration would be retained in full, and the government would have to manage a new individual account system and to ensure compliance for private plans. Businesses would have to keep track, pay period by pay period, of whether workers wanted to contribute to individual accounts; whether, for those who did, to deposit funds in the government system or in the private accounts; and, for those who chose the latter, which of many thousands of private fund managers the worker had selected.

National saving. Theoretically, because the plan would deny full inflation adjustments not only for Social Security benefits but also for the personal income tax and all indexed benefit programs except Supplemental Security Income, it would increase national saving. But in practice, Congress is not likely to permit income tax collections to rise over the years (the inevitable con-

SOCIAL SECURITY REPORT CARD — THE MOYNIHAN PLAN

Criteria	Grade
Adequacy, equity, and a fair return	F
Protection against risk	C+
Administrative efficiency	D
Increased national saving	D
Overall grade	D

sequence of not indexing the tax brackets, exemptions, and the standard deduction) or the purchasing power of entitlement benefits to fall. Thus the plan would lower national saving.

The Breaux-Gregg Plan

The plan proposed by Senators John Breaux (D-LA) and Judd Gregg (R-NH) and others would divert 2 percentage points of the current payroll tax to individual accounts. To cover that cost and to close the projected long-term deficit, the plan would cut Social Security benefits an average of 25–30 percent. At retirement, a worker would be required to convert enough of his or her account balance into an inflation-proof annuity to ensure that the annuity, plus the reduced Social Security benefit, would meet a minimum retirement income standard. The balance of the individual account could be withdrawn as needed by the retiree. A minimum benefit would be established equal to 60 percent of the poverty threshold for those with 20 years of covered earnings, rising to 100 percent of the poverty threshold for those with 40 years of earnings. A fail-safe mechanism would automatically keep the program in long-term balance.

Benefit adequacy and equity. The assured element of pension protection would be drastically curtailed under the Breaux-Gregg plan. Large Social Security benefit cuts are necessary because the plan would divert payroll taxes from Social Security into the individual accounts.

Protection against risk. The market risk of individual accounts would be moderate because investments would be limited to a few centrally managed index funds. The guaranteed minimum benefit would provide some protection to low earners if returns from their individual accounts turned out to be subpar, though over time productivity growth will push up real incomes while the poverty threshold will increase only at the pace of inflation. If many low and moderate earners received pensions based on the guaranteed minimum rather than on the Social Security benefit formula, the fundamental relationship between contributions (based on earnings) and benefits would be weakened, and political support for the system could diminish. The mandatory annuitization of a portion of the individual accounts would provide protection against outliving one's pension.

Administrative efficiency. The central administration and investment management of the personal accounts would keep costs down. Complexity would arise with the need to calculate the portion of each personal account to be annuitized and to administer both the annuity and the remaining balance.

National saving. Because it does not raise payroll taxes, the plan would not add much in the near term to national saving. Individual accounts would tend to add to national saving because they would not be considered good substitutes for IRAs or 401(k) plans.

Retain and Reform Social Security

The final approach to reform preserves the current defined-benefit system, tying pensions exclusively to each worker's past earnings and years of work, not to fluctuating asset prices.

The Ball Plan

Robert M. Ball, a former commissioner of the Social Security Administration, would restore projected long-term balance by raising revenues and cutting benefits modestly, as well as by diversifying the assets held by the trust fund reserves. Roughly half the projected long-term deficit would be closed by investing a portion of trust fund reserves (up to 40 percent by 2015) in the stock market.

Benefit adequacy and equity. The Ball plan would provide larger benefits than any of the other plans described, save the Feldstein plan. Vulnerable groups would be well protected.

Protection against risk. Because this plan would rely exclusively on defined-benefit pensions, it would spare workers exposure to the risks inherent in individual accounts. Annual cost-of-living adjustments would protect against inflation. The weakness of the Ball plan is that it does not solve the Social Security fiscal imbalance for the long run. The modest changes it proposes would allow Social Security to fall out of close long-run actuarial balance. We think current public distrust of the retirement system and of government in general makes it vital to adopt reforms that will restore financial balance and sustain it.

Administrative efficiency. The Ball plan would maintain the current low-cost administrative structure for taxes and benefits. Small added costs of investing trust fund reserves in equities should amount to no more than 1/100 of 1 percent of funds invested.

SOCIAL SECURITY REPORT CARD

Criteria	Grade
Adequacy, equity, and a fair return	C
Protection against risk	C
Administrative efficiency	C-
Increased national saving	B-
Overall grade	C+

THE BREAUX-GREGG PLAN

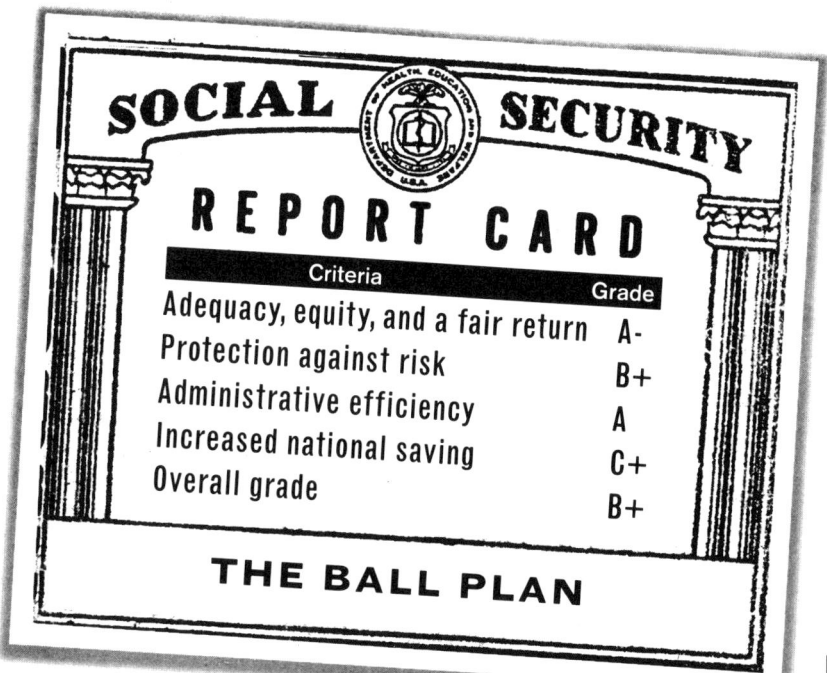

16. Should We Retire Social Security?

SOCIAL SECURITY REPORT CARD

THE BALL PLAN

Criteria	Grade
Adequacy, equity, and a fair return	A-
Protection against risk	B+
Administrative efficiency	A
Increased national saving	C+
Overall grade	B+

National saving. Because the Ball plan would both cut benefits and raise taxes only modestly, it would have little effect on national saving.

The Aaron-Reischauer Plan

Our own plan relies exclusively on a defined-benefit retirement system. It would cut benefits by about 8 percent on the average to boost reserve accumulation and raise national saving.

The plan's distinctive characteristic is the creation of a new Social Security Reserve Board, modeled on the Federal Reserve Board, that would manage all financial operations of Social Security. With multiple institutional safeguards in place to insulate the SSRB from political pressure, the board would invest Social Security reserves in excess of one and one-half year's benefits passively in a broad mix of private securities.

The operations of the SSRB would be removed from the budget presentations of the executive and legislative branches. Budget resolutions enacted each year to guide congressional action should exclude Social Security from aggregate totals.

Benefit adequacy and equity. Although our plan reduces benefits more than the Ball plan does, it does not cut pensions significantly for vulnerable groups such as the disabled. It would boost benefits for most surviving spouses. The new strategy for investing Trust Fund reserves would bring to people dependent on public pensions the higher yields made possible by a broad portfolio of public and private bonds and stocks.

Protection against risk. Our plan preserves the key advantage of defined-benefit pension plans by spreading risks broadly among the general population. Benefits would remain fully protected from inflation. The plan more than closes the long-term deficit, thus reducing uncertainty about future adjustment. It also incorporates a mechanism that would help to ensure that if the reformed program were ever to fall out of long-run actuarial balance, policymakers would enact corrective measures.

Administrative efficiency. Our plan maintains all the efficiencies of the current system.

National saving. Our plan would add moderately to national saving. It would isolate Social Security surpluses from the general budget process so that they are more likely than under the current budget rules to add up to national saving.

No Straight A Grades Here

No perfect way exists to reform the nation's mandatory retirement program. No plan, including our own, that cuts benefits or raises taxes merits a straight A grade. While investing Social Security's growing reserves, collectively or through individual accounts, in assets that have higher yields than government bonds can help, it cannot alone close the projected deficit. To finish the job, future retirees will have to accept smaller benefits than those promised under current law or future workers will have to pay higher taxes. The weightlifter's maxim, "no gain without pain" applies also to pension policy. The question is whose gain and whose pain?

SOCIAL SECURITY REPORT CARD

THE AARON-REISCHAUER PLAN

Criteria	Grade
Adequacy, equity, and a fair return	B+
Protection against risk	A
Administrative efficiency	A
Increased national saving	B+
Overall grade	A-

Unit 4

Unit Selections

17. **U.S. Monetary Policy: An Introduction,** FRBSF Economic Letter
18. **Central Banking in a Democracy,** Alan S. Blinder
19. **Is the Fed Slave to a Defunct Economist?** Evan F. Koenig
20. **Should the Fed Care about Stock Bubbles?** Paul Krugman
21. **Bank Mergers and the Big Money,** Charles Geisst
22. **The Stepchildren of Banking,** Richard A. Oppel Jr.
23. **Electronic Cash and the End of National Markets,** Stephen J. Kobrin

Key Points to Consider

❖ How is U.S. monetary policy used for the purpose of achieving national macroeconomic goals?

❖ Is monetary policy making subject to political influences? What might be done about this problem?

❖ Should the Federal Reserve pursue complete price stability? Explain.

❖ What role does "E-cash" play in an economy?

Links www.dushkin.com/online/

18. **Alan Greenspan's Tradeoff**
    http://www.pathfinder.com/fortune/1997/971208/fst5.html
19. **Federal Reserve Board**
    http://www.bog.frb.fed.us
20. **History of Money**
    http://www.ex.ac.uk/~RDavies/arian/llyfr.html
21. **Mark Bernkopf's Central Banks of the World: Central Banking Resources Center**
    http://patriot.net/~bernkopf

These sites are annotated on pages 4 and 5.

Money, Banking, and Monetary Policy

Money works, but it doesn't work miracles.—Paul Samuelson (1970 Nobel Laureate in Economics)

Compared to fiscal policy, monetary policy—the deliberate control of the money supply for the purpose of achieving macroeconomic goals—receives less attention in political debates and the media. Part of its apparent obscurity may be traced to differences in the manner in which the two policies are conducted: fiscal policy decisions are made by elected representatives in Congress following sometimes lengthy public debates, while monetary policies are determined by a small handful of Federal Reserve (Fed) officials meeting in closed session. In addition, the role of money in an economy is itself a fairly obscure topic for the average person; the effect of changes in the nation's money supply is generally less understood than, say, a tax cut, the effect of which can be felt immediately in a person's pockets. Nevertheless, monetary policy can have a powerful impact on a nation's economy.

The importance of monetary policy as a stabilizing instrument has increased significantly in recent years, as a ballooning federal deficit complicated the use of its major alternative, fiscal policy. The implementation of monetary policy requires the Federal Reserve to adjust what are known as "intermediate targets" (such as the money supply or short-term interest rates). These targets stand intermediate between certain ultimate objectives (such as high employment, low inflation, and so forth) and the instruments of monetary policy (including open market operations, discount rate policy, and reserve requirement changes). The intermediate targets are of interest not for their own sake, but for the close relationship they may bear to the ultimate goal of stabilizing the economy.

The unit begins with an article that offers insights into the major dimensions of U.S. monetary policy. What are the ultimate objectives of the Federal Reserve? What happens when these goals conflict? How does the Fed formulate its strategies, and how do its policies affect the economy?

The Federal Reserve is an unusual, hybrid government body that has little direct accountability to the American public. In "Central Banking in a Democracy," Alan Blinder asks: How can the economic fate of the nation be entrusted to such an institution?

The targets and instruments of monetary policy are the subject of the next two articles. First, Evan Koenig wonders if the Fed is slave to a "defunct economist." Some commentators have recently accused the Federal Reserve of pursuing a Keynesian policy of "fine tuning" the economy. As an alternative they advocate a policy of allowing output and employment to range freely, as long as inflation holds steady. Koenig argues that the Fed has, in fact, steered a middle course between these extremes.

An influential group of economists has argued that the only sensible inflation rate is no inflation at all. Paul Krugman asks: Should the Fed care if stock prices are climbing to record levels? (He reminds us of the importance of distinguishing between a stock market boom and a boom in real investment.)

Next, in "Bank Mergers and the Big Money" Charles Geisst assesses the usefulness of the Glass-Steagall Act, a 1933 U.S. law that prevents commercial banks from providing services in investment banking and insurance. Recent mergers within the banking and securities businesses are clearly in violation of the act's spirit, if not its text. Geisst cautions of the dangers of this arrangement.

The concluding two articles deal with the functions of money. In "The Stepchild of Banking" Richard Oppel Jr. explains why many people, especially in low-income neighborhoods, shy away from banks. He examines proposals for encouraging them to open bank accounts. Finally, Stephen Kobrin considers what the development of "E-cash" (or electronic money) might mean for the future of banking and U.S. monetary institutions.

U.S. Monetary Policy: An Introduction

U.S. monetary policy affects all kinds of economic and financial decisions people make in this country—whether to get a loan to buy a new house or car or to start up a company, whether to expand a business by investing in a new plant or equipment, and whether to put savings in a bank, in bonds, or in the stock market, for example. Furthermore, because the U.S. is the largest economy in the world, its monetary policy also has significant economic and financial effects on other countries.

The object of monetary policy is to influence the performance of the economy, as reflected in such factors as inflation, economic output, and employment. It works by affecting demand across the economy—that is, the population's willingness to spend on goods and services.

While most people are familiar with the fiscal policy tools that affect demand—such as taxes and government spending—many are less familiar with monetary policy and its tools. Monetary policy is conducted by the Federal Reserve System, the nation's central bank, and it influences demand mainly by raising and lowering short-term interest rates.

This *Economic Letter* is an introduction to U.S. monetary policy as it is currently conducted, and it answers a series of questions:
- How is the Fed structured to make monetary policy decisions?
- What are the Fed's goals?
- What tools does it use to implement its policies?
- How does monetary policy affect the U.S. economy?
- How does the Fed formulate strategies to reach its goals?

How Is the Federal Reserve Structured?

The Federal Reserve System (called the Fed, for short) is the nation's central bank. It was established by an Act of Congress in 1913 and consists of the seven members of the Board of Governors in Washington, D.C., and twelve Federal Reserve District Banks (for a discussion of the Fed's overall responsibilities, see *The Federal Reserve System: Purposes and Functions*).

The Congress structured the Fed to be independent within the government—that is, although the Fed is accountable to the Congress, it is insulated from day-to-day political pressures. This reflects the conviction that the people who control the country's money supply should be independent of the people who frame the government's spending decisions. Most studies of central bank independence rank the Fed among the most independent in the world.

What makes the Fed independent?

Three structural features make the Fed independent: the appointment procedure for governors, the appointment procedure for Reserve Bank Presidents, and funding.

Appointment procedure for Governors. The seven Governors on the Federal Reserve Board are appointed by the President of the United States and confirmed by the Senate. Independence derives from a couple of factors: First, the appointments are staggered to reduce the chance that a single U.S. President could "load" the Board with appointees; second, their terms of office are 14 years—much longer than elected officials' terms.

Appointment procedure for Reserve Bank Presidents. Each Reserve Bank President is appointed to a five-year term by that Bank's Board of Directors, subject to final approval by the Board of Governors. This procedure adds to independence because the Directors of each Reserve Bank are not chosen by politicians but are selected to provide a cross-section of interests within the region, including those of depository institutions, non-financial businesses, labor, and the public.

Funding. The Fed is structured to be self-sufficient in the sense that it meets its operating expenses primarily from the interest earnings on its portfolio of securities. Therefore, it is independent of Congressional decisions about appropriations.

How is the Fed "independent within government"?

Even though the Fed is independent of Congressional appropriations and administrative control, it is ultimately accountable to Congress and comes under government audit and review. The Chairman, other Governors, and Reserve Bank Presidents report regularly to the Congress on monetary policy, regulatory policy, and a variety of other issues and meet with senior Administration officials to discuss the Federal Reserve's and the federal government's economic programs.

Who makes monetary policy?

The Fed's FOMC (Federal Open Market Committee) has primary responsibility for conducting monetary policy. The FOMC meets in Washington eight times a year and has twelve members: the seven members of the Board of Governors, the President of the Federal Reserve Bank of New York, and four of the other Reserve Bank Presidents, who serve in rotation. The remaining Reserve Bank Presidents attend the meetings and contribute to the Committee's discussions and deliberations.

In addition, the Directors of each Reserve Bank contribute to monetary policy by making recommendations about the appropriate discount rate, which are subject to final approval by the Governors. (See "What Are the Tools of Monetary Policy?")

What Are the Goals of U.S. Monetary Policy?
Monetary policy has two basic goals: to promote "maximum" output and employment and to promote "stable" prices. These goals are prescribed in a 1977 amendment to the Federal Reserve Act.

What does "maximum" output and employment mean?
In the long run, the level of output and employment in the economy depends on factors other than monetary policy. These include technology and people's preferences for saving, risk, and work effort. So, "maximum" employment and output means the levels consistent with these factors in the long run.

But the economy goes through business cycles in which output and employment are above or below their long-run levels. Even though monetary policy can't affect either output or employment in the long run, it can affect them in the short run. For example, when demand contracts and there's a recession, the Fed can stimulate the economy—temporarily—and help push it back toward its long-run level of output by lowering interest rates. Therefore, in the short run, the Fed and many other central banks are concerned with stabilizing the economy—that is, smoothing out the peaks and valleys in output and employment around their long-run levels.

If the Fed can stimulate the economy out of a recession, why doesn't it stimulate all the time?
Consistent attempts to expand the economy beyond its long-run level will result in capacity constraints that lead to higher and higher inflation, without producing lower unemployment or higher output in the long run. In other words, not only are there no long-term gains from consistently pursuing expansionary policies, but there's also a price—higher inflation.

What's so bad about higher inflation?
High inflation can hinder economic growth. For example, when inflation is high, it also tends to vary a lot, and that makes people uncertain about what inflation will be in the future. That uncertainty can hinder economic growth in a couple of ways—it adds an inflation risk premium to long-term interest rates, and it complicates the planning and contracting by business and labor that are so essential to capital formation.

High inflation also hinders economic growth in other ways. For example, because many aspects of the tax system are not indexed to inflation, high inflation distorts economic decisions by arbitrarily increasing or decreasing after-tax rates of return to different kinds of economic activities. In addition, it leads people to spend time and resources hedging against inflation instead of pursuing more productive activities.

So that's why the other goal is "stable prices"?
Yes. Although monetary policy cannot expand the economy or reduce unemployment in the long run, it can stabilize prices in the long run. Price "stability" is basically low inflation—that is, inflation that's so low that people don't worry about it when they make decisions about what to buy, whether to borrow or invest, and so on.

If low inflation is the only thing the Fed can achieve in the long run, why isn't it the sole focus of monetary policy?
Because the Fed can determine the economy's average rate of inflation, some commentators—and some members of Congress as well—have emphasized the need to define the goals of monetary policy in terms of price stability, which is achievable. However, volatility in output and employment also is costly to people. In practice, the Fed, like most central banks, cares about both inflation and measures of the short-run performance of the economy.

Are the two goals ever in conflict?
Yes, sometimes they are. One kind of conflict involves deciding which goal should take precedence at any point in time. For example, suppose there's a recession and the Fed works to prevent employment losses from being too severe; this short-run success could turn into a long-run problem if monetary policy remains expansionary too long, because that could trigger inflationary pressures. So it's important for the Fed to find the balance between its short-run goal of stabilization and its longer-run goal of maintaining low inflation.

Another kind of conflict involves the potential for pressure from the political arena. For example, in the day-to-day course of governing the country and making economic policy, politicians may be tempted to put the emphasis on short-run results rather than on the longer-run health of the economy. The Fed is somewhat insulated from such pressure, however, by its independence, which allows it to achieve a more appropriate balance between short-run and long-run objectives.

Why don't the goals include helping a region of the country that's in recession?
Often enough, some state or region is going through a recession of its own while the national economy is humming along. But the Fed can't concentrate its efforts to expand the weak region for two reasons. First, monetary policy works through credit markets, and since credit markets are linked nationally, the Fed simply has no way to direct stimulus to any particular part of the country that needs help. Second, if the Fed stimulated whenever any state had economic hard times, it would be stimulating much of the time, and this would mean higher inflation.

But this focus on the well-being of the national economy doesn't mean that the Fed ignores regional economic conditions. Extensive regional data and anecdotal information are used, along with statistics that directly measure developments in the regional economy, to fit together a picture of the national economy's performance. This is one advantage to having regional Federal Reserve Bank Presidents sit on the FOMC: They are in close contact with economic developments in their regions of the country.

MONEY, BANKING, AND MONETARY POLICY

What Are the Tools of Monetary Policy?
The Fed can't control inflation or influence output and employment directly; instead, it affects them indirectly, mainly by raising or lowering short-term interest rates. The Fed affects interest rates mainly through open market operations and the discount rate, and both of these methods work through the market for bank reserves, known as the federal funds market.

What are bank reserves?
Banks and other depository institutions (for convenience, we'll refer to all of these as "banks") are legally required to hold a specific amount of funds in reserve. These funds, which can be used to meet unexpected outflows, are called reserves, and banks keep them as cash in their vaults or as deposits with the Fed. Currently, banks must hold 3–10% of the funds they have in interest-bearing and non-interest-bearing checking accounts as reserves (depending on the dollar amount of such accounts held at each bank).

What is the federal funds market?
From day to day, the amount of reserves a bank has to hold may change as its deposits change. When a bank needs additional reserves on a short-term basis, it can borrow them from other banks that happen to have more reserves than they need. These loans take place in a private financial market called the federal funds market.

The interest rate on the overnight borrowing of reserves is called the federal funds rate or simply the "funds rate." It adjusts to balance the supply of and demand for reserves. For example, an increase in the amount of reserves supplied to the federal funds market causes the funds rate to fall, while a decrease in the supply of reserves raises that rate.

What are open market operations?
The major tool the Fed uses to affect the supply of reserves in the banking system is open market operations—that is, the Fed buys and sells government securities on the open market. These operations are conducted by the Federal Reserve Bank of New York.

Suppose the Fed wants the funds rate to fall. To do this, it buys government securities from a bank. The Fed then pays for the securities by increasing that bank's reserves. As a result, the bank now has more reserves than it is required to hold. So the bank can lend these excess reserves to another bank in the federal funds market. Thus, the Fed's open market purchase increases the supply of reserves to the banking system, and the federal funds rate falls.

When the Fed wants the funds rate to rise, it does the reverse, that is, it sells government securities. The Fed receives payment in reserves from banks, which lowers the supply of reserves in the banking system, and the funds rate rises.

What is the discount rate?
Banks also can borrow reserves from the Federal Reserve Banks at their "discount windows," and the interest rate they must pay on this borrowing is called the discount rate. The total quantity of discount window borrowing tends to be small, because the Fed discourages such borrowing except to meet occasional short-term reserve deficiencies (see *The Federal Reserve: Purposes and Functions* for a discussion of other types of discount window borrowing that are unrelated to monetary policy).

The discount rate plays a role in monetary policy because, traditionally, changes in the rate may have "announcement effects"—that is, they sometimes signal to markets a significant change in monetary policy. A higher discount rate can be used to indicate a more restrictive policy, while a lower rate may signal a more expansionary policy. Therefore, discount rate changes are sometimes coordinated with FOMC decisions to change the funds rate.

What about foreign currency operations?
Purchases and sales of foreign currency by the Fed are directed by the FOMC, acting in cooperation with the Treasury, which has overall responsibility for these operations. The Fed does not have targets, or desired levels, for the exchange rate. Instead, the Fed gets involved to counter "disorderly" movements in foreign exchange markets, such as speculative movements that may disrupt the efficient functioning of these markets or of financial markets in general. For example, during some periods of disorderly declines in the dollar, the Fed has purchased dollars (sold foreign currency) to absorb some of the selling pressure.

Intervention operations involving dollars, whether initiated by the Fed, the Treasury, or by a foreign authority, are not allowed to alter the supply of bank reserves or the funds rate. The process of keeping intervention from affecting reserves and the funds rate is called the "sterilization" of exchange market operations. As such, these operations are not used as a tool of monetary policy.

How Does Monetary Policy Affect the Economy?
The point of implementing policy through raising or lowering interest rates is to affect people's and firms' demand for goods and services. This section discusses how policy actions affect real interest rates, which in turn affect demand and ultimately output, employment, and inflation.

What are real interest rates and why do they matter?
For the most part, the demand for goods and services is not related to the market interest rates quoted on the financial pages of newspapers, known as nominal rates. Instead, it is related to real interest rates—that is, nominal interest rates minus the expected rate of inflation.

Variations in expected inflation can make a big difference in interpreting the stance of monetary policy. In 1978, the nominal funds rate averaged 8%, but the rate of inflation was 9%. So, even though nominal interest rates were high, monetary policy actually was stimulating demand with a negative real funds rate of minus 1%.

By contrast, in early 1998, the nominal funds rate was 5% and the inflation rate was running at about 2%. This implied a positive 3% real funds rate. So the nominal funds rate of 8% in 1978 was more stimulative than the 5% nominal funds rate in early 1995.

How do real interest rates affect economic activity in the short run?

Changes in real interest rates affect the public's demand for goods and services mainly by altering borrowing costs, the availability of bank loans, the wealth of households, and foreign exchange rates.

For example, a decrease in real interest rates lowers the cost of borrowing and leads to increases in business investment spending and household purchases of durable goods, such as autos and new homes. In addition, lower real rates and a healthy economy may increase banks' willingness to lend to businesses and households. This may increase spending, especially by smaller borrowers who have few sources of credit other than banks. Lower real rates make common stocks and other such investments more attractive than bonds and other debt instruments; as a result, common stock prices tend to rise. Households with stocks in their portfolios find that the value of their holdings has gone up, and this increase in wealth makes them willing to spend more. Higher stock prices also make it more attractive for businesses to invest in plant and equipment by issuing stock. In the short run, lower real interest rates in the U.S. also tend to reduce the foreign exchange value of the dollar, which lowers the prices of the exports we sell abroad and raises the prices we pay for foreign-produced goods. This leads to higher aggregate spending on goods and services produced in the U.S.

The increase in aggregate demand for the economy's output through these various channels leads firms to raise production and employment, which in turn increases business spending on capital goods even further by making greater demands on existing factory capacity. It also boosts consumption further because of the income gains that result from the higher level of economic output.

How does monetary policy affect inflation?

Wages and prices will begin to rise at faster rates if monetary policy stimulates aggregate demand enough to push labor and capital markets beyond their long-run capacities. In fact, a monetary policy that persistently attempts to keep short-term real rates low will lead eventually to higher inflation and higher nominal interest rates, with no permanent increases in output or decreases in unemployment. As noted earlier, in the long run, output and employment cannot be set by monetary policy. In other words, while there is a trade-off between higher inflation and lower unemployment in the short run, the trade-off disappears in the long run.

Policy also can affect inflation directly through people's expectations about future inflation. For example, suppose the Fed eases monetary policy. If consumers and business people expect higher inflation in the future, they'll ask for bigger increases in wages and prices. That in itself will raise inflation without big changes in employment and output.

Doesn't U.S. inflation depend on worldwide capacity, not just U.S. capacity?

In this era of intense global competition, it might seem parochial to focus on U.S. capacity as a determinant of U.S. inflation, rather than on world capacity. For example, some argue that even if unemployment in the U.S. drops to very low levels, U.S. workers wouldn't be able to push for higher wages, because they're competing for jobs with workers abroad, who are willing to accept much lower wages.

This reasoning doesn't hold up too well, however, for a couple of reasons. First, a large proportion of what we consume in the U.S. isn't affected very much by foreign trade. One example is health care, which isn't traded internationally, and which amounts to about 14% of GDP.

Second, even when we consider goods that *are* traded internationally, the effect on U.S. prices is largely offset by flexible foreign exchange rates. Suppose the price of steel, or some other good, is lower in Japan than in the U.S. When U.S. manufacturers buy Japanese steel, they have to pay for it in yen, which they buy on the foreign exchange market. As a result, the value of the yen will climb relative to the dollar, and the cost of Japanese steel to U.S. firms will go up—even though the Japanese have not changed the (yen) price they charge.

How long does it take a policy action to affect the economy and inflation?

The lags in monetary policy are long and variable. The major effects of a change in policy on growth in the overall production of goods and services usually are felt within three months to two years. And the effects on inflation tend to involve even longer lags, perhaps one to three years, or more.

Why are the lags so hard to predict?

Since monetary policy is aimed at affecting people's demand, it's dealing with human responses, which are changeable and hard to predict.

For example, the effect of a policy action on the economy will depend on what people think the Fed action means for inflation in the future. If people believe that a tightening of policy means the Fed is determined to keep inflation under control, they'll immediately expect low inflation in the future, so they're likely to ask for smaller wage and price increases, and this will help to achieve that end. But if people aren't convinced that the Fed is going to contain inflation, they're likely to ask for bigger wage and price increases, and that means that inflation is likely to rise. In this case, the only way to bring inflation down is to tighten so much and for so long that there are significant losses in employment and output.

How Does the Fed Formulate Its Strategies?

The Fed's job of stabilizing output in the short run and promoting price stability in the long run is made more difficult by two main factors: the long and variable lags in policy, and the uncertain influences of factors other than monetary policy on the economy.

What problems do lags cause?

The Fed's job would be much easier if monetary policy had swift and sure effects. Policymakers could set policy, see its effects, and then adjust the settings until they eliminated any discrepancy between economic developments and the goals.

But with the long lags and uncertain effects of monetary policy actions, the Fed must be able to anticipate the effects of its policy actions into the distant future. To see why, suppose the Fed waits to shift its policy stance until it actually sees an increase in inflation. That would mean that inflationary momentum already had developed, so the task of reducing inflation would be that much harder and more costly in terms of job losses. Not surprisingly, anticipating policy effects in the future is a difficult task.

What problems are caused by other influences on the economy?

Output, employment, and inflation are influenced not only by monetary policy actions, but also by such factors as our government's taxing and spending policies, the availability and price of key natural resources (such as oil), economic developments abroad, financial conditions at home and abroad, and the introduction of new technologies.

In order to have the desired effect on the economy, the Fed must take into account the influences of these other factors and either offset them or reinforce them as needed. This isn't easy because sometimes these developments occur unexpectedly and because the size and timing of their effects are difficult to estimate.

The recent currency crisis in East Asia is a good example. Over the past year or so, economic activity in those countries has either slowed or declined, and this has reduced their demand for U.S. products. In addition, the foreign exchange value of most of their currencies has depreciated, and this has made Asian-produced goods less expensive for us to buy and U.S.-produced goods more expensive in Asian countries. By themselves, these factors would reduce the demand for U.S. products and therefore lower our output and employment. As a result, this is a factor that the Fed has had to consider in setting monetary policy.

Another example is the spread of new technologies that can enhance productivity. When workers and capital are more productive, the economy can expand more rapidly without creating inflationary pressures. In the last few years, there have been indications that the U.S. economy may have experienced a productivity surge, perhaps brought on by computers and other high-tech developments. The issue for monetary policymakers is how much faster productivity is increasing and whether those increases are temporary or permanent.

With all these uncertainties, how does the Fed know how and when its policies will affect the economy?

The Fed looks at a whole range of indicators of the future course of output, employment, and inflation. Among the indicators are measures of the money supply, real interest rates, the unemployment rate, nominal and real GDP growth, commodity prices, exchange rates, various interest rate spreads (including the term structure of interest rates), and inflation expectations surveys. Economic forecasting models help give structure to understanding the interplay of these indicators and policy actions. But these models are far from perfect—so policymakers rely on their own less formal judgments about indicators as well. Indeed, policymakers often disagree about how important one indicator is rather than another—and this isn't surprising, because the indicators can be hard to interpret, and they can even give contradictory signals.

To illustrate the difficulties of interpreting these indicators, consider the problems with three of the most prominent: the money supply measures (M1, M2, and M3), real interest rates, and the unemployment rate.

What are the problems of using the money supply as an indicator of future economic performance? Before much of the deregulation of the financial markets in the 1980s, measures of the money supply were pretty reliable predictors of aggregate spending; moreover, they could be controlled relatively well by the Fed. So the Fed paid special attention to them and to their annual target ranges during the 1970s and 1980s. In fact, from late 1979 to late 1982 the Fed explicitly targeted money on a short-term basis.

But the predictable relationship between the money supply and aggregate spending began to fall apart once financial markets were deregulated and new financial instruments were introduced. For example, consider M1, the narrowest monetary measure, which includes only currency and (fully) checkable deposits. Before deregulation, banks couldn't pay explicit interest on the deposits in M1, so people tended to keep only as much in them as they needed for their transactions; that made those deposits track spending pretty closely.

Once banks were allowed to pay explicit interest nationwide on checkable deposits, M1 no longer reflected spending so well because people started to leave money in those deposits over and above what they needed for transactions. Furthermore, once private financial markets started introducing instruments that competed with M1 deposits, some people shifted their funds to those instruments, and that also weakened the relationship between M1 and spending. Ultimately, the same kinds of deterioration occurred with the broader money supply measures, M2 and M3.

The Fed still establishes annual ranges for M2 and M3, as well as for total nonfinancial debt, as required by Congress. However, given the problems with the reliability of the aggregates, they have come to play a less central role in the formulation of monetary policy in the 1990s.

What are the problems with using real interest rates as indicators of future economic performance? Real interest rates are natural variables to consider as policy indicators, since they are influenced by the Fed and they are a key link in the transmission mechanism of monetary policy. But real interest rates are problematic as indicators of real GDP for at least two reasons.

First, it is not always obvious when real rates are "high" or "low." The reason is that real rates are figured as the nominal rate minus expected future inflation. The level of expected future inflation may be hard to estimate. Second, it also is not obvious how to determine the equilibrium real interest rate—that is, the rate that would be consistent with the full employment of labor and with real GDP being at its long-run level. This rate is needed as a benchmark to judge whether a given real interest rate is expansionary or contractionary.

The equilibrium real rate varies over time in ways that are difficult to measure or predict, and it depends on many factors, such as the productivity of investment, fiscal policy, tax rates, and preferences for risk and saving. So, unless real interest rates are extremely high or low relative to historical experience, it can be difficult to interpret the implications of observed market interest rates for future economic developments.

Why is it hard to pinpoint the natural rate of unemployment? The unemployment rate sometimes is used as an indicator of future inflation. In judging the inflationary implications of the unemployment rate, some economists focus on the so-called "natural rate" of unemployment as a benchmark. The natural rate is the umemployment rate that would occur when short-run cyclical factors have played themselves out—that is, when wages have had time to adjust to balance labor demand and supply. All else equal, if unemployment is below the natural rate, inflation would tend to rise; likewise, if unemployment is above the natural rate, inflation would tend to fall. But it is difficult to know what the natural rate of unemployment is, because it can change if the structure of the labor market changes. For example, the natural rate rose temporarily in the 1970s as more women sought jobs. And in recent years, some economists have argued that the natural rate has fallen because of worker "insecurity" stemming from rapid changes in the job skills needed by firms as computers and other new technologies were introduced.

Is that why policymakers look at so many indicators? Although all of the indicators mentioned above provide some useful information, none is reliable enough to be used mechanically as a sole target or guide to policy.

As a result, each FOMC policymaker must process all the available information according to his or her own best judgment and with the advice of the best research available. They then discuss and debate the policy options at FOMC meetings and try to reach a consensus on the best course of action.

Glossary of Terms

Capital market. The market in which corporate equity and longer-term debt securities (those maturing in more than one year) are issued and traded.

Central bank. Principal monetary authority of a nation, which performs several key functions, including issuing currency and regulating the supply of money and credit in the economy. The Federal Reserve is the central bank of the United States.

Depository institution. Financial institution that obtains its funds mainly through deposits from the public; includes commercial banks, savings and loan associations, savings banks, and credit unions.

Discount rate. Interest rate at which an eligible depository institution may borrow funds, typically for a short period, directly from a Federal Reserve Bank. The law requires that the board of directors of each Reserve Bank establish the discount rate every fourteen days subject to the approval of the Board of Governors.

Excess reserves. Amount of reserves held by an institution in excess of its reserve requirement and required clearing balance.

Equilibrium real interest rate. The level of the real interest rate that is consistent with the level of long-run output and full employment.

Federal funds rate. The interest rate at which banks borrow surplus reserves and other immediately available funds. The federal funds rate is the shortest short-term interest rate, with maturities on federal funds concentrated in overnight or one-day transactions.

Fiscal policy. Federal government policy regarding taxation and spending; set by Congress and the Administration.

Foreign currency operations. Purchase or sale of the currencies of other nations by a central bank for the purpose of influencing foreign exchange rates or maintaining orderly foreign exchange markets. Also called foreign-exchange market intervention.

Foreign exchange rate. Price of the currency of one nation in terms of the currency of another nation.

Government securities. Securities issued by the U.S. Treasury or federal agencies.

Gross Domestic Product (GDP). The total market value of a nation's output of goods and services. GDP may be expressed in terms of product—consumption, investment, government purchases of goods and services, and net exports—or, it may be expressed in terms of income earned—wages, interest, and profits.

Inflation. A rate of increase in the general price level of all goods and services. (This should not be confused with increases in the prices of specific goods relative to the prices of other goods.)

Inflationary expectations. The rate of increase in the general price level anticipated by the public in the period ahead.

Long-term interest rates. Interest rates on loan contracts—or debt instruments, such as Treasury bonds or utility, industrial, or municipal bonds—having maturities greater than one year. Often called capital market rates.

M1. Measure of the U.S. money stock that consists of currency held by the public, travelers checks, demand deposits, and other fully checkable deposits.

M2. Measure of the U.S. money stock that consists of M1, certain overnight repurchase agreements and certain overnight Eurodollars, savings deposits (including money market deposit accounts), time deposits in amounts of less than $100,000, and balances in money market mutual funds (other than those restricted to institutional investors).

M3. Measure of the U.S. money stock that consists of M2, time deposits of $100,000 or more at all depository institutions, term repurchase agreements in amounts of $100,000 or more, certain term Eurodollars, and balances in money market mutual funds restricted to institutional investors.

Market interest rates. Rates of interest paid on deposits and other investments, determined by the interaction of the supply of and demand for funds in financial markets.

Monetary policy. A central bank's actions to influence short-term interest rates and the supply of money and credit, as a means of helping to promote national economic goals. Tools of U. S. monetary policy include open market operations, discount rate policy, and reserve requirements.

4 ❖ MONEY, BANKING, AND MONETARY POLICY

Natural rate of unemployment. The rate of unemployment that can be sustained in the long run and that is consistent with constant inflation.

Nominal interest rates. Current stated rates of interest paid or earned.

Open market operations. Purchases and sales of government securities and certain other securities in the open market, through the Domestic Trading Desk at the Federal Reserve Bank of New York as directed by the Federal Open Market Committee, to influence short-term interest rates and the volume of money and credit in the economy. Purchases inject reserves into the banking system and stimulate growth of money and credit; sales do the opposite.

Productivity. The level of output per hour of work.

Real GDP. GDP adjusted for inflation. Real GDP provides the value of GDP in constant dollars, which is used as an indicator of the volume of the nation's output.

Real interest rates. Interest rates adjusted for the expected erosion of purchasing power resulting from inflation. Technically defined as nominal interest rates minus the expected rate of inflation.

Short-term interest rates. Interest rates on loan contracts—or debt instruments such as Treasury bills, bank certificates of deposit, or commercial paper—having maturities less than one year. Often called money market rates.

Total nonfinancial debt. Includes outstanding credit market debt of federal, state, and local governments and of private nonfinancial sectors (including mortgages and other kinds of consumer credit and bank loans, corporate bonds, commercial paper, bankers acceptances, and other debt instruments).

Suggested Reading

For an overview of the Federal Reserve System and its functions, see:

The Federal Reserve System: Purposes and Functions, 8th ed. Washington, DC: Board of Governors, Federal Reserve System, December 1994.

The Federal Reserve System in Brief. Federal Reserve Bank of San Francisco.

For further discussion on several of the topics covered here, see the following issues of the *FRBSF Economic Letter:*

Overview of monetary policy

94–27 "A Primer on Monetary Policy, Part I: Goals and Instruments," by Carl Walsh.
94–28 "A Primer on Monetary Policy, Part II: Targets and Indicators," by Carl Walsh.

Goals of monetary policy

93–21 "Federal Reserve Independence and the Accord of 1951," by Carl Walsh.
93–44 "Inflation and Growth," by Brian Motley.
94–05 "Is There a Cost to Having an Independent Central Bank?" by Carl Walsh.
95–16 "Central Bank Independence and Inflation," by Robert T. Parry.
95–25 "Should the Central Bank Be Responsible for Regional Goals?" by Timothy Cogley and Desiree Schaan.
97–01 "Nobel Views on Inflation and Unemployment," by Carl Walsh.
97–27 "What Is the Optimal Rate of Inflation?" by Timothy Cogley.
98–04 "The New Output-Inflation Trade-off," by Carl Walsh.

Monetary policy transmission mechanism

95–05 "What Are the Lags in Monetary Policy?" by Glenn Rudebusch.
95–23 "Federal Reserve Policy and the Predictability of Interest Rates," by Glenn Rudebusch.
97–15 "Job Loss During the 1990s," by Rob Valletta.
97–18 "Interest Rates and Monetary Policy," by Glenn Rudebusch.
97–29 "A New Paradigm?" by Bharat Trehan.
97–34 "Job Security Update," by Rob Valletta and Randy O'Toole.

Monetary policy strategies

93–01 "An Alternative Strategy for Monetary Policy," by John Judd and Brian Motley.
93–12 "Interest Rate Spreads as Indicators of Monetary Policy," by Chan Huh.
93–38 "Real Interest Rates," by Bharat Trehan.
93–42 "Monetary Policy and Long-Term Real Interest Rates," by Timothy Cogley.
94–13 "Monetary Policy in a Low-Inflation Regime," by Timothy Cogley.
97–35 "NAIRU: Is It Useful for Monetary Policy?" by John Judd.
98–07 "Is It Time to Look at M2 Again?" by Kelly Ragan and Bharat Trehan.
98–17 "Central Bank Inflation Targeting," by Glenn Rudebusch and Carl Walsh.
98–18 "U.S. Inflation Targeting: Pro and Con," by Glenn Rudebusch and Carl Walsh.
98–29 "The Natural Rate, NAIRU, and Monetary Policy," by Carl Walsh.

Central Banking in a Democracy

On September 26, 1996, Alan S. Blinder presented the following speech at the Federal Reserve Bank of Richmond. The text of the speech is printed below after J. Alfred Broaddus's introduction of the speaker.

Alan S. Blinder

Alan S. Blinder is a former Vice Chairman of the Board of Governors of the Federal Reserve System.

It is a pleasure to welcome all of you this afternoon for this latest program in our series of occasional lectures by distinguished economists on major economic policy issues. Largely for convenience, we hold these programs here at the Richmond Fed, and we are delighted to host them. But let me remind you that they are jointly planned and funded with the three university business schools here in Richmond. I'd like to introduce my colleagues in this endeavor: Dr. Al Altimus, Dean of the Lewis School of Business at Virginia Union University; Dr. Randolph New, Dean of the Robins School of Business at the University of Richmond; and Dr. Howard Tuckman, Dean of the School of Business at Virginia Commonwealth University. It's been a great pleasure working with these folks over the years and I think it's been a very productive collaboration. I would also like to recognize my colleague, Marvin Goodfriend, who is Senior Vice President and Director of Research here at the bank. Marvin is my principal adviser and has played a leading role in planning and putting on these programs in recent years.

It's a particular personal pleasure and an honor to introduce our speaker. Alan Blinder, to put it bluntly but accurately, is one of the most distinguished macroeconomists in the world today. He has done about everything any economist and even a leading economist would do. He earned a Ph.D. from a leading economics department, MIT. He has taught and is teaching at a top university, Princeton, which also happens to be his undergraduate alma mater. He has published numerous scholarly articles in professional journals, a leading economics textbook, and a number of other books, including a little gem on major economic policy issues called *Hard Heads, Soft Hearts*. Finally, he has served as an economic policymaker at the highest level. Early in his career, in the mid-'70s, he was briefly Deputy Assistant Director of the Congressional Budget Office when it was just getting started. More recently, of course, he was a member of the President's Council of Economic Advisers in the first year and a half of the Clinton Administration. In that capacity, he was a leading economic policy adviser to the Administration. Subsequently he was our colleague at the Fed, serving as Vice Chairman of the Board of Governors of the Federal Reserve System from June 1994 until he departed early this year to return to Princeton, where he is the Gordon S. Rentschler Memorial Professor of Economics. Some of you who have been attending these lectures regularly will remember that we had Alice Rivlin here not too long ago. She has now become the Vice Chairman of the Board of Governors. We wanted to give an equal opportunity to *former* Vice Chairmen of the Federal Reserve Board.

It's not an idle compliment when I say that as a veteran Fed employee, I greatly enjoyed Alan's all-too-brief tenure at the Fed. Let me share with you a little Fed secret. It's not about interest rates, but about the Federal Open Market Committee, which as you know is the main policymaking body in the

---

• The views expressed are those of the speaker and do not necessarily represent those of the Federal Reserve Bank of Richmond or the Federal Reserve System.

Fed. It's a strong and I believe effective committee, but it is not always a terribly lively committee. It was, however, a much livelier committee when Alan was part of it. He challenged us—and also helped us—to confront issues objectively with careful and solid economic analysis. He helped take the edge off the debates that we had in the committee during his tenure with keen and well-timed humor. And he raised the level of discussion in the committee during his tenure. I miss his input very much. It's good to have him back in Richmond. He was here about a year-and-a-half ago and gave a great lecture to the Virginia Bond Club. Please join me in welcoming back Dr. Alan Blinder.

Al, thank you very much for that fine introduction. I want to talk this afternoon about the role of the Federal Reserve in society in very broad terms and, along the way, to make a few rather more specific points. Then I will be glad to entertain questions about what interest rates will do next week, a subject about which I know nothing! But neither does anyone else, so we are all on an equal footing on the subject.

WHO DOES THE FED SERVE?

Relative to their economic and therefore social importance, central banks must be among the least well understood institutions in the entire world. For example, I have been told that millions of Americans still think that the Federal Reserve System is a system of government-owned forests and wildlife preserves where, presumably, bulls and bears and hawks and doves frolic together in blissful harmony. Having spent 19 months there, I can assure you that that is not the case. The Federal Reserve is an institution that touches almost everyone in America, plus many people outside America, but is itself touched or even seen by relatively few. But its traces are everywhere. Every time you pay or receive paper currency, you are using a "Federal Reserve Note"—a debt obligation of the Fed. Unbeknownst to most of you, your checks are also probably cleared through a regional Federal Reserve Bank; and, if you bank here in Richmond, through this regional Federal Reserve Bank.

When you read in a newspaper ad that a certain bank will pay you 5.7 percent on a certificate of deposit or you hear on television that an automobile company this week is offering 4.9 percent financing, you are seeing tangible evidence of the Fed's regulatory hand at work. Very few people have any idea that it is the Fed that tells banks and auto finance companies how to calculate and advertise those numbers. And even fewer know that the Fed doesn't always get it right!

The interest rates themselves, while set in free markets, are heavily influenced by the Fed's monetary policy. Most Americans these days know that, but few can tell you how that black magic is performed. Even fewer people understand how the Fed's interest rate decisions impact on the overall economy and therefore influence how many people will find jobs, how many will be laid off, how many businesses will succeed, how many will fail. Most economists will attest to the fact that the Fed has far more influence over these matters than the President and Congress.

The Federal Reserve System has a governance structure that is at least odd and perhaps even byzantine. While most countries in the world have one central bank, we have 12—the one here in Richmond and 11 others. These regional Federal Reserve Banks are, in a legal sense, private corporations. They have presidents, in this case Al Broaddus, and boards of directors. They even have shareholders. And while these corporations are extremely profitable—to the tune of over $20 billion a year for the 12 of them together—their shareholders do not reap the benefits. Instead, the Fed's prodigious profits are turned over to the United States Treasury—a very friendly gesture. Atop this organization of 12 putatively private corporations, there sits a seven-member Board of Governors in Washington, whose members are not elected by any of the stockholders, but rather are politically appointed. A very, very curious organizational structure.

So the question arises: Who does the Fed serve? Congress and the President? Most certainly not. Although the Fed is a creature of Congress, and its governors are all presidential appointees, the Fed does not exist to do their bidding. After all, that would make a mockery of the doctrine of central bank independence.

What about the banks? Well to some extent, the answer must be yes. The Fed is a bank for banks. It sells to these banks a variety of services, many of them in direct competition with private suppliers. The Fed is also deeply concerned with the health of the banking and payments system and will, when necessary, take strong steps to safeguard it. However, the Federal Reserve is also the supervisor of thousands of banks, either directly or indirectly, through their bank holding companies. (The Fed supervises all the bank holding companies.) It is a very odd arrangement when you think about it: The Fed is regulating its own customers. There are a lot of businesses in America that would like to regulate their own customers, but very few get to do that. In my view, it is a great mistake for the Federal Reserve to see itself as a service organization for the benefit of banks, however. It is a mistake that people in the Federal Reserve System make occasionally, but fortunately not very often.

Does the Fed serve the financial markets? As the nation's central bank, the Fed is naturally and certainly the ultimate guardian and protector of the entire financial system. In times of acute market distress, the Fed stands ready to play its classic role as lender of last resort. In more normal times, the Fed worries about such things as the integrity of the markets, financial fragility, speculative bubbles, the value of a dollar, and a host of other things. As I used to say when I was Vice Chairman of the Fed, we get paid, though not very much, to worry about *everything.*

But, in my view, none of these choices—not the President, not the Congress, not banks, not the financial markets—adequately describes the Fed's true constituency. In my view, that constituency can only be the entire nation. While I was on the Federal Reserve Board, I often said that I viewed myself as working for 260 million Americans. Given the central bank's broad reach and pervasive influence, no narrower constituency seemed appropriate. So I want to talk this afternoon about what the Federal Reserve does and should do to serve the national interest.

I think it would surprise most of you to learn that a time-and-motion study of the daily lives of Federal Reserve Governors would reveal that most of their efforts are devoted to bank regulatory issues, broadly defined. Most of this business is routine, extremely familiar, and intensely interesting to the banking industry, and totally unknown, deeply obscure, and generally quite boring to everybody else in society. This is the Federal Reserve that nobody knows. So as not to bore you with these matters, I will skip directly to the Federal Reserve that everybody knows, for nowhere is the Federal Reserve's public service role more visible than in the conduct of monetary policy. It is monetary policy that puts the Fed in the news constantly, and occasionally puts it in the middle of a political maelstrom.

If you don't live your life in the financial world, it is almost impossible to imagine how tightly focused the media and the markets are on the Federal Reserve. Fixated is not too strong a word. "Federal Reserve fetish" has not yet come into current use as a term of art, but I think it describes a lot of the behavior of the financial press and people in the financial markets. To the financial press, a Federal Reserve Governor is more engaging than a movie star. (Think about that one for a while!) When I was Vice Chairman of the Federal Reserve

18. Central Banking in a Democracy

Board, I simply came to expect to find 15, 20, or 25 reporters, plus several TV cameras, waiting any time I made a public appearance—no matter how boring my speech was going to be. (This, as you've noticed, doesn't happen to me anymore.)

Things were not always this way. The story is told that the only way President Kennedy could remember the difference between *monetary* policy and *fiscal* policy was that the letter "M" for monetary was also the first letter of the name of the Fed Chairman at that time, William McChesney Martin. Times have sure changed. I can assure you that President Clinton had no such problem, and neither did President Bush.

THE GOALS OF MONETARY POLICY

Just how is the Fed supposed to serve the national interest with this strange instrument called monetary policy? Under the terms of the Federal Reserve Act, as amended, Congress has directed the Fed to promote "maximum employment, stable prices, and moderate long-term interest rates." That sounds like three goals, but the phrase is often called the Fed's "dual mandate" because the interest rate objective is considered redundant. Price stability will almost certainly bring low long-term interest rates in its wake.

At this point, I need your indulgence for a very brief Economics 101 lecture on how monetary policy affects employment and inflation. It all works roughly as follows.

In the short run, employment is largely determined by total spending in the economy. Interest rates are one, though not the only, important determinant of that spending. So the Federal Reserve, via its effect on market rates of interest, exerts considerable indirect influence over employment and unemployment. But the process takes time. As economists put it, monetary policy works with long lags. While the lagged effects of monetary policy on unemployment are distributed through time—a little now, a little more the next quarter, and so on—it won't hurt you to think of them as taking about a year or two.

Changes in inflation, up or down, are largely determined by the balance between total spending, which is heavily influenced by monetary policy, and the economy's capacity to produce, which is not. If spending falls short of the economy's productive capacity, as happens in a recession, inflation will fall. If spending overshoots capacity, as sometimes happens in a boom, inflation will rise. But the lag from monetary policy decisions to inflation is even longer than the lag from monetary policy to employment because monetary policy first has to affect spending, and then spending must affect inflation. Think of the whole process—from a decision of the Federal Reserve on monetary policy to the reaction of inflation—as taking more than two years.

The central dilemma of monetary policy is this: Unless inflation is below the Federal Reserve's long-run target, which hasn't been true in a very long time, there is a short-run trade-off between the two goals—maximum employment and stable prices—that are set forth in the Federal Reserve Act. To push inflation lower, the Fed must make interest rates high enough to hold total spending below the economy's capacity to produce. But if it does that, the Federal Reserve will be reducing employment, contrary to the dictum to pursue "maximum employment." So monetary policy is forced to strike a delicate balance between the two goals. It is an excruciatingly difficult decision, with a great deal at stake. As a former holder of my former office once quipped, "That's why they pay them the big bucks!"

THE TRADE-OFF AND JACKSON HOLE

Early in my term as Vice Chairman of the Fed, I allegedly stirred up a controversy at a Federal Reserve conference in Jackson Hole, Wyoming, by acknowledging this trade-off explicitly. The context is important to an understanding of what happened, because the subject of that conference was *reducing unemployment*. Being a central banker at the time, I thought it was appropriate for me to address the role of central banks in that task. In my brief remarks, I noted that monetary policy actions have a profound effect on employment. I also suggested that a central bank could do its part to achieve low unemployment by pushing the nation's total spending up to the level of capacity, but not further. I observed that the Fed's dual mandate could reasonably be interpreted in precisely that way. So I endorsed that mandate as eminently reasonable instructions for the Congress to have given the Fed, rejecting the alternative of concentrating exclusively on price stability and ignoring unemployment.

Nothing I said at Jackson Hole that day was really controversial, and certainly nothing was original. My conceptualizations of monetary policy's role and of the trade-off between inflation and unemployment were totally conventional. My endorsement of the Fed's dual mandate meant that the Vice Chairman of the Federal Reserve was publicly endorsing the Federal Reserve Act. Now there's news for you! Furthermore, my implied "advice" to central bankers was fully consistent with the practices of central banks all over the world, regardless of what they preach. Indeed, I think a very fair academic critique of my little talk that day would have labeled it banal. Had a student in a course submitted that talk to me as a paper I think I would have said, "There is not an original idea here. You have to be able to do better than this."

About a dozen financial journalists were in the audience that day, and all but one of them heard it that way. But Keith Bradsher of *The New York Times* decided that he had just heard "a big story." I had, he was led to believe by some anonymous whispers, violated the sacred trust of central bankers by saying a few obvious things out loud. He told readers of *The Times* that I had publicly clashed with the Fed Chairman. That's funny; Alan Greenspan was sitting right there as I spoke, and he didn't hear it that way at all. I know, because the two of us had breakfast together the next morning, and he never indicated that I had said anything unusual—which I hadn't. No matter. On a slow news day in August Bradsher's story from Jackson Hole wound up on page one of *The New York Times.*

Media firestorms have a life of their own and, until you have been the subject of one, it is hard to imagine what they are like. For more than a month, a seemingly unending barrage of stories appeared in newspapers, magazines, over the financial wires, and even on TV and radio. I was made "controversial," which is one of the ways they try to stick the knife in you in Washington. The Fed, the public was told, had an outspoken new Vice Chairman who had broken several central banking taboos and publicly tangled with his Chairman. The hysteria reached a crescendo with truly a malicious attack published in both *Newsweek* and *The Washington Post* by Robert Samuelson, who decided—without ever bothering to call me up even once to talk about my views—that I was unfit both morally and intellectually to lead the Fed. One would be okay, but *both* morally and intellectually? Whoever said that serving in the government isn't fun?

I recount this episode not to dredge up the ghosts of irresponsible journalists' pasts, but for three reasons that are closely related to today's topic. The first is to give you a little window into what can happen when a Federal Reserve Governor publicly endorses the view that the Federal Reserve should be serving the national interest rather than just the parochial interests of the bond market. But I must insist that serving the national interest is the *only* correct way to conceptualize the Fed's mission; to me, the issue is not open to either compromise or debate.

The second reason is to tell you that I remain totally unrepentant and never retreated one inch from the position that I enunciated that day—not in public, and not inside the Federal Reserve. What

I said that day was true then, and it is true now. There is abundant evidence that Keynes was right back in the '30s when he said that modern industrial economies are not sufficiently self-regulating. They need a little help. Total spending sometimes roars ahead of productive capacity, which leads to accelerating inflation. And total spending sometimes lags behind productive capacity, leading to unemployment.

In principle, either fiscal policy—the government's taxing and spending policy—or monetary policy could serve as the balance wheel, propping up demand when it would otherwise sag and restraining it when it threatens to race ahead too rapidly. In practice, however, monetary policy is the only game in town nowadays. And when I say "in town," I don't mean just in Richmond or just in the United States—I mean all over the industrial world. The reason is the same here and in Europe: The need to reduce large fiscal deficits dictates that budget policy remain a drag on total spending for the foreseeable future, regardless of the state of the macroeconomy. With the fiscal arm of stabilization policy thereby paralyzed, a central bank that decides to concentrate exclusively on price stability is, in effect, throwing in the towel on unemployment.

So, to me, the argument for the Fed's dual mandate is both straightforward and convincing. The central bank exists to serve society. The public cares deeply about fluctuations in the pace of economic activity. And well-executed monetary policy has the power to mitigate fluctuations in employment. As the mathematicians say, "QED." Fortunately, almost all central bankers accept this argument nowadays, notwithstanding a great deal of misleading rhetoric to the contrary.

That leads me straight to the third reason for telling you the Jackson Hole story. As a citizen of a democracy, I have always found it intolerable for the government to deceive the governed. As a public servant, I also found it unconscionable. And I see no reason whatsoever why the central bank should have a special exemption from the requirement to level with the public.

CREDIBILITY

It is sometimes argued, to the contrary, that honest acknowledgment of the trade-off between unemployment and inflation, and of the central bank's concern with each, would rattle the financial markets—which want to believe that the central bank cares only about low inflation. This argument is nonsense. Both market participants and the financial press know the score and are far too sophisticated to be taken in by ritualistic rhetoric. I remember very well a conversation I had with a very smart financial reporter shortly after I left the Fed. He said that he has learned over the years to ignore what the Fed *says* and watch what it *does*. I had to concede that he was right, but it troubled me a great deal that the two would be so different. In my view, they should be a matched pair.

There is much talk at the Federal Reserve, as in the central banks all over the world, about the importance of *credibility,* which, according to the dictionary in my office, is "the ability to have one's statements accepted as factual or one's professed motives accepted as the true ones." Let me read the last phrase again: "one's professed motives accepted as the true ones." Precisely the point! Why is credibility considered so important?

The main reason, in my view, is that a central bank is a repository of enormous power over the economy. And if the central bank is independent, as the Federal Reserve is, this power is virtually unchecked. Such power is a public trust, assigned to the bank by the body politic through its elected representatives. In return, the citizens and their elected representatives have a right to expect—indeed to demand—that the bank's actions match its words. And matching deeds to words is, to me and to my dictionary, the hallmark of credibility.

CENTRAL BANK INDEPENDENCE

The Fed's role as the macroeconomic balance wheel is terribly important because it palpably effects people's lives. Stabilization policy is not something abstract; it is about how many jobs there will be, how many businesses will succeed. In my view, it is far and away the most important thing a central bank does for or to its society. And I felt that responsibility keenly every day that I served as Vice Chairman of the Fed, as I know Al Broaddus still does in his role as a member of the Federal Open Market Committee. Society, therefore, has a strong interest in seeing to it that the central bank does its job well. Evidence collected in recent years suggests that making the central bank more independent should help.

Before elaborating on this point, however, I need to define what I mean by an independent central bank—because there is no agreed-upon definition. To me, the term connotes two things.

The first is that the central bank is free to decide *how* to pursue its goals. This freedom does not mean that the Bank gets to select the goals on its own. On the contrary, in a democracy it seems not just appropriate, but virtually obligatory, that the political authorities should set the goals and then instruct—and I use that verb advisedly—the central bank to pursue them. If it is to be independent, the bank must have a great deal of discretion over how to use its instruments in pursuit of its assigned objectives. But it does not have to have the authority to set the goals by itself. Indeed, I would argue that giving the bank such authority would be an excessive grant of power to a bunch of unelected technocrats. In a democracy, the elected representatives of the people should make decisions like that. The central bank should then serve the public will.

The second critical aspect of independence, in my view, is that the central bank's decisions cannot be countermanded by any other branch of government, except under extreme circumstances. In our system of government, neither the President nor the Supreme Court can reverse a decision of the Federal Open Market Committee. Congress can, in principle, reverse such a decision, but only if it passes a law that the President will sign (or by overriding a presidential veto). This makes the Fed's decisions, for all practical purposes, immune from reversal; and, indeed, they never have been reversed. Without that immunity, the Fed would not really be independent, for its decisions would stand only as long as they did not displease someone more powerful.

In recent years, considerable empirical evidence has accumulated in support of the idea that macroeconomic performance is superior in countries that have more independent central banks. Researchers here and in other countries have developed several creative ways to measure central bank independence. Such measures include the bank's legal status, the rate of turnover of its leaders, the legal mandate in the bank's charter (for example, whether it is directed to pursue price stability), and answers to a questionnaire about its organizational structure. The clear weight of this evidence, and by now there is a lot of it, is that countries with more independent central banks have enjoyed lower average inflation without suffering lower average growth. This finding is, of course, completely consistent with economists' general view that, while there is a short-run trade-off between inflation and unemployment, there is no long-run trade-off.

These research results on the benefits of central bank independence raise a provocative question: Why is it that central banks possessing greater independence produce superior macroeconomic results on average? I want to suggest three reasons, all closely related.

First, as I emphasized in my brief Economics 101 lecture a couple of minutes ago, the effects of monetary policy come with long lags. So, to conduct monetary policy well, you must look far in the future and then wait patiently for the results. Farsightedness and patience, I dare say, are not the strong suits of the political process in a democracy. But they are absolutely essential to pursuing a successful monetary policy.

Second, and related to the time-horizon question, inflation-fighting has the characteristic cost-benefit profile of a long-term investment: You pay the costs of disinflation up front, and you reap the benefits—lower inflation—only gradually through time. So, if politicians were to make monetary policy on a day-to-day basis, they would be sorely tempted to reach for short-term gains at the expense of the future—that is, to inflate too much. Aware of this temptation, many governments wisely depoliticize monetary policy by delegating authority to unelected technocrats with long terms of office, thick insulation from the hurly-burly of politics, and explicit instructions to fight inflation.

Third, and related to this point about technocracy, the conduct of monetary policy is at least somewhat technical. It is a bit like shooting a rocket to the moon, though not nearly as exact. Very few elected officials in this or other countries have much understanding of how the monetary transmission mechanism works, of the long lags that I have mentioned, or of a variety of other technical details about monetary policy. So countries can probably get higher-quality monetary policy by turning the task over to trained technicians, subject, of course—and this is important in my view—to political oversight.

CENTRAL BANK INDEPENDENCE AND DEMOCRACY

At this point, a very deep philosophical question arises: Isn't all this profoundly undemocratic? Doesn't assigning so much power to unelected technocrats contradict some fundamental tenets of democratic theory? It is a legitimate question. My answer is: If you assign this power well, it needn't be antidemocratic. And I want to conclude this lecture with a detailed defense of that answer. The question is: How can an independent central bank be rationalized within the context of democratic government? My recipe comes in six parts.

First, we all know that, even in democracies, certain decisions are reserved to what is sometimes called the "constitutional stage" of government, rather than left to the daily legislative struggle. These are basic decisions that we do not want to revisit often; they should, therefore, be hard to re-

18. Central Banking in a Democracy

verse. So, for example, amending the U.S. Constitution requires much more than majority votes of both houses of Congress. The Founding Fathers thereby made it almost, but not quite, impossible to change certain basic provisions of law. And they meant it that way; it wasn't an accident.

Similarly with monetary policy. The Fed's independence, which derives from authority delegated by Congress, makes it very difficult, but not quite impossible, for elected officials to overrule or influence a monetary policy decision. Wise politicians made a once-and-for-all decision years ago to limit their own power in this way just as, for example, the Constitution made it very difficult to change the length of the President's term of office. The reasoning was precisely the same as that which led Ulysses to tie himself to the mast. He knew he would get better long-run results even though he wouldn't feel so good about it in the short run!

The second ingredient that helps make central bank independence consistent with democratic theory is something I emphasized earlier: The bank's basic goals are chosen by elected politicians, not by unelected technocrats. So, for example, when people suggest to me that the Fed should content itself with 3 percent inflation, I always answer, "the Federal Reserve Act, which is the law of the land, says 'stable prices,' not 'pretty low inflation.' " If the citizens think that is wrong, they should get the law changed. Until they do, the Federal Reserve should obey the law.

Third, the public has a right to demand honesty from its central bankers. This, again, is a point I made earlier in discussing the idea of credibility, which I defined as matching deeds to words. The central bank, in my view, owes this to the body politic in return for the broad grant of power it enjoys.

The fourth ingredient is closely related to this last point. I call it *accountability*, or perhaps just *openness*. Monetary policy actions have profound effects on the lives of ordinary people. In my view, a central bank in a democracy therefore owes these folks an explanation of what it is doing, why it is doing it, and what it expects to accomplish by its actions. As I often said while I was at the Fed, "It's their economy, not ours." By offering a reasonably full and coherent explanation of its actions, the central bank can remove much of the mystery that now surrounds monetary policy, enable interested parties to appraise its decisions contemporaneously, and then—importantly—allow outsiders to judge its success or failure after the fact, for the verdict of history is the only one that ultimately matters.

Let me assure you that greater openness is not a popular cause in central banking circles, where some see mystery as essential to effective monetary policymaking. Making the central bank more open and accountable, it is alleged, may subject it to unwelcome scrutiny that could threaten its independence.

I couldn't disagree with this argument more. In fact, I think it gets matters exactly backward. To me, public accountability is a moral corollary of central bank independence. In a democratic society, the central bank's freedom to act implies an obligation to explain itself to the public. Thus independence and accountability are symbiotic, not conflicting. Accountability legitimizes independence within a democratic political structure.

Nor, by the way, do I accept the claim, heard so much in central banking circles, that more accountability will harm the central bank—as long as the bank is independent. If the central bank makes good decisions, it should have no trouble explaining them to the public. If the Fed cannot articulate a coherent defense of its actions, maybe those decisions are not as good as it thinks. Indeed, being forced to articulate such a defense would probably be a good disciplinary device. Remember—and this is critical—I am talking here only about explaining the decisions after they are made, not putting them to a vote!

The Federal Reserve, tight-lipped as it is, is far from the worst offender in this regard. In fact, the Fed is probably more open and accountable than most central banks in the world. But the competition in this league is not very stiff—I think the New York Jets could win the championship in this particular league-and I believe the Federal Reserve could and should go much further. After all, we live in the most open society on the face of the earth, so just to say that we've beaten the world average is no great achievement for Americans.

The fifth ingredient in my democratic stew is that the leaders of the central bank should be politically appointed by the President, as is the current practice. When I went to the Federal Reserve Board in June 1994 as the first appointee of President Clinton, I joined Alan Greenspan, Mike Kelley, and John LaWare, who were originally sent there by President Reagan, and Larry Lindsey and Susan Phillips, who were appointed by President Bush. None of us was ever elected to anything. But Bill Clinton and George Bush and Ronald Reagan were. We obtained our political legitimacy from the men who appointed us, and they in turn got it the old-fashioned way—directly from the voters. That is as it should be.

Finally, the sixth ingredient—which I would argue should be present, but very rarely used: Central bank decisions should be reversible by the political authorities, but only under extreme circumstances. Reversal[s] should not be routine occurrences. As I've mentioned already, a Federal Reserve decision on monetary policy can, in principle, be overturned by an act of Congress. And Fed governors can be removed from office for good cause. These mechanisms have never been used in the history of the Federal Reserve; but America is wise to have them in place nonetheless. Delegated authority should be retrievable, not absolute.

A SUMMING UP

So, in summary, let us review how the Fed, or any other central bank for that matter, can best serve its nation with monetary policy.

To begin with, the central bank must always remember that it exists as a public institution chartered to serve the broad national interest, not the parochial interests of either the banking industry or the bond market. Often those interests coincide. But when they clash, the central bank should not hesitate before taking sides.

The highest calling of the central bank is to help stabilize the national economy. For if the bank should fail at this task, no one else will be around to pick up the pieces. In its role as macroeconomic steward, the Fed, I believe, should pursue two goals—both low unemployment and low inflation—not just one. That is what the people want and, in my view, the people have got it right.

A central bank can perform its monetary policy role better if it's independent from political manipulation, and that's probably why more and more governments around the world are granting their central banks independence these days.

Even though the Fed's independence looks superficially undemocratic, I believe it is consistent with democratic theory for several reasons: it is based on authority delegated by Congress; the basic goals of monetary policy are set legislatively; the leaders of the Fed are appointed by the President; and Congress retains ultimate control in case of dire emergency. But a central bank in a democracy has a duty to level with the public it serves, not to obfuscate. I used to ask some of my colleagues on the Federal Reserve staff in Washington what they would have thought if their father, every time he spanked them, had only said that he was doing it "to promote sustainable non-inflationary growth"— and nothing more. I don't believe that would have been considered good parenting, and I don't think it's good central banking. More fulsome explanation is appropriate.

A great Virginian, probably the greatest Virginian, once wrote, "Governments are instituted among men" (I'm sorry it was only men in those days) "deriving their just powers from the consent of the governed." It is very hard for the governed to give their consent if they don't have a clue about what is going on. Openness, accountability, and credibility are therefore, in my view, moral corollaries of central bank independence.

Furthermore, and finally, I dispute the notion that is so popular in some circles that monetary policy is best done amidst mystery, blue smoke, and mumbo jumbo. Central banks work their will through financial markets, and economists rarely argue that markets function better when they are less well informed. In my view, some small portion of the prodigious uncertainties over the effects of monetary policy exists because the markets have a hard time divining the Fed's intentions. This particular source of uncertainty can, and in my opinion should, be removed by greater openness. But that, I'm afraid, is a story for another lecture and another day.

Is the Fed Slave to a Defunct Economist?

JOHN MAYNARD KEYNES once stated that policymakers are "usually the slaves of some defunct economist." Well, according to a wide range of commentators, recently it's been Keynes himself who has held policymakers enthralled.[1] These commentators complain that the Fed has tried to "fine-tune" real activity—and that, in doing so, the Fed has imposed an artificial speed limit on the economy and kept the unemployment rate unnecessarily high. More specifically, Federal Reserve officials are accused of having relied too heavily on an analytical tool called the Phillips curve when deciding whether to raise the federal funds rate.

This article provides some historical perspective on the critics' complaints and evaluates the merits of their arguments. I argue that Fed policymakers would deserve censure if they behaved as the critics claim. However, the critics' accusations are largely without merit, and their own policy prescriptions are flawed.

Current Rates of Output Growth Are Not Sustainable

Over the past three years (1994:1–97:1), real GDP has grown at a 2.9 percent average annual rate. Over the past four quarters (1996:1–97:1), it has grown at a whopping 4 percent annual rate. The idea that growth at these rates can continue indefinitely is appealing but unrealistic. Chart 1 shows the relationship between real GDP growth and the change in the unemployment rate since the mid-1980s. For example, the point plotted in the extreme lower right-hand corner shows that real GDP rose by 7 percent in 1984, while the unemployment rate fell by 2 percentage points. More generally, the chart shows that the unemployment rate has tended to fall whenever GDP growth has much exceeded 2 percent. Indeed, the unemployment rate has declined in fully nine of ten years in which growth has exceeded 2 percent (the exception being 1992). In two of three years in which growth has fallen short of 2 percent, the unemployment rate has risen. In the exceptional year (1995), GDP growth fell below 2 percent by only 1 one-hundredth of a percentage point.

The implication is that GDP growth at recent rates must eventually drive unemployment to zero, unless productivity or the labor force begins to increase at a substantially faster clip than we have seen so far during this expansion.[2] Something is going to have to give, and that something is likely to be the growth rate of real GDP.

This conclusion leaves open the possibility that noninflationary growth of 2.5 percent or more is feasible over the next year or two. It's on the issue of whether strong growth can be sustained for another few years that reasonable people may disagree, depending on their beliefs about the nature of the short-term output–inflation trade-off.

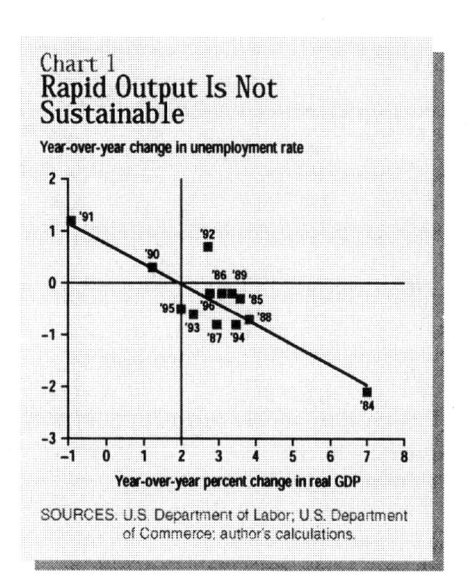

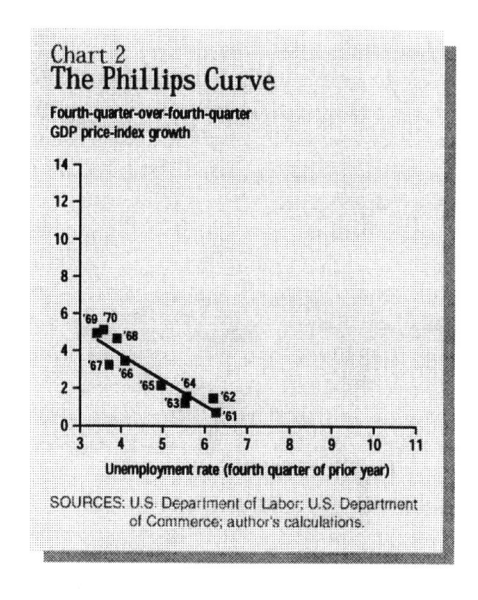

Chart 1
Rapid Output Is Not Sustainable

SOURCES: U.S. Department of Labor; U.S. Department of Commerce; author's calculations.

Chart 2
The Phillips Curve

SOURCES: U.S. Department of Labor; U.S. Department of Commerce; author's calculations.

The Phillips Curve

The downward sloping line shown in Chart 2, fitted to U.S. unemployment and inflation data from the 1960s, is called a Phillips curve. The Phillips curve is named after New Zealand-born economist Alban W. Phillips, who used British data to demonstrate that wage inflation tends to be high when the unemployment rate is low. Phillips' rationalization of this relationship was simple: the price of a good increases when the good is in high demand. Low unemployment rates are a symptom of high demand for labor, so low unemployment rates are associated with rapid increases in the price of labor. Economists often plot Phillips curves using product price inflation in place of wage inflation, because the two types of inflation tend to move together.

From 1958, when Phillips originally published his research, through the end of the 1960s, many economists believed that policymakers could choose any point along the Phillips curve and hold the economy there indefinitely. However, the 1970s forced people to rethink

From *Southwest Economy*, September/October 1997, pp. 5–8. © 1997 by the Federal Reserve Bank of Dallas. Reprinted by permission.

the Phillips curve. This reevaluation had two components, which I will discuss in turn.

Lesson 1: Changes in Inflation Expectations Shift the Phillips Curve

First, events of the 1970s increased appreciation for the importance of inflation expectations.[3] Milton Friedman and Edmund Phelps led the charge, arguing that monetary policy is like a drug for which the economy can build up a tolerance: larger and larger doses are required to achieve a given effect. Initially, an acceleration in money growth puts more real purchasing power in people's pockets. Increased sales mean more jobs, and unemployment falls. Consequently, the economy follows a path that looks a lot like the Phillips curve of the 1960s. However, as the rapid money growth continues, the economy begins to adapt to it. Eventually, wages and prices catch up to the money supply, and the stimulus to output and employment fades away. Only higher inflation remains. In Chart 3 (an updated version of Chart 2) we see a move to the right as we follow the economy from 1970 to 1971 and 1972. At first, Nixon's wage and price controls kept inflation down to 4 percent, but in 1973 inflation broke loose and a new round of stimulus began. By 1974 inflation was above 10 percent. Over the next 10 years—from 1974 through 1983—the economy stayed on a new, higher Phillips curve, representing a less favorable short-run trade-off between unemployment and inflation.

The reason for the shift in the Phillips curve was an increase in inflation expectations. In the 1960s, people thought that inflation would eventually stabilize at an annual rate of about 2 percent. From the mid-1970s to the mid-1980s, they acted as if inflation would eventually stabilize at an 8 or 9 percent annual rate. The increase in inflation expectations stemmed from policymakers' attempts to keep the unemployment rate artificially low.

The lowest unemployment rate that is consistent, over the long term, with *stable* inflation is called the nonaccelerating inflation rate of unemployment, or NAIRU. A typical NAIRU estimate is 6 percent. At unemployment rates below the NAIRU, there is a tendency for inflation expectations to rise. (Such was the experience of the early 1970s.) At unemployment rates above the NAIRU, there is a tendency for inflation expectations to fall.[4]

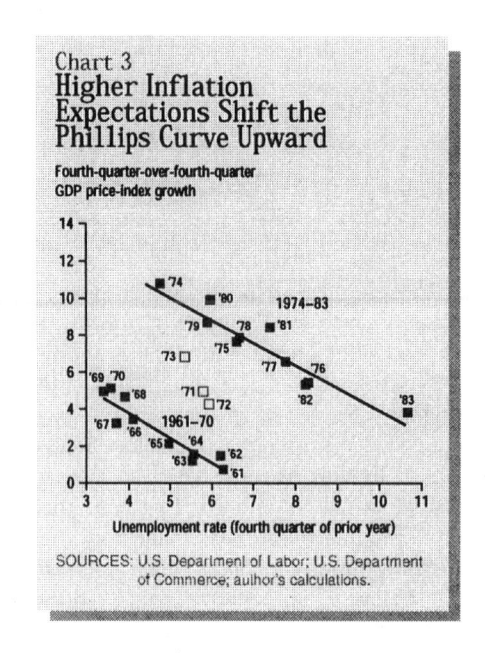

Unfortunately, you can't look up the value of the NAIRU in an encyclopedia, and it's not published in the *Wall Street Journal*. The NAIRU has to be estimated. A big part of the debate between those who believe that the Phillips curve remains a useful guide to policy and those who do not has to do with how good a handle we have on the NAIRU at any given moment.[5] That brings us to the second important lesson that economists learned during the 1970s.

Lesson 2: The NAIRU Varies Over Time—Not Always Predictably

The sharp oil price increases of the 1970s made it obvious to everyone that supply-side shocks can temporarily change the NAIRU and have an important impact on inflation. A supply shock is any disturbance that alters the amount of output that can be produced from given quantities of land, machinery and human effort. Supply-side shocks are also sometimes called productivity shocks. Aside from oil-price increases, the supply shocks that have received the most attention from macroeconomists are probably crop failures because of drought or flooding.

Just how important *are* supply shocks? That's the $64,000 question. Keynesians tend to view such shocks as infrequent and easily accounted for. It's this belief that drives their policy prescriptions. For if supply shocks don't shift the NAIRU around too much, so that its value can be pinned down, then the appropriate policy is obvious: get the unemployment rate to the NAIRU and keep it there. As a practical matter, the Keynesian prescription is for an unemployment rate of about 6 percent and GDP growth of about 2 percent.

Unfortunately for the Keynesians, more and more analysts are coming around to the view that supply-side shocks are so pervasive as to seriously limit the usefulness of the NAIRU as a policy guide. Even after accounting for food and energy shocks, NAIRU estimates vary substantially from year to year. Moreover, in any given year, the exact value of the NAIRU is not known with any confidence. Recent estimates suggest that the NAIRU is probably around 6 percent but could easily be as low as 4.5 percent or as high as 7.5 percent (Staiger, Stock and Watson 1997). Increasingly, analysts regard the NAIRU estimate *du jour* as a yellow caution sign rather than a red stoplight.

Has the Fed Been a Slave to the Keynesian View of the Phillips Curve?

If, as its critics assert, the Fed has been trying to hold the unemployment rate above some preconceived NAIRU, then it has bungled the job. As shown in Chart 4, the unemployment rate has fallen, more or less steadily, from a high of 7.7 percent in June 1992 to a low of 4.8 percent in July 1997. The unemployment rate was last above 6 percent three years ago (in July 1994) despite the fact that, for most of this period, 6 percent was the generally accepted estimate of the NAIRU. Clearly, the Fed

19. Is the Fed Slave to a Defunct Economist?

Chart 4
The Fed Has Not Been a Slave to the Phillips Curve

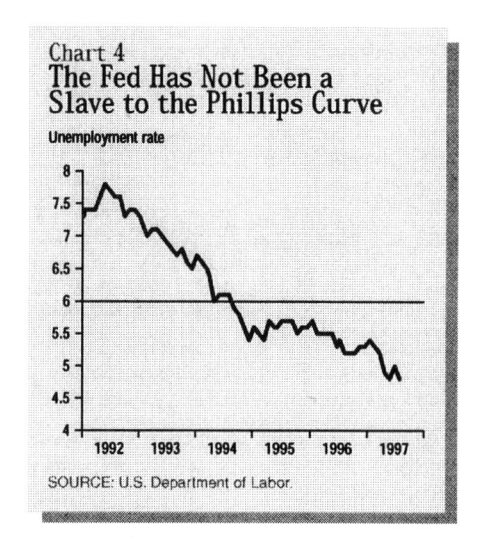

Unemployment rate

SOURCE: U.S. Department of Labor.

has not been slamming on the brakes. At most, the Fed has been occasionally tapping the brakes to slow the unemployment rate's descent.

It's revealing to look at the unemployment rate in combination with the inflation rate, rather than in isolation. As Chart 5 clearly shows, the short-run Phillips curve shifted down a notch during the mid-1980s in response to the persistently tough anti-inflation stance of the Volker Fed. Then, over the 10-year period from 1985 through 1994, unemployment and inflation varied pretty much as though people believed that inflation would eventually stabilize at around 4 percent. Since 1993, despite a falling unemployment rate, inflation has held steady. (Look at the points marked as stars.) It's beginning to look as though the Phillips curve has shifted yet again and that we're back in the 1960s, with expected inflation down around 2 percent. The challenge for policymakers is to ensure that we don't replay the *entire* 1960s inflation experience.

Why Has Inflation Been So Tame?

Three factors have contributed to the economy's strong inflation performance in recent years. First, we've benefited from a series of favorable supply shocks. These shocks have included innovations in health-care management that have held down medical cost inflation; the spread of cheaper, increasingly powerful computers and telecommunications devices; and increased competition because of deregulation and freer global trade. Second, a more uncertain and more flexible labor market may mean that the unemployment rate has become less useful as a measure of slack in the economy.[6] Finally, the Federal Reserve has conducted policy in a way that has convinced people that it is serious about preventing any significant resurgence of inflation.

How has Fed policy accomplished this task? Fed Chairman Alan Greenspan may have revealed the answer recently in a speech defending March's quarter-point hike in the federal funds rate. Greenspan said that "persisting—indeed increasing—strength in nominal demand for goods and services suggested to us that monetary policy might not be positioned appropriately to avoid a buildup in inflation pressures" (CitiCorp 1997). Note that Greenspan's statement focuses on the strength of the *nominal* demand for goods and services, not the real demand.

As shown in Chart 6, Federal Reserve policies have kept the level of nominal spending on a fairly steady 5 percent growth track over the past six years. Modest, steady spending growth is an attractive strategy to pursue in the face of uncertainty about the output–inflation trade-off. It is a strategy especially popular among economists trained in the monetarist tradition.

What's so great about a policy of steady spending growth? Since spend-

Chart 5
Is the Phillips Curve Shifting Yet Again?

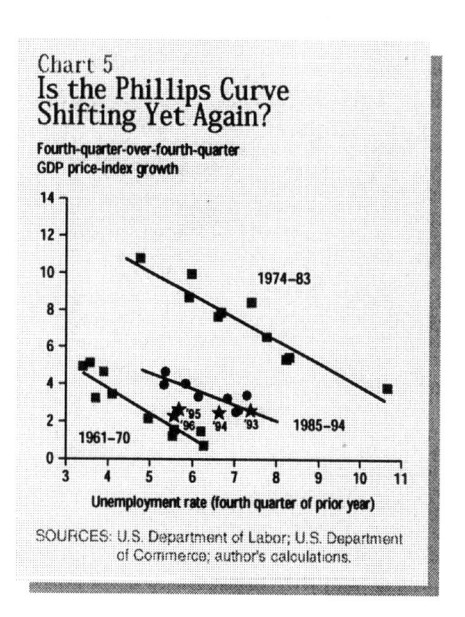

Fourth-quarter-over-fourth-quarter GDP price-index growth

SOURCES: U.S. Department of Labor; U.S. Department of Commerce; author's calculations.

Chart 6
Nominal Spending on a 5 Percent Growth Path

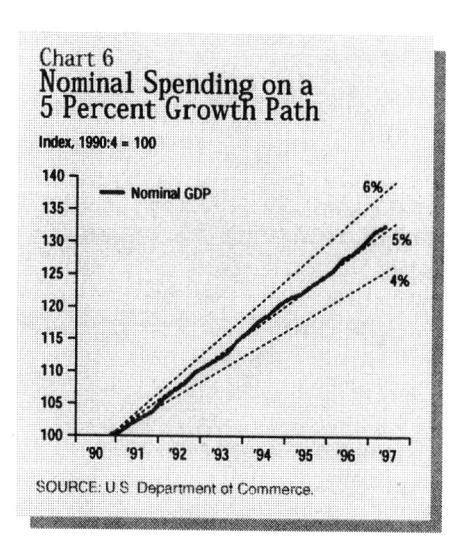

Index, 1990:4 = 100

SOURCE: U.S. Department of Commerce.

ing growth is the sum of real growth and inflation, a policy of steady spending growth does not preclude strong real growth, *provided* strong real growth is accompanied by low inflation. Turning this statement around, there is little danger that inflation will substantially accelerate under a policy of steady spending growth, for inflation can rise only to the extent that the economy's capacity for real growth falls.[7]

Survey results indicate that Federal Reserve policies during the 1990s have resulted in a gradual reduction in long-term inflation expectations. This reduction in expectations has undoubtedly contributed to the benign behavior of actual inflation in recent years.

Why Not Target Inflation Directly?

Many of the analysts who have been critical of the Fed seem to feel that the hallmark of a successful monetary policy is not stable output growth (the Keynesian view) and not low and stable spending growth (the monetarist view) but a stable inflation rate.[8] These commentators apparently believe that the Fed should allow output and employment to fluctuate arbitrarily, as long as inflation remains constant.

One problem with this approach is that inflation bounces around so much that a change in trend is often not apparent for six months to a year after it has begun.

Another problem is that the lags between the Fed's policy actions and their effects on inflation are considerable—most estimates put them at a year or more. When you add the time it takes for policy to change inflation to the time it takes to recognize that a change in policy is needed, trying to target the inflation rate is a little like trying to drive down a highway at 60 miles per hour in heavy fog, and—just to make things interesting—there's a five-second delay between when you apply the brakes and when the brakes are activated.

It's easy to call for inflation-rate targeting in a period when constant inflation is consistent with a booming economy. One has to wonder whether advocates of inflation-rate targeting will be equally vocal the next time we're hit with a major drought or a run-up in the price of oil, when holding inflation constant might require a recession.

The Fed and Its Critics

In summary, some commentators have accused the Federal Reserve of pursuing a Keynesian strategy. They claim that, in a mistaken effort to fine-tune real economic activity, the Fed has stifled output and employment gains that have their origins on the supply side.

The critics advocate an alternative policy—one that would allow output and employment to range freely, as long as inflation holds steady. Since they believe that supply-side shocks make the Phillips curve all but useless as a policy tool, the critics say the Fed should look to indicators of inflation expectations and to sensitive commodity prices for signs that inflation is about to accelerate.

In fact, the Fed has pursued a middle course. It has taken an eclectic approach to evaluating strain in the labor and product markets, neither rigidly enforcing a speed limit on real GDP growth nor panicking as the unemployment rate has fallen below 6 percent. It has allowed positive supply shocks to be reflected in higher output and employment but has restrained growth in nominal spending.

—Evan F. Koenig

Notes

[1] See, for example, Galbraith (1997) and Yardeni (1997a,b).

[2] For an elaboration of this argument, see Krugman (1996).

[3] The analysis that follows is developed more fully in Koenig and Wynne (1994).

[4] Just how quickly inflation expectations adjust and what information they respond to remain the subject of debate. In empirical work, most economists assume that expected inflation is just a weighted average of past actual inflation rates. Historically, this approximation does well, but in macroeconometrics, as in personal investing, "past performance is no guarantee of future results." The success of the standard approach may simply reflect the fact that to date we have seen no policy regime changes important enough to have had a major impact on Fed credibility.

[5] For a defense of the Phillips curve as a policy guide, see Meyer (1997a,b).

[6] For an elaboration, see Duca (1997) and Meyer (1997a).

[7] Thus, a policy of stabilizing nominal spending is a compromise between an output-stabilization policy and a price-level or inflation-stabilization policy. See Koenig (1995).

[8] Analysts expressing such views include Yardeni (1997a,b) and Kudlow (1997).

References

CitiCorp (1997), "Fed: Reaffirming the Move to a Tighter Stance," *Economic Week* 25 (May 19): 1.

Duca, John V. (1997), "A Tale of Three Supply Shocks, National Inflation and the Region's Economy," Federal Reserve Bank of Dallas *Southwest Economy*, Issue 2, 1–4.

Galbraith, James K. (1997), "Time to Ditch the NAIRU," *Journal of Economic Perspectives* 11 (Winter): 93–108.

Koenig, Evan F., and Mark A. Wynne (1994), "Is There an Output–Inflation Trade-Off?" Federal Reserve Bank of Dallas *Southwest Economy*, Issue 3, 1–4.

Koenig, Evan F. (1995), "Optimal Monetary Policy in an Economy with Sticky Nominal Wages," Federal Reserve Bank of Dallas *Economic Review*, Second Quarter, 24–31.

Krugman, Paul (1996), "Stable Prices and Fast Growth: Just Say No," *Economist*, August 31, 19–22.

Kudlow, Lawrence (1997), "In Search of an Enduring Standard," *Washington Times*, March 3, A12.

Meyer, Laurence H. (1997a), "The Economic Outlook and Challenges for Monetary Policy" (Remarks presented at the Charlotte Economics Club, Charlotte, North Carolina, January 16).

——— (1997b), "The Economic Outlook and Challenges Facing Monetary Policy" (Remarks presented at the Forecasters Club of New York, New York, April 24).

Staiger, Douglas, James H. Stock and Mark W. Watson (1997), "The NAIRU, Unemployment and Monetary Policy," *Journal of Economic Perspectives* 11 (Winter): 33–49.

Yardeni, Edward (1997a), "The Growth-Is-Good Case for Bonds," Deutsche Morgan Grenfell *Weekly Economic Analysis*, May 5, 1–5.

——— (1997b), "Deep Blue vs. Greenspan," Deutsche Morgan Grenfell *Weekly Economic Analysis*, May 19, 1–4.

ECONOMICS

Should the Fed Care About Stock Bubbles?

BY PAUL KRUGMAN

It was a time of unprecedented prosperity. And it was also a time of soaring stock prices, a time when the market became a national obsession. As more and more ordinary Americans began buying stocks, many responsible people became worried. True, some market gurus argued that changed fundamentals made the higher price levels reasonable—and those optimists had, of course, been right so far. But still there was a sense, almost a consensus, among sober heads that this was a classic bubble.

Even if stock prices had gone crazy, however, what if anything should be the policy response? Should the Fed raise interest rates and pop the bubble? Or would this simply bring on a recession? Anyway, if consumer prices are stable, should the central bank even care about asset inflation?

Like most debates in which nobody really knows the answer, this one became peculiarly intense and bitter. Those who wanted the bubble popped accused the other side of irresponsibility, warning that continued financial excesses would inevitably lead to a painful hangover. Their opponents argued that as long as there were no signs of inflation, to raise interest rates would be an act of pure spite and would itself bring on a gratuitous recession.

So even in times of prosperity, a central banker's lot is not a happy one. The funny thing is that 70 years later the great debate about the market and monetary policy, the one that raged in 1928 (bet you thought I was talking about current events—well, those too) remains unresolved. What, if anything, should the Fed do when it thinks the market has gone mad?

You can tell that this question has gotten Greenspan upset: He's so worried that he's become—it scares me to say this—comprehensible. Everyone knows he believes stock prices are too high. But the market is no more convinced now than it was the first time he warned about "irrational exuberance," back when the Dow was around 6500. So he can't seem to talk it down. Should he do more?

The answer, I'm almost convinced, is no: Leave the economy alone. But I'm not totally sure, so let me give both sides.

To start, let's assume Greenspan is right, that this *is* a bubble—that it isn't just the Internet stocks with infinite P/E ratios (because they haven't got, and may never get, any E) but stocks in general that are way out of line. Eventually the bubble will burst, and the "wealth effect" of that burst will pull down consumer spending. At that point we will have a recession if the Fed either doesn't or can't cut interest rates enough to keep the economy going.

Now, we know Greenspan will be fast on the trigger if it looks as if a recession is brewing, so the main danger is a collapse in consumer spending so deep that interest rate reductions are ineffective—sort of what happened to Japan. You might think that the big question, then, is whether this is at all likely for the U.S.

Actually, that's the wrong question. Say you're worried that after the Big Meltdown, Americans will be so discouraged that even zero interest won't keep them spending. That still doesn't mean things would necessarily have been better had the Fed raised rates when the market was high.

The thing to understand is that a stock market boom is not like a boom in physical investment—say, a boom in condominium construction. That kind of boom depresses future spending because it leaves behind a landscape littered with unsellable condos. But that isn't quite what happens when stocks surge: When the market value of Croesus.com doubles, that doesn't mean there will be an overhang of vacant dot-coms weighing down rental rates two years from now. It's paper gains today, paper losses tomorrow; who cares?

Advocates for pricking the market bubble have a few favorite scenarios. First, there's the "harder they fall" hypothesis: The higher stocks go now, the lower they will go—or the lower consumer spending will be for any given level of stock prices—when people return to reality. But that's more amateur psychology than serious analysis, and a poor basis for economic policy.

Ah, they say, but what about debt? Shouldn't Greenspan act to counter the defaults that could accompany a market crash? If consumers go deeply into debt to buy stock or to buy consumer goods because their market gains make them feel rich, this could depress spending later on. But really bad debt overhangs come when *businesses* (especially real estate developers) overborrow, which is not, as far as I can tell, a big problem in America right now.

Perhaps the most seductive argument for Greenspan's intervention in the market is the lesson that the past would seem to teach us: Didn't America's bubble in the 1920s, and Japan's in the 1980s, prepare the way for the economic crises that followed? Maybe—but it turns out that in both cases the central banks raised rates in an attempt to let the air out of markets, and thus may have helped precipitate the very slumps they feared.

So what should Greenspan do? Probably what he does best—i.e., nothing—and deal with the bubbles if and when they burst. Oh, and I wish he wouldn't worry so publicly: It makes me nervous when I understand what he's saying.

PAUL KRUGMAN *is a professor of economics at MIT.*

Bank Mergers and the Big Money

By Charles Geisst

THROUGHOUT THE 20th Century, most major regulations in the finance world have followed a crisis. After the stock market crash of 1929, Congress passed the Glass-Steagall Act, separating commercial banking from investment banking. Although financial leaders have complained about the law for years, it has never been repealed. Yet today, mergers within the banking and securities businesses are clearly in violation of the Glass-Steagall's spirit, if not its text. And the enormous mergers of the past week, once they are finalized, will make much of Glass-Steagall all but a dead letter.

The recent deals announced between Citicorp and the Travelers Group, BankAmerica and Nationsbank, and BancOne and First Chicago all are remarkable. Not only will they create a new dimension in banking by creating one-stop financial "supermarkets," but they would have been inconceivable as recently as 10 years ago. Congress has been reluctant to replace Glass-Steagall, but market forces have assumed its task. The new wave of mergers is the first actually to be driven by the current bull market—and by the assumption that the market will continue to climb. Euphoria is leading the way to corporate combinations rather than well-considered legislation.

It's hard, especially in the present giddy mood of the market, to predict what will happen over the long haul in the top-heavy financial service sector. But one thing is certain: Unless Congress steps in and establishes meaningful guidelines, the banking industry is in danger of plowing into unchartered territory. If banks and securities houses can merge without congressional approval, who is going to regulate these new mammoth financial institutions effectively? If the banks can pressure the Federal Reserve into having their own way, how can the public be assured that the safeguards built into the old banking laws will be observed?

Traditionally, the Glass-Steagall Act kept investment bankers out of commercial banking and vice versa. It also established FDIC deposit insurance, a critical consumer protection that has been neglected in the debate over revising the act. The entire banking community has come to rely upon insurance guarantees as a way to keep their customers secure. Occasionally, banks have also made bad loans on the assumption that the money was insured so no one really cared. The appeal of such safeguards helps explain why Congress cannot repeal Glass-Steagall so easily. But its reluctance to reform the act to allow a closer relationship between Wall Street and the banks has led the Federal Reserve to move discreetly into the vacuum.

Beginning in the late 1980s, the Fed under Alan Greenspan began allowing commercial banks like J.P. Morgan to underwrite corporate bonds and stocks, something banks had not done since 1933. Over the last 10 years, many of the larger banks have actively engaged in the securities business with the Fed's blessing. The Fed acted as the regulator of the bank holding companies. The assumption was that banking has changed so quickly that to continue to stop the banks from engaging in securities underwriting and trading would do them and the economy a disservice. Bigger became better. A large but quiet revolution was won quickly without a shot being fired. The Fed sanctioned what Congress was unwilling to countenance.

The same scenario played itself out in the commercial banking sector several years before this current trend. When banks were reeling under the weight of bad loans to developing countries in the 1980s, the Federal Reserve began to adopt a lenient policy toward banks merging across state lines. Merging across state lines had been illegal since 1927. American banks did not become truly national as a result, but they did begin to expand, often buying weaker sisters in other states on the verge of failing. This initial wave of interstate bank mergers opened the country to banks with larger ambitions. That was a far cry from the days when a New York City bank could not even branch into Long Island because of restrictive state laws. Three years ago, Congress finally acknowledged the inevitable and passed a new banking law allowing branching and expansion across state lines.

The problem now, however, is that the American banking system has been sucked into the raging bull market. And this rush into nationwide mergers involves more than the remarriage between commercial and investment banking—it has also brought life insurance into the banking orbit, another traditional hands-off area. Bankers argue that incorporating other financial services under their aegis is natural. Almost everyone else claims the opposite. Insurers do not want to give up their businesses to large banks any more than do most investment bankers.

Ironically, in a society that has been disavowing bigness in government over the last decade, business has taken the opposite tack. Bigger has become better, without question. But the escalation—and growing vertical integration—of financial services means we should start asking the question. Even Wall Street got caught up in its own hype and spin. Mergers make large fees for securities houses, who benefit every time a merger is announced. Now they themselves are increasingly becoming the targets of the acquisition-minded banks.

Although many toes have been stepped on in the recent binge, the whole issue comes down to size. The proposed BankAmerica/Nationsbank deal would create the largest bank in the country, with more than $500 billion in deposits. Advocates of expansion argue that the new institution would still not be truly national. For that to happen, a bank that stretched coast to coast, located in most if not all states, would need to be created. So what's the problem with creating mammoth banks that can compete with the large Japanese banks in terms of size?

It has always been a sore spot with American bankers that many of the largest banks in the world were Japanese. Huge amounts of savings poured into Japanese banks, quickly catapulting them to among the largest in the world. But the recent Japanese banking crisis proved that size alone was no guarantee against bad management. Sizeable loans losses in the entire industry have aggravated the Japanese recession, making it one of the longest running in the industrialized world. Slowly, the Japanese have begun—under a fair amount of American prodding—to liberalize their financial system. But liberalization itself is proceeding slowly because of the financial crisis. And no one can ensure that it will help cure the problem.

There is a lesson in the Japanese experience for American policymakers and financial leaders. Size does not necessarily spell success in the financial world. Selling all sorts of financial services under one roof has been a dream of bankers since the 1920s but has yet to succeed. And the public quickly is beginning to realize that larger banks are not necessarily efficient. Some evidence already exists that suggests banking costs rise rather than fall after a mega merger. Those benefits touted by the banks to justify mergers have not panned out. Banking is suddenly in danger of becoming a monopoly business—and that does not translate into lower fees for the consumer.

But policymakers should not be led by this current trend into allowing merger simply for merger's sake. The American experience with this sort of ad hoc growth is that it leads to financial crisis. The 1920s was one example; the fiasco among the S & Ls in the 1980s another. It is time to ask, "What's the rush?" before allowing the financial system to reinvent itself under its own power. One of the major sins of a bull stock market is that it often overlooks caution in favor of growth. Over the long term, we can't afford to be irrationally exuberant with something as critical as our national financial system.

Charles Geisst is professor of finance at Manhattan College and author of "Wall Street: A History" and "Investment Banking in the Financial System."

The Stepchildren of Banking

Efforts to Serve Low-Income Areas Appear to Sputter

By RICHARD A. OPPEL Jr.

Marilyn Vasquez quickly dismisses the notion that she would be better off using a bank. Local check cashers "don't ask for so much ID," said Ms. Vasquez, 20, a resident of the Bronx. "Banks are too much hassle."

She is not alone. Many people do not use banks, especially in low-income neighborhoods, citing inconvenience, high fees or a lack of branches nearby. But there is another reason: Banks often do not tell people that anyone can open a basic low-fee checking account.

More than one in eight families nationwide have no bank account, according to Government estimates. And while New York and New Jersey have broad-reaching "lifeline" laws requiring banks to offer low-cost accounts to anybody, few poor people take advantage of them. And similar laws in other states—including Illinois, Massachusetts, Minnesota, Rhode Island and Vermont—are even more limited.

Recent attempts to require low-cost accounts nationwide have been killed in Congress. This month, the House Banking Committee voted along party lines to exclude lifeline banking from a bill repealing the Glass-Steagall Act's barriers among the banking, securities and insurance industries. The Treasury Department, meanwhile, is working on a partial solution that would not require new legislation.

The middling success of low-cost checking in New York and elsewhere illustrates the difficulty of bringing the nation's poor into the banking mainstream. The banks' reluctance to promote the accounts has played a large role, but even those who say the laws are worthwhile cite other factors. Often, low-income people do not have enough identification to satisfy a bank, leaving no option but check cashers that charge fees. And some people face judgments, collections or other legal problems and do not want a financial record or simply have no money left after paying for basic needs.

"There was this naïve notion that if we could just have low-cost checking accounts, everyone would put money in the bank," said John P. Caskey, a Swarthmore College eco-

Bare-Bones Banking

Many people, especially in low-income neighborhoods, shy away from banks, blaming poor location, high fees and other obstacles to owning an account. Instead, they turn to check-cashing outfits, which have grown recently despite expensive transaction charges. To make the banking system more accessible, some states require banks to offer low-cost accounts.

	STATE WITH REQUIREMENTS FOR LOW-COST CHECKING ACCOUNTS	INITIAL DEPOSIT	MONTHLY FEE	WITHDRAWALS PER MONTH
ILLINOIS	Free for anyone age 65 or older.	$100 or direct-deposit sign-up	None	10
MASSACHUSETTS	Banks can offer them voluntarily in return for state Community Reinvestment Act credit.	$10	$3	8
NEW JERSEY	Banks are required to offer low-fee checking accounts.	$50	$3	8
NEW YORK	Banks are required to offer low-fee checking accounts.	$25	$3	8

OTHER STATE PROVISIONS

RHODE ISLAND	Basic savings accounts are free for people 17 and younger for accounts with a balance of $500 or less.
VERMONT	Regulators survey banks quarterly to insure that low-cost accounts are available. If they find that low-cost accounts are disappearing, the state can issue rules governing certain account charges.
MINNESOTA	Basic savings accounts are free with an average monthly balance of $50.

Sources: State banking departments; Federal Reserve Bank of New York

nomics professor and an expert on the financial habits of the poor. "Clearly that hasn't happened."

Such laws have "certainly had some incremental, positive effect," he said, but "the overall effect has been quite small."

Studies by consumer advocates have found that the poor can spend 4 to 10 times as much at check-cashing outlets as they would for basic accounts. But since New York enacted one of the toughest laws in the nation four years ago requiring banks to offer basic services to anyone for $3 a month, surprisingly few people have opened such accounts.

The state law says the most that banks can demand to open an account is $25 and that banks must keep the account open as long as a customer maintains a 1 cent minimum balance. It allows at least eight free withdrawals a month using checks or cash machines. For regular accounts, many large banks charge $9 or more a month, plus other fees, unless the customer carries at least a $1,500 balance.

"It's really sort of the hidden steal in banking in New York," said Russ Haven, legislative counsel at the New York Public Interest Research Group, a nonprofit research and advocacy organization. "Unfortunately, most consumers don't have any idea."

In a study last year, his group found that a third of bank employees did not mention low-cost options when customers asked about checking accounts. The group found that 4 of 10 banks posting information about account options did not include low-cost accounts, as required by state law. And calls to banks show they frequently emphasize higher-fee accounts and are often slow to mention—and occasionally deny altogether—that they offer low-cost accounts.

For certain, both New York and New Jersey residents have seen benefits. Regulators in New Jersey estimate that 700,000 residents now have low-cost accounts. But consumer advocates and researchers say the laws often have not helped many people they were intended for. Even New Jersey officials, who call their program a success, say the primary users are college students. They say they plan to push for more marketing in poorer areas.

A report published in a Federal Reserve Bank of New York journal last summer found that the laws had a limited impact bringing the working poor into banks and would not work better unless consumers were better informed.

"The banks are nightmares," said Bertha Lewis, head organizer for the Brooklyn chapter of the Association of Community Organizations for Reform Now. Commonly known as Acorn, the national group is pushing for improved lending in poor areas.

"You call branches," Ms. Lewis said, "and they don't know what you're talking about. There's no incentive for these banks to do this. This is the quietest law you never heard about."

Bankers say they comply with the law and defend their record of serving poor areas. **Chase Manhattan** says it has about 235,000 customers enrolled in low-cost accounts in New Jersey, New York and Connecticut. About half of them live in low- or moderate-income neighborhoods—the bank cannot say how many are actually low income—and many of the rest are college students. **Fleet Financial Group** says it has about 50,000 lifeline customers in New York City and Long Island. Citibank, the banking arm of **Citigroup,** declined to give a number.

Michael P. Smith, the president of the New York Bankers Association, called the program a success, but he added that it "was never designed to be a cure-all."

In Washington, Treasury officials are putting final touches on a plan they hope will give more than six million recipients of Federal benefits without accounts the option of having checks deposited directly into a new type of account at banks, credit unions and savings associations.

Nationally, industry representatives say most banks offer some form of basic account. But the most attractive accounts for consumers are vanishing quickly: In 1997, just 3 percent of banks offered free checking, a sharp drop from the 14 percent that offered it two years earlier, according to the Federal Reserve. In New York, only one bank in 77 offered it.

Mandatory low-cost banking grew out of fears that rising fees, as well as branch closings that often

Some say banks fail to inform customers about low-cost accounts.

follow bank mergers, would erode poor people's access to the banking system. Nationally, the number of banks, savings banks, savings and loans and credit union branches has dropped 4 percent in the last decade, according to Sheshunoff Information Services Inc., a research firm in Austin, Tex. In the same period, check-cashing outlets tripled to 7,000, according to industry estimates.

Indeed, the number of check-cashing stores has risen 11 percent in New York the last four years. And from 1994 to 1997, the value of checks cashed by outlets in New Jersey rose by one-fifth, to $3 billion.

But even with more check cashers, New York regulators have proposed raising the cap on fees to 1.4 percent of the amount of the check from 1.1 percent. Consumer groups say the increase will harm many poor people. But state banking regulators, relying in part on a report commissioned by the industry that argues that operating profit margins at check-cashing outlets had dropped to 18 percent in 1996 after holding steady at 22.5 percent from 1988 to 1993, say the increase is warranted.

Dollar Financial Group, which operates more than 400 check-cashing outlets in the United States and Canada, estimates that only 30 percent of its customers have bank accounts. It says it provides an advantage important to many low-income people. "These customers rely on their current income to cover immediate living expenses," the company explains in its annual report, "and cannot afford the delays inherent in waiting for checks to clear."

But even many people who might be willing to put up with delays often have little choice. In the poorest urban areas, entire ZIP codes have no banks. In parts of the South Bronx, for example, no banks exist "for 15 blocks in any direction," said Matthew Lee, executive director of Inner City Press-Community on the Move, which has challenged bank mergers.

And even where there are banks, customers at check-cashing outlets often do not know they have a lower-cost option. "There are a lot of people working around here under the impression you can't get" an account without high fees, said Denise Gunn, standing outside a check-cashing store on 149th Street near Third Avenue in the Bronx.

Mr. Haven, the New York public-interest lawyer, said bounced-check fees, always a concern for those with low balances, scare some people off. That factor will grow, he said, if state regulators approve a proposal to eliminate the $15 cap on such fees at state-chartered banks.

Some people, meanwhile, want to keep their financial lives private because they face debt collectors or child-support judgments or are earning off-the-books income. Ivan C. Lafayette, a Democratic Assemblyman whose Queens district includes a large immigrant population, adds that a number of immigrants rely on check cashers because they are unfamiliar with banks.

Some low-income residents find it impossible to produce enough identification to open accounts. In contrast, a study by the Consumer Federation of America found that only 8 percent of check-cashing stores required more than one formal ID.

Banks say they do inform customers about low-fee checking and have taken steps to preserve low-cost services in poorer areas. Chase says it loses millions of dollars a year offering low-cost accounts, which by agreement with New York officials cost $4 a month, not $3, but allow 10 withdrawals monthly.

New York banking regulators say they do not keep statistics on low-cost accounts. Evaluations in 1996 and 1997 "indicated that some bank personnel may not have been fully familiar" with their low-cost accounts, officials found. Last year, they said, a majority of the banks evaluated were complying fully.

Some groups are trying alternatives. Professor Caskey of Swarthmore points to an experiment in Los Angeles, where **Washington Mutual,** a large savings association, and Strategic Actions for a Just Economy, a community group, will begin a pilot program this year with about 1,000 welfare recipients. They will have checks deposited directly into accounts that have no minimum balance or monthly fees and that allow five free money orders a month.

Many participants are already more comfortable with money orders, the group says, and since money orders are prepaid, there is no risk of bouncing checks. The organization will also issue identification cards, using food stamp cards, apartment leases, utility bills and other documents for verification.

Others have their own ideas about how to improve low-cost checking, including making disclosure mandatory when bank employees discuss account options with customers. But with the powerful American Bankers Association and Republicans in Congress opposed to national low-cost banking laws, the Treasury Department may wind up playing the biggest role.

As part of a conversion from paper checks to electronically transferred benefit payments—expected to save $100 million annually—Treasury officials hope that by summer banks will offer new limited accounts for millions. Donald Hammond, the Treasury Department's Fiscal Assistant Secretary, said the department is "very committed to using this transition to try to bring people into the banking mainstream."

Electronic Cash and the End of National Markets

By Stephen J. Kobrin

Twenty-six years ago, Raymond Vernon's *Sovereignty at Bay* proclaimed that "concepts such as national sovereignty and national economic strength appear curiously drained of meaning." Other books followed, arguing that sovereignty, the nation-state, and the national economy were finished—victims of multinational enterprises and the internationalization of production. While sovereign states and national markets have outlasted the chorus of Cassandras, this time the sky really may be falling. The emergence of electronic cash and a digitally networked global economy pose direct threats to the very basis of the territorial state.

Let us begin with two vignettes. Fact: Smugglers fly Boeing 747s loaded with illicit drugs into Mexico and then cram the jumbo jets full of cash—American bills—for the return trip. Fiction: Uncle Enzo, Mafia CEO, pays for intelligence in the digital future of Neal Stephenson's novel *Snow Crash:* "He reaches into his pocket and pulls out a hypercard and hands it toward Hiro. It says 'Twenty-Five Million Hong Kong Dollars.' Hiro reaches out and takes the card. Somewhere on earth, two computers swap bursts of electronic noise and the money gets transferred from the Mafia's account to Hiro's."

The 747s leaving Mexico are anachronisms, among the last surviving examples of the physical transfer of large amounts of currency across national boarders. Most money has been electronic for some time: Virtually all of the trillions of dollars, marks, and yen that make their way around the world each day take the form of bytes—chains of zeros and ones. Only at the very end of its journey is money transformed into something tangible: credit cards, checks, cash, or coins.

Hypercards are here. Mondex, a smart card or electronic purse, can be "loaded" with electronic money from an automatic teller machine (ATM) or by telephone or personal computer using a card-reading device. Money is spent either by swiping the card through a retailer's terminal or over the Internet by using the card reader and a personal computer. An electronic wallet allows anonymous card-to-card transfers.

It is not just the current technology of electronic cash (e-cash) or even what might be technologically feasible in the future that presents policymakers with new challenges. Rather, policymakers must confront directly the implications of this technology—and, more generally, the emergence of an electronically networked global economy—for economic and political governance. As the U.S. comptroller of the currency, Eugene Ludwig, has noted, "There is clearly a freight train coming down the tracks. ... Just because it hasn't arrived yet doesn't mean we shouldn't start getting ready."

ELECTRONIC MONEY

Many different forms of "electronic money" are under development, but it is useful to look

---

STEPHEN J. KOBRIN is the director of the Lauder Institute of Management and International Studies and the William Wurster professor of multinational management at the Wharton School of the University of Pennsylvania. This paper develops themes raised at a discussion of electronic money at the 1997 annual meeting of the World Economic Forum in Davos, Switzerland.

at three general categories: electronic debit and credit systems; various forms of smart cards; and true digital money, which has many of the properties of cash.

Electronic debit and credit systems already exist. When a consumer uses an ATM card to pay for merchandise, funds are transferred from his or her account to the merchant's. Credit cards are used to make payments over the Internet. Computer software such as Intuit provides electronic bill payment, and it is but a short step to true electronic checks—authenticated by a digital signature—that can be transmitted to the payee, endorsed, and deposited over the Internet. Electronic debit and credit systems represent new, more convenient means of payment, but not new payment systems. A traditional bank or credit card transaction lies at the end of every transaction chain.

Smart cards and digital money represent new payment systems with potentially revolutionary implications. Smart cards are plastic "credit" cards with an embedded microchip. Many are now used as telephone or transit payment devices. They can be loaded with currency from an ATM or via a card reader from a telephone or personal computer, currency which can then be spent at businesses, vending machines, or turnstiles that have been equipped with appropriate devices. At this most basic level, a smart card is simply a debit card that does not require bank approval for each transaction; clearance takes place each day and the value resides in third-party accounts. There is no reason, however, that smart cards have to be limited in this way.

Banks or other institutions could provide value on smart cards through loans, payments for services, or products. The immediate transfer of funds between bank accounts is not necessary; units of value can circulate from card to card—and from user to user—without debiting or crediting third-party accounts. Assuming confidence in the creating institution, "money" could be created on smart cards and could circulate almost indefinitely before redemption.

Finally, electronic money can take true digital form, existing as units of value in the form of bytes stored in the memory of personal computers that may or may not be backed up by reserve accounts of real money. The money could be downloaded from an account, supplied as a loan or as payment, or bought with a credit card over the Internet. As long as digital cash can be authenticated *and* there is confidence in its continued acceptance, it could circulate indefinitely, allowing peer-to-peer payments at will. These are big "ifs," but they are well within the realm of the possible.

Imagine a world where true e-cash is an everyday reality. Whether all of the following assumptions are correct or even immediately feasible is unimportant; some form of e-cash is coming, and we need to begin the process of thinking about its as-yet-unexplored consequences for economic and political governance.

The year is 2005. You have a number of brands of e-cash on your computer's hard drive: some withdrawn from a bank in Antigua, some borrowed from Microsoft, and some earned as payment for your services. You use the digital value units (DVUs) to purchase information from a Web site, pay bills, or send money to your daughter in graduate school. Peer-to-peer payments are easy: You can transfer DVUs to any computer, anyplace in the world, with a few keystrokes.

Your e-cash is secure and can be authenticated easily. It is also anonymous; governments have not been able to mandate a technology that leaves a clear audit trail. Public-key encryption technology and digital signatures allow blind transaction; the receiving computer knows that the DVUs are authentic without knowing the identity of the payer. Your e-cash can be exchanged any number of times without leaving a trace of where it has been. It is virtually impossible to alter the value of your e-cash at either end of the transaction (by adding a few more zeros to it, for example).

DVUs are almost infinitely divisible. Given the virtually negligible transaction cost, it is efficient for you to pay a dollar or two to see a financial report over the Internet or for your teenager to rent a popular song for the few minutes during which it is in vogue. Microtransactions have become the norm.

E-cash is issued—actually created—by a large number of institutions, bank and nonbank. Electronic currencies (e-currencies) have begun to exist on their own; many are no longer backed by hard currency and have developed value separately from currencies issued by central banks. DVUs circulate for long periods of time without being redeemed or deposited. Consumer confidence in the issuer is crucial; as with electronic commerce (e-commerce) in general, brand names have become critical.

The early 21st century is described as a world of competing e-currencies, a throwback to the 19th-century world of private currencies. The better known brands of e-cash are highly liquid and universally accepted. It is a

Electronic Cash: A Glossary

Digital data: Information coded into a series of zeros and ones that can be transmitted and processed electronically.

Digital signature: A code that allows absolute authentication of the origin and integrity of a document, check, or electronic cash that has been sent over a computer network. A blind signature allows authentication without revealing the identity of the sender.

Disintermediation: The substitution of direct transactions for those that are mediated. The term originated when rising interest rates caused savings to be withdrawn from banks—whose interest rates were capped—and invested in money market instruments that were the direct debts of borrowers. Banks were disintermediated. In electronic commerce, the term refers to the rise of direct buyer-to-seller relationships over the Internet, disintermediating wholesalers and retail outlets.

Electronic money: Units or tokens of monetary value that take digital form and are transmitted over electronic networks. Digital Value Units are the basic units of denomination of electronic money; they may or may not correspond to units of national currency.

Encryption: The coding of information for security purposes, such as credit card numbers or electronic cash used over the Internet: Public-key encryption uses a mathematical algorithm comprising a pair of strings of numbers to encrypt and decrypt the data. For example, the sender would encrypt the data with the receiver's public key and the receiver would decrypt with his or her private key.

Internet: A global network of linked networks that allows communication and the sharing of information among many different types of computers. The World Wide Web is a graphical system on the Internet that allows rapid movement between documents and computers through the use of embedded (hypertext) links.

Smart card: A plastic card, similar to a credit card, containing a microchip that can be used to retrieve, store, process, and transmit digital data like electronic cash or medical information.

relatively simple matter for you to set up filters in your electronic purse to screen out e-currencies that you do not want to accept.

GOVERNANCE IN THE DIGITAL WORLD

E-cash and the increasing importance of digital markets pose problems for central government control over the economy and the behavior of economic actors; they also render borders around national markets and nation-states increasingly permeable—or, perhaps, increasingly irrelevant. In a world where true e-cash is an everyday reality, the basic role of government in a liberal market economy and the relevance of borders and geography will be drastically redefined.

While at first glance this concern appears to reflect a traditional break between domestic and international economic issues, in fact the advent of e-cash raises serious questions about the very idea of "domestic" and "international" as meaningful and distinct concepts. The new digital world presents a number of governance issues, described below.

- *Can central banks control the rate of growth and the size of the money supply?* Private e-currencies will make it difficult for central bankers to control—or even measure or define—monetary aggregates. Several forms of money, issued by banks and nonbanks, will circulate. Many of these monies may be beyond the regulatory reach of the state. At the extreme, if, as some libertarians imagine, private currencies dominate, currencies issued by central banks may no longer matter.

- *Will there still be official foreign exchange transactions?* E-cash will markedly lower existing barriers to the transfer of funds across borders. Transactions that have been restricted to money-center banks will be available to anyone with a computer. Peer-to-peer transfers of DVUs across national borders to not amount to "official" foreign exchange transactions. If you have $200 worth of DVUs on your computer and buy a program from a German vendor, you will probably have to agree on a mark-to-dollar price. However, transferring the DVUs to Germany is not an "official" foreign exchange transaction; the DVUs are simply revalued as marks. In fact, national currencies may lose meaning with the development of DVUs that have a universally accepted denomination. Without severe restrictions on individual privacy—which are not out of the question—governments will be hard-pressed to track, account for, and control the flows of money across borders.

- *Who will regulate or control financial institutions?* The U.S. Treasury is not sure whether existing regulations, which apply to both banks and institutions that act like banks (i.e., take deposits), would apply to all who issue (and create) e-cash. If non-financial institutions do not accept the extensive regulatory controls that banks take

as the norm, can reserve or reporting requirements be enforced? What about consumer protection in the event of the insolvency of an issuer of e-cash, a system breakdown, or the loss of a smart card?
- *Will national income data still be meaningful?* It will be almost impossible to track transactions when e-cash becomes a widely used means of payment, online deals across borders become much easier, and many of the intermediaries that now serve as checkpoints for recording transactions are eliminated by direct, peer-to-peer payments. The widespread use of e-cash will render national economic data much less meaningful. Indeed, the advent of both e-cash and e-commerce raises fundamental questions about the national market as the basic unit of account in the international economic system.
- *How will taxes be collected?* Tax evasion will be a serious problem in an economy where e-cash transactions are the norm. It will be easy to transfer large sums of money across borders, and tax havens will be much easier to reach. Encrypted anonymous transactions will make audits increasingly problematic. Additionally, tax reporting and compliance relies on institutions and intermediaries. With e-cash and direct payments, all sorts of sales taxes, value-added taxes, and income taxes will be increasingly difficult to collect. More fundamentally, the question of jurisdiction—who gets to tax what—will become increasingly problematic. Say you are in Philadelphia and you decide to download music from a computer located outside Dublin that is run by a firm in Frankfurt. You pay with e-cash deposited in a Cayman Islands account. In which jurisdiction does the transaction take place?
- *Will e-cash and e-commerce widen the gap between the haves and the have-nots?* Participation in the global electronic economy requires infrastructure and access to a computer. Will e-cash and e-commerce further marginalize poorer population groups and even entire poor countries? This widened gap between the haves and the have-nots—those with and without access to computers—could become increasingly difficult to bridge.
- *Will the loss of seigniorage be important as governments fight to balance budgets?* Seigniorage originally referred to the revenue or profit generated due to the difference between the cost of making a coin and its face value; it also refers to the reduction in government interest payments when money circulates. The U.S. Treasury estimates that traditional seigniorage amounted to $733 million in 1994 and that the reduction in interest payments due to holdings of currency rather than debt could be as much as $3.5 billion per year. The Bank for International Settlements reports that the loss of seigniorage for its 11 member states will be more than $17 billion if smart cards eliminate all bank notes under $25.
- *Will fraud and criminal activity increase in an e-cash economy?* At the extreme—and the issue of privacy versus the needs of law enforcement is unresolved—transfers of large sums of cash across borders would be untraceable: There would be no audit trail. Digital counterfeiters could work from anywhere in the world and spend currency in any and all places. New financial crimes and forms of fraud could arise that would be hard to detect, and it would be extremely difficult to locate the perpetrators. The task of financing illegal and criminal activity would be easier by orders of magnitude. E-cash will lower the barriers to entry and reduce the risks of criminal activity.

Most of the issues raised in the recent National Research Council report on cryptography's role in the information society apply directly to electronic cash. Secure, easily authenticated, and anonymous e-cash requires strong encryption technology. Anonymous transactions, however, cannot be restricted to law-abiding citizens. Encryption makes it as difficult for enforcement authorities to track criminal activity as it does for criminals to penetrate legitimate transmissions. Should privacy be complete? Or should law enforcement authorities and national security agencies be provided access to e-cash transactions through escrowed encryption, for example? What about U.S. restrictions on the export of strong encryption technology? E-cash is global cash; how can governments limit its geographic spread? Can they even suggest that strong encryption algorithms be restricted territorially?

GEOGRAPHIC SPACE VS. CYBERSPACE

A recent U.S. Treasury paper dealing with the tax implications of electronic commerce argues that new communications technologies have "effectively eliminated national borders on the information highway." It is clear from the paper's subsequent discussion, however, that the more fundamental problem is that electronic commerce may "dissolve the link between an income-producing activity and a specific location."

The source of taxable income, which plays a major role in determining liability, is defined geographically in terms of where the economic activity that produces the income is located. Therein lies the rub: "Electronic commerce doesn't seem to occur in any physical location but instead takes place in the nebulous world of 'cyperspace.'" In a digital economy it will be difficult, or even impossible, to link income streams with specific geographic locations. Digitalization is cutting money and finance loose from its geographic moorings. The framework of regulation that governs financial institutions assumes that customers and institutions are linked by geography—that spatial proximity matters. E-cash and e-commerce snap that link. What remains are systems of economic and political governance that are rooted in geography and are trying nonetheless to deal with e-cash and markets that exist in cyberspace. The obvious disconnect here will only worsen over time.

The geographical rooting of political and economic authority is relatively recent. Territorial sovereignty, borders, and a clear distinction between domestic and international spheres are modern concepts associated with the rise of the nation-state. Territorial sovereignty implies a world divided into clearly demarcated and mutually exclusive geographic jurisdictions. It implies a world where economic and political control arise from control over territory.

The international financial system—which consists of hundreds of thousands of computer screens around the globe—is the first international electronic marketplace. It will not be the last. E-cash is one manifestation of a global economy that is constructed in cyberspace rather than geographic space. The fundamental problems that e-cash poses for governance result from this disconnect between electronic markets and political geography.

The very idea of controlling the money supply, for example, assumes that geography provides a relevant means of defining the scope of the market. It assumes that economic borders are effective, that the flow of money across them can be monitored and controlled, and that the volume of money within a fixed geographic area is important. All of those assumptions are increasingly questionable in a digital world economy.

Many of our basic tax principles assume that transactions and income streams can be located precisely within a given national market. That assumption is problematic when e-cash is spent on a computer network. It is problematic when many important economic transactions cannot be located, or may not even take place, in geographic space.

The increasing irrelevance of geographic jurisdiction in a digital world economy markedly increases the risks of fraud, money-laundering, and other financial crimes. Asking where the fraud or money-laundering took place means asking Whose jurisdiction applies? and Whose law applies? We need to learn to deal with crimes that cannot be located in geographic space, where existing concepts of national jurisdiction are increasingly irrelevant.

The term "disintermediation" was first used to describe the replacement of banks as financial intermediaries by direct lending in money markets when interest rates rose. It is often used in the world of e-commerce to describe the elimination of intermediaries by direct seller-to-buyer transactions over the Internet. Many observers argue that e-cash is likely to disintermediate banks. Of more fundamental importance is the possibility that e-cash and e-commerce will disintermediate the territorial state.

To be clear, I argue that we face not the end of the state, but rather the diminished efficacy of political and economic governance that is rooted in geographic sovereignty and in mutually exclusive territorial jurisdiction. Questions such as, Where did the transaction take place? Where did the income stream arise? Where is the financial institution located? and Whose law applies? will lose meaning.

E-cash and e-commerce are symptoms, albeit important ones, of an increasing asymmetry between economics and politics, between an electronically integrated world economy and territorial nation-states, and between cyberspace and geographic space. How this asymmetry will be resolved and how economic and political relations will be reconstructed are two of the critical questions of our time.

What is to be Done?

The question asked here is not What is feasible? but What are the limits of the possible?

Whether the picture presented here is correct in all—or even some—of its details is unimportant. A digital world economy is emerging. Imagining possible scenarios is necessary if we are to come to grips with the consequences of this revolution.

The purpose here is to raise problems rather than to solve them and to imagine possible futures and think about their implications for economic and political governance. A digital world economy will demand increasing international cooperation, harmonizing national regulations and legislation, and strengthening the authority of international institutions.

The harmonization of national regulations will help to prevent institutions, such as those issuing e-cash, from slipping between national jurisdictions or shopping for the nation with the least onerous regulations. However, it will not address the basic problem of the disconnect between geographic jurisdiction and an electronically integrated global economy.

If it is impossible to locate transactions geographically—if the flows of e-cash are outside of the jurisdictional reach of every country—then the harmonization of national regulations will accomplish little. The basic problem is not one of overlapping or conflicting jurisdictions; it stems from the lack of meaning of the very concept of "jurisdiction" in a digitalized global economy.

The erosion of the viability of territorial jurisdiction calls for strengthened international institutions. It calls for giving international institutions real authority to measure, to control, and, perhaps, to tax. The Basle Committee on Banking Supervison—an international body of bank regulators who set global standards—could perhaps be given the authority to collect information from financial institutions wherever they are located and formulate and enforce regulations globally. Interpol, or its equivalent, may have to be given jurisdiction over financial crimes, regardless of where they are committed. That does not mean a world government; it does mean a markedly increased level of international cooperation.

The questions we must face are whether territorial sovereignty will continue to be viable as the *primary* basis for economic and political governance as we enter the 21st century and what the implications will be for the American economy—and Americans in general—if we refuse to cooperate internationally in the face of an increasingly integrated global economy.

Want to Know More?

A readable and knowledgeable introduction to the digital economy and the impact of "internetworking" on business and government can be found in Don Tapscott's *The Digital Economy* (New York: McGraw-Hill, 1996). Michael Dertouzos provides an evaluation of how the advent of the Information Age will transform how we live and learn, our business, and our national governments: *What Will Be* (San Francisco: HarperEdge, 1997). The June 12, 1995, issue of *BusinessWeek* featured an overview of smart cash, electronic money, and the issues they raise for business and government ("The Future of Money"). For a solid discussion of some of the technical aspects of e-cash and the public policy issues raised by its advent, see Steven Levy's "E-Money (That's What I Want)" in *Wired 2*, no. 12. The article also focuses on David Chaum, the founder of DigiCash, and his views on privacy vis-à-vis traceability. See Robert Teitelman & Stephen Davis's "How the Cash Flows," in *Institutional Investor* (August 1996), for a discussion of the digitalization of banking and finance at both the wholesale and the retail levels. The primary focus of the discussion is the impact of global electronic networks on traditional financial intermediaries and the regulatory process. If what you seek is a solid introduction to electronic money and the digitalization of finance in general and a thorough review of the regulatory issues raised, see "An Introduction to Electronic Money Issues," a paper prepared for the United States Department of the Treasury conference, "Toward Electronic Money and Banking: The Role of Government" (Washington, D.C.: September 19–20, 1996). Finally, read Raymond Vernon's seminal work, *Sovereignty at Bay* (New York: Basic Books, 1971). This time around, it might well be.

For links to Web sites that provide more useful information, visit FOREIGN POLICY's Web site at www.foreignpolicy.com.

Unit 5

Unit Selections

24. **Learning from the Big Booms,** Louis Uchitelle
25. **Yes, Virginia, There Will Be Recessions,** Business Week
26. **Productivity Gains Help Keep Economy on a Roll,** Louis Uchitelle
27. **Calculating the Price of Everything: The CPI,** Daniel Mitchell
28. **Overworked and Underemployed,** Barry Bluestone and Stephen Rose
29. **The Age-Adjusted Unemployment Rate: An Alternative Measure,** Robert Horn and Philip Heap

Key Points to Consider

❖ What is the present outlook for employment, price stability, and economic growth in the U.S. economy?

❖ Is there a the link between unemployment and inflation? Explain.

❖ In what ways are the Consumer Price Index and the U.S. unemployment rate flawed?

❖ How can Americans simultaneously be "overworked" and "underemployed"?

DUSHKIN ONLINE Links — www.dushkin.com/online/

22. **Business Cycle Indicators**
    http://www.globalexposure.com
23. **What's a Dollar Worth? CPI Calculation Machine**
    http://minneapolisfed.org/economy/calc/cpihome.html
24. **Economic Cycle Research Institute**
    http://www.businesscycle.com
25. **Employment Policy Foundation**
    http://www.epfnet.org
26. **WorkIndex**
    http://workindex.com

These sites are annotated on pages 4 and 5.

Employment, Prices, and the Business Cycle

Beware the economist who forecasted nine of the last five recessions. —Anonymous

Business cycles are a key feature of all market-based, capitalist economies. While no two cycles are identical (either in terms of their intensity or duration), they all share a common characteristic: a wave of expansion (or rising real Gross Domestic Product [GDP]) is always followed by a period of contraction (when real GDP falls)—which ultimately ends, and is followed by another expansion. Economists use many terms to characterize these events. The top of the expansion is sometimes called a "boom" or a "peak." If the subsequent contraction lasts for more than 6 months, it is officially known as a "recession." At the end of the recession there is a "trough," after which the economy expands again (the "recovery"). Whatever the terminology one employs, the "peak-contraction-trough-expansion" pattern is an essential fact of economic life.

Business cycles exert a powerful influence on modern economies. As real output rises, expansions can result in many thousands of new jobs for workers, which then shows up as a drop in the "unemployment rate" (the ratio of the number unemployed to the civilian labor force). New investment opportunities open up, leading to the creation of countless new business ventures. Unfortunately, history also shows that expansions are seldom risk-free; if they prove to be too vigorous, shortages of labor and other resources may develop. As the economy's output approaches capacity, pressures on wages and prices can develop, and the rate of inflation accelerates.

One of the more interesting macroeconomic questions is: How much output growth can an economy sustain without overheating? In the 1960s economists developed the notion that there was a close inverse relationship between unemployment and inflation. This theory (represented by what is called a "Phillips curve") holds that when the unemployment rate falls below some critical level, inflation accelerates. The exact nature of this relationship has been the topic of much debate in recent years. At one point it was believed that any drop in unemployment below 6 percent would trigger inflation. When (in the early 1990s) such a decline did occur—without any acceleration of inflation—some economists revised their estimate of the critical unemployment rate downward, to 5½ or even 5 percent. Recently, unemployment has dipped below 5 percent, and still nothing has happened to prices.

This unit begins with an article in which Louis Uchitelle offers some perspective on the "soaring nineties." He finds strong parallels with other periods of American prosperity (including the "roaring twenties" and the "fabulous fifties and sixties"). What is striking about each of these periods is that in each case the end came as a shock.

The steady, noninflationary growth of recent years has led some economists to ask: Does the dawning of the twenty-first century economy mean that we have seen our last recession? The next article says that the clear answer is no—one might as well ask whether a car can be built that never has an accident. History suggests that eras of rapid technological progress and productivity increases are often accompanied by economic volatility, not stability.

The current recovery is in its eighth year. Each year several million new jobs are added to the economy and the annual inflation rate is at its lowest level since World War II. Historical experience suggests that at this point in the recovery labor shortages and rising wages should be raising the inflation rate or shrinking profits. Yet neither is happening. In "Productivity Gains Help Keep Economy on a Roll" Louis Uchitelle explains the role that productivity improvements play in the current expansion.

Economic analysts and policymakers generally employ the Consumer Price Index (CPI) to track inflation. Recently, a debate has developed over the usefulness of this index. In "Calculating the Price of Everything: The CPI" Daniel Mitchell suggests that there are many plausible and reasonable versions of the CPI. He says that a variety of alternatives should be offered to meet the preferences of CPI users.

The essay "Overworked *and* Underemployed" then reports on two apparently competing trends in the U.S. work force: a substantial rise in the average work week coupled with a marked increase in part-time work by those unable to locate full-time employment (otherwise known as "contingent employment").

Finally, in "The Age-Adjusted Unemployment Rate: An Alternative Measure" Robert Horn and Philip Heap present an interesting perspective on the matter of measuring joblessness. They point out that the official rate does not take into account the fact that the age and sex composition of the labor force changes over time. Once such changes are allowed for, today's unemployment rate may not be as low as official statistics suggest.

Crash Course

Learning From the Big Booms

By LOUIS UCHITELLE

SUDDENLY, these are nervous times for prosperity fans. The stock market has the jitters; after going straight up all winter it has been stuck in place since April. The Asian economic boom, another great engine of American prosperity, is over. And the nation's economy shows signs of slowing.

Is this the beginning of the end of the Soaring Nineties? Who knows? There are plenty of economic seers in the land who, convinced that Americans are more efficient and productive than ever, see the good times rolling on.

Even the less sanguine say this may be the seventh inning rather than the ninth. But enough warning flags are up to invite comparisons with the other great periods of prosperity in modern history, and how they ended.

What is striking is that each of them—the Gilded Age in the late 19th century, the Roaring Twenties, the Fabulous Fifties and Sixties—ended suddenly, and in each case the end came as a shock. The same was true of the more ambiguous period of growth that ended with the stock market crash of 1987. The warning signs were there, but they were overlooked or minimized or simply beyond anyone's power to control.

"If you stood in 1928 and tried to imagine what the next decade would be like, you would never have imagined the Great Depression, and each period of prosperity has been like that," said Henry Kaufman, the Wall Street economist and consultant.

The Gilded Age, for example, ended with the financial panic of 1893. A weakening American currency frightened foreign investors, particularly the British, and they pulled out their money, helping to start a four-year depression.

The Roaring Twenties crashed with the stock market in 1929, and the Great Depression followed.

The Fifties and Sixties gave way to an unlikely combination of inflation and stagnant economic growth in the 1970's that shook American confidence.

Another stock market crash, in 1987, brought the decade of greed to a humbling conclusion.

Or did it really end? The bounceback in the 1990's, after a brief recession, brings some historians to the conclusion that the present decade is really an extension of the 1980's—half a generation of almost unbroken prosperity, particularly for upper-income people.

"What is remarkable about this era of prosperity is how long it has lasted and how entrenched the orthodoxy of free markets has become over all these years," said Alan Brinkley, the Columbia University historian. "We are really back to an age in which the reigning ideology is very close to laissez-faire, as it was in the Gilded Age."

That is one comparison. There are others. Implicit in them is the suggestion that the current era of prosperity can be prolonged by avoiding the mistakes that ended those earlier booms. Let's see.

The Gilded Age Dissolves in Panic

The Gilded Age, which lasted roughly 20 years, was born in the pell-mell economic growth after the Civil War. Railroads spread across the country. Steel mills blossomed, and other industries came into being. Their owners often turned to foreigners, particularly the British, to finance the projects.

Competition and over-expansion made these new industrialists vulnerable to bankruptcy. That, in turn, made the lenders nervous. And then a conflict over the value of the nation's currency finally pushed the lenders to call in their loans, which brought on the Panic of 1893.

The value of currency has, in different ways, been a source of trouble in nearly every period of prosperity. It is an issue in the maneuvering to prevent today's prosperity from running off the rails.

When dollars are scarce, their value rises. Reflecting this higher value, interest rates rise for borrowers, and prices drop for goods and services. The money, in effect, is worth more than what it buys.

One way to limit the supply is to pull dollars out of circulation, as the Federal Reserve sometimes does now. Another is to tie the dollar to gold, the practice in the Gilded Age, before there was a central bank.

A government pledges to convert each dollar into a fixed amount of gold. Since there was not that much gold available in the Gilded Age, the Government could not print that many dollars.

Virtually every government in the late 19th century adjusted its economy to the gold standard. In America, that galled farmers. They were a big part of the population, and they were desperate. Partly because of overproduction, prices for their crops kept falling. They needed low-interest credit, plenty of it, to keep going, and because of the gold standard they could not get it. Nor could they inflate their prices. The money, in limited supply, grew in value faster than their produce. Thousands of farmers lost their land.

Their solution was silver, which was much more abundant than gold. Under pressure from the populist farmers movement, Congress in 1890 authorized the Treasury to issue dollars backed by silver as well as gold. That greatly increased the money supply and made credit available at lower rates. But the dollar lost value. A "cheap" silver dollar could be converted into just as much gold as a dollar backed by gold.

The currency, in effect, was devalued, particularly in the eyes of lenders in Britain, a country on a pure gold standard. Nervous already from various bankruptcies, they called in their dollar loans and converted them into gold—behaving much as American and European lenders did last winter when they called in loans to South Korea and converted them back to hard currencies when that country's won fell in value.

President Grover Cleveland got the silver act repealed within months. But that did not lessen the concern that the dollar would be devalued. And as gold reserves fell below $100 million in April 1893, the panic was on.

The various players in this drama knew the potential consequences of their actions, historians explain, but given the passions and the political struggle, no one could stop the process.

That is the great lesson from the Gilded Age: the forces that unwind a prosperous era take on a life of their own. And that remains an issue over a century later, particularly in a world that still views a strong currency as a top priority.

The United States returned firmly to a gold standard only after the populist farmers' candidate, William Jennings Bryan, lost the 1896 presidential election to William McKinley. By then the depression had almost run its course. And a surge in the supply of gold, from new mines, brought relief to the farmers.

The Roaring Twenties End in Depression

The crash of 1929, the bursting of one of those speculative bubbles that have appeared periodically over the last three centuries, was probably inevitable. The Great Depression, however, might have been preventable. The 1987 crash demonstrated that the damage resulting from a stock market plunge can be limited. But that was by no means clear in the 1920's.

It was another decade of rapid expansion. New technologies appeared. New industries came into being. There were huge investments, eye-catching mergers and mass production of automobiles, appliances and other goods. Most significantly, millions of Americans, for the first time, participated in the stock market. The small investor had arrived.

The financial markets, in fact, were growing too rapidly for policymakers to fully grasp what was happening and develop ways to deal with the problems that would arise, notes Barry Eichengreen, an economist at the University of California at Berkeley.

The necessary safeguards—deposit insurance, bank regulation, stock trading rules, the Securities and Exchange Commission—came only in the 1930's. But

The belief endures that avoiding old mistakes will avert a crash.

they stand today as a safety net to mitigate the damage from a market crash, and from the bankruptcies and bank failures that accompany it.

The Federal Reserve, formed in 1913, was also groping. The panic of 1893 and another in 1907 had made the need for a central bank obvious. But its role as a lender of last resort and as a supplier of cheap credit in hard times would take years to develop. That role was fully in place in 1987, on the day after the stock market crash, when Alan Greenspan, the Fed's chairman, lowered interest rates and announced that the central bank stood ready to make credit available to keep the stock market and its players solvent.

"The Federal Reserve and its foreign counterparts were all groping in the 1920's toward an understanding of what a lender of last resort should do domestically," said Mr. Eichengreen, who is also an adviser to the International Monetary Fund. Now after the global financial crisis brought about by Asia's downfall, "We are groping toward trying to understand whether we need an international lender of last resort and, if so, how it should operate," Mr. Eichengreen added.

There was another problem pulling at the Fed after the 1929 crash, a replay of a theme that had been so important in the Panic of 1893. The Fed has been accused of responding to the crash by raising interest rates, thus restricting credit and demand in the teeth of the developing Depression—such behavior being just the opposite of what was needed.

But in fact the Fed vacillated, lowering rates at times, and deciding only in 1931 to push them up, said Charles Calomiris, an economist at Columbia University's Graduate School of Business.

What drove the Fed was England's decision to go off the gold standard. By raising interest rates, the Fed, in effect, made the dollar more valuable, which meant that dollar holders were less likely to convert their dollars to gold and once again deplete the nation's reserve.

24. Learning from the Big Booms

But the cost, once again, was a Depression.

"The commitment to the gold standard constrained how much the Fed could worry about managing—stimulating—demand," Mr. Calomiris said. That preference for a strong dollar may still be in play.

The Postwar Years

Never were two decades more prosperous in America than the 1950's and 1960's. Consumer demand, unfulfilled in the Depression and the war years, drove the economy. So did military spending. The United States became the supplier to a rebuilding world. Mass production and marketing made this the most productive era. As the nation's workers turned out more, their incomes rose. So they spent more, leaving the impression that the nation's output was limitless. It was not.

The costly Vietnam War and the Great Society programs strained the system. Prices, responding to shortages, began to rise in the late 1960's. The 1973 Arab embargo made oil prices shoot up, increasing inflation. Japan, Germany and other countries re-entered the marketplace, cutting into American sales.

That helped to reduce the rate at which the economy, productivity and incomes grew. None has ever recovered its old vigor, despite a considerable improvement in the last two years. Instead, upper-income people have been the big beneficiaries in the current era of prosperity. Corporate America, freed from many government constraints, argues that it is stronger because of the change. But whether the laissez-faire system that has emerged strengthens the nation's hand for the next crisis is anyone's guess.

The Japanese are under pressure to stimulate their economy by issuing more yen. But that weakens the yen, which creates problems for American and Asian exporters, straining these economies. What we need, Mr. Calomiris said, is a coordinated action in which the Federal Reserve agrees publicly to expand the American money supply. The goal would be to offset the Japanese action and keep currency values constant.

"Mr. Greenspan could announce no interest rate increases for six months," Mr. Calomiris said. "That would be an example of the kind of policy coordination that would be very effective."

And very uncharacteristic of the Federal Reserve.

PERSPECTIVE

YES, VIRGINIA, THERE WILL BE RECESSIONS

The U.S. economy has been growing for more than seven years. Even the widespread turmoil in Asia seems so far to have done nothing more than slow it down a bit. Does the dawning of the 21st Century Economy mean that we have seen our last recession?

The clear answer is no—you might as well ask whether a car can be built that never has an accident. Despite its current strength, the U.S. still could easily be sent into a downturn by any one of a number of different shocks. A collapse of the Japanese economy, say, could devastate U.S. financial markets and send the economy into a tailspin. Another steep plunge in the stock market, on top of the nearly 900-point drop in the Dow since July, could have an equally large negative impact by causing consumers to stop spending. Or the economy could be taken down by some unexpected event, just as the oil price shocks of the 1970s and the gulf war triggered recessions.

But even a deep recession or a stock market crash would not be a sign that the productivity gains of the 1990s are a myth, or that the 21st Century Economy is illusory. Quite the contrary—history suggests that eras of rapid technological progress and productivity increases are often accompanied by economic volatility, not stability.

Consider, for example, the first half of the 20th century, perhaps the most impressive period of technological progress yet seen. During this 50-year stretch, a series of breakthrough innovations—from autos to telephones—dramatically transformed the way people lived. And with the productivity of labor rising at an average rate exceeding 2% per year, living standards soared for almost everyone. Average real income per capita in 1950 was more than double that of 1900, and life expectancies rose from 47 years to 68 years, an incredible difference.

PLANT GROWTH. But that same 50-year stretch included the Great Depression and 11 smaller recessions. In particular, the Depression came right after the boom of the 1920s, a decade when manufacturing output per hour exploded by 63%. During the 1920s, the economy grew at a 6% annual rate, driven by the new technologies of the day: autos and radio. The number of autos on the road tripled during the decade, and by 1930 more than 40% of households had radio sets, up from virtually none at the beginning of the decade.

High productivity growth did not protect the country from the Great Depression. To the contrary: There is evidence that the productive capacity of the economy outran the ability of consumers to absorb the goods pouring out of the factories. This was particularly true in the auto industry, where producers such as General Motors Corp. and Ford Motor Co. competed for dominance by constantly building new factories in a bid for market share. "By the end of the 1920s, there was huge overcapacity in autos," notes Rick Szostak, an economic historian at the University of Alberta. "Once the auto market was saturated, there weren't other products to pick up the slack."

In some ways, there are uncomfortable parallels between the 1920s and 1990s. Today, a single sector, high tech, accounts for about 25% to 30% of growth—much the way a single sector, autos, drove growth in the 1920s. And it was softness in auto sales, starting in the summer of 1929, that helped trigger the stock market crash, just as today's stock market plummets whenever tech sales sag.

But other lessons from the 1920s and 1930s offer some assurance. Most economists agree that the initial downturn in 1929 was greatly worsened by bad policy decisions—notably an increase in protectionism, combined with a tight-money policy at the Federal Reserve Board. Most central bankers now understand that the right immediate response to a financial crisis in an otherwise sound economy is to pump money into the financial system rather than take it out.

The second lesson is that a powerful technology boom need not be stopped even by a deep downturn. From 1929 to 1937—through the worst of the Depression and a weak recovery—labor productivity actually rose 1.1% a year. By comparison, the recessions of the 1970s and 1980s—during an era of slow technological progress—produced devastating declines in productivity.

Indeed, the next downturn will provide a stern test for the 21st Century Economy. If productivity falls sharply during the next recession, that will suggest that the recent gains were only a temporary spike, and that the skeptics were correct. But if productivity continues to rise, that will be a clear sign that the 21st Century Economy is a good bet.

By Michael J. Mandel in New York

Productivity Gains Help Keep Economy on a Roll

By LOUIS UCHITELLE

DES MOINES—At the Maytag Corporation factory in nearby Newton, four young people stand around a large lazy susan, as if it were a coffee bar, assembling washing-machine doors. As the plastic door molds circle slowly by, each worker adds one metal part, and every 37 seconds a finished door comes off the revolving table.

The lazy-susan system is a triumph of productivity. The same four workers produce 90 more doors every hour than they used to, roughly a 15 percent improvement. Until last fall, each had assembled an entire door, one after another, in a much slower process. "I had to keep a full set of parts at every station," said Diana Brown, who now delivers them only to the central system.

Ms. Brown's pay, $18 an hour after 23 years at the plant, is nearly double that of her younger colleagues, and at 48 she sees herself as their "mother hen." Seniority indeed sets her apart. New hires now must start below union scale, marching to full pay through semiannual raises that show up in the nation's pay statistics, but without squeezing Maytag's profit.

As veterans like Ms. Brown retire, the new hires represent a larger share of the plant's 2,800 workers. The shift in the work force holds down the average wage, and Maytag's total labor costs.

"We are flattening our labor costs," said Leonard A. Hadley, chairman of Maytag. "It is problematic whether we can flatten labor costs over the long term. But short term, we are."

Maytag's experiences, like those of many corporations, help to explain the central puzzle of today's economy. Eight years into the current expansion, labor shortages and rising wages should be raising the annual inflation rate or shrinking profits. Yet neither is happening.

The annual inflation rate is only 1.6 percent, in sharp contrast to the last growth cycle, in the 1980's, when the rise in the Consumer Price Index reached 4.6 percent a year.

Nor are profits suffering noticeably, despite somewhat slower gains recently. By past standards, profits should be hurting, caught as they are between rising pay and stagnant prices. But many corporations have come up with numerous ways to dodge the bullet and confound the widely held view that inflation is an inevitable result of sustained prosperity.

How companies are managing this balancing act is abundantly evident here in central Iowa, not only at Maytag, which is based in Newton, but at two giant companies in Des Moines: the Principal Financial Group, which manages retirement plans for 43,000 companies, among other businesses, and Hy-Vee Food Stores Inc., a Midwestern supermarket chain with 179 stores. The tactics of these profitable companies—a manufacturer, a financial services firm and a retailer—are essentially the tactics of corporate America.

Productivity improvements play a growing role at all three companies in squeezing out more revenue for each hour of pay, and thus more profit. The lazy susan is just one of many examples that executives at the three companies pointed to during tours of their operations—changes that have raised the annual rate of improvement in the nation's productivity—the output of goods and services per worker—to 2 percent since 1995 from 1 percent in the early 90's. Other circumstances have also helped. Low interest rates, for example, saved Hy-Vee $1 million last year in debt payments.

The heart of the matter, however, lies in two gradual changes in behavior that have allowed corporations to forgo price increases in the face of intense global competition, yet raise wages and still make healthy profits. Normally by now, the Federal Reserve, fearing higher inflation, would have pushed up interest rates to slow the economy. It has not done so.

One key change is the increased corporate flexibility in manipulating labor costs. Maytag's below-scale starting wage is an example. Principal and Hy-Vee engage in another popular practice: "accordion" scheduling, the use of temporary workers and part-timers whose wages are up but whose hours are adjusted day to day—and even in the middle of a shift—so that an operation is never overstaffed.

"We call Manpower at 5 P.M. and have people in the next morning for any number of tasks," said Max F. Johnson, vice president for human resources of Principal, which since 1996 has nearly doubled the use of temporary help, such as telephone workers, computer operators, clerks and the like. "We are matching work to demand much more closely and less expensively."

Relocating Work And Other Strategies

Shifting work to lower-cost cities, a practice that has been popular for decades among manufacturers, is now common among service companies, too. Principal, for instance, shifts work, through computer transmissions, to offices in smaller cities like Waterloo and Ottumwa, Iowa, where wages are 5 to 10 percent lower than in Des Moines. Today, 36 percent of Principal's 4,000 employees in the pension division work outside Des Moines, up from 26 percent in 1993.

"Workers themselves are much less likely to resist such shifts," said Alan Krueger, a Princeton labor economist. "They no longer insist on maintaining wage scales across a company's various operations, or even see the need to do so. And when that breaks down, so does the pressure on prices that once came from across-the-board raises."

The other key means of relieving pressure on prices is through the introduction of fancier products and services. Because the Government lists these as new items rather than higher-priced variations of existing ones, they are not counted as price increases in the Consumer Price Index. If they were, the annual inflation rate, now 1.6 percent, would be over 3 percent, a study by Government economists found.

The washing-machine doors at the Maytag plant are for use in one

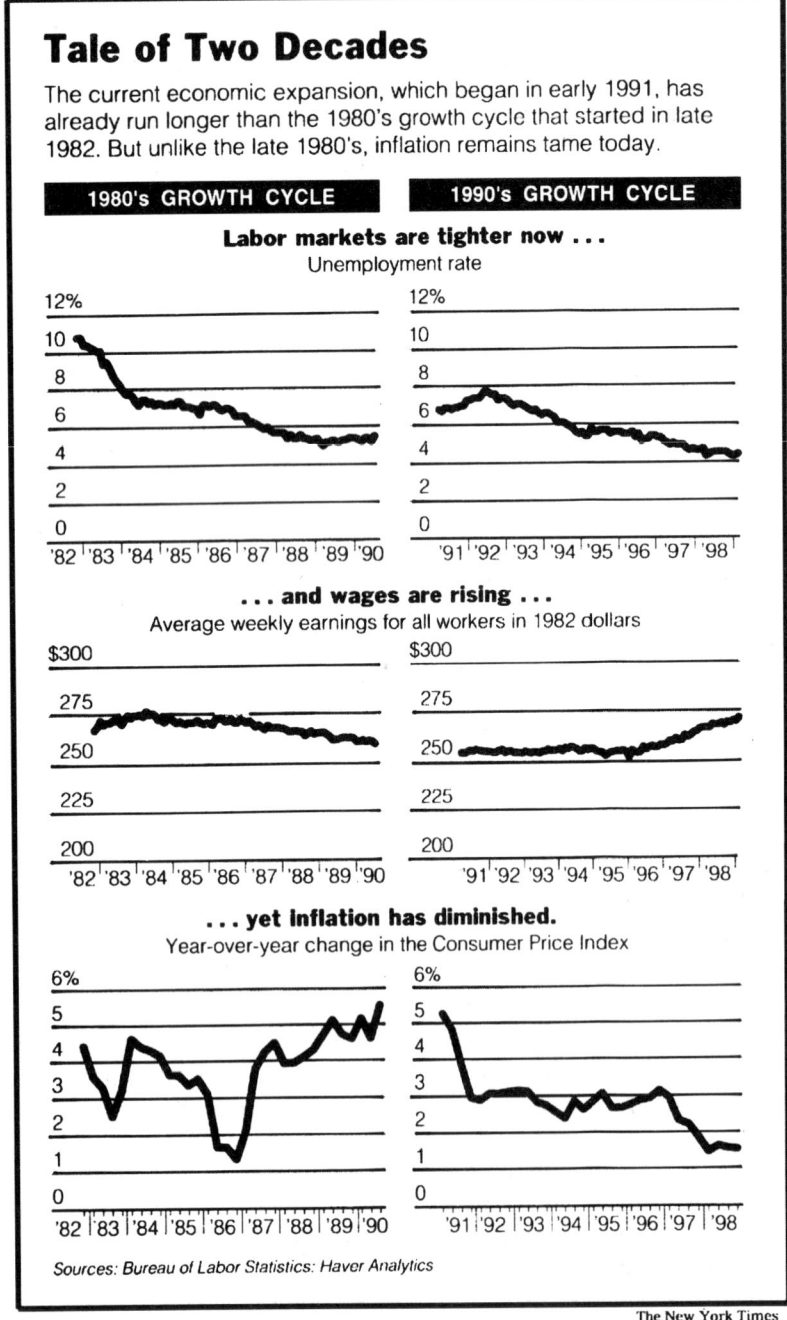

Tale of Two Decades

The current economic expansion, which began in early 1991, has already run longer than the 1980's growth cycle that started in late 1982. But unlike the late 1980's, inflation remains tame today.

1980's GROWTH CYCLE | **1990's GROWTH CYCLE**

Labor markets are tighter now . . .
Unemployment rate

. . . and wages are rising . . .
Average weekly earnings for all workers in 1982 dollars

. . . yet inflation has diminished.
Year-over-year change in the Consumer Price Index

Sources: Bureau of Labor Statistics; Haver Analytics

The New York Times

26. Productivity Gains Help Keep Economy on a Roll

of these new, upscale products—the Neptune, a front-loading, spin-action clothes washer that Maytag says removes stains better than other machines. The Neptune's price tag of $1,099 is $450 above Maytag's most expensive existing washer, and a big chunk of the price difference covers extra profit, not added cost.

"We have made a conscious effort to tilt the sales mix toward our premium brands," Mr. Hadley said. "They were 70 percent of our major appliance sales in 1998, up from 50 percent a decade ago. The goal is to keep driving up prices and profit margins with new features."

Cynthia Thompson, in a white chef's coat, is a soldier in this universal campaign. To find her in Hy-Vee's vast, softly lighted supermarket in West Des Moines, circle the outer perimeter where all the high-margin items are on display.

Go past the flower shop, the pharmacy, the cosmetics, the greeting card rack (grown to 140 feet in length from 12 in most stores a decade ago), the T-shirts, the Parisian and Italian white breads, the tortilla wrapped sandwiches, the special cuts of meat, the New York delicatessen salads (low cholesterol displayed in heart-shaped platters), the chilled and packaged dinners (a favorite is meatloaf with three side dishes), the salad bar, the Chinese food counter, the Italian takeout.

There, at the Italian Express station, Ms. Thompson, 37, who trained for a decade at Pizza Hut, presides over three full-timers and five part-timers—roughly the ratio for all of Hy-Vee's 42,000 workers. Her part-timers, teen-agers mostly, work accordion schedules, adjusting their hours to store traffic "to keep sales revenue per worker pretty steady," Ms. Thompson said, echoing the corporate strategy.

She and a friend who followed her from Pizza Hut handle the lunch traffic, their three biggest sellers being pepperoni, cheese and Italian sausage pizzas at $7.99 each. The lunch business has risen to $700 a day from $500 a few months ago, but Ms. Thompson has not added staff. She and her friend work a little harder, she said, to get the orders out—an extra effort that more than covers Ms. Thompson's recent 4 percent raise to well above $400 a week.

Dinner-hour sales are mostly packaged meals taken home and heated—meat lasagna for four ($12.99), pizzas ($2.25 to $10.99) and pastas ($4 to $6). "We try not to run up the cost by making labor-intensive foods," she said, ruling out, for example, pasta shells stuffed with several types of cheese.

The economics are straightforward. All the high-end items around the store's perimeter yield a margin of 30 to 70 cents above the cost of ingredients for each dollar of sales versus 20 to 30 cents for standard supermarket fare, the company says. Apply an overhead charge calculated at 24 cents per dollar of sales at the West Des Moines store and upscale merchandise becomes essential to profitability.

Payroll Grows But Profits Grow Faster

Last year, Hy-Vee's payroll, which was pushed up in part by a 21 percent increase in the minimum wage in 1997, rose at a faster rate than sales. But operating profits rose anyway. The reason was high-end merchandise. "Many of our stores are getting 25 percent of their revenues from these specialty items, and that is more than double what it was 10 years ago," said Ronald D. Pearson, chairman of Hy-Vee.

"People are doing well and trading up," he said. "They are buying ground beef with 90 percent lean meat at $2.50 a pound and not the 70 percent ground beef at $1 a pound that was popular five years ago. We hardly stock the 70 percent beef anymore."

But that raises some uncertainties. A sinking economy would reverse that trend, Mr. Pearson acknowledged, making those high-margin items a lot harder to sell.

Whatever the outlook, corporate America is not letting up in its ingenious strategies for holding down labor costs. Just watch John E. Beal in action at Principal Financial Group on a recent afternoon. A Blue Cross employee—Principal manages Blue Cross' 401 (k) plan—has called to apply for a $5,000 loan against his savings, and Mr. Beal, taking the call, suggests that the caller would get his loan more quickly if he used the push buttons on his phone rather than a live operator.

Tactfully, Mr. Beal walks the caller through Principal's "Teletouch" system, watching the progress on his computer screen. Midway through, the caller makes a mistake and Mr. Beal helps him undo the damage. "He had pressed the button for a biweekly repayment plan and he wanted bimonthly," Mr. Beal said.

Finally, all the right buttons are pressed and the loan application flows into Principal's computers, which automatically print out the necessary papers for mailing. Otherwise Mr. Beal would have had to handle the paperwork, at more cost.

The more difficult requests that come into Principal's call center in Des Moines are routed to people like Mr. Beal, whose college diploma hangs on a cloth partition wall near his computer. He earns $30,000—up 3.5 percent from his starting salary 13 months ago. New computer programs are gradually reducing the need for skilled operators like him. But for now, he pays for his own raises, in effect, by helping to herd toward automation the 2.9 million people in retirement plans managed by Principal.

The economics, as Principal lays them out, are clear. Human intervention, by Mr. Beal or any operator, costs $5.90 a call. Transactions that clients complete on their own by touch-tone phone are 45 cents, while those performed on the Internet come to 14 cents a hit. That is the big push now, switching the clientele to the Internet, which keeps a lid on the number of employees. "I had projected 250 people in our call centers by now," said

Michael J. Daugherty, assistant director of pension administration. "Teletouch and the Internet have held the number to 175."

More than 250 other employees, however, process paperwork that arrives by mail, including lists of monthly 401 (k) contributions that Principal's corporate clients have collected from their workers. The lists are scanned into Principal's computers and adjusted at various computer stations. To bypass this labor-intensive process, Principal has shifted 30,000 companies to Internet filing since mid-1997 and has notified some companies of a surcharge until they make the switch.

"We want to service the small company," said Daniel J. Houston, a Principal vice president, "but we need them to deliver electronically."

Of Efficiencies And Portfolios

How many more labor-saving efficiencies are still out there? Ask that of David McConnaughey, a Maytag vice president, and the answer comes back, intensely, "We have just begun." The executives at Hy-Vee and Principal are also believers. But sales are more problematic. And profits depend on them, too.

Prosperity enters here. If the economy slows, demand will fall for fancier, more profitable Maytag washing machines or Hy-Vee's high-end merchandise. Principal is similarly at risk; it charges clients a percentage of the pension money in their plans. That percentage has remained below 2 percent since 1995.

But if pricing is unchanged, revenue and profit are not. Both have risen as the total pension money managed by Principal has grown—through the monthly contributions and the rising stock market. Principal had 42 percent of the pension money invested in stocks late last year, up from 20 percent in 1994. A falling market would be a blow.

But in the era of Dow 10,000, stocks are not falling. Prosperity still reigns, and companies across America keep their balance—at least for now—between rising wages and steady prices.

Calculating the Price of Everything: The CPI

Daniel Mitchell

The author proposes a range of alternative CPIs. One estimate cannot satisfy all needs.

A cynic, Oscar Wilde observed a long time ago, "knows the price of everything and the value of nothing." More recently, many economists have become cynics about our official index of the price of (virtually) everything, the Consumer Price Index (CPI). The Boskin Commission in 1996 summarized most of the complaints about the CPI.[1] The commission argued that the CPI, as the Bureau of Labor Statistics (BLS) produces it, is beset by inflation overstatement. It identified two faults in the CPI: insufficient adjustment for product quality and lack of recognition of consumer substitution. The Boskin Commission also criticized the BLS for other technical deficiencies in the index. In the background of this debate loomed the fact that, by law, increases in the CPI cause social security payments and other government benefits to rise. And, because of indexation of income tax brackets, federal revenues increase with any rise in the index.

By no means do all economists agree with the criticisms of the CPI.[2] Nor are most familiar with the details of its construction. However, all economists and policy-makers should understand that continued debate about the index undermines public con-

---

DANIEL MITCHELL *is a professor at the Anderson Graduate School of Management and the Department of Policy Studies, School of Public Policy and Social Research, UCLA.*

fidence in official economic data. At various points, both Republicans and Democrats in Congress have threatened the BLS with extinction if it did not change its methodology. Republican Speaker of the House Newt Gingrich once proposed to "zero . . . out" the BLS if the agency did not alter the CPI to his liking. And so-called Blue Dog Democrats, led by Representative Charles W. Stenholm of Texas, once proposed mandating methodological changes.[3] If the Bureau of Labor Statistics makes changes in the CPI that move in the direction suggested by the Boskin Commission, the agency might be

> *My menu approach is based on the view that there are many plausible and reasonable versions of the CPI. A variety of alternatives should be offered to meet the preferences of CPI users.*

accused of kowtowing to political pressure. On the other hand, if the BLS does not make changes, the old complaints will continue and the agency will be seen as unresponsive.

I am proposing a resolution to the CPI controversy that is not related to the technical issues entailed in measuring quality or accounting for substitution, one that is also applicable to other official data series. I am suggesting that the CPI "problem" has been framed by an approach to official data that can only lead to continued conflict: the assumption that there is but one theoretically correct CPI. Even if perfection cannot be fully achieved in practice, proponents of this erroneous approach believe that statistical policy should at least aim at approximating a particular idealized index. My menu approach, in contrast, is based on the view that there are many plausible and reasonable versions of the CPI. I argue that a variety of alternatives should be offered to meet the preferences of CPI users.

Taylorism or Choice?

In the late nineteenth century, management guru Frederick W. Taylor argued that there was "one right way" for factory production tasks to be accomplished. By using "scientific" methods, that one right way could be both determined and imposed on factory workers. Nowadays, of course, the rigidity of Taylorism has fallen from grace in management circles. What is peculiar is that Taylorism should continue to be applied by knowledgeable economists to the quest for a single, perfect price index.

Economics, after all, is often defined as the science of *choice*. And Taylorism implies that there is no choice. Suppose that, for example, I were to argue that the public would be best served by having government and academic experts design an ideal automobile for consumers. Suppose that I further proposed thereafter that only one ideal model should be available. Most economists would recoil in horror at such a proposition. They would point to the varied preferences of automobile consumers. Some consumers prefer full-size cars; others want compacts. Some like sporty convertibles; others prefer utilitarian sedans. Why should a group of experts, however well-meaning or technically proficient, impose their will on others?

Taylorism and Official Data

If the one-right-way approach is not particularly appealing for automobiles, then consider the way major economic data series, including the CPI, are typically produced. Essentially, government experts—sometimes advised or critiqued by official task forces (such as the Boskin Commission)—design a methodology of data collection, assembly, and presentation. The end product is then presented to the public as the "official" Consumer Price Index (or Producer Price Index or gross domestic product [GDP] or other series). This approach to official statistics is simply "data-Taylorism." Why is Taylorism still the underlying methodology of official data?

There are several justifications for the current system of CPI production that might be cited. First, government has been perceived as a "neutral" source of data. A price index produced by, say, the American Association of Retired Persons might be suspect; perhaps such an index would be deliberately designed to exaggerate inflation and pump up social security benefits. Second, the government has the authority to compel or induce cooperation by data respondents. Absent such authority, failure to obtain cooperation could produce undesirable biases in data collection. Third, official statistics are public goods. Particularly for general indexes such as the CPI, it is not clear that there would be a sufficient private market to make collection and sale profitable. Even if the CPI were sold commercially, it would be difficult to prevent knowledge of it from being disseminated without payment.

Note, however, that these arguments basically support having the government as the primary collector and disseminator of major economic data such as the CPI. They do not speak to the issue of whether a *choice* of price indexes (or any other major series) should be provided by government statistical agencies. They do not support data-Taylorism.

Criteria for the CPI

Let me propose four criteria for the CPI that seem to characterize the needs of its varied users. The first three criteria are transparency, accordance with economic theory, and consistency, all objectives on which different users place differing weights. The fourth and final criterion is accuracy, a purported goal of all users. As will be seen, these criteria do not lead to a single CPI. Indeed, they can easily conflict with one another.

Transparency

The basic concept of the CPI should be transparent, that is, easy for those who are not economists, and who are affected by the CPI, to understand. For example, some union contracts have escalator clauses that gear wage adjustments to the CPI. And, as noted above, the CPI is used to index social security benefits as well other government benefits and to adjust income tax brackets.

The current CPI methodology, a Laspeyres index with weights based on the budget patterns of a "typical" consumer in some base period, is certainly transparent. It tells us what that consumer's buying habits in the base period would cost today.

If the CPI has risen by, say, 10 percent since the base period, it means that the basket of goods consumed back then costs 10 percent more now. What could be clearer? On the other hand, as many critics of the CPI have noted, this clarity comes at the cost of a departure from the economic theory of the consumer.

Accordance with Economic Theory

This criterion appears to have been the goal of the Boskin Commission, which argued that the CPI should approximate as closely as possible a true "cost of living" index. What model or theory did the Commission have in mind for its true cost of living index? Not surprisingly, the Commission was thinking of the textbook microeconomic model of a rational consumer making choices among products to maximize utility.

Most economists would acknowledge that the question of how much happiness money can buy is unanswerable in absolute terms. But they often believe (and teach) that it is possible to answer a less challenging question: How much money would I have to give you today to make you as happy as you were in some previous period? It is really that question that has guided criticisms of the CPI. The fixed-basket Laspeyres approach of the BLS does not provide the answer, critics note, because it denies the possibility of product substitution as relative prices shift. If the price of apples rises relative to the price of bananas, consumers can buy more bananas and fewer apples. They won't stick to the base-period basket and so can be made whole for inflation by an amount less than a fixed-basket index suggests. The make-whole amount, economists such as those on the Boskin Commission argue, should be the basis of the CPI.

A rise in the price of beer makes beer-drinkers worse off but has no effect on teetotalers. The average consumer is a cross between drinkers and teetotalers.

Unfortunately, standard economic theory offers less guidance to construction of a CPI than is often understood. Assume for the moment that the theory is an accurate representation of a single consumer at a moment in time. Assume that we have an index, which perfectly accords with theory. Even so, the index surely cannot simultaneously represent *all* consumers with their diverse incomes and tastes. A rise in the price of beer makes beer-drinkers worse off but has no effect on teetotalers. The average consumer is a cross between drinkers and teetotalers. If indexed social security benefits rose in response to beer prices, beer drinkers would be shortchanged. And teetotalers would receive a windfall. There is no theoretically correct way of adding up the conflicting welfare changes of these two groups in response to the adjustment. Consumer theory cannot even represent the *changing* tastes of a single consumer over time. It is premised on an unchanging utility function.

In short, a CPI based on the standard economic model is not a self-evident choice for all data users. Yet—imperfect though it actually is—such a theory-based CPI is certainly of interest for various purposes. Some users—certainly the members of the Boskin Commission—would like to see inflation measured that way. And if there is one fundamental axiom of economic theory, it is that there is no accounting for anyone's tastes.

Consistency

Macroeconomists and monetary policy-makers are often concerned with the relationship between inflation and the level of real economic activity. Generally, such users want to examine past relationships between inflation and activity, whether through econometric techniques or otherwise. These relationships are then used to predict the implications of current economic activity and policy. But if the measurement of inflation is constantly being changed, an acceleration or deceleration of inflation can be obscured. It becomes difficult to know if an observed acceleration or deceleration is a reflection of the actual trend in inflation or is merely a statistical artifact. Appropriate policy-making is made more difficult if measurement is based on a rubber yardstick. A consistently produced CPI facilitates the making of judgments about inflation trends.

Is the actual CPI produced using a constant methodology? In fact, it is not. During the 1990s, the BLS incorporated the following changes (among others) into the index, in part in response to the ongoing criticisms by economists of the CPI:

1991: Hedonic pricing introduced for apparel[4]
1991: Greater recognition of discount air fares
1992: Improved imputation methods for new product models
1994: Quality improvement recognized for reformulated gasoline
1995: Generic pricing recognized when drugs lose patent protection
1995: "Seasoning" procedures introduced for food to eliminate upward bias
1996: "Seasoning" extended to other products
1997: New procedures for pricing hospital services
1998: Hedonic pricing of home computers

These and other changes tended to produce lower rates of recorded inflation. And each change has a reasonable rationale behind it. As new procedures were being phased in, economists marveled about how much less inflation-prone the 1990s appeared, relative to earlier decades. Were they right? Or did the decisions of experts at the BLS and the criticisms of outside academics simply make it seem so? If consistency over time were a high priority of the data producers, we would not have to ask.

Accuracy

Finally, it is hard to quarrel with the virtue of data "accuracy." If accuracy is taken simply to mean the collection of precise data at the most detailed level, there is little controversy. When CPI data collectors record the price of bananas, we want them to ascertain the right price (although even defining the right price is more complicated than it sounds). Once we go beyond this level of detail, however, the concept of accuracy can be fuzzy. The myriad product and service prices that are gathered must be averaged together. Different weighting schemes will produce different results. Determining whether those schemes should be linear, geometric, fixed, chained, base-period, or end-period is at the heart of much of the CPI debate.

The product quality issue is often considered to be one of accuracy. Is the CPI accurately reflecting changes in the value of products that are the result of new product attributes? A newly purchased personal computer has more speed, memory, and other desirable features than one bought a decade ago. Surely it would be inaccurate simply to track the price of a personal computer over time without adjusting the selling price for quality change. But making that obvious point does not automatically suggest a precise methodology for adjusting the price.

Price adjustments for quality are inevitably subjective, even when performed with the elegance of regression analysis and hedonic pricing. As anyone who has ever run a regression knows, alternative—but reasonable—specifications produce alternative results. Ultimately, the price adjustment for quality change is a judgment call over which CPI users can disagree.

Consider Figure 1, which shows the change in the price of new cars from 1967 to 1997 as measured by four alternative indexes. The average nominal price of a new car has increased more than sixfold during that three-decade period. However, consumers have shifted to more expensive models during this period, exaggerating the seeming price increase. If we hold car quality constant, but recognize the added costs of mandated equipment (for safety and air pollution), the price increase would be a little over fourfold. If we assume that consumers value these mandates at cost, the increase is a bit under threefold. And if we assume that mandates and other quality changes are all valued by consumers at cost, the increase factor is about 2.6. It is this last assumption that is used by the BLS in the CPI component for new cars.

Surely, the range between 2.6 and 6+ is a wide one within which disagreement is possible about the appropriate methodology. For example, if mandated equipment is really valued at cost by consumers, why was it necessary to apply the mandate? Under this assumption producers would have offered the equipment and consumers would have bought it. In short, the measurement of quality is tricky.

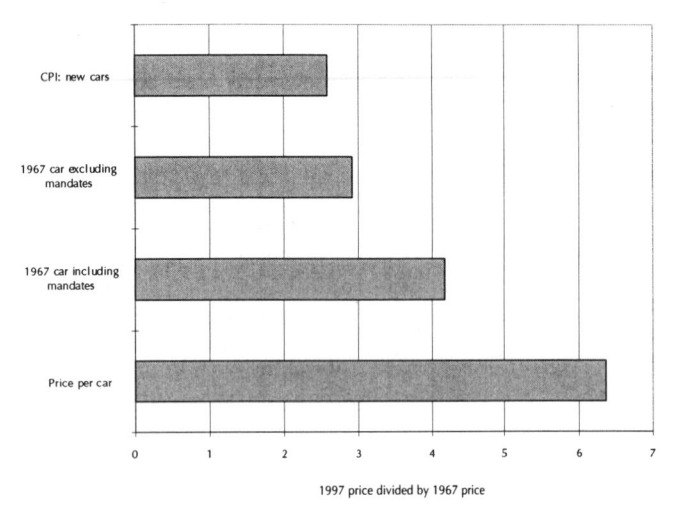

Figure 1. Alternative Measures of New Car Price Change: 1967–1997

Source: American Automobile Manufacturers Association.

A Menu Approach

Different users have different tastes with regard to transparency, accordance with theory, and consistency in the CPI. And while all users want the index to be accurate, there will inevitably be disagreement on what accuracy entails. The solution, therefore, is to respond as the private market does when there are different preferences for goods. In such a case, the private market typically offers a choice. Indexes should be offered to meet the preferences of different groups of users. The idea of a single, official CPI should be downplayed. Instead, users—even Congress, when it decides to index benefits or taxes—should be offered alternative CPIs. Users should make the choice of which index they will employ, not the Bureau of Labor Statistics.

Figure 2. Hypothetical Menu of Consumer Price Index Inflation Rates

What would this menu approach mean in practice? At present there are two CPIs offered, one weighted for "all urban consumers" (CPI-U) and the other for "urban wage earners and clerical workers" (CPI-W). In fact, however, there is only a slight weighting difference between the two, and they seldom give readings of inflation that diverge significantly. Under the menu proposal, CPI inflation would be presented in a matrix, something like that shown in Figure 2.

The hypothetical menu provides users with a choice of methodology, along both the substitution and quality control dimensions. On the vertical axis, users have a choice between a fixed-weight Laspeyres index—the current methodology, which has the advantage of transparency. The in-between option is a geometrically weighted index, along the lines that BLS has been publishing on an experimental basis. Such a weighting scheme arguably comes closer to the economic model of consumer choice. Finally, for those who want an even more elaborate index, a chained Fisher ideal of the type now used for the GDP deflator is offered.[5] This type of index most closely approximates the theoretical preferences of the Boskin Commission, but it is the least transparent. Try explaining to your grandmother that her social security adjustments are based on the chained geometric mean of a Laspeyres and Paasche index!

The market-basket updates that accompany the three options are also varied. They range from the current practice of updating the basket about every ten years to updating annually. Cases can be made for frequent and infrequent adjustments. Again, user preference is paramount.

Quality control—the horizontal axis of Figure 2—would also vary from modest to aggressive. The least aggressive approach would be that used before hedonic pricing began to make its way into the CPI. The in-between approach would be the current approach, as introduced in 1998. And the most aggressive would involve hedonic approaches to a broad range of products. Presumably, the members of the Boskin Commission would be most happy with the lower right corner of the matrix in Figure 2. Other users might pick another location. And all users, by studying the range of figures reported in the nine boxes, would have an indication of the sensitivity of the measured inflation rate to alternative approaches.

Of course, the menu of indexes offered could be different from Figure 2 along the two dimensions shown. There could be more or different options available. And there might be choices along other dimensions. For example, there has long been demand for a CPI based on the consumption habits of the elderly for purposes of social security indexation. While the BLS could not produce every possible variant, it could do more than it now does to meet user preferences. But doing so means abandoning data-Taylorism.

Political Advantages of a Menu Approach

When an index such as the CPI is used for resource allocation, it is inevitably subject to politicization. I have already noted the past threats against the BLS that have arisen in Congress to force changes in CPI methodology. That problem is built into the current Taylorist approach. If there is only one right official CPI, and if that one right index is used for budgetary indexation, politicians will inevitably want to influence the index's movements. (The current controversy over whether the year 2000 Census of Population should be based on a strict head count or employ sampling is another example of this tendency.) But if a menu of indexes is offered, including those that meet the criteria politicians say they want, then they are free to choose that version.

Of course, with a menu of indexes, there could be no hiding behind the BLS in making such choices. A politician who wanted to limit increases in social security benefits or to raise taxes could pick a version of the CPI expected to rise more slowly than others. He or she could cite the Boskin Commission and hope voters would buy the explanation. But the choice would be political and voters could then decide whether the selection made was what they wanted. Meanwhile, policy-makers concerned with inflation, professional economists, and wage-setters negotiating union contracts, could make their own choices of the CPI, unfettered by political vagaries.

Follow the Precedent

Is there any precedent for the menu approach for the CPI? To a limited extent, there is. The various underlying subcomponents of the CPI are offered—for example, food prices—along with the overall index. And certain subindexes are routinely published, such as the "core" CPI that excludes volatile energy and food prices. But all of these series are based on the same underlying methodology.

A better precedent for the menu approach is found in the unemployment rate data produced by the BLS, where variants are presented that deviate from the standard definition. For example, one variant includes an allowance for part-timers who are seeking full-time jobs. Another incorporates "discouraged" workers. This menu of unemployment rates was developed because over time the BLS found that it was the best way to meet complaints of arbitrariness in the official definition. Providing alternatives allowed critics to pick their preferred unemployment rate. My proposal is to extend the menu approach to the CPI and to other official data series.

Notes

1. Advisory Commission to Study the Consumer Price Index, "Towards a More Accurate Measure of the Cost of Living," *Daily Labor Report*, December 5, 1996, special report, pp. S10–S53.

2. For a detailed critique of the Boskin report, see Dean Baker, ed., *Getting Prices Right: The Debate Over the Consumer Price Index* (Armonk, NY: M.E. Sharpe, 1998).

3. "BLS Commissioner Says CPI Will Not Become Politicized," *Daily Labor Report*, February 23, 1995, pp. A1–A2; "Blue Dogs to Press for Downward CPI Change in 105th Congress, Stenholm says," *Daily Labor Report*, December 6, 1996, pp. A13–A14.

4. Hedonic pricing uses regression analysis to break a product down into attributes and applies implicit prices to each attribute. For example, attributes of a house could include lot size, number of bedrooms, neighborhood, age of the structure, and so on.

5. A chained Fisher ideal index requires end-period weights. Thus, it could not be offered monthly but could be offered annually once each year's consumption pattern was surveyed. This approach is used for the price deflators, which are part of the GDP accounts. Quarterly GDP deflator figures are fixed-weighted until the annual data are published.

UNRAVELING AN ECONOMIC ENIGMA

OVERWORKED *AND* UNDEREMPLOYED

BARRY BLUESTONE AND STEPHEN ROSE

Barry Bluestone is the Frank L. Boyden Professor of Political Economy at the University of Massachusetts at Boston and a senior fellow at the John W. McCormack Institute of Public Affairs.

Stephen Rose is Senior Research Economist at the Educational Testing Service.

At least since the 1980s people have said that they work "too hard"—that they are spending too much time on the job, with too little left for family, chores, or leisure. In 1991 this frustration became conventional wisdom thanks to Juliet Schor's best-seller, *The Overworked American*, which demonstrated that Americans worked an average of 163 more hours in 1990 than they had in 1970—or the equivalent of nearly an extra month of full-time work per year. According to Schor, men were working two and a half more weeks per year; women an average of seven and a half more weeks. These were startling statistics, reversing more than a century of gradual reduction in working time as society became richer and more productive. If Americans were working this much longer, then they were not only overworked by traditional U.S. standards, they were setting new world records.

But critics challenged Schor's data and pointed to a logical flaw in her argument. Today, more people work part-time because they can't find full-time work; more are temping or working as short-term independent contractors. Job insecurity is rampant, and other statistics show that the number of weekly hours on the typical job has actually shrunk steadily since World War II. It seemed implausible that Americans were simultaneously "overworked" and "underemployed," thus prompting the question: Were Schor and all the harried Americans who cheered her book's appearance wrong?

Not necessarily. It's possible, for instance, that we are mixing apples and oranges. The number of contingent jobs and average weekly hours refers to "jobs," not people. If individuals are moonlighting more—working multiple jobs in any given week—then the average workweek reported by employers can still shrink while the average workweek reported by workers can actually expand. It is also possible that one sector of the workforce is "overworked" while another portion is "underemployed."

But the real story turns out to be even more intriguing and complicated. Based on a new analysis of the data, we have found that Americans are indeed working longer than they once did, if not quite as much as Schor would have us believe. But, more importantly, we have also found that many Americans are both overworked and underemployed. Because of growing job instability, workers face a "feast and famine" cycle: They work as much as they can when work is available to compensate for short workweeks, temporary layoffs, or permanent job loss that may follow. What's more, while American families as a whole are putting in more time, that work isn't producing significant increases in living standards. For the typical two-breadwinner household, having both parents work longer hours may not mean an extra trip to Disney World or nicer clothes for school; more likely, it means keeping up car payments or just covering the costs of food and housing.

Multitasked

At one extreme are workers like Bill Cecil, a 50-year-old United Auto Worker member recently portrayed in the *Wall Street Journal*. Averaging four hours a day in overtime and volunteering to work seven days a week for most of the year, Cecil clocks an average of 84 hours a week at a Chrysler plant in Trenton, Michigan, where he works as a skilled millwright. In the past two years, Cecil's extraordinary work effort has paid off. He has averaged more than $110,000 a year in gross pay. Sacrificing, by his own admission, "freedom and time with family," he works as much overtime as the company will let him in order to help send his four kids to college, fill his lunch pail with lobster salad rather than luncheon meat, and underwrite his golf habit, which he indulges whenever a vacation or a layoff permits. While Bill Cecil's case is exceptional, 70 percent of the skilled-trades workers at his engine production facility are working at least some extra hours most weeks.

> Individuals may not be more overworked than before, but families certainly are.

28. Overworked *and* Underemployed

Increasing overtime is becoming more commonplace throughout the manufacturing industry. For the first four out of five post-World War II business cycles, average weekly hours of work for production and nonsupervisory workers in manufacturing remained roughly constant, varying only slightly between 40.1 and 40.4 hours. However, during the current business cycle, from 1989 to 1996, the average workweek has jumped to 41 hours—with average overtime reaching a post-World War II peak of 4.7 hours per week in 1994.

A *Fortune* magazine poll of Fortune 500 CEOs in 1990 found a similar tendency toward more work among executives. Sixty-two percent of CEOs reported their executives were working longer hours than they had ten years before. They reported that nearly nine out of ten of their high-level executives normally put in more than 50 hours a week while three-fifths of middle managers did the same.

Moonlighting is also on the rise. In 1979, 4.9 percent of U.S. workers reported working more than one job during the same workweek. By 1995, the percentage was up to 6.4 percent. Virtually all of this increase has occurred among women, who now represent nearly half of all multiple job holders. According to a recent survey sponsored by the *Washington Post*, the Kaiser Family Foundation, and Harvard University, two out of five families report they have sent an additional family member into the paid labor force or had an existing working member take on an additional job—simply because the family needed extra money.

Working more makes sense from both the employers' and the employees' perspectives. Manufacturing firms like Chrysler do not hesitate to schedule large amounts of overtime when product demand outstrips supply, even if it means paying time and a half, double time, or triple time during holidays, because it is still less expensive than covering the high fixed costs of recruitment, training, and possibly the underwriting of future severance pay associated with hiring new workers. For salaried white-collar employees who are exempt from hours regulations, the arithmetic is even simpler—the extra hours often cost the company nothing at all.

Fortune 500 CEOs and their executives say they need to put in overtime just to keep up with global competition and compensate for internal restructuring or middle-level management downsizing. But why would blue-collar workers so willingly give up leisure or family time? Schor has identified one factor, which she calls "capitalism's squirrel cage"—an "insidious cycle of work and spend" where people work long hours to support a material lifestyle always a bit beyond their reach. But that suggests the increased work hours are buying a rising standard of affluence, which is somewhat misleading. Indeed, a more compelling reason for extra work is the slowdown in wage growth during the past two decades. Between 1947 and 1973, real hourly wages for production and nonsupervisory employees rose by 79 percent. Since 1973 hourly wages have actually declined by more than 13 percent. For many workers, working longer hours is the only way to compensate for lower hourly wages.

Of course when pollsters ask people, "Would you like to work less?", most say "yes." But when pollsters include a caveat—that fewer working hours would mean less take-home pay—the answer changes sharply. Over the last 20 years, surveys with this appropriately worded question have been answered with great consistency: Approximately 60 percent say they prefer their current work schedule and pay. Of those who express a desire to change their working time, more people, by about three to one, express the desire to work longer rather than shorter hours.

Union negotiators in the U.S. know this, which is why they so rarely make reducing work time a priority in collective bargaining. In fact, many workers complain bitterly whenever management prerogative or union contract restrict overtime hours. In a "real experiment" on this issue, New York's state government in 1984 began allowing their workers to take voluntary reductions in work schedules without affecting their career statuses. The plan was flexible and permitted workers to move on and off "V-time." Since its inception, however, the program has never enrolled more than 2 percent of the workforce.

This expressed desire for more hours is consistent with the trend toward more contingent work. At the same time that many workers are looking to expand their number of working hours, the economy has shifted steadily from manufacturing to sectors like retail trade and services, where part-time work is more common. One estimate for 1995 places the total number of contingent workers (part-time, temporary, and contract workers) at close to 35 million—28 percent of the civilian labor force. Of these, 18 percent of the workforce or 23 million workers were part-time, working 35 hours or less per week. Smaller in absolute numbers, but growing much faster, is the temporary workforce,

> In what is supposed to be an "overworked" nation, the typical job is now part-time.

which between 1982 and 1995 more than tripled to 1.4 million workers. Manpower, Inc. now boasts it is the largest employer in America, submitting more W-2 forms to the Internal Revenue Service each year than any other firm. The number of contract and self-employed workers is also growing rapidly, indeed explosively. The U.S. General Accounting Office has reported that the number of individuals who are self-employed or working under personal contract was growing at more than 13 percent a year in the late 1980s. By 1988, 9.5 million Americans worked for themselves either full-time or as a supplement to regular or part-time employment.

A large proportion of the contingent workforce has chosen voluntarily to work part-time, as temporaries, or as independent contractors. Still, involuntary part-time employment is growing much faster than the voluntary variety. In 1973, 19 percent of total part-time employment was accounted for by individuals who wanted full-time jobs but could not find them. By 1993, this proportion was up to 29 percent. The incidence of involuntary part-time work is especially high among men. In 1985, one in four part-time women reported their part-time status was involuntary; nearly half of all part-time men did so.

For the labor force as a whole, these numbers begin to add up. Since 1994, the Bureau of Labor Statistics (BLS) has been compiling a new set of alternative measures of unemployment and underemployment—what the Labor Department calls "labor resource underutilization." In addition to the official unemployment rate, the BLS adds three types of "underutilized" workers: (1) those who have stopped looking for work only because they have become discouraged by their apparent job prospects; (2) those who are "marginally attached" to the civilian labor force; and (3) those who are working part-time only because they cannot find full-time jobs. The "marginally attached" include those who want and are available for a job and have recently searched for work, but have left the official labor force because of such constraints as child care or transportation problems.

The official unemployment rate in 1995 was 5.6 percent with an average of 7.4 million failing to find work each month. Adding discouraged workers to the total brings the "underemployment" rate up to 5.9 percent. Adding the "marginally attached" ups the rate to 6.8 percent. Finally, adding in the involuntarily part-time brings the rate to 10.1 percent. In what was a good year for the economy and employment growth, 1995, the total number of unemployed and underemployed workers reached nearly 13.5 million—one in ten of the total labor force.

All of these trends contribute to the decline in the average workweek reported by employers since at least World War II. As the chart on this page indicates (see "The Shrinking Workweek"), from 1947 to 1958 the average workweek was nearly 40 hours, the "full time" standard for much

THE SHRINKING WORKWEEK

Since World War II, the average workweek, as reported by employers, has declined.

Years	Average Week* In Hours
1947-1958	39.5
1959-1972	38.2
1973-1978	36.2
1979-1988	35.0
1989-1996	34.5

*Total private-sector employment

Source: Council of Economic Advisers, *Economic Report of the President, 1987*, Table B-41, and Council of Economic Advisers, *Economic Report of the President, 1996*, Table B-43.

of this century. In the most recent business cycle, the average workweek fell below 35 hours, the cutoff normally used to define a "part-time" job. Ironically, in what is supposed to be an "overworked" nation, the typical job is now part-time! Again, we should ask, "overworked," "underemployed," or perhaps both?

28. Overworked *and* Underemployed

WHOSE NUMBERS SHOULD WE BELIEVE?

Whether we believe that Americans are overworked or underemployed depends, in part, on whether we believe the work time data. Many economists question Juliet Schor's findings and its not hard to understand why: The idea that Americans are, on average, spending the equivalent of an extra month a year in paid work seems almost unbelievable.

But is it? According to one recent study, Schor's basic finding holds up, but her estimates of overwork appear somewhat exaggerated. Using data from the Current Population Survey, Larry Mishel and Jared Bernstein of the Economic Policy Institute have re-estimated annual work hours for various years. Their research confirms the general proposition of increased annual working hours, but for a comparable period (1973 to 1992) their estimate is only three-fifths as large as Schor's. They calculate that in 1973, the average workweek (for both employed and self-employed workers toiling in the public as well as the private sector) was 38.4 hours. The average work year was 43.2 weeks, yielding an annual estimate of 1,659 hours of work. By 1992, the average workweek had climbed by 0.6 hours while the average work year had increased to 45.2 weeks. Hence, annual average hours had risen to 1,759, an increase of 100 hours or 6 percent—but 63 hours less than Schor's estimate.

Yet even these more reasonable figures raise questions. Note that the steady decline in the average workweek reported by employers as shown in the "Shrinking Workweek" chart suggests that for average hours per job to decline while average hours per worker increases, there would have to be enormous increases in moonlighting. This seems implausible, because even with the recent increase in moonlighting, only 8 million workers out of a workforce of more than 125 million report holding more than one job.

The problem may be with the very survey data upon which Schor, Mishel, and Bernstein all rely. The estimates of hours worked come from the March Current Population Survey (CPS) for each year, which the U.S. Census Bureau and the Department of Labor compile annually. Among several dozen questions about labor market activity, the CPS asks respondents to report "hours worked last week" and "usual weekly hours of work last year." Individuals have only a few seconds to answer these questions. In making what may be a wild guess, particularly for those people

5 ❖ EMPLOYMENT, PRICES, AND THE BUSINESS CYCLE

INDIVIDUALS WORKING HARDER, AGAIN

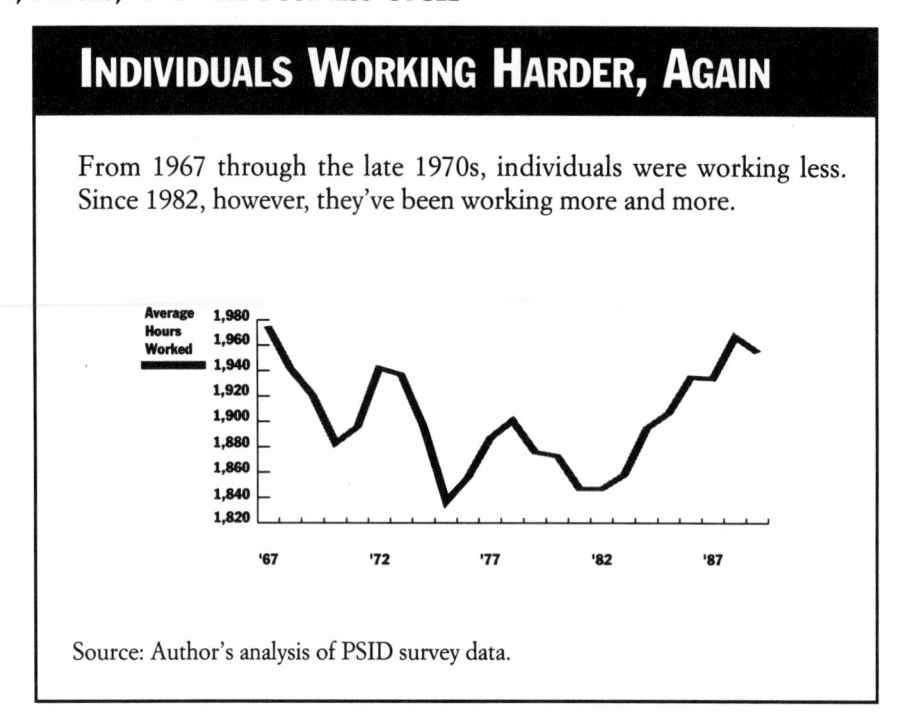

From 1967 through the late 1970s, individuals were working less. Since 1982, however, they've been working more and more.

Source: Author's analysis of PSID survey data.

whose hours vary substantially from week to week, the individuals frequently guess high. And the more harried and rushed they feel, the higher they guess. Could you account for the actual number of hours you spent working last week?

A more accurate measure of hours worked comes from special studies that target the work time issue by asking respondents to keep a 24-hour time diary of everything they do over a one- to two-day period. Such time diary surveys were first carried out by the University of Michigan Survey Research Center in 1965 and 1975, and then again by the University of Maryland in 1985. The accuracy of work time estimates derived from this survey approach is presumably superior to CPS measures for two reasons. First, the exercise's sole purpose is studying the use of time; second, respondents do not have to plum their memories for what they did a week ago or try to calculate instantly how many weeks they worked all of last year.

Sure enough, a comparison of CPS-estimated hours of work and diary entries suggests that people overestimate how much they work—and that the overestimates get bigger the more hours they put in. According to John Robinson of the University of Maryland and Ann Bostrom of Georgia Tech University, who studied the two sets of surveys, among those estimating 20 to 44 weekly hours, the CPS-type estimates were only slightly higher than the diary entries. But among workers claiming to "usually" work more than 55 hours per week, the gap was 10 hours or more per week. Robinson and Bostrom concluded that "the diary data suggest that only rare individuals put in more than a 55- to 60-hour workweek, with those estimating 60 or more hours on the job averaging closer to 53-hour weeks." Moreover, using the diary studies for 1965, 1975, and 1985, Robinson and Bostrom found a systematic increase in the size of the estimate gap over time. The gap rose from just one hour in 1965 to four hours in 1975 to six hours in 1985, which is more than enough to account for the alleged "overwork" that Schor and Mishel and Bernstein claim to have found.

When Robinson and Bostrom analyzed diaries for 1965, 1975, and 1985 more carefully, they found only small changes in hours worked among those who normally work 20 hours or more per week. Between 1965 and 1985, men's average hours declined by 0.7 hours per week from 47.1 to 46.4 hours, while working women's hours increased by the same amount (0.7) from 39.9 to 40.6 hours. If these numbers are believed, then the source of increased hours worked that Schor observed must be new entrants to the labor force—again, many of them women—and part-timers who have increased their part-time hours. Of course, whether this should be counted as "overwork" or not is a matter of deeply divided opinion.

SCHORING UP THE FINDINGS

What can we make of such sharply different findings? To answer this question, we decided to pursue still another approach, using yet another type of survey instrument. So far, all of the research on working hours has relied on data snapshots at different points in time using either the CPS or diary information. An alternative approach is to use longitudinal data—in other words, information about the same people gathered year after year—to track working hours. Using this information, we can follow the work time pattern of, say, a particular age group over several years—as one could with CPS data—or follow the same workers over time. Here we do both in order to provide completely new estimates of work time. We use the Panel Study of Income Dynamics (PSID), a data set of families that the University of Michigan Survey Research Center has been following since 1968. The long-running nature of the PSID permits a comparison of working time during two ten-year periods—the 1970s (1969–1979) and the 1980s (1979–1989). (These periods had similar growth rates in real output per person and in job creation, and each encompassed two complete business cycles. Hence, the comparison is a reasonable one to make.) We also combine the two decades of data to follow a particular age group (in this case, prime age workers with job experience) in order to derive typical trends in annual work hours for men and women, whites and blacks, and for segments of the population with differing amounts of schooling.

While the PSID does not provide the full detail nor perhaps the precision of hours estimates culled from the diary method, its data on hours worked is superior to that of the CPS. First, PSID asks respondents to detail their work experience by recalling how many days they were on vacation, on sick leave, on strike, or on leave due to other family members' illness. It then asks respondents to answer questions about regular hours of work per week and weeks worked on his or her main job. Then it poses the same questions concerning up to three other jobs respondents held during the year. Finally, all of this information is combined to yield an estimate of annual hours. Obviously, this approach suffers from recall problems, much as the CPS does, but the detail on each job presumably permits a better estimate.

The first part of our analysis is based on computing the average hours of work in each year from 1967 through 1989 for prime age workers (ages 25-54). In this case, we use the PSID as a series of cross sections where the sample individuals in each year vary as younger individuals enter the prime age group and aging workers leave it. We limit our sample in each year to those who reported hours of work, eliminating those from consideration who were out of the labor force in a given year. We generated separate estimates for men and women, and broke the findings down by race and by education. The graph on the preceding page ("Individuals Working Harder, Again") provides the results for all prime age workers.

There is clear evidence of variation related to the business cycle. Average hours dip sharply in 1970–71, in 1975, and then again during the steep 1981–82 recession. But overwhelming the business cycle is a U-shaped trend in hours of work. Average hours appear to decline through the early 1980s and then begin a sharp recovery throughout the decade. If we compare 1979 and 1989, the last two business cycle peaks, there does indeed appear to be an increase of 79 hours per year for the average worker. But over a longer period, this increase marks not so much a startling increase as a return to levels that prevailed in the late 1960s.

To obtain a more accurate estimate of the trend in hours, we ran a statistical exercise to control for the business cycle. Having done this, we find a small, but statistically significant, overall upward trend in annual hours for prime age workers as a group. The trend amounts to only 3.3 hours per year. Hence, over a 20-year period, we find a 66-hour increase in annual work—the equivalent of 1.5 weeks of full-time work per year. This is well below Schor's estimate of 163 hours and a third below that wh[ich] Mishel and Bernstein found. But, importantly, the trend is decidedly upward, in contrast to the essentially flat line Robinson and Bostrom found for the 1965–1985 period using the diary method.

Among men, working hours declined slightly, after we control for the business cycle. But for women, hours increased significantly. Indeed, our estimate of 18.8 additional hours per year translates into a 20-year total somewhat greater than even Schor's estimate. We also find significant differences in the hours trajectories by race. Reflecting trends well documented elsewhere, our estimate of a decline of 7.7 hours per year for black men translates into an average work year in the late 1980s more than 150 hours shorter than in the late 1960s. In 1989, we estimate that black men aver-

5 ❖ EMPLOYMENT, PRICES, AND THE BUSINESS CYCLE

MORE TOTAL HOURS . . .

Whatever the trends for individual workers, the change for families is clear: The average hours worked by husbands and wives have climbed steadily over the last two decades.

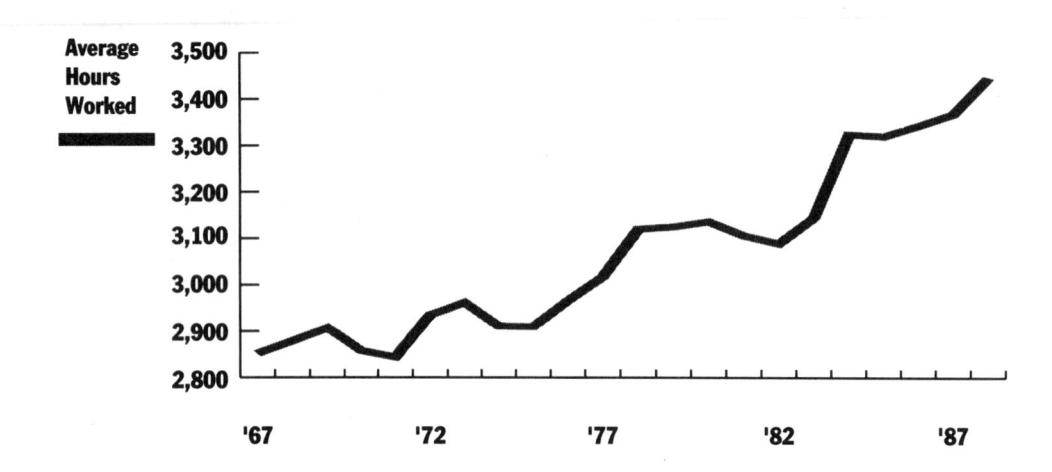

Source: Author's analysis of PSID survey data.

aged only 1,950 hours per year compared with just under 2,300 hours for white men. Higher unemployment rates are responsible for part of this difference. Shorter workweeks explain the remainder. This suggests that the continuing earnings gap between white and black men is only partly accounted for by differences in wage rates—the traditional measure of labor market "success." A large amount of the gap is also due to differences in hours worked. Wage rates matter, but what is really killing black men in the labor market is their inability to find full-time, full-year jobs as readily as their white counterparts.

The racial gap in hours worked among women shows an intriguing time pattern. On an annual basis, there appears to have been virtually no gap in work hours in 1967. The gap then widened significantly, so that by the mid-1970s black women were working almost 200 more hours per year than white women. White women caught up again, and by 1989 white and black women were working virtually the same amount. To close the gap, white women's cycle-adjusted hours had to rise substantially faster than that of black women. This is precisely what happened. Over 20 years, white women's annual hours increased by the equivalent of 10.3 weeks of full-time work, nearly double the 5.4 weeks for black women.

As a general rule, then, there has been a slight reduction in men's work hours and a large increase in women's hours. Given these trends, we can ask what has happened to family work effort as America has undergone the transition from the prototypical "Ozzie and Harriet" division of labor of the 1950s to the dual-career family of the 1980s and 1990s.

To investigate the trend in family work effort, we have estimated the combined hours of work for "prime age" families in which both husband and wife are working. The long-term trend is shown in the graph on this page ("More Total Hours..."). There is a clear and nearly unbroken trend toward much greater work effort, interrupted only modestly by the recessions of 1971, 1974–75, and 1980–1982. By 1988, prime age working couples were putting in an average of 3,450 hours per year in combined employment, up from 2,850 two decades before. (Data for family hours and earnings in our version of the PSID were incomplete for 1989, so we use 1988 as the end point for this analysis.)

Adjusting for business cycle effects, we calculate that for all husband-wife working couples, family work effort increased by more than 32 hours per year for each year of the 1970s and 1980s. Hence, in the span of just two decades, working husband-wife couples increased their annual market work input by a cycle-adjusted 684 hours or 4 months of full-time work. The typical dual-earner couple at the end of the 1980s was spending an additional day and half on the job every week. If individuals are not more overworked than before, families certainly are.

Increases in family work effort differ significantly depending on race and education. The increase in working hours among white working couples was 60 percent larger than the increase for black couples—a reflection of both the sharp decline in black men's hours and the large increase in white female work effort. More-educated working couples also increased their work effort more than those with less schooling. Those in which the husbands had at least undergraduate college degrees increased their combined work effort by nearly 730 hours compared to an increase of only 490 hours for couples headed by high school dropouts. The "overeducated" are the ones most "overworked."

Has this enormous increase in work effort paid off in terms of increased family earnings? The graph "... and for What?" shows our comparison of hours worked and earnings growth.

For prime age working couples as a group, combined real earnings rose by 18.5 percent between 1973 and 1988. (This represents an increase from $43,851 to $51,955 in 1989 dollars.) Most of this modest increase, however, did not come from improved wages, but from increased work effort. The 18.5 percent increase in real earnings was purchased with a 16.3 percent increase in hours worked. Over the entire 15-year period, the combined average husband-wife hourly wage increased by only 1.8 percent—the equivalent of a real hourly wage increase of less than 30 cents over the entire period, or 2 cents each year!

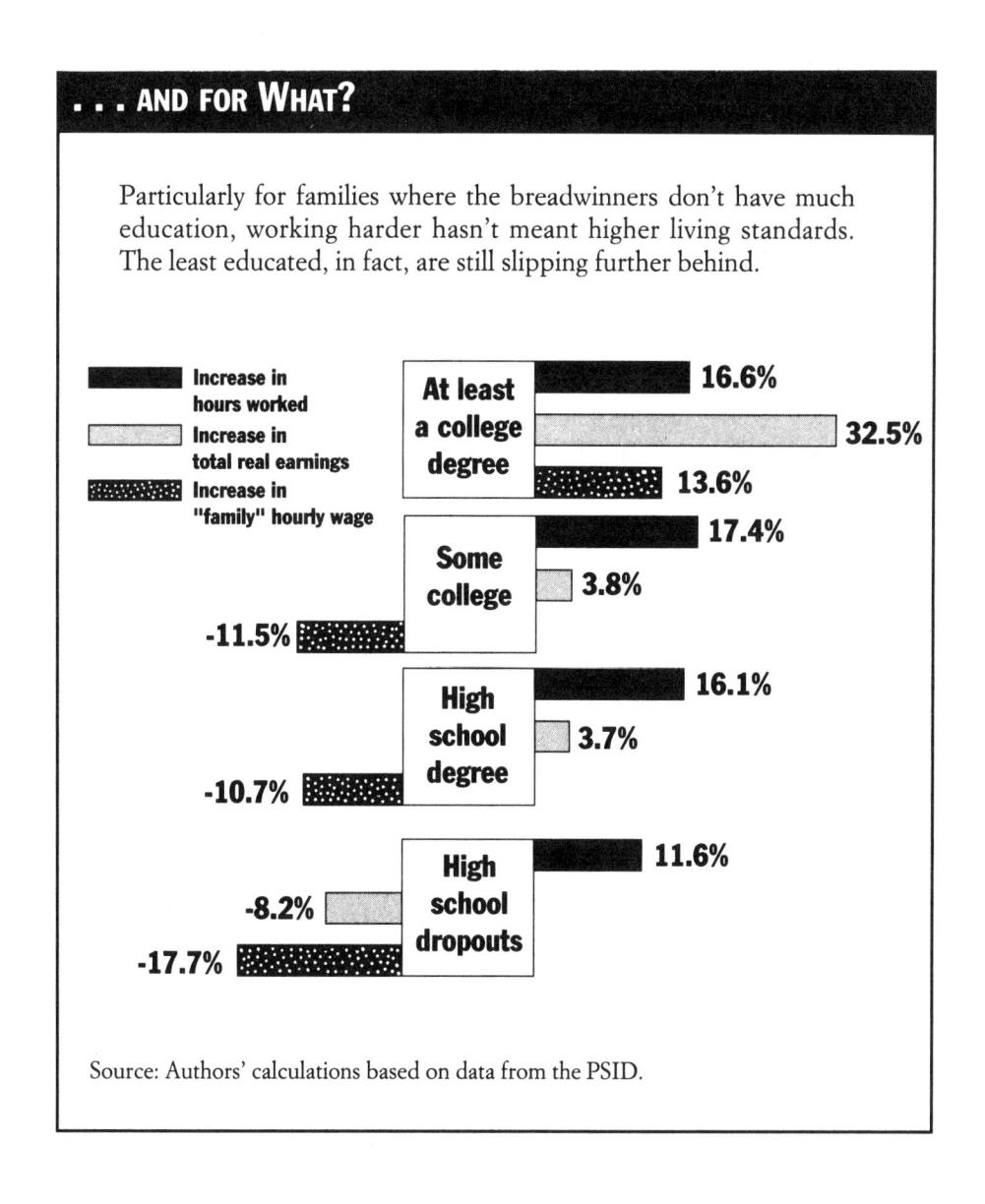

... AND FOR WHAT?

Particularly for families where the breadwinners don't have much education, working harder hasn't meant higher living standards. The least educated, in fact, are still slipping further behind.

Legend:
- Increase in hours worked
- Increase in total real earnings
- Increase in "family" hourly wage

At least a college degree
- 16.6%
- 32.5%
- 13.6%

Some college
- 17.4%
- 3.8%
- -11.5%

High school degree
- 16.1%
- 3.7%
- -10.7%

High school dropouts
- 11.6%
- -8.2%
- -17.7%

Source: Authors' calculations based on data from the PSID.

As such, Schor's "squirrel cage" does not appear to be far off the mark. American mythology holds that long hours will pay off in a steadily increasing standard of living; in other words, sacrificing time with family can pay for a dishwasher or microwave and, down the road, a more expensive college for one's children. Yet from a purely material perspective, all the extra hours from the "average" working family have yielded only a very modest improvement in the amount of goods and services they can buy.

But even this story is too sanguine for most families. When we break down the hours and earnings data by education group the tale gets even more depressing. Most Americans are not working harder so they can afford a fancier minivan; they're just trying to make payments on their old car or cover the rent. When you remove from the equation families headed by a worker with at least a college degree, it turns out that the enormous increase in work effort over the past 20 years has allowed families to maintain their old standard of living—but almost nothing more. For families headed by high school dropouts, the situation is the most dismal. Between 1973 and 1988, such families increased their annual work effort by nearly 12 percent yet ended up with 8 percent less annual income. For families headed by high school graduates or some college, work effort was up by 16 to 17.4 percent, producing less than a 4 percent increase in total earnings. These families are trapped in an *Alice in Wonderland* world, running faster and faster just to stay in the same place. For all of these families, the "family" hourly wage has fallen precipitously, by as much as 17 percent in the case of the high school dropout.

Of course, more work still pays off for one group: families headed by a college graduate. These families increased their work effort by about the same percentage as those headed by high school graduates or those with some college, yet their material consumption standard increased by nearly a full third between 1973 and 1988. Unfortunately, such well-educated families comprise less than a third of all American dual-income families.

Feasting Before the Famine

To this point, we have been concerned with trends in hours worked and earnings for particular demographic groups. We now shift our attention to an equally important issue. What can we say about the year-to-year variation in work hours for individual workers? This is of obvious importance given the debate over the apparent growth in job insecurity. If a worker is insecure about his job, then it is possible he may voluntarily work as much overtime as he can in order to cushion the blow of depressed income from future joblessness. Or, for that matter, he may work extra hours because he has to pay off credit card debts that accumulated in the last bout of underemployment.

To study this issue, we again separate the PSID into two ten-year time frames corresponding to the 1970s (1969-1979) and the 1980s (1979-1989). To focus on prime age workers, we restrict our analysis of each decade to individuals who began at ages 24 to 48 and ended the decade at ages 34 to 58. This prime age range provides a sample of those who, for the most part, are old enough to have completed their formal schooling and not old enough to have begun cutting back their work hours in anticipation of retirement.

To measure inter-year variation in work hours for these prime age workers, we have developed a special measure we call "Hi-Lo." This statistic measures the proportion of individuals in a group who, during a decade, experience at least one year in which they work more than 2,400 hours and at least one year of 1,750 hours or less. The "Hi" value is equivalent to an average workweek of approximately 46 hours or more. The "Lo" value is equivalent to less than 35 hours per week. These cutoffs correspond to common definitions of "overtime" work and "part-time" work.

According to our analysis, among all prime age males, nearly three out of ten workers (28 percent) had at least one year of substantial "overtime" and at least one year of significant "underemployment" during the 1980s. Compared to the 1970s, the proportion of such individuals experiencing such hours variation was up by nearly 8 percent.

For black men, the incidence of Hi-Lo variation is substantially higher than among white men, with 37 percent of black men experiencing this variety of "feast and famine" employment history. Those who have completed a high school diploma or college degree appear to experience less hours variation than those who drop out of high school or do not complete college.

But by the far the strongest indicators of the feast-or-famine syndrome emerge when we break the Hi-Lo numbers down according to earnings levels and the number of job changes. Among men in the lowest 20 percent of the earnings ladder, four out of ten experience Hi-Lo hours variation—more than double those in the top 20 percent. Those who have low earnings even when they are working full-time are the most likely to experience a feast-and-famine work life. Not surprisingly, those who change employers more often face the highest rates of Hi-Lo activity. More than half of prime age men who change employers at least four times in a decade face years of "overtime" and years of "underemployment." For women, the "overworked-underemployed" phenomenon expanded as well between the 1970s and 1980s. In the earlier decade, only 12 percent experienced such Hi-Lo work histories. In the 1980s, nearly 21 percent of women spent their lives on the work time roller coaster.

High school dropouts have seen a substantial rise in Hi-Lo activity between the two decades. But so have college graduates and the top-quintile earners. One might conjecture from these findings that those with the fewest skills and those in the ranks of middle managers have been particular victims of downsizing. Future research with the PSID should be able to provide more evidence to test this hypothesis.

Taken together, the results for men and women suggest that increased job instability has led to increased hours variability for men and increased hours and variability of work for women. While the data presented here cannot prove that male job instability causes men to work more overtime when it is available and at the same time increases women's workforce participation, the results are fully consistent with such a thesis. In short, we can conjecture that "underemployment" of men may be leading to "overwork" for families. Because Dad's work prospects are more uncertain than ever, Mom is working harder than ever before.

In the end, then, it turns out that both Schor and her critics were partially right. There is compelling evidence of both overwork and underemployment not only across the workforce, but for individual workers (particularly men) who may face bouts of full-time work interspersed with years in which part-time hours are the rule. In both the 1970s and the 1980s, more than one-quarter of men experienced a decade in which they worked at least one year of "overwork" (more than 46 hours per week) and at least one year of "underemployment" (less than 35 hours per week). How much of this is voluntary cannot be judged, but the finding is consistent with other research that shows growth in job instability and income insecurity. Adding to this evidence is our finding that those workers who change jobs more than four times in a decade are more than three times as likely to face bouts of "overwork" and "underemployment" as those who have at most one job change during the same period.

The reason for this overwork, ironically, turns out to be underemployment. Men are working overtime to compensate for expected job loss in the future. Women have expanded their work effort to cover for what otherwise would be a sharp reduction in family living standards.

What does this foreshadow for family and community? Americans will not find a better balance between work and leisure, between earning a living and spending time with loved ones, between wage earning and "civic engagement," until the economy provides long-term employment security and rising wages. If past is prologue, the last 25 years of U.S. labor market history should not make us sanguine about the possibilities.

There is serious political talk, now and then, about legislating shorter weeks. But no matter how much we may complain about being overworked and no matter how much we worry about latchkey kids, few American workers will support political action unless it is tied to a much broader set of policies aimed at improving material living standards along with more leisure.

FOR FURTHER READING

Rebecca Blank, "Are Part-Time Jobs Lousy Jobs?" In Gary Burtless, ed., *A Future of Lousy Jobs? The Changing Structure of U.S. Wages* (Brookings Institution, 1990).

John E. Bregger and Steven E. Haugen, "BLS Introduces New Range of Alternative Unemployment Measures," *Monthly Labor Review*, October, 1995.

Polly Callaghan and Heidi Hartmann, *Contingent Work: A Chartbook on Part-Time and Temporary Employment* (Economic Policy Institute, 1991).

Lawrence Mishel and Jared Bernstein, *The State of Working America 1994-95* (M.E. Sharpe, 1994).

John P. Robinson and Ann Bostrom, "The Overestimated Workweek? What Time Diary Measures Suggest," *Monthly Labor Review*, August, 1994.

Stephen J. Rose, "Declining Job Security and the Professionalization of Opportunity," Research Report No. 95-04, National Commission for Employment Policy, 1995.

Juliet Schor, *The Overworked American: The Unexpected Decline of Leisure* (Basic Books, 1991).

The Age-Adjusted Unemployment Rate: An Alternative Measure

Robert Horn and Philip Heap

If we adjust for the age of workers, today's unemployment rate does not look low at all.

The present state of the economy has led many economists and business writers to laud the "new economy," in which low and falling unemployment and low and falling inflation exist simultaneously.[1] Such pundits often cite the globalization of the economy, the relaxation of government regulations, and the eroding power of unions as reasons for sustained low inflationary economic growth. While not all observers predict the end of business cycles, many (who should know better) support the notion that sharp cyclical downturns are a thing of the past and unemployment rates can remain low without kindling inflationary fires in the economy. Even the recent economic turmoil in Asia and Russia has not dampened some observers' expectations of continued low inflationary growth.

The U.S. unemployment rate, which fell below 5 percent toward the end of last year, is low by recent historical standards. Professional economists, politicians, and reporters have long argued that the unemployment rate reported by the Bureau of Labor Statistics (BLS) is not an accurate measure of economic hardship or well-being because it does not differentiate among voluntary and involuntary part-time workers, multiple labor force participants in a household, underemployed workers, and so on. This brief essay argues that there is yet another reason the official BLS unemployment rate is not an accurate indicator of economic activity and ought to be called into question, and it presents an alternative measure of the unemployment rate.

ROBERT HORN is professor of economics and director of the Semester in Paris program, James Madison University. PHILIP HEAP is instructor of economics, James Madison University, and graduate student at the University of Virginia. The authors thank Lynn Turgeon, Hofstra University, and Ehsan Ahmed, James Madison University, for their useful comments on this paper.

Since unemployment rates vary by age and, to a lesser extent, by sex, changes in the relative importance of these groups in the labor force will affect measures of unemployment.

The reported unemployment rate does not take into account the fact that the age and sex composition of the labor force changes over time. The surge of young workers (baby boomers) into the labor force during the 1970s and early 1980s swelled the proportion of young workers in the labor force. Because young workers have consistently higher unemployment rates than do older workers, increases in the unemployment rate during this time may have been due more to changing population characteristics than flawed economic policy-making. Similarly, the decline in the unemployment rate during the mid- to late 1980s may be attributable more to the aging of the labor force than to the success of supply-side economics.[2] Perhaps the low reported unemployment rate we are currently experiencing warrants an alternative explanation as well.

This study uses an adjusted unemployment rate that "controls" for changes in the age and sex composition of the labor force by weighting the unemployment rate according to the respective sex and age share of the labor force in 1970.[3] The reported unemployment rate in 1970 was 4.9 percent—below what many economists' consider full employment. Between 1970 and 1997, the reported unemployment rate fell below 5 percent in only one other year, 1973. The labor force shares for 1970 and other selected years are presented in Table 1.

Table 1 shows that the composition of the labor force changed

29. Age-Adjusted Unemployment Rate

Table 1

Age and Gender Distribution of the Civilian Labor Force

Age group	1970 Men	1970 Women	1985 Men	1985 Women	1995 Men	1995 Women
16–19	4.8	4.0	3.6	3.3	3.1	2.8
20–24	6.9	5.9	7.2	6.5	5.6	4.8
25–44	26.2	14.1	28.8	22.8	28.6	24.3
45–64	20.1	14.5	14.7	10.7	15.1	13.0
65+	2.7	1.3	1.5	1.0	1.7	1.2

significantly between 1970 and 1995. For example, in 1970 teenaged workers comprised 8.8 percent of the labor force. By 1985 the teenage share of the labor force had declined to 6.9 percent, and by 1995 it had fallen even further, to 5.9 percent. Men aged 45 to 64 were 20.1 percent of the workforce in 1970, but only 15.1 percent in 1995. Women aged 25 to 44 increased their share of the workforce from 14.1 percent in 1970 to 24.3 percent in 1995. Since unemployment rates vary by age and, to a lesser extent, by sex, changes in the relative importance of these groups in the labor force will affect measures of unemployment.

Table 2 compares the adjusted unemployment rate with the BLS unemployment rate. The adjusted rates were below the reported rates in the early 1980s. This is consistent with the influx of the baby boomers into the labor market during this period, increasing the unemployment rate above what it would have been if labor force shares had remained constant. By the mid-1980s young workers had aged into prime low-unemployment ages and the unemployment rates of women had fallen relative

Table 2

Civilian Unemployment Rates

Year	Age Adjusted	BLS	Difference
1980	6.8	7.1	–0.3
1981	7.4	7.6	–0.2
1982	9.5	9.7	–0.2
1983	9.5	9.6	–0.1
1984	7.5	7.5	0.0
1985	7.2	7.2	0.0
1986	7.0	7.0	0.0
1987	6.3	6.2	0.1
1988	5.6	5.5	0.1
1989	5.5	5.3	0.2
1990	5.8	5.6	0.3
1991	7.1	6.8	0.3
1992	7.9	7.5	0.4
1993	7.3	6.9	0.4
1994	6.5	6.1	0.4
1995	6.0	5.6	0.4
1996	5.8	5.4	0.4
1997	5.4	4.9	0.5

to unemployment rates of men, negating any difference between adjusted and unadjusted rates.

Since the late 1980s, the aging of the workforce and the diminishing differential between reported unemployment rates of adult men and women have contributed to a lower reported unemployment rate.[4] The adjusted rate, which controls for changes in labor force shares, indicates that the unemployment rate in the 1990s would have been higher had the age structure of the workforce remained constant. In a sense, the aging of the workforce results in an understated BLS unemployment rate. The gap between the BLS rate and the adjusted rate, which was 0.4 percentage points per year from 1992 through 1996, increased to 0.5 percentage points in 1997.

This is a significant finding. It tells us that, had the age and sex distribution of the labor force *not* changed since the last time the economy operated at less than 5 percent unemployment, the unemployment rate would have been between 0.4 and 0.5 percentage points higher than it currently is. This difference may appear small until one considers that the total number of unemployed in the United States in 1997 was 6.7 million. If the unemployment rate had been 5.4 percent, the total number of unemployed would have been 7.4 million or an increase of close to 700,000 additional unemployed workers, a 10 percent increase in the reported unemployment rate.

The intention of this paper is not to dispute the strong performance of the U.S. economy in recent years. The combination of low inflation and (seemingly) low unemployment has given the United States economic bragging rights relative to most European economies, which remain burdened with high unemployment rates. The objective is simply to maintain that the widely held view that the U.S. economy is operating at an unemployment rate below full employment is flawed. The unemployment rate is low in part because groups that have historically had below-average unemployment rates are today a larger share of the workforce than they were before. An aging population has contributed to the lowering of the unemployment rate.

Finally, our results cast some doubt on the widely held view that the economy is operating near the nonaccelerating inflation rate of unemployment (NAIRU), the rate of unemployment at which inflation remains constant or does not accelerate.[5] If the age-adjusted unemployment rate is a better indicator of labor market "slack" than the reported unemployment rate, there remains room for further economic expansion without fear of accelerating inflation. Thus Federal Reserve Board chair Alan Greenspan can relax still more about the probability of higher inflation. Future discussions concerning the strengths and weaknesses of macroeconomic policy would be well advised not to overlook the importance of demographic changes on economic performance.

Notes

1. See, for example, Stephen B. Shepard, "The New Economy: What It Really Means," *Business Week* (November 17, 1997).
2. Robert N. Horn, "An Age-Adjusted Unemployment Rate," *Challenge* (July–August 1988), pp. 56–58.
3. This is similar to the "demographically adjusted unemployment rate" mentioned in the 1997 *Economic Report of the President* (p. 45). However, 1993 is used as the base year in those calculations. For reasons discussed below, we believe that 1970 is a more appropriate base year.
4. From 1990 to 1997, the reported unemployment rates of adult men and women (20 and over) were 5.5 percent and 5.3 percent, respectively.
5. The 1998 *Economic Report of the President* states that "a reasonable range for the NAIRU now has a midpoint of 5.4 percent."

Unit 6

Unit Selections

30. **Globalization and Its Discontents: Navigating the Dangers of a Tangled World,** Richard N. Haass and Robert E. Litan
31. **Why Trade Is Good for You,** The Economist
32. **Could It Happen Again?** The Economist
33. **Will Fair Trade Diminish Free Trade?** David M. Gould and William C. Gruben
34. **The Spotlight and the Bottom Line: How Multinationals Export Human Rights,** Debora L. Spar
35. **NAFTA: How Is It Doing?** Joe Cobb and Alan Tonelson
36. **Trade Policy at a Cross Roads,** I. M. Destler
37. **The United States Is Not Ahead in Everything That Matters,** John Schmitt and Lawrence Mishel
38. **The Euro: Who Wins? Who Loses?** Jeffry Frieden
39. **Russia Is Not Poland, and That's Too Bad,** Michael M. Weinstein
40. **Japan's Economic Plight: Fallen Idol,** The Economist
41. **The Other Crisis,** James D. Wolfensohn
42. **Changing Today's Consumption Patterns—for Tomorrow's Human Development,** United Nations Development Programme

Key Points to Consider

❖ How should America respond to the challenges of global competition?

❖ What is the principle of comparative advantage, and how might it be used to support the case for free trade? Why do nations protect their trade?

❖ Will efforts at economic integration such as NAFTA and the European monetary union succeed? Explain why, or why not.

❖ How do today's consumption patterns affect tomorrow's human development?

Dushkin Online Links

www.dushkin.com/online/

27. **European Union in the U.S.**
    http://www.eurunion.org
28. **Institute for International Economics**
    http://www.iie.com
29. **Inter-American Development Bank**
    http://www.iadb.org
30. **International Monetary Fund (IMF)**
    http://www.imf.org
31. **North American Free Trade Association (NAFTA)**
    http://www.itaiep.doc.gov/nafta/nafta2.htm
32. **Organization for Economic Cooperation and Development (OECD)**
    http://www.oecd.org
33. **Sustainable Development Organization**
    http://www.sustainabledevelopment.org
34. **UNCTAD**
    http://www.unctad.org
35. **WORLDLINK Glossary and Acronyms**
    http://www.worldlinkinternational.com/gloss.htm
36. **World Policy Institute**
    http://www.worldpolicy.org
37. **World Trade Organization (WTO)**
    http://www.wto.org

These sites are annotated on pages 4 and 5.

International Economics

Global free trade by 2010 would enhance the prosperity of all countries by underwriting the ultimate success for competitive liberalization. It would preclude the risk that regional arrangements could develop into hostile blocs. It would terminate any risk of North-South conflict by engaging both sets of countries in a cooperative multilateral enterprise that meets the needs of both. Such a vision should guide this area of international affairs as the world enters the 21st century.—C. Fred Bergsten ("Globalizing Free Trade," *Foreign Affairs*, May/June 1996).

Many of the world's most pressing economic problems are international in scope, involving the complex web of the trading and financial arrangements that link all countries in a global network. The world economy is in a period of rapid change. Over the last decade we have seen the end of the cold war; ambitious market reforms in what were formerly centrally-planned economies; an acceleration of the process of economic integration in the Americas, Western Europe, and the Pacific Rim; and increased use of protectionist measures by most major traders. How the United States responds to these challenges may well influence events in the world economy for many years to come.

The U.S. economy is extraordinarily resilient. Historically, it has consistently demonstrated an ability to adjust to change, to adapt new technologies, and to create new jobs. In absolute terms, the United States is presently the world's most important international trader: total U.S. exports and imports each exceed about a trillion dollars annually. In addition, the United States has for many years been able to enjoy the advantages of remaining relatively self-sufficient; it obtains just over 10 percent of all income from trade.

However, it is increasingly apparent that an important shift in power has occurred: the United States, once the world's predominant economic power, must now share the spotlight with Western Europe and East Asia. In this new multipolar world, America still appears to be the first among equals. But it no longer has the economic leverage or moral authority to dictate the course of world events.

We begin with a study by Richard Haass and Robert Litan of "Globalization and Its Discontents: Navigating the Dangers of a Tangled World." The global liberalization of trade has reduced barriers to the movement of goods and capital across national boundaries. But globalization has also created a series of problems, including job losses, increasing income inequality, and stagnant or deteriorating real wages.

"Why Trade Is Good for You" examines a key concept in international trade—known as "comparative advantage"—which explains why countries produce certain goods and services. If nations specialize according to their comparative advantage, they can prosper through trade regardless of how inefficient, in absolute terms, they may be in their chosen specialty. The comparative advantage principle is used to support the case for free trade.

For the past 25 years the biggest economic enemy in most countries has been inflation. Today, in most of the world, a greater danger may be deflation. In the next article *The Economist* asks: Could deflation happen again, and what might this mean for world trade?

In order to facilitate the liberalization of trade, most countries participate in the General Agreement on Tariffs and Trade (GATT). Substantial tariff reductions have occurred since the GATT's founding in 1947. Recently, however, policymakers have developed various forms of protection to "correct" for "unfair" trade by other countries. In the next article David Gould and William Gruben ask: Will fair trade diminish free trade?

Debora Spar then considers "The Spotlight and the Bottom Line: How Multinationals Export Human Rights." Traditionally, U.S. manufacturers of consumer products targeted for human rights violations abroad have turned the blame over to foreign subcontractors. Are voluntary codes of conduct an appropriate response to this problem?

The recent formation of the North American Free Trade Association (NAFTA) was marked by both extravagant promises about its benefits and by bloodcurdling warnings about its costs. In the following article Joe Cobb and Alan Tonelson ask: How is NAFTA doing? Next, I. M. Destler shows why favorable U.S. economic conditions provide a good opportunity for revising American trade policy. Then, in "The United States Is Not Ahead in Everything That Matters" John Schmitt and Lawrence Mishel use key measures of economic strength, including GDP per capita and productivity, to assert that Europe is doing every bit as well as the United States in the 1990s.

The unit continues with five articles that offer perspectives on individual countries and regions. In "The Euro: Who Wins? Who Loses?" Jeffry Frieden examines the potential impact of a common monetary policy on the economies of the European Union. Michael Weinstein explains how it happened that Poland and Russia have diverged economically so markedly over a decade. Next, *The Economist* focuses on "Japan's Economic Plight: Fallen Idol." Once feared for its economic strength, Japan today is feared for its weakness—and the harm its ailing system might do to the rest of Asia and the world.

In "The Other Crisis" James Wolfensohn argues that we must look beyond global financial crises to seek the long-term structural reforms needed to put the world's troubled economies back on the road to recovery. The unit concludes with a UN study that examines implications of the rapid growth of world consumption in the twentieth century for human development in the twenty-first century.

Globalization and Its Discontents

Navigating the Dangers of a Tangled World

Richard N. Haass and Robert E. Litan

The period immediately following the Second World War, which produced the Marshall Plan, NATO, and the U.S.-Japan security treaty, is rightly regarded as foreign policy's golden era. But it also saw the birth of comparably successful economic institutions—such as the International Monetary Fund, the World Bank, the General Agreement on Tariffs and Trade—designed to promote long-term prosperity through stable exchange rates, worldwide development, and open trade. Today these institutions are increasingly subject to criticism. The IMF, for instance, has come under attack for imposing drastic conditions in its "rescues" of Mexico in 1995 and Asia today. The World Trade Organization, formed in 1995 as the result of American calls for a body to resolve market-access disputes, has been attacked in this country for usurping America's sovereignty. And doubts abound about the role of development banks in an era of massive direct foreign investment.

The gap between the legacy of Bretton Woods and the economic and political demands of the modern world is growing. Much of this change is driven by rapid advances in, and thus lower costs of, communications, information flows, and travel. Official policy, much of it American, has played its part by reducing barriers to the movement of goods and capital across national boundaries. The result has been more intrusive and intense economic interaction—including the explosive growth of world capital markets, which led to the demise of fixed exchange rates—between a large and growing number of entities outside government control, a phenomenon that has come to be called "globalization."

But globalization has its problems. In some quarters it is seen as having caused the rapid flows of investment that moved in and out of countries as investor sentiment changed and were behind the Mexican and Asian financial crises. In the United States it is blamed for job losses, increasing income inequality, and stagnant or deteriorating real wages. Domestic discontent with globalization thwarted the passage last year of legislation that would have granted the president "fast track" authority to negotiate trade arrangements that Congress could not modify.

Globalization has become a target. Its dangers must be navigated successfully or the United States and others may be compelled to backtrack, diminishing the free movement of goods, services, and capital, which would result in slower growth, less technological innovation, and lower living standards.

RICHARD N. HAASS, Director of the Program in Foreign Policy Studies at the Brookings Institution, is the author of *The Reluctant Sheriff: The United States after the Cold War*. ROBERT E. LITAN, Director of Brookings' Program in Economic Studies, is coauthor of *Globaphobia: Confronting Fears about Open Trade*.

FREE-MARKET FOREIGN POLICY?

In this new world, poor economic policy-making, corrupt banking practices, dishonest accounting, and unrealistic currency alignments can have an impact on societies far removed. Although the United States, with its vast internal market, is considerably less "globalized" than other industrialized countries, millions of American jobs and billions of dollars are tied to economic developments elsewhere.

If there is consensus on the diagnosis, there is none on the prescription. There are at least three fundamentally different approaches to addressing the problems of the global economy.

The first embraces the free market and would abandon IMF-like rescue packages. It is motivated by the belief that the IMF lulls governments, investors, and lenders into recklessness. Emboldened by the prospect that the IMF will come to their rescue, they are free to act irresponsibly. In the words of George Shultz, William Simon, and Walter Wriston, IMF "interference will only encourage more crises." Mexico, in this view, led to Asia.

The laissez-faire, free-market approach looks good in the abstract because markets reward sound investments and regulatory practices and punish poor ones. In principle, it can provide incentives for investors to avoid overly risky investments and for governments to adopt prudent policies. To international free marketeers, safety nets destroy this incentive.

But this critique goes too far. Governments submitting to IMF rescue plans must often agree to wrenching reforms—not the kind of experience that invites other governments to be reckless. Similarly, investors in equity markets in Mexico and Asia were hit by depressed local stock prices and heavily devalued local currencies. The only parties that emerged relatively unscathed, and thus for whom the free market critique has some relevance, were certain creditors: holders of Mexican government debt during the Mexican crisis and banks in the recent Asian crisis.

The solution to this problem is not to remove the IMF—the international lender of last resort—but to develop ways to warn banks and other creditors that they will suffer in the event of a future crisis. During the Depression, Americans learned the cost of not having a functioning lender of last resort: a wave of bank and corporate failures, aggravated by a shortage of liquidity that the Federal Reserve failed to provide. The international equivalent of having no Fed is standing idly by while currencies plummet, countries run out of foreign exchange, trade and investment come to a halt, and crises in one region spread to others.

A hands-off approach would risk transforming limited crises into something much more costly. More than economics is at stake. Years of punishment by the marketplace are simply not acceptable when immediate strategic interests are involved, as they are, for example, in Mexico or South Korea. For better or worse, the United States cannot afford the collapse of countries vital to its national interest.

GOVERNING GLOBALIZATION

The second approach to taming the dangers of globalization could hardly be more different. It suggests the creation of new institutions to lend structure and direction to the global marketplace, complementing what is seen as the constructive but inadequate roles of the IMF and other bodies. For example, George Soros, arguing that "international capital movements need to be supervised and the allocation of credit regulated," has recommended creating the international equivalent of the United States' Fannie Mae, which guarantees residential mortgages for a fee. He calls for the establishment of an "International Credit Insurance Corporation" that would guarantee private sector loans up to a specified amount for a modest charge, while requiring that the borrowers' home countries provide a complete financial picture in order for them to qualify.

Henry Kaufman, a Wall Street economist, would go even further, creating a

"Board of Overseers of Major International Institutions and Markets" that would set minimum capital requirements for all institutions, establish uniform accounting and lending standards, and monitor performance. It would even discipline those who did not meet these criteria by limiting the ability of those who remained outside the system to lend, borrow, and sell.

Governments are sure to resist supranational bodies that so fundamentally challenge their sovereignty. Moreover, except for extreme crises when an IMF-like rescue is warranted, it is difficult to understand why international officials could determine how much credit to allocate better than the market. There is more than a little irony in applying the "Asian model" of centralization to the international economy just when the model has been so thoroughly discredited.

A third approach, which would leave the basic architecture of the international economy alone but still do some "remodeling," would involve a number of reforms designed to structure and discipline financial operations and transactions. This managed approach would eschew the heavy hand of international regulation but aim to maintain the element of risk essential to capitalism without removing the safety net provided by the IMF. This approach is closest to the manner in which the United States dealt with the savings and loan and banking crises of the 1980s: enacting legislation requiring shareholders to maintain a larger financial commitment to their banks while making it more difficult for regulators and policymakers to bail out large, uninsured depositors who could previously count on being protected. The challenge for the international community is to introduce the equivalent of the U.S. reforms at both the national and international levels.

Such reforms are already being worked on at the behest of the IMF. They include improving the supervision of financial institutions, instituting Western-style accounting practices in banks and corporations, and opening up markets to foreign investment. To ensure that these reforms are carried out, some other international body, such as the Bank for International Settlements or perhaps a nongovernmental organization, should issue regular "report cards" on individual countries' progress. In addition, the IMF must press countries to be forthcoming with accurate information about key financial data, including their current account positions, foreign exchange reserves, and short-term indebtedness to foreign creditors. Banks and investors will favor countries that are positively rated, and penalize or avoid those that are not. Governments and institutions will introduce desirable reforms lest they lose out.

More transparency and information is necessary but not sufficient for markets to avoid excesses. The challenge is to find effective ways of addressing the free market critique. A possible solution is for the IMF to condition its assistance on countries' penalizing all lenders of foreign currency in the event IMF intervention is required. In particular, the model legislation that each country could adopt would require (as long as an IMF rescue is in effect) that creditors automatically suffer some loss of their principal when their debt matures and is not rolled over or extended. This approach would discourage the sudden outflow of maturing debt when countries can least afford it. The threat of automatic loss in the event a country experiences economic crisis could underscore to banks and other creditors that their money is at risk and that they can no longer count on the IMF to bail them out. Creditors would respond, of course, by insisting on higher interest rates for borrowers with opaque or poorly capitalized balance sheets. But that is precisely the point: the price of loans should better reflect the risk of not getting repaid.

The Asian crisis demonstrates the need for more formal bankruptcy codes and mechanisms for restructuring the balance sheets of heavily indebted firms without necessarily shutting them down. Existing international institutions can assist countries in this area, as well as in strengthening bank supervision and accounting standards, but there is no need to establish a new international bankruptcy court or to vest existing international institutions with such powers. The United States has a bankruptcy code and process that handles insolvency of firms located here, even when they have foreign creditors. There is no reason why other countries cannot do the same thing.

THE HOME FRONT

To paraphrase former House Speaker Tip O'Neill, all economics is local. Policies promoting unfettered trade and investment will be rejected by Congress unless steps are taken to build a firm domestic political base. Once again, there are three approaches to choose from, running the gamut from laissez faire to heavy regulation. A pure market approach—one that would let the chips (and the workers) fall where they may—would be neither fair nor politically sustainable. Some sort of safety net is both desirable and necessary. At the same time, it would be foolish to try to insulate Americans from all of globalization's effects. It is impossible to protect jobs rendered obsolete by technological change and foreign competition. What lies between is a managed approach that helps workers cope with the consequences of globalization. It would both change and supplement existing programs and policies.

Since 1962, American policymakers have provided extended unemployment insurance to workers who can prove they were displaced primarily because of international trade. But this discourages workers from looking for employment, channeling them toward government training programs with little proven success. Moreover, it does not compensate workers for the cuts in pay they take even after finding new jobs. A more effective program would pay workers a portion of the difference between their wages at their previous and new jobs. This kind of earnings insurance would encourage workers to take new jobs even if they paid less, and offer the only real training that works—on the job. Workers could also be provided with benefits—health insurance, pensions, training, and unemployment insurance—that they could take with them when moving to a new employer.

Some will argue that portable benefits and earnings insurance are not enough. But globalization is a reality, not a choice. "You can run but you can't hide" might serve as the mantra for the age.

Those who urge us to hide by resurrecting barriers to trade and investment, with the ostensible aim of insulating Americans from the forces of globalization, would abandon America's commitment to the spread of markets and democracy around the world at precisely the moment these ideas are ascendant. Moreover, the potential economic and political cost would be enormous, depriving Americans of cheaper and in some cases higher quality goods and services, as well as denying them the opportunity to work at better paying jobs that depend on exports.

The real choice for governments is not how best to fight globalization but how to manage it, which will require creative policies both at home and abroad. It is ironic: the age of globalization may well be defined in part by challenges to the nation-state, but it is still states and governments—by the practices they adopt, the arrangements they enter into, and the safety nets they provide—that will determine whether we exploit or squander the potential of this era.

Why trade is good for you

A short tour of economic theory

ECONOMISTS are usually accused of three sins: an inability to agree among themselves; stating the obvious; and giving bad advice. In the field of international trade, they would be right to plead not guilty to all three. If there is one proposition with which virtually all economists agree, it is that free trade is almost always better than protection. Yet the underlying theory is not readily understood by non-economists. And the advice that follows from it—protection does not pay—is seldom wrong.

The argument for free trade is based on the theory of comparative advantage. This is one of the oldest theories in economics, usually ascribed to David Ricardo, an Englishman who wrote in the early 19th century. To see how it works, imagine two countries, East and West, which both produce two kinds of goods, bicycles and wheat. In a year, an Eastern worker can make two bikes or grow four bushels of wheat. A Westerner, however, can manage only one bushel or one bike. Each country has 100 workers, and initially both of their workforces are split evenly between the two industries. So East produces 200 bushels of wheat and 100 bicycles, whereas West produces 50 bushels and 50 bikes (see table 1, first panel).

Since East can produce both wheat and bicycles more cheaply than West, it has an absolute advantage in both industries. Even so, Easterners will benefit from trading with Westerners. This is because East is relatively more efficient at growing wheat, where it is four times as productive as West, than it is at making bikes, where it is only twice as productive. In other words, it has a comparative advantage in wheat. At the same time, West has a comparative advantage in making bikes, even though it has no absolute advantage in anything.

According to Ricardo's theory, both countries will be better off if each specialises in the industry where it has a comparative advantage, and if the two trade with one another. Specialisation increases world output. Suppose that East specialises in wheat growing, shifting ten workers from its bicycle factories to its fields, and producing 240 bushels and 80 bikes. West moves 25 workers from wheat farming into bike making, where its comparative advantage lies, and produces 75 bikes and 25 bushels. Global production rises (see second panel).

The point of economic activity, however, is not to produce but to consume. Both countries can enjoy more bikes and more wheat if they trade on terms at which both will gain. If East is going to import bikes, it will pay no more than two bushels in return (faced with a higher price, it would be better off moving workers back to the bike factory). Similarly, West will pay no more than one bike per bushel. Suppose that the "terms of trade", as economists call the ratio of export to import prices, are set at one-and-a-half bushels per bicycle, and that 33 bushels are traded for 22 bikes. The result (third panel) is that both countries are better off.

In essence, the theory of comparative advantage says that it pays countries to trade because they are different. West's relative deficiency in bike manufacture is less than in wheat farming. It is impossible for a country to have no comparative advantage in anything. It may be the least efficient at everything, but it will still have a comparative advantage in the industry in which it is relatively least bad. And even if a country were the most efficient in every industry, giving it an absolute advantage in everything, it could not have a comparative advantage in everything. In some industries, its margin would be more impressive than in others.

Economists' next argument for free trade is that opening up markets to foreign suppliers increases competition. Without free trade, domestic companies may have enjoyed mo-

31. Why Trade Is Good for You

Comparative arithmetic

Autarky	Wheat	Bicycles
East	200	100
West	50	50
Total	250	150
Specialisation	**Wheat**	**Bicycles**
East	240	80
West	25	75
Total	265	155
Trade	**Wheat**	**Bicycles**
East	207	102
West	58	53
Total	265	155

nopolies or oligopolies that enabled them to keep prices well above marginal costs. Trade liberalisation will undermine that market power. Competition should also spur domestic companies to greater efficiency because they will not be able to pass on the costs of slackness in higher prices.

In addition, free trade means that firms are no longer limited by the size of their home country, but can sell into bigger markets. In industries where average production costs fall as output increases, producing economies of scale, this means lower costs and prices. In such industries, trade also increases the variety of products on offer. If a car manufacturer, say, were limited to its home market, it would have a choice between producing small quantities of a number of models and large quantities of just a few, which could be produced more cheaply thanks to economies of scale. But given free trade, it would be able to produce more models because they could all be produced in large enough numbers.

All these arguments revolve around re-allocating resources to produce one-off improvements—what economists call the "static" gains from trade. But they think there are also "dynamic" gains to be had: freer trade can mean faster economic growth.

In recent years, theories of economic growth have become much more sophisticated. Although economists have long realised that productivity growth is a prime determinant of general economic growth, models of growth in the past made no attempt to explain productivity growth, but assumed that it was "exogenous" (caused by outside factors). Modern "endogenous" growth theories, however, do try to explain productivity growth.

Freer trade can play a part in this in a number of ways. For one, by making markets bigger it creates more scope for "learning by doing"—ie, for firms to become more efficient with repetition. Larger markets also offer bigger incentives for firms to invest in research and development. Moreover, trade disseminates knowledge and technology. Simply by participating in international markets, countries are exposed to other countries' techniques, and have an incentive to copy and improve on them.

All this can make the relationship between trade, technology and growth quite complicated. For example, freer trade does not necessarily mean faster growth all the time. If a country's comparative advantage lies in slow-growing, traditional industries, it may cut back its production in

An angelic mix

ECONOMIC theory strips the world of its complications in the hope of making sense of it. Real life is a lot messier, but economic theory can still help to explain it. Take a look, by way of illustration, at the trading activities of one city, Los Angeles, and the forces that have shaped it.

- **Luck.** LA's best-known export is films. Nowadays, this is easy enough to explain in terms of comparative advantage. California's lead in movie making is enormous. Initially, good light and fine weather may have helped, but other places had those too. Luck, a hundred years of practice and economies of scale probably mattered more.
- **Geography.** Thanks to a deep harbour on the Pacific coast, the twin ports of Los Angeles and Long Beach are the busiest in America and the third busiest in the world. Moving containers in and out of the ports and to and from the rest of America is a big business in itself. The Port of Los Angeles reckons that it supports over 250,000 jobs in southern California—more than one in 24 of the region's total.
- **People.** LA's location helps explain its rich ethnic mix. Besides Latinos, whites and blacks, this includes Chinese, Koreans, Vietnamese, Japanese, Indians and many others, creating an intricate pattern of international commerce. Linking up all these different networks can create further business. In El Monte, one of the LA conurbation's 88 municipalities, John Leung of Titan Group, a property company, plans a business park aimed at helping small LA companies find their way into international trade.
- **Technology.** The days when raw materials were produced in one country and turned into finished goods in another are long gone. The making of even the simplest goods is chopped up into a number of different stages, reflecting relative costs in different countries and falling international transport costs. Charlie Woo, chief executive of Megatoys, explains how a child's pinwheel, consisting of plastic sails pinned to a stick, is made in three different countries. The plastic is produced in America and cut to shape in China. The toy is then assembled in Mexico and shipped to LA for distribution.
- **Niches.** Some of LA's textile industry, explains Jack Kyser, a local economist, has gone south to Mexico in search of cheaper labour, but by no means all. Mexico is fine for run-of-the-mill jeans, but suppose that a smart department store quickly needs a new line of high-fashion dresses—perhaps just a few dozen, each selling for a few hundred dollars. A month or two later the style will be dead. The store might buy the dresses from one of the designers exhibiting in tiny spaces on 9th Street.

Many of those displaying here, explains Else Metchek of the California Fashion Association, are based in garages. Plenty more started up in them and moved on to greater things: one, launched 12 years ago, now turns over $85m a year. Even California style, however, has to accept a measure of globalisation. Knitwear production is so labour-intensive that it is moving abroad —not to Mexico, but to China.

other, faster-growing industries, so its growth rate may fall. But later on it will benefit from the technical advances of countries with a comparative advantage in faster-growing industries, which will give it better computers, more advanced drugs and so forth than if every country had tried to make everything for itself. Slower growth in the short run might therefore be balanced by faster growth in the long term.

Pinning down the link between freer trade and growth is not easy. One problem is how to measure the openness of a country's trade policy: trade barriers can take many different forms. Even so, there is good reason to believe that freer trade and faster growth generally go together.

Exceptions that prove the rule

So is free trade always the best policy? Not quite. One well-known exception is the "optimal tariff" imposed by countries that are big enough to exert an influence on the world prices of the goods they trade. By raising tariffs, they can significantly reduce world demand, cutting the world price of the good and tilting the terms of trade in their favour.

A second example, which came to prominence in the 1980s, is "strategic trade policy". In an industry with economies of scale, the imposition of a tariff, by reserving the home market for a domestic firm, allows the firm to cut its costs and, with luck, to undercut foreign rivals in overseas markets. Economists and politicians reckon that this might work in civil aircraft, semiconductors and cars.

However, it is rare for governments to be powerful enough to set optimal tariffs—and even rarer for them to have enough information to do so with pinpoint accuracy. They would need to be able to recognise a likely business proposition, and get their maths absolutely right. Even then, rival countries could follow suit, leaving them all worse off.

THE WORLD ECONOMY

Could it happen again?

For the past 25 years the biggest economic enemy in most countries has been inflation. Today, in most of the world, a greater danger may be deflation

MOST people take it for granted that prices will always rise, and understandably so. A 60-year-old American has seen them go up by more than 1,000% in his lifetime. Yet prolonged inflation is a recent phenomenon. Until about 60 years ago prices in general were as likely to fall as to rise. On the eve of the first world war, for example, prices in Britain, overall, were almost exactly the same as they had been at the time of the great fire of London in 1666.

Now the world may be reverting to that earlier normality. The prices of many things have fallen over the past 12 months or so. Not only computers and video players, whose prices have been declining for many years, but a wide range of goods—from cars and clothes to coffee and petrol—are, in many countries, cheaper than they were a year ago. It is conceivable that the world may be in for a new period of global deflation (meaning falling consumer prices) for the first time since the 1930s.

Talk of deflation is certainly at its highest level since then. The number of newspaper articles mentioning the D-word is running at more than 20 times the rate of a decade ago (see chart 1). Japan has been flirting with deflation for several years, but the complaint may be catching. Gary Shilling, an American economist, predicts in a new book*, that American consumer prices will fall by an average of 1-2% a year over the next decade. In Britain, the Centre for Economics and Business Research expects to see falling prices by 2002. Several pundits reckon that continental Europe is heading for deflation rather sooner.

Just how dangerous would that be? The answer is, it depends. In the 1930s, falling prices locked economies into a downward spiral, in which shrinking demand, deepening pessimism, financial distress and the apparent inability of governments to put things right led to economic collapse. But deflation can also take a friendlier form—when it is driven by rapid growth in productivity, for instance. Look around the world, and you see both kinds of deflation at work, and in some places a mixture of the two. That makes things horribly complicated for policymakers.

A long way down

Almost wherever you look though, you see falling prices. The cost of raw materials, for a start, is plunging. Oil prices have more than halved since the start of 1997; in the past two years, *The Economist*'s index of industrial-commodity prices has fallen by 30%. In real terms commodity prices are at their lowest since this index was first published a century and a half ago.

This long decline partly reflects technological progress that has boosted crop yields and mineral-extraction rates. But the most recent collapse in prices was largely triggered by the slump in East Asia, a big importer of raw materials. Producers in Latin America, Russia and South Africa have responded to lower prices by boosting output to keep up export revenues, but this has pushed prices lower still.

Producer prices have also fallen over the past 12 months in 14 of the 15 rich industrial economies that *The Economist* monitors each week in its indicator pages. Currency devaluations in East Asia released a flood of cheap manufactured goods on to world markets—to which Brazil will now add. Thanks to enormous overinvestment, especially in Asia, the world is awash with excess capacity in computer chips, steel, cars, textiles, ships and chemicals. The car industry, for instance, is already reckoned to have at least 30% unused capacity worldwide—yet new factories in Asia are still coming on stream.

Consumer-price inflation is also dropping, perhaps to an average of only 1% in the rich economies this year—the lowest for almost half a century (see chart 2 on next

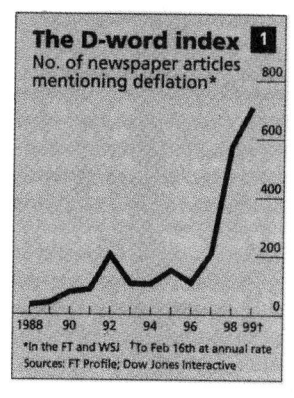

The D-word index [1]
No. of newspaper articles mentioning deflation*

*In the FT and WSJ †To Feb 16th at annual rate
Sources: FT Profile; Dow Jones Interactive

page). Consumer prices have fallen over the past year in Switzerland, Sweden, China, Hong Kong and Singapore. In the year to January, China's consumer prices fell by 1.2% and producer prices by 8%. The Chinese government has responded by introducing price controls—not to hold down prices, but to keep them up. As for Japan, its measured consumer-price inflation is slightly positive, but this reflects a distortion caused by a jump in food prices. In underlying terms, Japanese consumer prices are falling.

Even in Brazil, once famed for hyperinflation, consumer prices (as measured by Sao Paulo's FIPE index) fell by 1.8% last year. The devaluation of the *real* may now push up prices; but Brazil's deflation is likely to be exported to the rest of Latin America and beyond. And in the euro area consumer prices have been falling since the summer, although they are still up by 0.8% on a year ago. French and German inflation rates are teetering on the brink of deflation, at 0.3% and 0.5% respectively.

---
* "Deflation", by Gary Shilling, Lakeview Publishing Company.

Official consumer-price indices in any case overstate inflation rates because they fail to take full account of improvements over time in the quality of goods (today's cars or televisions have many more features than 20 years ago), and because the weights given to different goods and services tend to be out of date. The overstatement is usually reckoned to be up to one percentage point a year. So any country with measured inflation of less than 1% may, in reality, be experiencing falling prices.

However, all these numbers need to be treated with care. "Deflation", like many economic concepts, is a widely misunderstood and often misused term. Its proper definition is a persistent fall in the general price level of goods and services; it is not to be confused with a decline in prices in one economic sector, or with a fall in the inflation rate (which is known as disinflation). Thus falling commodity prices do not, of themselves, constitute deflation—they are a shift in relative prices that reduces real incomes in producing countries and boosts them in importing countries. Likewise a fall in manufacturing prices is not deflation if it is offset by rising prices for services. In America, for example, the average price of goods has fallen over the past year, but the prices of services have risen by 2.5%, to produce an overall (measured) consumer-price inflation rate of 1.6%.

Kill or cure
Deflation is not necessarily bad. Indeed, productivity-driven deflation, in which costs and prices are pushed lower by technological advances or by deregulation, is beneficial, because lower prices lift real incomes and hence spending power. In the last 30 years of the 19th century, for example, consumer prices fell by almost half in America, as the expansion of railways and advances in industrial technology brought cheaper ways to make everything; yet annual real growth over the period averaged more than 4%.

Today, the computer and telecoms revolutions are similarly pushing down costs. By reducing barriers to entry and making price information more widely available, the Internet is pushing down the prices of goods ranging from cars to books, and of services from insurance to air travel. The arrival of Europe's single currency will also increase price competition in the euro area. A study by ING Barings concludes that this might trim a quarter of a percentage point off the euro area's annual inflation rate over the next five years. Further downward pressure on prices in Europe and Japan has also been caused by deregulation of electricity and telephones. All these sources of deflation are good for economies, not bad.

Deflation is dangerous, on the other hand, when it reflects a sharp slump in demand, excess capacity and a shrinking money supply—as in the early 1930s. In the four years to 1933, American consumer prices fell by 25% and real GDP by 30%. Runaway deflation of this sort can be much more damaging than runaway inflation,

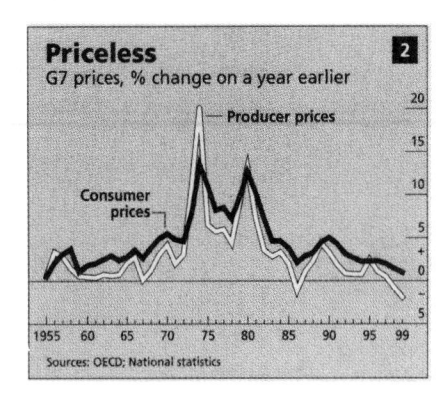

Priceless [2]
G7 prices, % change on a year earlier

Sources: OECD; National statistics

because it creates a vicious spiral that is hard to escape.

Thus, the expectation that prices will be lower tomorrow may encourage consumers to delay purchases, depressing demand and forcing firms to cut prices by even more. Falling prices also inflate the real burden of debt, causing bankruptcies and bank failures. That makes deflation particularly dangerous for economies that have large corporate debt—such as Japan's. Most serious of all, deflation can make monetary policy ineffective: nominal interest rates cannot be negative, so real rates can get stuck too high.

Today's deflation comes in both benign and malign guises. New technology and deregulation are pushing down prices of many goods and services around the globe, which should be good for most economies. But weak demand is also creating harmful deflationary pressures in some countries. A good way to detect this is to look at countries' "output gaps": the difference between actual output and output at full capacity.

Japan's output gap is forecast to widen to a record 7% of GDP this year. The country is on the brink of a vicious deflationary spiral, with falling prices swelling companies' real debts and keeping real interest rates high. The rest of East Asia also has huge spare capacity. Even if growth resumes this year, Thailand's GDP is unlikely to regain its level of 1996 until 2001. If so, output will in total have fallen by almost one-third relative to productive potential (as measured by the economy's trend growth rate of 7%). Meanwhile, China has 40% excess capacity in manufacturing.

None of this excess capacity is likely to be shut down quickly, because cash-strapped firms have an incentive to keep factories running, even at a loss, to generate income. The global glut is pushing prices relentlessly lower. Devaluation cannot make excess capacity disappear; it simply shifts the problem to somebody else. But in the process, global demand will contract as emerging economies are forced to raise interest rates to deter capital outflows.

The European Union has been running a modest, though persistent, output gap of around 2% of GDP for several years, but this is likely to widen in 1999 if, as widely forecast, growth falls below trend. The American economy, in contrast, is running above its productive potential. Indeed, without the recent fall in oil and commodity prices, America's inflation rate would have risen, forcing the Federal Reserve to raise interest rates. America may be enjoying some deflation of the benign variety, as a result of information technology and increased competition; but booming consumer spending and double-digit money-supply growth suggest that it will not, at least in the near future, suffer from malign deflation.

Fear of falling
Only a handful of economies are clearly experiencing true deflation. Even Japan, despite dreadful policy errors, has not experienced declines in prices as bad as those in the 1930s. America and Europe have so far benefited from cheaper import prices. Indeed, most countries are now simply enjoying price stability. This should help, not harm future growth. Yet the risk of outright deflation has clearly increased. A sharp slowdown in America or Europe could easily send overall price levels falling for the first time since the 1930s.

There are several causes for concern:
• Global excess supply is unprecedentedly high. **Output gaps** are tricky to measure, but *The Economist*'s best guess is that the world output gap is approaching its biggest since the 1930s (see chart 3 on next page). Deflation could occur even without a contraction in global output. All that is needed is a protracted period of growth below trend, which causes the output gap to widen and hence the inflation rate to fall, until it eventually turns negative. Thus, even if Asia's growth picks up this year and next, but (as widely expected) remains below trend, the region's output gap will continue to widen.
• **Nominal GDP growth** in the G7 economies looks set to fall this year to around 2.5%—close to its slowest rate since the second world war. (Japan's nominal GDP fell by 3.4% in the year to the third quarter of 1998). This suggests that, on a global level, policy is too tight. Ideally, in a developed economy, a central bank that has the medium-term goal of price stability should aim for nominal GDP growth of 4-5%. This allows room for long-term growth of 2-3% and inflation of 1-2%.
• A third danger is that **lower commodity prices**, while boosting real incomes in most rich economies, are hurting producers in the already troubled emerging economies. This may not be a zero-sum game.

Cash-starved emerging economies are likely to cut spending faster than rich countries spend their windfall.

• But the biggest risk of all is a **failure to adjust** on the part of policymakers, workers, companies and investors, all of whom are used to coping with high inflation, not deflation. In past periods of benign deflation, as in the late 19th century, everyone was used to the notion of falling prices. But today, few have had any such experience—making the risk of mistakes much greater.

For instance, in response to calls for lower interest rates, the European Central Bank (like the Bank of Japan before it) has retorted that European interest rates are already at record low levels. But real interest rates, which rise as inflation falls, are nowhere near their record lows.

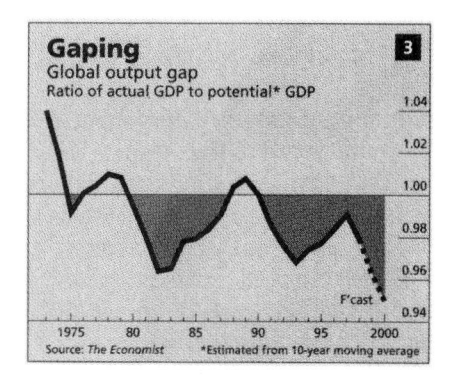

Workers also need to learn the new rules of the game. If unions continue to demand big annual wage increases—Germany IG Metall is currently seeking a pay rise of 6.5%—despite flat or falling prices, firms may have no alternative but to cut jobs. And falling goods prices could also provoke trade friction. Cheaper imports of manufactured goods from Asia, say, could trigger renewed protectionism in America and Europe, further depressing world growth.

Deflation is especially painful for debtors. Not only does the real burden of debt rise, but falling property prices also reduce the value of collateral, forcing banks to write down debts. It is worrying, therefore, argues Ian Harwood, an economist at Dresdner Kleinwort Benson, that since deflation was last experienced on a global scale, the level of private debt has risen sharply, thanks to a combination of financial deregulation with years of inflation that made borrowing attractive. Total private-sector debt is now around 130% of GDP in America and 200% in Japan, compared with less than 100% of GDP in America in 1928.

Companies too will find it hard to adjust to falling prices. Wages rarely fall, so deflation tends to squeeze profit margins. This may explain why surveys in Europe and America suggest that businessmen are so much gloomier than consumers: deflation tends to be good news for consumers, but bad news for companies. It is often easy to increase profits by raising prices in inflationary times; when there is deflation, the only way is to cut costs.

Deflation could be a particular problem for property, retailing and financial markets. Inflationary times favour property investment: inflation erodes the real value of a mortgage and delivers capital gains. In a world of falling prices, buying a house becomes less attractive than renting. Deflation also squeezes retailers' profits, because wages (a big chunk of total costs) are less flexible downwards than prices. Retailers will also see volume and profit margins squeezed as consumers delay purchases in the hope that prices will fall.

As for financial markets, consider only the alarming gap between investors' expectations of American profits, which are said to support current share prices on Wall Street, and the more likely actual path of profits as global deflationary pressures squeeze American firms. Total American profits have already fallen slightly over the past year.

Indeed this could be the factor that finally bursts America's stockmarket bubble. And when that happens, and America's consumer-spending boom goes into reverse, the economy could quickly be dragged into recession, increasing the risk that the world as a whole might tip into a period of outright deflation or even slump.

Time to reflate

There seems little likelihood that prices will ever fall by anything like as much as in the 1930s. Prices and wages are today much stickier, especially in services (which account for a far bigger chunk of economies), and policymakers reckon, post-Keynes, that they now understand better how to use monetary and fiscal weapons to prevent deflation. Yet Japan shows that the threat of deflation is real even in a modern economy if policymakers blunder.

Inflation, as Milton Friedman once said, "is always and everywhere a monetary phenomenon". So it is with deflation. It can be prevented by appropriate policies. Overly tight monetary policies, and the straitjacket imposed by the gold standard, were largely to blame for the prolonged deflation in the 1930s.

So how to respond to today's deflationary risks? The widening output gap and sluggish nominal GDP growth are both signals that monetary policy in the G7 economies, taken as a whole, is too tight. Not in America, certainty; but both Europe and Japan are operating below normal capacity. Yet oddly, as John Makin, an economist at the American Enterprise Institute, points out, these economies have done less to ease monetary policy since the middle of last year than America, whose economy least needed a boost.

Japan's monetary conditions have, in effect, tightened as a result of higher bond yields and a stronger yen, though policymakers are trying to reverse these. In the euro area, nominal short-term interest rates have been cut, but real rates are barely any lower than they were last June, because inflation has fallen. American real interest rates, in contrast, have fallen by two-thirds of a percentage point.

The world economy is, in short, precariously balanced on the edge of a deflationary precipice. Policymakers still have ample time to use their monetary and fiscal weapons to prevent deflation. The danger for some central bankers is that, having for now seen off the threat of inflation, they rest on their laurels and fail to confront the possibility of deflation. That would be foolish indeed. For history has shown that once deflation takes hold, it can be far more damaging than inflation.

Article 33

Will Fair Trade Diminish Free Trade?

By David M. Gould and
William C. Gruben*

While trade agreements since the first GATT round in 1947 have reduced tariffs dramatically, new forms of protection have exploded. In particular, policymakers in many countries have developed protection to correct for "unfair" trade by other nations. Allegations of dumping – the act of selling goods for a lower price abroad than in the home or other markets – have been the prime justification for this raising protectionism. But antidumping laws have been applied so broadly that they have become a simple means of avoiding competition. The central question addressed in this article is whether the new World Trade Organization will stem the rising tide of antidumping suits that has weakened global free trade.

THE SUCCESSFUL COMPLETION of the Uruguay Round of the General Agreement on Tariffs and Trade (GATT) that created of the World Trade Organization (WTO) in January 1995 has generated much optimism about the future of world trade, and with good reason. The trade accord not only eliminated tariffs on many goods, but it was also the first GATT-round accord to address intellectual property rights, trade in services, and agricultural subsidies. The WTO estimates that the volume of world trade in goods grew by 8 percent in 1995, four times the growth of world GDP. In fact, during the 1990s, international trade has routinely grown far faster than world output, an indication that national economies are becoming ever more closely linked. The WTO now includes 127 members; another thirty countries, including China and Russia, want to join.

In such an environment, it may seem strange to question the global commitment to free trade. But postwar history shows that, while trade agreements have reduced some forms of protectionism, new forms have been invented that at least partially replace them. At the same time that GATT reduced tariffs on manufactured goods from an average rate of about 40 percent in 1947 to about 3.8 percent now (Figure 1), the United States and other countries were refining disguised forms of protectionism. Increasingly complicated nontariff administrative procedures and laws began to regulate the flow of trade.

**Figure 1
Tariffs in Industrial Countries**

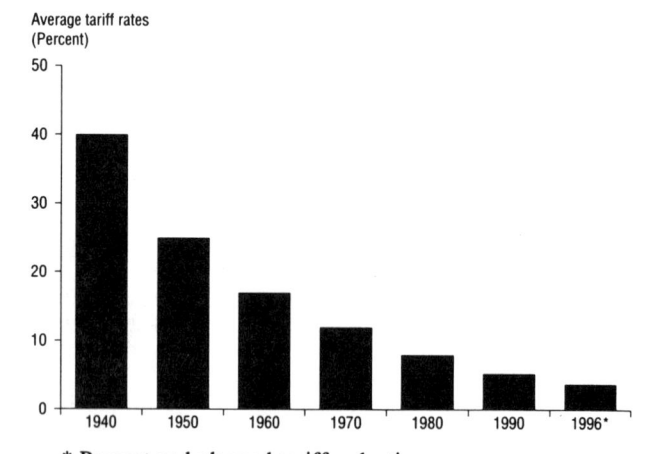

Average tariff rates (Percent)

* Present and planned tariff reductions.
Source: Stoeckel, Pearce, and Banks (1990): WTO (1996).

More specifically, policymakers have developed contingent trade protection to "correct" for "unfair" trade by other countries. The most often alleged unfair trading practice is *dumping* – the act of selling goods for a lower price abroad than in the home or other markets or selling at below average total costs. During the 1960s, GATT member countries initiated fewer than twelve antidumping actions per year. By the late 1970s, the United States alone averaged more than

---

* David M. Gould is Senior Economist and Policy Advisor and William C. Gruben is Assistant Vice President, Federal Reserve Bank of Dallas, TX

thirty-five cases per year. As Figure 2 shows, in the first half of the 1990s, the number of cases outstanding across the four most frequent users of antidumping laws (the European Union, the United States, Canada, and Australia) has been increasing, particularly in the United States. Many developing countries (e.g., Argentina, Brazil, India, Mexico, and South Africa) have joined the escalating use of antidumping laws. The four major users represented 82 percent of the antidumping measures enforced in July 1995, but only 51 percent of the cases initiated between 1994-95 (Messerlin 1996).

Figure 2
Antidumping Actions Outstanding
Mid-years, 1981-95

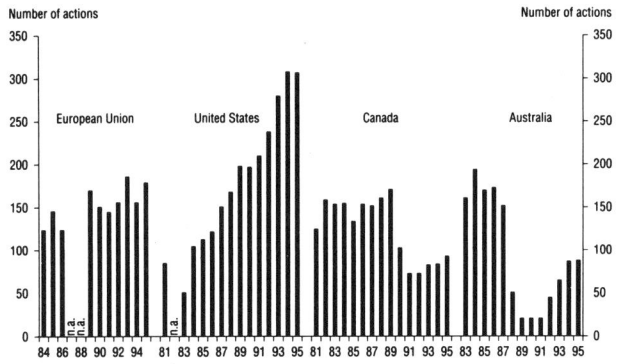

Source: WTO and GATT Annual Reports up to 1995.

Past GATT agreements have included rough guidelines for using antidumping duties, but the WTO has codified these guidelines more fully than any previous GATT accord. Moreover, these codifications greatly resemble those of U.S. law.

The central question addressed in this article is whether the WTO will stem the rising tide of administered trade regulations that has weakened the trend toward liberalized trade around the world. Because the WTO adopted many aspects of U.S. fair trade laws, we use the U.S. experience as a benchmark to glimpse what the future may hold for world trading.

WHEN IS TRADE UNFAIR?

The express intention of fair trade laws is to prevent foreign sellers from pricing and selling anticompetitively or predatorialy in your country. For example, if foreign exporters sell for less in the United States than at home, U.S. laws and rules accommodate U.S. efforts at retaliation. But is this notion of unfair trade really unfair?

Economists often deny that below-cost prices or foreign export subsidies mean unfair trade. After all, if foreign firms want to sell cheaply in the United States, why should U.S. consumers not be allowed the obvious benefit? This argument recognizes the benefits to consumers, but dismisses the effects of unfair trading on some domestic producers and ignores other arguments against unfair trading practices. Moreover, as Bhagwati (1988) notes, "A free trade regime that does not rein in or seek to regulate artificial subventions will likely help trigger its own demise."

But how does one assess whether foreign exporters are pricing predatorily? Messerlin (1996) has formulated criteria to determine whether foreign exporters are credible predators. Are foreign exporters enjoying individual market shares large enough to make them potential predators in the domestic market? Is their share of the domestic market growing fast enough to suggest that over one or more years they will have a dominant position? Can foreign predators, once they capture a market, ensure monopoly profits by keeping domestic firms out of the market?

In spite of the widespread allegations of predatory behavior, Shin (1992) found that only 5.7 percent of 282 U.S. antidumping cases studied between 1980-89 might involve it. Bourgeois and Messerlin (1993) found similar results for the European Union.

In the concrete world of politics and economic interests, government policies in support of antidumping laws typically place the concerns of import-competing industries over those of consumers and of producers who use imports. An analysis of eight antidumping duties imposed by the United States between 1989 and 1990 showed that for each $1 gained by the protected industries, the U.S. economy as a whole lost $3.60, on average (Anderson 1993). In a 1995 report, the U.S. International Trade Commission found that the net cost of antidumping and countervailing duties in only one year, 1991, amounted to $1.59 billion, or 0.03 percent of U.S. gross domestic product (USITC 1995).

Whether or not predatory pricing is a practice that fair trade laws are supposed to address, the laws have been applied so broadly they often seem to have been a means of avoiding competition. Antidumping laws share many attributes of pure protectionism.

WHY FAIR TRADE LAWS DO NOT ALWAYS WORK

Contrary to popular notions about dumping, under present U.S. and WTO law, dumping is not defined as selling below cost in order to capture markets. Dumping is simply selling at a lower price in the foreign market than in other markets or selling at below average total costs. Antidumping actions do not require evidence of predatory behavior, or intentions to monopolize, or of any other efforts to drive competitors out of business.

U.S. antidumping laws of the past placed the burden of proof on the accusing industry. Over time, Congress has dropped the requirement of intent and instead has focused on the prevention of injury to domestic firms (Murray 1991). The burden of proof no longer falls on the accusing industry but upon the industry or firm that is accused. Foreign firms are presumed guilty until proven innocent.

Under current U.S. law, any industry can approach the Department of Commerce and the International Trade Commission (ITC) and claim foreigners are pricing exports lower in the United States than at home. The Department of Commerce investigates the case, and the ITC determines whether material injury has occurred. Antidumping duties are imposed when foreign merchandise is sold in the United States for less than "fair" value. A duty is assessed equal to the amount by which the estimated foreign market value exceeds U.S. price.

While antidumping laws are not inconsistent with the desire to keep trade fair, their current application permits liberal interpretation of what is and what is not fair trade. Below we discuss some of the procedural problems with antidumping laws.

PROBLEMS WITH THE APPLICATION OF U.S. ANTIDUMPING LAWS

In the application of antidumping law, small changes can make big differences. Juggling the procedures for constructing fair market prices, for identifying injury to a domestic industry, or for gathering information from foreign firms can substantially change the law's impact. Over the years, in response to domestic pressures to protect particular industries, these procedures have often changed in order to increase the likelihood of finding against foreign producers and for domestic complainants.

This pattern is not isolated to the United States. With time, countries as diverse as Canada, Poland, and Mexico have converged in their antidumping procedures. By considering how antidumping laws have been applied in the United States, it is possible to assess how the WTO will affect their future use across a broader set of countries. This list explains some of the most often cited problems with the past application of U.S. antidumping laws. As will be discussed, some of these practices continue.

1. *Pricing below average costs.* The 1974 Tariff Act broadened antidumping law to prohibit foreign exporters from pricing below average total costs of production. Such pricing is not only legal for domestic firms, but is typical when sales are weak or when firms are launching new products. Prohibiting foreign firms from doing what domestic firms do creates a bias toward finding dumping when it would not be found otherwise.
2. *Constructed prices.* If the Department of Commerce suspected that 10 percent or more of an exporter's sales were below average total costs, these sales were excluded from the determination of "fair market value." If the Department of Commerce believed that 90 percent or more of an exporter's sales were below average total costs, all relevant foreign market information on actual sales was omitted and an artificial price was constructed. In calculating the foreign price, standard assumptions were used for normal profits (a minimum markup of 8 percent over total costs), production costs, general and administrative expenses (a markup of 10 percent over the cost of production) and exchange rates. Sometimes dumping could be found even when the price of the foreign product was higher in the United States than in the country of origin. The 8 percent profit rule punished foreign producers for running lower profit margins. Almost any antidumping duty could be justified.
3. *Data requirements.* When a U.S. firm charged a foreign competitor with dumping, the Department of Commerce requested detailed cost information from the foreign competitor. Just the volume of data the U.S. government required of foreign firms in such cases could be a deterrent to trade. The Department of Commerce could present an accused foreign firm with a questionnaire as long as 100 pages that requested specific accounting data on individual sales in the home market; data on sales to the United States; and all the detailed data needed to adjust for tariffs, shipping, selling, and distribution costs. Information had to be recorded and transmitted to the Department of Commerce in English and in a computer-readable format within a short deadline stipulated under the U.S. statutes (Murray 1991, 34).
4. *Averaging foreign but not domestic prices.* The procedure involved averaging foreign prices over a period of time and comparing this average with individual U.S. domestic transactions to determine if dumping had occurred. Comparing average foreign prices with individual U.S. domestic transactions can lead to a finding of dumping even if domestic and foreign prices are exactly the same every day.
5. *Price margins.* Considering the substantial room for error in calculating foreign prices, the price differentials, or margins, that define dumping were strikingly small. In the United States, a foreign industry was typically subject to antidumping findings if it sold its products for less than 99.5 percent of what was estimated as fair market value. Because 99.5 percent of fair market value is 0.5 percent less than 100 percent, this rule was called the 0.5-percent *de minimis* rule.
6. *Review.* In spite of problems in the methodology of calculating antidumping duties, once an antidumping duty is imposed, it may remain in force for years without periodic review of whether the foreign country had ceased dumping.

THE WTO: A NEW DIRECTION?

The new antidumping regulations of the WTO are important for at least two reasons. First, to the degree that the new agreement harmonizes regulations across countries, it will result in greater transparency and will restrain arbitrary implementation. Second, the Uruguay Round of the GATT Agreement outlawed voluntary export restraints, a popular from of disguised protectionism. With this avenue closed, more countries that want to restrict imports while enjoying the low tariff benefits of WTO membership will likely turn to antidumping. In both of these senses the WTO indeed represents a new direction.

Not only does the WTO impose more uniformity, but it impedes some of the United States' and other countries' tactics that – while consistent with antidumping regulations – were arguably protectionist. In spite of these clear and concrete movements toward trade liberalization and transparency, some of the new rules are ambiguous enough to allow countries (certainly the United States) to honor the letter of the WTO rules while ignoring the spirit of free trade.

AREAS WHERE PROTECTIONIST BIAS HAS FALLEN: NEW WTO VS. OLD U.S. LAW

Among the most criticized U.S. antidumping procedures was the construction of "fair market" prices when actual market prices were available. As noted, the Commerce Department could "construct" a foreign "market" price if it suspected that 10 percent of a foreign firm's sales were below some estimate of average total cost of production. Opportunities for abusing this procedure had meant that using constructed prices increased the likelihood of a finding of illegal dumping (Baldwin and Moore, 1991). Under the new WTO rules, constructed prices are still legal but are subject to more restrictions. As a result, U.S. officials can now use completely constructed foreign market prices only if 20 percent (versus the pre-WTO 10 percent) of a foreign firm's sales are below some estimate of its cost of production.

Moreover, in constructing fair market value, the arbitrary 8 percent mark-up on total costs for profit and 10 percent mark-up on manufacturing costs for general and administrative expenses are prohibited. The WTO Antidumping Code requires that general and administrative costs and profit be based on the experience of the producer or exporter under investigation. Under amended U.S. law, if such information is unavailable (as may be expected when prices "must" be constructed), average general and administrative costs and profits of other exporters or producers under investigation, or of other exporters or producers of merchandise in the same general category are to be used.

The WTO also affected the U.S. 0.5 percent *de minimis* rule. Under this rule, a foreign firm that was found to have sold in the United States for as little as 0.5 percent less than some estimate of fair market value would be subject to antidumping duties. The WTO contains a 2 percent *de minimis* rule that supersedes the 0.5 percent rule. The U.S. is pledged to honor the letter of this increased *de minimis* rule but has found a way of interpreting the relevant article to limit its coverage somewhat.

The WTO also addressed the problem of comparing average foreign market prices to individual domestic sales. Recall that, according to this procedure, individual prices in the United States were compared with average foreign prices. This meant that any price fluctuations of an import during an investigation could generate an affirmative dumping finding, i.e., if an imported product's price happened to change at all during the investigations, it would on at least one day fall below the total-period average as a matter of simple arithmetic. Just as every human being cannot have above-average intelligence, there will likewise always be one price that is below the average price.

In most cases under the WTO, governments pursuing antidumping investigations agree to compare average foreign prices with average domestic prices and individual foreign sales with individual domestic sales. However, even under the WTO, some provisions sanction the apples-to-oranges comparison of average prices to individual prices. The WTO sanctions this practice when a government investigates charges of spot dumping, a dumping category that involves brief dips below fair market prices.

The new dispute settlement mechanism also contains elements that can thwart protectionism. Previously, when a country illegally imposed an antidumping duty on another country, GATT had little power to investigate the case, let alone discipline the country. Any country, including the country acting illegally, could stop the investigation process. Moreover, even if the case proceeded to a finding of illegality, no discipline could have been imposed upon the offending country unless the country itself agreed.

In contrast, the WTO does not require the offending country to agree either to its investigation or discipline. Moreover, if a country does not implement a WTO panel's recommendations within a certain period, the country that was harmed can seek authorization to retaliate.

Among the most significant moves toward limiting administered protection is the new sunset rule that requires a review of injury each five years after an antidumping order is issued, i.e., antidumping actions can no longer continue indefinitely without further review, as has been common in some countries, including the United States.

More generally, the WTO enhances freer trade through greater transparency and due process. The agreement makes the antidumping duty laws more specific, permitting exporters to form more concrete and accurate expectations about the criteria for fair pricing. The agreement more fully defines avenues for dispute settlement, which also increase the likelihood of freer trade and can lower the risk to traders.

AREAS WHERE PROTECTIONIST BIAS HAS NOT CHANGED

While the WTO has reduced the protectionist bias in the areas mentioned above, in spite of some clear limitations, in other areas it has had a smaller effect. The extensive documentation that the U.S. Department of Commerce and other countries have historically imposed on foreign producers accused of dumping is not addressed by the WTO. In the United States, for example, the requirement that foreign firms complete around 100 pages of documentation in a tight time frame, in English, and in a computer-readable format, is not likely to change as a result of any current agreements. The WTO does not reduce countries' opportunities to impose what some have charged are unreasonable and arbitrary demands on foreign producers.

In spite of outward appearances to the contrary, another area in which the new agreement has not changed much is in the determination of injury. Traditionally, if the amount of "dumped" imports is not great enough to inflict some measure of material injury to an industry, then antidumping duties were not legal under GATT. But the definition of material injury was ambiguous and broadly subject to each country's interpretation. The typical interpretation was that any foreign sales that displace domestic sales were cause for injury.

In contrast, the WTO defines the line at which dumped imports are to be considered negligible (i.e., too small to be injurious and therefore not subject to antidumping duties). The volume of dumped imports defined as negligible is less than 3 percent of total imports of the product or, if more than one country is subject to a dumping complaint, 7 percent of total imports. If a Japanese automobile maker is selling inexpensive cars in the United States and is alleged to be dumping, but sales of its cars are less than 3 percent of total imports, no duties will be assessed against its exports.

This new negligibility rule has, as of yet, not proven much of a constraint upon judgments of injury and it may be less restrictive to protectionists than past U.S. rules. Consider the case of a foreign firm that is sole exporter of some product to the United States. Suppose, in this hypothetical case, that U.S. manufacturers make so much of a similar product that the foreign exporter's sales account for only a 0.0001 percent share of the U.S. market. Under the new accord, a dumping suit may be filed against this firm because its share of total imports of this product is 100 percent, even though its share of the domestic market is only 0.0001, i.e., the negligibility requirement is 3 percent of total imports, not 3 percent of the total market.

It is hard to know if firms will file complaints about dumping at such a trivial level in the future. It does appear possible that, if such a 3-percent of imports negligibility requirement had been deemed sufficient to determine injury in the past, the number of injury determinations would have been greater than they, in fact, were. Finger (1994, 7) suggests that, had the WTO 3-percent criterion been the sole standard for evaluating the steel dumping petitions, injury would have been ruled in every case that the United States International Trade Commission rejected in July 1993.

Another protectionist detail of the WTO rules involves the legitimization of a much criticized European Union procedure for investigating antidumping. Administering authorities are permitted to calculate profit margins based on selected sales instead of following generally accepted accounting principals. The exaggerated profit figures are then used to inflate dumping margins, the differences between what are calculated as prices in the producer country and what are calculated as prices in the importing country. The presence of dumping and the appropriateness of damages and penalties are, of course, assessed on the basis of this margin.

Moreover, even though the WTO rules seem to reduce protectionism, it is clear that the United States has made efforts to turn these rules against free trade. We have already noted that the U.S. interprets the WTO price comparison rules to continue to allow apples-to-oranges comparisons in certain cases. In addition, although we have discussed changes in the *de minimis* rule as signifying reduced protectionist opportunities, the changes apply to antidumping investigations. U.S. legal language makes a distinction between investigations, which occur prior to a determination of dumping, and reviews, which occur thereafter. Accordingly, U.S. law still allows the 0.5 *de minimis* standard for the purpose of collecting estimated duty deposits from alleged violators. In addition, U.S. government memoranda make clear that efforts will be made to minimize the trade liberalizing effects of the sunset rule.

Although the WTO dispute settlement mechanism has simplified the process of disciplining countries that abuse the antidumping laws, there is little the WTO can actually do besides make recommendations. As with the old GATT agreement, even a recommendation to discipline may not be implemented. Moreover, the dispute settlement mechanism will preclude WTO panels from imposing their own judgments of fact or law on national antidumping authorities when the authorities have acted according to their own laws (U.S. Department of Commerce 1994). Finger and Fung (1993, 1) note that since July of 1993, only five GATT panels were able to determine illegal antidumping actions, but not one of these actions has since been lifted.

Table 1 presents a summary of the assessed effects of WTO on U.S. antidumping actions. As the table summarizes, the overall effect of the accord on U.S. fair trade laws appears to be a modest reduction in the opportunities they offer for out-and-out protectionism.

CONCLUSION

By all measures, commerce is becoming more globalized. The growth of world trade and investment has outstripped the growth of world income since GATT negotiations began in 1947. This long-term trend is unlikely to be reversed, in spite of the weak improvement in the WTO's ability to curtail the rapid growth of antidumping duties and other forms of administered protection. The benefits of open markets and international trade are now too apparent for most nations to ignore.

What persists, however, is the misconception that the purpose of trade accords is not to open one's own markets to imports, but to pry open other nations' markets for exports. The opening of home markets is usually seen as a concession to others, not (as economic logic suggests) as a good thing in itself because it benefits local consumers and makes both national and world economies work more efficiently.

Because of this bias, self-interested groups have been able to move quietly and swiftly under the cloak of "fair trade" to raise trade barriers in order to protect their market niche. A serious problem is that, as more transparent forms of protectionism are noticed and then negotiated away, self-interested groups devise replacements that are less transparent, such as antidumping laws and other nontariff barriers. The economic cost of antidumping laws is not merely the size of outstanding duties but also the cost of deterring potential trade. Like other sets of regulations, it creates incentives for manipulation and back-door harassment.

Perhaps the best strategy is not to modify the current fair trade laws but abandon them altogether and instead utilize more transparent forms of temporary protection, such as safeguard measures, to satisfy the demand for protection and ease the transition to a more liberalized trade environment. If anticompetitive behavior, such as cartels, monopolies, or predation are overriding concerns, then an international antitrust policy (like a domestic antitrust policy) can be drafted that treats domestic and foreign firms equivalently.

FOOTNOTES

[1] The use of data requests as a form of harassment is not peculiar to the United Sates. In 1991, Mexico filed an antidumping case against U.S. denim producers and gave them fifteen days to fill out a twenty-five page, detailed report on accounting and production processes. The report had to be in Spanish and in computer-readable format.

[2] Indeed, for the purposes of the Uruguay Round, the European Union and the Unites States formed a "nonaggression pact" whose purpose was to "resist all changes in antidumping rules that would make the system less trade restrictive (Horlick and Shea, 1995, p.a2)."

Table 1
Effects of WTO Rules on U.S. Antidumping Actions

New Rule	Effect
Five-year sunset rule on antidumping duties. After five years, dumping duties will be terminated unless a new review takes place.	Reduces the likelihood of permanent protection being granted to industries when foreign dumping is no longer present.
The level below which dumping margins will be ignored (the *de minimis* rule) rises from 0.5 percent to 2.0 percent.	Slightly reduces the number of the most frivolous antidumping investigations.
Level at which sales below cost are considered substantial rises from 10 percent to 20 percent.	Slightly decreases the number of cases in which foreign market price information is disregarded. May limit frivolous antidumping findings.
Defines a preference for comparing average domestic prices with average foreign prices or individual domestic prices with individual foreign prices. However, countries can still compare averages with individual prices when spot dumping is alleged.	Slightly decreases opportunity to find dumping when prices are identical in the foreign and home markets.
GATT panels cannot impose their judgments on a country when the country, in its finding of dumping, has acted in an unbiased and objective manner.	May slightly increase the opportunity to find dumping.
Dumped imports from all countries will not be considered injurious to domestic firms if they constitute less 7 percent of total imports.	Unlikely to have a significant effect on dumping actions.

[3] McGee (1995) argues that there is nothing to prevent domestic producers in the United States from arguing that the 10 percent general and administrative cost markup and the 8 percent profit markup should continue whenever they constitute, in the vernacular of antidumping, the "best information available."

[4] As in the case of the *de minimus* margins, the United States interprets the Uruguay Round Antidumping Code rules on average-to-average comparisons to apply only to the investigation phase. In the review phase, which is explained in the previous note, the United States interprets the Code to allow it to revert to the old apples-to-oranges rule if it so chooses.

[5] Indeed, some antidumping actions have been in force without reconsideration for decades.

[6] In the past, both the World Bank and the International Monetary Fund have sanctioned and at times even encouraged assistance-seeking development countries to enact antidumping rules, although antidumping is no longer encouraged.

[7] In this context, it is important to understand fully the meaning of the term "review." An importer that has been found to have dumped is required to deposit estimated dumping duties with the U.S. Customs at the time goods subject to an antidumping order enter the United States. These estimated duties are on the difference between some measure of foreign selling price vs. a measure of U.S. selling price. The final duty is assessed later, after a review to determine the actual selling margin. Note that the review is a procedure that takes place after the initial determination of dumping.

[8] See, for example, Palmeter (1995), pp. 73-4.

[9] For a much fuller elucidation of this issue, see Magee, Brock and Young's (1994) discussion of the voter information paradox. According to this theory, as voter opposition to protectionism becomes increasingly sophisticated, political parties respond with higher equilibrium levels or more opaque distortions.

REFERENCES

Anderson, Keith B. (1993), "Antidumping Laws in the United States – Use and Welfare Consequences," *Journal of World Trade* 27 (April): 99-117.

Baldwin, Robert E., and Michael O. Moore (1991), "Political Aspects of the Administration of the Trade Remedy Laws," in *Down in the Dumps: Administration of the Unfair Trade Laws*, Richard Boltuck and Robert E. Litan, eds. (Washington, DC: Brookings Institution).

Bhagwati, Jagdish (1988), *Protectionism* (Cambridge, MA: MIT Press).

Bourgeois, Jacques H.J., and Patrick A. Messerlin (1993) "Competition and EC Antidumping Regulations," Institut d'Etudes Politiques de Paris. mimeo.

Finger, J. Michael (1994), "The Subsidies-Countervailing Measures and Antidumping Agreements in the Uruguay Round Final Act," mimeo, World Bank.

_____ (1992), "Dumping and Antidumping: The Rhetoric and the Reality of Protection in Industrial Countries," *World Bank Research Observer* 7 (July): 121-43.

_____, and K.C. Fung (1993), "Will GATT Enforcement Control Antidumping," *Policy Research Working Paper* no. 1232, World Bank, December.

_____, H. Keith Hall, and Douglas R. Nelson (1982), "The Political Economy of Administered Protection," *American Economic Review* 72 (June): 452-66.

Hindley, Brian and Patrick A. Messerlin (1996), *Antidumping Industrial Policy: Legalized Protectionism in the WTO and What to Do about It*, (Washington, DC: The AEI Press).

Horlick, Gary N. and Eleanor C. Shea (1995), "The World Trade Organization Antidumping Agreement,"*Journal of World Trade* 29 (February): 5-32.

Magee, Stephen, William Brock, and Leslie Young (1989), *Black Hole Tariffs and Endogenous Policy Theory: Political Economy in General Equilibrium* (New York: Cambridge University Press).

McGee, Robert W. (1995), "Antidumping Laws in the Twenty-First Century," in *International Business in the Twenty-First Century*, Khosrow Fatemi and Susan E.W. Nichols, eds.(Laredo, TX: International Trade and Finance Association).

Messerlin, Patrick A. (1996), "Competition Policy and Antidumping Reform: An Exercise in Transition," in *The World Trading System: Challenges Ahead*, Jeffrey J. Schott, ed. (Washington, DC: Institute of International Economics).

Murray, Tracy (1991), "The Administration of the Antidumping Duty Law by the Department of Commerce," in *Down in the Dumps: Administration of the Unfair Trade Laws*, Richard Boltuck and Robert E. Litan, eds. (Washington, DC: Brookings Institution).

OECD (1996), *OECD Economic Outlook* (Paris: Organization for Economic Cooperation and Development), June.

Palmeter, N. David (1995), "United States Implementation of the Uruguay Round Antidumping Code." *Journal of World Trade* 29 (June): 39-82.

Shin, Hyun Ja (1992), "Census and Analysis of Antidumping Actions in the United States," Princeton University, mimeo.

Stoeckel, Andres, David Pearce, and Gary Banks (1990), *Western Trade Blocs* (Canberra, Australia: Center for International Economics).

U.S. Department of Commerce (1994), *Uruguay Round Update* (Washington, DC: Office of Multilateral Affairs, International Economic Policy, U.S. Department of Commerce), January.

USITC (1995), *The Economic Effects of Antidumping and Countervailing Duty Orders and Suspension Agreements*, Publication 2900, (Washington, DC: U.S. International Trade Commission), June.

WTO (1996), *Annual Report 1996* (Geneva: World Trade Organization), August.

The Spotlight and the Bottom Line

How Multinationals Export Human Rights

Debora L. Spar

In 1996 Kathie Lee Gifford made front-page news. The well-liked television personality had lent her name to a discount line of women's clothing that, it was discovered, had been made by underage Central American workers. That same year, the Walt Disney Company was exposed contracting with Haitian suppliers who paid their workers less than Haiti's minimum wage of $2.40 a day. Nike and Reebok, makers of perhaps the world's most popular athletic footwear, were similarly and repeatedly exposed.

In all these cases, the companies accused were U.S. manufacturers of consumer products. They were being targeted for human rights violations committed abroad not by their own managers or in their own plants but by the subcontractors who produced their products in overseas facilities. Traditionally, the corporate response to this subcontractor problem has been predictable, if unfortunate. U.S. firms have argued that they cannot realistically or financially be held responsible for the labor practices of their foreign suppliers. "The problem is, we don't own the factories," a Disney spokesperson protested. "We are dealing with a licensee."

Recently, though, this attitude has started to change. As a direct result of heightened human rights activism, sharper media scrutiny, and the increased communication facilitated by the Internet, U.S. corporations are finding it difficult to sustain their old hands-off policy. Under pressure, they are beginning to accept responsibility for the labor practices and human rights abuses of their foreign subcontractors.

CODES OF CONDUCT

Much of this new activity clusters around the promulgation of voluntary codes of conduct. In just the past several years, U.S. industry has proposed and accepted a rash of codes. In 1996 Labor Secretary Robert Reich launched a "No Sweat" campaign designed to force foreign garment makers to comply with U.S. labor laws and to expose retailers who might be purchasing garments made under sweatshop conditions. This was followed by the widespread publication of a Labor Department "Trendsetter" list of retailers that had publicly agreed to "demonstrate a commitment" to U.S. labor laws and to monitor the working conditions under which their garments were produced. In August 1996 the White House established an Apparel Industry Partnership, which devised a workplace code of conduct defining decent and humane working conditions, applicable to all participating companies as well as to their overseas contractors. To ensure that the code became more than a public relations

---

DEBORA L. SPAR is Associate Professor of Business Administration at Harvard University's Graduate School of Business Administration.

exercise, members of the Partnership also proposed that the code's adherents open their facilities to periodic inspections by independent monitors. Even more striking is Social Accountability 8000, an ambitious attempt to compel firms to comply with a certifiable set of labor and human rights standards, launched last year by the Council on Economic Priorities and a group of influential companies. SA8000 rests on market acceptance, not legal coercion. Firms would comply with the standards and the monitoring necessary to ensure compliance simply to win certification. Already, the retail giants Toys 'R' Us and Avon have announced their intent to demand that all their suppliers become SA8000-certified.

It is easy, perhaps, to be cynical about these codes. Prominent critics such as Louis Henkin of Columbia Law School have charged that they carry less weight than legal standards and lack bite. But it is not clear that such skepticism is warranted. In fact, codes of conduct have already begun to be a significant factor in the pursuit of human rights. By changing the calculus of U.S. firms doing business abroad, codes can change their behavior.

CAUGHT IN THE ACT

The logic follows a pattern that one might call the spotlight phenomenon. When U.S. corporations go abroad, they take more than their capital and technology with them. They also take their brand names, their reputations, and their international images. They bring in their wake the scrutiny of U.S.-based activist groups and the international media. When U.S. corporations are caught engaging in unfair or abusive practices, these groups spring into action, casting a shadow of scorn. To some extent, the process echoes the familiar muckraking of decades past, but the combination of an increasingly global economy and ever-more sophisticated and diverse communication channels has recently expanded the reach of even small-scale critics. On the Internet, grassroots activism has, quite literally, been electrified. Using inexpensive electronic mailing campaigns, human rights groups can reach a far wider audience than in the past, drawing supporters from across national borders to mobilize consumer boycotts or political action campaigns. Once these campaigns reach the public arena, the perpetually hungry media brings attention to even small stories—especially those pitting giant U.S. corporations against hapless foreign workers.

Although this new form of muckraking creates its own potential hazards, it also affects the basic calculus of an investing firm. Suddenly, the advantages of lower-cost labor or lower-cost inputs from more abusive suppliers must be weighed against the crush of negative publicity, the cost of public relations, and the possibility of consumer protests. For consumer products firms, the impact is particularly intense since highly visible brand names provide an ideal target for smear campaigns and other public attacks.

At the moment, public awareness of human rights issues is not fully decisive in the marketplace. Customers still seem to favor brand, price, and quality over perceptions of humane treatment and social responsibility. But these preferences are starting to change. In a 1995 survey, 78 percent of respondents said that they would prefer to shop at retail stores that had committed themselves to ending garment worker abuse; 84 percent said they would pay an extra $1 on a $20 item to ensure that the garment had been made in a worker-friendly environment. Similar results appeared in a 1996 survey—only this time, nearly 24 percent said that retailers and not just manufacturers should take responsibility for preventing the use of sweatshop labor. Such polls do not, of course, necessarily predict consumer behavior, but they do seem to show a heightened awareness of human rights issues and a newfound eagerness to hold manufacturers and retailers accountable for their behavior.

As public concern coalesces around issues of human rights, the promulgation of codes and standards completes the spotlight phenomenon. Once firms have adhered to publicly acknowledged standards, they magnify the effect of their own violations. So long as firms could argue that subcontractors were beyond their reach, they could limit the public fallout from findings of abuse. With codes in place, however, firms can no longer hide behind an arm's length relationship of indifference. Once they have agreed to comply, they will be forced to—not by the sanction of law but by the sanction of the market. Firms will cut off abusive suppliers or make them clean up because it is now *in their financial interest* to do so. The spotlight does not change the morality of U.S. multinational managers. It changes their bottom-line interests.

A RACE TO THE TOP

Already, early evidence supports the potency of the spotlight phenomenon. When reports surfaced that Reebok was purchasing soccer balls stitched by 12-year-old Pakistani workers, the firm sprang into action. It created a new central production facility in Pakistan and established a system of independent monitors. Eager to retain its image as a strong supporter of human rights around the world, Reebok affixed new "Made without Child Labor" labels to its soccer balls. The Gap also bowed dramatically to public pressure. After several high-profile protests in 1995, including one at a Manhattan store, The Gap signed an agreement with the National Labor Committee committing itself to independent third-party monitoring of its overseas suppliers. Starbucks Coffee, generally regarded as one of the most socially progressive U.S. firms, was heavily picketed in 1995 by activists demanding that the company keep closer tabs on the Guatemalan plantations from which it buys some of its coffee beans. The chain eventually complied, issuing a revised code of conduct and specific action plans for all of its supplier countries.

Recently, the spotlight has focused most frequently on Burma, whose ruling junta, the State Peace and Development Council, is one of the world's most repressive regimes. Facing mounting criticism of their presence in Burma, Levi Strauss, Macy's, Liz Claiborne, and Eddie Bauer all pulled their operations out of the country. So did oil giants Texaco and Amoco, even though just six months earlier Amoco's president had described Burma as one of his firm's most promising new regions for exploration. A spokesman for Eddie Bauer neatly captured the changed calculus facing the firms. "After months of researching the situation," he announced, "we deemed that the political climate and growing opposition to trade in Burma posed a potential threat to our future manufacturing opportunities." In other words, they were leaving purely for commercial reasons. The spotlight had made its way to their bottom line.

What makes this dynamic even more powerful is the potential for cooperation and collective action. The problem for competing firms is that the force of the market makes it difficult for any single company to pay higher wages or insist on superior labor standards. Of course, some firms do so out of conviction; others do so because they have a higher-quality or niche product that enables them to pass cost increases on to their consumers. Yet in the aggregate, the familiar problem of "free riders" remains. If one firm pays the higher wage or refuses to do business with an exploitative low-cost subcontractor, it risks losing market share to more callous competitors. Thus, multinationals have long been able to rationalize their use of low-wage labor or abusive subcontractors by appealing to the unstoppable force of global competition. If they held to higher standards, they claim, their rivals would instantly overwhelm them. Theoretically, the only way to solve this free-rider problem is through collective action. If all firms—or at least a good majority of the larger ones—adhere to the same standard, none is individually penalized. Collective action can thus force a race to the top rather than the much-heralded race to the bottom. What changes the direction of this race is the combined force of codes and publicity. Firms adhere to the higher standard because public attention forces them to do so. And the more companies adhere, the easier it is for even the low-profile or sluggish to join.

The Burma withdrawals showcased this collective dynamic. Once Levi Strauss pulled out, it was easier for Macy's and Liz Claiborne to follow. Collective action was also a major component of Reebok's approach to Pakistan. Before proceeding with its child-labor-free campaign, the company obtained approval and support from both the World Federation of Sporting Goods Industry and the U.S.-based Sporting Goods Manufacturers Association. When Reebok refused to sell balls made with child labor, so did all of its competitors. None, then, were left at a commercial disadvantage—and all collectively left themselves vulnerable to the scrutiny of the spotlight. As pressure for codes continues to mount, and as firms such as Price Waterhouse and Kroll Associates eagerly offer to perform audits of firms' compliance with the codes, such cases will probably proliferate. In the process, human rights are likely to improve.

STRANGE BEDFELLOWS

Human rights and U.S. multinational corporations are traditionally considered unlikely bedfellows. By nature, firms are not in the business of promoting human rights abroad, and advocates of human rights have typically disdained corporations rather than embracing them. When Washington has pursued a human rights agenda, U.S. firms have historically been little more than the awkward instrument of U.S. policy: their activities are denied to rogue states as retribution for human rights abuses.

But perhaps there is another way to think about multinational involvement. In some cases and industries, the natural impact of U.S. firms may well be to hinder the development of human rights. Sometimes multinationals funnel capital to repressive states or abuse the labor force they find at their disposal. Sometimes their presence cements the power of dictators or helps suppress opposition groups. Earlier this century, for example, United Fruit helped mastermind a coup in Guatemala; ITT played a key role in overthrowing the popularly elected government of Salvador Allende in Chile; and U.S. mining and oil companies forged cozy relationships with dictatorial regimes across Africa. But overall and empirically there is little to suggest that U.S. investment is inherently bad for human rights in the developing world. If anything, the available evidence indicates that the presence of U.S. multinationals usually corresponds to an improvement in human rights. This relationship certainly does not prove that U.S. investment *causes* human rights to be more respected, but neither does it give any credence to predictions of exploitation and malfeasance. Investment by U.S. firms may well help move human rights in a positive direction.

It would be absurd to advocate investment by U.S. firms as a panacea for the human rights abuses that pepper the globe. A multitude of ills can only be addressed through diplomacy, persuasion, or sometimes force. But there are things that multinationals, especially U.S. multinationals, can do. Simply by following their own interests, they may influence the local environment in positive ways. They bring jobs, capital, technology, know-how, management techniques, labor relations, and administrative structures that are unlikely to depart too dramatically from U.S. standards. These working standards will nearly always be higher than those that prevail in the local developing economy.

Finally, U.S. multinationals bring with them the glare of public scrutiny and the changes it can induce in an increasingly global marketplace. When local producers in Vietnam, Pakistan, or Honduras exploit their work force, few in the West hear of it, especially if the products are not exported to Western markets. But when those same producers become suppliers to Reebok, Levi Strauss, or Walt Disney, their actions make headlines in the United States. Changing their behavior becomes, increasingly, a bottom-line concern of Reebok, Levi Strauss, and Disney.

Under these circumstances, the old Leninist link between multinational firms and foreign exploitation seems outmoded or even contradictory. Rather than having an interest in subverting human rights, corporations—particularly high-profile firms from open and democratic societies—may well see the commercial benefits of promoting human rights. It is ironic, and certainly not obvious. But in a world marked by international media and transnational activism, U.S. multinationals could be—indeed, may already be—a powerful instrument in the pursuit of human rights.

NAFTA: How A Successful Agreement

by Joe Cobb

During the heated debate about the North American Free Trade Agreement (NAFTA) in 1993, many claims and counterclaims were made about job losses.

Ross Perot coined the famous sound bite "a giant sucking sound" to describe American jobs going south. Now the evidence is in. Hundreds of thousands of U.S. jobs have *not* been destroyed, and the U.S. manufacturing base has *not* been weakened.

Instead, U.S. exports and employment levels have risen significantly as total trade among the NAFTA countries has increased, and the average living standards of American workers have improved. The general unemployment rate declined to 5.3 percent in 1996 from 6.8 percent in 1993.

In 1996, U.S. global trade (exports plus imports) totaled $1.765 trillion—over 23 percent of U.S. GDP, compared with 10 percent in 1970. The Office of the U.S. Trade Representative (USTR) has estimated that by the year 2010, trade will represent about 36 percent of U.S. GDP. Today, more than 11 million U.S. jobs depend on exports, 1.5 million more than in 1992. Roughly a quarter of U.S. economic growth during the Clinton administration has been due to export expansion.

Total North American trade increased $127 billion during NAFTA's first three years, from $293 billion in 1993 to $420 billion in 1996, a gain of 43 percent. Canada and Mexico are already the top two U.S. trading partners, but if the post-NAFTA increase in trade with them had been with a single country, it would make that country the fourth-largest U.S. trading partner.

In 1996, U.S. exports to Canada and Mexico, at $190 billion, exceeded U.S. exports to any other area of the world, including the entire Pacific Rim or all of Europe. Mexico and Canada purchased $3 of every $10 in U.S. exports and supplied $3 of every $10 in U.S. imports in 1996.

While NAFTA involves both Canada and Mexico, the controversy in 1993 was whether adding Mexico would have bad effects for the American worker. But obviously, the economic growth from increased trade with Mexico has not hurt. U.S. exports to Mexico are up 37 percent from 1993, reaching a record $57 billion in 1996.

During NAFTA's first three years, 39 of the 50 states increased their exports to Mexico, and 44 states reported a growth in exports to Mexico during 1996, as the pace of U.S. exports to that country accelerated.

According to the U.S. Department of Commerce, U.S. exports to Mexico in the fourth quarter of 1996 were growing at an annualized rate of $64 billion. Moreover, U.S. market share in Mexico increased from 69 percent of total Mexican imports in 1993 to 76 percent in 1996.

Total two-way trade between the United States and Mexico was nearly $130 billion. During this period, U.S. exports to Canada also increased by $134 billion, or 33 percent. Total two-way trade between the United States and Canada was $290 billion in 1996.

A close look at the numbers shows there is a U.S. trade deficit with both Canada and Mexico, but the success of NAFTA once again proves there is nothing wrong with trade deficits, as economists have taught for over 200 years. The combined U.S. trade deficit with Canada and Mexico increased from $9 billion in 1992 to $39.9 billion in 1996. But since 1992, the U.S. economy has created 12 million new jobs (net). Man-

(continued on page 160)

Is It Doing?

A Failed Approach

by Alan Tonelson

In 1992, Bill Clinton won the presidency in part by making a very quotable, trenchant point about George Bush's economic record. Everything that was supposed to be going up, he and Al Gore emphasized repeatedly, was going down. And everything that was supposed to be going down was going up.

Five years later, a similar point can be made about NAFTA, the North American Free Trade Agreement completed by the Clinton administration in late 1993. In fact, few public policy initiatives in recent memory have so mercilessly and consistently mocked their champions' predictions.

Today, NAFTA supporters want to extend the treaty's terms to the rest of the Western Hemisphere, starting with Chile. Early this fall, the administration is expected to submit to Congress its request for fast-track authority for these and a series of other major trade talks. But the cracked crystal ball of NAFTA lobbyists in and out of government should call into question not only their credentials as analysts but their entire approach to economic globalization.

NAFTA was advertised as nothing less than a godsend to the United States, Canada, and Mexico—a boon not only to broad-based prosperity throughout North America but for social progress and political stability in Mexico in particular.

By the entirely reasonable Clinton-Gore up-down standards, however, NAFTA's results have been positively perverse—except for the big U.S. multinational corporations that dominate North American trade flows.

The impact of NAFTA and NAFTA-style globalization has been especially damaging in the United States and Mexico, whose recent trade record will understandably be the focus of Congress' upcoming NAFTA expansion debate.

Since NAFTA's late-1993 signing, median wages in the United States and Mexico are down, as is employment in manufacturing, which generates an economy's highest-paying jobs on average.

The U.S. trade deficit with Mexico, on the other hand, is way up. So are flows of illegal drugs and immigrants from Mexico into the United States—even though NAFTA was supposed to make Mexico so prosperous that its people would be able to earn a decent living by staying home and out of criminal activity. And despite NAFTA's ostensible national security dimension—preventing chaos on America's southern border—social and political instability in Mexico are way up, too, as is anti-Americanism.

NAFTA supporters point to two of their own rising indicators to score the agreement as a success: the simple post-NAFTA expansion of trade within North America and the continued healthy levels of U.S. exports to Mexico despite the peso collapse and subsequent Mexican depression.

Expanded trade, however, is at best a peculiar measure of economic policy success. In the first place, most of the U.S.-Mexico trade expansion has come in the form of rising U.S. imports from Mexico.

Rising imports, of course, can be a sign of national economic health, and bilateral trade deficits are not always bad or even important. But in America's current circumstances, the jump in imports from Mexico is adding significantly to a U.S. global deficit that sets new records every year. That deficit persists despite the vaunted competitive comeback

(continued on page 161)

(continued from page 158)

ufacturing employment grew from 16.9 million jobs in 1992 to 18.3 million in 1993, an increase of 1.4 million net new jobs.

The U.S. Department of Labor lists more than 110,000 U.S. workers as certified for training assistance under NAFTA's Trade Adjustment Assistance Program, which indicates that Perot was not entirely wrong. Those Americans lost their jobs because of NAFTA. But the negative impact of NAFTA each week must have been very small if only 110,000 jobs is the total after three years.

Although 110,000 families were hit hard by NAFTA, the job-loss rate in the United States, as reported by the number of new unemployment insurance claims,

■

Total two-way trade between the United States and Mexico was nearly $130 billion.

■

is normally about 350,000 every week. Moreover, the U.S. economy currently creates more than 110,000 new jobs (net) in about two weeks. On the positive side of the employment issue, U.S. exports to NAFTA countries currently support 2.3 million U.S. jobs, according to the USTR.

A study by economist Richard Nadler, who reviewed U.S. standards of living before and after NAFTA was launched in 1994, found that the rate of increase in personal wealth has more than tripled since NAFTA was implemented.

His review measured the improvement in three ways: First, growth in disposable personal income, adjusted for inflation, averaged 1.89 percent annually in 1994–95, compared with 0.25 percent annually 1990–93. Second, personal consumption expenditures grew by an inflation-adjusted 1.76 percent annually during 1994–95, compared with 0.56 percent a year in 1990–93.

Finally, inflation-adjusted GDP per capita grew by 1.79 percent annually in 1994–95, compared with only 0.23 percent during 1990–93. Of course, there was a recession in 1990–91, which slowed down the economy in the pre-NAFTA period, but perhaps NAFTA has helped prevent a recession since then.

INVESTMENT BOOM

The major complaint against NAFTA by organized labor during the 1993 controversy over adopting the treaty was the fear that new investments would be made south of the border instead of in U.S. factories. There has indeed been an investment boom in Mexico, but the inflow has not seemed to have any depressing effect on the United States.

NAFTA has encouraged U.S. and foreign investors with apparel and footwear factories in Asia to relocate their production operations to Mexico. This diversion of investment from Asia to Mexico "saved the heavier end of clothing manufacture in the United States: the textile mills," according to Nadler.

NAFTA has been very good for the traditional southern textile states like North Carolina and Alabama, as well as for major U.S. agricultural states such as Montana, Nebraska, and North Dakota, whose politicians in Congress typically opposed it.

The investment boom in Mexico has been a major source of new demand for U.S. manufacturers of capital goods. The largest post-NAFTA gains in U.S. exports to Mexico have been in such high-technology manufacturing sectors as industrial machinery, transportation and electronic equipment, plastics and rubber, fabricated metal products, and chemicals.

A recent economic analysis published by the U.S. Federal Reserve Bank of Chicago concludes that NAFTA will lead to output gains for all three participant countries. The study concluded that, under NAFTA, the sustained annual growth rate of the three economies is permanently higher than it would be otherwise.

Mexico's GDP is predicted to rise by an added factor of 3.26 percent, U.S. GDP by 0.24 percent, and Canada's GDP by 0.11 percent. These gains are roughly twice as large as those predicted by previous forecasts of NAFTA's potential for accelerated growth in North American trade, output, and employment.

In general, bilateral Mexican-North American trade should increase about 20 percent as a result of NAFTA. This projected growth also means more U.S. jobs and a higher standard of living for American workers.

One of NAFTA's main purposes was to "lock in" the process of economic and political reform in Mexico, which started in the late 1980s. Mexico's membership in NAFTA, the World Trade Organization, the Asia-Pacific Economic Cooperation forum, and the Organization for Economic Cooperation and Development has created international commitments and linkages that politicians in Mexico cannot ignore.

Mexico's constitution was amended in 1996 to make the electoral process more transparent and independent of the government. These reforms had a dramatic effect on July 6, 1997, when opposition parties obtained a majority in Mexico's congression-

35. NAFTA: How Is It Doing?

Exceeding Expectations

★ The average living standards of American workers have improved, and the general unemployment rate declined to 5.3 percent in 1996.

★ U.S. exports to Latin America and the Caribbean increased by 110 percent from 1990 to 1996.

★ The sustained annual growth rate of the United States, Canada, and Mexico is consistently higher than it would be otherwise.

al elections for the first time. There can be no doubt that NAFTA is a major factor in Mexico's transformation toward a free-market democracy on the U.S.-Canadian model.

The proposals to expand NAFTA to include Chile and other countries of the Western Hemisphere are questioned by doubters, but the evidence is already clear. As a market for U.S. goods, the Western Hemisphere already is nearly twice as large as the European Union and nearly 50 percent larger than Asia. The Western Hemisphere accounted for 39 percent of U.S. goods exports in 1996 and was the only region in which the United States recorded a trade surplus in both 1995 and '96.

Moreover, while U.S. goods exports to the world generally increased 57 percent from 1990 to 1996, U.S. exports to Latin America and the Caribbean (excluding Mexico) increased by 110 percent during the same period. If current trends continue, Latin America alone will exceed Japan and western Europe combined as an export market for U.S. goods by the year 2010.

There should be no doubts about the success of NAFTA. Although only three years old, this international trade agreement has far exceeded the expectations of its advocates back in 1993. Even though three years may seem like too little time to reach any final judgments about NAFTA, it already is clear that critics of this agreement have been wrong on all counts.

Joe Cobb is president of the Trade Policy Institute in Washington, D.C.

★★★★★★★★★★★★★

(continued from page 159)

of American industry during the 1990s, a historically weak dollar, and unimpressive recent relative growth rates.

Although macroeconomists have assured us that the gap would close, the Fed now judges the economy's overall growth rate is being cut by about a third. In fact, significantly reducing America's global trade deficit might actually enable the U.S. economy to grow fast enough to push up real wages for most Americans—something that hasn't happened on a sustained basis since 1973.

Just as important, expanded trade per se has no place as a major goal of U.S. foreign economic policy. It is simply a means to an end. The raison d'être of any economic policy is encouraging a healthy and sustained rise in living standards for the vast majority of Americans. Failure to meet this goal dwarfs any other economic achievements, whether low inflation, expanded productivity, rising stock markets, or even strong overall growth.

INTRA-COMPANY TRADE

As for the levels of U.S. exports to Mexico, a look beneath the surface reveals how misleading such aggregate figures can be. According to a UCLA study commissioned by the Clinton administration itself, post-NAFTA U.S.-Mexican trade has been driven "almost entirely" by the growth of intra-company trade.

Such exports, which represent a large (more than one-third) and growing share of overall goods exports, do more to destroy good jobs than to create them. The reasons can be complex, but the export argument is so central to the pro-NAFTA case that they are worth examining in some detail.

Traditional goods exports—

161

6 ❖ INTERNATIONAL ECONOMICS

NAFTA supporters offer a superficially convincing alibi for Mexico's ills, blaming them entirely on the peso crash, not the trade treaty.

Unsatisfactory Results

✪ NAFTA's results have been negative—except for the big U.S. multinational corporations.

✪ Median wages in the United States and Mexico are down, as is employment in manufacturing.

✪ Flows of illegal drugs and immigrants from Mexico into the United States are high.

which consist of sales of finished products from U.S. companies to unrelated customers abroad—boost American employment by expanding a company's customer base and thus require increased production and often more employees to meet the new demand. U.S. intra-company exports, for their part, consist of the shipments of parts and components of finished products from individual companies' U.S.-based factories to their overseas factories.

These foreign facilities perform further manufacturing or final assembly work. From the standpoint of creating high-paying manufacturing jobs for Americans, such exports are a growing problem, because in most cases the assembly or further manufacturing used to be done in this country.

Intra-company exports can still produce U.S. jobs in net if shipping some production abroad helps U.S. businesses increase final overseas sales or recapture markets at home—say, by enabling companies to customize their products to suit local tastes in new markets.

But much of the new U.S. manufacturing investment abroad is in countries like Mexico, whose people are generally too poor to buy what they make, and/or that are trying to export their way to national prosperity and thus artificially depress consumption. Moreover, the figures for U.S. industries like autos—where U.S. investment has been enormous—indicate that very little of what they produce in Mexico is exported outside North America.

Instead, much of the U.S. multinationals' foreign output gets sent right back to America for final sale. And since virtually no U.S. industries with big American payrolls have won back much domestic market share since NAFTA's signing, it's clear that intra-company trade amounts to America largely exporting to itself. This means that most of the new production in countries like Mexico is simply replacing production in the United States.

Exactly how much do U.S. multinationals produce abroad for eventual sale back to the United States? Only the companies and Washington know for sure. But the former want to keep this information secret—largely to avoid a public relations nightmare.

The latter simply swallows the corporate line about the need to protect trade secrets. In the case of Mexico, however, the scale of this ersatz exporting can be measured by looking at Mexican government figures. They tell us that, currently, 62 percent of all U.S. exports to Mexico are eventually reexported back to the United States—up from 40 percent before NAFTA.

When Vice President Gore debated Ross Perot in 1993 on the treaty's merits, he used booming new Mexican Wal-Marts as symbols for the huge new Mexican consumer market he claimed NAFTA would open for American companies and workers alike. A better symbol would be Mexican autoworkers performing sophisticated, highly productive manufacturing work that used to be done in America—at one-eighth the wage.

MEXICO'S CRISIS

NAFTA supporters offer a superficially convincing alibi for Mexico's ills, blaming them entirely on the peso crash, not the trade treaty. But they conveniently overlook the role played by NAFTA-style economic liberalization policies in triggering Mexico's crisis—principally, hooking Mexico on inflows of foreign capital that the country's corrupt leaders could sustain politically only by overvaluing their currency and artificially increasing the average Mexican's purchasing power. In addition, any U.S. administration failing to anticipate such an extraordinary event is obviously not competent to make Mexico policy to begin with.

The NAFTA lobby also insists that without the treaty, high-paying manufacturing jobs would continue to flee overseas—only they would wind up in East Asia, where manufacturers use far fewer U.S.-made inputs and therefore far fewer U.S. workers. They're right, but their point unwittingly indicts the broader globalization approach they favor.

In the world created by these policies:

• where the U.S. permits many of its biggest trading partners to shut out competitive American-made goods;

• where American companies therefore have little choice but to remain competitive by cutting costs through outsourcing to low-wage countries;

• and where the enormous U.S. market remains wide open to goods carrying American brand names but produced in countries where cheap and even child and slave labor is abundant, where unions are violently repressed, and where job safety and serious environmental-regulations protections are virtually unknown;

it is indeed better to use NAFTA to encourage production in Mexico rather than in China or Indonesia. Yet simply accepting these conditions ultimately condemns American workers and their foreign counterparts to a global race to the bottom in terms of wages and working conditions.

Replacing the failed NAFTA approach to North American trade alone will not turn globalization into a winner for workers at home and abroad. But with the fast-track debate looming this fall, it's the ideal place to start.

Alan Tonelson is a research fellow at the U.S. Business and Industrial Council Educational Foundation, a business-related research organization.

TRADE POLICY AT A CROSS ROADS

BY I.M. DESTLER

FOR U.S. TRADE POLICY, the past quarter-century is not without irony. Its first 20 years were replete with economic troubles, real and perceived: "oil shocks" and double-digit inflation in the 1970s; the "twin deficits" of budget and trade in the 1980s; unemployment, the productivity slowdown, and stagnation in workers' take-home pay; the growing challenge from Japan. Yet over these same two decades, the United States maintained and reinforced its open-market international trade policies, with two unprecedented global agreements (the Tokyo Round and the Uruguay Round under the General Agreement on Tariffs and Trade), the North American Free Trade Agreement, and other liberalization initiatives.

In the past five years, by contrast, the U.S. economic situation has turned astonishingly rosy. Inflation and unemployment are both at or near their 25-year lows. Productivity is rising, as are workers' real incomes. The budget deficit and the Japanese threat are both history. Yet since the beginning of 1995, U.S. trade policy has been on hold. For the better part of three years President Bill Clinton sent no proposal to Congress to renew the "fast-track" negotiating authority granted to all his predecessors since Gerald Ford. When he finally did so, and lobbied hard for it in the fall of 1997, his overture was spurned. When House Speaker Newt Gingrich pressed for approval last September, the vote was negative.

Today U.S. producers and consumers are exceptionally well positioned to gain from global trade. Federal government action can enhance these gains, particularly by negotiating with other nations to achieve further mutual reductions in trade barriers. But no agenda for U.S. trade policy can be credible in 1999 unless it recognizes and takes account of the political forces that led to today's stalemate.

Diplomatic Success, Political Stalemate

Bill Clinton inherited two landmark trade initiatives: NAFTA, signed by President George Bush in 1992, and the GATT Uruguay Round, initiated under Ronald Reagan. In an uphill battle, Clinton won congressional approval of NAFTA in November 1993—after negotiating side agreements with Canada and Mexico on labor and environmental issues. His U.S. Trade Representative, Mickey Kantor, closed the Uruguay Round deal a month later, and Congress approved its implementing legislation in December 1994.

The United States concluded 1994 with two new trade-liberalizing commitments. In November, leaders of the Asia Pacific Economic Cooperation Forum (APEC) agreed to free trade among themselves by 2010 (2020 for the less developed members). In December Western Hemisphere nations pledged to negotiate a Free Trade Area of the Americas by 2005.

The years that followed saw further progress in trade liberalization under the auspices of the World Trade Organization, the permanent global institution created during the Uruguay Round. Three new sectoral negotiations carrying over from the Uruguay Round were successfully concluded: information technology in December 1996, basic telecommunications services in February 1997, and financial services in December 1997. The WTO's Dispute Settlement Understanding also got off to a credible start. The United States became the most active complainant and won most of its cases.

The United States also remained active in bilateral trade matters, striking agreements with Japan on autos and China on intellectual property. But U.S. negotiators were undercut by the expiration of fast track, the law that allows them to make credible commitments to reduce U.S. trade barriers in exchange for market-opening commitments by U.S. negotiating partners.

I.M. Destler is director of the Center for International and Security Studies at the Maryland School of Public Affairs and a visiting fellow at the Institute for International Economics. This article is drawn from the author's chapter in Setting National Priorities *(Brookings, forthcoming).*

Fast track is Washington's solution to a bedrock constitutional dilemma. The president and his executive branch can negotiate all they like, but Congress makes U.S. trade law. Other nations know that our highly independent legislature will not necessarily deliver on executive promises. So in negotiations where broad-ranging commitments to open markets are exchanged, they refuse to bargain seriously unless U.S. officials can assure that Congress will write their concessions into U.S. statutes. Fast track offers that assurance, with its promise that Congress will vote up or down, within a defined time period, on legislation submitted by the president to implement specific trade agreements.

> **The U.S. market remains open. The U.S. economy is in exceptionally good shape, recent signs of weakness notwithstanding. But U.S. Trade policy is in serious trouble.**

Congress first granted fast-track authority in 1974 and renewed it five times thereafter. When APEC members and the Western Hemisphere nations agreed to free trade in 1994, the prevailing assumption was that the U.S. president would be granted that authority to carry out his nation's side of the bargain. So it was also with the follow-on agenda of the WTO involving intellectual property, government procurement, and agriculture. But President Clinton will shortly enter his sixth year without fast-track authority, and near-term prospects for its enactment are not good.

The trouble began with a 1994 proposal by USTR Mickey Kantor for a broad, seven-year fast-track extension as part of the Uruguay Round implementing legislation. Building on the NAFTA side agreements and seeking to mend trade policy relations with wounded Democratic constituencies, Kantor proposed that "labor standards" and "trade and the environment" be among the seven "principal trade negotiating objectives" for which fast track would be employed. Organized business objected vehemently, as did free-trade Republicans. Compromise was

36. Trade Policy at a Cross Roads

never reached, and the administration did not include fast track in the bill.

In 1995, the House Ways and Means Committee, under its new Republican chairman Bill Archer (R-TX), approved a fast-track bill. But sporadic negotiations with Kantor, centering on the labor-environment language, were unsuccessful. In early 1997 the Senate Finance Committee leadership joined its House counterparts in pressing for a White House fast-track proposal. But differences over labor and the environment had hardened. Many Democrats wanted these issues to be central to future trade negotiations; almost all Republicans took the opposite position.

The president's heart lay with his Democratic allies. And there were strong general arguments for linkage: trade undeniably affected both workers and the environment, and trade policy needed to broaden its domestic support. But the Clinton administration had been pressing these connections since it came to office and meeting strong international resistance, particularly from developing nations that saw the trade-labor linkage in particular as disguised protectionism. After postponing a decision for months, Clinton went where the votes were, toward the Republican majority. He proposed legislation in September 1997 with severe limits on coverage of labor and environmental issues. He counted on his persuasive powers, as witnessed earlier with NAFTA, to bring victory. But despite 11th-hour, one-on-one lobbying, the president gained support from only 43 House Democrats, just 21 percent of the total.

Faced with House defeat, Clinton asked House Speaker Newt Gingrich—a strong fast-track supporter—to adjourn for the year without a vote. Gingrich complied. But when Clinton—concerned over Democratic divisions—failed to renew his proposal in 1998, Gingrich brought it to a vote anyway, urged on by business and farm interests and Republican partisans. The result was a debacle—180 votes for and 243 against. Just 29 Democrats voted yes, and 71 Republicans were opposed.

The Current Situation

The U.S. market remains open. The U.S. economy is in exceptionally good shape, recent signs of weakness notwithstanding. But U.S. trade policy is in serious trouble. The core reason is what stymied fast track: the impact of globalization and Americans' differences about how to respond. Growing U.S. engagement in the world economy has had important effects on Americans' welfare and their economic institutions. On balance, the impact is favorable, and the flexibility and innovativeness of U.S. firms and workers augur well for the future. But anxieties are widespread.

Caught in the middle are Democrats concerned about increasing inequality in U.S.

income distribution, the weakening of labor unions, and the impact of economic activity on the environment. Many see globalization as inevitable and trade as, on balance, a good thing. But they also see losers, particularly among their core constituencies, and they see weak and declining U.S. programs to help these losers. They favor strengthening the safety net at home, but they also argue for moves toward globalization of norms on labor and environmental standards. These "trade and . . ." issues blocked fast track in 1997, and the lines hardened when Gingrich tried to force matters in 1998.

Traditional business protectionism, by contrast, was barely visible in the fast-track fight. But a surge in steel imports has now triggered a strong industry campaign for relief, and other industries may follow. For the strength of the dollar, and the Asian financial crisis, have brought a rise in the volume of imports comparable to the unprecedented surge of the early 1980s. Throughout the Clinton administration, the overall U.S. merchandise trade deficit has been rising: from $131 billion in 1993 to $198 billion in 1997 and a projected $250 billion for 1998. Over the first two years, the actual impact on the U.S. economy was muted: the increase in the *quantity* of imports was less than the increase in *value,* as a decline in the dollar led to a modest rise in import prices. But in 1995 the dollar began rising, and since then, with import prices falling, the increased quantity of imports has been greater than the dollar figures show.

The final piece of bad news for U.S. trade policy has been the global financial crisis, compounded by the collapse of confidence in Japan. Both have shifted administration legislative attention from fast track to replenishment of IMF resources, which Congress finally granted last October.

Political and economic circumstances today are therefore less auspicious than those under which Clinton's fast-track campaign failed in late 1997. Yet the arguments remain strong for renewing the U.S. policy of leadership in international trade liberalization.

Why Trade Liberalization Still Makes Sense

The economic case for open trade begins with the gains from specialization. We trade because we can get more of the goods and services we value by devoting our energies to what we can do well and using the proceeds to purchase what others are good at making (or doing). Lowering U.S. import barriers increases opportunities to trade, and thus the gains from trade.

Trade also offers dynamic benefits by encouraging deployment of America's resources, including creative human talent, in innovative, knowledge-intensive industries, leading to increased productivity and a larger "economic pie" for distribution within the nation. A final economic advantage of U.S. trade liberalization is the leverage it provides in getting other nations to reciprocate.

The economic case for active trade-negotiating policy is particularly strong vis-à-vis countries with which we trade substantially—those in North America, East Asia, and Europe. APEC encompasses the first two, so liberalization under its auspices offers great potential. Economic gains are maximized in global negotiations under the auspices of the WTO, simply because their successful conclusion brings substantial barrier reduction by the preponderance of U.S. trading partners.

> It is reasonable and proper to debate what U.S. negotiating priorities should be. But failure to engage is not reasonable, for globalization is coming, ready or not.

By economic criteria, U.S. trade with the remainder of the Western Hemisphere is less critical. But trade plays a particularly constructive *political* role in U.S. relations with today's Latin America. Democratization and economic reforms have led most of those nations to reverse the longstanding priority given to "nonintervention in internal affairs" and national economic autonomy. Their agreement to a Free Trade Area of the Americas is widely viewed as the triumph of the deepening of engagement with the United States and with each other. It is a powerful source of U.S. leverage, particularly on economic issues but beyond them as well.

Trade policy also has substantial domestic political importance. The stance our government, particularly Congress, takes is a potent symbol of Americans' attitudes toward engagement in the global economy. Openness and readiness to negotiate are signs of confidence. Ambivalence and stalemate suggest pessimism about our capacity to handle the new challenges. Moreover, U.S. trade policy reflected bipartisan consensus as recently as the Uruguay Round vote of 1994. Restoring that consensus is important for effective policy in the future.

Finally, to the degree that Americans are genuinely concerned about trade's impact on social norms and conditions at home as well as abroad, international trade negotiations remain the primary means of shaping the terms of globalization. It is reasonable and proper to debate what U.S. negotiating priorities should be. But failure to engage is not reasonable, for globalization is coming, ready or not.

Breaking the Stalemate

Without fast track, President Clinton and his successor will be unable to negotiate significant new trade agreements. And their hands will be tied in their exercise of broader international economic leadership. Much of the recent argument over fast track has been symbolic, for no one can claim that important new trade-related labor and environmental understandings are available to the United States if only Congress would authorize their pursuit. Thus many in the trade policy community see these issues as a no-win diversion, a move into territory guaranteed to stir domestic controversy with little chance of international achievement. Yet trade *does* affect the plight of workers. Trade *does* affect the environment. If means are not available to address these effects, advocates of these causes will oppose trade liberalization.

At the same time, the trade agenda can easily become overloaded with "related" issues for which there is little prospect of meaningful agreement. Seeking to do everything may assure doing nothing. And for some in the labor-environment coalition, this may be the objective.

If the matter at stake were a central trade negotiation with major, visible costs to the United States for not joining it promptly, a House majority could probably have been squeezed out in 1997 or 1998. But the agenda is scattered—FTAA, APEC, WTO sectoral talks—and the costs of delay to U.S. interests are initially modest. Thus it will be difficult for the administration and its allies to win by resubmitting the old bill and "trying harder." Yet waiting until 2001 and a new presidency means two more years of U.S. trade policy weakness, of hardening ideological lines at home, of leaving the agenda and the gains to other nations or allowing the global and regional trade regimes to drift.

Bill Clinton appears to recognize all this—he has spoken repeatedly of the need to "do the hard work of building a bipartisan coalition" on trade "when Congress returns next year." What follows is a suggested approach aimed at winning some significant negotiating authority next year, with prospects of more thereafter.

The United States will host, late in 1999, the next Ministerial Conference of the WTO. Clinton should establish a goal of enacting trade legislation by that date. He should restate his maximum agenda—fast track under the time-tested formula, granted for a number of years, covering regional FTAs as well as global negotiations. He should negotiate a timetable with legislative leaders—a presidential proposal sometime in March, perhaps, with House action by midsummer and Senate consideration thereafter.

Most important, the president should signal his readiness to compromise on specifics by launching a dialogue with leaders on both sides of the ideological divide, including members of Congress and representatives of private organizations. This dialogue should address three central, intertwined issues: the specific negotiations to be authorized, the means for addressing the "trade and . . . " issues, and the means for coping with the costs of globalization. Each might be addressed by a working group organized by the administration but reaching beyond it.

A working group on the specific negotiations, for example, could be headed by the U.S. Trade Representative, Charlene Barshevsky. The current global agenda consists primarily of WTO sectoral negotiations. They have been generally less controversial than the regional agenda, where the U.S. debate has centered on NAFTA and its legacy. Until fast-track advocates in the proposed working group can make a stronger case about NAFTA than they have to date, the group would likely confirm greater support for the global than for the regional negotiations.

The group on "trade and . . . " issues should be headed by a senior figure outside the administration known for sympathy for the two central concerns—labor and the environment—and for trade liberalization. The group should include representatives of the business, labor, and environmental communities who are prepared to be pragmatic about one another's perspectives and to explore how much they might be accommodated. The hope would be to develop an action agenda for international negotiating goals and means acceptable to most Republicans and attractive to many Democrats.

A final group would address the costs of globalization to Americans who are hurt by it. Its head might be a sympathetic member of Congress or a prominent former member, such as Bill Bradley. The lack of a strong program to help the trade losers has been a major weakness in the Clinton administration's position, for a positive adjustment policy for workers at home would respond much more effectively to their plight than any conceivable agreements on labor standards overseas. The longstanding U.S. Trade Adjustment Assistance program has lost credibility because of modest funding and perceived ineffectiveness in worker retraining. A possible alternative would be a program of "earnings insurance" offsetting a portion of workers' losses in pay that result from trade-liberalizing agreements.

The goal of such a dialogue is to broaden support for trade policy and address trade's often-disruptive impacts on American society. It could lead to any one of a number of policy outcomes, from development of a narrow fast-track bill for negotiations with broad support (probably WTO sectoral), with dialogue continuing on the thornier issues; to enactment of broad fast-track authority together with new programs for those hurt by trade and economic changes; to a law combining immediate fast-track authority for certain negotiations with an expedited procedure under which the president could seek it for others. Realistically, one would hope to build a consensus approach that would win, eventually, significant support within the environmental community and the backing of some labor sympathizers.

It would be best for U.S. trade policy if Congress were to grant comprehensive fast-track negotiating authority immediately. But this is not likely, nor is it essential. What is essential is for the president, Congress, and key societal groups to engage in a process that leads to step-by-step granting of negotiating authority as it addresses, step by step, the concerns of critics. The process must begin soon and continue through the 2000 elections. For, left to itself, the presidential primary dynamic will only make matters worse, as Democrats compete for union favor and Republicans joust for endorsement by values conservatives sympathetic to linking trade and abortion policy or trade and religious freedom.

Anxieties over globalization have brought stalemate to the U.S. trade policy agenda. But the exceptional current condition of the American economy offers an unusually favorable climate for addressing these anxieties. If not now, when?

Article 37

The United States Is Not Ahead in Everything That Matters

John Schmitt and Lawrence Mishel

Many people now argue that labor market rigidities are making Western Europe less competitive. But by key measures of economic strength, including GDP per capita and productivity, Europe is doing every bit as well as the United States in the 1990s.

Low unemployment in the United States—just 4.3 percent at present—has spawned triumphalism here and envy in Europe. According to the standard view, the United States can thank its "dynamism" and flexibility for its current good fortune. Europe, on the other hand, should blame its record unemployment rates on rigid labor market institutions (unions and high minimum wages, for example) and the burden of large welfare states. That the United States has considerably lower unemployment than Europe is both true and enviable. However, this statement, which is the primary basis for recent U.S. triumphalism, is a narrow and incomplete comparison. This article assesses some of the key claims made about the economic performance of the United States and the other advanced countries by presenting internationally comparable data on a broad range of economic indicators. We analyze both what the indica-

JOHN SCHMITT is a labor ecomomist at the Economic Policy Institute (EPI). LAWRENCE MISHEL is EPI's research director. They are, with Jared Bernstein, authors of The State of Working America 1998–99 *(Ithaca: Cornell University Press, 1998).*

tors tell us about the leading advanced economies' performance in the 1990s relative to earlier periods and what they tell us about performance of the "U.S. model" relative to economies with stronger labor-market institutions including trade unions, minimum wages, and social benefits.

Specifically, we evaluate the economies of the Group of Seven (G7) industrialized democracies in three areas: first, their ability to generate goods and services; second, their ability to create employment; and, third, their ability to generate an equitable growth in earnings.

To summarize the main findings:

- In all the G7 economies—including the United States—growth in gross domestic product (GDP) per capita has been slower in the 1990s than it was in the 1970s and 1980s. Despite widespread praise of U.S. dynamism, per capita GDP growth in the United States in the 1990s through 1997 has been slower than that of Germany and Japan and only about equal to rates in the United Kingdom, France, and Italy.

- In all the G7 economies except Germany and Italy, productivity growth has been slower in the 1990s than it was in the 1970s and 1980s. The United States and Canada have had the lowest productivity growth rates among the G7 economies in the 1980s and 1990s.

- High, sustained productivity growth has allowed many European economies to catch up to the higher productivity levels of the United States. Recent data from the Conference Board estimate that the economies of France, western Germany, the Netherlands, and Belgium are, on average, as productive as the U.S. economy.

- In all the G7 economies—including the United States—job creation rates are slower in the 1990s than they were in the 1970s and 1980s. The deceleration in job creation rates has been sharpest in Canada and the United States.

- In all the G7 economies except the United States, unemployment has been higher in the 1990s than in the 1970s and 1980s.

- In all the G7 economies except the United States, real compensation growth has been slower in the 1990s than it was in the 1970s and the 1980s. The improvement in the United States in the 1990s reflects a switch from declines in real compensation in the 1980s to what are essentially stagnant compensation levels in the 1990s.

Generating Goods and Services

The first set of indicators measures the capacity of each economy to generate goods and services for its population. Table 1 demonstrates that, among the G7 countries, the GDP growth rate during the 1990s (1989–97) has generally been lower than during the 1970s (1973–79) and the 1980s (1979–89). The one exception is Germany, which led the G7 countries in GDP growth in the 1990s with a 2.5 percent annual growth rate, up from a 1.8 percent annual growth rate in the 1980s. The United States (2.2 percent) and Japan (2.0 percent) are the second- and third-fastest growing economies among the G7. The remaining four economies all have growth rates below 2.0 percent per year, with Italy (1.2 percent) growing at the slowest pace.

When population growth rates across countries differ widely, however, the growth rate in GDP may paint a misleading picture of the economy's capacity to provide goods and services for its population. Table 1, therefore, also reports annual growth rates in GDP per capita. Again, with the exception of Germany,

Table 1

Real Gross Domestic Product, Annual Average Growth Rates, 1973–1997

	1973–79		1979–89		1989–97	
	GDP	GDP per capita	GDP	GDP per capita	GDP	GDP per capita
G7						
United States	3.5	2.5	2.7	1.8	2.2	1.1
Japan	4.6	3.5	3.8	3.2	2.0	1.7
Germany	2.9	3.1	1.8	1.7	2.5	1.8
France	3.5	3.0	2.3	1.8	1.5	1.0
Italy	3.6	3.1	2.4	2.3	1.2	1.0
United Kingdom	2.4	2.4	2.4	2.2	1.6	1.2
Canada	4.9	3.7	3.1	1.9	1.5	0.2
Other Advanced OECD						
Australia	3.5	2.3	3.3	1.8	2.7	1.5
Austria	3.7	3.8	2.1	2.0	2.3	1.2
Belgium	3.2	3.0	1.9	1.8	1.6	1.2
Denmark	2.5	2.2	1.8	1.8	2.3	2.0
Finland	3.3	2.9	3.7	3.3	0.6	0.1
Ireland	4.9	3.4	3.1	2.7	6.0	5.7
Netherlands	3.1	2.4	1.9	1.3	2.6	1.9
New Zealand	1.7	0.8	2.4	1.8	2.0	0.8
Norway	4.8	4.3	2.6	2.2	3.7	3.2
Portugal	4.8	2.9	2.9	2.6	2.2	2.3
Spain	3.8	2.7	2.8	2.3	2.0	1.8
Sweden	2.0	1.7	2.0	1.8	0.9	0.2
Switzerland	1.1	1.3	2.1	1.6	0.5	-0.5

Source: Authors' analysis of OECD data.
Note: Data for 1997 are OECD projections.

growth rates across the G7 countries are all lower in the 1990s than in the 1970s or 1980s. Growth in GDP per capita growth is strongest in Germany (1.8 percent per year) and Japan (1.7 percent). Rapid population growth in the United States lowers the growth rate in GDP per capita there to 1.1 percent per year, about the same rate as in the United Kingdom (1.2 percent), France (1.0 percent), and Italy (1.0 percent). Canada's moderate GDP growth rate and fast population growth rate leave it with a 0.2 percent per year growth rate in GDP per capita in the 1990s.

The most important determinant of the growth of GDP per capita is the growth rate of productivity—the output of goods and services per hour worked in the economy. Productivity growth is a fundamental indicator of an economy's capacity to improve its efficiency. Estimates made by the Organization for Economic Cooperation and Development (OECD) of the annual average growth in labor productivity in the business sector for twenty OECD countries from 1960 through 1996 (not shown) demonstrate that among the G7 countries, productivity growth rates were generally lower in the 1979–96 period than in the earlier two periods (1960–73 and 1973–79). The four economies with the fastest productivity growth in the 1979–96 period were Japan (2.2 percent per year), France (2.2 percent), Italy (2.1 percent), and the United Kingdom (1.8 percent). Over the same period, Canada (1.0 percent) and the United States (0.8 percent) experienced the slowest productivity growth in the G7.

The Conference Board productivity estimates in Table 2 are broadly consistent with the OECD data: a substantial slowdown in productivity growth rates in recent years, with Japan and the European G7 economies experiencing faster productivity growth rates than the United States and Canada did in the 1980s and 1990s. The Conference Board data also allow us to go beyond the growth in productivity to look at the actual level of output of goods and services across international economies. Historically, economists have argued that slower productivity in the United States was due to the country's lead in technological innovation: Other economies had relatively easy-going "catch-ups" to the more technologically advanced United States. The most recent data from the Conference Board, however, suggest that the United States no longer has the world's most productive economy. Table 2 also reports Conference Board estimates of real GDP per hour worked in 1960, 1973, 1987, and 1995, using the U.S. output level as the benchmark in each year. In 1960 and 1973, productivity levels in the other G7 countries were generally about two-thirds the level in the United States. The gap narrowed considerably between 1973 and 1987 and again between 1987 and 1995. By 1995, real output per hour worked in two G7 economies, France (102) and western Germany (101), had surpassed the level in the United States (100). Two other European economies, the Netherlands (98) and Belgium (97), were not far behind. A recent study by the Bureau of Labor Statistics (BLS) for 1996 confirms that other advanced countries have caught up to the United States in productivity.

Critics of European economies often argue that the "rigidities" in those economies have robbed them of the dynamism that is supposed to be evident in the United States. Data on the two most important measures of economic dynamism—growth in GDP per capita and productivity—however, give no support to this view. During the 1990s, Germany and Japan have experienced per capita GDP growth well above that of the United States. In fact, per capita GDP growth in the United States in the 1990s has not been distinguishable from that of the United Kingdom, France, or Italy. With respect to productivity, all the G7 economies except Canada have outperformed the United States, usually by a substantial margin. While economists have historically downplayed faster productivity growth in Europe and Japan as evidence only that it is easier to follow than to lead, new data on international productivity levels suggest that many European economies have narrowed or eliminated the productivity gap with the United States. Whatever liabilities a developed welfare state, broad social protections, and strong unions may represent for a country, no evidence exists to suggest that these institutional arrangements lead to slower economic or productivity growth.

Generating Employment

The second set of indicators describes the ability of each economy to generate employment opportunities for its population. According to OECD data in Table 3, the United States led the G7 in job creation between 1989 and 1997, with an average annual job creation rate of 1.2 percent. Over the same period, Japan and Canada expanded employment at 0.8 percent per year; France and the United Kingdom saw no change in employment; and

Table 2

Real Gross Domestic Product per Hour Worked

	As percent of U.S. level in each year				Average annual growth rate		
	1960	1973	1987	1995	1960–73	1973–87	1987–95
G7							
United States	100	100	100	100	2.9	1.2	0.9
Japan	21	45	58	68	9.3	3.2	2.9
Germany*	52	69	84	101	5.2	2.7	3.3
France	54	73	96	102	5.3	3.3	1.7
Italy	40	64	78	90	6.7	2.7	2.8
United Kingdom	58	66	79	84	3.9	2.6	1.8
Canada	79	79	86	85	2.8	1.9	0.7
Other Advanced OECD							
Australia	73	70	77	76	2.5	1.9	0.8
Austria	44	64	79	83	5.9	2.9	1.5
Belgium	49	68	89	97	5.5	3.3	2.1
Denmark	48	63	68	74	5.0	1.8	2.0
Finland	37	55	64	74	6.1	2.4	2.8
Ireland	31	42	59	84	5.5	3.9	5.4
Netherlands	58	77	95	98	5.3	2.8	1.4
New Zealand	—	—	—	—	—	—	—
Norway	48	56	76	88	4.2	3.6	2.7
Portugal	22	37	40	38	7.2	1.8	0.5
Spain	23	44	57	70	8.1	3.1	3.7
Sweden	58	73	78	79	4.7	1.7	1.1
Switzerland	71	76	76	86	3.4	1.3	2.4
OECD (excluding the United States)	47	61	73	80	5.5	2.6	2.2

Source: Conference Board (1997).
*Data refer to western Germany only.

Table 3

Employment, Annual Average Growth Rates, 1979–1997

	1979–89	1989–97*
G7		
United States	1.7	1.2
Japan	1.1	0.8
Germany	0.4	–0.2
France	0.2	0.0
Italy	0.2	–0.4
United Kingdom	0.6	0.0
Canada	2.0	0.8
Other Advanced OECD		
Australia	2.4	1.0
Austria	0.0	0.6
Belgium	0.0	0.0
Denmark	0.5	0.1
Finland	0.9	–1.6
Ireland	–0.5	2.7
Netherlands	0.7	1.8
New Zealand	0.1	1.8
Norway	0.8	0.8
Portugal	1.3	–0.3
Spain	0.1	0.2
Sweden	0.6	–1.6
Switzerland	1.8	0.2
European Union	0.0	0.0

Source: Authors' analysis of OECD data.
* Data for 1997 are OECD projections.

Germany (–0.2 percent per year) and Italy (–0.4 percent) saw employment fall. Separate employment data from the BLS show a similar pattern in the 1990s.

We can judge these job-creation rates along two dimensions: first, how the recent rates compare with the historical experience of each country; and, second, how the rates in individual countries compare to others in the same time period. Although the United States has outperformed the rest of the G7 in the 1990s, its performance has been lackluster by its own historical standards. For instance, the OECD data (Table 3) show a deceleration in U.S. employment growth from 1.7 percent per year in 1979–89 to 1.2 percent in 1989–97. At the same time, the other G7 economies also experienced a deceleration in job growth in the 1990s relative to the 1980s, with the worst deceleration in Canada. The mildest slowdown occurred in Japan, where employment growth fell from 1.1 percent per year to 0.8 percent between the 1980s and 1990s.

Although the United States created jobs at a faster rate than the other G7 nations in the 1990s, three OECD countries outdid the United States over the period: Ireland (2.7 percent annual rate), the Netherlands (1.8 percent), and New Zealand (1.8 percent).

International comparisons of employment growth, like GDP growth, are sensitive to international differences in population (and, thereby, labor force) growth. Table 4, therefore, reports U.S. BLS estimates of the "employment-to-population rate"—the share of the working-age population in each country that has a job—in selected years from 1967 through 1996. In 1967, the employment rates for men in G7 countries were about 80 percent (the exception is Italy at 73.9 percent). Between 1967 and 1979, and again between 1979 and 1996, the share of men in employment fell in every G7 country, including the United States. This decrease reflects greater participation in postsecondary education and earlier retirement, as well as diminished employment opportunities for men. Between 1989 and 1996, the employment rates fell least in Japan (–0.2 percentage points) and the United States (–1.6). Declines were larger for Canada (–6.2), western Germany (–5.8), the United Kingdom (–4.7), France (–3.6), and Italy (–3.4).

The pattern of employment rates is different for women. First, in every country in every year, employment rates were lower for women than men, generally reflecting women's nonmarket responsibilities. Second, rather than falling over the 1967–96 period, women's employment rates rose in all G7 countries except France. Between 1979 and 1996, women's employment rates increased most in the United States (8.5 percentage points), Canada (6.8) and the United Kingdom (4.8). Increases were smaller in Germany (2.8), Japan (2.0), and Italy (1.1). Women's employment rates fell slightly in France (–0.2). During the 1990s, however, the movement toward higher female employment rates generally decelerated and even turned negative in some cases. Women's employment rates grew in the United States (1.7 percentage points), western Germany (1.5), and the United Kingdom (1.0). They were basically unchanged in Japan (0.3) and fell in Canada (–1.6), France (–0.9), and Italy (–0.2).

The unemployment rate has been at the center of the current debate over economic policy. Table 5 shows the unemployment

Table 4

Employment Rates for Civilians

	Employment rate[a]					Change	
	1967	1973	1979	1989	1996	1979–89	1989–96
Men							
G7							
United States	78.0	75.5	73.8	72.5	70.9	–1.3	–1.6
Japan	80.0	80.8	78.2	75.1	74.9	–3.1	–0.2
Germany[b]	78.2	75.3	69.8	65.9	60.1	–3.9	–5.8
France[c]	77.7	74.2	69.6	61.2	57.6	–8.4	–3.6
Italy[d]	73.9	69.3	66.3	59.9	56.5	–6.4	–3.4
United Kingdom[c]	81.5	79.1	74.5	70.4	65.7	–4.1	–4.7
Canada	76.3	74.3	73.4	71.4	65.2	–2.0	–6.2
Other Advanced OECD							
Australia	83.8	81.8	75.3	71.9	67.9	–3.4	–4.0
Netherlands[c]	n.a.	77.3	74.3	65.0	66.9	–9.3	1.9
Sweden[c]	78.9	75.1	73.7	70.9	61.8	–2.8	–9.1
Women							
G7							
United States	39.0	42.0	47.5	54.3	56.0	6.8	1.7
Japan	48.9	46.8	45.7	47.4	47.7	1.7	0.3
Germany[b]	38.0	39.1	38.4	39.7	41.2	1.3	1.5
France[c]	37.2	39.2	40.5	41.2	40.3	0.7	–0.9
Italy[d]	25.3	24.5	27.3	28.6	28.4	1.3	–0.2
United Kingdom[c]	40.7	43.4	45.3	49.1	50.1	3.8	1.0
Canada	35.1	39.1	45.3	53.7	52.1	8.4	–1.6
Other Advanced OECD							
Australia	36.6	40.9	40.7	48.6	50.4	7.9	1.8
Netherlands[c]	n.a.	27.3	29.2	37.4	44.9	8.2	7.5
Sweden[c]	45.6	50.3	57.2	61.7	54.2	4.5	–7.5

Source: Authors' analysis of Bureau of Labor Statistics, "Comparative Civilian Labor Force Statistics, Ten Countries, 1959–96" (September 1997), tables 4 and 5.
[a]Total employment as a percentage of working-age population.
[b]Data for western Germany; 1996 column is preliminary figure for 1994.
[c]Data for 1996 are preliminary.
[d]Data in 1996 column are preliminary data for 1995.

rates in 1979, 1989, and 1997, as reported by the national statistical agencies of twenty OECD countries ("Common"). Between 1979 and 1996, unemployment rates increased in all G7 countries except the United States. These unemployment rates, which the OECD refers to as "commonly used" rates, however, rely on various national definitions of unemployment and employment that are not necessarily consistent over time or across countries.

Table 5, therefore, also displays the OECD's estimates of "standardized" unemployment rates using the internationally recognized, search-based definition of unemployment. For most countries, the switch to the international definition makes little difference, either because these countries' national definition is close to the international standard or because the national unemployment count is a good proxy for one conducted using the international definition.

For the United Kingdom and Germany, however, the standardized and commonly used definitions produce different accounts of the unemployment history of the last two decades. In the United Kingdom, which uses a claimant-based definition (i.e., the unemployed are defined as those receiving unemployment benefits) for its official unemployment rate, the commonly used definition consistently understates unemployment. The bias is large in 1979 (4.7 percent standardized rate compared to a 4.0 percent official rate); grows larger by 1989 (7.3 percent stan-

Table 5

Comparing Unemployment Rates, 1996: Commonly Used Versus Standardized Definitions

	1979 Common	1979 Standard	1989 Common	1989 Standard	1996 Common	1996 Standard
G7						
United States	5.8	5.8	5.3	5.3	5.4	5.4
Japan	2.1	2.1	2.3	2.3	3.4	3.4
Germany	—	—	—	—	10.3	8.9
Western Germany	3.2	2.7	6.9	5.6	—	7.2
France	5.8	5.3	9.3	9.3	12.3	12.4
Italy	7.8	5.8	10.2	10.0	12.1	12.0
United Kingdom	4.0	4.7	6.1	7.3	8.0	8.2
Canada	7.5	7.5	7.5	7.5	9.7	9.7
Other Advanced OECD						
Australia	6.1	6.1	6.1	6.2	8.5	8.6
Austria	1.8	—	4.3	—	6.3	4.4
Belgium	7.5	9.1	9.4	7.5	12.8	9.8
Denmark	6.2	.	9.3	7.4	8.8	6.9
Finland	6.0	6.5	3.5	3.3	16.3	15.3
Ireland	7.1	—	15.1	14.7	11.9	11.6
Netherlands	3.6	5.8	6.9	6.9	6.7	6.3
New Zealand	1.8	—	7.1	7.1	6.1	6.1
Norway	1.9	2.0	4.9	5.0	4.9	4.9
Portugal	8.2	—	5.1	4.9	7.3	7.3
Spain	8.6	7.7	16.7	17.2	22.2	22.1
Sweden	2.1	2.1	1.5	1.6	8.1	10.0
Switzerland	0.3	—	0.5	—	4.7	—

Sources: Except western Germany: *OECD Economic Outlook*, 62 (December 1997): A24; Annex tables 21, 22. Western Germany: U.S. Department of Labor, Bureau of Labor Statistics, "Unemployment Rates in Nine Countries, Civilian Labor Force Basis Approximating U.S. Concepts, Seasonally Adjusted, 1975–1997" (December 1997).

dardized compared to 6.1 percent official); and falls substantially by 1996 (8.2 percent standardized, 8.0 percent official).

Differences between the standardized and national definitions also affect the German case, which is further complicated by the effects of unification. The OECD data for western Germany show that the German national definition overstates the unemployment rate in 1979 (3.2 percent official, 2.7 percent standard) and 1989 (6.9 percent official, 5.6 percent standard). This is also true in 1996 for Germany as a whole, when the national definition put unemployment at 10.3 percent compared to the 8.9 percent standardized rate. At the same time, the standardized rate for Germany in 1996 is the weighted average of unemployment rates in eastern and western Germany. According to BLS data, the standardized unemployment rate in western Germany (excluding the former East Germany) in 1996 was 7.2 percent, 1.7 percentage points lower than the national average. Conclusions about the underlying strength of the German economy based on the unemployment rate in western Germany (7.2 percent in 1996) differ from those based on the standardized rate for the country as a whole (8.9 percent) and especially from those based on the commonly used national definition (10.3 percent). To put this in perspective, the standardized unemployment rate in western Germany in 1996 was one percentage point lower than the figure for the United Kingdom—and just 1.8 percentage points above the U.S. rate. The trend since 1996, however, has been a further widening of the unemployment gap between the United States and Germany.

To sum up, job creation rates were slower in the 1990s than in the 1980s in all G7 countries, with the sharpest decelerations in Canada and the United States. While the United States led the G7 in employment creation in the 1990s, the U.S. performance—even including the strong results in 1997—has still been well below that of the 1970s and 1980s. Recent U.S. job growth has also been slower than in some other OECD countries, most notably the Netherlands. Job growth in the 1980s and 1990s has not been fast enough in any of the G7 countries, including the United States, to prevent a decline in the employment rates for men. At the same time, the United States, Canada, and the United Kingdom have had more success than other G7 economies in incorporating women into the labor market. Japan continues to enjoy the lowest unemployment rates in the G7 countries, but the United States is the only G7 economy where unemployment was lower in 1996 than in 1979 or 1989.

The unemployment data generally support the view that European economies with strong labor market institutions such as trade unions, minimum wages, and social benefits have high unemployment rates, but simple comparisons of international unemployment rates can be misleading. The commonly used definition of unemployment in Germany in 1996, for example, puts unemployment there at 10.3 percent. The standardized unemployment rate puts it at 8.9 percent, and when eastern Germany is excluded, the standardized rate falls to 7.2 percent. The data also show a wide range of unemployment rates even among countries with similar labor market institutions: Denmark and the Netherlands, for example, have much lower unemployment rates than France and Italy.

Earnings Growth and Distribution

Finally, we examine the ability of each economy to generate equitable growth in labor income. Table 6 shows the annual, real growth in compensation—that is, wage or salary plus benefits—per employee for twenty OECD countries from 1979 through 1996. Among the G7 countries, real compensation growth was generally slower in the 1989–96 period than it was in 1979-89. In the 1990s, real compensation grew fastest in France (1.1 percent per year), followed by Japan (0.7 percent), Italy (0.7 percent), the United Kingdom (0.5 percent), and Canada (0.5 percent). Over the same period, real compensation was close to stagnant in the United States (0.1 percent) and Germany (–0.1 percent).

The estimates in Table 6 refer to annual compensation and have not been adjusted to control for changes in the average hours worked each year. Since annual hours have grown in the United States while they have fallen elsewhere, the data in Table 6 understate the degree to which real hourly compensation grew faster in other advanced countries relative to the United States.

Table 7 examines the growth of earnings inequality over the 1980s and 1990s among all workers (the data for men and women separately show the same trends), using data on full-time employees in all sectors of the economy. The table measures inequality as the ratio of earnings of high-wage workers (those making more than 90 percent of the total workforce) to the earnings of low-wage workers (those making more than only 10 percent of the workforce). By this measure, in the early 1980s, Canada and the United States were the most unequal of the OECD countries. The ratio of earnings of the "ninetieth-percentile worker to those of the tenth-percentile worker (the "90–10

Table 6

Real Compensation per Employee in the Business Sector, Annual Average Growth Rates, 1979–1996

	1979–89	1989–96
G7		
United States	–0.3	0.1
Japan	1.4	0.7
Germany	1.2	–0.1
France	1.1	1.1
Italy	1.4	0.7
United Kingdom	2.1	0.5
Canada	0.5	0.5
Other Advanced OECD		
Australia	0.3	0.6
Austria	1.9	1.3
Belgium	0.9	1.7
Denmark	0.3	1.6
Finland	3.0	2.3
Ireland	1.6	1.4
Netherlands	0.0	0.4
New Zealand	0.1	–0.8
Norway	0.4	1.4
Portugal	0.1	3.5
Spain	0.1	1.8
Sweden	1.3	0.8
Switzerland	1.7	0.7

Source: EPI analysis of OECD data.

---

ratio") was 4.01 in Canada and 3.65 in the United States, well above most of the rest of the economies in the table. As the last two columns of the table indicate, inequality grew steadily in the United States throughout the 1980s and 1990s. As a result, by the mid-1990s, the United States had surpassed Canada as the OECD country with the highest degree of earnings inequality among full-time workers.

The pattern of changes in inequality in the rest of the OECD economies was complex. In the 1980s, inequality grew in the United Kingdom (4.9 points per year), Canada (4.4), Japan (1.5), Australia (1.3), and Finland (1.2). It was relatively flat in Sweden (0.9), Austria (0.6), France (0.4), Denmark (0.4), and Norway (–0.7). And it fell sharply in Italy (–7.8) and Germany (–3.8). In the 1990s, inequality grew sharply in Italy (16.0) and Portugal (13.9) and less in New Zealand (5.3), Austria (2.9), Sweden (1.5), Belgium (1.4), and the United Kingdom (1.1, a significant deceleration from the 4.9 points of the 1980s). Over the same period, inequality changed relatively little in Switzerland (0.9), Australia (0.8), and the Netherlands (–0.3), and actually declined in Canada (–5.2), Finland (–3.7), Germany (–3.5), France (–3.2), and Japan (–2.4). In short, since the end of the 1970s, earnings inequality has grown substantially in the United States, the United Kingdom, and New Zealand, but has fluctuated within a much narrower band in most of the rest of the more regulated OECD economies.

In cross-country comparisons the rise of earnings inequality in the United States (and the United Kingdom) and the relative stability of the earnings distribution elsewhere is frequently linked to the pattern of rising unemployment in Europe. In this analysis, various forces such as technology and globalization have increased the relative demand for skilled (i.e., highly educated) workers and lowered relative demand for "unskilled" workers. The "flexibility" of U.S. labor markets in allowing

37. United States Is Not Ahead

wages of the unskilled to fall and, therefore, for earnings inequality to grow is said to have allowed unemployment of unskilled workers to remain low in the United States. In contrast, in this view, European labor-market institutions, such as strong collective bargaining systems, high minimum wages, and strong labor and social protections, have prevented the wage structure from responding to external (primarily technological) forces, thereby inducing high unemployment for unskilled workers.

Table 8 assesses this claim about the causes of higher European unemployment—that Europe's labor-market institutions, such as strong unions, high minimum wages, and generous benefits, have priced less-skilled workers out of jobs. If this were the case, we would expect the unemployment rates of less-educated workers and better-educated workers to be relatively close to one another in the United States, where relatively weak unions, low minimum wages, and stingy benefits would have less of an effect on the employment prospects of less-educated workers (that is, wages can fall so as to promote more jobs for the less skilled). Conversely, we would expect the unemploy-

Table 7

Trends in Overall Earnings Dispersion Ratio of Ninetieth- to Tenth-Percentile Earnings

	1979[a]	1989[b]	1995[c]
G7			
United States			4.39
Japan	3.01	3.16	3.02
Germany	2.69	2.46	2.32
France	3.24	3.28	3.28
Italy	2.94	2.16	2.80
United Kingdom	2.79	3.28	3.38
Canada	4.01	4.45	4.20
Other Advanced OECD			
Australia	2.74	2.87	2.92
Austria	3.45	3.51	3.66
Belgium	—	2.33	2.25
Denmark	2.14	2.18	—
Finland	2.46	2.57	2.38
Ireland	—	—	—
Netherlands	—	2.61	2.59
New Zealand	2.89	2.92	3.04
Norway	2.06	2.16	—
Portugal	—	3.49	4.05
Spain	—	—	—
Sweden	2.04	2.12	2.13
Switzerland	—	—	2.72

Source: EPI analysis of *OECD Employment Outlook* (July 1996): 61–62, table 3.1.

[a] Data for this year or for earliest available year. For Austria, Denmark, Finland, Norway, and Sweden data refer to 1980; for Canada data refer to 1981; for Germany data refer to 1983; for New Zealand data refer to 1984.
[b] For Canada and New Zealand data refer to 1988; for Norway data refer to 1987.
[c] Data for this year or for latest available year. For Belgium, Germany, Italy, Portugal, and Sweden data refer to 1993; for Austria, Canada, Finland, France, Japan, New Zealand, and the Netherlands data refer to 1994.

---

ment rates of less-educated and better-educated workers to be relatively farther apart in Europe, where labor market institutions would, by conventional thinking, disproportionately hurt job creation for less-educated workers. The data in Table 8 run completely counter to the conventional expectation. The unemployment rate for less-than-high-school-educated workers in the United States in 1994 was 3.9 times higher than for college-educated workers. The ratio of less-educated to better-educated unemployment rates was lower in seventeen of the remaining

Table 8

Unemployment Rates by Education Level, 1994

	Unemployment rate[a]			Ratio of	
	Less than High school	High school	College	Less than High school/ college	High school/ college
G7					
United States	12.6	6.2	3.2	3.9	1.9
Japan	—	—	—	—	—
Germany[b]	13.9	8.8	5.4	2.6	1.6
France	14.7	10.5	6.8	2.2	1.5
Italy	8.4	7.5	6.4	1.3	1.2
United Kingdom	13.0	8.3	3.9	3.3	2.1
Canada	14.3	9.0	7.3	2.0	1.2
Other Advanced OECD					
Australia	10.2	6.9	4.5	2.3	1.5
Austria	4.9	2.8	1.7	2.9	1.6
Belgium	12.5	7.1	3.7	3.4	1.9
Denmark	17.3	10.0	5.3	3.3	1.9
Finland	22.7	16.4	8.5	2.7	1.9
Ireland	18.9	9.7	4.9	3.9	2.0
Netherlands	8.2	4.8	4.3	1.9	1.1
New Zealand	9.3	5.3	2.9	3.2	1.8
Norway	6.5	4.7	2.3	2.8	2.0
Portugal	6.0	6.2	2.5	2.4	2.5
Spain	21.3	19.4	15.0	1.4	1.3
Sweden	8.8	7.6	3.6	2.4	2.1
Switzerland	5.1	3.4	3.0	1.7	1.1
Average (excluding the United States)	12.9	9.3	6.2	2.3	1.6

Source: Authors' analysis of data from *OECD Employment Outlook* (July 1997): 175–76, table D.

[a] Standardized rate.
[b] Eastern and western Germany.

---

eighteen countries in the table (Ireland had the same ratio as the United States). Thus, it appears that Europe's strong labor-market institutions have not contributed to relatively higher unemployment rates among less-educated workers compared to the United States. If anything, the European institutions appear to be associated with substantially lower relative unemployment rates for less-educated workers.

Conclusions

Economists have grown reluctant to compare recent economic performance with that of the "golden age" from the end of World War II through the first oil shock in 1973. Even by the lower standards of the 1970s and the 1980s, however, all the G7 economies appear to be experiencing difficulties in the 1990s. In all the G7 countries, growth in GDP (except Germany), GDP per capita, productivity (except Germany and Italy), and employment (including the United States) are lower in the 1990s than they were in the 1980s. In all the G7 countries, employment rates for men were lower in 1997 than they were in 1979 or 1989, and overall unemployment rates, except in the United States, were higher. In all the G7 countries, real compensation growth in the 1990s has been at or below its rate in the 1980s (except the United States, where real compensation in the 1990s has grown a mere 0.1 percent per year). While ongoing cyclical upswings in some G7 countries in the 1990s may yet improve overall performance for that decade, the gaps with the 1970s and 1980s are probably too large to close in what remains of this decade or these business cycles. By the same token, the performance of the United States, which is probably near the top of its current business cycle, is only likely to deteriorate further.

The international data provide little support for the contention that U.S.-style labor-market reform will make European economies more dynamic. With the exception of Canada, the other G7 economies already match or exceed U.S. rates of per capita GDP growth in the 1990s. All already exceed U.S. productivity growth rates. Data from the Conference Board even suggest that, by the mid-1990s, several European economies had achieved productivity levels on a par with the United States.

Nor do the data hold out much hope that the "U.S. model" can spur job growth in European economies. U.S. labor-market institutions were unable to prevent a significant deceleration in the U.S. job-creation rate in the 1990s relative to the 1980s or in the 1980s relative to the 1970s. They were also unable to prevent a decline in the employment rates for men, despite absolute declines in real compensation in the 1980s and large increases in male earnings inequality. The European economy that has most emulated the United States in the past two decades, the United Kingdom, has not created a single job, on net, in the decade of the 1990s. Meanwhile, economies with much stronger labor-market institutions, such as Australia, Canada, and the Netherlands, have created jobs during the 1980s or 1990s at rates comparable to those of the United States.

At the same time, U.S.-style labor-market reform does seem to be implicated in widening earnings inequality since the end of the 1970s, with large increases in both the United States and the United Kingdom.

The Euro: Who Wins? Who Loses?

by Jeffry Frieden

Europe's economic and monetary union (EMU) is the result of 25 years of political battles among and within the continent's nations. Several times—most notably in the early 1980s and again in the early 1990s—the European Union (EU) nearly tore itself apart as it attempted to stabilize the fluctuations of the European countries' different currencies and move toward a single currency. In the end, supporters of a common currency won.

In January 1999, 11 European countries will adopt the euro. For three years, they will use the common currency instead of their existing national currencies for large-scale trade and payments. Then, in 2002, euro coins and notes will take the place of national currencies in everyday circulation—that is, in the wallets and minds of Europeans.

With the end of the battle over a common currency, Europeans have a more momentous, and more contentious, task before them: to agree on a common monetary policy for Europe's disparate countries, regions, and groups and to manage the political clashes that this process of agreement will unleash. The struggle for control of Europe's most important tool for economic policy pits powerful conflicting interests against one another. And these skirmishes are likely to have substantial effects on the European economy, and on the course of European integration in general.

JEFFRY FRIEDEN *is professor of government at Harvard University and editor (with Barry Eichengreen) of* Forging an Integrated Europe *(University of Michigan Press, 1998).*

MONETARY UNION'S POLITICAL ROOTS

Economists agree almost unanimously that the purely economic benefits of establishing a monetary union do not outweigh the costs (see box "The Economics of Currency Unions"). This conclusion may be open to question, but even skeptics agree that political factors have been paramount in the drive for monetary union.

But politics encompasses many different things. Three principal factors made the euro attractive and feasible:

- **The quest for anti-inflationary credibility.** Under a single currency, countries with relatively high inflation, such as Italy and Finland, could tie their currencies to that of a low-inflation country, such as Germany, to help reinforce perceptions about their commitment to bringing inflation down.
- **Broader links to European integration.** Once the quest for a zone of monetary stability in Europe was under way, countries that were not participating worried that they would be excluded from other initiatives and, thus, be relegated to second-class citizenship within the EU.
- **Support from powerful business interests.** The prospect of exchange-rate stability and a single currency won the solid backing of most large corporations and banks in Europe. Big businesses believed that removing the uncertainties of currency fluctuations would help them realize the full promise of a single European market, and

give them a larger effective home base from which to confront outside competitors. These three forces were strong enough to carry 11 EU members through to EMU. And they will almost certainly be strong enough to carry the Euro-11—and maybe even a few more countries—through to full implementation of the single currency in 2002.

Of course, the transition to full currency union between now and 2002 might run into difficulties. Why might one of the Euro-11 drop out? The countries involved vary greatly in their economic structures and problems, a principal reason why many economists doubt the wisdom of undertaking the EMU enterprise in the first place. A monetary policy that might be right for France and Germany could prove very costly for Spain or Portugal. Spain's current unemployment of 19 percent—and youth unemployment of around 40 percent—might become politically intolerable, and national attempts to reduce it may seem inconsistent with the tight monetary policy of the new European Central Bank (ECB). A strong euro that increases the price of Europe's exports and cheapens the cost of its imports might drive Portuguese manufacturers to the wall, and the ECB might refuse to weaken the common currency to make Portuguese knitwear more competitive.

Overblown expectations about the economic consequences of EMU may aggravate these transitional tensions. After years of slow growth, high unemployment, and worsening social problems, many Europeans hope that EMU will point the way toward greater prosperity. But the new central bank is likely to argue that it cannot solve decade-long structural problems, and that attempts to use looser monetary policy to stimulate the economy will only lead to a new round of inflation. Should raised expectations clash with restrictive ECB policy, some national publics might rethink their support for the euro.

But it would take severe economic and political difficulties to shake any of the current EMU members loose from the euro. Their concerns about being left out of a central EU institution, losing the continued support from big business, and walking away from the years of hard work that got them into Europe's monetary club in the first place will probably pull all of the euro zone through to 2002.

Identifying Winners and Losers

Up to this point, the French, Germans, Italians, and others have debated whether they should join EMU. Domestic supporters and opponents have clashed over a particular country's adherence to monetary union, as often happens in national disputes over trade or social policy.

From now on, however, the question facing Europeans is not national but continental in nature: What Europe-wide policy will their new joint central bank follow? The answer will reflect the push and pull among Europe's various interest groups, the pressures of public opinion in different countries, and complex calculations about costs and benefits.

Two dimensions of debate will come to the fore. The first is internal, the ECB's making of a "domestic" monetary policy. Although the euro zone is not one country, it will be for monetary purposes, and it will face the usual problems confronted by national monetary policymakers. Here, the tradeoff will lie between sustaining the region's

Lower Prices, Fewer Jobs
Average Rates of Unemployment and Inflation in the European Union

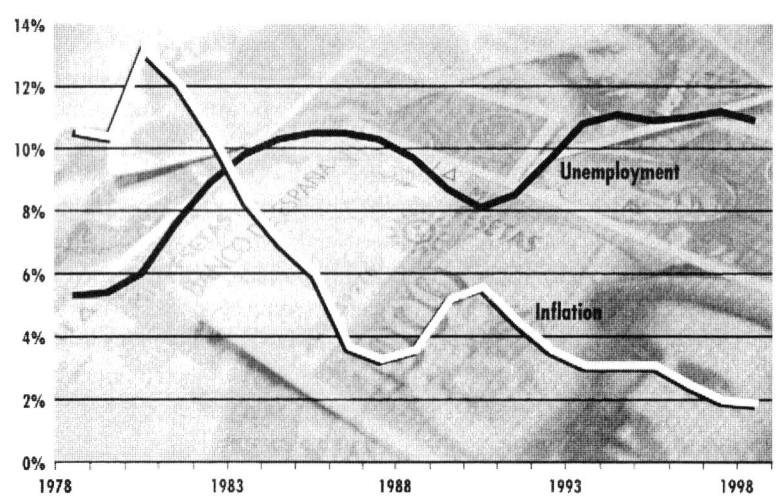

Note: 1997–98 figures are projected. Data from European Union member states at indicated year.
Source: *OECD Economic Outlook* (Paris: Organization for Economic Cooperation and Development, June 1998).

current low inflation and stimulating growth and employment. The difficulties inherent in this tradeoff are compounded by the extraordinary diversity of European economic conditions and interests.

Some of the EU's most influential groups and countries place extremely high value on very low inflation. For years, all potential EMU members have had to follow the lead of the German central bank—the Bundesbank, one of the most tough-minded guardians of financial probity in the world—even at the expense of other political and economic concerns. Lowering the ECB's inflation-fighting guard would incur the wrath of the continent's central bankers, who are backed by most of its banks and big businesses.

Then again, there is strong public sentiment throughout Europe behind lowering interest rates to deal with slow growth and high unemployment, even if doing so means incurring somewhat higher inflation. The region has lived with double-digit joblessness for a decade, with the unemployment rate reaching well above 20 percent in some countries. The roots of Europe's high and persistent unemployment are buried deep in its social and political structure—there is no easy solution. Although monetary policy cannot do much to fix what is broken in Europe's labor markets, the Bundesbank's nearly single-minded pursuit of zero inflation has probably slowed growth and raised unemployment across the continent.

In fact, one reason why EMU has garnered strong support in Europe is that it will transfer control of European monetary policy from the hard-money Bundesbank to the presumably less-extreme ECB. Labor unions around Europe will register their dissatisfaction if the ECB shows too little concern for the growth and employment effects of policies. Small businesses and mortgage holders are also likely to want low interest rates.

The second fault line for Europeans is external: namely, ECB policy toward the value of the euro in foreign exchange markets. In this case, they must choose between having a euro that rivals the dollar as an international currency and a weaker euro that makes European goods more competitive with those of other continents.

Europe's financial press has been filled with hopeful predictions that the euro will challenge the dollar for use in official currency reserves and in international trade and investment. This strengthened status, of course, requires a currency that inspires international confidence—that is, a robust euro, one not subject to sudden and unexpected fluctuations.

A strong common currency is also attractive to European financial markets. After all, the powerful position of U.S. banks and corporations is related to the dominant global position of the dollar. The widespread use of the dollar in international payments and investment almost certainly increases demand for the services of U.S. banks, while the denomination of most world trade in dollars probably gives American exporters a competitive edge. Many European businesses hope that international faith in the euro will translate into similar international success for Europe's financiers and investors by making it easier and more attractive for foreigners to use European banks and buy European goods and services.

But a strong euro will make foreign products cheap relative to European ones. For this reason, there are

Europe's Monetary Politics: Who Benefits?

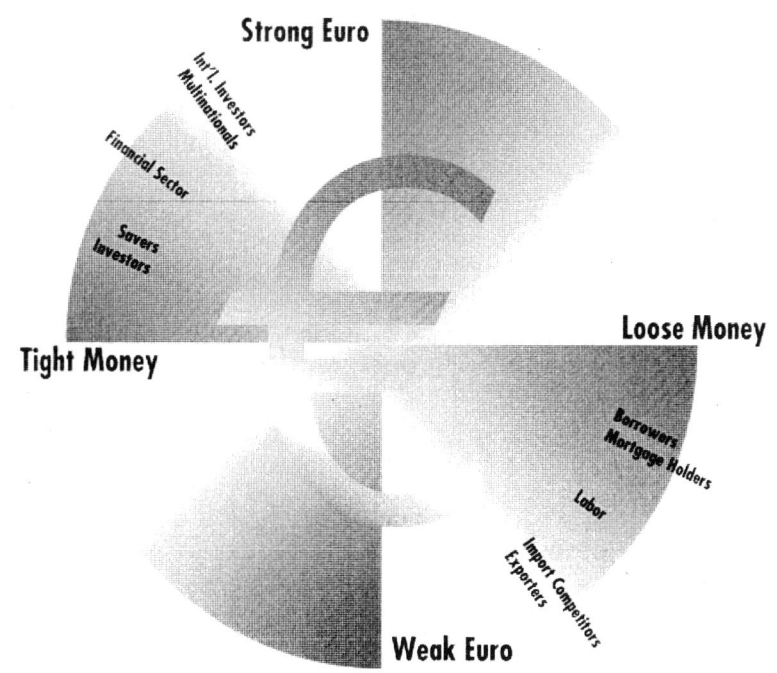

Strong Euro: Int'l Investors, Multinationals, Financial Sector, Savers, Investors

Tight Money

Loose Money: Borrowers, Mortgage Holders, Labor, Import Competitors, Exporters

Weak Euro

The Economics of Currency Unions

Economic analysis of the national costs and benefits of a currency union is based on the theory of Optimal Currency Areas (OCA) developed more than 30 years ago by the pioneering American economist Robert Mundell and others.

In this view, two countries should merge their currencies if two criteria are satisfied:

First, there is no need for an independent monetary policy. If countries are economically identical, they gain nothing from having different moneys and monetary policies. But if countries are likely to face different conditions, they should devise their own responses. A rise in world oil prices has opposite effects on oil exporters and oil importers; each might react best to the increase with different monetary policies in place. Then again, if two countries face similar, externally determined conditions, they do not need separate currencies. This existence of correlated exogenous shocks would satisfy the first OCA criterion.

Second, there is no possibility of effective independent monetary policy. If Texas tried to have a different monetary policy from the rest of the United States, its tight integration into the rest of the U.S. market—especially by way of migration and capital flows—would quickly counteract Texas policy. This second OCA criterion is associated with the existence of factor mobility, especially the mobility of labor. That is, if labor is very mobile between two countries, then having separate currencies will be of little use.

In applying this theoretical framework to economic and monetary union (EMU), most economists have compared Europe with the United States. They have found that the countries of the European Union (EU) vary more than the regions of the United States, and that labor is much less mobile within Europe than within the United States. Thus, economists have overwhelmingly concluded that the EU is not an optimal currency area and that EMU cannot be justified on standard economic grounds.

There are two principal objections to this conclusion. The first objection is that the economic costs and benefits of EMU have been mismeasured, largely because it is difficult to measure long-term ("dynamic") effects with accuracy. Currency union might dramatically increase trade and investment in ways that are hard to anticipate, thus increasing the efficiency of Europe's economies.

The second is that economists have focused solely on whether EMU will increase aggregate social welfare. There may be other legitimate economic concerns, such as how to reduce volatility, and legitimate social and political ones as well, such as how to further economic integration.

Both objections have merit. Most economists remain convinced, however, that establishing a monetary union will be very costly and the benefits of doing so limited or unknown.

—J.F.

---

powerful pressures to keep the euro from appreciating against the dollar and other currencies. Thus, Europe's exporters and import competitors are a force against encouraging or allowing the euro to strengthen, a trend that could be especially troublesome as more and more goods from Asia and other low-wage regions push into European and third country markets.

Of course, the two dimensions of monetary politics are tightly linked. More restrictive policies mean higher interest rates and a stronger euro; more stimulative policies mean lower interest rates and a weaker euro. The interrelationship of internal and external policies—and their connections to trade, fiscal, and other policies—only make tough choices even harder.

Although monetary policy is complex and the outcomes associated with it cannot be forecast perfectly, we can identify a general lineup of winners and losers from the different monetary policy stances. In principle, of course, nobody likes inflation or a weak currency; the question then is how much importance should be placed on fighting inflation or strengthening the euro, given that both imply raising interest rates and the relative prices of European goods on world markets.

A strong euro and tight money suggest a priority on international confidence in the currency and low inflation. The two tend to go hand-in-hand: High interest rates to keep inflation down will make the currency more attractive and raise its price (exchange rate). Europe's big international investors, banks, and corporations are focused on the strength and reliability of the currency, and the stability of monetary conditions "at home" in the euro zone. Europeans with savings will certainly benefit if interest rates are high and inflation is kept in check, but a strong anti-inflationary stance and an emphasis on the currency's international standing typically come at the expense of employment and the competitive position of those producing for export markets or competing with imports.

A weak currency and loose money are associated with aggressively using the exchange rate to help Europeans compete with foreign producers and using interest rates to stimulate a sluggish economy. Low interest rates too are important to borrowers as well, especially to those with home mortgages to pay. The labor movement is also a good example of a powerful constituency that supports the idea of accepting a little more inflation in the interest of stimulating the economy.

Of course, some groups will find themselves torn. European exporters want a currency that is both reliable and weak; they may have to choose one or the other. Those manufacturers that produce goods whose price is not a major competitive factor—luxury cars or high-quality electronics, for example—probably find currency stability more important than a depreciated euro. But Europeans who make products that underpricing can drive out of the market—clothing, shoes, steel—care much more about the currency's value.

Conflicts to Come

The ECB thus faces pressures from the outset that cannot all be satisfied. It is not hard to design a popular monetary policy when the economy is growing and incomes are rising, but in times of trouble, whatever the ECB does will be unpopular with some of its constituents.

The three most obvious potential scenarios for conflict among Europe's competing interests are the following:

Recession

The European economy—or portions of it—tumbles. Recession-ravaged countries, regions, and groups—weary of stagnation—demand that the ECB help them. Monetary hardliners—wary of inflation—insist that the recession is a local problem or a necessary corrective and that the inflationary alternative is far worse. If the ECB responds to those in trouble with expansion, foreign-exchange traders could desert the euro, causing a debilitating currency crisis. If the ECB holds firm, its resolve could cause a political backlash aimed at reining in the central bank or otherwise altering European policy.

Localized Financial Crisis

One of Europe's notoriously weak financial systems, say that of Spain, is threatened by a wave of bank failures. The national authorities are unable or unwilling to foot the enormous bill needed to stave off bank runs and incipient panic. They turn to the ECB, demanding a loosening of monetary policy to help their banks. Perhaps they even insist that the ECB and its member central banks provide short-term loans to the troubled Spanish banking system.

The ECB could bail out its bankrupt member. This course would be unpopular in countries unaffected by the crisis, for the bailout might mean raising inflation elsewhere and sending other people's money to Spain. And the bailout might itself encourage a run on other weak banks, now that the ECB has set the precedent of making bad loans good.

Or the ECB could ignore the local crisis and let Spain pay the consequences. This alternative risks Spanish resentment of the central bank and its partners. And it also risks the transmission of the crisis to the rest of the euro zone, for financial panic in one region of a currency union can rarely be segregated from the rest.

Crisis Abroad

The Japanese economy continues to slump, the Asian crisis worsens, and the American bull market comes to an abrupt end. Collapse on Wall Street causes a wave of bank failures in North America and a new debt crisis in Latin America. Asian, Latin American, and North American producers raise barriers to foreign goods and ship their unsold products to Europe at fire-sale prices.

Europe's leading banks and corporations see in this crisis an ideal opportunity for them to supplant their Japanese and American rivals and for the euro to take its place as the most reliable currency in the world. They, along with the continent's central bankers, call for the ECB to redouble its commitment to monetary rectitude. But many European manufacturers and farmers are being devastated by the flood of cheap imports and lost access to foreign markets. They demand that the euro be allowed to decline in value to keep pace with the dollar and yen. Meanwhile, Europe's key financial and commercial centers want a strong euro, while low-wage manufacturing and farming regions need a

6 ❖ INTERNATIONAL ECONOMICS

> ## Is EMU Geopolitical?
>
> Some analysts ascribe geopolitical roots to Europe's economic and monetary union (EMU). They argue that France wanted EMU to bind Germany to its Western partners after the end of the Cold War. Germany agreed, despite its misgivings about a single currency, to prove its commitment to the Western alliance.
>
> This argument is weak at best. Plans for a common currency for Europe go back to the late 1960s when, if anything, it was French links to NATO that were in doubt. The project developed and solidified during the height of the Cold War when German fealty to the alliance was not in question. In fact, the German government has long been one of the most enthusiastic supporters of monetary union.
>
> In any event, so complex and unprecedented a process as EMU seems a strange way to cement a strategic military partnership. There are easier and more direct ways to encourage military collaboration, such as the act of military collaboration itself.
>
> —J.F.

weak currency. The ensuring battle pits north against south, city against countryside.

None of these scenarios is novel: For most large countries, including the United States, these constraints have been central to macroeconomic policy for years. But they have not been faced by the EU as an entity, for it has not had a currency or monetary policy—until now. With the inauguration of EMU and the euro, the EU will have to deal with cross-cutting social and political demands that it cannot meet without calling one or another of its central commitments—free trade, price stability, economic growth, employment creation—into question.

The Myth of Independence

In theory, this European clash of interests should not matter, for the ECB is supposedly above politics. Its constitution is designed to make it mimic the hard-line Bundesbank. And yet the new central bank will have to be sensitive to the desires and demands of Europe's businesses, labor unions, politicians, and others. If it strays too far from the preponderance of opinion and interests in the EU, it will be brought to heel. The manner is as yet undetermined—perhaps via national government threats that are channeled to or through "their" bank board members, or the European Parliament's incipient oversight, or back-channel influence from the European Commission—but the ECB will definitely be unable to ignore the opinions of powerful Europeans.

Any lingering doubts about the ultimate arbiters of European policy were put to rest at the very birth of the ECB. In April of this year, the French government insisted that the banks' first president, Willem (Wim) Duisenberg, serve only half his term and then resign in favor of a Frenchman, Jean-Claude Trichet. The French were able to override the desires of all other EMU members and of the overwhelming majority of central bankers in a carefully structured political deal.

This episode was meaningless in a practical sense, since Duisenberg and Trichet are virtually indistinguishable as central bankers. The true lesson—and, probably, the true reason for French insistence on a political deal—was symbolic. It demonstrated conclusively that the ECB serves at the sufferance of member states and their political leaders.

This circumstance is nothing new for central banks: An apolitical central bank is an oxymoron. But the ECB faces the difficult task of finding balance among much more disparate regions and interests than is the case in most countries. As a novel creature, it is desperate to establish its credibility with financial markets. Meanwhile, the ECB will be a brand-new player on the international economic scene, drawn immediately into the maelstrom of international financial diplomacy and emerging-market bailouts. And the institutional uncertainties of the new monetary union will make the political obstacles that the ECB has to negotiate more treacherous.

The formal structure and responsibilities of the ECB are clear. Like most central banks, it has a governing board that meets periodically to decide how to react to economic conditions. It can use a variety of instruments to intervene in financial markets to raise or lower interest rates, and to raise or lower the value of the euro. Central bankers are busy working out the technical details of how the ECB will in fact operate, but essential political considerations remain unclear.

National central banks have the backing of national political authorities. Typically, they are semiautonomous agents of the government, who are required to report periodically. However, there is no "government" of EMU, no analogue to the national governments to which national central banks are responsible.

The Euro in Real Life

In 2002, governments in the European Union (EU) will have six months to replace approximately 13 billion bank notes and 80 billion coins. Finns accustomed to bank notes of one size may need new billfolds to accommodate euro notes of seven different sizes.

Millions of vending machines will have to be adapted for new coins; so will pay phones, parking meters, cash dispensers, and slot machines. In Germany alone, the cost of updating coin-fed machines is expected to be half a billion dollars.

Cash will increasingly give way to plastic. "Smart cards" with microprocessors and memory chips will make transactions in euro easier for banks, merchants, and customers.

Price differences will level out. Euro pricing will make it easier for customers to compare the cost of identical goods in different countries. One likely result: Coca-Cola will no longer cost twice as much in Germany as in Spain, or half as much in France as in Belgium. Extreme price differences across Europe—estimated at 65 percent for ketchup, 115 percent for chocolate, and 155 percent for beer—will shrink. Catalog and Internet sales will soar.

Many businesses will not translate prices into exact euro equivalents. Rather, they will likely round up or down, based partly on what makes for a more psychologically attractive price. For example, a product priced in April 1998 at 99.95 FF for its under-one-hundred-FF appeal would have been valued at 15.38 euro—a figure that lacks similar psychological punch. As a result, merchants may change not just pricing but product sizes.

Freed from having to pay currency exchange commissions, cross-border travelers will have more money to spend. Currently, a tourist in Europe with $1,000 who visits 15 countries, changes his or her money in each of them, but buys nothing can end up with only $500. With the elimination of commissions, Europe's exchange bureaus will lose almost $2 billion by 2010. Tourists will save an average of $13 per cross-border visit within the EU as a result of the unified currency.

In other words, there is a void at the center of Europe's new monetary institution.

In addition to formal lines of responsibility, successful central banks rely on informal relations with politicians and financial markets that usually take years or decades to develop. If monetary policy appears too much in thrall to private banks, it risks a reaction from popular political representatives. But if monetary policy seems too politically motivated, it loses the confidence of financial markets.

Since the 1930s, the American central-banking compromise has meant a Federal Reserve System dominated by the financial sector and tempered by congressional oversight. Although uncomfortable for all parties most of the time, the balance has dampened strife over monetary policy.

The ECB, however, lacks established lines of communication with both financial markets and the European public. It will take time for a system of accountability to financial markets and politicians to develop. In the United States, control of the Fed was hotly disputed and uncertain for more than 20 years after its 1913 founding. A stable compromise was arrived at only in the mid-1930s.

Contested monetary institutions can have two disastrous effects. The first is paralysis in a crisis, as nobody has the authority to act forcefully. The Great Depression of the 1930s was probably exacerbated by Fed dithering—the result of political dissension among the New York Fed, regional reserve banks, the Fed Board in Washington, Congress, and others.

A second effect of central-banking institutions with unclear lines of accountability, authority, and communication is excessive influence by those with informal ties to the central bank, generally private financiers. And the perception that monetary policy has slipped away from public control into the hands of the financial markets can cause a powerful political backlash.

For the foreseeable future, the ECB is likely to lack the political ability to act decisively. And it will probably be called on to do so—either because of local financial difficulties or fundamental disagreements over European monetary policy. Moreover, incomplete mechanisms for ECB political accountability will aggravate the underlying difficulties of the new central bank's job.

WHAT TO EXPECT

None of this is to say that EMU is a bad idea or that it is doomed to failure. In fact, it is likely to have many positive effects and has political support that is broad and deep enough to ensure that it will probably endure any but the gravest of difficulties.

The political realities of today's EU will define the future of the euro. One of these political realities is that almost any possible monetary stance will excite opposition from powerful Europeans. There are important constituencies that favor tight and loose money and a strong and a weak euro. This dynamic is no different from what happens in any country, from Australia to Zambia. The novelty of EMU is that the pulling and hauling among different sectors is multiplied many times by the great diversity of Europe's economies and by the even greater diversity of European political and social organizations and institutions.

The ECB will be unable to rely on broad consensus over monetary policy. Especially in times of stagnation or crisis, it will be the focus of intense political pressure from business, labor, governments, and regions with divergent interests.

Another political reality is that the ECB will have to take these political pressures into account. The new central bank will need to find a way to address the legitimate concerns of its European constituents, varied as they might be. The ECB's response to the winners and losers of Europe's monetary experiment will determine the future course of the euro and of European integration.

The European Central Bank

The new European Central Bank (ECB) was established on June 1, 1998, and is headquartered in Frankfurt, Germany. It is the centerpiece of the European System of Central Banks. The ECB is responsible for the conduct of monetary policy in the countries that are full participants in Europe's economic and monetary union (EMU): Austria, Belgium, Finland, France, Germany, Ireland, Italy, Luxembourg, the Netherlands, Portugal, and Spain.

National central banks continue to exist, although they have little autonomy in implementing ECB monetary policy. Some maintain important responsibilities for such national policies as financial regulation.

The ECB is governed by three bodies: the Executive Board, Governing Council, and General Council. The Executive Board has six members and is headed by the ECB president and vice-president. These six individuals are appointed to eight-year terms by agreement among EU member governments, with some input from the European Parliament. The first set of six, appointed in May 1998, have staggered terms to ensure that they do not all leave office at the same time.

The president of the ECB is Willem (Wim) Duisenberg, a veteran Dutch central banker. The French government held up Duisenberg's appointment until it had obtained a commitment from him (which he denies publicly) to step down after four years in favor of Jean-Claude Trichet, the current head of the French central bank.

The Governing Council is made up of the six executive board members along with the governors of the constituent central banks (11 as of now). It will probably be the principal decision-making body of the ECB. The General Council includes the central bank governors of those EU member countries that are not part of EMU (four at present), but it is unlikely to play a major role in monetary policy decisions.

Typically, a national central bank is required to make periodic reports to its government or parliament. The ECB does not have so specific a line of responsibility, although it is expected to provide regular accounts of its actions to the EU's principal decision-making bodies: the European Commission, European Council, and European Parliament. To compensate somewhat for this lack of direct accountability, the 11 EMU countries have established an informal consultative group, the Euro-11, which will discuss common economic policy problems and issues.

—J.F.

WANT TO KNOW MORE?

EMU is the product of recent economic and political developments. Daniel Gros and Niels Thygesen, two strong supporters of EMU, present this historical context in their book, *European Monetary Integration,* (London: Longman, 1998). Readers should also consult *Forging an Integrated Europe* (Ann Arbor: University of Michigan Press, 1998), edited by Barry Eichengreen and Jeffry Frieden.

Peter Kenen, one of the best-informed academic observers of EMU, offers a summary of the issues in his book *Economic and Monetary Union in Europe: Moving Beyond Maastricht* (Cambridge: Cambridge University Press, 1995). Charles Wyplosz wrote his well-respected article "EMU: Why and How It Might Happen" (*Journal of Economic Perspectives,* Fall 1997) when many observers were just beginning to take the prospect of EMU seriously. For a more recent and extended analysis, read the articles collected in *The New Political Economy of EMU* (New York: Rowman and Littlefield, 1998), edited by Frieden, Gros, and Erik Jones. In his paper *Europe's Gamble* (Washington: Brookings Institution Press, 1997), leading macroeconomist Maurice Obstfeld discusses the potential for economic and political problems in a functioning EMU.

Russia Is Not Poland, and That's Too Bad

By MICHAEL M. WEINSTEIN

PUT aside for a moment the frightening crash of the ruble and the collapse of Russia's stock and bond markets last week. They are symptoms of something larger — a deformed economy in which the Government sets business taxes that few firms ever pay, enterprises promise wages that employees never see, loans go unpaid, people barter with pots, pans and socks and shady dealing runs rampant.

It didn't have to be this way. The Russians need only look to Poland to behold the better road untraveled. Poland too began the decade saddled with paltry living standards bequeathed by a sclerotic, centrally controlled economy run by discredited Communists. It reached out to the West for help creating monetary, budget, trade and legal regimes, and unlike Russia it followed through with sustained political will. It now ranks among Europe's fastest-growing economies.

Key to Poland's steady success have been two policy decisions, and discussing them helps to illuminate by contrast what is going wrong in Russia.

First, Poland adopted what might be called the Balcerowicz rule, named after

> Russia stifled the free-market chaos of the kiosks. Now it's left with only chaos.

Leszek Balcerowicz, the Finance Minister who masterminded Poland's market reforms. Mr. Balcerowicz invited thousands of would-be entrepreneurs to sell, within loose limits, anything they wanted anywhere they wanted at whatever price they wanted. Economists called this liberalization. The Poles called it competition.

The Balcerowicz rule helped break the chokehold of Communist-dominated, state-owned enterprises and Government bureaucracies over economic activity. Also, encouraging small start-ups denies organized crime opportunities for large prey.

When Poland broke away from communism, Western economists had wrung their hands trying to figure out what to do with its sprawling state-owned factories, which operated more like social welfare agencies than production units. The solution, it turned out, was benign neglect. Rather than convert factories, the Poles allowed them to shrivel. Workers peeled away to set up retail shops and other small enterprises largely free of Government interference.

The second major decision was scarier. Poland forced insolvent firms into bankruptcy, preventing them from draining resources from productive parts of the economy. That also ended a drain on the Federal budget by firms that had to be propped up by one disguised subsidy or another.

There were moments when the post-Communist Government in Russia appeared headed in the same direction. In early 1992, the Yeltsin Government embraced the Balcerowicz rule. Russians were invited to take to the streets and set up kiosks and curbside tables, selling whatever they wanted at whatever price consumers would pay. But then Communist antibodies, in the form of the oligarchs who controlled the state-owned factories and natural resources, were activated. They detected foreign tissue and attacked. Local governments buried the Balcerowicz rule, imposing licensing and other requirements and eventually strangling start-ups. Professor Marshall Goldman of Harvard points to revealing comments by Viktor S. Chernomyrdin, the off-again, on-again Prime Minister whom President Boris N. Yeltsin restored to his post last week. Mr. Chernomyrdin observed that street vendors were an unattractive, chaotic blight on a proud country. The Russian authorities cracked down.

Snuffed Out

The impact was severe. Anders Aslund, a former adviser to the Russian Government now at the Carnegie Endowment for International Peace, estimates that since the middle of 1994, the number of enterprises in Russia has stagnated. In a typical Western economy, he estimates, there is 1 business for every 10 residents. In Russia, the ratio is 1 for every 55.

By snuffing out start-ups, Russia lost the remarkable device by which Poland drained workers out of worthless factories into units that could produce the goods that people wanted to buy.

Russia not only stifles start-ups; it also props up incompetents. It tolerates businesses that cannot pay taxes or wages. They survive because of systems of barter and mutual forbearance of loans and taxes. Suppliers engage in round-robin lending by which everyone owes money to someone and no one ever pays up. That too throws a lifeline to insolvent firms.

Russian factories continue to churn out steel and other products that no one needs. One measure of the deformity is that Russia is littered with factories employing 10,000 or more workers. In the United States, such factories are a rarity. The effect is to keep alive concerns that chew up $1.50 worth of resources in order to turn out a product that is worth only $1 to consumers. Economists call this "negative value added." Ordinary folk call it economic suicide.

Oligarchs

Russia, of course, was not like Poland before or after communism. History matters. Poland could let its relatively small number of mega-factories wither, confident that workers could be absorbed in fast-growing small enterprises. Russia's officials had no such confidence about absorbing the workers from its numerous, gigantic state-owned factories.

Unlike communism in Poland, Soviet communism went back 70 years, obliterating private property and extinguishing memory of a time when ordinary people ran independent shops. There was also, Mr. Goldman points out, a vibrant civic culture in Poland in the early 1990's that equated the freedom of markets with freedom from the Soviets. There was no such unambiguous response in Russia.

Yet Clifford Gaddy of the Brookings Institution makes the point that where start-ups were encouraged, namely Moscow, they thrived. Still, when Prime Minister Sergei V. Kiriyenko in recent months threatened to close down insolvent firms, the oligarchs rose up and forced Mr. Yeltsin to drive his Prime Minister out of office. The problem was not that Russia had no choices. It made the wrong ones.

The West played a decisive role in Poland, but, it now appears, not in Russia. Poland invited Western economists and investment bankers to help design and execute its reform package. The West also provided timely aid to smooth over the painful adjustment of economic reconstruction. The Poles used the aid as promised, to pay for bold reform.

Russia too received Western aid. But, it now appears, the money did more to postpone reforms than to provoke them. Over the years, the West extracted grudging promises from the Russian Government to undertake this or that pro-market reform. The promises were never fulfilled. Western money permitted the Russians to preserve subsidies that keep the economy, such as it is, on life support.

Grand Bargain

This too might have been otherwise. Early in Mr. Yeltsin's reign, Professor Jeffrey Sachs of Harvard, a major architect of the Polish reforms and a former Yeltsin adviser, organized a lobbying campaign for a grand bargain, by which the West would provide substantial aid early if Mr. Yeltsin would implement tough market reforms. The West dithered and the moment was lost. Whether the bargain would have convinced the Russians to follow the Poles' course rather than their own is unclear. But by the time the West did crank up aid, the economy had foundered, people had soured on reform and opponents of an economic overhaul had erected high hurdles. Today Russia is paying the price. A government that clamped down on reform in part because it produced chaotic, messy streets now oversees an economy that is a chaotic mess.

JAPAN'S ECONOMIC PLIGHT

Fallen idol

Japan was once feared for its economic might. Today it is feared for its economic weakness—and the harm its ailing system might do to the rest of Asia and the world. Just how sick is Japan?

SOON, and for the first time, Japan will have a higher jobless rate than America—a telling moment in the shifting fortunes of the two economies. While America continues to enjoy rapid growth, Japan is in recession. The country's GDP fell by an annualised 5.3% in the three months to March—much more than expected and the second consecutive quarterly fall. Its banks are creaking under their burden of bad loans; this week the yen hit an eight-year low of ¥147 against the dollar, before joint intervention by America and Japan pulled it back; the unemployment rate, with further to rise, already stands at a post-war high of 4.1%.

Things will probably get worse before they get better. Consumer and business confidence is severely depressed. Worries about jobs and the fragility of financial institutions is likely to cause families to save more and spend less in coming months, adding to fears of a self-reinforcing deflationary spiral. Firms, struggling under a mountain of debt and excess capacity, are slashing investment, and exports to the rest of Asia are falling. Over the next year or so more firms will go bust, unemployment will climb, and the scale of the banks' problems may well turn out to be even worse than has been admitted so far. If the recession in the rest of Asia deepens or if America's economy—tripped by a sharp fall on Wall Street, say—falls suddenly into recession, then Japan's economic prospects will look grimmer still.

What a transformation. Ten years ago, anybody predicting that America would grow faster than Japan and have lower unemployment would have been called a fool. Then, Japan's economic superiority was seen not as a momentary or cyclical thing but as something inseparable from its "model". In particular, the blueprint for Japan Inc was based on close links between firms, banks and government officials. These arrangements sheltered managers from impatient shareholders and foreign competition, allowing them to take a long view. Anglo-Saxon capitalism, obsessed with the short term, didn't stand a chance.

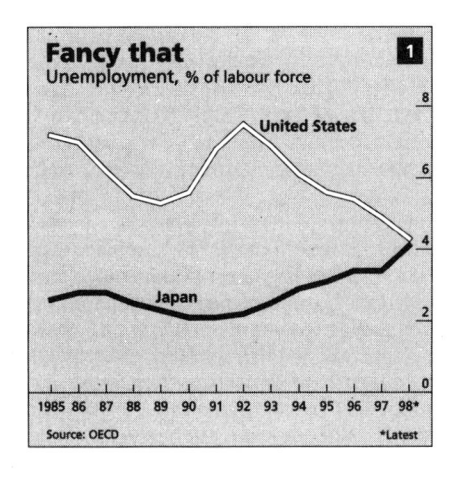

Now, many trace Japan's failure back to that same financial root. Under ministry guidance, banks kept weak firms in business, they say, in the end undermining the entire economy. Echoing the earlier logic, the country's current condition is again seen not as a temporary thing but as something that is so deeply embedded as to be almost inevitable. Unless Japan abandons its distinctive model, it will stagnate (or worse) indefinitely.

Economists love to extrapolate. America's current phase of strong non-inflationary growth is expected to continue indefinitely—just as its previous underperformance, relative to Japan, was regarded as permanent. In the same way, many commentators see no way out of Japan's difficulties. Bad as these are, however, they are not as bad as they are often made out to be. The mood of much of today's commentary, which sees a grim future for Japan however far into the future you look, is too bleak.

Japan's recession is likely to grow worse in the short term—but maybe not much worse. Beyond the short term, Japan's prospects are brighter than many currently expect. In the midst of financial crisis, the short term can seem like an age, and people determined to panic will find no consolation in looking further ahead. But the open-minded may indeed find some consolation there—not to mention a better basis for their economic forecasts.

Demand or supply?

A first question is whether Japan's downturn is due to deep structural defects or merely to inadequate demand. Many claim that Japan's weak growth of 1.3% a year, on average, over the past six years is largely the fault of stifling regulation and weak industrial management, which in turn have bred widespread inefficiency and a dwindling return on capital. Some conclude that Japan's potential output (what the economy could produce if its capacity were fully employed) has been growing at no more than 1% a year of late, compared with 3-4% a year in the 1980s. If this were true, stimulating demand in the economy would be to little purpose. The only way to spur growth would be to embark on wide-ranging deregulation and structural reform—a process that would take years, however determinedly it was followed. In this case, the medium-term outlook would indeed be bleak.

Undeniably, Japan's structural defects

6 ❖ INTERNATIONAL ECONOMICS

(especially excessive borrowing by firms to invest in projects with low returns) have worsened its problems. But most of the blame for the country's stagnation lies with the government's failure to boost demand. The authorities made a series of errors in monetary and fiscal policy. They were too reluctant to raise public borrowing and cut interest rates in the early 1990s, after Japan's financial bubble burst, and then much too quick to tighten fiscal policy again last year.

Viewed from the supply-side, the answer is the same. In any economy, growth in potential output depends on the growth in the labour force and rising productivity. Japan's labour-force growth has slowed from just over 1% a year in the 1980s to around 0.5% in the 1990s, and the workforce is expected to decline in the next century. On the other hand, economic rigidities have not worsened over the past decade (if anything, they may have eased, thanks to some deregulation), so there is no reason to suppose that underlying growth in productivity has fallen sharply. Indeed, productivity growth in manufacturing has averaged 3% during the past five years, exactly the same as in the 1980s.

On this basis, Japan's potential output is probably still growing by around 2% a year. Since actual growth has been less than this over the past six years, the economy now has a sizeable "output gap"—meaning that it could grow faster for several years without encountering bottlenecks. This is another way of saying that the problem is (lack of) demand, not supply.

Fiscal follies

At this point one faction of the pessimists makes a different argument: supposing that demand is indeed part of the problem, they say, the government is powerless, for one reason or another, to use fiscal and monetary policy to address it. The government did in fact announce a fiscal stimulus of about 2% of GDP in April; and interest rates are currently set at a historic low of 0.5%. But it makes no difference, according to this view: neither easy money nor public spending can prevent Japan being sucked into a deflationary spiral.

As it happens, Japan is not yet in fact suffering from a full-scale deflation. True, producer prices fell 1.7% in the year to May and the prices of equities and land are falling. But a one-off drop in prices due to cheaper imports from Asia, lower oil prices or deregulation in telecommunications is not the same as "deflation". Producer prices are falling in lots of other rich economies, thanks to lower commodity prices. Japanese consumer prices in the aggregate are not yet declining, nor are wages.

There is a danger that Japan may indeed drift towards deflation—but macroeconomic policy ("demand management")

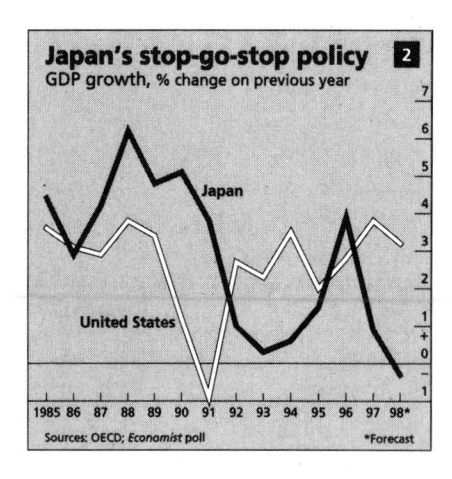

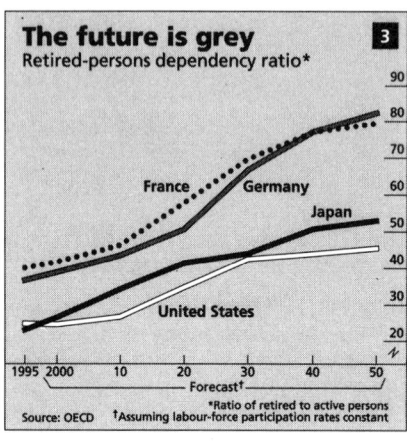

Japan's stop-go-stop policy 2
GDP growth, % change on previous year

Sources: OECD; *Economist* poll *Forecast

The future is grey 3
Retired-persons dependency ratio*

Source: OECD *Ratio of retired to active persons
†Assuming labour-force participation rates constant

can prevent this. It is true that interest rates cannot go much lower, but monetary policy can stimulate the economy in other ways. One is through the exchange rate. The 20% drop in the yen against the dollar over the past year will help not only to boost exports but, more important, to raise import prices and prevent deflation. It will also make Japanese assets look cheaper by international standards and therefore more attractive to foreign buyers.

The argument that fiscal policy is impotent is also flawed. Umpteen packages over the past five years have, it is claimed, failed to boost the economy. But if the impact appeared modest, so was the stimulus. Ministers overstated the scale of their packages by including measures without a direct impact on growth (such as lending by government agencies and the front-loading of previously planned public works). The actual amount injected into the economy over the past five years—through increased public works or tax cuts—was only one-third of all the measures announced by the government*. Much of the deterioration in Japan's budget—from a general-government surplus of 1.5% of GDP in 1992 to a deficit of

----

* For details see "How Much is Enough for Japan?", by Adam Posen, to be published by the Institute for International Economics in July.

3% last year—reflected the automatic fall in tax revenues due to the downturn.

Also, to measure the effects of any stimulus you need to look not just at actual growth rates, but at what growth would otherwise have been. Given the plunge in equity and property prices, the 85% rise in the yen between 1990 and 1995 and the troubles in East Asia, Japan's output would have been expected to fall sharply. A large stimulus in 1995-96 did deliver GDP growth of 3.9% in 1996 (see chart 2). But then the government was too eager to contain borrowing: it tightened policy prematurely in 1997 and the economy slowed.

Might fiscal policy be failing now for new reasons? One common argument is that public-sector debt (at almost 100% of GDP) has climbed too high, especially if you take account of increasing future pension liabilities as the population ages. This implies that taxes will have to rise sharply in future—and, in turn, that far-sighted households will therefore save any tax cut rather than spend it. However, long-term government bond yields of only 1.2% hardly suggest that investors are worried about the scale of government borrowing.

In any case, Japan's future pensions bill needs to be put in context. According to the OECD, the ratio of retired people to the labour force will not rise as much in Japan as in Germany or France (see chart 3). Japan also has more room to raise taxes: its tax burden is only 32% of GDP, compared with 45-50% in continental Europe.

Debtors' prison

A more plausible reason to think that Japan's recession might get much worse is the sorry state of its banking system. This will not neutralise the effects of a fiscal stimulus entirely (as the experience of 1995-96 showed), but it may be enough to dampen them. The banks' overhang of bad loans—estimated at ¥80 trillion, or 12% of GDP—serves as a brake on new lending, and thus on demand. Also, the bad debts raise anxieties about the security of the banking system, further undermining consumer confidence. The debts need to be acknowledged in all their awfulness, and written off.

The government has persistently shied away from that—although it is wrong to accuse it of doing nothing at all. In a policy u-turn in February it announced a ¥30 trillion plan to strengthen deposit insurance and to help banks write off bad loans. As yet, little of this has been used, and rumours about banks or life insurers in trouble continue to rattle the markets. Doubts remain over how the money will be used—foolishly, to bail out insolvent banks, or wisely, to support sound ones? But at least money is now available both to prevent a severe interruption of credit and, should the need arise, to reduce the risk of system-wide failure if more banks go under.

40. Japan's Economic Plight

On balance, if—and it is a big if—the immediate storm in global markets can be weathered, Japan's current recession is likely to prove short-lived. The government's latest fiscal stimulus, its biggest yet, combined with the weaker yen, will boost growth strongly in the second half of this year. Calculations by Dresdner Kleinwort Benson suggest that a 10% fall in the yen will boost GDP by 1.7% by 1999—roughly the same amount as the fiscal package itself.

Unfortunately, this has to fill a deepening hole left by the slump in exports to the rest of Asia. Two-fifths of Japan's exports go to the region, equivalent to 4.2% of its GDP, compared with only 2.4% of GDP bound for America and Germany. It seems likely that the slump in East Asia will knock up to 2% off Japan's GDP this year. Taking all this into account, the Japanese economy is likely at best to see output broadly unchanged, year on year, in 1998.

If demand merely stabilises in emerging East Asia next year, then Japan's exports will not fall much further. Some of Japan's current fiscal stimulus will also make itself felt in 1999, so the economy could enjoy a reasonable recovery. But further fiscal measures will still be required. It is essential to avoid repeating last year's mistake of tightening policy too soon.

Policy will need to be kept loose, ideally combining tax cuts with tax reform. A review of taxes is promised after the Upper House elections in July. Cuts in marginal income-tax rates combined with a broadening of the tax base would both boost spending and make the economy more efficient. Japan's top rate of income tax, 65%, is currently the highest among the rich economies. This is likely to be cut to 50%.

The reform agenda

Given sufficient resolve, the government has the means to close the output gap. But it should take steps, in addition, to speed the growth of the economy's productive capacity: demand-side measures and supply-side measures do not exclude each other. Again, the government has made more of a start in regulatory reform, for instance, than it is given credit for. Much more remains to be done, but telecommunications, retailing, transport and energy have all seen deregulation of various kinds. And in April Japan's "Big Bang" began to set its financial sector free.

Relaxing the laws controlling large stores has already increased competition by encouraging rapid growth in the number of big supermarkets and foreign retailers. Deregulation in the oil industry—allowing more oil imports and self-service stations—has sharply reduced petrol prices. The cost of telephone calls has fallen thanks to liberalisation. Since the mobile-phone market was set free in 1994, rates have plummeted and the number of phones has jumped from 2m in 1994 to nearly 40m.

In other ways too, the platform for faster productivity growth is already in place. Japan's labour market is not as rigid as Germany's, say. Wages are more flexible—thanks to the larger part played by bonuses—and trade unions are weaker. In some industries, lifetime employment can make it hard for firms to cut costs—but only about one-fifth of all workers in their 40s is actually in lifetime employment.

Indeed, by international standards, Japan does not measure up that badly. Its rate of return on capital may be a lot less than America's—a fact that has attracted attention lately—but it is no worse than in many European economies. The World Economic Forum's latest ranking of competitiveness puts Japan in 12th place, well above France and Germany (22nd and 24th, respectively). To be sure, continental Europe is hardly a model to aspire to—but then again nobody is condemning continental Europe to perpetual stagnation. Indeed, France and Germany are now enjoying relatively brisk growth.

The biggest supply-side obstacle to future growth may no longer be (if it ever was) excessive regulation or inflexible labour markets, but a corporate culture that finds it easy to tolerate low returns and difficult to tolerate outright failure. If the economy's return on capital is to improve, it will be necessary to close ailing companies more promptly. This is the aspect of the Japanese model which now matters most—and may be the most difficult to change. But recession, financial liberalisation and the squeeze on banks are all playing their part.

Traditionally, managers have faced little pressure to improve their return on assets. Most of their capital came from banks which also held equity in the firm. Troubled firms could stay in business by borrowing more. But as bad loans erode their capital, banks are starting to say "no" to companies, or to charge higher risk premiums. Firms are being forced to turn to the bond market and—thanks to this year's financial deregulation—compete with foreign firms to attract capital.

As markets tumble and commentators tear their hair, it is difficult to accept that Japan's recession may have useful side-effects of this kind—but that makes it no less true. Kevin Hebner, an analyst at SBC Warburg, points to several promising signs. For instance, companies are starting to offer stock-option schemes to managers, giving them an incentive to pursue shareholders' interests. More firms are setting explicit targets for return on equity. And some companies have announced plans to buy back shares, as a way to improve that return.

In the new climate, the threat of takeover may also start to play its part in spurring efficiency. Firms have traditionally been protected by their relationship with their bank and by cross-shareholdings held by friendly companies. But as friendly firms themselves face financial pressure, some are demanding a better return, or, desperate for cash, are selling some of their shareholdings to financial institutions. Recent cross-border M&A activity such as the deal between Travelers and Nikko and current talks between Daimler Benz and Nissan Diesel is just the start. Opaque company accounts remain an obstacle to a vigorous market for corporate control—but next year the country is moving to international accounting standards which will improve disclosure.

If all this works, mind you, it will hurt. These new pressures will encourage firms to cut costs, shed labour and use assets more efficiently. In the short term that means plant closures, rising unemployment, and hence more gloomy headlines about Japan's economic prospects. But creative destruction will help Japan to raise its return on capital. Redundancies and bankruptcies are evidence that the economic adjustment mechanism is working at last. Capitalism, you might say, is finally coming to Japan. Pity it had to be the hard way.

Article 41

The Other Crisis

The global financial crisis will be overcome, says the head of the World Bank, but we must look beyond to find peace and stability.

By James D. Wolfensohn

We are living in a period of global crisis. The crisis may not be fully developed yet, but there is the possibility that it will extend further—and the auguries suggest that it will. In East Asia, more than 20 million people fell back into poverty last year, and growth is likely to be halting and hesitant for several years to come. Russia is beset by economic and political crisis—caught between two systems, and comfortable with neither. Japan, the world's second-largest economy, has a government committed to economic reform, and yet it is still in recession.

The crisis started in Thailand in June 1997 and spread to Korea and Indonesia, and the International Monetary Fund and others put

JAMES D. WOLFENSOHN is president of the World Bank Group. This article is adapted from his remarks to The Conference Board on Oct. 14, 1998.

together large financial packages to try and restore confidence to that part of the world. Instead, we have seen 7 percent growth go to 7 percent *negative* growth, in addition to great increases in unemployment. Japan, a country that we have seen for a long time as an engine of the area, now has 2 percent negative growth and serious problems in the financial sector.

It is clearly an issue of importance to everybody that Japan put itself on a more stable path in terms of its financial system and on a more stable path toward growth. It matters because 20 percent of the region's trade goes to Japan and 50 percent of the financing comes from Japan. Moreover, Japan is a major center of commodity prices, which affects not just that region but other parts of the world. The first thing to realize is that the solution will not be just financial stimulus—not even the $30 billion that the Japanese have offered to help re-stimulate the East Asian economies.

I have tried in the past to indicate that finance and mathematics are not the single solution to financial crises. No amount of money is instantly going to put in place the long-term structural reform necessary to put these economies back on the road to recovery; nor will it change the atmospherics, the traditions, or the activities in Asia in the ways that Asians themselves are asking for them to be changed.

Asia needs a reform of the financial system: a transparent financial system, with appropriate supervision and control, and a bankruptcy law that works. It needs quicker and more effective judicial systems, and a reform of governance and regulation. It needs accounting practices in industry that are at international levels, the elimination of corruption, and a properly rewarded civil service.

This is not a description of Asia as we know it today. As we look at the crisis, we need to remember that it won't be fixed by dollars. We're talking about massive cultural change throughout the region, and this is not something that can be fixed overnight. Countries cannot supervise banking systems unless they have supervisors. They cannot seek clarity in terms of reporting from banks unless they have bank officers who know how and what to report. They cannot have bankruptcy laws unless some are written, unless they have judges, unless they have a procedure to administer them. They cannot have social systems that function unless some are established and people know how to work with them.

This is a task and a challenge of several years, at best—all within a framework of a macroeconomic policy that works. But it's a challenge or task not just of finance. It's a human challenge. It's a task of building social systems, of putting the right structures in place.

The Unanswered Question

These problems aren't limited to Asia. We have great difficulties in governance in Russia as well. Last year, the World Bank was meeting with Finance Minister Anatoly Chubais and his team and many others whom we thought were a team of reformers. They're all gone. We now have Mikhail Zadornov, who is the vestige of a reformer, but in an environment in which it is extremely difficult for us to know what the policy is. We have in Russia not such a tremendous financial problem in terms of the world GDP, but we surely have an immense social problem and an immense political problem. And since underlying the resolution of these problems is going to be the restoration of confidence, we have a serious issue facing us in Russia, which has effects on other countries, from Turkey to Central Asia.

Recently, of course, all the talk has been about what is happening in Latin America. We have seen Brazil's reserves drop from $75 billion to $50 billion, and that is after a $20 billion inflow—meaning there was a movement of $45 billion of funds in Brazil. And the question is: Is Latin America next? By most measures, it should not be. We have a remarkable group of presidents and finance ministers throughout Latin America, and they've taken a lot of the necessary steps.

The significant problem in the region is a lack of confidence. There are people betting: Is there going to be a devaluation in Country X? And if there is, shouldn't I get my money out now? This sort of guesswork is moving international funds around the world with a lack of confidence based not on an individual country-by-country analysis, but on the issue of which are the developing and transitional economies, and the numbers show it.

Two years ago, we had a flow in excess of $300 billion from the developed world to the developing and transition economies. In the last year, that amount has probably dropped by more than $150 billion, and there's a very good possibility it will drop even further in the coming year. Of that loss, at least $100 billion is a reduction in bank financing, and probably $40 billion is in terms of bond investment.

That kind of money is not easily replaced, particularly when the banks around the world are themselves gun-shy, looking only at their share prices and the recent activities in terms of hedge funds. This means we have a global reduction in liquidity, in addition to an outflow of funds from countries, which is very difficult to estimate but could easily be another $100 billion.

We have, then, a reduction in liquidity between $200 billion and $300 billion. We have a pressure on the marketplace that cannot be met by the international financial institutions alone. Those institutions can surely try to stabilize the global economy, but if there is a lack of confidence in the private sector and from investors, they can't put up an amount of money that can stabilize the situation or replace those flows of funds.

In the 30 or 40 meetings I had in October with ministers and leaders of countries, I was fascinated to see that it is not just the so-called crisis countries that have problems; the well-off countries are also being excluded from the international financial arena. It's costing them 10 percent to 20 percent more to borrow in the market, and countries cannot afford to borrow at 20 percent. But that isn't even the problem. The real issue is that the money isn't available.

Where the money will come from is the unanswered question that we're all facing in terms of the flows of funds, and the liquidity squeeze that is going on around the world. The squeeze cannot be dealt with by the international institutions alone; it also requires a private sector that is prepared to bear its responsibility and not just take off and run for the hills, or it will create the very problems that we're all seeking to avoid.

These are some of the issues that we're dealing with, and they don't lend themselves to easy solutions. Nevertheless, the IMF has done an extremely good job in trying to mobilize capital to establish a framework in which confidence can be restored. But we face new challenges, because you cannot have a reduction of credit, a tying-in of expansion, a reduction in growth, and still have a healthy, growing world. It just isn't possible.

We've seen trade reduced from 9 percent growth two years ago, to 5 percent this last year, and projected to be 2 percent next year. So trade is not growing. As for 1999 projections for the global GDP, the best estimates that I've seen so far speak of a 2 percent global growth. That's not a lot of growth.

The Real Crisis

Behind the financial problems, and the financial packages designed to solve them, lies a major social problem. We have 3 billion people in the world who live on less than $2 a day, and 1.3 billion who live on less than $1 a day. We have 1.5 billion people who don't have access to clean water, and another 2 billion people who don't have power. We're losing forests at the rate of an acre a second. We are despoiling our environment. We are adding 85 million people a year to our planet. In another 30 years, we're going to need twice the food, with no greater arable land.

In the past year, there have been nuclear tests in India and Pakistan, the threat of war in Eritrea and Ethiopia, and terrorist bombs in Kenya and Tanzania. There has been the impact of El Niño, with its full devastating force falling most heavily on the poor. In Bangladesh, floods kept two-thirds of the nation under water for more than two months, setting back many of the recent social and economic gains. In China, the flooding of the Yangtze River region caused an estimated 3,500 deaths and 200 million lives dislocated.

These factors add up to a human drama that very rarely makes headlines. In the past year, I have seen a mother in Mindanao pull her child out of school, haunted by the fear that he will never return; a family in Korea, with a mid-size scrap-metal business, made destitute through lack of credit; a father in Jakarta paying a moneylender three times his salary in interest, not knowing how he will ever work himself free; a child in Bangkok condemned to work the streets, a child no longer. While we talk of financial crisis, the human pain of poverty is all around us.

Too often, we have focused on economics, without sufficient understanding of the social, political, environmental, and cultural aspects of society. We need a new framework to evaluate the macroeconomic performance of each country—a framework that considers the progress in structural reforms necessary for long-term growth, that includes the human and social accounting, and that deals with the status of women, rural development, indigenous people, and progress in infrastructure.

At the World Bank, we have been restructuring our existing portfolios to ensure a sharp focus on priority programs that can reach poor communities quickly. We are working to keep children in school, by supporting a program in Indonesia that provides scholarships for 2.5 million children; creating jobs in Thailand through a new social fund; and putting frameworks in place for social protection in Korea through a series of structural adjustment loans. Only by balancing the need for drastic change with protecting the poor can we bring the international financial community and local citizens with us.

The Next Phase

While it is easy to focus on Korea, Thailand, Indonesia, problems in Malaysia, and maybe a problem in Brazil or Argentina or Russia, we can't escape from the inevitable global and social issues, which existed before the crisis and which we didn't adequately deal with then. But at least then there was growth. The developing and the transitional world is at about $6 trillion, about 20 percent of global GNP. In another 20 years, it will be 35 percent, because it is that world that is growing at a much faster rate—twice the rate of the developed world.

Our interest in the developing world is in terms of more than economic self-interest. We have a deep interest in terms of environment; in terms of global stability; in terms of migration. We have many interconnected interests, whether in crime, or drugs, or health. Yet somehow these issues just drop off the agenda when we're thinking in financial terms about the latest crisis.

We will somehow get through these financial crises. Korea will come back. Thailand will come back. We will solve $60 billion of private debt in Indonesia. Even Russia will come back. Latin America will come back. It's a question of when. And it's a question of with what pain, and I can't answer that.

But I urge you to think beyond that to the human drama that is going on, to the global drama that is inevitable and that you need to keep in mind when you're thinking about these problems.

If we handle it right, we have an enormous opportunity. We can have a singular world, where our children have the possibility of having interconnections with developed and transitional economies in many ways. We at the World Bank have linked 400 high schools on the Internet. It's amazing to see kids from Alaska working with kids in the Cote d'Ivoire. We're running global universities by satellite. In the jungles of Brazil, Indians are using satellites and talking to other villagers hundreds of miles away about the environment—they can't read, but they can run a satellite.

This world is becoming a fascinating place, and in terms of trade and investment and environment it presents enormous possibilities. But what it needs is a change in all of our perceptions. It needs us to look beyond this crisis and to think globally, not perhaps for ourselves but certainly for the next generation. And that is what we're trying to do at the Bank.

One way or another, I'm sure we'll get through it. We will restore liquidity, growth will come back, and we will all heave a huge sigh of relief. But remember to set that against the much broader issue of the state in which the world finds itself in terms of environment, in terms of humanity, and in terms of peace and stability. Those are the real issues.

OVERVIEW

Changing today's consumption patterns —for tomorrow's human development

World consumption has expanded at an unprecedented pace over the 20th century, with private and public consumption expenditures reaching $24 trillion in 1998, twice the level of 1975 and six times that of 1950. In 1900 real consumption expenditure was barely $1.5 trillion.

The benefits of this consumption have spread far and wide. More people are better fed and housed than ever before. Living standards have risen to enable hundreds of millions to enjoy housing with hot water and cold, warmth and electricity, transport to and from work—with time for leisure and sports, vacations and other activities beyond anything imagined at the start of this century.

How do these achievements relate to human development? Consumption is clearly an essential means, but the links are not automatic. Consumption clearly contributes to human development when it enlarges the capabilities and enriches the lives of people without adversely affecting the well-being of others. It clearly contributes when it is as fair to future generations as it is to the present ones. And it clearly contributes when it encourages lively, creative individuals and communities.

But the links are often broken, and when they are, consumption patterns and trends are inimical to human development. Today's consumption is undermining the environmental resource base. It is exacerbating inequalities. And the dynamics of the consumption-poverty-inequality-environment nexus are accelerating. If the trends continue without change—not redistributing from high-income to low-income consumers, not shifting from polluting to cleaner goods and production technologies, not promoting goods that empower poor producers, not shifting priority from consumption for conspicuous display to meeting basic needs—today's problems of consumption and human development will worsen.

But trend is not destiny, and none of these outcomes is inevitable. Change is needed—and change is possible.

In short, consumption must be shared, strengthening, socially responsible and sustainable.
- *Shared.* Ensuring basic needs for all.
- *Strengthening.* Building human capabilities.
- *Socially responsible.* So the consumption of some does not compromise the well-being of others.
- *Sustainable.* Without mortgaging the choices of future generations.

Human life is ultimately nourished and sustained by consumption. Abundance of consumption is no crime. It has, in fact, been the life blood of much human advance. The real issue is not consumption itself but its patterns and effects. Consumption patterns today must be changed to advance human development tomorrow. Consumer choices must be turned into a reality for all. Human development paradigms, which aim at enlarging all human choices, must aim at extending and improving consumer choices too, but in ways that promote human life. This is the theme of this report.

Trend is not destiny—change is possible

The 20th century's growth in consumption, unprecedented in its scale and diversity, has been badly distributed, leaving a backlog of shortfalls and gaping inequalities.

Consumption per capita has increased steadily in industrial countries (about 2.3%

42. Changing Today's Consumption Patterns

annually) over the past 25 years, spectacularly in East Asia (6.1%) and at a rising rate in South Asia (2.0%). Yet these developing regions are far from catching up to levels of industrial countries, and consumption growth has been slow or stagnant in others. The average African household today consumes 20% less than it did 25 years ago.

The poorest 20% of the world's people and more have been left out of the consumption explosion. Well over a billion people are deprived of basic consumption needs. Of the 4.4 billion people in developing countries, nearly three-fifths lack basic sanitation. Almost a third have no access to clean water. A quarter do not have adequate housing. A fifth have no access to modern health services. A fifth of children do not attend school to grade 5. About a fifth do not have enough dietary energy and protein. Micronutrient deficiencies are even more widespread. Worldwide, 2 billion people are anaemic, including 55 million in industrial countries. In developing countries only a privileged minority has motorized transport, telecommunications and modern energy.

Inequalities in consumption are stark. Globally, the 20% of the world's people in the highest-income countries account for 86% of total private consumption expenditures—the poorest 20% a minuscule 1.3%. More specifically, the richest fifth:
- Consume 45% of all meat and fish, the poorest fifth 5%.
- Consume 58% of total energy, the poorest fifth less than 4%.
- Have 74% of all telephone lines, the poorest fifth 1.5%.
- Consume 84% of all paper, the poorest fifth 1.1%.
- Own 87% of the world's vehicle fleet, the poorest fifth less than 1%.

How rewarding is today's pattern of consumption in terms of human satisfaction? The percentage of Americans calling themselves happy peaked in 1957—even though consumption has more than doubled in the meantime.

Despite high consumption, poverty and deprivation are found in all industrial countries and in some they are growing. This year's Report presents a new index of poverty in industrial countries—a multidimensional measure of human deprivation, on the same lines as the human poverty index presented in *Human Development Report 1997* for developing countries but more appropriate to the social and economic conditions of the industrial countries.

The new human poverty index (HPI-2) shows that some 7–17% of the population in industrial countries is poor. These levels of deprivation have little to do with the average income of the country. Sweden has the least poverty (7%), though ranked only thirteenth in average income. The United States, with the highest average income of the countries ranked, has the highest population share experiencing human poverty. And countries with similar per capita incomes have very different levels of human poverty. The Netherlands and the United Kingdom, for example, have HPI-2 values of 8% and 15%, despite similar income levels.

HPI-2 shows conclusively that underconsumption and human deprivation are not just the lot of poor people in the developing world. More than 100 million people in rich nations suffer a similar fate. Nearly 200 million people are not expected to survive to age 60. More than 100 million are homeless. And at least 37 million are without jobs, often experiencing a state of social exclusion. Many conclusions about deprivation apply to them with equal force.

Ever-expanding consumption puts strains on the environment—emissions and wastes that pollute the earth and destroy ecosystems, and growing depletion and degradation of renewable resources that undermines livelihoods.

Runaway growth in consumption in the past 50 years is putting strains on the environment never before seen.
- The burning of fossil fuels has almost quintupled since 1950.
- The consumption of fresh water has almost doubled since 1960.
- The marine catch has increased fourfold.
- Wood consumption, both for industry and for household fuel, is now 40% higher than it was 25 years ago.

193

6 ❖ INTERNATIONAL ECONOMICS

Rapid consumption growth for some, stagnation for others, inequality for all—with mounting environmental costs

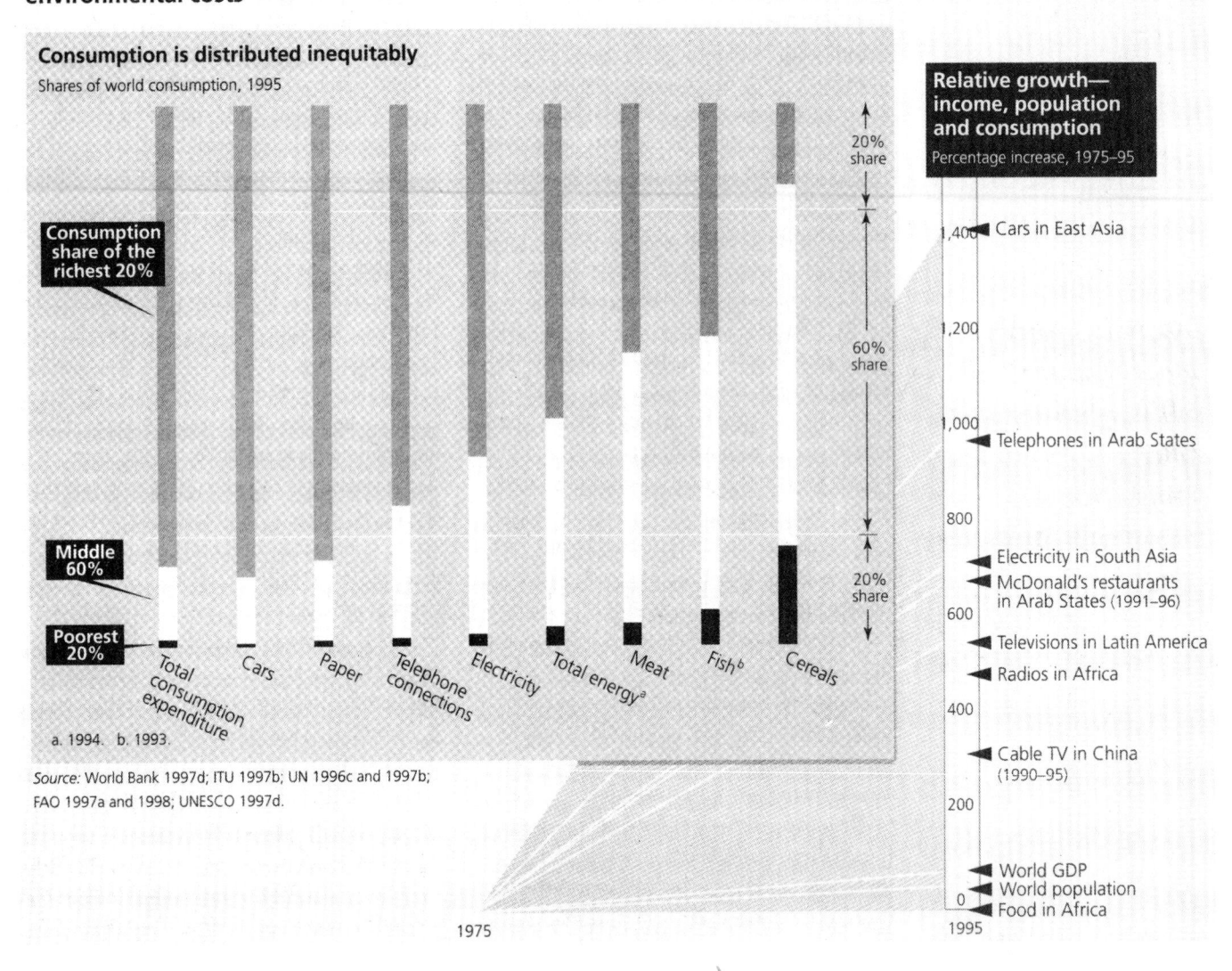

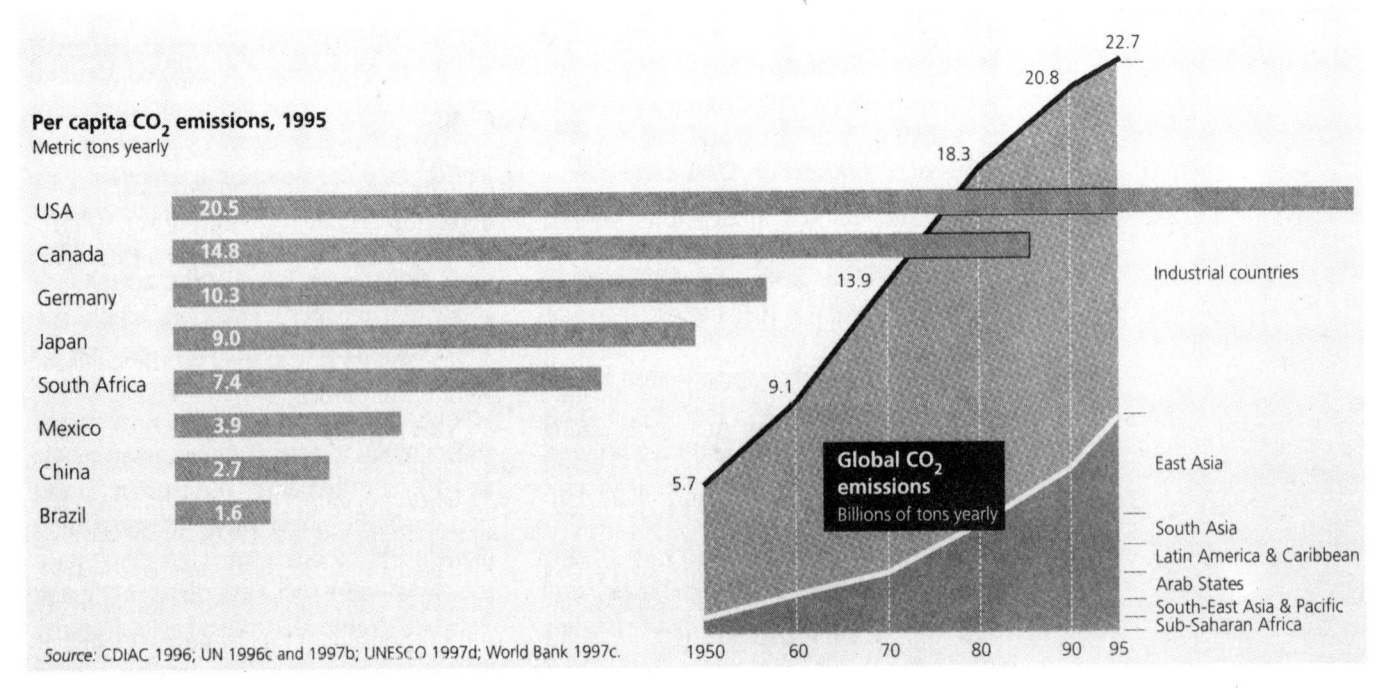

Consumption is distributed inequitably
Shares of world consumption, 1995

- Consumption share of the richest 20%
- Middle 60%
- Poorest 20%

Categories: Total consumption expenditure, Cars, Paper, Telephone connections, Electricity, Total energy[a], Meat, Fish[b], Cereals

20% share / 60% share / 20% share

a. 1994. b. 1993.

Source: World Bank 1997d; ITU 1997b; UN 1996c and 1997b; FAO 1997a and 1998; UNESCO 1997d.

Relative growth—income, population and consumption
Percentage increase, 1975–95

- 1,400 — Cars in East Asia
- 1,200
- 1,000 — Telephones in Arab States
- 800 — Electricity in South Asia
- McDonald's restaurants in Arab States (1991–96)
- 600 — Televisions in Latin America
- Radios in Africa
- 400 — Cable TV in China (1990–95)
- 200
- 0 — World GDP / World population / Food in Africa

1975 — 1995

Per capita CO$_2$ emissions, 1995
Metric tons yearly

Country	Value
USA	20.5
Canada	14.8
Germany	10.3
Japan	9.0
South Africa	7.4
Mexico	3.9
China	2.7
Brazil	1.6

Global CO$_2$ emissions
Billions of tons yearly

Values: 5.7, 9.1, 13.9, 18.3, 20.8, 22.7

Regions: Industrial countries, East Asia, South Asia, Latin America & Caribbean, Arab States, South-East Asia & Pacific, Sub-Saharan Africa

1950 — 60 — 70 — 80 — 90 — 95

Source: CDIAC 1996; UN 1996c and 1997b; UNESCO 1997d; World Bank 1997c.

42. Changing Today's Consumption Patterns

Poor people and poor countries bear many costs of unequal consumption

Yet growth in the use of material resources has slowed considerably in recent years, and much-publicized fears that the world would run out of such non-renewable resources as oil and minerals have proved false. New reserves have been discovered. The growth of demand has slowed. Consumption has shifted in favour of less material-intensive products and services. Energy efficiency has improved. And technological advance and recycling of raw materials have boosted efficiency in material use, now growing more slowly than economies. Call this dematerialization. The per capita use of basic materials such as steel, timber and copper has stabilized in most OECD countries—and even declined in some countries for some products.

So, non-renewables are not the urgent problem. It is two other crises that are nudging humanity towards the "outer limits" of what earth can stand.

First are the pollution and waste that exceed the planet's sink capacities to absorb and convert them. Reserves of fossil fuels are not running out, but use of these fuels is emitting gases that change the ecosystem—annual carbon dioxide (CO_2) emissions quadrupled over the past 50 years. Global warming is a serious problem, threatening to play havoc with harvests, permanently flood large areas, increase the frequency of storms and droughts, accelerate the extinction of some species, spread infectious diseases—and possibly cause sudden and savage flips in the world's climates. And although material resources may not be running out, waste is mounting, both toxic and non-toxic. In industrial countries per capita waste generation has increased almost threefold in the past 20 years.

Second is the growing deterioration of renewables—water, soil, forests, fish, biodiversity.

• Twenty countries already suffer from water stress, having less than 1,000 cubic metres per capita a year, and water's global availability has dropped from 17,000 cubic metres per capita in 1950 to 7,000 today.

• A sixth of the world's land area—nearly 2 billion hectares—is now degraded as a result of overgrazing and poor farming practices.

• The world's forests—which bind soil and prevent erosion, regulate water supplies and help govern the climate—are shrinking. Since 1970 the wooded area per 1,000 inhabitants has fallen from 11.4 square kilometres to 7.3.

• Fish stocks are declining, with about a quarter currently depleted or in danger of depletion and another 44% being fished at their biological limit.

• Wild species are becoming extinct 50–100 times faster than they would naturally, threatening to tear great holes in the web of life.

The world's dominant consumers are overwhelmingly concentrated among the well-off—but the environmental damage from the world's consumption falls most severely on the poor.

The better-off benefit from the cornucopia of consumption. But poor people and poor countries bear many of its costs. The severest human deprivations arising from environmental damage are concentrated in the poorest regions and affect the poorest people, unable to protect themselves.

• A child born in the industrial world adds more to consumption and pollution over his or her lifetime than do 30–50 children born in developing countries.

• Since 1950 industrial countries, because of their high incomes and consumption levels, have accounted for well over half the increase in resource use.

• The fifth of the world's people in the highest-income countries account for 53% of carbon dioxide emissions, the poorest fifth for 3%. Brazil, China, India, Indonesia and Mexico are among the developing countries with the highest emissions. But with huge populations, their per capita emissions are still tiny—3.9 metric tons a year in Mexico and 2.7 in China, compared with 20.5 metric tons in the United States and 10.2 in Germany. The human consequences of the global warming from carbon dioxide will be devastating for many poor countries—with a rise in sea levels, Bangladesh could see its land area shrink by 17%.

- Almost a billion people in 40 developing countries risk losing access to their primary source of protein, as overfishing driven by export demand for animal feed and oils puts pressure on fish stocks.
- The 132 million people in water-stressed areas are predominantly in Africa and parts of the Arab states—and if present trends continue, their numbers could rise to 1–2.5 billion by 2050.
- Deforestation is concentrated in developing countries. Over the last two decades, Latin America and the Caribbean lost 7 million hectares of tropical forest, Asia and Sub-Saharan Africa 4 million hectares each. Most of it has taken place to meet the demand for wood and paper, which has doubled and quintupled respectively since 1950. But over half the wood and nearly three-quarters of the paper is used in industrial countries.

The poor are most exposed to fumes and polluted rivers and least able to protect themselves. Of the estimated 2.7 million deaths each year from air pollution, 2.2 million are from indoor pollution, and 80% of the victims are rural poor in developing countries. Smoke from fuelwood and dung is more dangerous to health than tobacco smoke, but every day women have to spend hours cooking over smoky fires.

Leaded petrol, used more in developing and transition economies than in industrial countries, is crippling human health, permanently impairing the development of children's brains. In Bangkok up to 70,000 children are reported to be at risk of losing four or more IQ points because of high lead emissions. In Latin America around 15 million children under two years of age are at similar risk.

These environmental challenges stem not only from affluence but also from growing poverty. As a result of increasing impoverishment and the absence of other alternatives, a swelling number of poor and landless people are putting unprecedented pressures on the natural resource base as they struggle to survive.

Poverty and the environment are caught in a downward spiral. Past resource degradation deepens today's poverty, while today's poverty makes it very hard to care for or restore the agricultural resource base, to find alternatives to deforestation, to prevent desertification, to control erosion and to replenish soil nutrients. Poor people are forced to deplete resources to survive; this degradation of the environment further impoverishes them.

When this reinforcing downward spiral becomes extreme, poor people are either forced to move in increasing numbers to ecologically fragile lands. Almost half the world's poorest people—more than 500 million—live on marginal lands.

The poverty–environmental damage nexus in developing countries must be seen in the context of population growth. In the developing world pressures on the environment intensify every day as the population grows. The global population is projected to be 9.5 billion in 2050, with more than 8 billion in developing countries. To feed this population adequately will require three times the basic calories consumed today, the equivalent of about 10 billion tons of grain a year. Population growth will also contribute to overgrazing, overcutting and overfarming.

How people interact with their environment is complex. It is by no means simply a matter of whether they are poor or rich. Ownership of natural resources, access to common properties, the strength of communities and local institutions, the issue of entitlements and rights, risk and uncertainty are important determinants of people's environmental behaviour. Gender inequalities, government policies and incentive systems are also crucial factors.

In recent times environmental awareness has been increasing in both rich and poor countries. The rich countries, with greater resources, have been spending more on environmental protection and clean-up. The developing countries, though they have fewer resources, have also been adopting cleaner technologies and reducing pollution, as in China.

The world community has also been active on environmental problems that directly affect poor people. Such areas include desertification, biodiversity loss and exports of hazardous waste. For example, the Convention on Biological Diversity has

Competitive spending and conspicuous consumption turn the affluence of some into the social exclusion of many

42. Changing Today's Consumption Patterns

near-universal signature, with over 170 parties. The Convention to Combat Desertification has been ratified by more than 100 countries. But the deterioration of arid lands, a major threat to the livelihoods of poor people, continues unabated.

And there are other immediate environmental concerns for poor people, such as water contamination and indoor pollution, that have yet to receive serious international attention. Global forums discuss global warming. But the 2.2 million deaths yearly from indoor air pollution are scarcely mentioned.

Rising pressures for conspicuous consumption can turn destructive, reinforcing exclusion, poverty and inequality.

Pressures of competitive spending and conspicuous consumption turn the affluence of some into the social exclusion of many. When there is heavy social pressure to maintain high consumption standards and society encourages competitive spending for conspicuous displays of wealth, inequalities in consumption deepen poverty and social exclusion.

Some disturbing trends:
- Studies of US households found that the income needed to fulfil consumption aspirations doubled between 1986 and 1994.
- The definition of what constitutes a "necessity" is changing, and the distinctions between luxuries and necessities are blurring. In the 1980s Brazil, Chile, Malaysia, Mexico and South Africa had two to three times as many cars as Austria, France and Germany did when they were at the same income level 30 years earlier.
- Household debt, especially consumer credit, is growing and household savings are falling in many industrial and developing countries. In the United States households save only 3.5% of their incomes, half as much as 15 years ago. In Brazil consumer debt, concentrated among lower-income households, now exceeds $6 billion.

Many voice concerns about the impact of these trends on society's values—and on human lives. Do they further deepen poverty as households compete to meet rising consumption standards—crowding out spending on food, education and health? Do these patterns motivate people to spend more hours working—leaving less time for family, friends and community?

And is globalization accelerating these trends in competitive spending and rising standards?

Globalization is creating new inequalities and new challenges for protecting consumer rights

Globalization is integrating consumer markets around the world and opening opportunities. But it is also creating new inequalities and new challenges for protecting consumer rights.

Globalization is integrating not just trade, investment and financial markets. It is also integrating consumer markets. This has two effects—economic and social. Economic integration has accelerated the opening of consumer markets with a constant flow of new products. There is fierce competition to sell to consumers worldwide, with increasingly aggressive advertising.

On the social side local and national boundaries are breaking down in the setting of social standards and aspirations in consumption. Market research identifies "global elites" and "global middle classes" who follow the same consumption styles, showing preferences for "global brands". There are the "global teens"—some 270 million 15- to 18-year-olds in 40 countries—inhabiting a "global space", a single pop-culture world, soaking up the same videos and music and providing a huge market for designer running shoes, t-shirts and jeans.

What are the consequences? First, a host of consumption options have been opened for many consumers—but many are left out in the cold through lack of income. And pressures for competitive spending mount. "Keeping up with the Joneses" has shifted from striving to match the consumption of a next-door neighbour to pursuing the life styles of the rich and famous depicted in movies and television shows.

Second, protecting consumer rights to product safety and product information has

197

become complex. Increasingly, new products with higher chemical content, such as foods and medicines, are coming on the market. When information is not adequate, or safety standards are not strictly enforced, consumers can suffer—from pesticides that are poisonous, from milk powder that is contaminated.

At the same time the consumer receives a flood of information through commercial advertising. An average American, it is estimated, sees 150,000 advertisements on television in his or her lifetime. And advertising is increasing worldwide, faster than population or incomes. Global advertising spending, by the most conservative reckoning, is now $435 billion. Its growth has been particularly rapid in developing countries—in the Republic of Korea it increased nearly threefold in 1986–96, in the Philippines by 39% a year in 1987–92. In 1986 there were only three developing countries among the 20 biggest spenders in advertising. A decade later there were nine. And in spending relative to income, Colombia ranks first with $1.4 billion, 2.6% of its GDP.

Poor countries need to accelerate their consumption growth—but they need not follow the path taken by the rich and high-growth economies over the past half century.

Not only have consumption levels been too low to meet basic needs for more than a billion people, their growth has often been slow and interrupted by setbacks. In 70 countries with nearly a billion people consumption today is lower than it was 25 years ago. It cannot be raised without accelerating economic growth—but growth has been failing many poor people and poor countries. Despite the spectacular growth of incomes for many people in Asia, only 21 developing countries worldwide achieved growth in GDP per capita of at least 3% each year between 1995 and 1997—the rate needed to set a frame for reducing poverty.

Some suggest that developing countries should restrain their consumption in order to limit environmental damage. But this would mean prolonging the already scandalously deep and extensive deprivation for future generations.

Developing countries today face a strategic choice. They can repeat the industrialization and growth processes of the past half century, and go through a development phase that is inequitable, and creates an enormous legacy of environmental pollution. Or they can leapfrog to growth patterns that are:
- Pro-environment, preserving natural resources and creating less pollution and waste.
- Pro-poor, creating jobs for poor people and households and expanding their access to basic social services.

If poor countries can leapfrog in both consumption patterns and production technologies, they can accelerate consumption growth and human development without the huge costs of environmental damage. They can incorporate many of the available technologies that are not only less environmentally damaging but clean—solar energy, less energy-intensive crop production, cleaner paper production technologies.

Leapfrogging technologies will enhance the prospects for development by saving the huge costs of environmental clean-up that many countries are now incurring. The cost savings will go beyond the direct costs of cleaning up old toxic sites, scrubbing coal power plants and so on. Health care costs linked to environmental damage can also be saved. And leapfrogging will bypass the lock-in that can result from inappropriate infrastructure development.

Some argue that the scope for cheap, effective and politically less contentious antipollution policies is very limited in poor countries. This is a myth. Many actions have already been taken. And further options exist:
- Higher yields can be achieved through more intensive agricultural methods rather than more fertilizers and pesticides.
- Phasing out lead in petrol costs only 1–2 cents per litre for the refinery, as Mexico and Thailand have shown.
- Solar power and compact fluorescent lightbulbs can increase efficiency fourfold and reduce the need for rural electricity grids.

Developing countries today can leapfrog to growth patterns that are pro-environment and pro-poor

42. Changing Today's Consumption Patterns

- Clean four-stroke engines can be made compulsory for motorcycles and three-wheelers, as Thailand has done.

These show what is possible. But to realize the potential, more needs to be done to develop and apply innovations.

Affluent societies in industrial countries also face strategic choices. They can continue the trends in consumption of the past decade. Or they can shift to consumption that is pro-people and pro-environment.

Continuing past trends would increase industrial countries' consumption by four- to fivefold over the next half century. Some argue that growth must be slowed and consumption downsized. But the real issue is not growth of consumption but its impacts on people, the environment and society. If societies adopt technologies that diminish the environmental impact of consumption, if patterns shift from consuming material goods to consuming services, growth can help, not hinder, moves to sustainability. The strategic choices of rich countries as the world's dominant consumers, will be critical in determining the future.

AGENDA FOR ACTION

Five goals are central:
- Raise the consumption levels of more than a billion poor people—more than a quarter of humanity—who have been left out of the global expansion of consumption and are unable to meet their basic needs.
- Move to more sustainable consumption patterns that reduce environmental damage, improve efficiency in resource use and regenerate renewable resources—such as water, wood, soils and fish.
- Protect and promote the rights of consumers to information, product safety and access to products that they need.
- Discourage patterns of consumption that have a negative impact on society and that reinforce inequalities and poverty.
- Achieve more equitable international burden-sharing in reducing and preventing global environmental damage and in reducing global poverty.

The key is to create an enabling environment for sustainable consumption—where both consumers and producers have the incentives and options to move towards consumption patterns that are less environmentally damaging and less socially harmful. People care about the impact of consumption on their own health and safety—and the broader impact on the environment and society. But they are caught up in a system of limited choices and opportunities and perverse incentives. Here's a seven-point agenda for action.

1. Ensure minimum consumption requirements for all—as an explicit policy objective in all countries.

"Everyone has the right to a standard of living adequate for the health and well-being of himself and his family, including food, clothing, housing and medical care and necessary social services ... Everyone has the right to education" (Universal Declaration of Human Rights). These principles of universalism and human rights acknowledge the equal rights of everyone—women, men and children—without discrimination. They demand governance that ensures that all have enough to eat, that no child goes without education, that no human being is denied access to health care, safe water and basic sanitation and that all people can develop their potential capabilities to the full extent.

Strong public action is needed to meet these goals. This means a mix of public provisioning in basic social services and an enabling environment and incentive system for private and voluntary action. It means:
- Strong public policies to promote food security—ranging from conducive monetary, fiscal, commercial and pricing policies to institutions and incentives to promote local production and distribution.
- Priority public expenditures for basic social services—education, health, safe water, basic sanitation. Not only should services be expanded, but access should be made more equitable. Studies in many countries show that access favours the better-off rather than the poor, and urban rather than rural populations.
- Infrastructure for transport and energy to provide affordable and efficient services

Consumption levels of over a billion poor people must be raised

for people, not just economic growth. This means, for example, public transport, paths for bicycles and pedestrians and energy from renewable sources in rural areas.
- Incentives to develop "poor people's goods"—low-cost housing materials, energy-saving equipment and food storage systems.
- Institutions and legal frameworks that secure people's rights to housing, to common property, to credit.

John Kenneth Galbraith wrote 40 years ago about private affluence amid public squalor. Far from narrowing, the contrasts have grown, and to them are added private and environmental squalor.

2. Develop and apply technologies and methods that are environmentally sustainable for both poor and affluent consumers.

Human development can be sustained with purposeful action. The challenge is not to stop growth. It is to change the patterns of consumption and production, using new technologies to achieve greater efficiency and to reduce waste and pollution. Many such technologies are already in production or on the drawing board.

Sustainable growth of consumption and production depends on major advances in cleaner, material-saving, resource-saving and low-cost technologies. Also needed are consumption options that are environmentally friendly and low cost and affordable for the poor. But many do not yet exist—these need to be invented. And those that exist need to be better marketed—goods that use less energy and fewer renewables (water and wood), that create less waste and pollution and that are low in cost. Such options may be available in some countries—the zero-emission car, for example—but not worldwide, or they may be only at the experimental stage. Public expenditure on research and development in energy has declined by a third in real terms since the early 1980s. Moreover, less than 10% goes to energy efficiency improvements. The rest goes largely to fossil fuel and nuclear energy development. The case is strong for firms and governments to support more technological development and application.

Rather than attempting to pick and promote winning technologies, governments can help create a dynamic marketplace to perform that task more effectively. The state can require all energy providers—public and private—to supply a fixed minimum share of energy from renewable sources—either by generating it themselves or by purchasing it from other providers. This approach both ensures the introduction of renewable energy sources in the market and stimulates innovation of more efficient and lower-cost technologies.

The benefits of cleaner technologies have been well demonstrated, as with the reduction of material use in OECD countries. Many technological solutions already exist for environmentally friendly goods, but current pricing structures undervalue environmental costs and benefits—and thus reduce market incentives. Increased public support for further research and development could accelerate the pace of technological progress.

There is a particular need for technologies to meet the requirements of the poor. About 2 billion people in developing countries lack access to electricity. Meeting this need through clean, renewable sources of energy can reduce poverty and indoor air pollution. The sun and wind are available at no cost to villages that have little hope of being connected to electricity grids. Windpower, now the world's fastest-growing source of energy, meets only 1% of global demand. India aims by 2012 to provide 10% of its electricity from renewables, which could provide half the world's energy by the middle of the next century.

Perhaps most important among technologies for the poor are those for agricultural production in ecologically marginal environments. Improvements in food production in much of Asia and Latin America would not have been possible without the green revolution—the scientific breakthroughs that provided high-yielding varieties of rice, wheat and maize. The world average yield of these crops has more than doubled over the past 20 years. But this did not happen in areas of lower rainfall and in the more fragile ecological zones, where

A second green revolution is needed—primarily to benefit the world's poorest

42. Changing Today's Consumption Patterns

people subsist on millet and sorghum—and on cattle, sheep and goats. The world average yield of millet and sorghum increased by only 15% over the past two decades.

A second green revolution is needed for these people, among the world's poorest. But this should not just repeat the first revolution—it needs to aim both at increasing yields and incomes and at preserving and developing the environmental base.

The private sector has a critical role too—not just to meet the challenges of social responsibility but to produce environmentally friendly, poverty-reducing goods. The market for environmental goods alone is estimated at $500 billion. But for the private sector to act, it needs the right signals from prices and incentives in the market.

3. Remove perverse subsidies and restructure taxes to shift incentives from consumption that damages the environment to consumption that promotes human development.

Many developing countries use subsidies—on staple foods and basic energy supplies, for example—to help poor people survive and reduce poverty. Yet at the same time, most countries tax employment and subsidize pollution and environmental damage directly and indirectly. Such "perverse" subsidies are particularly common in the sectors of energy, water, road transport and agriculture. Total subsidies worldwide in these four sectors are estimated at $700–900 billion a year. They are also often distributionally regressive, benefiting mostly the wealthy—often political interest groups—while draining the public budget.

The absolute amount of subsidies is about twice as large in the OECD countries as in the rest of the world. In the OECD countries agriculture is most heavily subsidized (more than $330 billion), followed by road transport ($85–200 billion). In developing and transition economies the largest subsidies go to energy ($150–200 billion) and water ($42–47 billion). In the words of the Earth Council, "the world is spending hundreds of billions of dollars annually to subsidize its own destruction."

Removing perverse subsidies and imposing environmental taxes can promote equitable growth

Environmental taxes—charging for pollution, congestion and depletion—have proved highly effective in both industrial and developing countries. They have been widely used in Western Europe and are the well-accepted core of green tax reforms—the Swedish air pollution tax and the Dutch water pollution tax, for example. But not just in Europe. Malaysia's effluent charges and Singapore's automobile taxes are well established and effective.

In Europe the social costs of environmental damage, unaccounted and unpaid, are estimated to average more than 4% of GDP. Estimates for the United States range from 2% to 12%. Users are encouraged to make excessive and wasteful use of road transport, with private cars most underpriced and most environmentally damaging.

Removing perverse subsidies that encourage environmental damage, lower economic efficiency and benefit the wealthy—and imposing environmental taxes instead—can be a catalyst for reducing inequalities and poverty and improving the prospects for equitable growth. Environmental taxes raise revenues that can be used to spend on environmental protection, to reduce taxes on labour, capital and savings or to improve access to social services for poor people.

The policy instruments described above present a win-win opportunity for changing consumption patterns to reverse environmental damage and increase the consumption of the poor. Removing water subsidies, for example, would reduce water use by 20–30%—and in parts of Asia by as much as 50%. That would make it possible, without large, environmentally destructive water development projects, to supply safe drinking water to most of the 1.3 billion people now lacking it.

Another example: congestion charges can finance improvements in public transport and expand transport options. They can ease congestion, save time, lower the costs of public transport and, usually, improve the distribution of income. Road transport subsidies in developing countries amount to $15 billion. The increased involvement of the private sector in financing, building and operating public transport systems in the

1990s is creating pressure to reduce road subsidies and increase user fees. Argentina cut subsidies to suburban rail systems by $25 million between 1993 and 1995 when it privatized the operation of urban transport.

The benefits of a shift from taxing employment to taxing pollution and other environmental damage could be considerable. An OECD study on Norway suggests that a revenue-neutral shift would reduce unemployment while encouraging recycling and reducing environmental damage.

More and more countries are realizing that old policies and subsidies have adverse consequences. Thus energy subsidies in developing countries have fallen from more than $300 billion in the early 1990s to about $150–200 billion today. Environmental taxes are multiplying. But perverse subsidies are still huge, and environmental taxes have reached nowhere near their potential. Even in the Nordic countries, where some of the most interesting experiments are being carried out, pollution taxes and congestion charges raise only about 7% of government revenues.

4. Strengthen public action for consumer education and information and environmental protection.

The expansion of consumer choice has little significance if choices are based on wrong or misleading information. Strong public action to protect consumer rights is needed to offset vastly unbalanced information flows dominated by commercial advertisements.

Consumer rights must be defended through:
- Strict standards for consumer health and safety.
- Product labelling about the content and proper use of products and their environmental and social impact.
- Information and awareness campaigns about potential health hazards, such as smoking tobacco and the improper use of feeding formula for infants.

Advertising can serve positive purposes, but controls are needed, especially on television advertising targeting young children. Sweden bans television advertising directed at children under 12.

Where price incentives are inadequate, environmental laws and regulations are needed. Skilfully devised, controls can be enabling for the consumer, not restricting. But implementation is as important as legislation. Strong institutions, free from corruption, are needed to enforce regulations in such areas as rights to land, security of tenure in housing and accurate information on consumer goods to protect the interests of poor people.

Regulation and market interventions can be mutually reinforcing. Sometimes regulation is needed to initiate action that can later be taken further with price incentives. At other times price incentives can be used to make a start—with regulation later to ensure wider compliance, especially after fostering social acceptance.

A new approach that has gained considerable interest and momentum in recent years is self-regulation through publicizing information on industrial polluters. This encourages the production of information about pollution generation, both as a source of incentive for behavioural change and as a benchmark for subsequent regulation. A well-known example is the US Toxic Release Inventory, which requires businesses to report the amounts of toxic materials that they put into the environment. Many companies respond by reducing pollution to preserve their reputations.

5. Strengthen international mechanisms to manage consumption's global impacts.

Environmental damage crosses borders. So do shifts in consumption patterns and habits. Poverty and inequality are issues of global magnitude and thus cannot be tackled by nations singly. They require international action.

International responsibilities for ensuring the sustainability of natural resource use have been debated in numerous forums. The Kuala Lumpur Meeting of the Parties to the Basel Convention on the Ban on Hazardous Waste agreed to ban the export

Consumer rights must be protected from unbalanced information flows

of such waste to poor countries. Both the Convention on Biological Diversity and the Convention on International Trade in Endangered Species of Wild Flora and Fauna have been quite successful.

Although some of these agreements sometimes fall short of expectations and ideals, they are steps in the right direction. The recent Kyoto Meeting on the United Nations Framework Convention on Climate Change has set industrial country targets for emissions of carbon dioxide and proposed a Clean Development Mechanism to assist developing countries. Both the financing and the institutional arrangement for this mechanism must be dealt with by the global community. Another problem that needs to be addressed: the continuing decline of official development assistance and the mounting unsustainable debt of poor countries.

Many global instruments to tackle environmental and poverty issues are under-developed—such as environmental trading permits, debt swaps and fair trade schemes. These instruments tend to be double-edged swords, however, and need to be carefully negotiated so that they do not penalize poor nations and make them even poorer. Trading environmental permits should not mean permanently giving away the rights of developing countries. A coordinating global institution in the form of the proposed international bank for environmental settlements is needed to develop and manage these instruments equitably.

Strong civil society alliances should be built to protect consumer rights

6. Build stronger alliances among the movements for consumer rights, environmental protection, poverty eradication, gender equality and children's rights.

Consumer groups have been a powerful force for protecting consumer rights worldwide. They have helped remove unsafe products from the market and promote proper labelling and the supply of safe and low-cost goods.

Now consumers increasingly are using the power of their purses to push the interests of communities even halfway around the globe. Studies in Europe show that consumers are willing to pay price premiums of 5–10% for products that are more environmentally sound (in production, operation and disposal).

Businesses are responding to consumer demand for cleaner, safer products. Evidence from Eastern Europe shows that firms exporting to the European Union tend to have cleaner production processes than firms that produce for the domestic markets, which are less environmentally demanding.

Conventional wisdom assumes that environmental damage is a necessary consequence of economic growth. This is wrong. Environmental damage is a drain on economic growth, and it is possible to pursue a path to growth that does not damage the environment.

Poverty eradication, environmental sustainability, consumer rights protection—all these build on one another. Eradicating poverty does not require growth that ignores consumer rights or destroys the environment. Quite the opposite. Protecting consumer rights and protecting the environment are necessary for eradicating poverty and reducing inequalities.

There is great potential for building closer alliances among the environmental movement, the women's movement, the movement for children, consumer groups and pressure groups against poverty. Already their central concerns show great convergence. Stronger alliances are needed—and possible—if each movement emphasizes the common need for human development. United and mobilized together, these groups can achieve much more.

7. Think globally, act locally. Build on the burgeoning initiatives of people in communities everywhere and foster synergies in the actions of civil society, the private sector and government.

The growing number and strength of consumer and environmental movements around the world—including the 2,000 town and city Agenda 21s that have been prepared—reflect the commitment of people to taking collective action. Many opinion surveys show that people place a higher value on community and family life than on acquiring material possessions. And many people are asking how they can give more emphasis to human concerns.

Some 100 countries have prepared national human development reports, assessing their present situations and drawing conclusions on actions to achieve more human patterns of development. Most of these plans have analysed needs in the critical areas of education, health and employment, often linking them with opportunities for generating resources from reduced military spending.

These initiatives in many cases are the outcomes of successful alliances of the government, institutions of civil society and international organizations.

Progress has also been made in the area of sustainable consumption and a cleaner environment as a result of civil pressure, public action and private sector responses. The instruments: eco-taxes and subsidy removal, stiff environmental regulations backed by penalties, community efforts for better management of common resources (erosion control, reforestation) and more equitable provisioning of public infrastructure and services.

This shows what is possible. It also shows that support exists for a cleaner environment, a more equitable society and the eradication of poverty. Individuals, households, civil society groups, governments and private businesses—all have a role, and together their complementary efforts can build even more energy and synergy for action.

• • •

In the poorer countries many priorities in consumption still need to be addressed. Increases in consumption should be planned and encouraged—but with attention to nurturing the links, to making sure that the increases contribute to human development and to avoiding extremes of inequality. Forward-looking perspectives are also needed—to avoid infrastructure and institutions that may lock a country into unsustainable or socially dysfunctional consumption.

In the better-off countries—most of the industrial countries and some of the richer developing countries—the challenge is different. The priority to eradicate poverty and ensure the basic needs of all remains. Indeed, the failure of the richest countries to do that is a scandal. But as general living standards rise and the proportion in poverty falls, the balance of attention in economic and social policy needs to shift. Increasingly, the policy focus needs to move towards enlarging the options for patterns of consumption in which human creativity can be lived out and carried forward with diversity and fulfilment, with most of the population at comfortable levels of consumption, well above the margins of subsistence. These policies need to be combined with those of the environment and human development.

Recent experiences give considerable hope, with more evidence showing that changes in consumption patterns towards sustainable poverty reduction are possible.

Hope brings challenge. The high levels of consumption and production in the world today, the power and potential of technology and information, present great opportunities. After a century of vast material expansion, will leaders and people have the vision to seek and achieve more equitable and more human advance in the 21st century?

Increases in consumption must also nurture links to human development

Documents

TOTAL OUTPUT, INCOME, AND SPENDING
GROSS DOMESTIC PRODUCT

In the fourth quarter of 1998, according to revised estimates, current-dollar gross domestic product (GDP) rose 6.9 percent (annual rate), real GDP (GDP in chained 1992 dollars) rose 6.0 percent, and the implicit price deflator rose 0.8 percent.

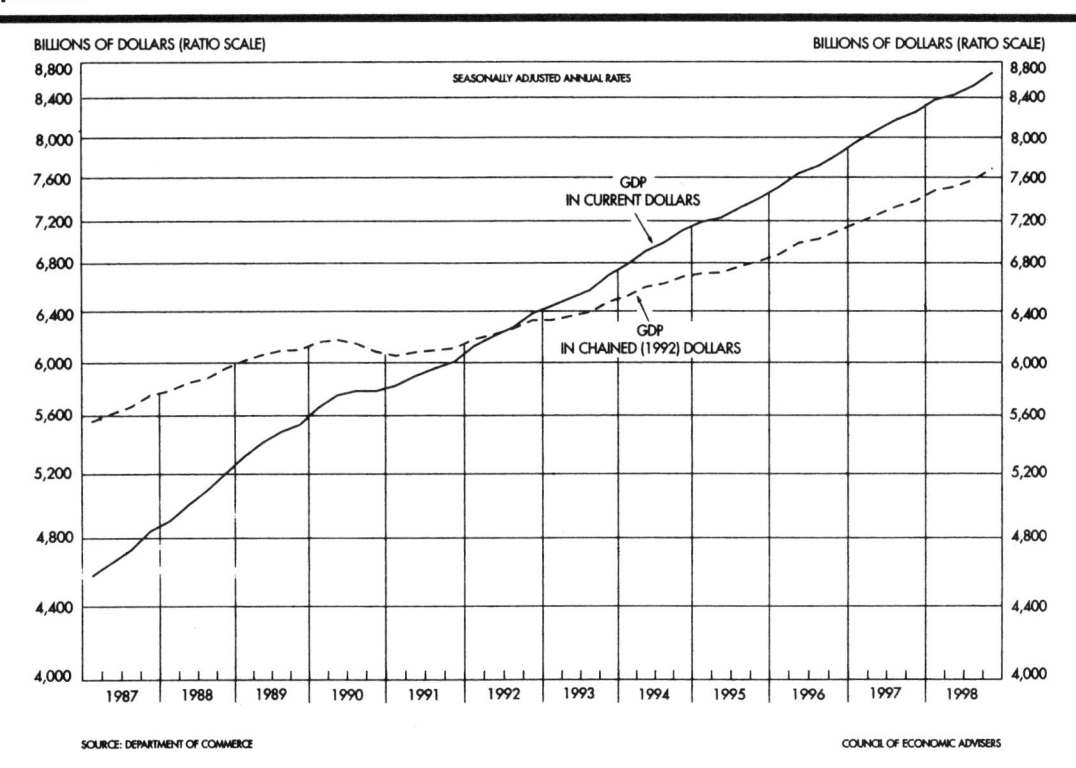

[Billions of current dollars; quarterly data at seasonally adjusted annual rates]

Period	Gross domestic product	Personal consumption expenditures	Gross private domestic investment	Net exports	Exports	Imports	Total	Federal Total	National defense	Non-defense	State and local	Final sales of domestic product	Gross domestic purchases [1]	Addendum: Gross national product
1990	5,743.8	3,839.3	799.7	−71.3	557.3	628.6	1,176.1	503.6	373.1	130.4	672.6	5,735.8	5,815.1	5,764.9
1991	5,916.7	3,975.1	736.2	−20.5	601.8	622.3	1,225.9	522.6	383.5	139.1	703.4	5,919.0	5,937.2	5,932.4
1992	6,244.4	4,219.8	790.4	−29.5	639.4	669.0	1,263.8	528.0	375.8	152.2	735.8	6,237.4	6,274.0	6,255.5
1993	6,558.1	4,459.2	876.2	−60.7	658.6	719.3	1,283.4	518.3	360.7	157.7	765.0	6,537.6	6,618.8	6,576.8
1994	6,947.0	4,717.0	1,007.9	−90.9	721.2	812.1	1,313.0	510.2	349.2	161.0	802.8	6,885.7	7,037.9	6,955.2
1995	7,269.6	4,953.9	1,043.2	−83.9	819.4	903.3	1,356.4	509.1	344.4	164.7	847.3	7,238.9	7,353.5	7,287.1
1996	7,661.6	5,215.7	1,131.9	−91.2	873.8	965.0	1,405.2	518.4	351.0	167.4	886.8	7,629.5	7,752.8	7,674.0
1997	8,110.9	5,493.7	1,256.0	−93.4	965.4	1,058.8	1,454.6	520.2	346.0	174.3	934.4	8,043.5	8,204.3	8,102.9
1998ʳ	8,511.0	5,807.9	1,367.1	−151.2	959.0	1,110.2	1,487.1	520.6	340.4	180.2	966.5	8,451.6	8,662.2	8,490.5
1995: I	7,170.8	4,862.5	1,058.9	−94.7	787.8	882.5	1,344.1	512.3	346.1	166.2	831.8	7,111.8	7,265.5	7,189.3
II	7,210.9	4,931.5	1,029.6	−108.0	803.4	911.4	1,357.8	511.7	348.1	163.6	846.2	7,185.6	7,318.9	7,233.3
III	7,304.8	4,986.4	1,030.6	−74.5	835.1	909.6	1,362.3	511.2	345.5	165.7	851.1	7,287.7	7,379.3	7,313.2
IV	7,391.9	5,035.3	1,053.6	−58.4	851.5	909.9	1,361.4	501.2	337.9	163.3	860.2	7,370.4	7,450.3	7,412.6
1996: I	7,495.3	5,108.2	1,075.3	−75.7	856.6	932.3	1,387.5	517.1	350.3	166.8	870.4	7,479.1	7,571.0	7,515.0
II	7,629.2	5,199.0	1,118.3	−94.0	863.0	957.0	1,406.0	523.1	355.6	167.4	882.9	7,600.6	7,723.2	7,643.3
III	7,703.4	5,242.5	1,167.9	−115.5	861.4	976.9	1,408.6	519.0	351.3	167.7	889.6	7,653.6	7,818.9	7,708.6
IV	7,818.4	5,313.2	1,166.0	−79.6	914.2	993.8	1,418.8	514.6	346.7	167.9	904.2	7,784.6	7,898.0	7,829.0
1997: I	7,955.0	5,402.4	1,206.4	−93.3	930.2	1,023.5	1,439.4	517.0	341.1	175.9	922.4	7,895.2	8,048.2	7,952.4
II	8,063.4	5,438.8	1,259.9	−86.8	961.1	1,047.9	1,451.5	522.9	349.1	173.8	928.6	7,979.9	8,150.2	8,062.3
III	8,170.8	5,540.3	1,265.7	−94.7	981.7	1,076.4	1,459.5	521.0	347.1	173.9	938.5	8,116.2	8,265.5	8,162.0
IV	8,254.5	5,593.2	1,292.0	−98.8	988.6	1,087.4	1,468.1	520.1	346.5	173.6	947.9	8,182.6	8,353.3	8,234.9
1998: I	8,384.2	5,676.5	1,366.6	−123.7	973.3	1,097.1	1,464.9	511.6	331.6	180.0	953.3	8,288.7	8,508.0	8,369.4
II	8,440.6	5,773.7	1,345.0	−159.3	949.6	1,108.9	1,481.2	520.7	339.8	180.9	960.4	8,401.3	8,599.9	8,421.8
III	8,537.9	5,846.7	1,364.4	−165.5	936.2	1,101.7	1,492.3	519.4	343.7	175.7	972.9	8,480.9	8,703.4	8,510.9
IVʳ	8,681.2	5,934.8	1,392.4	−156.2	976.8	1,133.0	1,510.2	530.7	346.4	184.3	979.5	8,635.5	8,837.4	8,660.0

[1] GDP less exports of goods and services plus imports of goods and services.

Source: Department of Commerce, Bureau of Economic Analysis.

DISPOSITION OF PERSONAL INCOME

According to revised estimates, per capita disposable personal income in chained (1992) dollars rose at an annual rate of 3.1 percent in the fourth quarter of 1998.

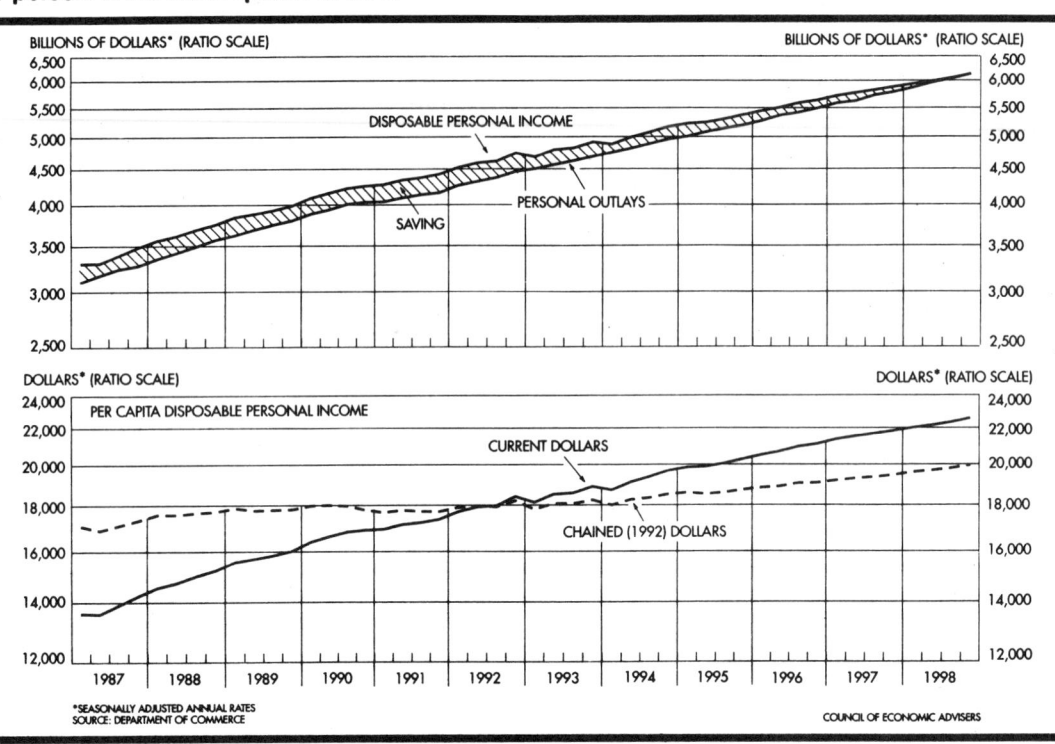

Period	Personal income	Less: Personal tax and nontax payments	Equals: Disposable personal income	Less: Personal outlays [1]	Equals: Personal saving	Disposable personal income in billions of chained (1992) dollars	Per capita disposable personal income, Current dollars	Per capita disposable personal income, Chained (1992) dollars	Per capita personal consumption expenditures, Current dollars	Per capita personal consumption expenditures, Chained (1992) dollars	Percent change in real per capita disposable personal income	Saving as percent of disposable personal income	Population, including Armed Forces overseas (thousands) [2]
	Billions of dollars						Dollars				Percent		
1991	4,965.6	624.8	4,340.9	4,097.4	243.5	4,483.5	17,179	17,744	15,732	16,249	-1.2	5.6	252,680
1992	5,255.7	650.5	4,605.1	4,341.0	264.1	4,605.1	18,029	18,029	16,520	16,520	1.6	5.7	255,432
1993	5,481.0	690.0	4,791.1	4,580.7	210.3	4,666.7	18,558	18,077	17,273	16,825	.3	4.4	258,161
1994	5,757.9	739.1	5,018.9	4,842.1	176.8	4,772.9	19,251	18,308	18,093	17,207	1.3	3.5	260,705
1995	6,072.1	795.0	5,277.0	5,097.2	179.8	4,906.0	20,050	18,640	18,822	17,499	1.8	3.4	263,194
1996	6,425.2	890.5	5,534.7	5,376.2	158.5	5,043.0	20,840	18,989	19,639	17,894	1.9	2.9	265,579
1997	6,784.0	989.0	5,795.1	5,674.1	121.0	5,183.1	21,633	19,349	20,508	18,342	1.9	2.1	267,880
1998 r	7,126.1	1,098.3	6,027.9	6,000.2	27.7	5,348.5	22,304	19,790	21,490	19,068	2.3	.5	270,258
	Seasonally adjusted annual rates												
1995: I	5,979.5	767.2	5,212.3	4,997.4	214.9	4,883.0	19,876	18,621	18,542	17,371	1.7	4.1	262,235
II	6,030.3	795.7	5,234.7	5,070.6	164.0	4,876.0	19,915	18,551	18,762	17,476	-1.5	3.1	262,847
III	6,093.5	799.0	5,294.5	5,132.1	162.4	4,909.1	20,091	18,628	18,922	17,544	1.7	3.1	263,527
IV	6,185.0	818.3	5,366.8	5,188.8	178.0	4,956.1	20,316	18,761	19,061	17,602	2.9	3.3	264,169
1996: I	6,284.3	849.7	5,434.6	5,261.1	173.5	4,992.0	20,533	18,860	19,299	17,727	2.1	3.2	264,680
II	6,390.0	893.3	5,496.7	5,356.2	140.5	5,018.4	20,722	18,919	19,600	17,894	1.3	2.6	265,258
III	6,476.7	899.4	5,577.3	5,405.2	172.2	5,072.8	20,976	19,079	19,717	17,934	3.4	3.1	265,887
IV	6,549.8	919.7	5,630.1	5,482.5	147.6	5,089.0	21,127	19,096	19,938	18,021	.4	2.6	266,491
1997: I	6,666.7	955.6	5,711.2	5,575.8	135.4	5,130.8	21,391	19,217	20,235	18,178	2.6	2.4	266,987
II	6,743.6	975.8	5,767.9	5,616.0	151.9	5,167.5	21,558	19,315	20,329	18,213	2.1	2.6	267,545
III	6,820.9	999.0	5,821.8	5,723.3	98.5	5,198.4	21,709	19,385	20,660	18,447	1.5	1.7	268,171
IV	6,904.9	1,025.5	5,879.4	5,781.2	98.2	5,235.8	21,871	19,478	20,807	18,529	1.9	1.7	268,815
1998: I	7,003.9	1,066.8	5,937.1	5,864.0	73.0	5,287.1	22,046	19,632	21,078	18,770	3.2	1.2	269,309
II	7,081.9	1,092.9	5,988.9	5,963.3	25.6	5,321.5	22,192	19,719	21,394	19,010	1.8	.4	269,867
III	7,160.8	1,108.4	6,052.4	6,039.8	12.6	5,364.1	22,373	19,829	21,612	19,155	2.3	.2	270,523
IV r	7,257.9	1,124.9	6,133.1	6,133.6	-.6	5,421.2	22,604	19,980	21,873	19,334	3.1	0	271,331

[1] Includes personal consumption expenditures, interest paid by persons, and personal transfer payments to rest of the world (net).
[2] Annual data are averages of quarterly data, which are averages for the period.

Source: Department of Commerce (Bureau of Economic Analysis and Bureau of the Census).

SOURCES OF PERSONAL INCOME
Personal income rose $39.7 billion (annual rate) in February, following an increase of $46.6 billion in January. Wages and salaries increased $28.3 billion in February, following an increase of $31.5 billion in January.

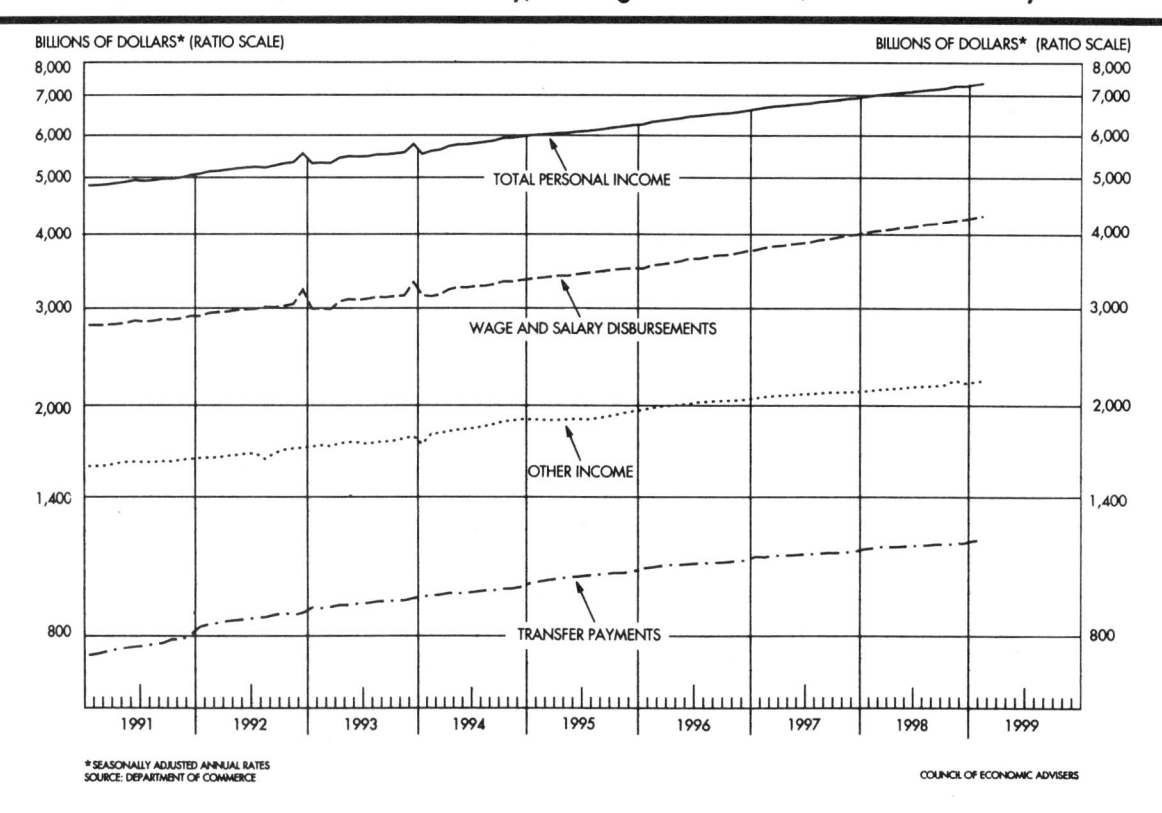

CORPORATE PROFITS
In the fourth quarter of 1998, according to current estimates, corporate profits before tax fell $12.4 billion (annual rate) and profits after tax fell $4.8 billion.

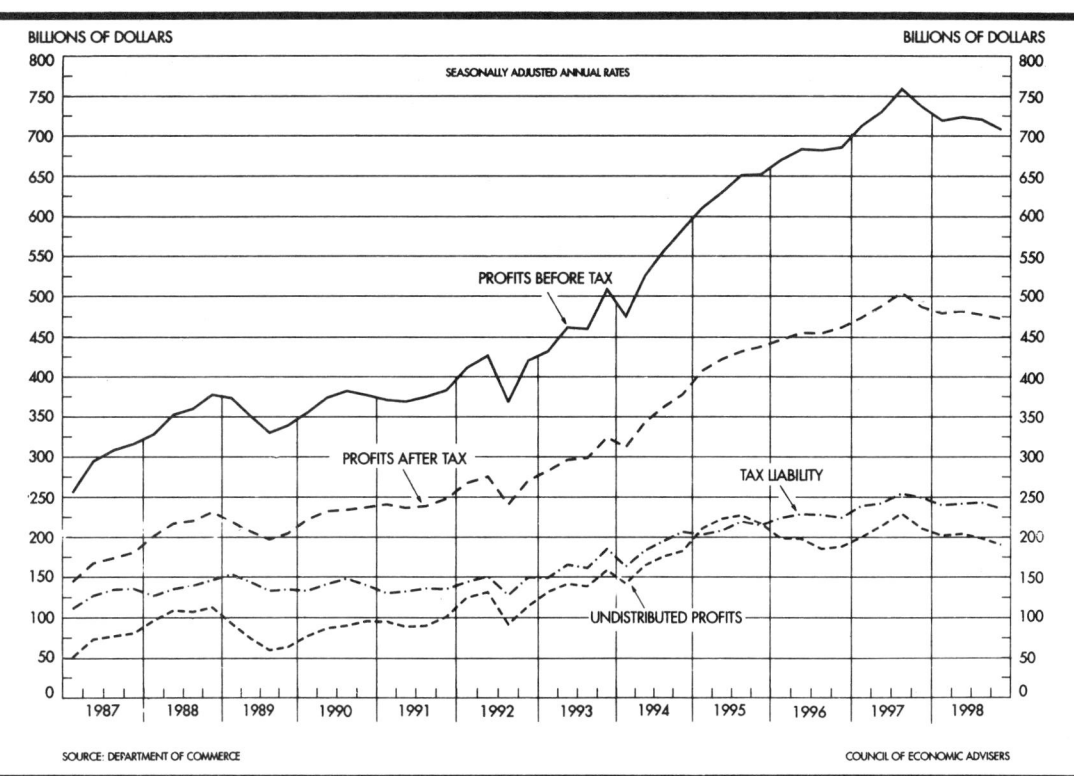

CONSUMER PRICES—ALL URBAN CONSUMERS

In February, the consumer price index for all urban consumers rose 0.1 percent seasonally adjusted and not seasonally adjusted. The index was 1.6 percent above its year-earlier level.

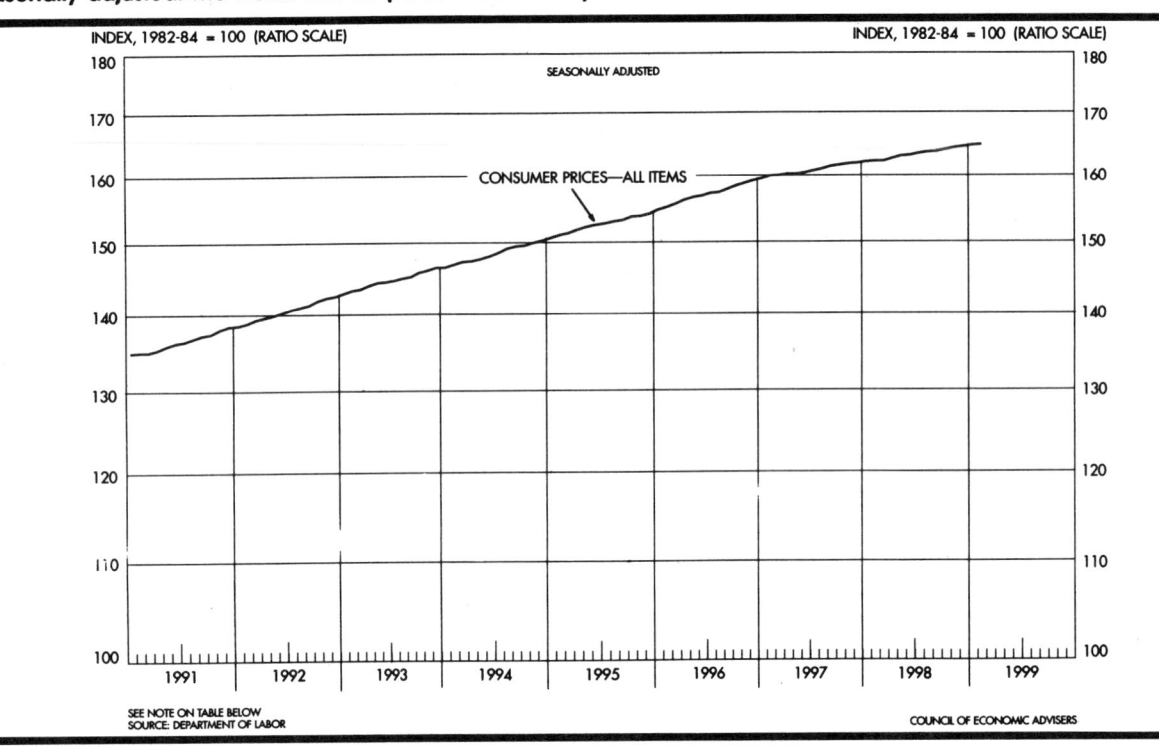

[1982–84=100, except as noted; monthly data seasonally adjusted, except as noted]

Period	All items[1] Not seasonally adjusted (NSA)	All items[1] Seasonally adjusted	Food	Housing Total[1]	Shelter Total[1]	Shelter Rent of primary residence	Shelter Owners' equivalent rent (12/82 =100)	Fuels and utilities	Apparel	Transportation Total[1]	Transportation New cars	Transportation Motor fuel	Medical care	Energy[2]	All items less food and energy
Rel. imp.[3]	100.0	....	15.4	39.8	30.3	7.0	20.5	4.7	4.8	17.0	....	2.5	5.7	6.3	78.3
1989	124.0	....	125.1	123.0	132.8	132.8	137.4	107.8	118.6	114.1	119.2	88.5	149.3	94.3	129.0
1990	130.7	....	132.4	128.5	140.0	138.4	144.8	111.6	124.1	120.5	121.0	101.2	162.8	102.1	135.5
1991	136.2	....	136.3	133.6	146.3	143.3	150.4	115.3	128.7	123.8	125.3	99.4	177.0	102.5	142.1
1992	140.3	....	137.9	137.5	151.2	146.9	155.5	117.8	131.9	126.5	128.4	99.0	190.1	103.0	147.3
1993	144.5	....	140.9	141.2	155.7	150.3	160.5	121.3	133.7	130.4	131.5	98.0	201.4	104.2	152.2
1994	148.2	....	144.3	144.8	160.5	154.0	165.8	122.8	133.4	134.3	136.0	98.5	211.0	104.6	156.5
1995	152.4	....	148.4	148.5	165.7	157.8	171.3	123.7	132.0	139.1	139.0	100.0	220.5	105.2	161.2
1996	156.9	....	153.3	152.8	171.0	162.0	176.8	127.5	131.7	143.0	141.4	106.3	228.2	110.1	165.6
1997	160.5	....	157.3	156.8	176.3	166.7	181.9	130.8	132.9	144.3	141.7	106.2	234.6	111.5	169.5
1998	163.0	....	160.7	160.4	182.1	172.1	187.8	128.5	133.0	141.6	140.7	92.2	242.1	102.9	173.4
1998: Feb	161.9	162.1	159.5	158.7	179.6	169.8	185.5	128.4	132.8	142.5	140.9	96.9	239.0	104.8	172.2
Mar	162.2	162.1	159.5	159.0	180.0	170.3	186.0	128.7	132.5	141.9	140.9	94.0	239.7	103.6	172.4
Apr	162.5	162.5	159.6	159.6	180.6	170.8	186.6	129.0	132.7	141.8	141.0	93.2	240.5	103.4	172.9
May	162.8	162.9	160.4	159.9	181.2	171.3	187.1	128.8	132.9	141.7	140.3	93.3	241.4	103.3	173.3
June	163.0	163.0	160.4	160.1	181.6	171.8	187.6	128.4	133.1	141.4	140.0	92.5	242.1	102.7	173.5
July	163.2	163.3	160.9	160.4	181.9	172.2	188.1	128.3	132.7	141.8	140.7	92.2	242.7	102.5	173.8
Aug	163.4	163.5	161.3	160.7	182.5	172.8	188.6	127.9	134.0	141.6	141.2	90.6	243.7	101.5	174.2
Sept	163.6	163.6	161.4	161.0	183.2	173.3	189.1	127.1	133.2	141.1	140.8	89.1	244.4	100.3	174.5
Oct	164.0	163.9	162.2	161.3	183.7	173.8	189.6	126.8	133.2	141.3	140.5	89.8	244.9	100.4	174.8
Nov	164.0	164.2	162.4	161.8	184.3	174.4	190.0	127.2	133.1	141.1	140.5	88.6	245.4	100.1	175.0
Dec	163.9	164.4	162.5	162.0	184.6	174.9	190.6	127.0	132.3	140.6	140.6	86.4	246.1	99.0	175.6
1999: Jan	164.3	164.6	163.3	161.9	184.6	175.3	190.8	126.8	130.8	140.4	140.6	86.4	246.9	98.8	175.7
Feb	164.5	164.7	163.5	162.1	184.9	175.6	191.3	127.1	130.6	140.2	139.9	86.1	247.5	98.8	175.8

[1] Includes items not shown separately.
[2] Household fuels—gas (piped), electricity, fuel oil, etc.—and motor fuel. Motor oil, coolant, etc. excluded beginning 1983.
[3] Relative importance, December 1998.

NOTE.—Data beginning January 1999 reflect a change in CPI index formula calculation and other changes in methodology. See Bureau of Labor Statistics news release *Consumer Price Index* dated February 19, 1999 for details.

Source: Department of Labor, Bureau of Labor Statistics.

REAL PERSONAL CONSUMPTION EXPENDITURES

[Billions of chained (1992) dollars, except as noted; quarterly data at seasonally adjusted annual rates]

Period	Total personal consumption expenditures	Durable goods				Nondurable goods					Services			Retail sales of new passenger cars and light trucks (millions of units)
		Total durable goods	Motor vehicles and parts	Furniture and household equipment	Other	Total nondurable goods	Food	Clothing and shoes	Gasoline and oil	Fuel oil and coal	Other	Total services [1]	Housing	Medical care	
1991	4,105.8	462.0	193.2	177.0	91.8	1,302.9	659.6	215.9	103.4	10.8	313.2	2,341.0	635.2	621.6	12.3
1992	4,219.8	488.5	206.9	189.4	92.3	1,321.8	660.0	225.5	106.6	10.9	318.8	2,409.4	646.8	646.6	12.8
1993	4,343.6	523.8	218.9	207.8	97.2	1,351.0	675.3	234.2	108.7	10.7	322.1	2,468.9	654.7	655.3	13.9
1994	4,486.0	561.2	230.0	229.4	102.3	1,389.9	687.9	247.1	109.8	10.7	334.3	2,535.5	674.3	662.1	15.0
1995	4,605.6	589.1	230.6	251.2	109.0	1,417.6	689.5	260.1	114.3	11.2	343.1	2,599.6	688.6	675.0	14.7
1996	4,752.4	626.1	235.0	277.5	117.1	1,450.9	692.6	276.1	116.0	11.2	356.7	2,676.7	700.9	686.6	15.0
1997	4,913.5	668.6	239.3	307.7	127.7	1,486.3	699.3	288.4	117.9	10.3	373.0	2,761.5	717.4	701.7	15.0
1998 r	5,153.3	737.1	259.6	347.3	138.5	1,544.1	718.0	310.3	119.9	9.6	390.3	2,879.5	735.0	723.2	15.5
1995: I	4,555.3	575.2	227.4	242.6	106.5	1,410.4	689.5	256.4	113.5	10.4	340.9	2,570.4	684.9	669.1	14.8
II	4,593.6	583.5	229.5	246.6	108.7	1,415.9	689.6	258.4	114.2	11.4	342.8	2,594.8	687.0	673.0	14.5
III	4,623.4	595.3	232.6	254.1	110.3	1,418.5	688.9	262.1	114.3	11.3	342.7	2,610.3	689.7	677.2	14.8
IV	4,650.0	602.4	232.8	261.4	110.5	1,425.6	690.0	263.5	115.3	11.7	346.0	2,622.9	692.7	680.9	15.0
1996: I	4,692.1	611.0	235.9	265.0	112.3	1,433.5	691.1	268.0	114.7	11.9	348.9	2,648.5	695.7	679.5	15.1
II	4,746.6	629.5	237.9	277.7	117.0	1,450.4	693.4	276.4	116.2	11.1	355.0	2,668.4	698.6	685.6	15.1
III	4,768.3	626.5	232.8	280.0	117.6	1,454.7	691.4	279.8	116.0	11.3	358.2	2,688.1	702.6	687.7	15.0
IV	4,802.6	637.5	233.3	287.2	121.5	1,465.1	694.3	280.3	117.0	10.6	364.8	2,701.7	706.7	693.5	14.9
1997: I	4,853.4	656.3	239.1	296.2	125.8	1,477.9	699.4	286.0	116.7	9.8	368.3	2,722.1	711.2	694.8	15.3
II	4,872.7	653.8	230.8	303.7	125.9	1,477.1	697.3	283.3	118.3	10.4	369.9	2,743.6	715.1	698.6	14.5
III	4,947.0	679.6	244.4	312.7	128.5	1,495.7	700.6	291.9	118.4	10.7	377.0	2,775.4	719.5	704.2	15.3
IV	4,981.0	684.8	242.7	318.1	130.8	1,494.3	699.9	292.3	118.1	10.1	376.8	2,804.8	723.9	709.4	14.8
1998: I	5,055.1	710.3	247.8	335.8	135.1	1,521.2	706.8	307.4	118.5	9.2	383.5	2,829.3	728.7	714.9	15.3
II	5,130.2	729.4	258.9	339.3	138.6	1,540.9	716.3	311.4	118.4	9.7	389.2	2,866.8	732.7	721.6	16.0
III	5,181.8	733.7	252.6	352.0	139.1	1,549.1	718.9	309.8	121.1	9.9	393.4	2,904.8	737.1	725.3	14.7
IV r	5,246.0	775.0	279.3	362.1	141.0	1,565.1	730.1	312.5	121.5	9.5	395.2	2,917.2	741.5	730.8	16.2

[1] Includes other items, not shown separately.

NOTE.—Because of the formula used for calculating real GDP, the chained (1992) dollar estimates for the detailed components *do not add* to the chained-dollar value of GDP or to any intermediate aggregates.

Source: Department of Commerce, Bureau of Economic Analysis.

CONSUMER CREDIT

[Billions of dollars; seasonally adjusted]

Period	Consumer credit outstanding (end of period)				Net change in consumer credit outstanding [1]			
	Total	Automobile	Revolving	Other [2]	Total	Automobile	Revolving	Other [2]
1989: Dec [3]	779.0	290.8	211.2	277.0	(4)	(4)	(4)	(4)
1990: Dec	789.3	283.5	238.6	267.2	10.3	-7.3	27.4	-9.8
1991: Dec	777.2	263.4	263.7	250.1	-12.1	-20.1	25.1	-17.1
1992: Dec	779.9	262.7	278.2	239.1	2.7	-.7	14.5	-11.0
1993: Dec	839.1	288.1	310.0	241.1	59.2	25.4	31.8	2.0
1994: Dec	960.7	327.9	365.6	267.2	121.6	39.8	55.6	26.1
1995: Dec	1,095.7	364.2	443.2	288.3	135.0	36.3	77.6	21.1
1996: Dec	1,181.9	392.3	499.5	290.1	86.2	28.1	56.3	1.8
1997: Dec	1,233.1	413.4	531.1	288.6	51.2	21.1	31.6	-1.5
1998: Dec r	1,299.2	447.0	560.5	291.7	66.1	33.6	29.4	3.1
1998: Jan	1,235.5	415.3	533.0	287.1	2.4	1.9	1.9	-1.5
Feb	1,240.5	416.7	535.3	288.4	5.0	1.4	2.3	1.3
Mar	1,247.3	419.8	539.4	288.2	6.8	3.1	4.1	-.2
Apr	1,251.8	421.2	541.8	288.7	4.5	1.4	2.4	.5
May	1,254.2	422.6	541.2	290.4	2.4	1.4	-.6	1.7
June	1,263.5	425.5	545.3	292.7	9.3	2.9	4.1	2.3
July r	1,269.2	428.3	543.4	297.5	5.7	2.8	-1.9	4.8
Aug r	1,276.2	432.7	548.3	295.3	7.0	4.4	4.9	-2.2
Sept r	1,283.6	435.6	551.7	296.3	7.4	2.9	3.4	1.0
Oct r	1,294.9	437.8	557.6	299.5	11.3	2.2	5.9	3.2
Nov r	1,296.6	442.4	556.5	297.7	1.7	4.6	-1.1	-1.8
Dec r	1,299.2	447.0	560.5	291.7	2.6	4.6	4.0	-6.0
1999: Jan r	1,314.5	454.1	566.7	293.7	15.3	7.1	6.2	2.0
1999: Feb p	1,323.2	459.3	569.0	294.9	8.7	5.2	2.3	1.2

[1] For year-end data, change from preceding year-end; for monthly data, change from preceding month.
[2] Outstanding loans for mobile homes, education, boats, trailers, vacations, etc., plus non-installment credit.
[3] Data newly available in January 1989 result in breaks in many series between December 1988 and subsequent months.
[4] Because of breaks in series, net change not available.

Source: Board of Governors of the Federal Reserve System.

Share of Aggregate Income Received by Each Fifth and Top 5 Percent of Households by Race and Hispanic Origin of Householder: 1977 to 1996

[Households as of March of the following year. Income in 1996 CPI-U adjusted dollars. Data for the years 1977 through 1986 were revised in March 1996.]

Year and race	Number (1,000)	Upper limit of each fifth (dollars) Lowest	Second	Third	Fourth	Lower limit of top 5 percent (dollars)	Share of aggregate income Lowest	Second	Third	Fourth	Highest	Top 5 percent	Mean income (dollars)	Gini ratio
ALL RACES														
1996	101,018	14,768	27,760	44,006	68,015	119,540	3.7	9.0	15.1	23.3	49.0	21.4	47,123	0.455
1995[1]	99,627	14,825	27,709	43,242	67,047	116,337	3.7	9.1	15.2	23.3	48.7	21.0	46,265	0.450
1994[2]	98,990	14,214	26,679	42,454	66,530	116,268	3.6	8.9	15.0	23.4	49.1	21.2	45,665	0.456
1993[3]	97,107	14,080	26,797	42,122	65,475	113,618	3.6	9.0	15.1	23.5	48.9	21.0	44,983	0.454
1992[4]	96,426	14,091	26,996	42,384	64,870	110,736	3.8	9.4	15.8	24.2	46.9	18.6	43,435	0.434
1991	95,699	14,501	27,648	42,704	65,386	111,051	3.8	9.6	15.9	24.2	46.5	18.1	43,685	0.428
1990	94,312	15,006	28,405	43,457	66,271	113,741	3.9	9.6	15.9	24.0	46.6	18.6	44,901	0.428
1989	93,347	15,305	29,102	44,729	67,960	116,093	3.8	9.5	15.8	24.0	46.8	18.9	46,210	0.431
1988	92,830	15,096	28,515	44,439	67,101	113,583	3.8	9.6	16.0	24.3	46.3	18.3	45,116	0.427
1987[5]	91,124	14,917	28,314	44,197	66,797	111,775	3.8	9.6	16.1	24.3	46.2	18.2	44,763	0.426
1986	89,479	14,828	28,321	43,742	66,024	111,986	3.9	9.7	16.2	24.5	45.7	17.5	44,034	0.425
1985[6]	88,458	14,582	27,490	42,319	63,881	106,830	4.0	9.7	16.3	24.6	45.3	17.0	42,383	0.419
1984	86,789	14,497	27,037	41,537	62,820	105,088	4.1	9.9	16.4	24.7	44.9	16.5	41,474	0.415
1983[7]	85,290	14,178	26,423	40,514	61,276	101,764	4.1	10.0	16.5	24.7	44.7	16.4	40,014	0.414
1982	83,918	13,983	26,276	40,308	60,183	100,290	4.1	10.1	16.6	24.7	44.5	16.2	39,896	0.412
1981	83,527	14,210	26,180	40,742	60,252	98,041	4.2	10.2	16.8	25.0	43.8	15.6	39,681	0.406
1980	82,368	14,405	26,881	41,198	60,434	98,182	4.3	10.3	16.9	24.9	43.7	15.8	40,155	0.403
1979[8]	80,776	14,861	27,638	42,458	61,693	100,639	4.2	10.3	16.9	24.7	44.0	16.4	41,460	0.404
1978	77,330	14,839	27,893	42,179	61,423	98,956	4.3	10.3	16.9	24.8	43.7	16.2	41,212	0.402
1977	76,030	14,431	27,060	41,040	59,831	96,724	4.4	10.3	17.0	24.9	43.6	16.1	39,970	0.402
WHITE														
1996	85,059	16,000	29,440	46,000	70,200	122,647	3.9	9.2	15.2	23.2	48.4	21.1	48,994	0.446
1995[1]	84,511	15,937	29,296	45,196	69,117	120,346	4.0	9.3	15.3	23.3	48.1	20.7	48,109	0.442
1994[2]	83,737	15,544	28,585	44,358	68,813	119,719	3.8	9.2	15.1	23.2	48.6	21.1	47,678	0.448
1993[3]	82,387	15,510	28,393	43,975	67,594	116,616	3.9	9.3	15.3	23.3	48.2	20.7	46,999	0.444
1992[4]	81,795	15,656	28,740	44,386	67,099	113,309	4.1	9.7	15.9	24.1	46.2	18.4	45,397	0.423
1991	81,675	16,008	29,069	44,702	67,438	113,940	4.1	9.9	16.0	24.1	45.8	17.9	45,530	0.418
1990	80,968	16,562	30,011	45,303	68,396	116,805	4.2	10.0	16.0	23.9	46.0	18.3	46,712	0.419
1989	80,163	16,731	30,866	46,817	69,855	118,992	4.1	9.8	16.0	23.8	46.3	18.7	48,134	0.422
1988	79,734	16,657	30,527	46,449	69,061	116,316	4.1	10.0	16.2	24.1	45.6	18.0	47,041	0.416
1987[5]	78,519	16,574	30,386	46,131	69,051	114,255	4.1	10.0	16.3	24.2	45.5	17.9	46,676	0.415
1986	77,284	16,366	30,021	45,759	68,244	114,883	4.1	10.1	16.4	24.3	45.1	17.2	45,867	0.415
1985[6]	76,576	15,951	29,164	44,038	65,869	109,687	4.2	10.2	16.5	24.4	44.7	16.8	44,123	0.411
1984	75,328	15,794	28,709	43,370	64,654	107,752	4.3	10.3	16.6	24.6	44.2	16.2	43,185	0.405
1983[7]	74,170	15,753	28,192	42,234	63,034	105,466	4.4	10.4	16.6	24.6	44.1	16.1	41,675	0.404
1982	73,182	15,427	27,942	41,877	62,346	103,071	4.4	10.4	16.8	24.6	43.9	15.9	41,541	0.403
1981	72,845	15,678	28,003	42,490	61,994	101,001	4.5	10.5	17.0	24.8	43.2	15.3	41,344	0.397
1980	71,872	15,823	28,625	42,906	62,074	100,584	4.5	10.6	17.1	24.7	43.1	15.5	41,776	0.394
1979[8]	70,766	16,239	29,574	44,102	63,502	103,730	4.4	10.6	17.0	24.6	43.4	16.2	43,094	0.396
1978	68,028	16,215	29,288	44,141	62,876	102,043	4.5	10.6	17.1	24.6	43.2	16.1	42,740	0.394
1977	66,934	15,640	28,798	42,631	61,692	99,304	4.5	10.6	17.2	24.7	43.0	15.8	41,531	0.394

See footnotes at end of table.

Share of Aggregate Income Received by Each Fifth and Top 5 Percent of Households by Race and Hispanic Origin of Householder: 1977 to 1996--Con.

[Households as of March of the following year. Income in 1996 CPI-U adjusted dollars. Data for the years 1977 through 1986 were revised in March 1996.]

Year and race	Number (1,000)	Upper limit of each fifth (dollars)				Lower limit of top 5 percent (dollars)	Share of aggregate income						Mean income (dollars)	Gini ratio
		Lowest	Second	Third	Fourth		Lowest	Second	Third	Fourth	Highest	Top 5 percent		
BLACK														
1996	12,109	8,790	17,720	30,000	49,502	85,000	3.1	8.0	14.5	23.7	50.7	21.7	32,460	0.479
1995[1]	11,577	8,648	17,399	29,536	47,663	82,188	3.2	8.2	14.8	24.2	49.6	20.2	31,298	0.468
1994[2]	11,655	7,996	16,723	28,395	48,429	85,507	3.0	7.9	14.3	24.3	50.5	20.1	30,977	0.477
1993[3]	11,281	7,774	15,820	27,145	45,604	82,041	3.0	7.7	14.3	23.7	51.3	21.1	29,566	0.484
1992[4]	11,269	7,325	15,397	27,164	45,057	78,721	3.1	7.8	14.7	24.8	49.7	19.1	28,461	0.470
1991	11,083	7,545	16,086	28,176	46,180	79,079	3.1	7.8	15.0	25.2	48.9	18.3	28,849	0.464
1990	10,671	7,750	16,485	28,811	46,938	83,150	3.1	7.9	15.0	25.1	49.0	18.5	29,788	0.464
1989	10,486	7,979	16,803	29,121	48,082	83,005	3.2	8.0	15.0	24.9	48.9	18.2	30,361	0.461
1988[5]	10,561	7,879	15,915	28,112	47,838	81,766	3.3	7.7	14.6	24.7	49.7	18.7	29,811	0.468
1987	10,192	7,754	16,021	27,623	46,226	80,799	3.3	7.9	14.8	24.4	49.7	19.3	29,227	0.468
1986	9,922	7,576	16,142	27,969	46,490	79,768	3.2	8.0	15.0	25.1	48.8	18.2	28,964	0.464
1985[6]	9,797	7,997	16,040	27,108	44,851	75,849	3.5	8.3	15.2	25.0	48.0	17.5	28,194	0.450
1984	9,480	7,865	15,403	25,886	38,055	74,629	3.6	8.4	15.0	24.7	48.3	17.4	27,131	0.450
1983[7]	9,243	7,561	14,825	25,205	42,357	71,725	3.6	8.3	15.2	25.2	47.8	16.9	26,041	0.448
1982	8,916	7,666	15,189	25,577	41,186	66,935	3.6	8.6	15.3	25.5	47.0	16.9	25,844	0.442
1981	8,961	7,857	15,049	25,085	42,128	69,656	3.8	8.6	15.3	25.4	46.9	16.1	25,870	0.440
1980	8,847	8,043	15,618	25,737	42,190	70,908	3.7	8.7	15.4	25.3	46.9	16.6	26,633	0.439
1979[8]	8,586	8,502	16,462	26,927	44,526	72,089	3.9	8.8	15.5	25.4	46.3	16.1	27,568	0.433
1978	8,066	8,619	16,504	27,893	44,164	73,559	4.0	8.7	15.6	25.3	46.4	16.3	27,956	0.431
1977	7,977	8,689	15,889	26,067	42,204	69,823	4.2	9.2	15.5	24.9	46.3	16.7	26,790	0.425
HISPANIC ORIGIN [9]														
1996	8,225	11,000	19,800	31,000	49,560	86,000	3.8	9.0	14.7	23.1	49.5	21.5	34,005	0.457
1995[1]	7,939	10,295	18,593	29,753	47,667	82,671	3.8	8.9	14.8	23.3	49.3	20.8	32,122	0.455
1994[2]	7,735	10,294	19,163	30,734	49,190	87,078	3.7	8.7	14.8	23.3	49.6	21.0	33,436	0.459
1993[3]	7,362	10,815	19,545	30,490	48,110	83,065	3.9	9.1	15.1	23.1	48.7	20.4	32,890	0.447
1992[4]	7,153	10,736	19,906	31,093	48,893	82,923	4.0	9.4	15.7	24.1	46.9	18.1	32,232	0.430
1991	6,379	11,082	20,736	32,325	50,376	86,399	4.0	9.4	15.8	24.3	46.5	17.7	33,260	0.427
1990	6,220	11,505	21,008	32,695	50,419	86,685	4.0	9.5	15.9	24.3	46.3	17.9	33,579	0.425
1989	5,933	11,859	22,146	34,518	53,958	89,838	3.8	9.5	15.7	24.4	46.6	18.1	35,419	0.430
1988	5,910	10,897	20,955	33,184	51,534	87,734	3.7	9.3	15.6	24.2	47.2	19.0	34,474	0.437
1987[5]	5,642	10,841	20,717	32,589	51,363	87,477	3.7	9.1	15.5	24.1	47.6	19.2	34,233	0.441
1986	5,418	11,166	20,615	32,926	51,605	85,777	4.0	9.5	15.9	24.8	45.8	16.5	33,174	0.424
1985[6]	5,213	10,645	19,685	31,707	48,849	81,296	4.1	9.5	16.1	24.8	45.6	16.5	31,822	0.418
1984	4,883	10,598	20,084	32,455	48,711	80,271	3.9	9.5	16.2	25.0	45.3	16.6	31,907	0.420
1983[7]	4,666	10,239	19,691	30,838	47,007	77,319	4.2	9.7	16.3	24.9	44.9	16.0	30,512	0.413
1982	4,085	10,707	19,695	30,735	46,816	76,274	4.2	9.6	16.2	24.7	45.3	16.7	30,743	0.417
1981	3,980	11,974	21,071	32,630	48,759	78,340	4.5	10.3	16.7	24.8	43.6	15.3	31,995	0.398
1980	3,906	11,740	20,834	32,070	48,622	78,583	4.4	10.2	16.4	24.9	44.1	16.0	31,788	0.405
1979[8]	3,684	12,722	22,390	33,924	49,869	81,630	4.6	10.5	16.6	24.6	43.7	15.9	33,458	0.396
1978	3,291	12,552	22,547	33,242	48,997	76,644	4.7	10.7	16.9	24.9	42.8	15.4	32,407	0.385
1977	3,304	12,413	21,425	31,422	47,045	74,456	4.9	10.8	16.9	24.7	42.8	15.4	31,194	0.383

NOTE: It appears that between the years 1977 and 1986 negative amounts were included in the aggregate. These data were revised to maintain comparability with the majority of years where negative amounts were treated as zeros.

[1]Full implementation of the 1990 census-based sample design and metropolitan definitions, 7,000 household sample reduction, and revised race edits.
[2]Introduction of 1990 census-based sample design.
[3]Data collection method changed from paper and pencil to computer-assisted interviewing. In addition, the March 1994 income supplement was revised to allow for the coding of different income amounts on selected questionnaire items. Limits either increased or decreased in the following categories: earnings increased to $999,999; social security increased to $49,999; supplemental security income and public assistance increased to $24,999; veterans' benefits increased to $99,999; child support and alimony decreased to $49,999.
[4]Implementation of 1990 census population controls.
[5]Implementation of a new March CPS processing system.
[6]Recording of amounts for earnings from longest job increased to $299,999. Full implementation of 1980 census-based sample design.
[7]Implementation of Hispanic population weighting controls and introduction of 1980 census-based sample design.
[8]Implementation of 1980 census population controls. Questionnaire expanded to show 27 possible values from 51 possible sources of income.
[9]Persons of Hispanic origin may be of any race.

EMPLOYMENT, UNEMPLOYMENT, AND WAGES

STATUS OF THE LABOR FORCE

In March, employment fell by 111,000, and unemployment fell by 344,000.

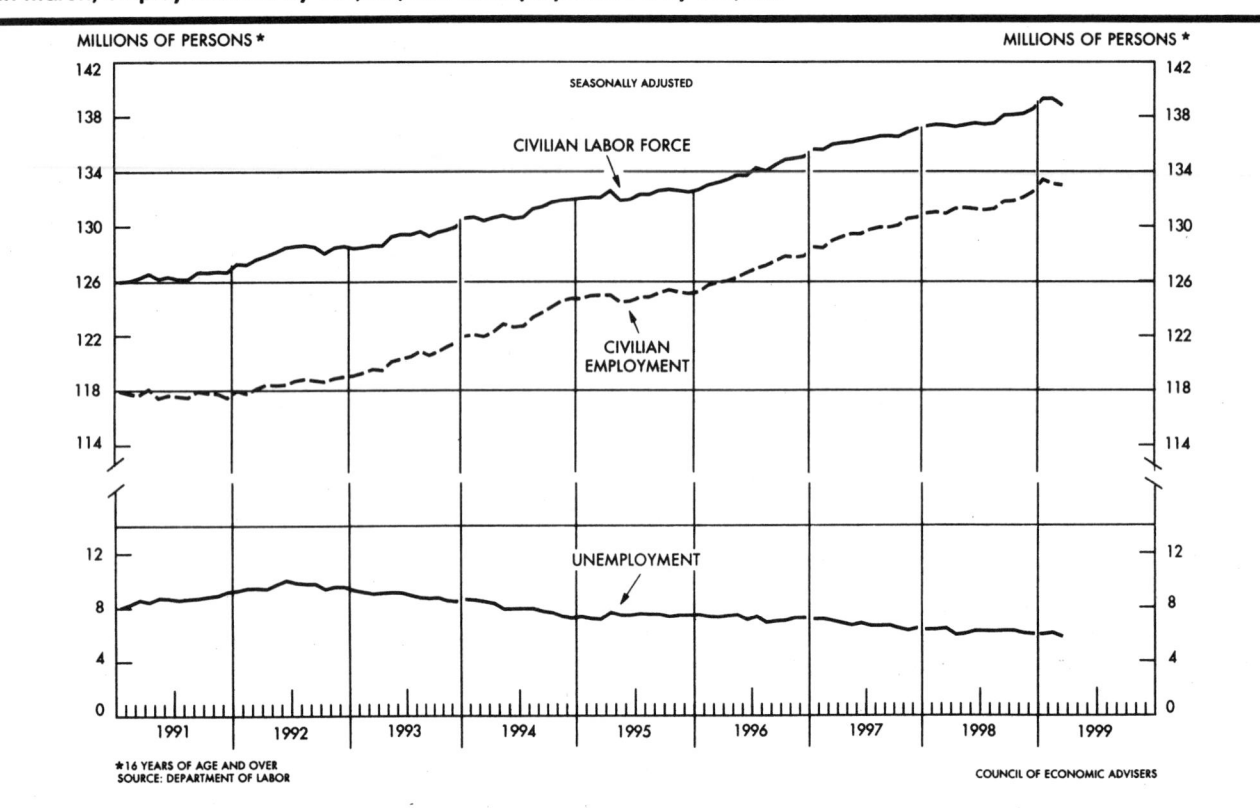

SELECTED UNEMPLOYMENT RATES

In March, the unemployment rate fell to 4.2 percent from 4.4 percent in February.

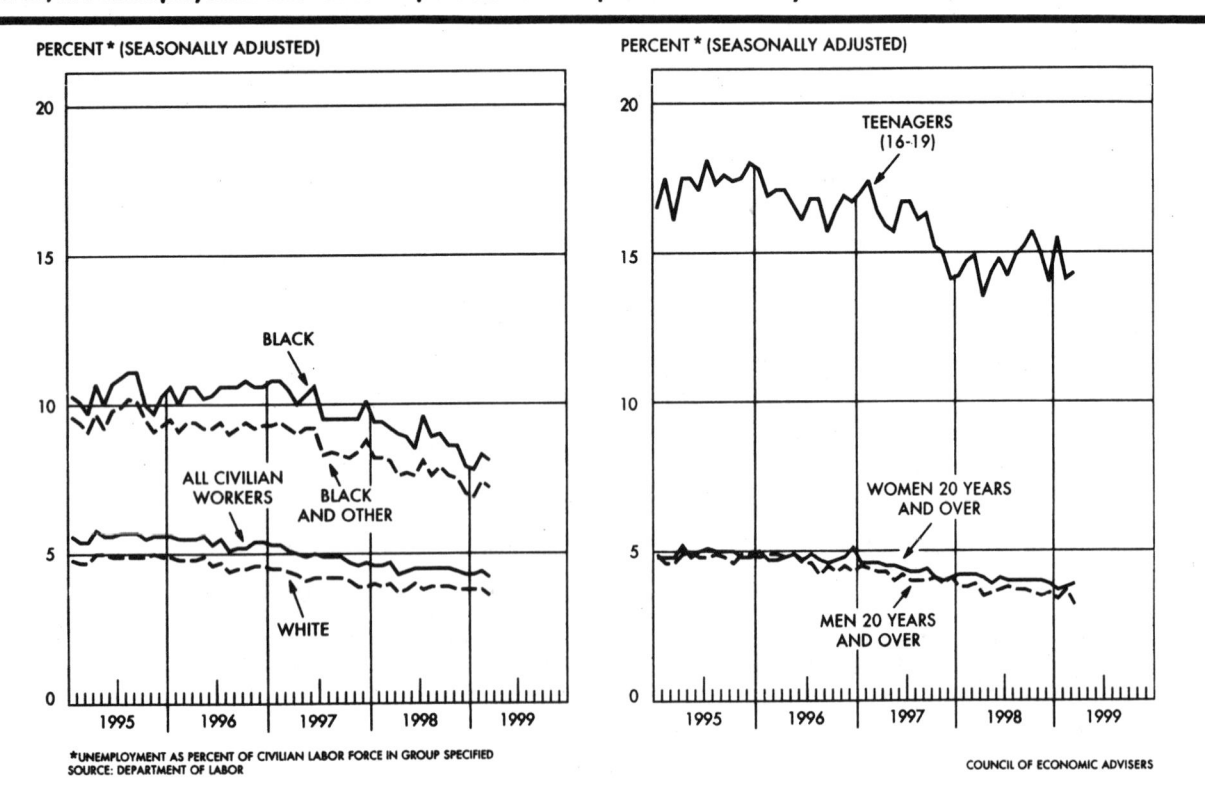

AVERAGE WEEKLY HOURS, HOURLY EARNINGS, AND WEEKLY EARNINGS
PRIVATE NONAGRICULTURAL INDUSTRIES

[For production or nonsupervisory workers; monthly data seasonally adjusted]

Period	Average weekly hours - Total private nonagricultural [1]	Average weekly hours - Manufacturing Total	Average weekly hours - Manufacturing Overtime	Average gross hourly earnings - Total private nonagricultural [1] Current dollars	Average gross hourly earnings - Total private nonagricultural [1] 1982 dollars [2]	Average gross hourly earnings - Manufacturing	Average gross weekly earnings - Total private nonagricultural [1] Current dollars	Average gross weekly earnings - Total private nonagricultural [1] 1982 dollars [2]	Average gross weekly earnings - Current dollars Manufacturing	Average gross weekly earnings - Current dollars Construction	Average gross weekly earnings - Current dollars Retail trade	Percent change from a year earlier, total private nonagricultural Current dollars	Percent change from a year earlier, total private nonagricultural 1982 dollars
1989	34.6	41.0	3.8	$9.66	$7.64	$10.48	$334.24	$264.22	$429.68	$513.17	$188.72	3.8	−1.0
1990	34.5	40.8	3.6	10.01	7.52	10.83	345.35	259.47	441.86	526.01	194.40	3.3	−1.8
1991	34.3	40.7	3.6	10.32	7.45	11.18	353.98	255.40	455.03	533.40	198.48	2.5	−1.6
1992	34.4	41.0	3.8	10.57	7.41	11.46	363.61	254.99	469.86	537.70	205.06	2.7	−.2
1993	34.5	41.4	4.1	10.83	7.39	11.74	373.64	254.87	486.04	553.63	209.95	2.8	−.0
1994	34.7	42.0	4.7	11.12	7.40	12.07	385.86	256.73	506.94	573.00	216.46	3.3	.7
1995	34.5	41.6	4.4	11.43	7.39	12.37	394.34	255.07	514.59	587.00	221.47	2.2	−.6
1996	34.4	41.6	4.5	11.82	7.43	12.77	406.61	255.73	531.23	603.33	230.11	3.1	.3
1997	34.6	42.0	4.8	12.28	7.55	13.17	424.89	261.31	553.14	623.57	241.03	4.5	2.2
1998	34.6	41.7	4.6	12.77	7.75	13.49	441.84	268.11	562.53	642.53	254.63	4.0	2.6
1998: Feb	34.7	42.0	4.8	12.59	7.69	13.42	436.87	266.71	563.64	640.53	249.11	4.3	3.1
Mar	34.6	41.8	4.8	12.63	7.71	13.46	437.00	266.79	562.63	631.40	249.70	3.7	2.6
Apr	34.5	41.4	4.5	12.70	7.73	13.44	438.15	266.84	556.42	636.62	252.30	4.1	2.7
May	34.7	41.8	4.6	12.73	7.74	13.47	441.73	268.53	563.05	635.36	253.75	4.3	2.7
June	34.6	41.8	4.6	12.76	7.75	13.47	441.50	268.23	563.05	633.98	253.17	4.6	3.1
July	34.6	41.7	4.6	12.79	7.76	13.42	442.53	268.36	559.61	652.29	255.50	4.5	3.0
Aug	34.6	41.7	4.6	12.85	7.78	13.52	444.61	269.30	563.78	651.80	256.07	3.8	2.4
Sept	34.4	41.6	4.5	12.87	7.79	13.57	442.73	268.00	564.51	636.29	256.94	3.4	2.3
Oct	34.6	41.7	4.5	12.90	7.79	13.57	446.34	269.69	565.87	652.58	257.54	3.8	2.5
Nov	34.5	41.7	4.5	12.94	7.80	13.58	446.43	269.26	566.29	649.90	256.65	3.2	1.8
Dec	34.6	41.7	4.5	12.98	7.81	13.58	449.11	270.39	566.29	664.39	258.39	3.5	2.0
1999: Jan ʳ	34.5	41.6	4.6	13.03	7.83	ʳ13.63	449.54	269.99	ʳ567.01	ʳ664.58	259.84	3.0	1.3
Feb ʳ	34.6	41.6	4.5	13.06	7.84	13.66	451.88	271.40	568.26	659.45	261.92	3.4	1.8
Mar ᵖ	34.5	41.6	4.5	13.09	....	13.70	451.61	....	569.92	648.96	260.42	3.3	....

[1] Also includes other private industry groups shown on p. 14.
[2] Current dollar earnings divided by the consumer price index for urban wage earners and clerical workers (CPI-W) (on a 1982=100 base).

Source: Department of Labor, Bureau of Labor Statistics.

EMPLOYMENT COST INDEX—PRIVATE INDUSTRY

Period	Index (June 1989 = 100) Total compensation	Index (June 1989 = 100) Wages and salaries	Index (June 1989 = 100) Benefits [1]	Percent change from 3 months earlier Total compensation	Percent change from 3 months earlier Wages and salaries	Percent change from 3 months earlier Benefits [1]	Percent change from 12 months earlier Total compensation	Percent change from 12 months earlier Wages and salaries	Percent change from 12 months earlier Benefits [1]
	Not seasonally adjusted									
1989: Dec	102.3	102.0	102.6	....	....	....	4.8	4.1	6.1
1990: Dec	107.0	106.1	109.4	....	....	....	4.6	4.0	6.6
1991: Dec	111.7	110.0	116.2	....	....	....	4.4	3.7	6.2
1992: Dec	115.6	112.9	122.2	....	....	....	3.5	2.6	5.2
1993: Dec	119.8	116.4	128.3	....	....	....	3.6	3.1	5.0
1994: Dec	123.5	119.7	133.0	....	....	....	3.1	2.8	3.7
1995: Dec	126.7	123.1	135.9	....	....	....	2.6	2.8	2.2
1996: Dec	130.6	127.3	138.6	....	....	....	3.1	3.4	2.0
1997: Dec	135.1	132.3	141.8	....	....	....	3.4	3.9	2.3
1998: Dec	139.8	137.4	145.2	....	....	....	3.5	3.9	2.4
	Seasonally adjusted						Not seasonally adjusted		
1995: Mar	124.4	120.6	133.9	0.7	0.7	0.3	2.9	2.9	2.9
June	125.3	121.5	134.6	.7	.7	.5	2.8	2.9	2.6
Sept	126.1	122.4	135.3	.6	.7	.5	2.6	2.8	2.1
Dec	126.9	123.2	136.0	.6	.7	.5	2.6	2.8	2.2
1996: Mar	127.7	124.4	136.1	.6	1.0	.1	2.7	3.2	1.6
June	128.8	125.6	137.0	.9	1.0	.7	2.9	3.4	1.7
Sept	129.7	126.5	137.8	.7	.7	.6	2.9	3.3	1.8
Dec	130.6	127.4	138.6	.7	.7	.6	3.1	3.4	2.0
1997: Mar	131.4	128.5	138.8	.6	.9	.1	3.0	3.4	2.0
June	132.6	129.7	139.7	.9	.9	.6	2.9	3.3	2.0
Sept	133.7	131.0	140.4	.8	1.0	.5	3.2	3.6	2.0
Dec	135.1	132.5	141.7	1.0	1.1	.9	3.4	3.9	2.3
1998: Mar	136.0	133.6	142.1	.7	.8	.3	3.5	4.0	2.3
June	137.2	134.9	143.2	.9	1.0	.8	3.5	4.0	2.6
Sept	138.7	136.6	144.2	1.1	1.3	.7	3.8	4.3	2.6
Dec	139.7	137.6	145.1	.7	.7	.6	3.5	3.9	2.4

[1] Employer costs for employee benefits.

NOTE.—The employment cost index is a measure of the change in the cost of labor, free from the influence of employment shifts among occupations and industries.

Data exclude farm and household workers.

Source: Department of Labor, Bureau of Labor Statistics.

FEDERAL FINANCE

FEDERAL RECEIPTS, OUTLAYS, AND DEBT

In the first 5 months of fiscal 1999, there was a deficit of $27.5 billion, compared with a deficit of $56.0 billion a year earlier.

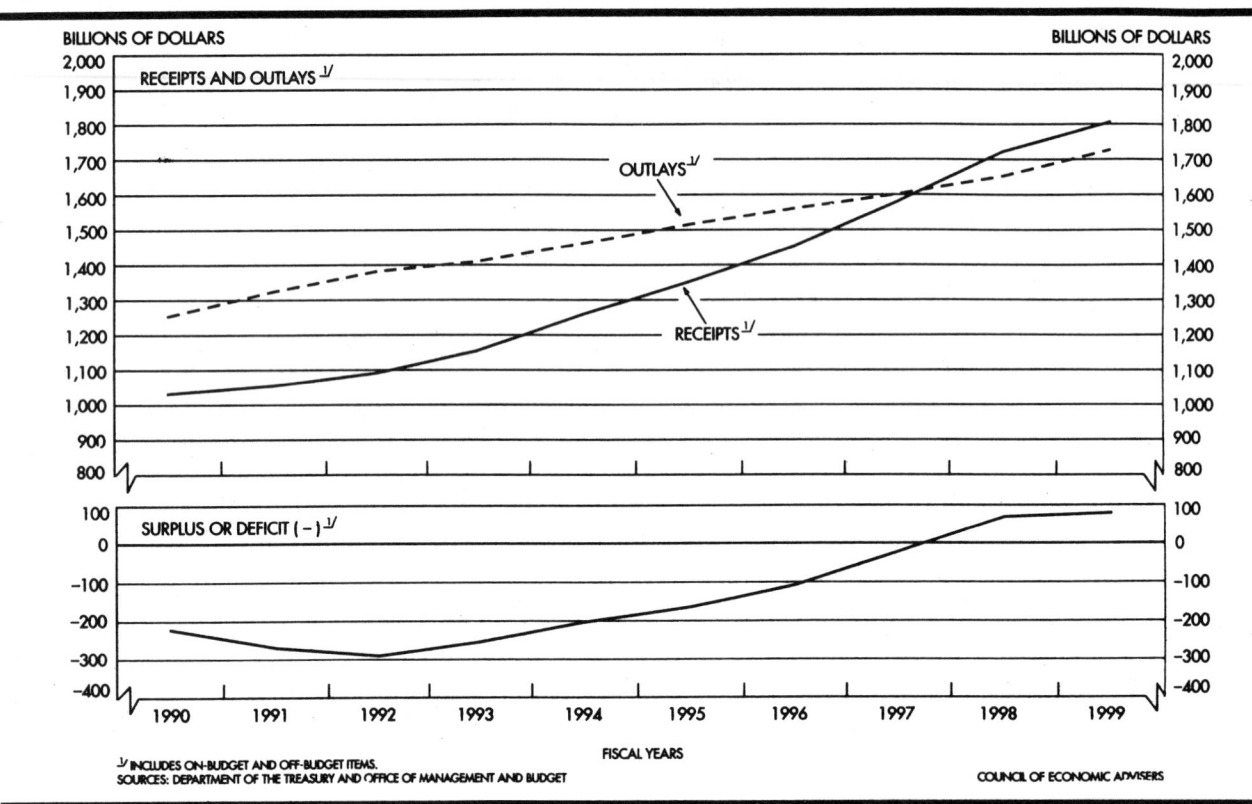

[Billions of dollars]

Fiscal year or period	Total Receipts	Total Outlays	Total Surplus or deficit (−)	On-budget Receipts	On-budget Outlays	On-budget Surplus or deficit (−)	Off-budget Receipts	Off-budget Outlays	Off-budget Surplus or deficit (−)	Federal debt (end of period) Gross Federal	Federal debt (end of period) Held by the public
1982	617.8	745.8	−128.0	474.3	594.4	−120.1	143.5	151.4	−7.9	1,137.3	919.8
1983	600.6	808.4	−207.8	453.2	661.3	−208.0	147.3	147.1	.2	1,371.7	1,131.6
1984	666.5	851.9	−185.4	500.4	686.1	−185.7	166.1	165.8	.3	1,564.7	1,300.5
1985	734.1	946.4	−212.3	547.9	769.6	−221.7	186.2	176.8	9.4	1,817.5	1,499.9
1986	769.2	990.5	−221.2	569.0	807.0	−238.0	200.2	183.5	16.7	2,120.6	1,736.7
1987	854.4	1,004.1	−149.8	641.0	810.3	−169.3	213.4	193.8	19.6	2,346.1	1,888.7
1988	909.3	1,064.5	−155.2	667.8	861.8	−194.0	241.5	202.7	38.8	2,601.3	2,050.8
1989	991.2	1,143.7	−152.5	727.5	932.8	−205.2	263.7	210.9	52.8	2,868.0	2,189.9
1990	1,032.0	1,253.2	−221.2	750.3	1,028.1	−277.8	281.7	225.1	56.6	3,206.6	2,410.7
1991	1,055.0	1,324.4	−269.4	761.2	1,082.7	−321.6	293.9	241.7	52.2	3,598.5	2,688.1
1992	1,091.3	1,381.7	−290.4	788.9	1,129.3	−340.5	302.4	252.3	50.1	4,002.1	2,998.8
1993	1,154.4	1,409.4	−255.0	842.5	1,142.8	−300.4	311.9	266.6	45.3	4,351.4	3,247.5
1994	1,258.6	1,461.7	−203.1	923.6	1,182.4	−258.8	335.0	279.4	55.7	4,643.7	3,432.1
1995	1,351.8	1,515.7	−163.9	1,000.8	1,227.1	−226.3	351.1	288.7	62.4	4,921.0	3,603.4
1996	1,453.1	1,560.5	−107.5	1,085.6	1,259.6	−174.0	367.5	300.9	66.6	5,181.9	3,733.0
1997	1,579.3	1,601.2	−21.9	1,187.3	1,290.6	−103.3	392.0	310.6	81.4	5,369.7	3,771.1
1998	1,721.8	1,652.6	69.2	1,306.0	1,335.9	−29.9	415.8	316.6	99.2	5,478.7	3,719.9
1999 (estimates)	1,806.3	1,727.1	79.3	1,362.3	1,404.0	−41.7	444.0	323.1	121.0	5,614.9	3,669.7
Cumulative total, first 5 months:[1]											
Fiscal year 1998	646.9	703.0	−56.0	484.5	580.1	−95.5	162.4	122.9	39.5	5,474.3	3,810.5
Fiscal year 1999	683.7	711.3	−27.5	510.2	586.7	−76.4	173.5	124.6	48.9	5,574.7	3,722.6

[1] Data from current issue *Monthly Treasury Statement.*

NOTE.—Data (except as noted) are from *Budget of the United States Government, Fiscal Year 2000,* issued February 1, 1999.

Sources: Department of the Treasury and Office of Management and Budget.

U.S. INTERNATIONAL TRANSACTIONS

In the fourth quarter of 1998, the goods deficit fell to $62.3 billion, from $64.9 billion in the third quarter. The current account deficit fell to $63.8 billion in the fourth quarter, from $65.7 billion in the third quarter. (Data for 1998 revised.)

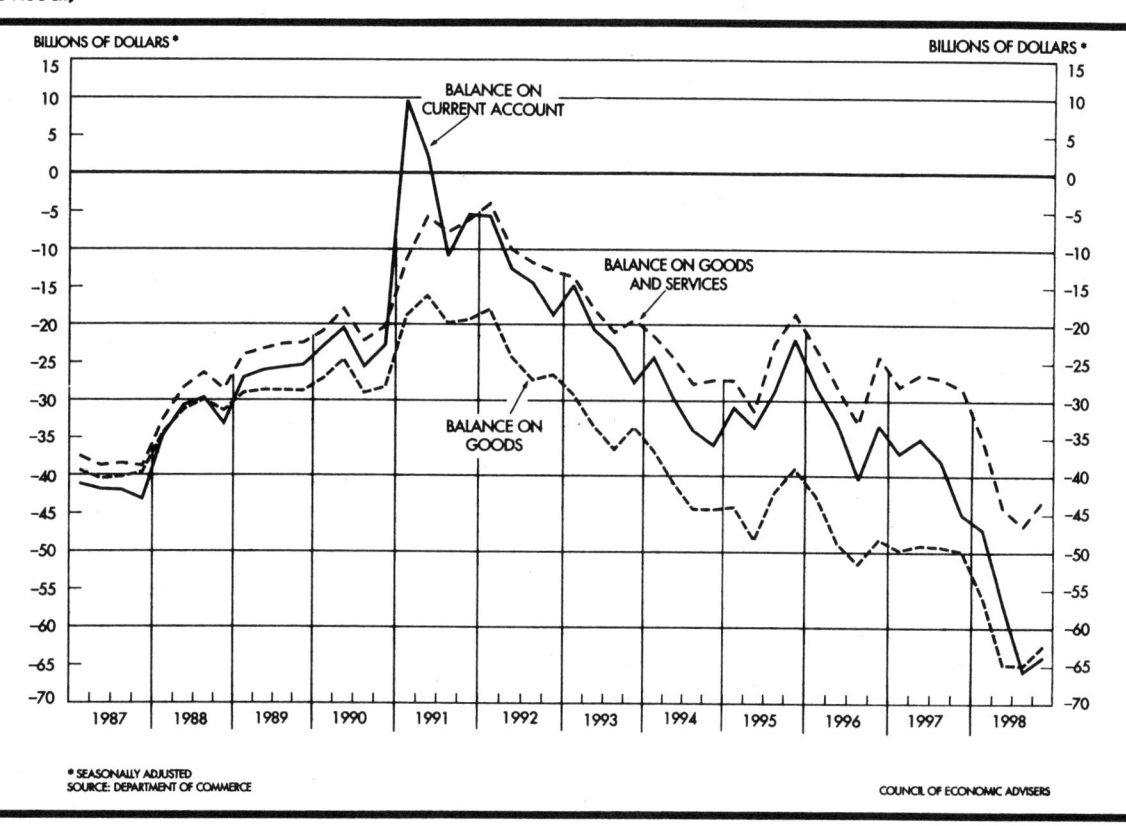

[Millions of dollars; quarterly data seasonally adjusted, except as noted. Credits (+), debits (−)]

Period	Goods[1] Exports	Imports	Net balance	Net military transactions[2,3]	Net travel and transportation receipts	Other services, net	Balance on goods and services	Receipts on U.S. assets abroad	Payments on foreign assets in U.S.	Net	Balance on goods, services, and income	Unilateral transfers, net[4]	Balance on current account
1989	362,120	−477,365	−115,245	−6,749	3,551	26,245	−92,197	153,659	−138,639	15,020	−77,177	−26,963	−104,139
1990	389,307	−498,337	−109,030	−7,599	7,501	27,999	−81,129	163,324	−139,149	24,174	−56,955	−34,669	−91,624
1991	416,913	−490,981	−74,068	−5,274	16,561	31,851	−30,931	141,408	−119,891	21,517	−9,414	5,032	−4,383
1992	440,352	−536,458	−96,106	−1,448	19,969	38,899	−38,685	125,003	−102,462	22,541	−16,144	−35,230	−51,374
1993	456,832	−589,441	−132,609	1,269	19,714	39,686	−71,939	126,702	−102,754	23,948	−47,991	−38,142	−86,133
1994	502,398	−668,590	−166,192	2,495	16,305	46,479	−100,913	157,742	−141,263	16,479	−84,434	−39,391	−123,825
1995	575,845	−749,574	−173,729	4,769	21,772	47,297	−99,891	203,844	−184,569	19,275	−80,616	−34,638	−115,254
1996	611,983	−803,320	−191,337	4,684	24,969	53,110	−108,574	213,196	−198,960	14,236	−94,338	−40,577	−134,915
1997	679,325	−877,279	−197,954	6,781	22,670	58,297	−110,206	241,787	−247,105	−5,318	−115,524	−39,691	−155,215
1998 p	671,055	−919,040	−247,985	4,072	14,176	60,623	−169,114	242,615	−265,094	−22,479	−191,593	−41,855	−233,448
1996: I	150,855	−193,467	−42,612	748	5,769	12,994	−23,101	51,997	−46,638	5,359	−17,742	−10,473	−28,215
II	152,130	−200,965	−48,835	993	6,548	13,090	−28,204	51,801	−47,826	3,975	−24,229	−8,777	−33,006
III	151,253	−202,806	−51,553	1,105	4,345	13,025	−33,078	53,058	−51,327	1,731	−31,347	−9,043	−40,390
IV	157,745	−206,082	−48,337	1,838	8,307	14,001	−24,191	56,340	−53,168	3,172	−21,019	−12,284	−33,303
1997: I	163,499	−213,222	−49,723	1,542	5,944	14,107	−28,130	57,581	−57,567	14	−28,116	−8,874	−36,990
II	169,240	−218,336	−49,096	2,191	5,711	14,679	−26,515	61,271	−60,811	460	−26,055	−9,035	−35,090
III	172,302	−221,598	−49,296	1,945	5,414	14,832	−27,105	62,551	−64,095	−1,544	−28,649	−9,445	−38,094
IV	174,284	−224,123	−49,839	1,103	5,600	14,677	−28,459	60,384	−64,631	−4,247	−32,706	−12,337	−45,043
1998: I r	171,190	−227,223	−56,033	1,527	4,401	14,733	−35,372	62,546	−64,764	−2,218	−37,590	−9,428	−47,018
II r	164,543	−229,321	−64,778	1,043	3,990	15,510	−44,235	61,925	−65,271	−3,346	−47,581	−9,390	−56,971
III r	163,414	−228,313	−64,899	829	2,406	15,167	−46,497	58,480	−67,645	−9,165	−55,662	−10,032	−65,694
IV p	171,908	−234,183	−62,275	673	3,379	15,213	−43,010	59,663	−67,417	−7,754	−50,764	−13,001	−63,765

[1] Adjusted from Census data for differences in timing and coverage; excludes military.
[2] Transfers under U.S. military agency sales contracts (exports) minus direct defense expenditures (imports).
[3] Quarterly data are not seasonally adjusted.
[4] Includes transfers of goods and services under U.S. military grant programs.
See p. 37 for continuation of table.

Glossary

Absolute advantage: A condition that exists when one producer can produce a product more efficiently than the first producer. The two producers benefit when each produces the product in which it has an absolute advantage and trades part of its output for the other product.

Affirmative action program: A program devised by employers to increase their hiring of women and minorities; frequently mandated by government regulations.

Aggregate concentration: A measure of the proportion of the total sales of all industries accounted for by the largest firms in the country. There is no common standard for measuring the aggregate concentration ratio.

Aggregate demand: The total effective demand for the nation's total output of goods and services.

Aggregate supply: The total amount of goods and services available from all industries in the economy.

Allocation: A decision as to what is to be produced with the resources of an economy or who is to get what is produced.

Alternative indicators: A more realistic measures of economic progress than the traditional Gross National Product (GNP). GNP tells only how much a nation is producing, but not whether it is using up nonrenewable resources.

Annually balanced budget: A budgetary principle calling for the revenue and expenditures of a government to be equal during the course of a year.

Antitrust legislation: Laws that prohibit or limit monopolies or monopolistic practices.

Appropriate technology: A term used by economist E. F. Schumacher to describe methods and techniques that will render the highest productive capacity with the smallest possible level of resource usage.

Arbitrage: The simultaneous buying and selling of two or more currencies in different markets for purposes of gain. The most prevalent forms are exchange and interest rate.

Area chart: A chart in which filled areas compare the magnitude of data series, frequently over time.

Authoritarian (state) socialism: A command economy in which all of the means of production are in the hands of the state and decision making is centralized.

Automatic stabilizers: Changes in government payments and tax receipts that automatically result from fluctuations in national income and act to aid in offsetting those fluctuations.

Automatic transfer services (ATS): A type of account that provides for the depository institution to automatically transfer funds from the depositor's savings account to her or his checking account when it has been drawn down.

Automation: Production techniques that adjust automatically to the needs of the processing operation by the use of control devices.

Average costs: Total costs divided by the number of units produced.

Average propensity to consume (APC): The percentage of after-tax income that, on the average, consumers spend on goods and services.

Average propensity to save (APS): The percentage of after-tax income which, on the average, consumers save.

Average revenue: Can be computed by dividing total revenue by the number of units produced and sold.

Average total cost of production (ATC): The cost of all the inputs used per unit of output.

Average variable cost of production (AVC): The cost of all the variable inputs used per unit of output.

Balance of payments: An annual summary of all economic transactions between a country and the rest of the world during the year.

Balance of trade: The net deficit or surplus in a country's merchandise trade; the difference between merchandise imports and exports.

Bar chart: A chart, similar to a column chart turned on its side, used to compare sizes and amounts or emphasize differences in amounts, usually at the same point in time.

Barrier to entry: An obstacle to the entry of new firms into an industry.

Barter: Direct exchange of goods and services without the use of money.

Base period (base year): The reference period for comparison of subsequent changes in an index series; set equal to 100.

Basic deficit: The excess of import-type transactions over export-type transactions in a country's current, long-term capital and noninduced, short-term capital movements in the balance of payments.

Benefits principle: Levy of a tax on an individual to pay the costs of government service in proportion to the individual's benefit from the service.

Bilateral trade negotiations: Trade negotiations between two countries only.

Black market: Transactions that evade government controls and taxation, and are thus illegal.

Bond: A long-term, interest-bearing certificate issued by a business firm or by a government that promises to pay the bond holder a specified sum of money on a specified date.

Boycott: Refusal by consumers to buy the products or services of a firm.

Break-even point: The output level of a firm where total revenue equals total costs (TR = TC).

Buddhist economics: Popularized by British economist E. F. Schumacher, it is the systematic study of how to attain given ends with the least possible means. The aim is to maximize human well-being with a minimum of consumption.

Business cycles, phases: The phases of change an economy usually experiences from slump to recovery. The four typical phases used to describe economic activity in industrial nations are: depression, recovery, recession, and prosperity.

Business transfer payments: Outlay by business for which no good or service is exchanged, such as excise taxes, payouts under deferred compensation arrangements, gifts, and donations.

Capital: The means of production, including factories, office buildings, machinery, tools, and equipment; alternatively, it can mean financial capital, the money to acquire the foregoing and employ land and labor resources.

Capital consumption allowances: The costs of capital assets consumed in producing GNP.

Capital equipment: The machinery and tools used to produce goods and services.

Capital gains: Net income from the sale of an asset, such as stocks.

Capital output ratio: The ratio of the cost of new investment goods to the value of the annual output produced by those investment goods.

Capital saving: The effect of an innovation or invention that lowers the share of capital (inventory, property, or money) relative to the share of labor used in a business or industry. (An example of a capital-saving device would be the use of leased equipment in business.)

Capital stock: The actual amount of physical capital and inventories in existence at a given time, or, in terms of business organizations, a source of funds used for capital.

Capitalism: An economic system based on the right of private ownership of most of the means of production, such as businesses, farms, mines, and natural resources, as well as private property, such as homes and automobiles.

Cartel: An industry in which the firms have an agreement to set prices and/or divide the market among members of the cartel.

Celler-Kefauver Act: The 1950 law that amends sections of the Clayton Act, which forbade mergers through stock acquisition only.

Central bank: A government institution that controls the issuance of currency, provides banking services to the government and to the other banks, and implements the nation's monetary policy; in the United States the Federal Reserve System acts as the central bank.

Central planning: A method of resource allocation in which top leadership makes the major decisions on production, distribution, and coordination.

Centrally directed (command) economy: An economic system in which the basic questions of what, how, and for whom to produce are resolved primarily by governmental authority.

Certificate of deposit (CD): A deposit of a specified sum of money for a specified period of time that cannot be redeemed prior to the date specified.

Chart: A graphic representation of statistical data or other information.

Check: A written order to a depository institution to pay a person or institution named on it a specified sum of money.

Circular flow diagram: A schematic drawing showing the economic relationships between the major sectors of an economic system.

Civil Aeronautics Board (CAB): A semi-independent regulatory body that is responsible for the economic regulation of commercial air transportation.

Civil Rights Act of 1964: Federal legislation declaring it unlawful to discriminate against a person on the basis of race, sex, or age.

Clayton Antitrust Act: Adopted in 1914 as a companion law to the Sherman Antitrust Act, it prohibits price discrimination by a seller where the effect may injure competitors; tying contracts and exclusive dealerships where the effect lessens competition; acquisition of stock of a rival business where the effect is to reduce competition; and interlocking directorates among competing firms of a certain size.

Collective bargaining: A process by which decisions regarding the wages, hours, and conditions of employment are determined by the interaction of workers acting through their unions and employers.

Collectivization: The process of consolidating small or individual holdings into larger, cooperatively run enterprises.

Collusion: An agreement or conspiracy, usually secret, among nominal competitors to engage in anticompetitive practices in violation of antitrust laws.

Commodity: An economic good.

Commodity markets: Large-scale, organized exchanges, similar to stock markets, where vast quantities of goods are exchanged.

Communism: According to Karl Marx, the last stage of economic development after the state has withered away and work and consumption are engaged in communally; today frequently used to designate state socialist economies.

Comparative advantage: Gains from international trade are maximized when each nation specializes in the production of those goods in which its comparative advantage is greatest (or comparative disadvantage least).

Complement: A product that is employed jointly in conjunction with another product.

Computer-integrated manufacturing (CIM): A system of integrating all the operations of different departments in a plant by means of a central computer and a network of workstation computers.

Concentration ratio: A measure of the extent to which a market or industry is dominated by a few firms. The most widely used concentration ratios are those published by the Commerce Department as part of the various censuses of business.

Conglomerate merger: The joining of two firms that do not produce the same good or service (or close substitutes) or outputs at different stages of the same production process.

Conspicuous consumption: The practice of consuming goods or services far beyond one's needs to demonstrate wealth, power, and success. Thorstein Veblen coined the phrase in *Theory of the Leisure Class* (1899).

Constant dollar GNP (Real GNP): The value of GNP adjusted for changes in the price level since a base period.

Constant value: Refers to a national income account adjusted for price changes. What remains is a dollar measure that changes only because of changes in the quantities of goods and services.

Consumer equilibrium: The condition in which consumers allocate their income in such a way that the last dollar spent on each good or service and the last dollar saved provide equal amounts of utility.

Consumer Price Index (CPI): A statistical measure of changes in the prices of a representative sample of urban family purchases relative to a previous period.

Consumer Product Safety Commission (SPSC): A semi-independent federal agency created in 1972 to establish mandatory safety standards for products and to monitor the design, construction, contents, performance, and labeling of consumer products. A five-member commission, appointed by the president and confirmed by the Senate, which develops regulations to enforce standards and imposes product bans.

Consumer sovereignty: The theory that states that, in a free-market economy, the consumer determines which goods and services will be produced.

Consumer surplus: The difference between the total utility received from a product and the total market value of that product. The surplus is received by the consumer, but not at the expense of the producer.

Consumer tastes and preferences: Individual liking or partiality for specific goods or services.

Consumption: The amount spent by households on currently produced goods and services.

Consumption-investment mix: The percentage of shares of the national product going respectively to consumption and investment.

Convergence hypothesis: Contends that market economies and command economies are both changing in the direction of becoming identical.

Cooperative: Producer and worker cooperatives are associations in which the members join in production and marketing and share the profits. Consumer cooperatives are associations of consumers engaged in retail trade, sharing the profits as a dividend among the members.

Corporation: A business enterprise that is chartered by a state government or, occasionally, by the federal government to do business as a legal entity.

Correspondent bank: A bank in another city or country that a bank has an arrangement with to provide deposit transfer or other services.

Cost of living adjustment (COLA): A frequently used provision of labor contracts that grants wage increases based on changes in the consumer price index; often referred to in negotiations as the "escalator clause."

Cost of living index: *See* Consumer price index.

Cost-benefit analysis: A comparison of all the costs of a project to the value of the benefits of that project.

Cost-push inflation: A continuing rise in the general price level that results from increases in production costs.

Creative financing: Any new method to raise capital for an enterprise without use of bank loans, stock offerings, or other conventional steps. Also, the myriad new methods developed because of high interest rates for financing house purchases.

Credit card: An economic instrument extended by businesses and banks that allows the acquisition of something of value in exchange for the promise to return its equivalent (payment) at some time in the future.

Crowding out: The term given to the effect government has in reducing the amount of financial capital available for private investment.

Currency: That part of the money supply consisting of coins and paper bills.

Currency appreciation: An increase in the value of a country's currency relative to other currencies as a result of a decrease in its supply relative to the demand for it.

Currency depreciation: A decline in the value of a country's currency as a result of an increase in its supply relative to the demand for it.

Current value: Gross National Product is normally defined in terms of current market value, or the quantities of various outputs—final goods and services—multiplied by their respective prices and summed together.

Cyclical balanced budget: A budgetary principle calling for balancing the budget over the course of a complete business cycle rather than in a particular fiscal or calendar year; over the course of the cycle, tax receipts and expenditures would balance.

Cyclical unemployment: The lack of work that occurs because the total effective demand for goods and services is insufficient to employ all workers in the labor force.

Debit card: An economic instrument issued by the creditor that shows the amount of debt to be incurred.

Deficit: A negative balance after expenditures are subtracted from revenues.

Deflation: A decrease in the general level of prices or an increase in the value of money in terms of goods and services.

Demand: The relationship between the quantities of a good or service that consumers desire to purchase at any particular time and the various prices that can exist for the good or service.

Demand curve: A graphic representation of the relationship between price and quantity demanded.

Demand deposits (checking accounts): Liabilities of depository institutions to their customers that are payable on demand.

Demand schedule: A table recording the number of units of a commodity demanded per unit of time at various money prices.

Demand theory: A plausible explanation of the manner in which purchasers of commodities respond to price changes. It is an empirical fact that consumers purchase more of a good or service at a low price than at a high price.

Demand-pull inflation: A continuing rise in the general price level that occurs when aggregate demand exceeds the full-employment output capacity of the economy.

Democratic (liberal) socialism: An economic system that combines state ownership of at least some of the means of production and a set of democratic political institutions.

Depository institutions: Financial institutions that maintain deposit account obligations to customers; includes commercial banks, savings banks, savings and loan associations, and credit unions.

Depreciation: Reduction in value, quality, and usefulness of a fixed asset (plant or equipment) because of physical deterioration, destruction, or obsolescence resulting from technological development.

Depression: *See* Business cycles, phases.

Deregulation: The process of eliminating government regulations and reducing the scope and power of regulatory bodies.

Derived demand: *See* Factor demand.

Design for manufacturability and assembly (DFMA): A system of designing products in which the design engineers consult with manufacturing personnel during the designing process to avoid designs that will be difficult or costly to manufacture.

Devaluation: A decrease in the value of a country's currency relative to other currencies due to an official government reduction in the exchange rate under a fixed rate system.

Diagram: A graph that shows the relationship between two or more variables that may or may not have values that can actually be measured; a graphic model.

Differentiated competition: An industry in which there are a large number of firms producing similar but not identical products; sometimes called monopolistic competition.

Differentiated products: Similar but not identical products produced by different firms.

Diminishing marginal utility: *See* Demand theory.

Diminishing returns: *See* Law of diminishing returns.

Direct controls: Government control of individual prices and wages, prohibiting increases without the authorization of the controlling agency.

Direct relationship: A relationship between two variables in which their values increase and decrease together.

Discount rate: The interest rate charged by the Federal Reserve on loans to depository institutions.

Discounting: Assigning a present value to future returns; making a loan with the interest subtracted in advance from the principal.

Discretionary fiscal policy: Fiscal policy measures activated by overt decisions.

Disposable income: The amount of after-tax income that households have available for consumption or saving.

Diversification: The process in which a business firm increases the variety of products it produces and sells, either by introducing new products into the same product line or market, or by going into new product lines or markets.

Dumping: Occurs when a nation sells export products in foreign countries more cheaply than the same products are sold domestically.

Dynamic efficiency: Efficiency over a period of time with changing resources and levels of technology.

Earned income: Wages, salaries, and other employee compensation, plus earnings from self-employment.

Earned income tax credit (EITC): A federal tax credit for poor families with earnings that offset their tax liabilities and, for the poorest, provides a tax subsidy.

Econometrics: A subdiscipline of economics that describes the ways in which statistics and modeling can be combined to explain economic relationships. Such a model relates economic theory to actual economic events.

Economic concept: A word or phrase that conveys an economic idea.

Economic good: Any good or service that sells for a price; that is, not a free good.

Economic growth: An increase in the production capacity of the economy.

Economic imperialism: The practice of expansionism where control of a country is maintained through economic power rather than through political action or military force.

Economic model: A simplified representation of the cause and effect relationships in a particular situation. Models may be in verbal, graphic, or equation form.

Economic profits: Earnings on invested capital that are in excess of the normal rate of return.

Economic rent: Any payment to an owner of a productive resource that is an amount in excess of the payment needed to keep the resource in its current use.

Economic surplus: A margin of output over and above consumption needs that can be allocated to investment for intensive growth.

Economies of scale: Decreasing costs per unit as plant size increases.

Effective demand: The desire and the ability to purchase a certain number of units of a good or service at a given price.

Efficiency: Maximizing the amount of output obtained from a given amount of resources used for a given amount of output.

Elastic (demand): A demand condition in which the relative size of the change in quantity demanded is greater than the size of the price change.

Elasticity ratio: A measurement of the degree of the response of a change in quantity to a change in price.

Employee involvement (EI): Various programs for incorporating hourly-wage workers in decision making; may involve decisions on production methods, work scheduling, purchase of capital equipment, etc.

Entrepreneur: A business innovator who sees the opportunity to make a profit from a new product, new process, or unexploited raw material and then brings together the land, labor, and capital to exploit the opportunity, risking failure.

Environmental Protection Agency (EPA): A department within the executive branch charged with enforcing the nation's laws relating to the improvement and maintenance of a good environment.

Equal Employment Opportunity Commission (EEOC): An independent federal agency established in 1965 to prohibit employment discrimination on the basis of race, color, national origin, religion, sex or physical limitation. The enforcement body for the equal employment provisions of the Civil Rights Act of 1964.

Equation of Exchange: *See* Quantity equation.

Equilibrium: Applies to virtually all economic units in the economy, to the relationships among them, and to the economy as a whole; when aggregate demand is just equal to aggregate supply. Equilibrium positions occur in three levels of economic analysis—analysis of individual decision makers, market analysis, and analysis of an entire economic system.

Equilibrium price: The price at which the quantity of a good or service offered by suppliers is exactly equal to the quantity that is demanded by purchasers in a particular period of time.

Equilibrium quantity: The quantity of a good that the producers are willing to supply and the consumers are willing to purchase at a given price.

Equity (housing): The owner's share of the value of property or other assets, net of mortgages or other liabilities.

Excess demand: Occurs when a commodity price is below the equilibrium.

Excess reserves: Reserves of depository institutions over and above the legally required minimum on deposit with the Federal Reserve.

Excess supply: Occurs when a commodity price is above the equilibrium.

Exchange rate: The value of a nation's currency measured in the number of units of a foreign currency for which it can be exchanged.

Excise taxes: A tax on a particular type of good or service; a sales tax.

Export (X): Domestically produced good or service sold abroad.

Extensive growth: Economic growth that results from an increase in population and in proportionate quantities of other factor inputs; does not generally raise a country's standard of living.

External costs: Costs of the production process that are not carried by the producer unit or by the purchaser of the product and are therefore not taken into consideration in production and consumption decisions. Air pollution represents an external cost of production.

External economies: Benefits that accrue to parties other than the producer and purchaser of the good or service; benefits for which payment is not collected.

Externalities: Exists when the decisions of the producers or consumers of a good or service impose direct costs or benefits on persons or firms other than the decision maker. Also called spillover effects, neighborhood effects, or external costs or benefits.

Factor demand: The demand for a factor of production, not because it directly provides utility, but because it is needed to produce finished products that do provide utility.

Factor incomes: The return to factors of production as a reward for productive activity.

Factor market: A market in which resources and semifinished products are exchanged.

Factor share: The part of national income received by a particular factor of production.

Factors of production (factor inputs): Land, labor, and capital, synonymous with production inputs.

Fair Labor Standards Act: The federal Wage and Hours law adopted by Congress in 1938 that set a minimum wage for most American workers. It also mandates overtime pay beyond an eight-hour work day or over 40 hours a week.

Fed: Federal Reserve System.

Fed Board of Governors: The governing body of the Federal Reserve System consisting of seven members appointed by the president for 14-year terms.

Federal Communications Commission (FCC): An independent federal agency that regulates radio and television broadcasting and interstate and foreign telephone and telegraph services. A seven-member commission, appointed by the president to seven-year terms, grants broadcast licenses and regulates common carriers in the communications industry.

Federal Deposit Insurance Corporation (FDIC): A U.S. government agency that insures deposits up to $100,000 in savings and commercial banks if a participating bank fails.

Federal funds market: The market among depository institutions for temporary transfer of excess reserves from one institution to another.

Federal Open Market Committee: A committee consisting of the Federal Reserve Board and the presidents of five regional Federal Reserve banks that decides on the purchase or sale of government securities by the Federal Reserve to implement monetary policy.

Federal Reserve Board of Governors: The governing body of the Federal Reserve System consisting of seven members appointed by the U.S. president for 14-year terms.

Federal Reserve System (Fed): The central bank of the United States; a system established by the Federal Reserve Act of 1913 to issue paper currency, supervise the nation's banking system, and implement monetary policy.

Federal Trade Commission (FTC): The federal agency responsible for enforcement of antitrust laws in conjunction with the Antitrust Division, Department of Justice. The FTC, with a five-member governing board and national network of offices, attempts to counter deceptive actions and practices and anticompetitive behavior among business through its regulations.

Financial capital: The money to acquire the factors of production.

First-tier wage industry: An industry in which both the firms and the unions have extensive market power, and as a result wages in the industry are above the average for all industries.

Fiscal federalism: Tax collection and disbursement of funds by a higher level of government to lower jurisdictions.

Fiscal policy: The use of federal government spending, taxing, and debt management to influence general economic activity.

Fixed costs: Production costs that do not change with changes in the quantity of output.

Food and Drug Administration (FDA): An agency within the U.S Health and Human Services (HHS) Department that is responsible for the protection of the public from health hazards posed by harmful or mislabeled foods, cosmetics, medical devices, and drugs.

Foreign sector: Economic transactions with nations abroad.

Foreign-exchange market: A set of institutions, including large banks in the world's financial centers, private brokers, and government central banks and other agencies, that deal in the exchange of one country's money for another's.

Fourth world: The poorest countries of the underdeveloped regions that do not have intensive growth or any valuable export resources.

Free enterprise: A microeconomic concept referring to a business firm privately owned and operated for profit. Under the free enterprise system most of the goods and services are provided by the private sector.

Free good: A production or consumption good that does not have a direct cost.

Free trade: International trade that is unrestricted by government protectionist measures.

Freely fluctuating exchange rates: An exchange-rate system by which the relative values of different currencies are determined by demand and supply rather than by government fiat.

Frictional unemployment: The lack of work that occurs from time lost changing jobs.

Fringe benefits: Nonwage returns to workers for labor services; includes time off with pay for holidays, vacations, and sick leave, retirement benefits, health care, and similar benefits.

Full employment: Employment of nearly everyone who desires to work. In practice, an unemployment level of not more than 4–5 percent is considered full employment.

Full employment aggregate demand: The level of total effective demand that is just sufficient to employ all workers in the labor force.

Full Employment and Balanced Growth Act (1978): A federal law enacted by Congress that set forth national goals for employment, economic growth, and development.

Functional finance: The use of fiscal policy to stabilize the economy without regard to the policy's effect on a balanced government budget.

Functional income distribution: The shares of total income distributed according to the type of factor service for which they are paid, e.g., rent as a payment for land, wages for labor, and interest for capital.

Gandhian economics: Gandhi developed economics that combined ethics with economics in order to maximize the welfare of all. His system was committed to the pursuit of truth (dharma) rather than self-interest (artha).

General Agreement on Tariffs and Trade (GATT): An organization established in 1947 composed of most non-Communist nations. GATT negotiations have periodically reduced tariffs for all member nations under the most-favored-nation principle, which extends any tariff concession that one nation extends to another to all participating countries.

Giveback: Withdrawal of a labor benefit prior to the end of a collective bargaining agreement by mutual agreement of the employer and the union, normally to avoid closure of plants due to business losses.

Gold standard: A monetary system under which a country defines its currency as a given weight of gold. The system provides a mechanism by which anyone can exchange any form of domestic currency and gold at that official value and does not interfere with domestic or international movement of gold. By 1936, all countries had abandoned the gold standard.

Government spending (G): Spending by the various levels of government on goods and services, including public investment.

Great Depression: A period of worldwide economic crisis during the 1930s that closed banks, created 25 percent unemployment, and led to government intervention in the U.S. economy.

Great Leap Forward: A 1958 attempt by the Chinese leadership to accelerate the rate of economic development by maximizing investment in industrial growth, which resulted in an economic and food crisis.

Gross Domestic Product (GDP): The sum of the values of all goods and services produced within the country during the year.

Gross National Product (GNP): The sum of the values of all goods and services produced by residents of the country during the year, including earnings on foreign investments and excluding foreign investments in this country.

Gross investment or gross private domestic investment (I): Private sector spending on capital equipment, increased stocks of inventories, and new residential housing.

Headcount index: The percentage of the population below the poverty line.

High technology: Production processes that utilize modern techniques and are capital-intensive with a large investment in equipment per worker.

Horizontal merger: The joining of two firms that produce the same good or service, or close substitutes.

Household: An economic unit consisting of an individual or a family.

Human capital: Labor that is literate, skilled, trained, healthy, and economically motivated.

Hyperinflation: A condition in which prices rise faster and faster and people spend more money before it buys less; also known as runaway inflation.

Hypothesis: A tentative explanation of an event; used as a basis for further research.

Implicit interest: Income that derives from the use of capital but is not paid as interest but rather as a part of accounting profits.

Implicit wages: Income that is the result of labor input but is not received in the form of wages or salaries, but in some other form such as net proprietor's income (profits).

Import (M): Good or service purchased from foreign suppliers.

Import-competing industry: A domestic industry that produces the same or a close substitute good that competes in the domestic market with imports.

Incentive: A motivation to undertake an action or to refrain from undertaking an action; in a market economy profits are the incentive to produce.

Income: The return to a factor of production as a reward for productive activity.

Income effect: The change in demand of a good or service as a result of a change in the consumer's income.

Incomes policy: Any policy that has an effect on real income, the purchasing power of individuals' money incomes.

Increasing costs: A rise in average production costs as the quantity of output of the good increases.

Index number: A percentage or ratio of two observations, the denominator being the base item in a cross section or the base period in a time series. The observations could be prices, quantities, or values.

Index of leading economic indicators: An index that includes 12 economic variables that have been found to have a historical tendency to precede the turning points of the level of Gross National Product. The index is a composite of those 12 indicators.

Indexing: A system of adjusting incomes in line with inflation.

Indicative planning: A method used by governments to improve the performance of the economy by providing economic information in the form of forecasts or targets for industries and, possibly, providing incentives for selected industries.

Indicators: Statistical time series, or groups of series, used by economists to predict future economic activity. Most indicators may be categorized as coincident, lagging, or leading.

Indirect taxes: Taxes that are ultimately paid in full or in part by someone other than the business from which the tax is collected; not income taxes.

Individual Retirement Accounts (IRA): A personal savings investment account on which income taxes are not paid until the money is withdrawn at or after age $59\frac{1}{2}$ or death.

Industrial production index: A monthly measurement of physical output, compiled and published by the Board of Governors of the Federal Reserve System.

Industrial Revolution: Dramatic technological and social changes that occurred in the nineteenth century that altered economies, began the process of mass production and led to the modern industrial age.

Industry consortium: A combination of firms in an industry to carry out a common purpose.

Inelastic Demand: A demand condition in which the relative size of the change in the quantity demanded is less than the size of the price change.

Infant industry argument: The contention that it is economically justified to provide trade protection to a new industry's early stages of growth until it can compete with established foreign rivals.

Inflation: A continuously rising general price level, resulting in a loss of the purchasing power of money.

Infrastructure: An economy's stock of capital—much of it publicly owned—that provides basic services to producers and consumers. Includes highways, electric power, water supplies, educational facilities, health services, etc.

In-kind income: Income in a form other than money.

Institutions: Decision-making units, established practices, or laws.

Intensive growth: Economic growth that results from increased productivity and raises a country's standard of living.

Interdependence: The relationship between individuals and institutions in a country or between countries that arises because of specialization of production.

Interest: A factor payment for the use of capital.

Internalize external costs: The process of transforming external costs into internal costs so that the producer and consumer of a good pay the full cost of its production.

International Monetary Fund (IMF): An organization established in 1946 to assist in the operation of the world monetary system by regulating the exchange practices of countries and providing liquidity to member countries that have payment problems.

Interstate Commerce Act of 1887: Nineteenth-century law enacted by Congress to curb monopolistic and discriminatory shipping practices to railroads and to prohibit arrangements among competing railroads for sharing traffic and earnings. The law also created an Interstate Commerce Commission.

Interstate Commerce Commission (ICC): A regulatory body established in 1887 to regulate railroads, interstate trucking, inland water transport, and other transportation firms.

Inventories: The value of finished and semifinished goods and raw materials in the hands of producers and distributors.

Inverse relationship: A relationship between two variables in which the value of one decreases as the value of the other increases.

Investment (I): Spending by businesses on currently produced goods in national income accounting and development economics; in finance, the purchase of stocks, bonds, and other titles to property.

Invisible hand: A concept used by Adam Smith that states that individuals who freely pursue their own self-interests will automatically promote the interests of society.

Job action: A concerted action by employees to disrupt production or distribution in order to put pressure on employers to grant concessions.

Junk bonds: Bonds that are issued paying higher than normal interest rates because they have a greater risk of default.

Jurisdictional dispute: Conflicts between unions as to which one shall represent a certain group of workers.

Just-in-time: A system that provides for raw materials and subassemblies to be delivered by suppliers to the location where they will be processed at the time they are needed rather than being stored in inventories.

Keogh Plan: A tax-sheltered retirement account for those who are self-employed.

Keynesian economics: The body of macroeconomic theories and policies that stem from the model developed by John Maynard Keynes.

Kinked demand curve: An analytical approach using certain assumptions to explain price rigidity in oligopolistic markets.

L: A measure of the money supply that includes M3 plus commercial paper, savings bonds, and government securities with maturities of 18 months or less.

Labor: All human resources including manual, clerical, technical, professional, and managerial labor.

Labor force: All members of the working-age population who are either employed or seeking or awaiting employment.

Laffer curve: An economic model developed by economist Arthur Laffer that purports to show a relationship between marginal tax rates and the level of total tax revenue.

Laffer effect: The impact of cutting marginal tax rates postulated by economist Arthur Laffer who says the release of revenue into the economy will stimulate new production and therefore result in more tax revenues at lower rates.

Laissez-faire: A concept of nonintervention by government developed by the eighteenth-century French physiocrats in reaction against mercantilism and incorporated into classical economic writings by Adam Smith and others.

Land: All natural resources, including fields, forests, mineral deposits, the sea, and other gifts of nature.

Law of demand: The quantity demanded of a good or service varies inversely with its price; the lower the price the larger the quantity demanded, and the higher the price the smaller the quantity demanded.

Law of diminishing returns: The common condition in which additional inputs produce successively smaller increments of output.

Law of supply: The quantity supplied of a good or service varies directly with its price; the lower the price the smaller the quantity supplied, and the higher the price the larger the quantity supplied.

Leading indicator: An economic measurement or time series of one aggregate of economic activity that precedes a change in total economic activity. Leading indicators include new durable goods orders, average weekly state unemployment insurance claims, and new building permits.

Learning curve: A diagram showing how labor productivity or labor costs change as the total number of units produced by a new plant or with new technology increases over time.

Less developed countries (LDCs): Nonindustrialized countries, primarily located in Africa, Asia, or Latin America, generally characterized by poverty income levels, a labor force primarily employed in agriculture, extensive underemployment, illiteracy, and high rates of population growth.

Leverage: A concept used to describe the effect of an increase in sales or the price on a firm's profits. There are two kinds of leverage: operating leverage, which looks at the ratio of fixed costs for a firm, and financial leverage, which is defined as the proportion of the firm's assets that have been raised by borrowing.

Limited liability: A legal provision that protects individual stockholders of a corporation from being sued by creditors of the corporation to collect unpaid debts of the firm.

Line graph: A graph in which points on a line show the relationship of two variables.

Liquidity: The degree of ease with which an asset can be converted into cash without appreciable loss in value.

Long run: A period of time long enough for all factors of production to be variable (but not so long, however, that the basic technology in use can be changed).

Long-term capital: Direct investment in plant and equipment or portfolio investments in stocks and bonds.

Lorenz curve: A diagram showing the distribution of income among groups of people; an indicator of the degree of inequality of income distribution.

Macroeconomics: The area of economic studies that deals with the overall functioning of an economy, total production output, employment, and the price level.

Marginal analysis: An analytical technique frequently used in economics in which small increments in quantities are examined.

Marginal cost: The addition to total cost from the production of an additional unit of output.

Marginal revenue: The rate at which total revenue varies as sales quantity varies and can be thought of as the difference in revenue between selling an additional unit and not selling that unit.

Marginal tax rate: The incremental tax burden due to an incremental change in the tax base.

Marginal utility: The amount of satisfaction a consumer derives from consuming one additional unit (or the last unit consumed) of a particular good or service.

Marginalist school: A significant development in Neoclassical economic theory that led to the market theory of supply and demand, the acceptance of the equilibria concept and possible expansion of economic theory through the use of differential calculus.

Market: *See* Marketplace.

Market concentration: A measure of the number of firms in an industry.

Market economy: An economic system in which the basic questions of what, how, and for whom to produce are resolved primarily by buyers and sellers interacting in markets.

Market system: An economic system that relies predominantly on a market mechanism to determine allocation of scarce resources, production techniques, pricing, distribution of goods and services to members of society, and so on.

Marketplace (market): A network of dealings between buyers and sellers of a resource or product (good or service); the dealings may take place at a particular location or they may take place by communicating at a distance with no face-to-face contact between buyers and sellers.

Marxism: An economic theory and philosophy named for Karl Marx (1818–1883), the founder of "scientific" socialism and leader of the revolutionary movement to overturn capitalism. Marxian economics use the labor theory of value wherein the value of the commodity consists of capital (raw materials and depreciation), variable capital (labor), and surplus value (profit).

Maximum profit level: The output level of a firm where the revenue from one additional unit of production (marginal revenue) is equal to the cost of producing that unit (marginal cost).

Medicaid: A federally subsidized, state-administered program to pay for medical and hospital costs of low-income families.

Medium of exchange: *See* Money.

Mercantilism: A doctrine that dominated policies in many countries from the sixteenth to the eighteenth centuries, which held that exports should be maximized and imports minimized to generate an inflow of gold, and exports of machinery and technology should be prohibited to prevent competition from foreign producers.

Merger: A contractual joining of the assets of one formerly independent business firm with another, frequently by the purchase by one company of a controlling share of the stock of another company.

Merit goods: Result when intellectually or morally elite groups override individual preferences.

Microeconomics: The area of economic studies that deals with individual units in an economy, households, business firms, labor unions, and workers.

Minimum wage laws: Federal or state laws that prohibit employers from paying less than a specified hourly wage to their employees.

Mixed economy: An economic system in which the basic questions of what, how, and for whom to produce are resolved by a mixture of market forces with governmental direction and/or custom and tradition.

Model: A simplified representation of the cause and effect relationships in a particular situation. Models may be in verbal, graphic, or equation form.

Monetarism: Economic theory that emphasizes the importance of changes in the money supply and their impact on the aggregate economy. Closely linked to economist Milton Friedman, monetarism employs the equation of exchange (PQ = MV) as an analytical device.

Monetarists: Those who believe that changes in the money supply have a determinative effect on economic conditions.

Monetary Control Act: Officially known as the Deposit Institutions and Monetary Control Act of 1980, the law extended the Federal Reserve Board's control over the economy and lifted some restrictions on savings deposits.

Monetary policy: Actions of the Federal Reserve Board to produce changes in the money supply, the availability of loanable funds, or the level of interest rates in an attempt to influence general economic activity.

Money: A commodity that is accepted by common consent in payment for goods and services and as settlement of debts and contracts.

Money market mutual fund: An investment fund that pools the assets of investors and puts the cash into debt securities that mature in less than one year; short-term bank

CDs, commercial paper of corporations, 6-month Treasury bills.

Money multiplier: The ratio of the maximum increase in the money supply to an increase in bank reserves. Determined by the required reserve ratio.

Money supply: There are four measures of the money supply used by the Federal Reserve System. M1 is the narrowest definition with L the broadest in scope:

- *M1:* A measure of the money supply that includes currency in circulation, demand deposit accounts, negotiable order of withdrawal (NOW) accounts, automatic transfer savings (ATS) accounts, traveler's checks, and checkable money market accounts.
- *M1-A:* A measure of the money supply that includes currency in circulation and demand deposit accounts in commercial banks only.
- *M1-B:* A measure of the money supply that includes currency in circulation and checkable deposit accounts in commercial banks, savings banks, savings and loan associations, and credit unions.
- *M2:* A measure of the money supply which includes M1 plus savings deposits, small time deposits (CDs), and certain money market mutual funds.
- *M3:* A measure of the money supply which includes M2 plus large time deposits (CDs).
- *L:* M3, plus other liquid assets such as term Euro-dollars held by non bank U.S. residents, bankers' acceptances, commercial paper, Treasury bills and other liquid government instruments, and U.S. savings bonds.

Monopolistic pricing: Setting a price above the level necessary to bring a product to market by restricting the supply of the product.

Most-favored-nation clause: Any tariff reduction (called tariff concession) that one member grants to another that must also be extended to other members.

Multilateral trade negotiations: Simultaneous trade negotiations between a number of countries.

Multinational company: A firm based in one country with operations in one or more additional countries.

Multiplier: The ratio of the ultimate increase in income, caused by an initial increase in spending, to that initial increase.

National debt: The amount of money owed by the government of a country through the practice of borrowing.

National economic plan: A plan drawn up by a national planning board or agency covering a specific period of time setting forth economic goals to be achieved and providing for actions in the public and private sectors to achieve these goals.

National income (NI): The total of all incomes earned in producing the Gross National Product.

National income accounts: The collective name for various macroeconomics measurements such as GNP and national income.

National Labor Relations Board: Independent regulatory agency empowered to prevent and remedy unfair labor practices by employers or by union organizations and to ensure fair union representation.

Nationalized industries: Industries that have been transformed from private to public ownership.

Natural monopoly: An industry in which the economies of scale are so extensive that a single firm can supply the whole market more efficiently than two or more firms could; natural monopolies are generally public utilities.

Natural rate hypothesis: The hypothesis that there is a long-run level of real gross national product (GNP) that exists independent of the inflation rate.

Near money: Assets with a specified monetary value that can be readily redeemable as money; savings accounts, certificates of deposit, and shares in money market mutual funds.

Negative Income Tax: An income maintenance plan that would provide a guaranteed minimum income for eligible families with no other income, and a supplement for families with incomes below a predetermined level.

Negotiable Order of Withdrawal (NOW) Accounts: Savings and loan bank customer accounts on which checks can be drawn.

Neomercantilists: Contemporary advocates of mercantilist trade policies to restrict imports, maximize exports of consumer products, and restrict exports of capital equipment and technology to prevent competition from foreign producers.

Net exports (X × M): The value of goods and services exported minus the amount spent on imported goods and services.

Net value: The market value of a worker's output after subtracting the other production costs, such as raw materials.

Nonearned income: Dividends, interest, capital gains, and other nonlabor income.

Nontariff barriers: Restrictions on imports resulting from requirements for special marking, test, or standards enforced on imported goods or the time delays in clearing them for importation.

Normal rate of return: The rate of earnings on invested capital that is normal for a given degree of risk.

Occupational Safety and Health Administration (OSHA): An agency of the U.S. Department of Labor created to encourage employers and employees to reduce workplace hazards and enforce on-the-job safety and health standards.

Oligopoly: A shared monopoly in which there is no explicit agreement among the firms.

Open-market operations: The purchase or sale of government securities by the Federal Reserve to implement monetary policy.

Opportunity cost: Real economic cost of a good or service produced measured by the value of the sacrificed alternative.

Partnership: A nonincorporated business enterprise with two or more owners.

Patent: A form of property rights giving an inventor of a new product design or process (or the owner of the patent, if sold) the sole legal right to use, not use, or dispose of the invention.

Per capita real income: Individual personal income, mostly wages, stated in noninflationary monetary units. It is calculated by dividing the total national income (or GNP) by the population size.

Perfect competition: *See* Pure competition.

Perfectly elastic (demand): A demand condition in which the quantity demanded varies from zero to infinity when there is a change in the price.

Perfectly inelastic (demand): A demand condition in which there is no change in the quantity demanded when price changes.

Personal consumption expenditures (C): Spending by households on goods and services.

Personal income distribution: The pattern of income distribution according to the relative size of people's income.

Phillips curve: A statistical relationship between increases in the general price level and unemployment.

Planned obsolescence: The practice of producing goods or services that are deliberately designed to limit use, thereby requiring replacement or repair.

Population density: The average number of people per unit of land area.

Poverty gap: The aggregate income shortfall of the poor as a percentage of aggregate consumption.

Poverty line: The family income level below which people are officially classified as poor.

Predatory business practice: Any action on the part of a firm carried out solely to interfere with a competitor.

Price discrimination: Selling a product to two different buyers at different prices where all other conditions are the same.

Price elasticity of demand: The relative size of the change in the quantity demanded of a good or service as a result of a small change in its price.

Price indexes: Indicators of the general level of prices and attempts to average price changes of individual goods and services into a composite that will reflect the net effect of all the price changes upon the general level of prices. *See also* Consumer Price Index; Producer Price Index.

Price leadership: A common practice in shared monopoly industries by which one of the firms in the industry, normally one of the largest, changes its prices, and the other firms follow its lead.

Price level: The average level of money prices, a general indicator of the state of the economy.

Price stability: A constant average level of prices for all goods and services.

Priority sectors: Those parts of the economy that decision makers want to expand most rapidly and therefore favor with scarce inputs.

Privatization: The process of selling government assets to private buyers and/or relinquishing government services to the private sector.

Producer Price Index (PPI): Replaced the Wholesale Price Index as the most important monthly measure of prices at the wholesale level. PPI is really three indexes: one for producer finished goods, one for intermediate, and one for crude commodities. The PPI usually refers to the finished goods index.

Product differentiation: A device used by business firms to distinguish their product from the products of other firms in the same industry.

Product market: A market in which finished goods and services are exchanged.

Production inputs: The factors of production used in producing a good or service.

Production possibility frontier (PPF): Frequently used by economists to explain the costs to the economy of producing more of one good in terms of the resultant lost quantities of other goods.

Productivity: A ratio of the amount of output per unit of input.

Profits: The net returns after subtracting total costs from total revenue. If costs are greater than revenue, profits are negative.

Progressive income tax: A tax rate that increases as the income on which the tax is based grows larger.

Progressive tax system: A system of taxation based on increasing marginal tax rates at higher levels of income.

Promissory note (IOU): A written obligation to pay a specified amount at a specified time.

Property tax: A tax levied on real estate, including the land and structures on it.

Proportional tax: A levy that takes the same proportion in taxes from low and high incomes.

Proprietorship: A business enterprise with a single private owner.

Prosperity: See Business cycles, phases.

Protectionism: Measures taken by the government in order to limit or exclude imports that compete with domestic production.

Protectionist measures: Actions taken by the government in order to limit or exclude imports that compete with domestic production.

Public utility: An industry that produces an essential public service such as electricity, gas, water, and telephone service; normally, a single firm is granted a local monopoly to provide the service.

Public Utility Commission: A regulatory body whose members are appointed by government to set rates and services provided by public utility firms.

Pure competition: A condition prevailing in an industry in which there are such a large number of firms producing a standardized product that no single firm can noticeably affect the market price by changing its output; also an industry in which firms can easily enter or leave.

Pure monopoly: An industry in which there is only one firm.

Pure public good: A good or service that is collectively consumed.

Quality-of-work-life program: An activity that attempts to improve the workplace environment of a business, encourage employee participation and counter worker alienation and absenteeism.

Quantity demanded: The amount of a good or service that consumers would purchase at a particular price.

Quantity equation (equation of exchange): The quantity of money (M) times the velocity of its circulation (V) equals the quantity of goods and services transacted (T) times their average price (P), normally written PQ = MV.

Quantity theory of money: See Quantity equation.

Quota: A limit on the quantity or value of a good that can be imported in a given time period.

Rate discrimination (price discrimination): Charging different customers different rates for services of equal production cost.

Rate level: The general level of rates (prices) of a regulated company.

Real capital: The buildings, machinery, tools, and equipment used in production.

Real flow: Involves the physical movement of goods and services and/or the use of factors of production.

Real income: See Price level.

Real interest rate: The quoted interest rate calculated on an annual basis and adjusted for changes in the purchasing power of money during the duration of the loan.

Real investment: The purchase of business structures and capital equipment; investment measured in dollars of constant value to adjust for inflation.

Real output: The value of output adjusted for changes in prices; the volume of output.

Recession: See Business cycles, phases.

Reciprocal Trade Agreement Act (1934): Federal law in effect from 1934 to 1962 that empowered the president to reduce tariff barriers by as much as 50 percent on a reciprocal basis with other countries through negotiated treaties. Extended 11 times, the law enabled the United States to reduce tariffs by more than 75 percent.

Recovery: See Business cycles, phases.

Regressive tax: A levy that takes a higher proportion from low incomes in taxes than it takes from high incomes.

Residual accounts: Short-term capital transfers and monetary gold transactions that compensate for the imbalance in a country's basic balance in its international payments.

Resources: The inputs that are used in production. Includes natural resources (minerals, timber, rivers), labor (blue collar, white collar), and capital (machinery, buildings).

Revaluation: An increase in the value of a country's currency relative to other currencies due to an official government increase in the exchange rate under a fixed rate system.

Revenue: The receipts from sales of goods and services.

Sales tax: A tax levied on the value of a good or service when exchanged.

Say's Law: A theory of the French economist J. B. Say, which holds that when goods or services are produced, enough income is generated to purchase what is produced, thereby eliminating the problem of overproduction.

Scarcity: The limited resources for production relative to satisfy the wants and needs of all the people in the world.

Scientific method: A procedure used by scientists to develop explanations for events and test the validity of those explanations.

Securities and Exchange Commission (SEC): Independent federal agency established under the Securities Exchange Act of 1934 that regulates brokers, investment companies, stock exchanges and the actions of corporate officers in the securities industry.

Shared monopoly: An industry in which there are only a few firms; more specifically, an industry in which four or fewer firms account for more than 50 percent of industry sales.

Sherman Antitrust Act: The 1890 antitrust law that makes restraint of trade and other monopolistic practices such as price fixing unlawful.

Shift in demand: A change in the quantity of a good or service that would be purchased at each possible price.

Shift in supply: A change in the quantity of a good or service that would be offered for sale at each possible price.

Short run: A period of time so short that the amount of some factor inputs cannot be varied.

Short-term business cycles: Fluctuations in economic activity, particularly prices, production, and employment.

Social indicators: Noneconomic statistics that reflect a country's standard of living.

Social Security: A federal program of social insurance, introduced in 1935, that now provides retirement, disability, and medical care to eligible participants.

Socialism: An economic system that involves state ownership of the means of production, equitable distribution of incomes, and economic planning.

Specialization: Concentrating the activity of a unit of a production resource—especially labor—on a single task or production operation. Also applies to the specialization of nations in producing those goods and services that their resources are best suited to produce.

Speculators: People who purchase goods or financial assets in anticipation that prices will rise and they can sell at a profit; speculators can also speculate on a fall in prices.

Stagflation: A term created to describe a situation of simultaneous economic stagnation, high unemployment, and inflation.

State (authoritarian) socialism: A command economy in which virtually all of the means of production are in the hands of the state and decision making is centralized.

Stationary state: A condition of no change; a static economy with no growth.

Statistics: The data on economic variables; also the techniques of analyzing, interpreting, and presenting data.

Stock option: The right to purchase a specific amount of a corporation's stock at a fixed price. Often part of the compensation package for a company's top executives.

Strike: A collective refusal by employees to work.

Structural unemployment: The lack of work that occurs because of changes in the basic characteristics of a market, such as a new substitute product, a change in consumer tastes, or new technology in production.

Substitution effect: *See* Law of demand.

Supply: The relationship between the quantities of a good or service that sellers wish to market at any particular time and the various prices that can exist for the good or service.

Supply curve: A graphic representation of the relationship between price and quantity supplied.

Supply schedule: A table recording the number of units of a good or service supplied at various possible prices.

Supply-side economics: An approach to macroeconomic problems that focuses on the importance of increasing the supply of goods and services.

Surplus: A positive balance after expenditures are subtracted from revenues.

Taft-Hartley Act: A federal law, also known as the Labor-Management Relations Act of 1947, that seeks a balance of power between labor and management, protects the public from economic harm in labor disputes, and allows the president injunction powers in strikes that threaten the public safety and well-being. The law restrains the power of unions by amending the Wagner Act of 1935.

Tariff quota: A combination of a limited quantity or value of a good that can be imported free of duty or at a low tariff and high tariffs imposed on amounts exceeding the limit.

Tariffs: Taxes placed on imports either by value (ad valorem duty) or per unit of quantity (specific duty); also, the whole schedule of a country's import duties.

Technology: The body of skills and knowledge that comprises the processes used in production.

Terms of trade: The ratio of average export prices to average import prices.

Theory of the firm: In microeconomics, the analysis of the decision-making process of firms—all firms are assumed to maximize profits. In economic theory, a firm is defined as any organizationally separate production unit.

Third World: The underdeveloped, nonaligned nations in Asia, Africa, and Latin America.

Time series: The changes in the values of a variable over time; a chart in which time—generally years—is one of the variables.

Total cost: The sum of fixed cost and variable cost.

Total revenue: The sum of receipts from all of the units sold; price × quantity.

Total utility: The amount of satisfaction a consumer derives from all of the units of a particular good or service consumed in a given time period.

Trade adjustment assistance: Supplementary unemployment payments to workers who have lost their jobs because of import competition and assistance to firms in shifting to other types of production.

Trade balance: Exports minus imports (net exports).

Trade-off: The choice between alternative uses for a given quantity of a resource.

Traditional economy: An economic system in which the basic questions of what, how, and for whom to produce are resolved primarily by custom and tradition.

Transfer payments: Expenditures for which no goods or services are exchanged. Welfare, Social Security, and unemployment compensation are government transfer payments.

Treasury bill: A short-term, marketable, federal government security with a maturity of one year or less.

Trust: A combination of producers in the same industry under one direction for the purpose of exerting monopoly power.

Unbalanced growth: Directing a country's capital resources into one or a limited number of industries to promote growth in those industries at a more rapid rate than growth of industry in general.

Underemployed: Workers who cannot obtain full-time employment or who are working at jobs for which they are overqualified.

Unfavorable balance of trade: The deficit in a country's merchandise trade when imports during the year are greater than exports.

Union shop: A firm in which all workers must belong to the union that represents their bargaining unit.

Unit of measurement (standard of value or unit of account): A common denominator of value in which prices are stated and accounts recorded.

Unitary elasticity (demand): A demand condition in which the relative change in the quantity demanded is the same as the size of the price change.

Urbanization: Migration of the population from rural areas to cities.

Utility: The amount of satisfaction a consumer derives from consumption of a good or service.

Value added: The difference between the value of a firm's sales and its purchases of materials and semifinished inputs.

Variable: A quantity—such as number of workers, amount of carbon dioxide, interest rate, amount of cropland, etc.—whose value changes in relationship to changes in the values of other associated items.

Variable costs: *See* Average variable cost of production.

Velocity of money circulation (V): The average rate at which money changes hands.

Venture capitalist: An individual or firm that provides financing for new business ventures for a share in the returns if the business succeeds.

Vertical equity: Fair differentiations of treatment of individuals at different levels.

Vertical merger: The joining of two firms in which the output of one firm is an input of the other firm.

Vertically integrated: Separate divisions of one company producing the different stages of a product and marketing their output to one another.

Vicious circle of poverty: The pattern of economic stagnation that results from a lack of surplus of production to invest in capital goods to increase productivity.

Wage (salary): A factor payment for labor service.

Welfare economics: A branch of economic study concerned with how an economic system attempts to maximize the welfare of its people; studies the principles by which alternative economic objectives can be ranked in terms of social welfare.

Welfare state (democratic socialism): An economic system that is committed to the security of its population in the areas of income, health care, job security, and providing for old age.

Wholesale Price Index (WPI): Replaced by the Producer Price Index in 1978; it was one of the best known of the price indexes. A statistical composite measure of price movements in wholesale, or primary, markets.

Workfare: A program that requires nonexempt welfare recipients to work at public service jobs for a given number of hours a month.

World Bank (International Bank for Reconstruction and Development—IBRD): A specialized agency of the UN that began operations in 1945 first to help countries rebuild facilities destroyed in World War II and subsequently to help finance development of the LDCs.

SOURCES

The Encyclopedic Dictionary of Economics, Fourth Edition, 1991. Dushkin/McGraw-Hill, Guilford, CT 06437.

The Study of Economics: Principles, Concepts, and Applications, Turley Mings, 1995. Dushkin/McGraw-Hill, Guilford, CT 06437.

Index

A

Aaron-Reischauer plan, to reform Social Security, 73
accuracy, CPI and, 119
advertising, 202
age-adjusted unemployment rate, 132–133
Amoco, 155
antidumping laws, free trade and, 146–152
Apparel Industry Partnership, 153
Arrow, Kenneth, 22
Asia Pacific Economic Cooperation Forum (APEC), 165
Asian economic crisis, 189; IMF and, 46
Aslund, Anders, 183
assets, debts and, 45
"asymmetric information," 22
auto industry, 112; deflation and, 143

B

Balcerowicz, Leszek, 183
Ball plan, to reform Social Security, 72–73
bank reserves, 78
BankAmerica, 97, 98
banking: economic stagnation in Japan and, 186–187; function of, in democracy, 83–90; low-cost, 99–101; mergers in, 97–98
Basle Committee on Banking Supervision, 107
Basel Convention on the Ban on Hazardous Waste, 202–203
Beal, John E., 115
Bernstein, Jared, 125, 127
biotechnology, 10
Blank, Rebecca M., 46–47
Blaug, Mark, 13
blue-collar workers, 123
"Board of Overseers of Major International Institutions and Markets," 137–138
Bostrom, Ann, 126, 127
Bradsher, Keith, 86, 87
Brazil, 143, 189
Breaux-Greggs plan, to reform Social Security, 72
budget deficit, 28–29; high interest rates and, 48–49
Buffett, Warren, 30
Bundesbank, 177
Bureau of Economic Analysis (BEA), 28–29, 31
Bureau of Labor Statistics (BLS), 124, 132; CPI and, 117–121
Burma, human rights and, 155, 156
Bush, George, 89

C

Canada, NAFTA and, 158–163
carbon dioxide, 195, 203
cascading taxes, 59
Chase Manhattan, 100, 101
check cashers, 99, 101
checking, low-cost, and low-income neighborhoods, 99–101
Chernomyrdin, Viktor S., 183
Cleveland, Grover, 111
climate change, 195, 197, 203
Clinton, Bill, 89, 165, 166–167
codes of conduct, human rights for multinational corporations and, 153–155
collective action, human rights policies of multinational corporations and, 155–156
comparative advantage, 140–142
Congressional Budget Office (CBO), 33, 83
consistency, CPI and, 119
Constitution, U.S., banking and, 88–89
Consumer Price Index (CPI), measurement of, 117–121
consumer rights, 197–198, 202
consumption patterns, human development and, 192–204
consumption taxes, 59, 60
contingent workers, underemployment and, 122–131
Convention on Biological Diversity, 196–197
Convention to Combat Desertification, 197
Council of Economic Advisers, *Economic Report of the President for 1998* by, 44–47
Council of Economic Priorities, 154
CPI. *See* Consumer Price Index
CPI-U, 120
CPI-W, 120
currencies, electronic, 102–107

D

Debreu, Gerard, 22
debts: assets and, 45; deflation and, 145
deficit. *See* budget deficit
deforestation, changing consumption patterns and, 195, 196
deflation, 143–145
demand, economic stagnation in Japan, 185–186, 187
democracy, function of banking in, 83–90
depreciation deduction, transition relief in flat tax and, 61
digital value units (DVUs), 103
discount rates, 78
disposable income, taxes and, 50–57
Dollar Financial Group, 100–101
Dornbusch, Rudgier, 21, 23
drug trade, underground economy and, 32, 33
Duisenberg, Willem, 180, 182
dumping, free trade and, 146–152

E

economic and monetary union (EMU), in the European Union, 175–182
Economic Report of the President, 1998 (Council of Economic Advisers), 44–47
economic Web sites, 24–25
Eddie Bauer, 155
Eichengreen, Barry, 155
electronic cash, 102, 103, 106, 107
electronic commerce, 103, 105, 106
electronic currencies, 102–107
encryption, 104, 105
"endogenous" growth theories, 141
EMU. *See* economic and monetary union
environmental issues: Council of Economic Advisers on, 47; influence of consumption patterns on human development, 192–204
environmental taxes, 201
euro, 175–182
Europe, 168–174; monetary union in, 175–182
European Central Bank (ECB), 176, 179, 180–181, 182
European Union (EU), monetary union and, 175–182
excess capacity, deflation and, 144
Executive Board, of European Central Bank, 182
"exogenous" growth theories, 141

F

Fair, Ray C., 25
fair trade, free trade and, 146–152
Fairmodel, 25
"fast-track" negotiating authority, 164, 165
federal funds market, 78
Federal Reserve Board, 28, 33, 91–94, 111; banking and, 83–90, 97; stock bubbles and, 95–96
Federal Reserve System, 76–82
Feld, Alan, 65
Feldstein plan, to reform Social Security, 69–70
Feldstein, Martin, 19, 20
Fischer, Stanley, 21, 23
fish stocks, changing consumption patterns and, 195
flat tax, 58–62, 65
Fleet Financial Group, 100
FOMC (Federal Open Market Committee), 76–77, 78
foreign direct investment (FDI), 29–30
Foundations of Economic Analysis (Samuelson), 22
free trade, 146–152; NAFTA and, 158–163; theory of comparative advantage and, 140–142; U.S. policy on, 164–167
"free-rider" problem, human rights practices of multinational corporations and, 155–156
Friedman, Milton, 20

225

"funds rate," 78

G

game theory, 22
Gap, The, 155
GATT (General Agreement on Tariffs and Trade), 146–152, 165
GDP (Gross Domestic Product), 28
General Agreement on Tariffs and Trade (GATT), 146–152, 165
General Council, of European Central Bank, 182
"general equilibrium" proof, 22
General Theory of Employment, Interest, and Money (Keynes), 14, 19
geography, comparative advantage and, 141
Gilbert, Robert, 25
Gilded Age, 110–111
Glass-Steagall Act, bank mergers and, 97
global warming, changing consumption patterns and, 195, 197, 203
globalization, 136–139; free trade and, 146–152; impact of consumption patterns on human development and, 192–204; New Economy and, 8–12
Godley, Wynne, 41
Goffe, Bill, 24–25
gold standard, 110, 111
Governing Council, of European Central Bank, 182
Gramlich, Edward, 70–71
Great Depression, 111, 112
Greenspan, Alan, 19, 86, 93, 95–96, 97, 111
Gregg, Judd, 72

H

Hadley, Leonard A., 113, 115
human poverty index (HPI-2), 193
human rights, multinational corporations and, 153–157
hypercards, 102
Hy-Vee Food Stores Inc., 113–114, 115, 116

I

Illinois, low-cost banking laws in, 99
IMF (International Monetary Fund), 136, 137, 138; Asian economic crisis and, 46
immigration, underground economy and illegal, 32
income inequality, 30; consumption patterns and, 192–204; in Europe vs. U.S., 172–173
increasing-returns model, of Paul Krugman, 22
independence, of central banks and democracy, 88–90

Individual Account plan, to reform Social Security, 70–71
inflation, 77, 79; Phillips curve and, 92–94
interest rates, 78–79; budget deficits and, 48–49
Internal Revenue Service (IRS), 31, 50
"International Credit Insurance Corporation," 137
International Monetary Fund. *See* IMF
International Trade Commission (ITC), 148, 150
Internet, 103, 106; economic Web sites and, 24–25
intra-company trade, NAFTA and, 161–162
ITT, 157

J

Japan: banking industry in, 98, 186–187; economic stagnation in, 185–187, 188–189
job-creation rates, in Europe vs. U.S., 170–172
"jurisdiction," 107

K

Kantor, Mickey, 165
Kaufman, Henry, 137–138
Keynes, John Maynard, 13–15, 19, 20, 22, 33, 86–87
Kiriyenko, Sergei V., 184
Krugman, Paul, 21, 22, 23
Kuala Lumpur Meeting of the Parties to the Basel Convention on the Ban on Hazardous Waste, 202–203
Kyoto Meeting on the United Nations Framework Convention on Climate Change, 203

L

Labor Department, human rights and, 153
lazy-susan system, productivity at Maytag Corporation and, 113
leaded gasoline, 196, 198
Levi Strauss, 155, 156
"lifeline" laws, low-cost banking and, 99–101
Liz Claiborne, 155, 156
Lucas, Robert, 20–21, 22, 23

M

Macy's, 155, 156
Malthus, Thomas, 14, 21
Martin, Bill, 41
Marx, Karl, 21–22
Massachusetts, low-cost banking laws in, 99
Maytag Corporation, 113, 114–115, 116
mergers, in banking industry, 97–98

Mexico: NAFTA and, 158–163; peso crisis in, 162–163
Mill, James, 14
Minnesota, low-cost banking laws in, 99
Mishel, Larry, 125, 127
Mondex, 102
M1, 80
Monetary History of the United States (Friedman and Schwartz), 20
monetary policy, 20; Federal Reserve System and, 76–82
moonlighting, underemployment and, 122–131
Morgenstern, Oskar, 22
mortgage interest deduction, flat tax and, 61
Moynihan plan, to reform Social Security, 71–72
multilateral agreement on investments (MAI), 46
multinational corporation (MNCs), human rights and, 153–157
multitasking, underemployment and, 123–125

N

NAFTA (North American Free Trade Agreement), debate over success of, 158–163, 165, 167
National Bureau of Economic Research (NBER), 21
national savings, 29, 41
Nationsbank, 97, 98
"natural rate of unemployment," 81
New Economy, effect of technological innovation and globalization on, 8–12
New Jersey, low-cost banking laws in, 99, 100
New York, low-cost banking laws in, 99, 100
Nike, 153
nominal funds rate, 78–79
nonaccelerating inflation rate of unemployment (NAIRU), 45, 92–93

O

Okun's Law, 36
Omnibus Budget Reconciliation Act of, 1993, 50, 51
open market operations, 78
Optimal Currency Areas (OCA), theory of, 178
"optimal tariffs," 142
Organization for Economic Cooperation and Development (OECD), economic Web site of, 25
output gaps: deflation and, 144; economic stagnation in Japan and, 186, 187

P

Palatine High School, 25

Panel Study of Income Dynamics (PSID), 127, 129, 130, 131
paper money, underground economy and, 32
part-time workers, 114; underemployment and, 122–131
Pearson, Ronald D., 115
permit-trading program, for sulfur dioxide, 47
Personal Security Accounts (PSA) plan, to reform Social Security, 68, 69
peso crisis, in Mexico, 162–163
Phillips, Alban W., 20, 91
Phillips curve, 91–94
Poland, 183–184
pollution, consumption patterns and, 195–196
poverty. See income inequality
price stability, 77
Principal Financial Group, 113–114, 115–116
product quality, CPI and, 117, 120, 121
product safety, consumer rights and, 197–198, 202
productivity, 112, 113–116; comparative advantage and, 140–142; deflation and, 144; measuring changes in, 30; in New Economy, 8–12
protectionism, free trade and, 146–152

Q

quality, product, and CPI, 117, 120, 121

R

race, family work effort and, 130
Reagan, Ronald, 89
real interest rates, 78, 79
recessions, 112
Reebok, 153, 155, 156
refund delay of 1985, 51, 54, 55–56
Reich, Robert, 153
Resources for Economists on the Internet, 24–25
Revenue Act of 1964, 51, 52, 53–54
Revenue and Expenditure Control Act of 1968, 51, 52, 54–55
Rhode Island, low-cost banking laws in, 99
Ricardo, David, 14, 140
Rippe, Richard, 41
Roaring Twenties, 111
Robinson, John, 126, 127

Romer, Paul, 21, 22
Russia, 183–184, 188, 189

S

Sachs, Jeffrey, 19, 23, 184
sales taxes, 59, 65
Samuelson, Paul, 13, 20, 22
Samuelson, Robert, 86
Sargent, Thomas, 20
savings and loan (S&L) crisis, 29
savings, national, 29, 41
Say, Jean-Baptiste, 13–15, 20
Schlossberg, Gary, 31
Schor, Juliet B., 122–131
Smith, Adam, 13, 21, 63
Social Accountability 8000 (SA8000), 154
social policy, Council of Economic Advisers on, 46–47
Social Security, plans to reform, 68–73
Solow, Robert M., 14, 20
Soros, George, 137
Spain, 176
Starbucks Coffee, 155
State Peace and Development Council, of Burma, 91
Stiglitz, Joseph, 22
stock bubble, Federal Reserve Board and, 95–96
Strategic Actions for a Just Economy, 101
subsidies, environment and, 201
sulfur-dioxide permit-trading program, 47
Summers, Larry, 19, 22, 23, 46
supply, economic stagnation in Japan and, 185–186, 187
supply-side shocks, 92, 93, 94

T

Tariff Act of 1974, 148
tariffs, 142
Tax Foundation, 66
tax rebate of 1975, 51, 54, 55, 56
Tax Reform Act of 1986, 62
taxes: consumer spending and, 50–57; consumption, 59, 60, 65; environmental, 201; flat, 58–62, 65; loss of, in underground economy, 31–33; reform of, and simplicity, 63–65; sales, 59–65; studies on burden of, 66–67; value-added, 59
Taxpayer Relief Act, 62
Taylor, Frederick, 118
technological unemployment, 16

technology, 112; comparative advantage and, 141; deflation and, 143, 144; New Economy and, 8–12
temporary workers, 114
Texaco, 155
Theory of Optimal Currency Areas (OCA), 178
Thompson, Cynthia, 115
Tobin Tax, 46
trade. See free trade
transition relief, flat tax and, 61
transparency, CPI and, 118
Treatise on Political Economy (Say), 13
Trichet, Jean-Claude, 180, 182

U

underemployment, 122–131
underground economy, 31–33
unemployment, 81; age-adjusted rate of, 132–133; rate of, and Phillips curve, 91, 92; technological, 16; in U.S. vs. Europe, 170–172
unions, labor: euro and, 177; underground economy and, 32–33
United Fruit, 157
US Toxic Release Inventory, 202

V

value-added taxes (VATs), 59
Vermont, low-cost banking laws in, 99
von Neumann, John, 22

W

Washington Mutual, 101
water stress, changing consumption patterns and, 195, 196
Wealth of Nations, The (Smith), 13, 21, 63
Web sites, economic, 24–25. See also Internet
White House Economic Statistics Briefing Room, 25
white-collar workers, 123
World Bank, 190
World Trade Organization (WTO), 136, 146–152, 165, 166–167

Y

Yellen, Janet, 44, 45
Yeltsin, Boris, 183, 184

AE Article Review Form

We encourage you to photocopy and use this page as a tool to assess how the articles in **Annual Editions** expand on the information in your textbook. By reflecting on the articles you will gain enhanced text information. You can also access this useful form on a product's book support Web site at **http://www.dushkin.com/online/.**

NAME: DATE:

TITLE AND NUMBER OF ARTICLE:

BRIEFLY STATE THE MAIN IDEA OF THIS ARTICLE:

LIST THREE IMPORTANT FACTS THAT THE AUTHOR USES TO SUPPORT THE MAIN IDEA:

WHAT INFORMATION OR IDEAS DISCUSSED IN THIS ARTICLE ARE ALSO DISCUSSED IN YOUR TEXTBOOK OR OTHER READINGS THAT YOU HAVE DONE? LIST THE TEXTBOOK CHAPTERS AND PAGE NUMBERS:

LIST ANY EXAMPLES OF BIAS OR FAULTY REASONING THAT YOU FOUND IN THE ARTICLE:

LIST ANY NEW TERMS/CONCEPTS THAT WERE DISCUSSED IN THE ARTICLE, AND WRITE A SHORT DEFINITION:

We Want Your Advice

ANNUAL EDITIONS revisions depend on two major opinion sources: one is our Advisory Board, listed in the front of this volume, which works with us in scanning the thousands of articles published in the public press each year; the other is you—the person actually using the book. Please help us and the users of the next edition by completing the prepaid article rating form on this page and returning it to us. Thank you for your help!

ANNUAL EDITIONS: Macroeconomics 00/01

ARTICLE RATING FORM

Here is an opportunity for you to have direct input into the next revision of this volume. We would like you to rate each of the 42 articles listed below, using the following scale:

1. **Excellent: should definitely be retained**
2. **Above average: should probably be retained**
3. **Below average: should probably be deleted**
4. **Poor: should definitely be deleted**

Your ratings will play a vital part in the next revision. So please mail this prepaid form to us just as soon as you complete it. Thanks for your help!

RATING / ARTICLE

1. Meeting the Challenge of the New Economy
2. The Accidental Inventor of Today's Capitalism
3. Economic Possibilities for Our Grandchildren
4. What in the World Happened to Economics?
5. Statistics and Even Lore of the Dismal Science
6. State of the Union: Black Holes in the Statistics
7. The Economy You Can't See
8. How Fast Can the U.S. Economy Grow?
9. Hell No, We Won't Save!
10. The Economic Report of the President for 1998: A Review
11. Reflections on the Balancing Act
12. The Tax Man Cometh: Consumer Spending and Tax Payments
13. The Flat Tax in Theory and Practice: Simple, Efficient, Fair. Or Is It?
14. Why Are Taxes So Complicated, and What Can We Do about It?
15. Are Americans Really Overtaxed?
16. Should We Retire Social Security?: Grading the Reform Plans
17. U.S. Monetary Policy: An Introduction
18. Central Banking in a Democracy
19. Is the Fed Slave to a Defunct Economist?
20. Should the Fed Care about Stock Bubbles?
21. Bank Mergers and the Big Money
22. The Stepchildren of Banking
23. Electronic Cash and the End of National Markets
24. Learning from the Big Booms
25. Yes, Virginia, There Will Be Recessions
26. Productivity Gains Help Keep Economy on a Roll
27. Calculating the Price of Everything: The CPI
28. Overworked *and* Underemployed
29. The Age-Adjusted Unemployment Rate: An Alternative Measure
30. Globalization and Its Discontents: Navigating the Dangers of a Tangled World
31. Why Trade Is Good for You
32. Could It Happen Again?
33. Will Fair Trade Diminish Free Trade?
34. The Spotlight and the Bottom Line: How Multinationals Export Human Rights
35. NAFTA: How Is It Doing?
36. Trade Policy at a Cross Roads
37. The United States Is Not Ahead in Everything That Matters
38. The Euro: Who Wins? Who Loses?
39. Russia Is Not Poland, and That's Too Bad
40. Japan's Economic Plight: Fallen Idol
41. The Other Crisis
42. Changing Today's Consumption Patterns—for Tomorrow's Human Development

(Continued on next page)

229

ANNUAL EDITIONS: MACROECONOMICS 00/01

BUSINESS REPLY MAIL
FIRST-CLASS MAIL PERMIT NO. 84 GUILFORD CT

POSTAGE WILL BE PAID BY ADDRESSEE

**Dushkin/McGraw-Hill
Sluice Dock
Guilford, CT 06437-9989**

NO POSTAGE
NECESSARY
IF MAILED
IN THE
UNITED STATES

ABOUT YOU

Name _____ Date _____

Are you a teacher? ☐   A student? ☐
Your school's name

_____

Department

_____

Address _____ City _____ State ____ Zip ____

School telephone # _____

YOUR COMMENTS ARE IMPORTANT TO US!

Please fill in the following information:
For which course did you use this book?
_____

Did you use a text with this *ANNUAL EDITION*? ☐ yes ☐ no
What was the title of the text?
_____

What are your general reactions to the *Annual Editions* concept?
_____

Have you read any particular articles recently that you think should be included in the next edition?
_____

Are there any articles you feel should be replaced in the next edition? Why?
_____

Are there any World Wide Web sites you feel should be included in the next edition? Please annotate.
_____

May we contact you for editorial input? ☐ yes ☐ no
May we quote your comments? ☐ yes ☐ no